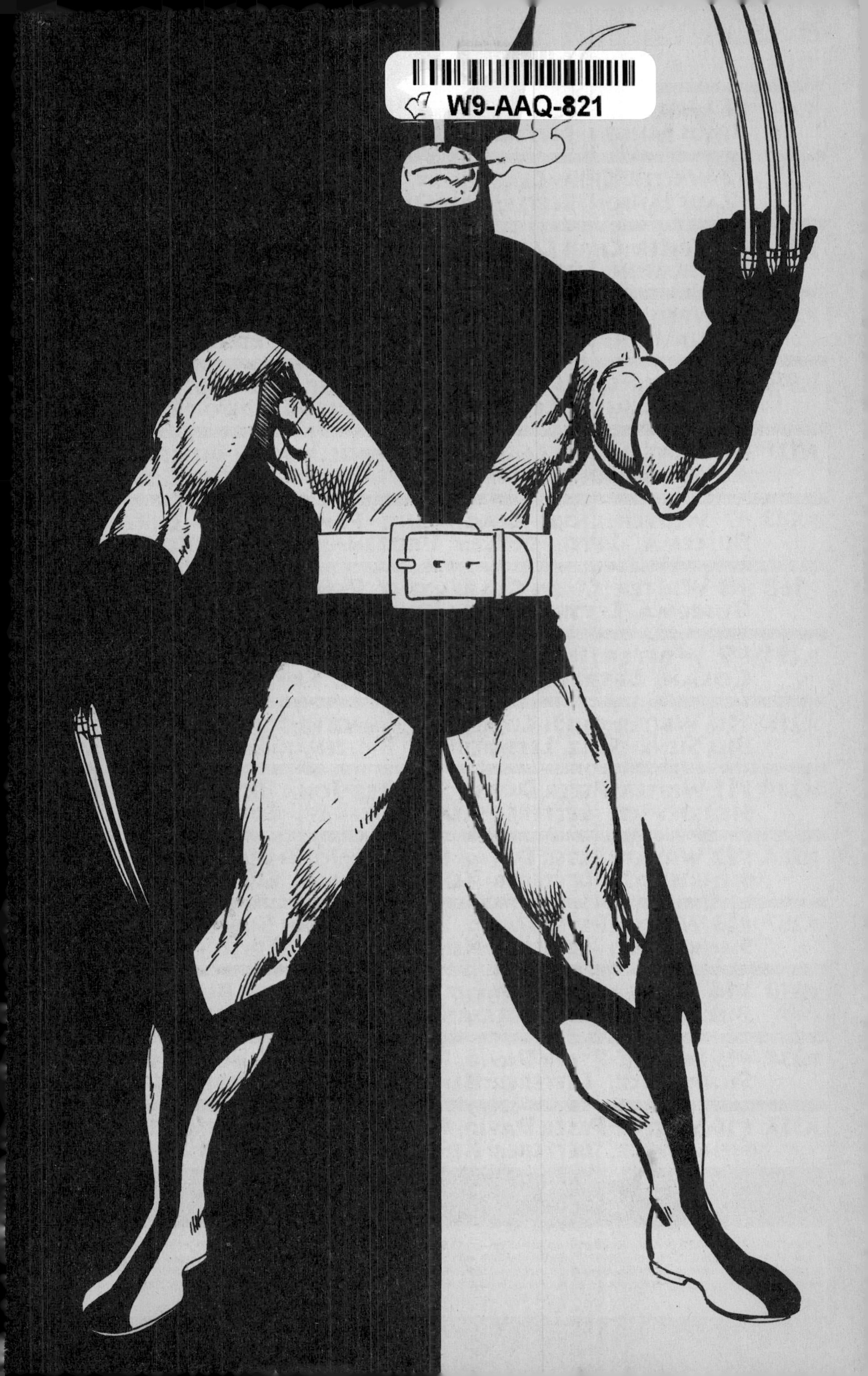

C R E D I T S

ESSENTIAL WOLVERINE® Originally published in magazine form as WOLVERINE #1-#23. Published by MARVEL COMICS; 387 PARK AVENUE SOUTH, NEW YORK, N.Y. 10016. Copyright © 1988, 1989, 1990 Marvel Characters, Inc. All rights reserved. WOLVERINE (including all prominent characters featured in this issue and the distinctive likenesses thereof) is a trademark of MARVEL CHARACTERS, INC. No part of this book may be printed or reproduced in any manner without the written permission of the publisher. Printed in the U.S.A. First Printing, 1996. ISBN #0-7851-0257-4. GST #R127032852.

REPRINT CREDITS

DAN HOSEK-Reptrint Editor

MATT IDELSON-Supervising Editor

BOB HARRAS-Editor In Chief

NGHIA LAM & JASON RODRIGUEZ-New Cover Art

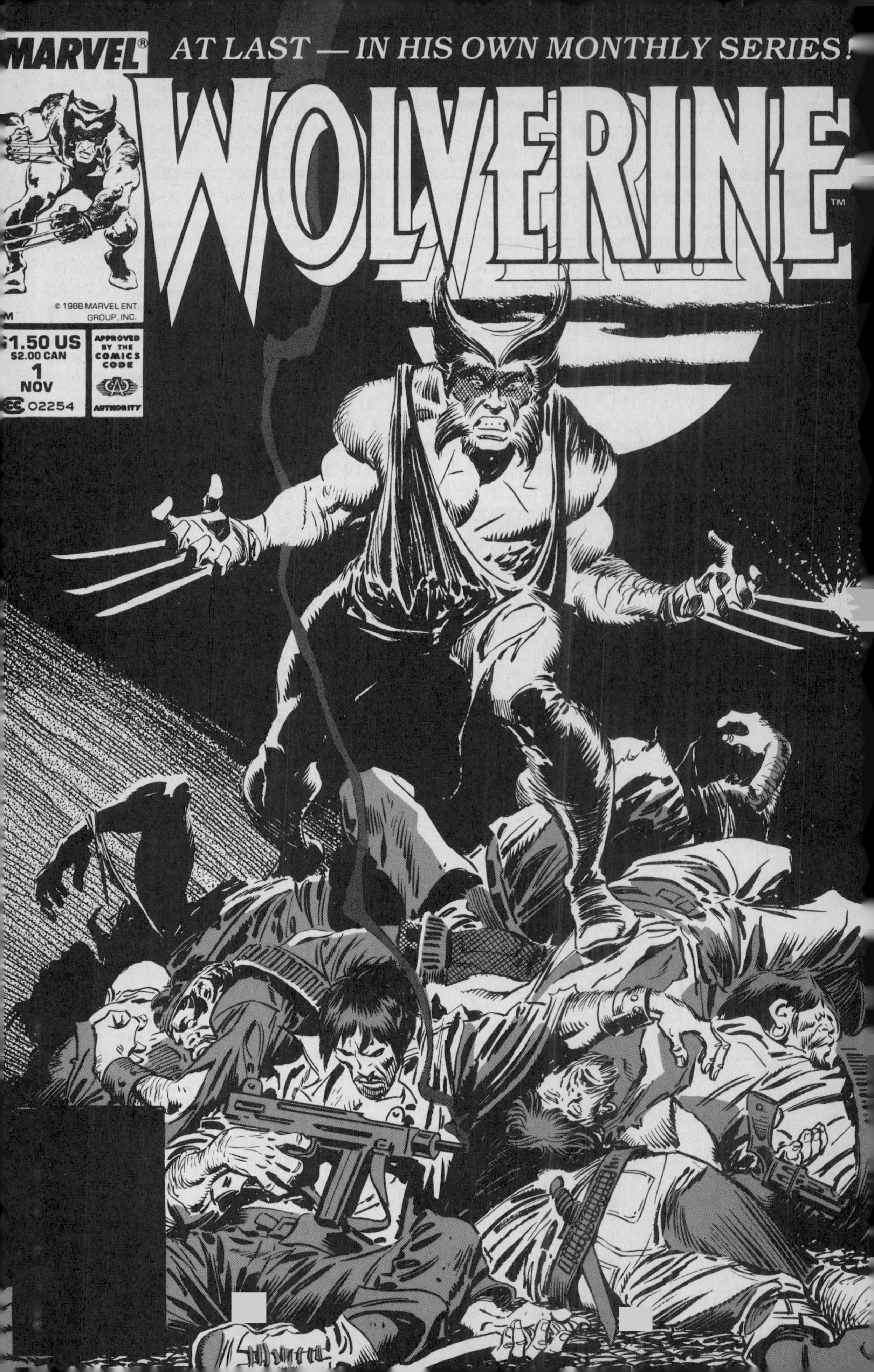
MARVEL®
AT LAST — IN HIS OWN MONTHLY SERIES!
WOLVERINE™
© 1988 MARVEL ENT. GROUP, INC.
$1.50 US
$2.00 CAN
1
NOV
02254
APPROVED BY THE COMICS CODE AUTHORITY

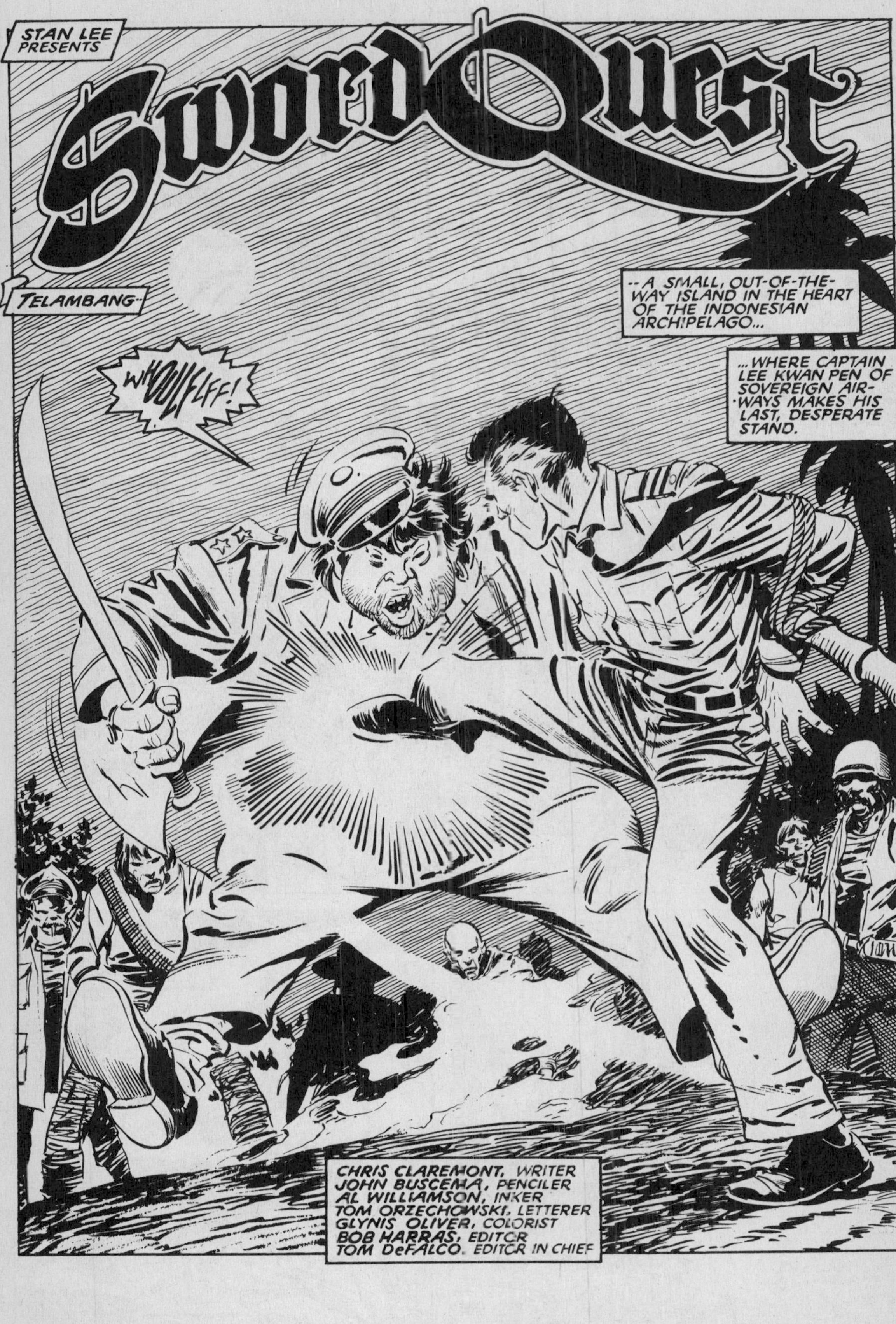
STAN LEE PRESENTS
SWORD QUEST
TELAMBANG--
--A SMALL, OUT-OF-THE-WAY ISLAND IN THE HEART OF THE INDONESIAN ARCHIPELAGO...
...WHERE CAPTAIN LEE KWAN PEN OF SOVEREIGN AIR-WAYS MAKES HIS LAST, DESPERATE STAND.
WHOOLFFF!
CHRIS CLAREMONT, WRITER
JOHN BUSCEMA, PENCILER
AL WILLIAMSON, INKER
TOM ORZECHOWSKI, LETTERER
GLYNIS OLIVER, COLORIST
BOB HARRAS, EDITOR
TOM DeFALCO, EDITOR IN CHIEF

FATSO CALLS HIMSELF BANAPUR KHAN.

PRINCE OF PIRATES.

OUWHWWCH!

MOSTLY, HIS RIFFRAFF OUTFIT PREYS ON BOAT PEOPLE-- REFUGEES FLEEING CAMBODIA AND VIETNAM-- STRIPPING THEM OF EVERYTHING THEY POSSESS OF VALUE.

DEPENDING ON THEIR MOOD...

...BANAPUR'S CREW GENERALLY KILLS THE MEN...

...DO WORSE TO THE WOMEN.

AN' THEN SELL ANYONE WHO SURVIVES...

...TO THE LOCAL SLAVE TRADERS.

CAP*TAIN*!?!

HOLY MOTHER HAVE MERCY...

BLESSED BUDDHA RECEIVE HIS SOUL...

WE'RE GONNA DIE WE'RE GONNA DIE WE'RE GONNA DIE

EV'RYBODY DIES, BOO'FUL. BUT WE'LL MAKE REAL SURE...

...Y'ALL HAVE A FUN TIME...

...B'FORE IT'S YOUR TURN.

CHIEF'S SLIPPIN', MATE. THAT FLYBOY HAD HIM ONNA ROPES.

YOU READY TO CHALLENGE HIM THEN, ROGER? DI'N'T THINK SO.

SO! WHICH OF YOU LOVELY LADIES...

...WISHES TO HELP ME CELEBRATE MY GLORIOUS VICTORY?

NOW NOW-- DON'T BE SHY--

--AM I SUCH AN OGRE?

AND IF I AM...

...D'YOU THINK IT WISE...

...TO MAKE ME ANGRY?

A HALF-CENTURY AGO...

...WHEN THE DUTCH RULED THIS NEIGHBORHOOD...

...THEY BUILT AN EMERGENCY AIRSTRIP ON TELAMBANG. IN ALL THAT TIME, NO ONE HAD EVER USED IT...

...UNTIL EIGHT DAYS AGO...

...WHEN SOVEREIGN FLIGHT 49 DISAPPEARED.

TWENTY-ONE CREW, A HUNDRED-EIGHTY PASSENGERS.

MOST OF 'EM BEYOND MY HELP.

FIRST THING I FOUND AFTER COMING ASHORE...

...WAS THEIR MASS GRAVE.

PIRATES ARE CARELESS AN' COCKY.

THEY DON'T EXPECT TROUBLE.

GLRYXKK

THERE'S JUST THE ONE GUARD, OUT BY THE PLANE.

THEN, THERE'S NONE.

THE USUAL TRIP WIRES AN' BOOBY TRAPS.

NO TROUBLE AT ALL...

... FOR ME TO PASS.

SAME GOES FOR THE PERIMETER PATROLS AT THE VILLAGE PROPER.

LIKE THE PLANE SQUAD, THEIR MINDS AREN'T ON THEIR JOB...

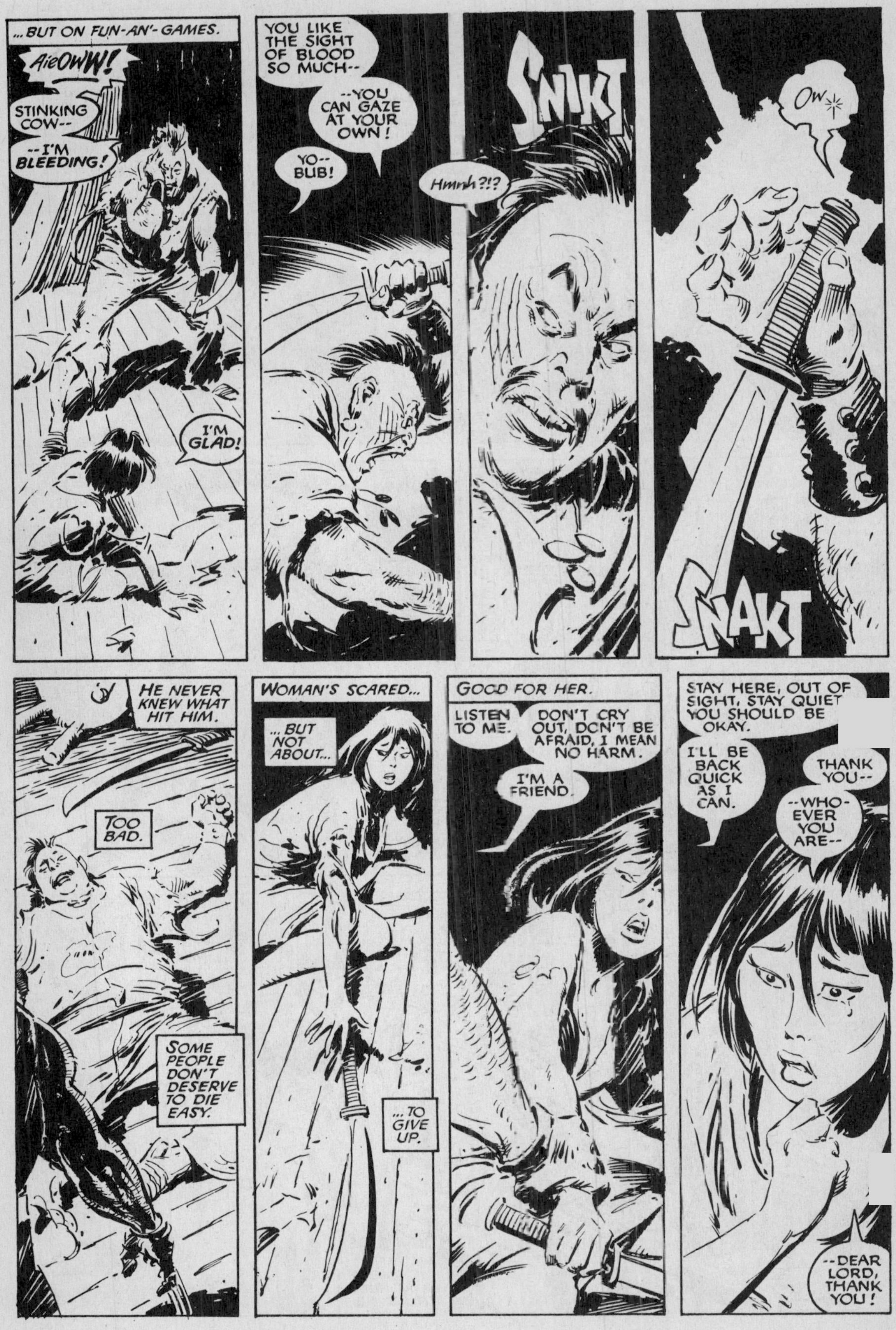
...BUT ON FUN-AN'-GAMES.
AieOWW!
STINKING COW--
--I'M BLEEDING!
I'M GLAD!
YOU LIKE THE SIGHT OF BLOOD SO MUCH--
--YOU CAN GAZE AT YOUR OWN!
YO--BUB!
SNIKT
Hmnh?!?
OW
SNAKT
HE NEVER KNEW WHAT HIT HIM.
TOO BAD.
SOME PEOPLE DON'T DESERVE TO DIE EASY.
WOMAN'S SCARED...
...BUT NOT ABOUT...
...TO GIVE UP.
GOOD FOR HER.
LISTEN TO ME.
DON'T CRY OUT, DON'T BE AFRAID, I MEAN NO HARM.
I'M A FRIEND.
STAY HERE, OUT OF SIGHT, STAY QUIET YOU SHOULD BE OKAY.
I'LL BE BACK QUICK AS I CAN.
THANK YOU--
--WHO-EVER YOU ARE--
--DEAR LORD, THANK YOU!

I'M HOMING ON A SPECIFIC SCENT.

FOLLOWED IT FROM PLANE TO VILLAGE...

... FINALLY TO THIS HUT.

A BREATH TELLS ME I'M ALMOST TOO LATE, A LOOK CONFIRMS IT.

SNKT!

KOJIMA?

< KOJIMA NOBURO, CAN YOU HEAR ME? > *

< WHO... SPEAKS? I... >

< ... KNOW THAT VOICE? >

*TRANSLATED FROM THE JAPANESE:- BOB

< IT IS LOGAN. >

< LIAR! >

< A CHEAP TRICK-- AND I WILL NOT... BE DECEIVED. >

< LOGAN IS... DEAD. >

< THEN CONSIDER ME A GHOST. >

HE'LL HAVE NO TROUBLE DOING THAT, STRANGER...

... BECAUSE WHEN WE'RE THROUGH...

... A GHOST IS WHAT YOU'LL TRULY BE!

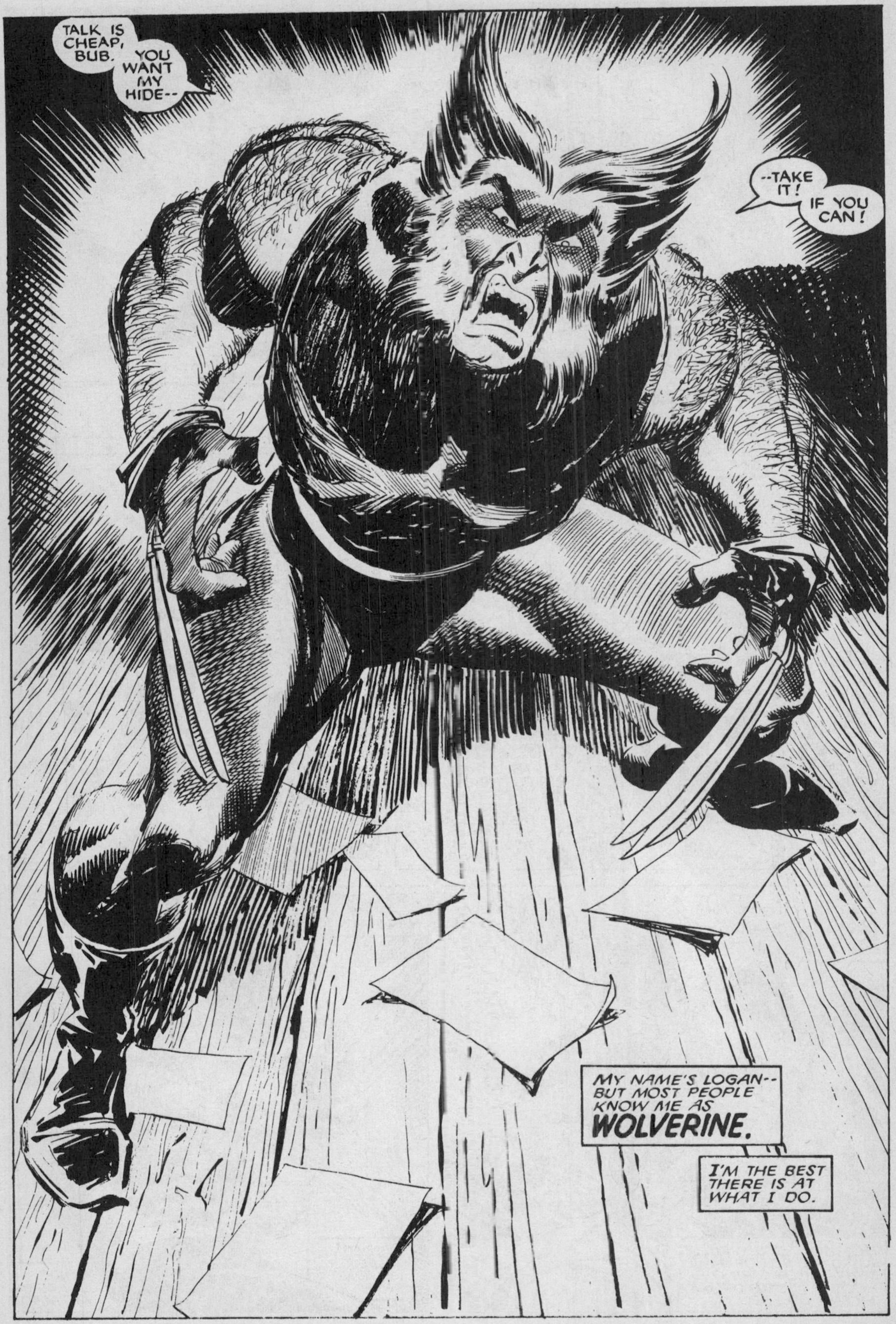
TALK IS CHEAP, BUB.
YOU WANT MY HIDE--
--TAKE IT!
IF YOU CAN!
MY NAME'S LOGAN-- BUT MOST PEOPLE KNOW ME AS WOLVERINE.
I'M THE BEST THERE IS AT WHAT I DO.

BUT WHAT I DO BEST...

...ISN'T VERY NICE.

I FIGURE ABOUT A HUNDRED PIRATES, GIVE OR TAKE A FEW.

REAL RATRACE CUTTHROAT LOW-LIFES, WHO PROBABLY CONSIDER THEMSELVES AS ROUGH-AN'-TOUGH AS MEN CAN BE.

MY KIND'A CROWD...

...MY KIND'A ODDS.

I ALMOST FEEL SORRY FOR 'EM.

I GOT 'IM, I GOT 'IM!

BUDDA BUDDA BUDDA

HOTSHOT POPS A FULL 40-ROUND BOX OF 9-MIL MY WAY, NOT CARING A HOOT IF HIS UZI DROPS FRIEND OR FOE...

...SO LONG AS HE NAILS ME.

THE BULLETS BURN LIKE FIRE.

WOULD'VE KILLED ANYONE ELSE.

THEY JUST MAKE ME MAD.

WHICH IS WHEN THINGS GET OUTTA HAND.

Y'SEE, I'M A MUTANT--

--BORN WITH A PARAHUMAN, SUPER-EFFICIENT HEALING FACTOR...

..THAT CAN DEAL WITH ANY ILLNESS OR POISON...

...OR WOUND.

MAKES ME WAY STRONGER'N NORMAL, FASTER, TOUGHER.

MAKES MY SENSES KEENER'N ANY ANIMAL'S.

IN ADDITION, MY BONES ARE LACED WITH ADAMANTIUM-- THE STRONGEST METAL KNOWN--

--SO THEY'RE VIRTUALLY UNBREAKABLE.

DON'T KNOW HOW THAT HAPPENED...

...OR WHO'S RESPONSIBLE--

-- DON'T MUCH CARE ANY-MORE.

I AM WHAT I AM.

TOO BAD FOR THESE CLOWNS.

FINALLY, I HAVE CLAWS.

SIX OF 'EM, THREE IN EACH HAND-- EXTENDING FROM BIONIC HOUSINGS IMPLANTED IN MY FOREARMS.

BLADES ARE PURE ADAMANTIUM, HONED SO KEEN THEY'LL CUT THROUGH ANYTHING.

SAVED MY BUTT TOO MANY TIMES TO COUNT.

USUALLY, I'M RESTRAINED ABOUT USING 'EM.

SKRAM!

NOT TONIGHT.

WHILE EVERYBODY'S FIGHTING... ...THIS IS MY BEST CHANCE TO ESCAPE.

BUT THEN-- WHAT OF MR. KOJIMA-- AND THE OTHERS...?

I'M PART OF THE FLIGHT CREW-- EVEN IF I'M ONLY A STEWARDESS-- THE PASSENGERS ARE MY RESPONSIBILITY.

I CAN'T DESERT THEM.

OH-- POOR MR. KOJIMA--

--WHAT DID THEY WANT...

...TO MAKE THEM TORTURE YOU SO?

NOBURO KOJIMA IS THE PERSONAL SECRETARY OF THE WOMAN I LOVE, MARIKO YASHIDA-- HEAD OF ONE OF JAPAN'S MOST POWERFUL NOBLE HOUSES--

--SOON AS I HEARD HE WAS ON THE MISSING PLANE...

...I STARTED SEARCHING.

MORE I DISCOVERED, ALONG THE WAY...

...THE GRIMMER I GOT.

I'M AN X-MAN.

MUTANTS LIKE ME, BAND OF SUPER HEROES. GOOD PEOPLE. IDEALISTS. DREAMERS-- FOREVER LOOKING FOR THE BEST IN OTHERS.

WITH THEM, KILLING IS A LAST RESORT.

WITH ME, IT'S SECOND-NATURE.

KIAI!

THUK

I TAKE THE WORLD AS IT IS, AN' GIVE BETTER THAN I GET.

KTANG!

?!?!

COME AT ME WITH A SWORD.

I'LL MEET YOU WITH A SWORD.

YOU WANT MERCY.

SHOW A LITTLE, FIRST.

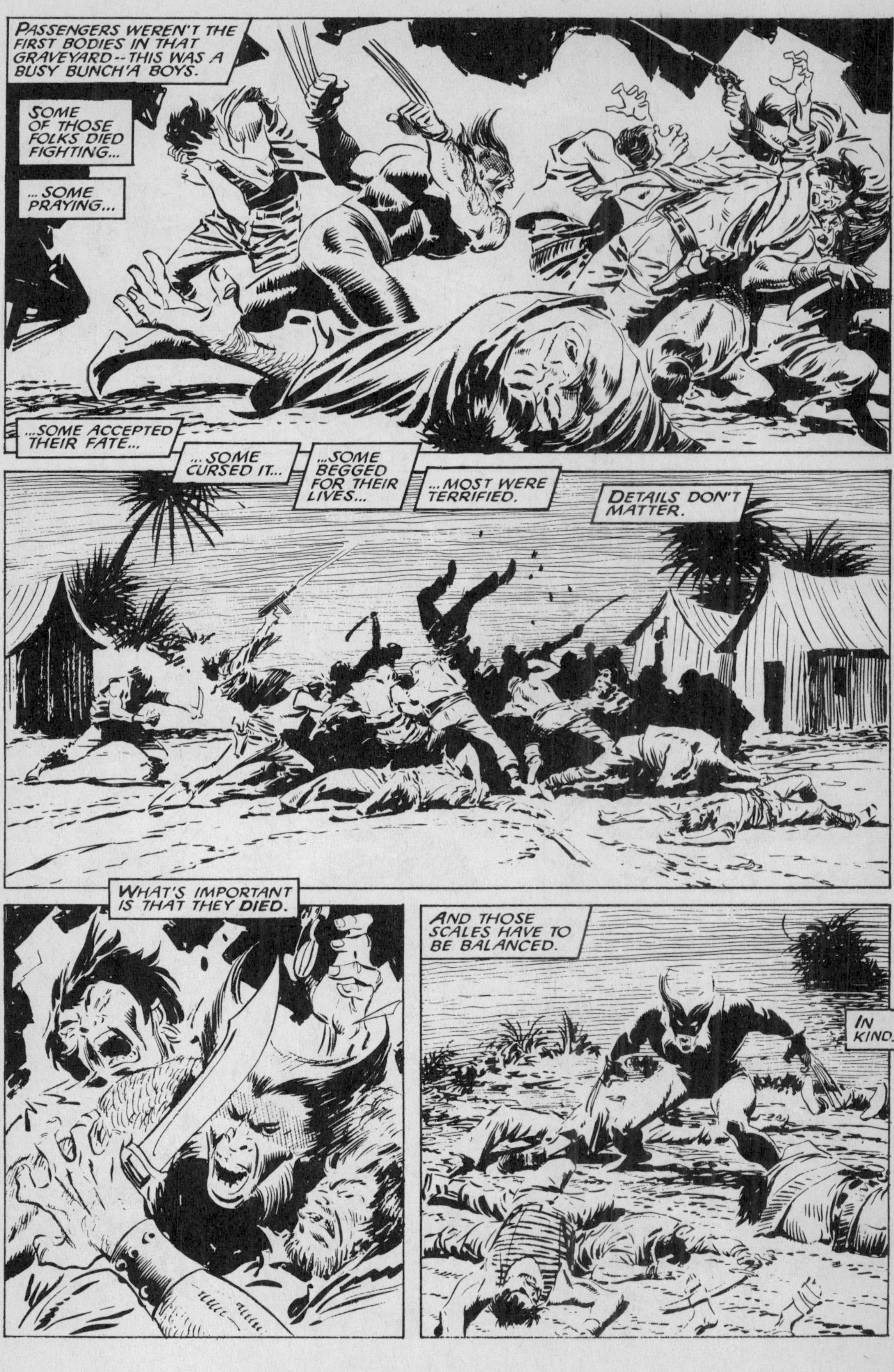
PASSENGERS WEREN'T THE FIRST BODIES IN THAT GRAVEYARD--THIS WAS A BUSY BUNCH'A BOYS.
SOME OF THOSE FOLKS DIED FIGHTING...
...SOME PRAYING...
...SOME ACCEPTED THEIR FATE...
...SOME CURSED IT...
...SOME BEGGED FOR THEIR LIVES...
...MOST WERE TERRIFIED.
DETAILS DON'T MATTER.
WHAT'S IMPORTANT IS THAT THEY DIED.
AND THOSE SCALES HAVE TO BE BALANCED.
IN KIND.

CHEONG?

LAL??

AMRAM SINGH ???

HANRAHAN?!

KRAUSE--

--ANSWER ME, YOU RENEGADE LEGIONNAIRE DOG--

--ROHMER!

IS ANYONE THERE?!

THIS ISN'T FUNNY--

--STOP FOOLING ABOUT--

--ANSWER ME!

I'M HERE.

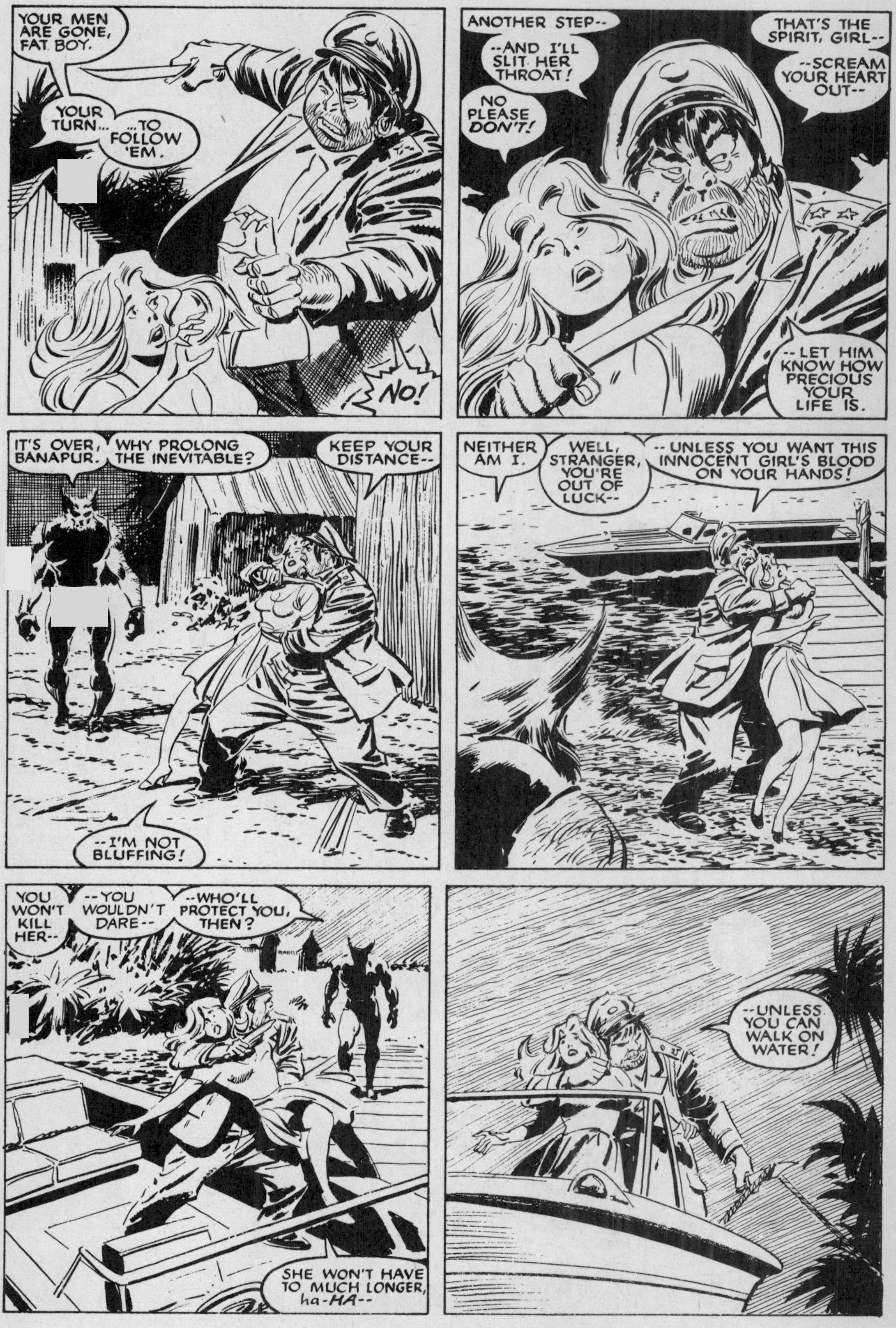

YOUR MEN ARE GONE, FAT BOY.
YOUR TURN... ...TO FOLLOW 'EM.
NO!
ANOTHER STEP--
--AND I'LL SLIT HER THROAT!
NO PLEASE DON'T!
THAT'S THE SPIRIT, GIRL--
--SCREAM YOUR HEART OUT--
--LET HIM KNOW HOW PRECIOUS YOUR LIFE IS.
IT'S OVER, BANAPUR.
WHY PROLONG THE INEVITABLE?
KEEP YOUR DISTANCE--
--I'M NOT BLUFFING!
NEITHER AM I.
WELL, STRANGER, YOU'RE OUT OF LUCK--
--UNLESS YOU WANT THIS INNOCENT GIRL'S BLOOD ON YOUR HANDS!
YOU WON'T KILL HER--
--YOU WOULDN'T DARE--
--WHO'LL PROTECT YOU, THEN?
SHE WON'T HAVE TO MUCH LONGER, ha-HA--
--UNLESS YOU CAN WALK ON WATER!

SHE'S SERVED HER PURPOSE, BANAPUR, LET HER GO.

WHY SHOULD I DO SO FOOLISH A THING?

SHE'LL KEEP ME COMPANY ON THE ROAD.

AND BRING A PRETTY PRICE FROM THE SLAVERS.

SO LONG, SUCKER!

COCKY SONUVAGUN FIGURES HE'S HOME FREE...

...THAT NOTHING CAN STOP HIM.

I KNOW BETTER.

I'LL GATHER MORE MEN-- PLENTY AVAILABLE-- AND COME AFTER YOU, STRANG ✳

BLAM!

LIGHT ONSHORE BREEZE...

...CARRIED THE STEWARDESS'S SCENT TO ME...

...AS WELL AS THE FACT SHE HAD A GUN.

THAT WAS FOR CAPTAIN LEE.

HE WAS A GOOD MAN.

I WISH I'D BEEN IN TIME TO SAVE HIM.

I WISH I'D BEEN ABLE TO SAVE 'EM ALL--

--INSTEAD OF AVENGE THEM.

BUT, IN MY LINE O' WORK, WISHES DON'T COUNT FOR MUCH.

< YOU NEED NOT PRETEND, MY LORD, I KNOW I AM DYING. >

< I MERELY PRAY THAT I DO SO... >

< ..WITH HONOR. >

< THE PIRATES, LOGAN-SAN-- EMPLOYED BY THE CULT OF THE BLACK BLADE! >

< THEY WANTED... THE MURAMASA SWORD! >

< LADY MARIKO... NEVER IMAGINED... CULT STILL ACTIVE-- OR SO POWERFUL! >

< FANATICS... STOP AT NOTHING... TO REGAIN THEIR... SACRED TALISMAN. >

< COURIERS... BRINGING IT FROM AMERICA... >

< ...ARRIVING MADRIPOOR AIRPORT... TOMORROW... >

< ...IN DEADLY DANGER! >

< THE COURIERS, KOJIMA-SAN-- WHAT ARE THEIR NAMES?! >

< TOO LATE FOR ME, MY LORD, BUT THE COURIERS... >

< ... MORE THAN THEIR LIVES... AT STAKE... >

< ... LOGAN-SAN, IF THE LEGENDS ARE TRUE... >

< ...THAT SWORD OF EVIL... >

< ... CAN CORRUPT... >

< ... CONSUME... >

< ...THEIR souls... >

I'LL DO WHAT I CAN, MY FRIEND.

AND GET THE WORD TO LADY MARIKO...

...THAT YOU SERVED HER FAITHFULLY AND WELL...

...AND DIED, A TRUE SAMURAI!

CULT GOES BACK CENTURIES-- SOME SAY TO THE BIRTH OF JAPAN-- LAST BIG RESURGENCE WAS IN THE 'TWENTIES, AS PART OF THE PRE-WAR RISE OF JAPANESE MILITARISM.

MADRIPOOR HERALD

TUES AUGUST 17 1986   35¢

SKYLINER HIJACKED

SURVIVORS OWE LIVES TO MYSTERY SAVIOR

PAGE 2

MacARTHUR'S COUNTER-INTELLIGENCE CREW SUPPOSEDLY TOOK CARE OF 'EM, DURING THE OCCUPATION.

THOUGHT WE DID A PRETTY GOOD JOB.

LIVE AN' LEARN.

SOVEREIGN AIRWAYS ANNOUNCES THE ARRIVAL AT MADRIPOOR AIRPORT...

...OF CONCORDE FLIGHT ONE FROM LOS ANGELES.

BEEN HERE THE WHOLE FLAMIN' DAY.

MEETING EVERY FLIGHT, SCOOPING OUT THE ARRIVING PASSENGERS.

AS IMPORTANTLY, CHECKING OUT THE PEOPLE MEETING THEM.

CUSTOMS AND IMMIG

NAME, PLEASE?

SO FAR, NO JOY.

LINDSAY McCABE.

ARE YOU AMERICAN?

BORN AND BRED, FROM SAN FRANCISCO.

YOUR PROFESSION?

ACTRESS

AND YOUR REASON FOR VISITING THE PRINCIPALITY OF MADRIPOOR?

TOURIST.

PASS, THEN. I HOPE YOU ENJOY YOUR STAY.

ME, TOO! I SURE AIM TO GIVE IT MY BEST SHOT!

SHE'S THE ONE!

BINGO!

THIS IS TROUBLE-- I KNOW THE GIRL. AND WORSE, SHE KNOWS WOLVERINE.

WHEN THE X-MEN WERE IN SAN FRAN A WHILE BACK, WE STAYED WITH HER AN' HER ROOMMATE, PRIVATE EYE JESSICA DREW.

AS FAR AS LINDSAY-- AN' THE WORLD-- ARE CONCERNED, THE X-MEN ARE DEAD. IF SHE RECOGNIZES ME, OUR SECRET'S BLOWN.

WHOOPS!

FORTUNATELY, I'VE CHANGED A LOT...

...SINCE WE LAST MET.

CAREFUL, FELLA-- WATCH WHERE YOU'RE GOING!

BEG PARDON, MISSY.

NO REACTION, NOT EVEN A FLICKER.

SO FAR, SO GOOD.

AN' THAT BRIEF CONTACT ENABLED ME TO GET A LOCK ON HER SCENT.

TAXI

IMPERIAL HOTEL, PLEASE.

I CAN FOLLOW HER ANYWHERE.

OTHERS HAVE THE SAME IDEA.

LOCAL MUSCLE. RENT-A-PUNKS, HIRED FOR THE JOB, JUST LIKE BANAPUR'S PIRATES.

AS EASILY TAKEN CARE OF.

SNIKT-SNAKT!

THE TIRE'S FLAT!

LOUSY, STINKING, IMPORTED PIECE OF JUNK!

CHANGE IT, YOU FOOL!

HURRY, WE'LL LOSE HER!!

SO MUCH FOR THEM.

CITY OF MADRIPOOR'S SPLIT BASICALLY IN TWO...

...ALONG MOSTLY ECONOMIC LINES...

...EACH HALF REPRESENTING THE MOST ABSOLUTE OF EXTREMES.

HIGHTOWN--ON THE PEAKS OVERLOOKING THE PORT AND LOWTOWN-- CONTAINS WEALTH BEYOND THE WILDEST DREAMS OF AVARICE. AND LUXURY TO MATCH.

WOW, oh WOW!

THIS IS ONE CLASSY HOTEL!

CONSIDERED BY MANY, MISS, TO BE THE FINEST IN THE WORLD.

I CAN SEE WHY.

THIS IS SO WILD AND WONDERFUL-- I FEEL LIKE DOROTHY, GONE TO OZ--

--HALF-SCARED I'LL WAKE UP AND DISCOVER IT'S ONLY A DREAM.

THANK HEAVEN SOMEONE ELSE IS FOOTING THE BILL.

I BET MY WHOLE BANK ACCOUNT WOULDN'T COVER A SINGLE NIGHT HERE.

YOUR SUITE, MISS!

HEY-- SORRY TO BE SUCH A BABBLER, IT'S JUST I'M SO EXCITED, WHAT AN ADVENTURE--!

PLEASE, MY DEAR, DON'T STOP TALKING ON OUR ACCOUNT.

INDEED, IT'S IN YOUR BEST INTERESTS...

...TO TELL US EVERYTHING WE DESIRE TO KNOW.

I BEG YOUR PARDON?!

INSIDE, GIRL!

BEHAVE YOURSELF-- DO AS YOU'RE TOLD--

--OR YOU WON'T LIVE TO REGRET IT!

HEY--

--WHAT IS THIS--

--WHO ARE YOU PEOPLE?!

THE LESS YOU KNOW...

...THE GREATER YOUR LIFE EXPECTANCY.

CONSIDER YOURSELF A MOUSE-- Ms. McCABE--

...IN THE JAWS OF THE TIGER!

NOTHING HERE!

NOT IN THIS ONE, EITHER!

AND THESE ARE ALL HER BAGS!

GIMME A BREAK, FELLAS.

CUSTOMS ALREADY DID THIS.

WHERE IS IT?!

WHERE IS WHAT?

DON'T PLAY GAMES, GIRL!

YOU ARE THE COURIER--

--WHERE HAVE YOU HIDDEN THE BLACK BLADE?!

PARDON ME ALL TO BLAZES...

...FOR BUTTIN' IN...

KRAKOOM!

...BUT THAT'S NO WAY TO TREAT A LADY.

THESE AREN'T LOCAL TALENT.

CULT, POSSIBLY-- AN' FROM THE WAY THEY REACT TO MY ENTRANCE, TOP PROFESSIONALS.

FOOL! YOUR INTRUSION HAS SIGNED...

...YOUR DEATH WA*AIEEEEYAIE!*

OTHER GUY'S QUICK ON THE DRAW.

NO PROBLEM.

KTHUD!

BUT THE GUN TAKES A BAD BOUNCE.

MY CLAWS COULD END THIS FRACAS ON THE SPOT.

BUT THEY'D ALSO BLOW MY COVER.

BETTER, FOR NOW, TO PLAY THINGS COOL AND LEAVE THE "DRAGON LADY" WITH THE UPPER HAND.

DON'T MOVE, STRANGER. I HAVE THE GUN.

BIG DEAL...

--I HAVE THE *LAMP!*

OW!

OKAY, MISTER--

--HOW 'BOUT YOU MAKE LIKE A GENTLE-MAN...

...BEFORE SOMETHING HAPPENS WE'LL BOTH REGRET.

MR. *EASTWOOD* TAUGHT ME HOW TO USE THIS THING, BUT I'M NO EXPERT, AND TARGETS DON'T BLEED AND I'M NOT SCARED STIFF WHEN I SHOOT AT 'EM.

WHICH MEANS, IT WON'T TAKE MUCH TO MAKE THIS GO OFF.

IN CASE YOU HADN'T NOTICED, DARLIN'...

...I'M THE ONE WHO CAME TO YOUR RESCUE.

THEY'RE THE BAD GUYS.

I'M ON YOUR SIDE.

YOU'RE THE MAN FROM THE AIRPORT, WHO BUMPED INTO ME.

YUP. KOJIMA SENT ME.

I'D PREFER HEARING THAT FROM HIM.

CAN'T. HE'S DEAD.

FLIGHT GOT HIJACKED A WEEK AGO, BY THE SAME OUT-FIT WHO'S AFTER YOU NOW.

DEAD? A *WEEK* AGO?!

BUT THAT'S IMPOSSIBLE-- I SPOKE TO HIM YESTERDAY, BEFORE LEAVING SAN FRANCISCO!

WHOEVER YOU SPOKE TO, MISSY, IT WASN'T HIM.

BUT JESSIE-- MY PARTNER-- SHE'S THE ONE CARRYING THE SWORD--

--SHE'S ON HER WAY TO *MEET* HIM!

WHICH MEANS, SHE COULD WELL BE ON HER WAY...

...TO HER OWN *FUNERAL.*

NEXT:

The Black Blade

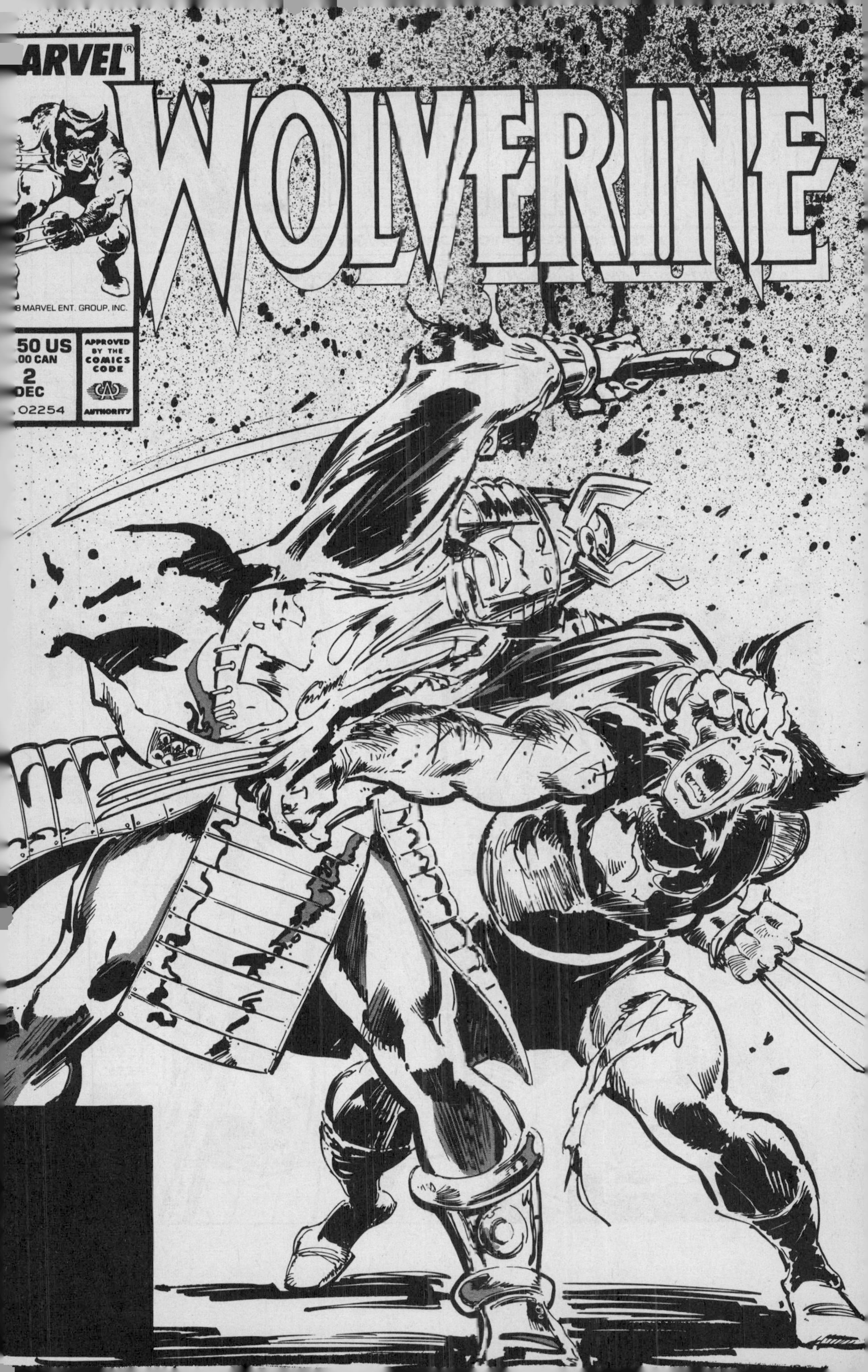
MARVEL
WOLVERINE
8 MARVEL ENT. GROUP, INC.
50 US
.00 CAN
2
DEC
02254
APPROVED BY THE COMICS CODE AUTHORITY

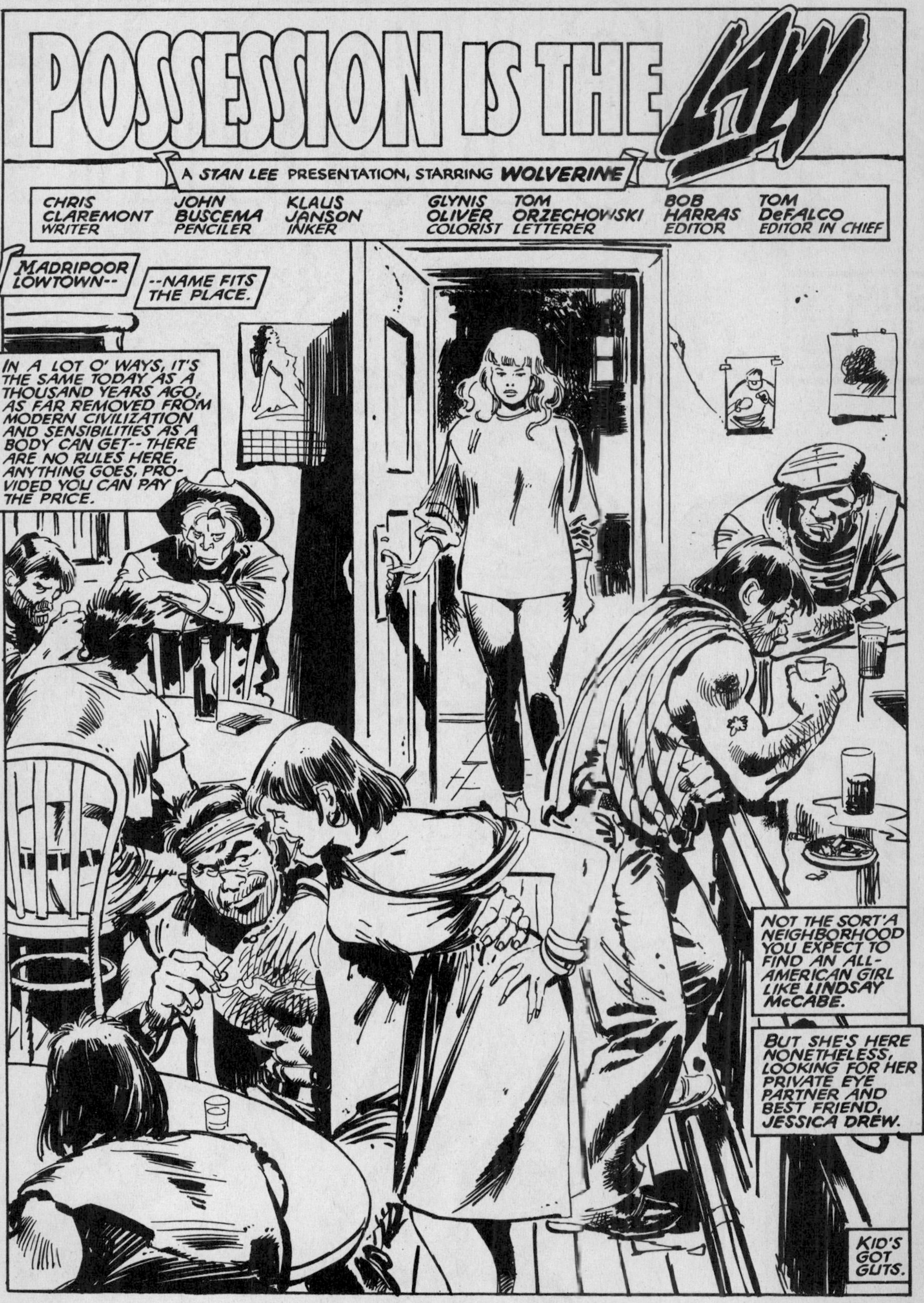

POSSESSION IS THE LAW
A STAN LEE PRESENTATION, STARRING WOLVERINE
CHRIS CLAREMONT WRITER
JOHN BUSCEMA PENCILER
KLAUS JANSON INKER
GLYNIS OLIVER COLORIST
TOM ORZECHOWSKI LETTERER
BOB HARRAS EDITOR
TOM DeFALCO EDITOR IN CHIEF
MADRIPOOR LOWTOWN--
--NAME FITS THE PLACE.
IN A LOT O' WAYS, IT'S THE SAME TODAY AS A THOUSAND YEARS AGO, AS FAR REMOVED FROM MODERN CIVILIZATION AND SENSIBILITIES AS A BODY CAN GET-- THERE ARE NO RULES HERE, ANYTHING GOES, PROVIDED YOU CAN PAY THE PRICE.
NOT THE SORT'A NEIGHBORHOOD YOU EXPECT TO FIND AN ALL-AMERICAN GIRL LIKE LINDSAY McCABE.
BUT SHE'S HERE NONETHELESS, LOOKING FOR HER PRIVATE EYE PARTNER AND BEST FRIEND, JESSICA DREW.
KID'S GOT GUTS.

TROUBLE IS, IN A DUMP LIKE THIS... ...COURAGE DON'T COUNT FOR MUCH.

SHE'S YOUNG, SHE'S BLOND, SHE'S CLEAN--

--THAT MAKES HER FLAMIN' NEAR UNIQUE IN LOWTOWN...

...A PEARL BEYOND PRICE.

MOMENT SHE'S INSIDE, LOCAL JOYBOYS MAKE THEIR MOVE.

SHE DOESN'T NEED TO KNOW THE LANGUAGE TO UNDERSTAND WHAT'S BEIN' SAID...

...OR THAT THEY WON'T TAKE "NO" FOR AN ANSWER.

WHICH IS WHERE I COME IN.

KID'S WITH ME.

THAT A PROBLEM FOR YOU BOYS?

DIDN'T THINK SO.

NICE CROWD.

I WARNED YOU NOT TO COME.

THIS IS WHERE OUR CONTACT ARRANGED TO MEET JESSIE...

...HOW BAD CAN IT BE?

DON'T ANSWER, OKAY?

BRAINS, TOO-- GOTTA GIVE HER CREDIT-- SHE KNOWS NOW THAT "CONTACT" WAS AN IMPOSTOR, WHICH MEANS HE CHOSE HERE BECAUSE IT'S AN IDEAL PLACE TO TAKE THE MERCHANDISE AN' LEAVE THE COURIER'S BODY BEHIND.

COPS WON'T DO ANYTHING ABOUT IT, LOCALS WON'T CARE.

HERE'S YOUR USUAL, PATCH.

I'LL HAVE THE SAME.

I'D RECONSIDER THAT, IF I WERE YOU.

YOU FIGURE I CAN'T HANDLE IT?

A BODY SHOULD KNOW ITS LIMITATIONS, MISS.

AN' TEST 'EM, MISTER...

...EVERY CHANCE IT GETS.

YOUR FUNERAL.

HOUSE SPECIAL, SWEETIE.

DRINK IT AN' DROP!

WE'LL SEE!

WE SURE WILL.

NEED A HAND, SWEETIE?

Whoops!

NO WAY! I CAN MAKE IT BACK UP...

...ON MY OWN!

SAME AGAIN, OKAY?

WHATEVER I HAVE TO!

Whew! WOW! NICE KICK! TASTY, TOO!

WHAT'RE YOU TRYIN' TO PROVE?

I DON'T BELIEVE IT!

ASIDE FROM ME, PATCH IS THE ONLY ONE COULD EVER HANDLE THAT CONCOCTION.

YOU SHOULD HANG AROUND MOVIE CREWS ON LOCATION, THERE ARE REAL HARD-CASE BOOZERS.

ONE TIME, SHOOTING IN BAJA, THEY CAME UP WITH HOME-BREW THAT MAKES THIS TASTE LIKE MILK.

'COURSE, HAVING A MISSPENT SUBURBAN YOUTH HELPS.

IF IT ISN'T A TRADE SECRET...

...WHAT'S IN IT?

LITTLE O' THIS, LITTLE O' THAT-- SOME GIN, SOME VODKA, SCOTCH FOR KICK...

...SODA FOR COLOR, PLUS

YEAH-- HOW'D YOU KNOW?

THAT'S *LONG ISLAND ICED TEA.* RITE OF PASSAGE IN HIGH SCHOOL WAS GETTING SICK AS DOGS ON THAT STUFF.

YOU FROM 'ROUND THERE, SWEETIE?

MASSAPEQUA. BERNER HIGH.

AMITYVILLE HIGH!

WHY, WE'RE PRACTICALLY NEIGHBORS!

I'M BELLE.

LINDSAY, HEY, YOU KNOW THE BOATHOUSE, ON MERRICK ROAD--?

DO I EVER--! WHY, ONCE...

HATE TO INTERRUPT CLASS REUNION, LADIES, BUT SOME OF US ARE HERE ON BUSINESS.

YEAH. RIGHT. SORRY. FORGOT. LATER, BELLE, OKAY?

WHAT'S OUR NEXT MOVE, "PATCH"?

YOU STAY DOWN HERE...

...WHILE I LOOK FOR JESSICA.

THE HECK I WILL.

I'M COMING WITH YOU, BUB!

YOU, GIRL, ARE DOIN' WHAT YOU'RE TOLD.

LISTEN TO YOURSELF-- YOU'RE MORE'N HALFWAYS LOOPED.

I RUN INTO TROUBLE, I CAN'T AFFORD A ZONED OUT SPACE CADET AT MY BACK. SURE WAY TO GET SOMEONE KILLED.

BELLE, I'M TRUSTING YOU-- LOOK AFTER HER.

NO PROBLEM, PATCH. SHE'LL BE FINE.

OF ALL THE MACHO, ARROGANT--!

WHO THE HECK D'YOU THINK YOU *ARE,* BUB?!

PROB'LY THE BEST FRIEND YOU'LL *EVER* HAVE IN THIS TOWN, SWEETIE.

Humph!

I DON'T NEED HIM.

I CAN TAKE CARE OF MYSELF.

ON SECOND THOUGHT...

...*uh,* BELLE...

CAN YOU TEND BAR?

I'M A *PROFESSIONAL* ACTRESS--

--SOME DAYS IT FEELS...

...LIKE I WAS *BORN* TENDING BAR!

IT'S HOW YOU PAY THE BILLS BETWEEN GIGS.

THEN HOP ON OVER...

AS SOON DONE AS SAID.

WHERE'S PATCH? HE SHOULD SEE THIS--

--I'LL SHOW HIM *LOWWUP!*

VERY NICE, DEAR. DEFINITELY OLYMPIC CALIBER.

WOW-- GUESS I *AM* BOMBED!

I'M SORRY, I MADE A MESS. I *AM* A MESS!

SO FIRST WE CLEAN *YOU* UP.

AND THEN YOU CLEAN *THIS* UP.

PATCH, PEOPLE CALL ME-- --AS GOOD A NAME AS ANY--

...SINCE I CAN'T USE MY OWN.

WORLD BELIEVES WOLVERINE TO BE DEAD.

AIN'T ABOUT TO CHANGE THAT NOTION.

FOR ME, THIS CAPER BEGAN WITH A SKYJACKED 747 AND A DYING FRIEND...

...CULT OF THE BLACK BLADE...

...FANATICS... STOP AT NOTHING TO REGAIN THEIR SACRED TALISMAN...

...COURIERS... BRINGING IT FROM AMERICA...

... IN DEADLY DANGER!

LOCAL PIRATES HAD BEEN HIRED TO BRING DOWN THE PLANE.

IN THE PROCESS, THEY SLAUGHTERED MOST OF THE PASSENGERS AN' CREW.

I PUT 'EM OUT OF BUSINESS.

THE NEXT DAY, AT MADRIPOOR INTERNATIONAL, WHEN THE 'STATES FLIGHT ARRIVED, I WAS WAITING.

COURIER TURNED OUT TO BE LINDSAY.

BAD JOSS-- SHE KNEW ME FROM THE OLD DAYS.

IF SHE RECOGNIZED ME AS WOLVERINE, MY COVER WOULD BE TOTALLY BLOWN.

BY THE WAY THINGS TURNED OUT, I HAD TO TAKE THE CHANCE.

THE CULT WAS WAITING AT HER HOTEL.

WITHOUT ME, THEY'D HAVE KIDNAPED HER-- OR WORSE.

SO HERE I AM, MIDDLE OF THE FLAMIN' NIGHT, CRUISIN' THIS FLEAPIT JOYHOUSE, TRYIN' TO SPOT A SCENT I BARELY REMEMBER...

...AN' HOPIN' THAT WHEN I FIND JESSICA DREW--

-- WHO WAS ACTUALLY CARRYIN' THE TALISMAN, WHILE LINDSAY PLAYED THE DECOY--

--SHE'LL STILL BE ALIVE, AN' WHOLE.

BUT AS IT TURNS OUT...

...I DON'T NEED JESSIE'S SCENT...

...TO TELL ME WHICH IS THE RIGHT ROOM...

...OR THAT I'M TOO LATE.

IN THE HANDS OF A MASTER...

...THERE'S PROBABLY NO DEADLIER SINGLE-COMBAT WEAPON IN THE WORLD, IN ALL HISTORY...

...THAN THE DAI-KATANA, THE JAPANESE SAMURAI SWORD.

THESE BRAVOS LEARNED THAT THE HARD WAY.

NOW, IT'S MY TURN...

...TO FOLLOW IN THEIR FOOTSTEPS...

...AND FACE THE LION IN ITS DEN.

BUT BEFORE ANYTHING CAN HAPPEN...

KRA KOW!

IF YOU VALUE YOUR LIFE, GAIJIN...

...STAND ASIDE AND INTERFERE NO LONGER...

...IN AFFAIRS THAT ARE NONE OF YOUR CONCERN.

I KNOW THE ARMOR, I KNOW THE WEAPON, I KNOW THE MAN-- ONLY TOO WELL-- KENUICHIO HARADA.

THE SILVER SAMURAI.

WORSE, HE KNOWS ME. AN' HATES MY GUTS.

JUST WHAT THIS CAPER FLAMIN' NEEDS.

GOT NO IDEA WHAT HE WANTS WITH THE MURAMASA SWORD. DON'T MUCH CARE, EITHER.

I'M NOT ABOUT TO LET HIM TAKE IT.

PROBLEM IS, WORLD BELIEVES ME--AS WOLVERINE, ALONG WITH THE REST O' THE X-MEN--TO BE DEAD. THAT'S HOW WE WANT THINGS.

SAMURAI RECOGNIZES ME. OUR COVER'S BLOWN.

KWUD.

SO I CAN'T FIGHT LIKE MYSELF.

PROBLEM WITH THAT IS, ANY LESS'N MY BEST...

...GIVES HARADA THE ADVANTAGE.

KA-ROWWW

HE'S A MUTANT, SAME AS ME.

MY POWER'S A HEALING FACTOR.

HIS IS TO CHANNEL ENERGY THROUGH HIS SWORD BLADE...

...THAT ENABLES IT TO CUT THROUGH ANYTHING.

INCLUDING, HE LIKES TO BOAST, MY ADAMANTIUM LACED SKELETON.

ONE WAY TO END THIS, QUICK AN' SURE, BEFORE IT GOES THAT FAR.

I COULD "POP" MY CLAWS. HE WON'T BE EXPECTING THAT.

HE'LL BE DEAD BEFORE HE KNOWS IT.

BUT HE'S A WARRIOR, AND IN HIS OWN WAY, AN HONORABLE MAN.

LIKE ME.

SO I FIGHT FAIR.

AN' PAY THE PRICE.

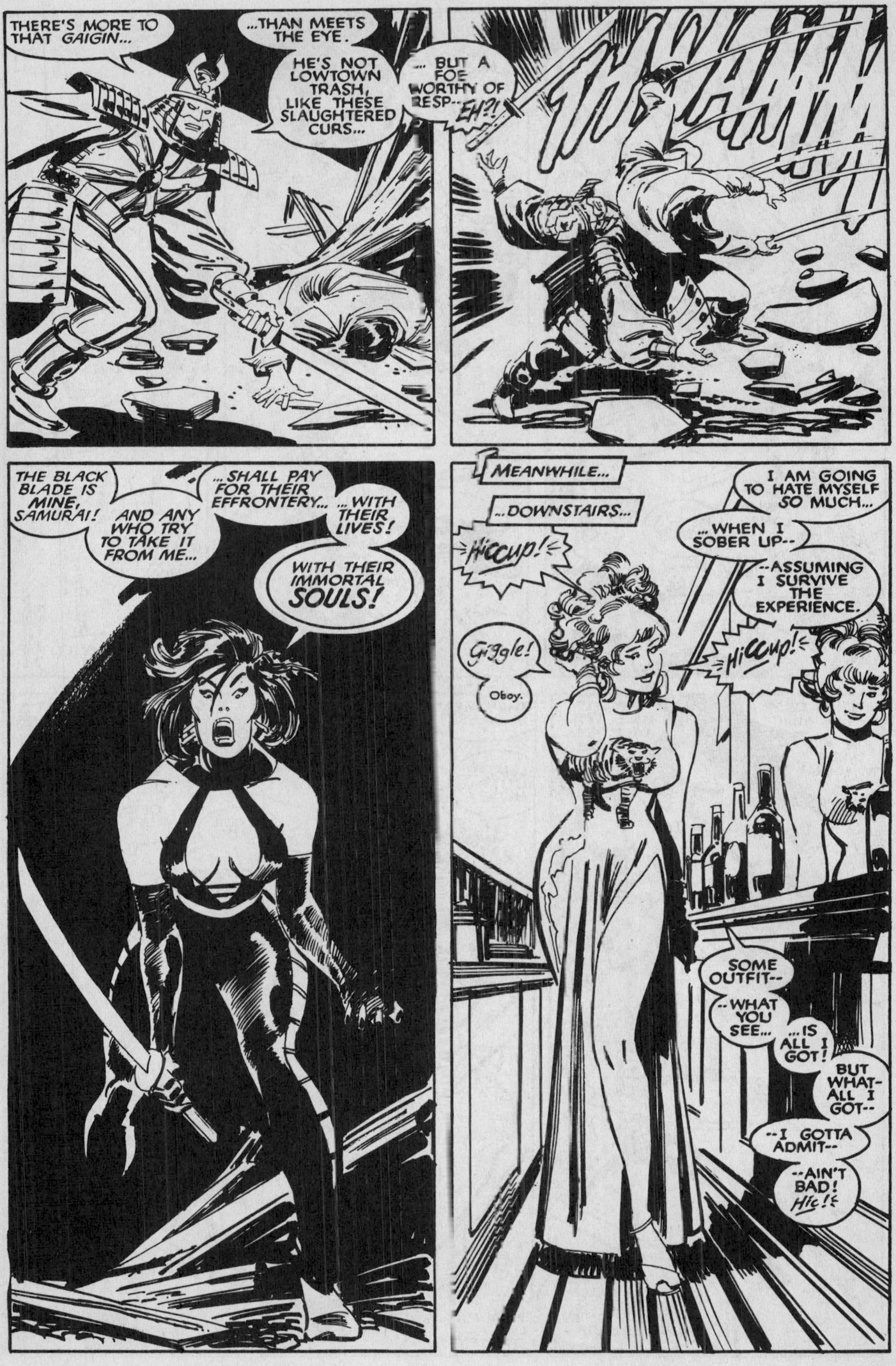
THERE'S MORE TO THAT GAIGIN...
...THAN MEETS THE EYE.
HE'S NOT LOWTOWN TRASH, LIKE THESE SLAUGHTERED CURS...
... BUT A FOE WORTHY OF RESP-- EH?!
THE BLACK BLADE IS MINE, SAMURAI!
AND ANY WHO TRY TO TAKE IT FROM ME...
...SHALL PAY FOR THEIR EFFRONTERY...
...WITH THEIR LIVES!
WITH THEIR IMMORTAL SOULS!
MEANWHILE...
...DOWNSTAIRS...
Hiccup!
I AM GOING TO HATE MYSELF SO MUCH...
...WHEN I SOBER UP--
--ASSUMING I SURVIVE THE EXPERIENCE.
Giggle!
Oboy.
Hiccup!
SOME OUTFIT--
--WHAT YOU SEE...
...IS ALL I GOT!
BUT WHAT-ALL I GOT--
--I GOTTA ADMIT--
--AIN'T BAD! Hic!

WHAT THE--?!

HEY-- A FIGHT!

JOIN IN?

TAKE SIDES?

TAKE BETS!

FOR ALL THY SKILL, SAMURAI-- --THY VAUNTED POWER-- --THOU'RT NO MORE A MATCH FOR ME...

...THAN THOSE OTHERS.

HOLY COW-- THAT'S JESSICA!?!

WHY'S SHE DRESSED LIKE THAT, AND TALKING SO STRANGELY?!

WHAT HAPPENED TO PATCH?!!

JESSICA DREW, HEAR ME!

I'VE NO WISH TO HARM YOU--!

WORDS WILL NOT SAVE YOU, FOOL!

AND THAT NAME IS OF NO MORE IMPORT TO THE MISTRESS OF THE BLACK BLADE...

...THAN THE LIFE IT REPRESENTS.

THEY MEAN BUSINESS!

WRECK THE PLACE!

AIN'T WORTH MY NECK TO PLAY THE HERO!

THAT'S WHY THEY CALL A GUN AN "EQUAL- IZER," ROSCOE.

LEMME OUTTA HERE!

LET 'EM!

GANGWAY!

THEY FIGHT PRETTY GOOD, RUFE.

BLACK BLADE.

OUTFIT IN TOWN'S OFFERIN' SERIOUS BUCKS FOR IT, NO QUESTIONS ASKED.

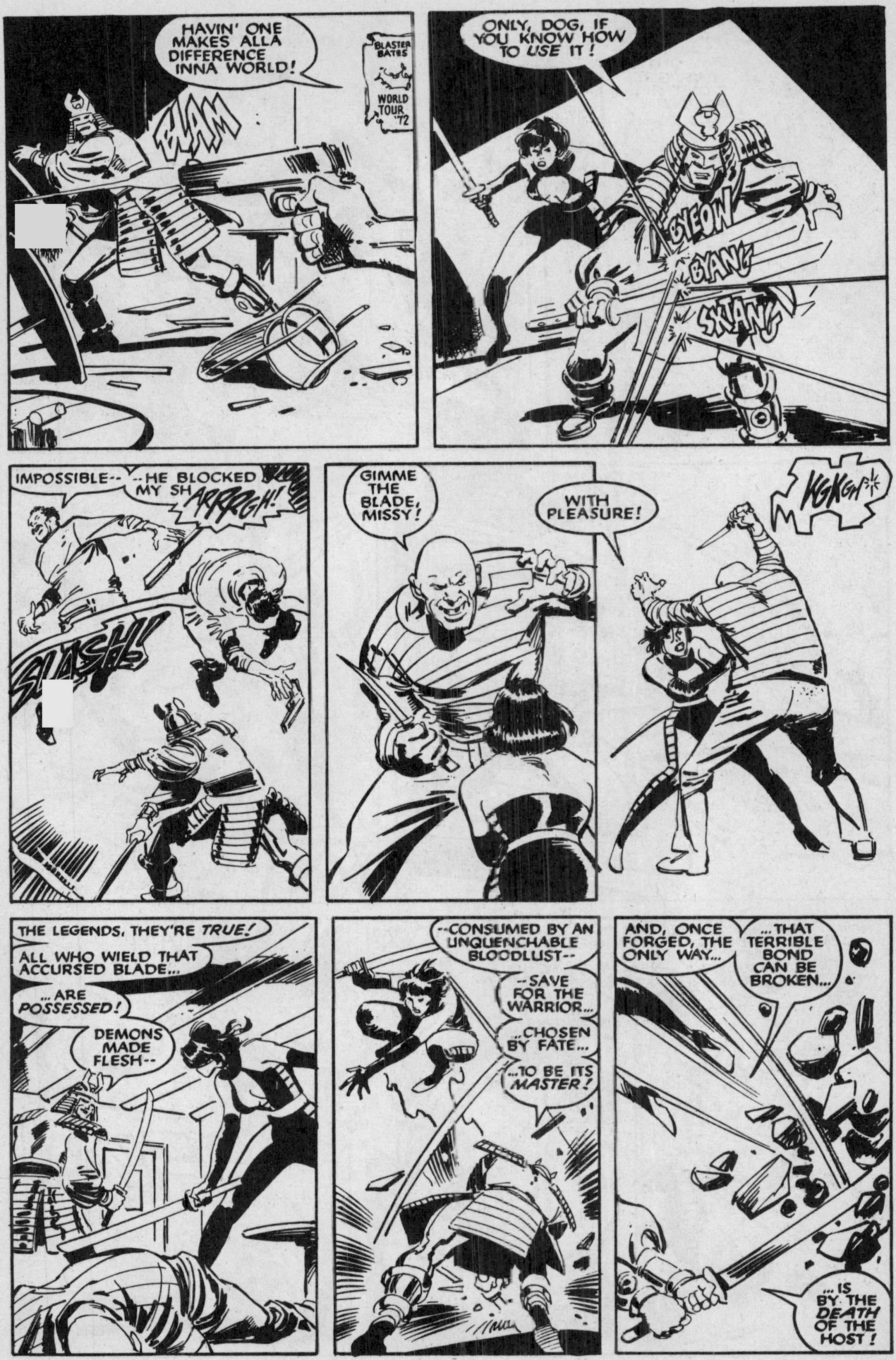
HAVIN' ONE MAKES ALLA DIFFERENCE INNA WORLD!
BLASTER BATES WORLD TOUR '72
BLAM
ONLY, DOG, IF YOU KNOW HOW TO USE IT!
GYEOW
BYANG
SKANG
IMPOSSIBLE--
--HE BLOCKED MY SH ARRRGH!
SLASH!
GIMME THE BLADE, MISSY!
WITH PLEASURE!
THE LEGENDS, THEY'RE TRUE!
ALL WHO WIELD THAT ACCURSED BLADE...
...ARE POSSESSED!
DEMONS MADE FLESH--
--CONSUMED BY AN UNQUENCHABLE BLOODLUST--
--SAVE FOR THE WARRIOR...
...CHOSEN BY FATE...
...TO BE ITS MASTER!
AND, ONCE FORGED, THE ONLY WAY...
...THAT TERRIBLE BOND CAN BE BROKEN...
...IS BY THE DEATH OF THE HOST!

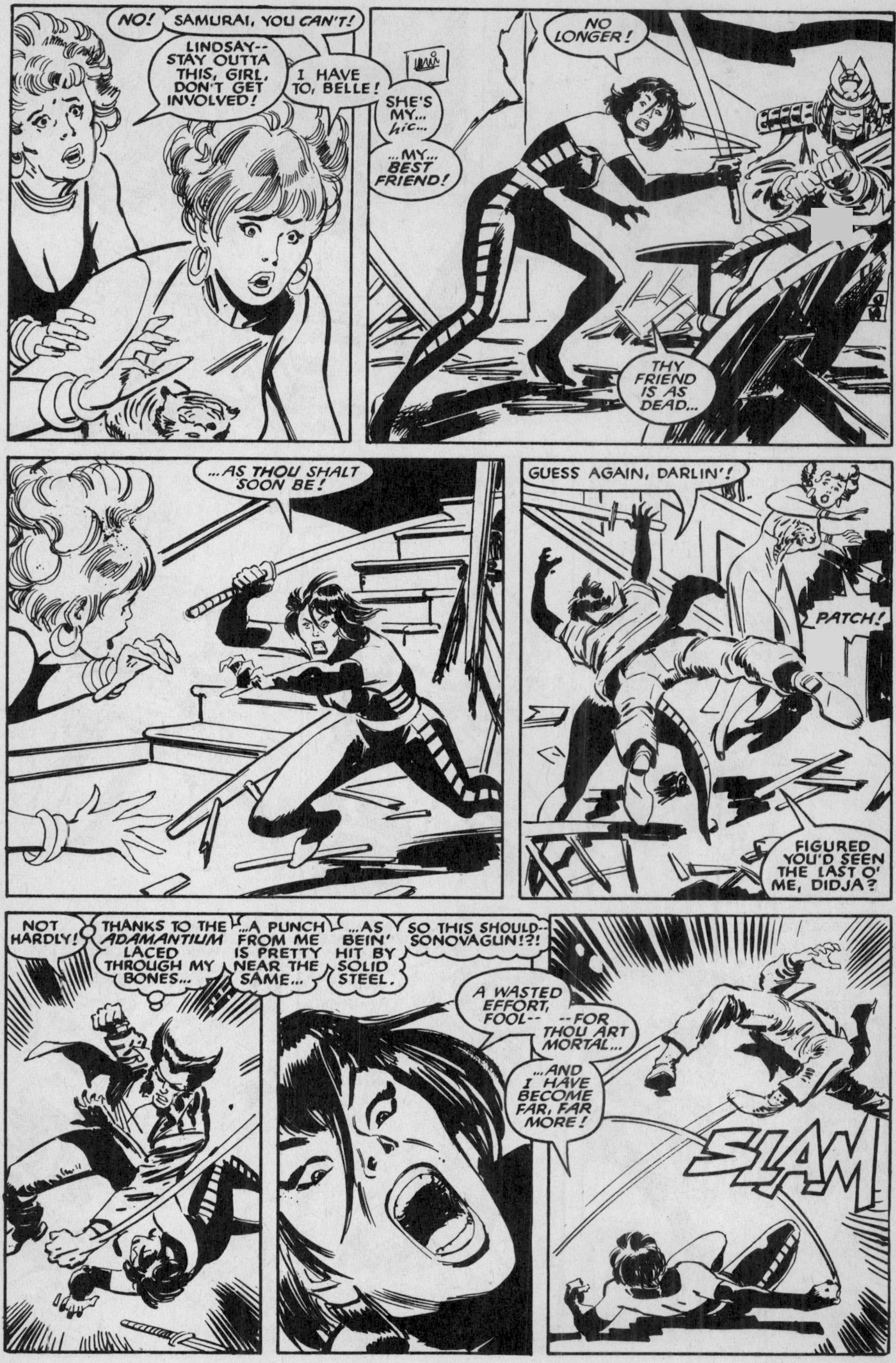
NO!
SAMURAI, YOU CAN'T!
LINDSAY-- STAY OUTTA THIS, GIRL, DON'T GET INVOLVED!
I HAVE TO, BELLE!
SHE'S MY... hic...
...MY... BEST FRIEND!
NO LONGER!
THY FRIEND IS AS DEAD...
...AS THOU SHALT SOON BE!
GUESS AGAIN, DARLIN'!
PATCH!
FIGURED YOU'D SEEN THE LAST O' ME, DIDJA?
NOT HARDLY!
THANKS TO THE ADAMANTIUM LACED THROUGH MY BONES...
...A PUNCH FROM ME IS PRETTY NEAR THE SAME...
...AS BEIN' HIT BY SOLID STEEL.
SO THIS SHOULD-- SONOVAGUN!?!
A WASTED EFFORT, FOOL--
--FOR THOU ART MORTAL...
...AND I HAVE BECOME FAR, FAR MORE!
SLAM

WHAT NOW, HOTSHOT?! I HARDLY PULLED THAT PUNCH...

...DIDN'T FAZE HER A BIT.

SAMURAI AIN'T FARIN' MUCH BETTER.

I'M A LONER-- BY NATURE AN' PROFESSION.

I DON'T HAVE MANY FRIENDS.

MEANS I TEND TO CHERISH THE FEW I MAKE.

JESSICA DREW'S ON THAT LIST.

BUT IF HER PERSONALITY-- HER SELF-- HER SOUL--

--HAS BEEN CONSUMED BY THE SWORD...

...THEN KILLIN' HER NOT ONLY BECOMES NECESSARY...

SNIKT

...IT'S AN ACT OF MERCY.

BUT IN THE MEANTIME, UNTIL I KNOW FOR SURE, I GOT OTHER CARDS TO PLAY.

FIGHT'S CLEARED THE BAR, THERE'S NO ONE TO SEE ME USE MY CLAWS.

THEY'LL CUT ANYTHING...

...SO IT'S NO PROBLEM AT ALL TO END THE FIGHT...

...BY BRINGIN' DOWN THE HOUSE!

BLESSED AMATERASU--!?!

I FIGURE THE SAMURAI'S ARMOR'LL PROTECT HIM.

WON'T BREAK MY HEART IF IT DOESN'T.

I'M GAMBLIN' WHATEVER FORCE IS SUPER-CHARGIN' JESS'LL PROTECT HER, TOO.

IT DOES.

REAL WELL.

SHE ISN'T EVEN SCRATCHED.

IN THE BLINK OF AN EYE...

...SHE'S UP A WALL...

...AN' GONE.

YOU OKAY, McCABE?!

WHO... LOWERED THE BOOM?

LOWTOWN'S AS RATTY AS IT IS OLD.

DON'T TAKE MUCH TO BRING A BUILDING DOWN.

JESSICA-- SHE MAY BE TRAPPED!

NO SUCH LUCK.

STAY PUT. I'LL FOLLOW HER TRAIL.

AND WHEN YOU FIND HER?

I'LL DO WHAT I HAVE TO.

LIKE I SAID, A SMART GIRL. SHE KNOWS WHAT I MEAN.

I ONLY HOPE SHE HAS SENSE ENOUGH...

...NOT TO INTERFERE.

SOMEBODY'S PINNED UNDER THE RUBBLE.

HEY-- I COULD USE A HAND HERE, CLEARING AWAY THE MESS!

NICE CROWD-- ALL THEY DO IS WATCH AND MAKE =hic= REMARKS.

SAME TO YOU, FELLAS!

UGH-- DRESS IS SO TIGHT--

...I CAN HARDLY BREATHE...

...OR BEND OVER!

HOBOY! THE SAMURAI'S SWORD. AND-- SURPRISE, SURPRISE--

--THE MAN HIMSELF!

REMEMBER ME?

YOUR LADY FRIEND, VIPER, NEARLY KILLED ME.

AND THE PAIR OF YOU TRIED YOUR BEST TO DO THE SAME TO JESSIE. *

*IN SPIDER-WOMAN #'S 42-44 -- BOB "BEFORE MY TIME" HARRAS.

WHERE'S YOUR PARTNER?

WE HAVE PARTED COMPANY. TO ME, SHE IS AS ONE DEAD.

THEN MAYBE... ...YOU SHOULD...

...JOIN HER!

TROUBLE IS, I DON'T HAVE A KILLER INSTINCT.

YOU SPARED MY LIFE.

I'M ALREADY REGRETTING IT.

MY SWORD, IF YOU PLEASE.

A LIFE FOR A LIFE, SAMURAI--

--JESSICA'S FOR YOURS.

MS. McCABE--!

THE FLOOR--

--COLLAPSING--!

I HAVE YOU--!

A LIFE FOR A LIFE, Ms. McCABE--

--NOW WE STAND EVEN.

LIKE HECK WE DO --hic--

--WHY ARE YOU HERE, WHAT DO YOU WANT?!

THE BLACK BLADE. NO MORE... ...NO LESS.

ALL I WANT IS JESSICA BACK, THE WAY SHE WAS, ALIVE AND WHOLE.

YOU KNOW NOT WHAT YOU ASK.

I DON'T CARE!

YOU ARE IN NO POSITION TO MAKE DEMANDS...

...AND IN LESS OF ONE TO ENFORCE THEM.

TRY ME.

D'YOU WANT ME TO BEG? FINE-- NAME YOUR PRICE-- oh, SPIT!

GREAT! JUST WHEN THEY'RE NOT NEEDED...

...THE COPS ARRIVE.

Oh, SPARE ME!

GO WITH THEM. THIS IS WARRIOR'S WORK.

YOU ARE MAD, WOMAN.

YOU BETCHA! C'MON, LET'S SCRAM WHILE WE CAN.

IN THE OLD DAYS, JESS HAD SUPER-POWERS, WENT BY THE NAME SPIDER-WOMAN.

SHE HAD STRENGTH, AGILITY, SHE STUCK TO WALLS AND CEILINGS, PLUS SOME OTHER HANDY TALENTS.

GRAPEVINE SAID, SHE LOST 'EM ALL AWHILE BACK.*

*IN AVENGERS #241--BbmtH!

BIG FLAMIN' DEAL--SAME GRAPEVINE SAYS THE X-MEN ARE DEAD.

WHICH MAKES THIS CAPER THAT MUCH MORE DANGEROUS.

I THOUGHT I HAD KILLED THEE, UPSTAIRS AT THE BAR.

SWORD CUT ME DEEP. BLEEDIN' STOPPED, BUT IT STILL HURTS LIKE SIN.

YOU TRIED.

YOU AREN'T THE FIRST.

THIS TIME, WARRIOR, I'LL MAKE CERTAIN.

JESS DOESN'T MOVE LIKE HERSELF. SHE COMES AT ME WITH THE STANCE, THE GRACE OF A SAMURAI.

CAN'T HELP WONDERIN' WHAT WENT INTO THAT BLADE...

...TO MAKE IT ABLE TO DO THIS?

IF I DO NOTHING ELSE...

...I SWEAR...

...I'LL SMASH THAT SWORD TO BITS.

O'COURSE...

...TO DO THAT...

KIAI!

...I HAVE TO BE ALIVE.

SHOK

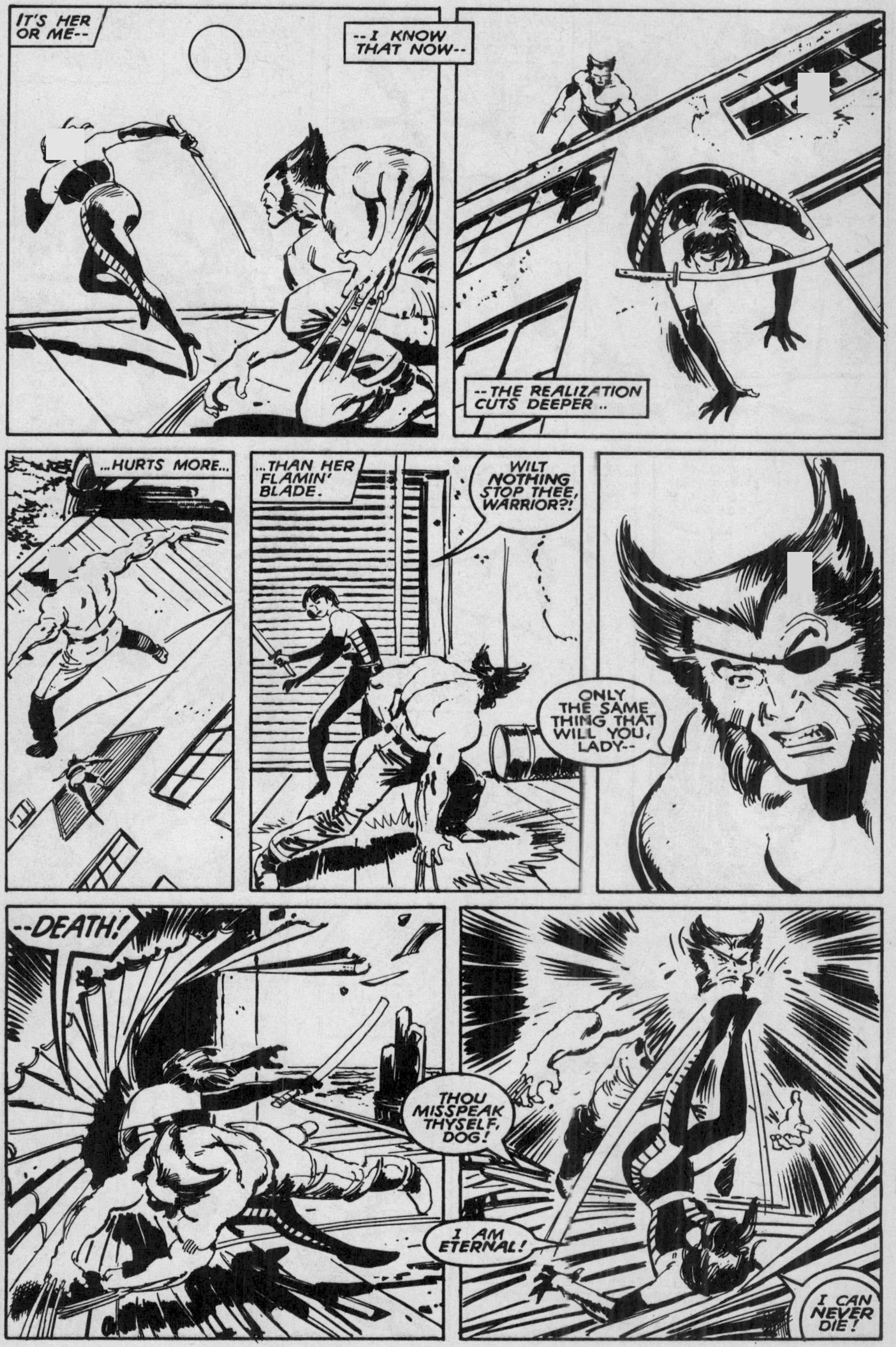
IT'S HER OR ME--
--I KNOW THAT NOW--
--THE REALIZATION CUTS DEEPER ..
...HURTS MORE...
...THAN HER FLAMIN' BLADE.
WILT NOTHING STOP THEE, WARRIOR?!
ONLY THE SAME THING THAT WILL YOU, LADY--
--DEATH!
THOU MISSPEAK THYSELF, DOG!
I AM ETERNAL!
I CAN NEVER DIE!

ONLY THE VESSEL IS MORTAL. WHEN ONE IS USED UP...

...I SIMPLY WAIT TO FIND ANOTHER.

MY ADAMANTIUM CLAWS...

INDEED, THEY STRIKE SPARKS...

...THAT IGNITE THE SAWDUST ON THE FLOOR.

...DON'T EVEN CHIP HER BLADE.

WAREHOUSE IS PILED HIGH WITH FLAMMABLES. WHEN THEY CATCH, PLACE'LL GO UP LIKE A BOMB.

COULDN'T CARE LESS.

THERE'S A PART OF ME, I DON'T LET SURFACE OFTEN --THOUGH SOMETIMES I CAN'T STOP IT-- THAT'S MORE ANIMAL THAN MAN.

A WILD BERSERKER RAGE...

...THAT WIPES AWAY ALL RATIONALITY.

WHEN IT HITS...

...I'M CONSUMED AS WHOLLY AND COMPLETELY AS THE BLACK BLADE HAS JESSICA.

I KILL, PURELY AN' SIMPLY...

...UNTIL THERE'S NOBODY LEFT TO KILL.

IT TAKES ME NOW.

MAYBE JESS REALIZES THAT...

...BECAUSE SHE "RABBITS" FOR THE ROOF.

I'M RIGHT BEHIND HER.

WHICH IS EXACTLY WHAT SHE WANTS.

SKIN BREAKS.

BONES DON'T.

SHE TRIES AGAIN.

WHICH IS EXACTLY WHAT I WANT.

FIRST I'LL TAKE THE BLADE FROM HER.

THEN, THE LIFE.

...I'LL GRIEVE.

LATER, WHEN I'M SANE AGAIN...

NO!

BUT...

SUCH SPIRIT I HAVE NEVER KNOWN!

REJOICE, WARRIOR--

--FOR THOU AND I ARE FATED...

...TO BE ONE!

NO!

WHY FIGHT, DEVIL-MAN...

...WHAT "IN THY HEART AND SOUL...

...THOU KNOW'ST THINE OWN DESIRE?!

THERE, ON THE ROOF-- SAMURAI, WE'VE FOUND THEM--

--BUT LOOK AT JESSICA--

--oh MY LORD, WE'RE TOO LATE!

TRUE, LINDSAY.

BUT I FEAR...

"...NOT IN THE WAY YOU THINK."

LET THE WORLD TREMBLE--

--LET ALL WHO LIVE BEWARE--

--FOR, AT LONG LAST, THE BLACK BLADE HAS A MASTER...

...WORTHY OF THE NAME!

...THE BOND THAT'S BEEN FORGED...

AND WITH THIS WOMAN'S SACRIFICE...

...CAN NEVER BE BROKEN!

NEXT:
The Black Blade!

A WOLVERINE Gallery

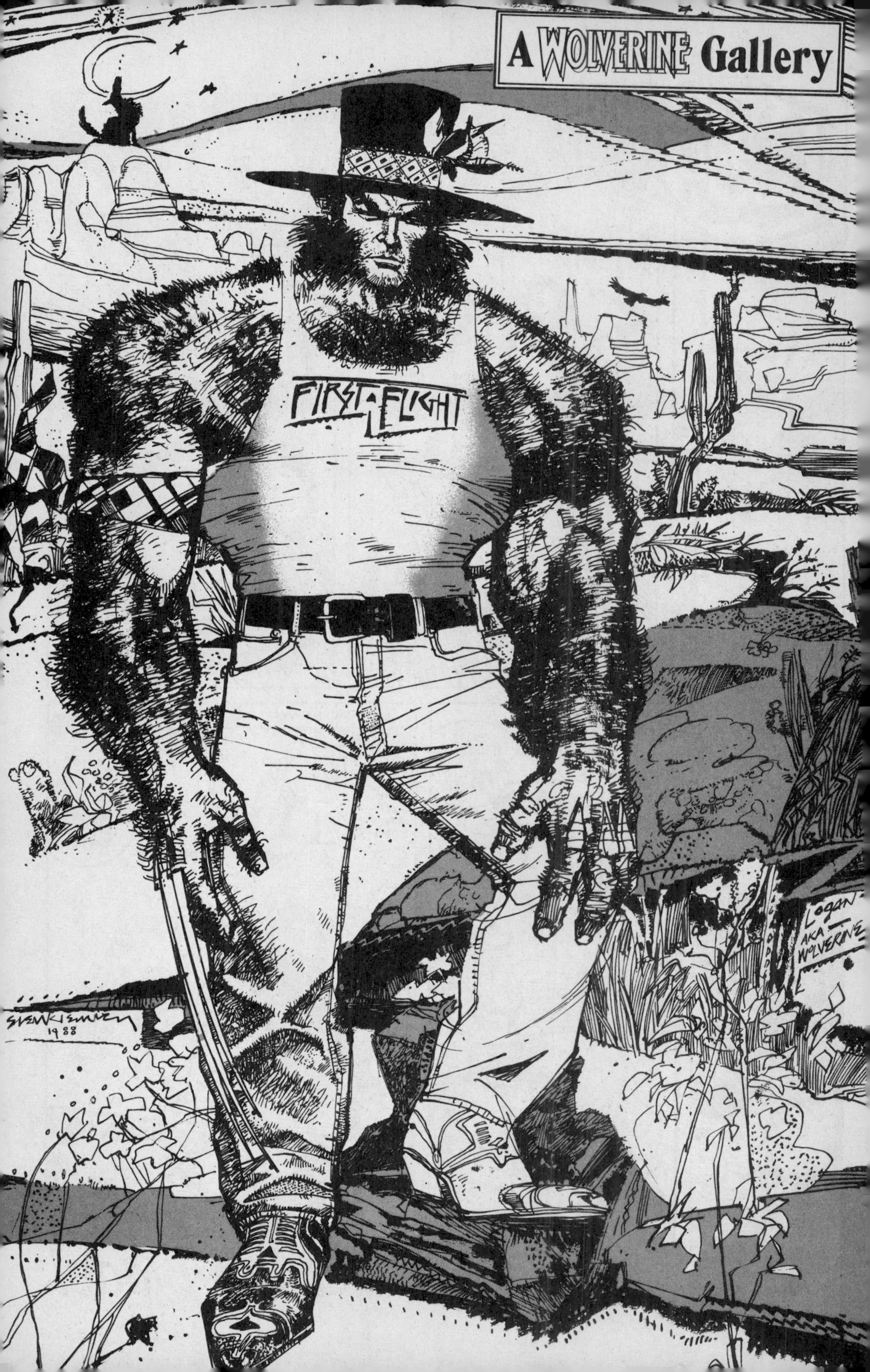
FIRST FLIGHT
Logan AKA WOLVERINE
SIENKIEWICZ 1988

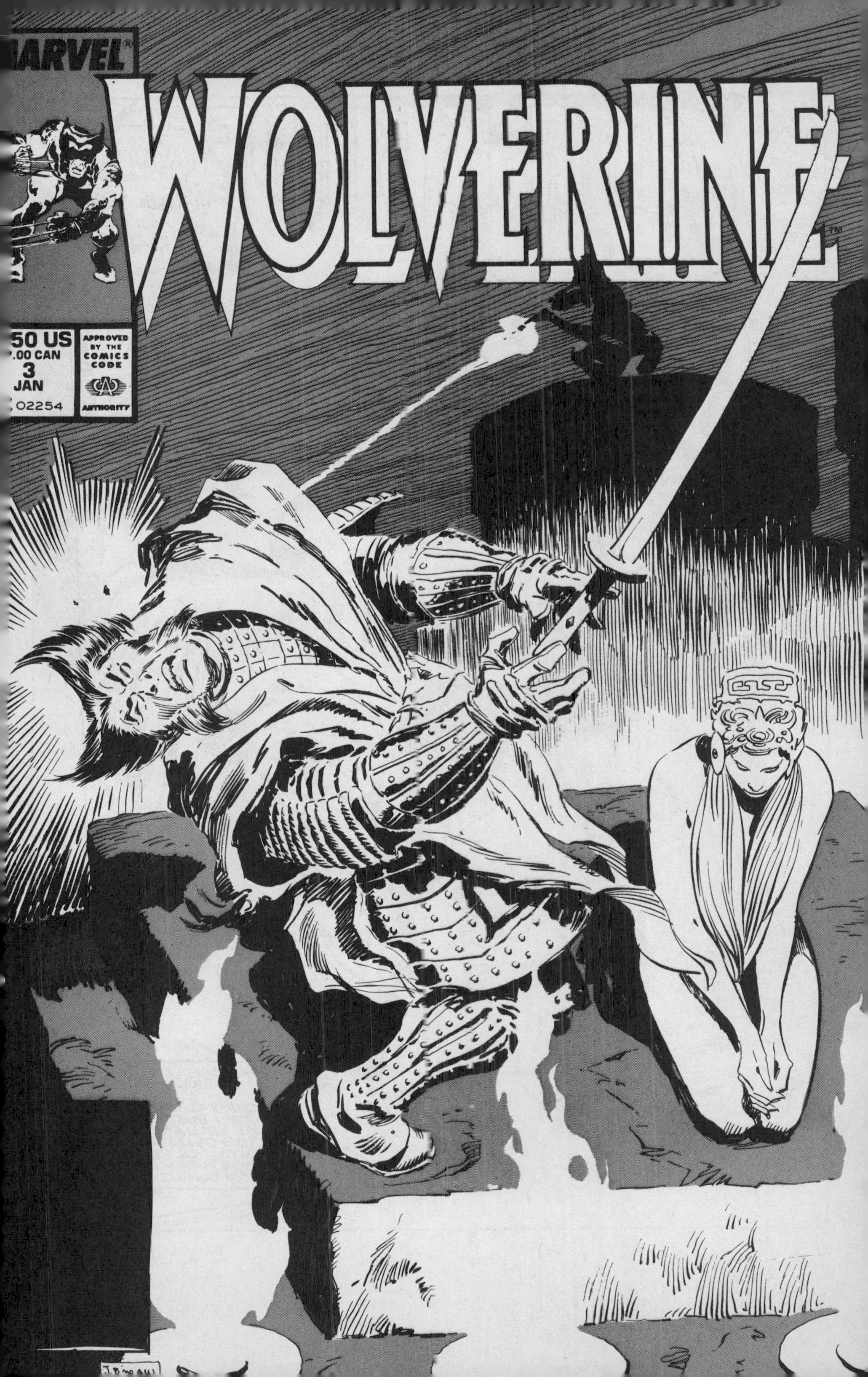
MARVEL
WOLVERINE
50 US
.00 CAN
3
JAN
02254
APPROVED BY THE COMICS CODE AUTHORITY

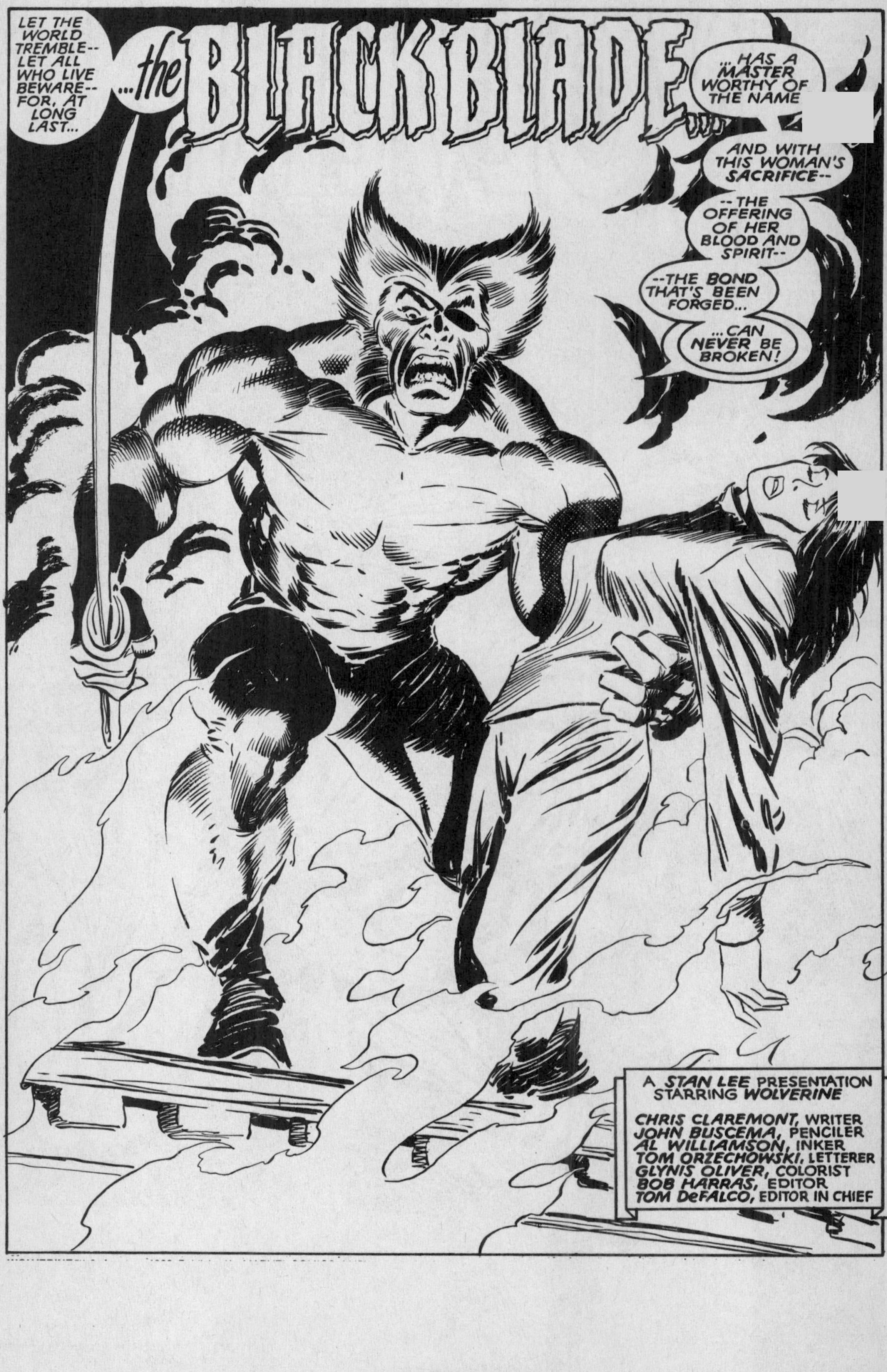
LET THE WORLD TREMBLE-- LET ALL WHO LIVE BEWARE-- FOR, AT LONG LAST...
...the BLACKBLADE...
...HAS A MASTER WORTHY OF THE NAME
AND WITH THIS WOMAN'S SACRIFICE--
--THE OFFERING OF HER BLOOD AND SPIRIT--
--THE BOND THAT'S BEEN FORGED...
...CAN NEVER BE BROKEN!
A STAN LEE PRESENTATION STARRING WOLVERINE
CHRIS CLAREMONT, WRITER
JOHN BUSCEMA, PENCILER
AL WILLIAMSON, INKER
TOM ORZECHOWSKI, LETTERER
GLYNIS OLIVER, COLORIST
BOB HARRAS, EDITOR
TOM DeFALCO, EDITOR IN CHIEF

THE WARRIOR HAS BEEN *POSSESSED* BY THE BLADE'S EVIL, *LINDSAY McCABE...*

...JUST AS YOUR COMPANION, *JESSICA DREW,* WAS BEFORE HIM.

SAMURAI --hic--

--WE'VE GOT TO DO SOMETHING!

THE WOMAN'S FATE IS SEALED, MORTALS--

--AS IS YOUR OWN...

...SHOULD YOU BE FOOL ENOUGH TO INTERFERE!

NO!

HE JUMPED INTO THE FLAMES!

JESSIE!

LINDSAY-- THE WAREHOUSE-- THE *FIRE!*

I DON'T CARE! SHE'S MY *BEST* FRIEND! I WON'T ABANDON HER!!

ARE YOU MAD--

--THE BUILDING'S *COLLAPSING!*

AIAIEEE

YOUR LOYALTY-- AND COURAGE-- DO YOU MORE CREDIT, WOMAN... ...THAN YOUR BRAINS!

MY DRESS-- IT'S *BURNING!*

HOLD STILL! I'LL CUT YOU FREE!

SLASH

WHAT ARE YOU DOING?! LET ME GO!

WHEN WE'RE SAFE, NOT BEFORE!

LET ME GO, YOU JERK-- --MY FRIEND'S INSIDE THERE-- --LET ME GO!

IF SHE IS, LINDSAY, THEN SHE IS DEAD. NO! NO NO NO PLEASE NO oh no

BUT IF SIMPLY SLAYING HER WAS PATCH'S AIM... ...HE'D HAVE DONE IT THEN AND THERE.

I SUSPECT RETURNING TO THE FIRE WAS NO ACT OF SUICIDE...

...BUT HIS WAY OF COVERING HIS TRAIL. MOST EFFECTIVELY.

HE MEANS TO SACRIFICE JESSICA, THAT MUCH IS CLEAR... ...BUT WE'VE NO WAY OF KNOWING WHEN, OR WHERE.

NOT NECESSARILY, PAL.

'CAUSE I THINK --hic-- I GOT US... ...AN ACE IN THE HOLE.

YOU LOOK SURPRISINGLY WELL, O'DONNELL.

WHY-- ONE WOULD HARDLY CREDIT THAT YOU'D RECENTLY BEEN A "GUEST"...

--OF THE LATE, UNLAMENTED CRIMELORD ROCHE, AND HIS INQUISITOR.*

*AS SEEN IN MARVEL COMICS PRESENTS #7-10. --Bob.

PRINCESS BAR

I GOT RESCUED--

--NO THANKS TO THE GOOD OFFICES OF MY OLD FRIEND, THE CHIEF OF POLICE.

REGRETTABLY, IN THAT IMBROGLIO, MY HANDS WERE TIED.

I KNOW. I UNDERSTAND. NO HARD FEELINGS.

YOUR GRACIOUSNESS SHAMES ME.

BY THE BY, I'M TOLD YOU AND THE PRINCESS BAR HAVE TAKEN ON A, SHALL WE SAY, "SILENT PARTNER?"

CARE TO ELABORATE? NO??

PERHAPS SOME OTHER TIME.

WE HAD QUITE A SPECTACULAR FIRE TONIGHT...

... THAT DESTROYED A DOCKLAND WAREHOUSE.

QUITE SPECTACULAR, IT WAS--

--COMING HOT ON THE HEELS, AS IT WERE, OF A PITCHED BATTLE...

... THAT LEVELED A NEARBY JOYHOUSE.

WOULD ANYONE PRESENT CARE TO ASSIST ME WITH THOSE INQUIRIES?

WELL.

THEN.

THE HOUR IS LATE.

AND THIS DAY HAS BEEN A LONG ONE.

PAST TIME I WAS HOME AND IN BED.

UNTIL TOMORROW, O'DONNELL.

PERHAPS, BY THEN, YOU--

--OR YOUR... FRIENDS--

--WILL HAVE SOME NEWS.

ENCHANTÉ, Ms. McCABE-- À DEMAIN.

YOU *KNOW* ME?

MY DEAR, I AM THE *CHIEF* OF POLICE. I KNOW *EVERYONE* IN MADRIPOOR.

JUST AS I LIKE TO KNOW...

...EVERYTHING THAT'S HAPPENING.

AU REVOIR, MES AMIS.

UNTIL TOMORROW.

THAT WAS BRILLIANT.

YOU SMASH A FAIR CHUNK OF LOWTOWN TO BITS...

...THEN WALTZ IN HERE...

...JUST AS THE CHIEF GRILLS ME FOR INFORMATION.

HEY! WE'D HAVE USED THE BACK ENTRANCE-- *BURP!*--SORRY--

--IF WE'D KNOWN WHERE IT WAS!

HE RECOGNIZED ME. I AM WANTED THE WORLD OVER.

WHY DIDN'T HE *ARREST* ME?

HIS INSTINCTS TELL HIM THIS IS MORE THAN A SIMPLE PUNCH-UP.

BUT HE'S ALSO A MAN WHO LIKES RESULTS. IF HE DOESN'T GET HIS ANSWERS, WE'RE ALL OF US IN FOR IT.

SO WHAT HAPPENED? WHERE'S *PATCH*?!

...THE SWORD POSSESSED HIM, HE MEANS TO SACRIFICE Ms. DREW.

WE HAVE TO FIND HIM, AN' STOP HIM.

...AND I COULDN'T TELL YOU WHERE TO *BEGIN* TO LOOK.

IT'S A BIG ISLAND. I *LIVE* HERE...

LINDSAY SAYS YOU HAVE THREE CULTISTS PRISONER IN YOUR CELLAR.

MIGHT THEY NOT BE PERSUADED TO COOPERATE?

FAT CHANCE, MATE. THEY'RE FANATICS, THE TOUGHEST HARDCASES I'VE EVER SEEN. THEY'LL DIE FIRST.

Awhwh-- I BET YOU JUST HAVEN'T ASKED THEM...

...AS *NICELY* AS I WILL.

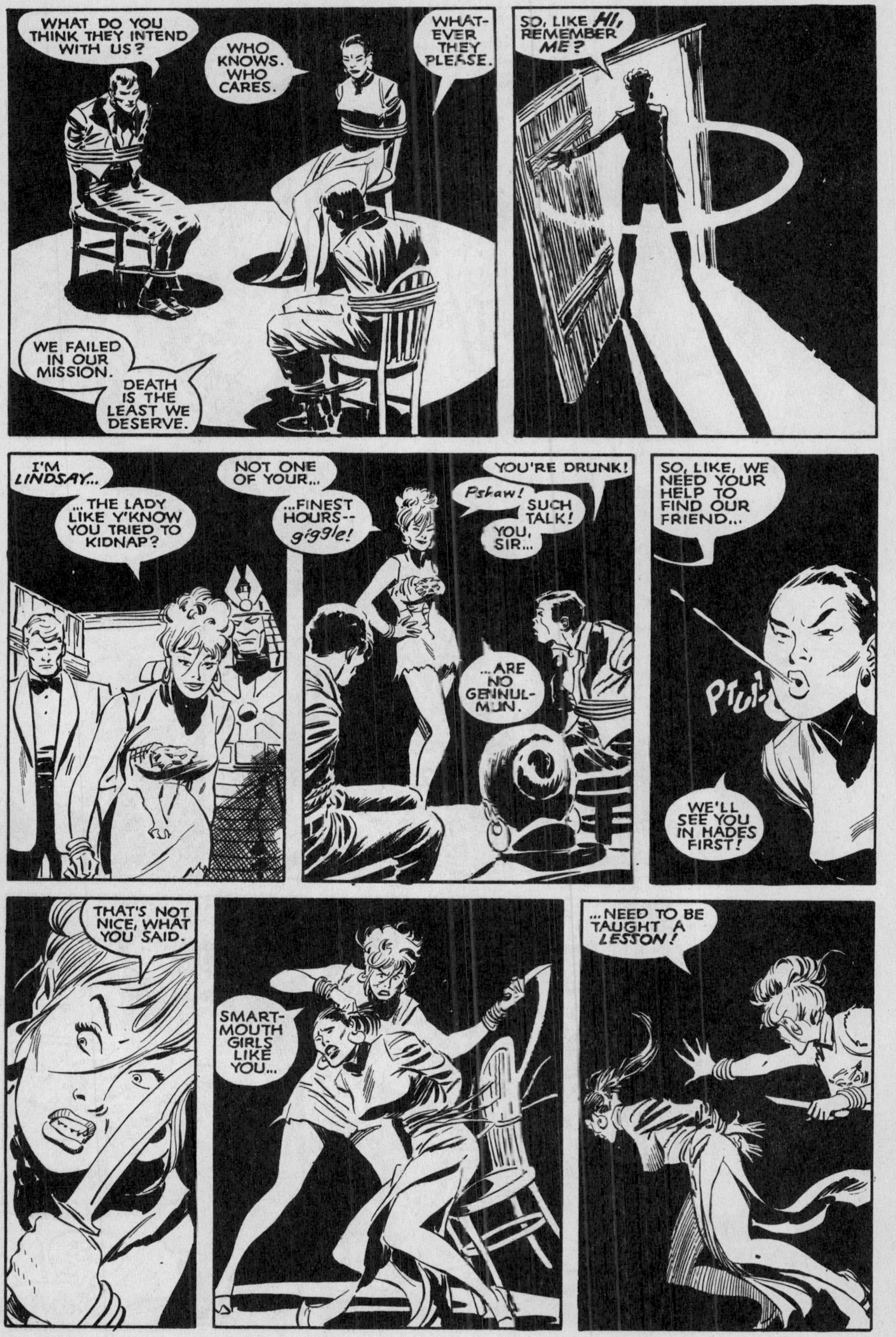
WHAT DO YOU THINK THEY INTEND WITH US?
WHO KNOWS. WHO CARES.
WHAT-EVER THEY PLEASE.
WE FAILED IN OUR MISSION.
DEATH IS THE LEAST WE DESERVE.
SO, LIKE HI, REMEMBER ME?
I'M LINDSAY...
...THE LADY LIKE Y'KNOW YOU TRIED TO KIDNAP?
NOT ONE OF YOUR...
...FINEST HOURS-- giggle!
YOU'RE DRUNK!
Pshaw! SUCH TALK!
YOU, SIR...
...ARE NO GENNUL-MUN.
SO, LIKE, WE NEED YOUR HELP TO FIND OUR FRIEND...
PTUI!
WE'LL SEE YOU IN HADES FIRST!
THAT'S NOT NICE, WHAT YOU SAID.
SMART-MOUTH GIRLS LIKE YOU...
...NEED TO BE TAUGHT A LESSON!

WHAT IS THIS--?!

--WHAT'S THE WOMAN DOING?!!

SHE'S CRAZY--

THAT KNIFE-- --THE LOOK ON HER FACE--

-- SAMURAI, SHE ISN'T FOOLING!

SO MUCH, THE BETTER.

PERHAPS THEN, THEY WILL TAKE HER SERIOUSLY.

Ohhhh, SWEETIE-BABY...

...THIS IS GONNA BE SOoo MUCH FUN!

I'M PUTTING A STOP TO-- ?!!?

THIS IS LINDSAY'S PLAY, O'DONNELL.

AS YOU VALUE YOUR OWN LIFE...

...TRUST HER.

BY THE SACRED BLADE--

MEI YIN-- DEFEND YOURSELF!

-- IF I WERE FREE--!

DON'T BE SO EAGER TO BE A MARTYR, HONEY...

...YOU'LL GET YOUR CHANCE--

--AND PROBABLY A LOT SOONER THAN YOU THINK! BUT IN THE MEANTIME...

...LADIES FIRST!

LISTEN, TSUBORO--

--SHE'S BEATING MEI YIN TO DEATH!

SLAP
BOP
CHUNT CHUNT
CRAK!

SAMURAI, THINGS ARE OUT OF HAND!

I NEVER DREAMED THE GIRL HAD THIS IN HER!

NOR DID I.

IT IS A... REVELATION

YAAARRGGGH*

THAT SCREAM--! SO HORRIBLE--!

MEI YIN?!?

FOR THE LOVE OF HEAVEN, ANSWER-- MEI YIN!?!

Heh Heh heh Heh heh heh

THAT WAS FUN!

Giggle

THE LADY heh WOULDN'T TELL heh heh ME WHAT I WANTED TO KNOW.

NOW SHE CAN'T.

BUT I DON'T MIND REALLY.

BECAUSE THAT GIVES ME THE CHANCE...

...TO PLAY WITH YOU.

NO!

BLESSED ANCESTORS, I'LL TALK, I'LL TALK!

ONLY PLEASE PLEASE PLEASE I BEG YOU KEEP HER AWAY FROM ME!

OKAY, McCABE...

--YOU'VE DONE YOUR PART.

...SHOW'S OVER--

I'LL TAKE THE KNIFE...

...AND HANDLE THINGS FROM HERE.

Oh--

--POO!

WELL, IF THEY DON'T COOPERATE, O'DONNELL--

--IF THEY HOLD BACK IN THE SLIGHTEST--

--THEN I'LL BE BACK!

YOU HEARD THE LADY.

YOU WANT TO SAVE YOURSELVES--

--YOU KNOW WHAT TO DO.

I SAW. I HEARD.

I DO NOT BELIEVE.

YOU KNOW ME, THEY DON'T.

Whew!

BET O'DONNELL DIDN'T REALIZE HOW RIGHT HE WAS WHEN HE CALLED THIS A "SHOW."

AND THE BEST PERFORMANCE ALWAYS TAKES A LOT OUT OF YOU.

THIS WAS A DECEPTION?

YOU BET! SOME OF THE SLAPS WERE REAL...

...BUT THE CRIES WERE ALL ME, FAKING THE WOMAN'S VOICE, ESPECIALLY THE SCREAM AT THE END, I WAS REAL PROUD OF THAT.

AND THE BLOOD?

STAGE BLOOD--FROM O'DONNELL'S MAKE-UP STORES THAT HIS DANCERS USE.

THEN-- THE WOMAN IS NOT DEAD?

OF COURSE SHE ISN'T, WHAT KIND OF A FIEND D'YOU TAKE ME FOR?!!

SILLY ME--THAT WAS THE WHOLE POINT OF THE EXERCISE, TO CONVINCE THEM I REALLY WAS A FIEND.

BOY, IF THE PRODUCER OF "SORORITY SLASHER" HAD ONLY SEEN THIS...

...I BET HE'D HAVE CAST ME IN THE LEAD FOR SURE!

HIS LOSS. YOU WERE SUPERB.

DARN STRAIGHT!

BETTER, MUCH BETTER! NOTHING LIKE A SHOWER, AND A CHANGE OF CLOTHES...

...TO MAKE A BODY FEEL A BIT MORE *HUMAN.*

THE *SILVER SAMURAI*-- --NEVER SEEN HIM WITHOUT HIS ARMOR-- --FUNNY, *HE* LOOKS HUMAN, TOO.

NO LESS IMPRESSIVE, THOUGH.

IS THIS WHAT THEY MEAN...

...ABOUT THE SWORD...

...BEING THE EXTENSION OF THE MAN?

I DON'T MEAN TO INTRUDE, SAMURAI.

I'VE NEVER SEEN YOU IN ACTION--

--ONLY HEARD ABOUT IT FROM JESSICA.

YOU'RE PRETTY DARN SUPERB YOURSELF.

IS THIS A "MAGIC" BLADE, AS WELL? I'VE HEARD IT CAN CUT THROUGH ALMOST ANYTHING.

THIS? COMPARED TO THE MURAMASA SWORD, IT IS *NOTHING.*

THE "MAGIC" YOU SPEAK OF HAS NOTHING TO DO WITH THE WEAPON, IT IS OF THE *MAN.*

I AM WHAT IS CALLED A *MUTANT.*

I GENERATE THE CUTTING ENERGY WITHIN MY OWN BODY, THE *SWORD* MERELY GIVES IT FOCUS.

FOR MY PURPOSES, ONE OF THE FACSIMILE *KATANAS* SOLD THROUGH MAIL ORDER MAGAZINES WOULD SERVE AS WELL.

THEN WHAT MAKES THIS *BLACK BLADE* SO SPECIAL?

THE CREATION OF A TRUE SWORD IS AS MUCH A SPIRITUAL ACT AS A PHYSICAL ONE.

THE SMITH IMBUES THE METAL WITH A PIECE OF HIS SOUL, JUST AS THE WARRIOR CONSECRATES IT WITH HEART AND LIFESBLOOD.

NONE BEFORE MURAMASA EVER CREATED SUCH BLADES, NONE AFTER EVER WANTED TO.

THE SWORD WAS THE ULTIMATE PRODUCT OF HIS BRILLIANCE--

--PERHAPS IT ALSO BECAME INFECTED WITH HIS MADNESS AS WELL.

HE SOUGHT HIS WHOLE LIFE TO CRAFT THE PERFECT BLADE...

...THE TRANSCENDENT, TERRIBLE BEAUTY THAT DESTROYS ALL IT TOUCHES.

MIGHT NOT THE BLADE ITSELF HAVE A SIMILAR DREAM--

--TO BE THE PERFECT WEAPON?

SEARCHING THROUGH THE AGES...

...FOR THE WARRIOR WORTHY TO WIELD IT?

TOO FLIPPIN' METAPHYSICAL FOR ME, MATE.

OCCASIONALLY, YOU ENGLISH ARE TOO ICONOCLASTIC FOR YOUR OWN GOOD.

A PRACTICAL PEOPLE, THAT'S US.

BUT IF YOU'RE RIGHT, IT'S FOUND IT'S MAN--

-- IN PATCH.

NO.

THE BLADE MASTERS HIM. THAT IS NOT HOW IT SHOULD BE.

"DOESN'T MATTER. YOU CAN SORT THINGS OUT, FACE TO FACE."

"I LOOK FORWARD TO THAT."

"BET YOU DO."

"CULT'S HIDEOUT IS AN OLD HIGHLAND TEMPLE, BLEEDIN' MILES OUT IN THE BOONIES, PROVERBIAL MIDDLE O' NOWHERE.

"WE'VE NO TIME TO WASTE. CEREMONY'S KEYED TO THE FULL MOON-- AND THE LAST ONE OF THIS MONTH IS TONIGHT!"

YOU WERE RIGHT-- IT'S THE KIND OF PLACE INDY JONES WOULD LOVE.

NO SIGN OF LIFE, THOUGH.

TEMPLE LOOKS DESERTED.

ONLY ONE WAY TO FIND OUT FOR CERTAIN.

I'LL TAKE THE POINT.

NO, O'DONNELL.

YOU STAY BEHIND, LINDSAY AND I WILL GO

SAY WHAT?!?

WHILE I DEAL WITH THE CULT AND PATCH...

...YOU CAN RESCUE JESSICA.

THAT'S NUTS-- O'DONNELL CAN DO IT BETTER...

...IT'S HIS LINE OF WORK!

PERHAPS. BUT I DO NOT KNOW HIM. I DO NOT KNOW YOU, LINDSAY-- AND YOUR CAPABILITIES.

AS IMPORTANTLY, JESSICA KNOWS YOU.

SHE WILL FOLLOW YOU WITHOUT HESITATION.

FINALLY, SHOULD WE FAIL...

...O'DONNELL IS BEST ABLE...

...TO DEAL WITH THE AUTHORITIES...

...AND AVENGE OUR DEATHS.

GEEZ-- THAT'S A COMFORTING THOUGHT.

HATE TO SAY IT, DUCKS...

...BUT HE MAKES SENSE.

BETTER TAKE THIS.

MODIFIED HECKLER & KOCH...

...WITH A LOWLIGHT SNIPER-SCOPE.

YOU KNOW YOUR WEAPONS...

...AND FROM THE LOOKS OF THINGS...

...HOW TO USE 'EM.

YOU'RE CHOCK-FULL OF SURPRISE, MS. McCABE.

I DID A SEASON ON "TOUR OF DUTY." THERE WERE ARMY TROOPERS AND VIETNAM VETS ACTING AS TECHNICAL ADVISERS. I LIKED HANGING OUT WITH THEM.

THEY LIKED SHOWING OFF THEIR HARDWARE AND EXPERTISE.

NICE THING ABOUT ACTING IN MOVIES.

YOU GO ALMOST ANYWHERE, LEARN TO DO JUST ABOUT EVERYTHING.

ALWAYS INTERESTING, DISCOVERING WHAT'LL COME IN HANDY.

THIS ISN'T THE MOVIES, LINDSAY, IT'S REALITY.

I START THINKING ABOUT THAT, O'DONNELL...

...I'LL START SCREAMING.

BE SEEING YOU!

NOT TO WORRY LUV--

--YOU'LL DO FINE.

THIS IS AN IDEAL PERCH.

YOUR FIELD OF FIRE COVERS THE ENTIRETY OF THE TEMPLE FLOOR.

HEADS UP-- IT'S SHOWTIME!

STANDING ROOM ONLY CROWD.

THEY CARRY ON A TRADITION ESTABLISHED BY THE SWORD'S VERY CREATION.

AS THE BLACK BLADE TOOK ITS FIRST LIFE IN THE SPRING...

...THE BEGINNING OF THE YEAR...

...SO ARE ALL THE CULT'S SACRIFICES EXECUTED AT DAWN--

--THE BEGINNING OF THE DAY.

I CANNOT FIGHT MY WAY THROUGH SO MANY TO THE ALTAR...

...IN TIME TO PREVENT PATCH FROM SLAYING JESSICA--

--THAT, LINDSAY, MUST BE YOUR JOB.

YOU MUST KILL PATCH...

...BEFORE HE KILLS YOUR FRIEND.

I'M NOT A KILLER.

BUT IF I DON'T--!

"THE CELEBRANT'S WEARING THE SWORD--

--IT MUST BE PATCH.

"AND THERE'S JESS!"

"SHE DRUGGED, OR UNDER SOME SPELL, OR WHAT?

"AIR'S SO STINKING THICK WITH INCENSE-- HOW CAN THOSE PEOPLE EVEN BREATHE DOWN THERE--

"--AND THEIR CHANTING-- ENOUGH ALREADY--

"--MAKES MY HEAD HURT."

"YOU MUST KILL PATCH...

"...BEFORE HE KILLS YOUR FRIEND."

SO EASY TO SAY, SAMURAI-- --MURDER'S YOUR TRADE.

GOTTA STOP SHAKING-- --JESSIE'S DEPENDING ON ME--

--IT'LL MAKE ME MISS!

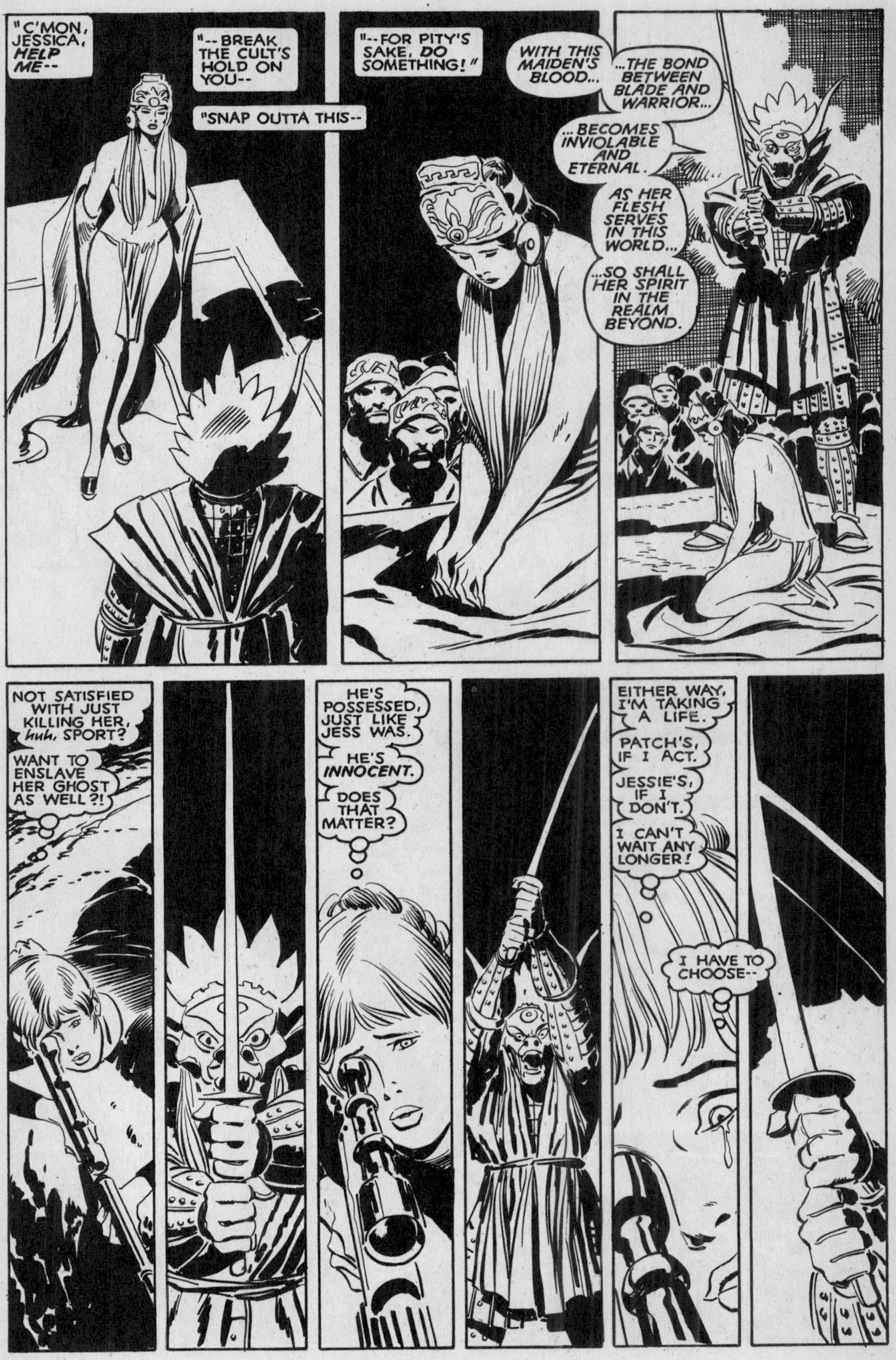
"C'MON, JESSICA, HELP ME--
"--BREAK THE CULT'S HOLD ON YOU--
"SNAP OUTTA THIS--
"--FOR PITY'S SAKE, DO SOMETHING!"
WITH THIS MAIDEN'S BLOOD...
...THE BOND BETWEEN BLADE AND WARRIOR...
...BECOMES INVIOLABLE AND ETERNAL.
AS HER FLESH SERVES IN THIS WORLD...
...SO SHALL HER SPIRIT IN THE REALM BEYOND.
NOT SATISFIED WITH JUST KILLING HER, huh, SPORT?
WANT TO ENSLAVE HER GHOST AS WELL?!
HE'S POSSESSED, JUST LIKE JESS WAS.
HE'S INNOCENT.
DOES THAT MATTER?
EITHER WAY, I'M TAKING A LIFE.
PATCH'S, IF I ACT.
JESSIE'S, IF I DON'T.
I CAN'T WAIT ANY LONGER!
I HAVE TO CHOOSE--

--NOW!

BLAM

I DID IT. I DID IT! I KILLED HIM!

STOP WHINING, YOU NINNY!

JESSIE'S STILL DOWN THERE!

WHAT YOU'VE DONE DOESN'T MEAN BEANS...

...IF YOU DON'T GET HER OUT!

AN INTRUDER! AN ASSASSIN!

THE LORD OF THE BLACK BLADE HAS BEEN SLAIN!

SEARCH THE TEMPLE--

--FIND HIS SLAYER--

-- THAT WE MAY REPAY HIM IN KIND!

PEACE, DOGS!

IF YOU VALUE YOUR PULING, PATHETIC LIVES...

...LEAVE THIS PLACE!

THE SILVER SAMURAI!

HE, TOO, SEEKS THE SACRED BLADE.

TO ARMS, BRETHREN!

THIS IS HIS DOING!

GIVE THIS RENEGADE THE ANSWER HE DESERVES!

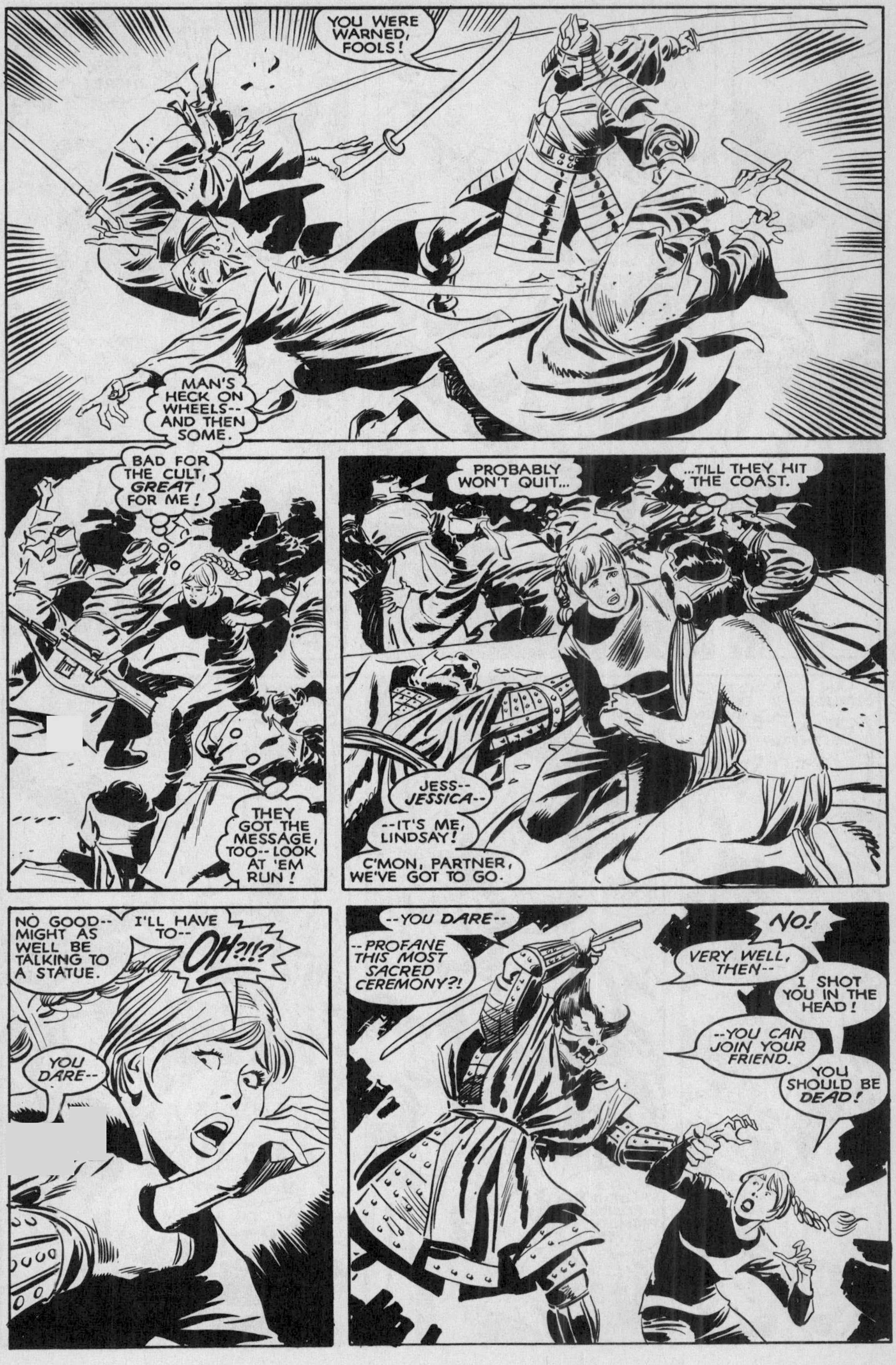
YOU WERE WARNED, FOOLS!
MAN'S HECK ON WHEELS-- AND THEN SOME.
BAD FOR THE CULT, *GREAT* FOR ME!
THEY GOT THE MESSAGE, TOO-- LOOK AT 'EM RUN!
PROBABLY WON'T QUIT...
...TILL THEY HIT THE COAST.
JESS-- *JESSICA*--
--IT'S ME, LINDSAY!
C'MON, PARTNER, WE'VE GOT TO GO.
NO GOOD-- MIGHT AS WELL BE TALKING TO A STATUE.
I'LL HAVE TO--
OH?!!?
YOU DARE--
--YOU *DARE*--
--PROFANE THIS MOST SACRED CEREMONY?!
NO!
VERY WELL, THEN--
I SHOT YOU IN THE HEAD!
--YOU CAN JOIN YOUR FRIEND.
YOU SHOULD BE *DEAD*!

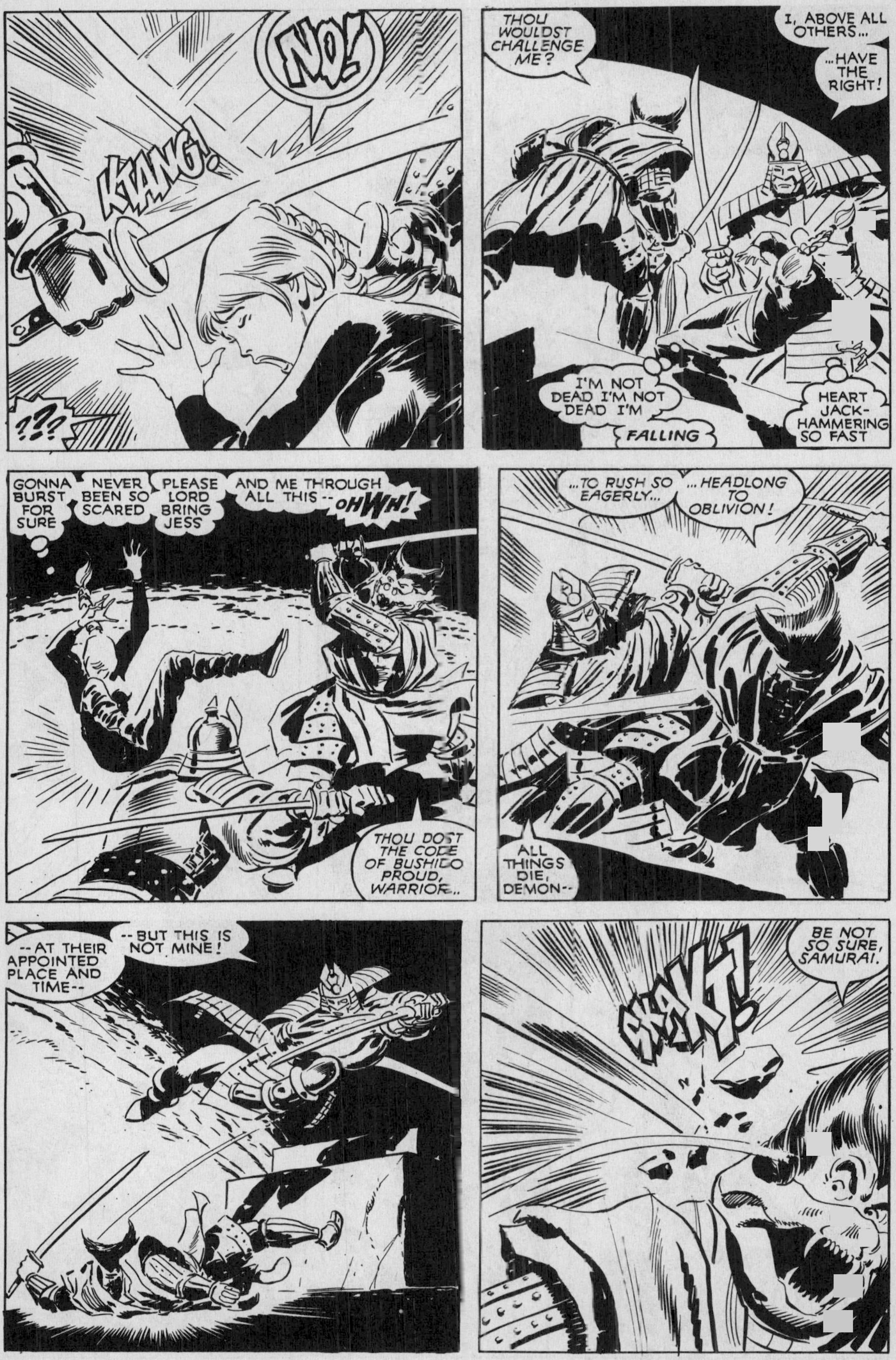
NO!
KTANG!
???
THOU WOULDST CHALLENGE ME?
I, ABOVE ALL OTHERS...
...HAVE THE RIGHT!
I'M NOT DEAD I'M NOT DEAD I'M
FALLING
HEART JACK-HAMMERING SO FAST
GONNA BURST FOR SURE
NEVER BEEN SO SCARED
PLEASE LORD BRING JESS
AND ME THROUGH ALL THIS -- OHWH!
THOU DOST THE CODE OF BUSHIDO PROUD, WARRIOR..
...TO RUSH SO EAGERLY...
...HEADLONG TO OBLIVION!
ALL THINGS DIE, DEMON--
--AT THEIR APPOINTED PLACE AND TIME--
--BUT THIS IS NOT MINE!
SKAKT!
BE NOT SO SURE, SAMURAI.

I AM THE FIRE IN THE SOUL...

...OF HIM WHO MADE ME--

--AND OF ALL THOSE WHO'VE WIELDED ME...

...DOWN THROUGH THE AGES--

SKYANG!

--WHAT MATCH ART THOU, MORTAL, FOR THAT?!

THWAK

GOOD POINT.

NO SENSE RUNNING, THOUGH--

--EVEN IF JESS WAS IN ANY SHAPE TO.

SAMURAI WINS, THERE'S NO NEED.

IF HE LOSES--

--oh, NO!

BEHOLD, WARRIOR-- ALL HAS COME TO PASS...

...AS I FORETOLD.

NO!

I WON'T LET YOU KILL HIM!

BLAM

IN THAT CASE, WOMAN...

...SINCE THOU WILT PERSIST IN INTERFERING...

MY RIFLE--!?!

...I MUST NEEDS DISPOSE OF THEE FIRST.

CARELESS, DEMON-- --TO TURN YOUR BACK-- --ON A FOE NOT YET SLAIN!

AN OVERSIGHT MOST SPEEDILY AND SIMPLY...

...RECTIFIED!

KTHOW

BY HEAVEN-- --HIS FISTS...

...STRIKE LIKE BATTERING RAMS!

MY ARMOR... ...BARELY ABLE...

...TO WITHSTAND...

THOU ART A VALIANT FOE, SAMURAI. THEREFORE THOU HAST EARNED A WARRIOR'S DEATH.

BY MY BLADE RATHER THAN BLUDGEONING BLOWS.

I SALUTE THEE-- --AND THY COMPANION!

AS I CLAIM... ...AS I TAKE... ...McCABE... DREW-- --FRIENDS!

THE BLACK BLADE CALLS NONE "FRIEND"-- --IT IS A LAW UNTO ITSELF!

FORGED IN BLOOD--

--CONSECRATED TO DEATH--

--MAYBE... ...SO...

...BUT NOT BY MY HANDS!

NOT WITH MY BODY! I'M A FREE MAN!!

I WON'T BE... ...ANYBODY'S SLAVE!

SHOK!

PATCH-- --HOLY COW, IS HE--

--JESSIE! OH GEEZ, NOT YOU, TOO!

McCABE...

...YOU AN' YOUR PARTNER... ...OKAY?

GOT ONE FLAMIN' BEAUT OF A HEADACHE, GIRL... ...THANKS TO YOU. BUT UNDER THE CIRCUMSTANCES... ...I'M NOT COMPLAININ'.

MY LORD-- IT WASN'T A DREAM!

GETTIN' BETTER ALL THE TIME, PATCH. AND YOU?

GLAD THERE ARE NO HARD FEELINGS.

HEY, SAMURAI, WE HIT THE JACKPOT WITH THIS CAPER-- --WOULDJA BELIEVE IT? A HAPPY ENDING... ...ALL 'ROUND...

AT LAST-- --AT LAST-- --THE *SILVER SAMURAI* HAS HIS BLADE...

...OF *DESTINY!*

NOT OVER.

NOT YET.

MY BODY BLOCKS HARADA'S VIEW AS I *"POP"* MY CLAWS. DUNNO IF I CAN NAIL HIM...

...BUT I HAVE TO TRY.

THEN, SURPRISINGLY...

NOTHING'S HAPPENING!

NO CHANGE IN CLOTHES OR SPEECH-- YOU AREN'T *POSSESSED!*

EVIDENTLY NOT. AS I HOPED. THE *BLACK BLADE* HAS FINALLY FOUND ITS FATED MASTER, THE WARRIOR CHOSEN FOR IT BY *KARMA.*

FIGURES. BLACK BLADE...

...FOR A BLACK-HEARTED ROGUE.

WHO BETTER TO CONTROL A *DEMENTED* BLADE, MY FRIEND, THAN AN EQUALLY DRIVEN MAN? PERHAPS, IN THE PROCESS, BOTH WILL FIND *SALVATION.* AND *PEACE.*

YOU SHOULD HAVE REMEMBERED, *"PATCH"*, THAT IF A MAN ALREADY *POSSESSES* A BLADE -- ESPECIALLY ONE OF *HONOR* --

--THERE IS *NO ROOM* IN HIS SOUL FOR ANOTHER.

FAREWELL.

FATES WILLING, WE SHALL *NOT* MEET AGAIN.

WHAT'S THAT MEAN?

NEVER YOU MIND, GIRL. *PRIVATE* BUSINESS.

THERE'S A LOT OF HISTORY, AND BLOOD, BETWEEN ME AND THE *SAMURAI.*

IN SPITE OF THAT, I FIND MYSELF WISHING HIM WELL.

BY THE WAY, McCABE. *NICE* SHOT.

I'M GLAD I *MISSED.*

HAH! ME, I'M GLAD THAT WAS A *THICK* MASK...

...WITH A *THICKER SKULL* BENEATH.

BEEN A *HECKUVA* NIGHT, LADIES...

...LET'S GO HOME AN' CELEBRATE THE *DAWN!*

NEXT: **BLOODSPORT!**

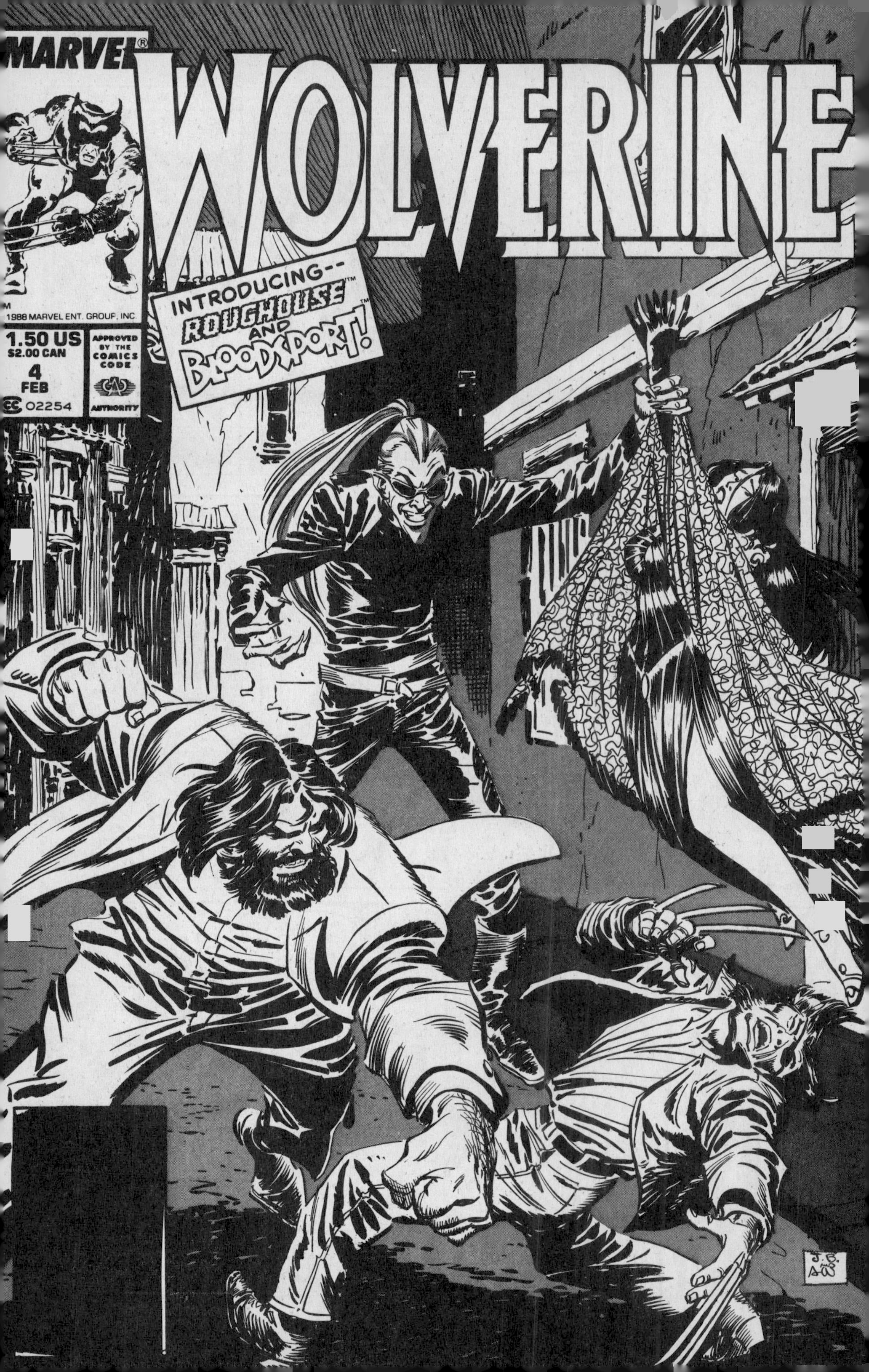
MARVEL®
WOLVERINE
© 1988 MARVEL ENT. GROUP, INC.
1.50 US
$2.00 CAN
4
FEB
02254
APPROVED BY THE COMICS CODE AUTHORITY
INTRODUCING-- ROUGHOUSE™ AND BLOODSPORT!™
J.B. AW

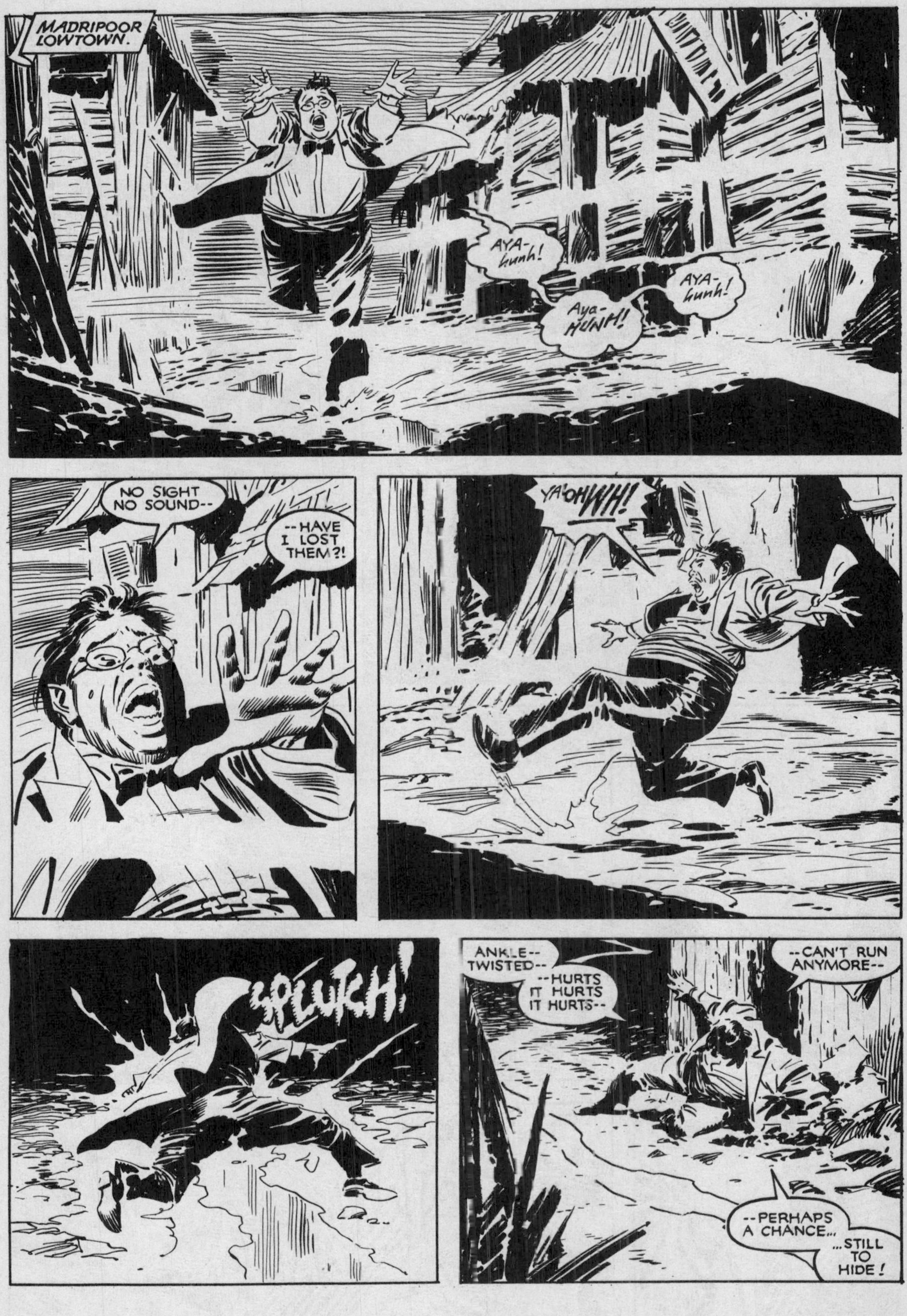
MADRIPOOR LOWTOWN.
AYA-hunh!
AYA-hunh!
Aya-HUNH!
NO SIGHT NO SOUND--
--HAVE I LOST THEM?!
YA'OHWH!
SPLUTCH!
ANKLE-- TWISTED--
--HURTS IT HURTS IT HURTS--
--CAN'T RUN ANYMORE--
--PERHAPS A CHANCE...
...STILL TO HIDE!

WE LET YOU *RUN*, LITTLE MAN!

SKBAM!

YII!

BUT YOU CAN'T HIDE HA HA HA

THAT'S A NO-NO. HA HA

SPOILS OUR GAME, DON'T'CHA SEE? HA

MADMAN! POSSESSING THE POWER... ...TO LEVEL A HOUSE...

...WITH A SINGLE BLOW!

Ah Hah Aiow

CHEST BURNING

ALL MY AIR

LEAVING NONE FOR ME TO BREATHE

CHANCELLOR RANJAMARYAM.

NO PLEASE TELL ME WHAT YOU WANT

I'LL PAY ANY PRICE

I BEG YOU

SPARE ME

WE ARE MEN OF HONOR, CREATURES OF DUTY.

OUR SERVICE IS ALREADY PLEDGED.

AND THE ONLY COIN THAT DREAD LORD WILL ACCEPT FOR THIS EVENTIDE'S WORK...

...IS THY LIFE.

AYAYAAAAAAAAAA

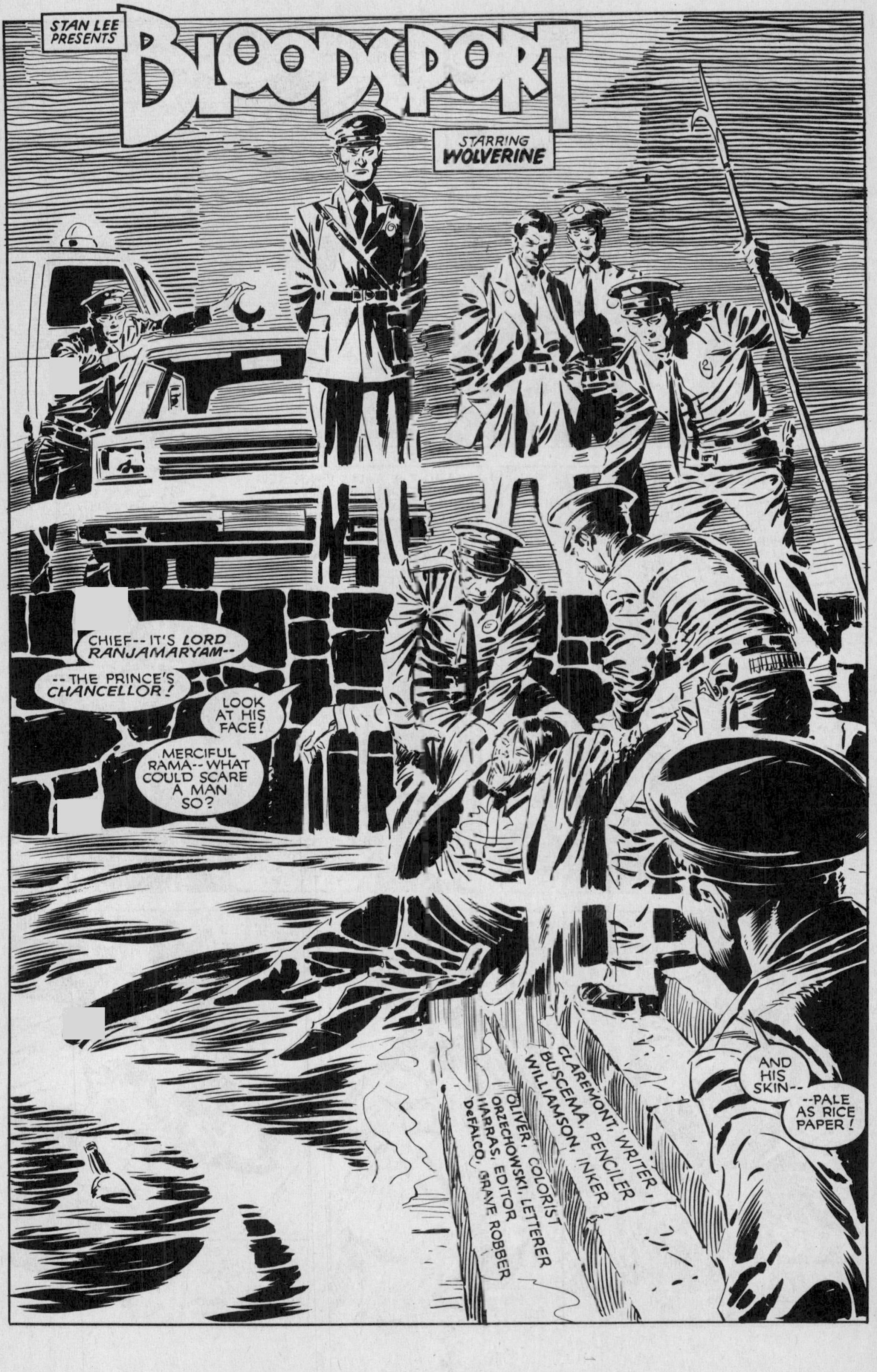
STAN LEE PRESENTS
BLOODSPORT
STARRING WOLVERINE
CHIEF-- IT'S LORD RANJAMARYAM--
--THE PRINCE'S CHANCELLOR!
LOOK AT HIS FACE!
MERCIFUL RAMA-- WHAT COULD SCARE A MAN SO?
AND HIS SKIN--
--PALE AS RICE PAPER!
CLAREMONT, WRITER
BUSCEMA, PENCILER
WILLIAMSON, INKER
OLIVER, COLORIST
ORZECHOWSKI, LETTERER
HARRAS, EDITOR
DeFALCO, GRAVE ROBBER

SO TELL ME, TAI-- --THIS WHERE YOU CONSCIENTIOUSLY ROUND UP ALL THE "USUAL SUSPECTS"?

AN EXERCISE IN FUTILITY, FRIEND *PATCH*-- --EITHER AS SERIOUS SUGGESTION... ...OR AN ATTEMPT AT HUMOR.

IN THIS INSTANCE, I'LL WAGER WE COULD INTERROGATE EVERY "SUSPECT" IN MADRIPOOR...

...AND LEARN NOTHING.

AND PLEASE, SPARE ME THE TRADITIONAL: "I JUST HAPPENED TO BE IN THE NEIGHBORHOOD."

I MIGHT AS PERTINENTLY INQUIRE, ON THE OTHER HAND, WHAT YOU ARE DOING HERE?

HEARD THE RADIO CALL REQUESTING YOUR PRESENCE.

FIGURED ANYTHING WORTH DRAGGING YOU OUTTA BED WAS WORTH A LOOK-SEE.

ANY OBJECTIONS TO MY TAKING A GANDER AT THE BODY?

CHIEF-- WHY DO YOU ALLOW THAT FOREIGNER SUCH LIBERTIES?!

BECAUSE, DETECTIVE, IN MATTERS SUCH AS THESE...

"...PATCH HAS A SPECIAL-- I MIGHT SAY, UNIQUE-- EXPERTISE."

I LIKED RANJA.

HE KNEW MORE BAWDY SONGS EVEN THAN ME.

AND WAS AS DEADLY AT POKER...

...AS CHESS.

HE USED PEOPLE-- THAT WAS HIS JOB--

--BUT HE TRIED ALONG THE WAY TO HURT AS FEW AS POSSIBLE, AND HELP AS MANY.

THERE ARE WORSE EPITAPHS.

WELL?

SORRY. NOTHIN' THERE YOU PROBABLY DIDN'T SPOT FOR YOURSELF.

A LIE, O' COURSE, BUT I CAN'T TELL TAI ANY MORE WITHOUT JEOPARDIZING MY COVER.

YOU LOGGIN' THIS AS MURDER?

UNTIL PERSUADED OTHERWISE.

RUMOR HAS IT, THE CHANCELLOR PLANNED TO RECOMMEND TO THE PRINCE THAT HE ACKNOWLEDGE T'GER AS THE NEW CRIMELORD.

YOU FIGURE SOMEBODY OBJECTED AN' ACED RANJA TO PREVENT IT?

A PLAUSIBLE SCENARIO. AND A DANGEROUS ONE.

EVEN THE MOST POWERFUL OF MEN WOULD NOT DARE ASSAULT THE PRINCE'S HOUSEHOLD WITHOUT SANCTION.

THIS IS A TIME, MY FRIEND, WHEN AMBITION RUNS HOT AS FEVER.

SO LONG AS THE CRIMELORDS SAVAGE ONLY THEIR OWN, I AM FREE TO LOOK THE OTHER WAY.

STEP BEYOND THOSE BOUNDS-- DISTURB THE GENERAL TRANQUILITY OF THE STATE-- AND I WILL DO WHATEVER IS REQUIRED TO PUT AN END TO IT.

IN SUCH CIRCUMSTANCES, PATCH, DUTY REQUIRES I HAVE NO FRIENDS.

FAIR WARNING. PROBLEM IS, WE BOTH KNOW ANYBODY WHO'LL KILL THE CHANCELLOR WON'T MIND AT ALL ADDING THE CHIEF OF POLICE TO HIS LIST.

SOUTH SEAS SKYWAY

MIGHT AS WELL QUIT STRUGGLIN', BUCKO.

ON THIS LONELY LITTLE AIRSTRIP OF YOURS, AIN'T NOBODY AROUND TO HEAR YOU SCREAM.

AAGKGH!

AN' THE ONLY WAY YOU'RE GETTIN' LOOSE...

GAGKH!

...IS IF I LET YOU GO.

THE QUESTION S, SIRRAH...

...WILT THOU BE ALIVE WHEN HE DOES SO?

BRAZ

MY EXCEEDING BOISTEROUS COMPANION CALLS HIMSELF *ROUGHOUSE.*

I AM *BLOODSPORT.*

WE ARE HERE TO INFORM THEE THAT A NEW ORDER HATH ARRIVED ON *MADRIPOOR.*

AND THOU ART *ARCHIBALD CORRIGAN,* PROPRIETOR OF *SOUTH SEAS SKYWAYS.*

EMBRACING IT WILL PROVE MUTUALLY PROFITABLE-- FOR THEE AND OUR EMPLOYER BOTH, IT WOULD GUARANTEE WEALTH BEYOND THY WILDEST DREAMS.

DENYING IT, HOWE'ER-- AS OTHERS HAVE DONE, TO THEIR COST--

-- WILL GUARANTEE ONLY THY *GRAVE.*

A'IERRRGH!

FLY NO MORE FOR TYGER.

THE WENCH'S DAY IS DONE, HER NINE LIVES ALL BUT USED UP.

THY FEALTY, AVIATOR, BELONGS NOW TO OUR GENERAL--

--OR, MY CORRIGAN...

...THY *HEART* BELONGS TO *ME.*

TAI HAS HIS WAY OF INVESTIGATIN' A CRIME, I HAVE MINE.

WHEN I KNELT BESIDE RANJA'S BODY, IT WAS TO GET A LOCK ON HIS SCENT.

THEN, I BACK-TRAILED ALONG THE CANAL...

...'TIL I FIND WHERE HE WAS DUMPED IN.

PAIR OF BRUISERS DID THE DEED.

A WILD-- DISTURBING, ENTICING, FAMILIAR-- ALIEN-NESS TO THEIR SCENT...

...ONLY I CAN'T QUITE PLACE FROM WHERE.

JUDGING FROM THE MESS THEY LEFT BEHIND, THOUGH...

...THEY'RE NEITHER OF 'EM TO BE TAKEN LIGHTLY.

MADRIPOOR'S A SOCIETY WHERE ASSASSINATION AND KIDNAP FOR PROFIT ARE FACTS OF LIFE.

RANJA NEVER LEFT HIS PALACE WITHOUT TWO CARS OF ARMED BODYGUARDS FOR COVER.

AN' THE COMPOUND ITSELF IS LACED WITH THE BEST DEFENSES MONEY CAN BUY.

BUT SOMEONE GOT IN, AN' GOT RANJA OUT WITHOUT ANYBODY BEING THE WISER.

NO PROBLEM FOR ME.

THIS KIND'A CAPER IS WOLVERINE'S STOCK IN TRADE--

--MADE EASIER BY THE FACT THAT I'M A MUTANT, WITH PHYSICAL SENSES SO NATURALLY ACUTE I FUNCTION AS WELL IN PITCH-DARKNESS AS BROAD DAYLIGHT.

TABLE SET FOR TWO.

STANDS TO REASON. RANJA WAS A PLAYER.

WARNED HIM MORE'N ONCE THAT'D BE HIS DOWNFALL. HE LAUGHED HIS LAUGH AN' SAID, "PERHAPS, MY DEAR FRIEND, BUT WHAT A WAY TO GO."

CARELESS LADY. SHE LEFT A HANDKERCHIEF.

I KNOW THE SCENT...

...AND WITH THAT BREATH...

...THIS MESS GETS A WHOLE LOT MORE COMPLICATED.

HIGHTOWN'S AS FLASH AS LOWTOWN IS SHABBY, RACING HEADLONG INTO THE 21st CENTURY...

...WHILE ITS SHORESIDE COUNTERPART STAYS STUBBORNLY ANCHORED IN THE PAST.

THERE ARE FORTUNES IN BOTH PLACES.

IT'S JUST, THE ONES IN HIGHTOWN ARE MORE OBVIOUSLY EASY TO FIND.

THE SOVEREIGN BILLS ITSELF AS THE FINEST HOTEL IN THE WORLD.

CERTAINLY, THE MOST EXPENSIVE. THE RATES ON THE TRIPLEX *IMPERIAL* PENTHOUSE WOULD BANKRUPT SOME COUNTRIES.

THE CURRENT GUEST HAS AN OPEN-ENDED LEASE.

HIM, I'LL DEAL WITH LATER.

RIGHT NOW, MY INTEREST'S EXCLUSIVELY IN...

KARMA!

< NOT A MOVE, GIRL, NOT A SOUND-- AND IF YOU TRY TO USE YOUR POWER TO *POSSESS* ME... >

< ...YOU'LL BE *DEAD* BEFORE THAT THOUGHT CAN BECOME ACTION. >

MY VIET'S RUSTY, BUT SHE GETS THE MESSAGE.

< THIS SUITE'S RENTED TO *GENERAL NGUYEN NGOC COY.* WHO IS HE? >

< MY UNCLE. >

< BUT-- WHO ARE YOU?! >

< HOW IS IT YOU KNOW ME?!! >

< MY BUSINESS. WHAT'S HE WANT IN MADRIPOOR? >

< WHAT HE ALWAYS DOES-- *POWER.* >

< AND YOU HELP HIM?! >

< I HAVE SWORN MYSELF TO HIS SERVICE. >

< WHY? >

< THAT IS MY BUSINESS. >

< YOU WERE WITH CHANCELLOR RANJAMARYAN EARLIER TONIGHT. >

< HE'S DEAD. MURDERED. >

< SOMEONE OR SOMETHING SUCKED THE BLOOD RIGHT OUT OF HIM. YOU'RE INVOLVED. QUESTION IS... >

< ...ARE YOU RESPONSIBLE? >

< BETTER SORT OUT WHICH SIDE OF THE LINE YOU STAND ON, MS. XIAN COY MANH-- >

< --THE GOOD OR THE BAD, THE YIN OR THE YANG-- >

< --AND BE PREPARED TO TAKE THE CONSEQUENCES. >

NO!

NEXT DAY. LOWTOWN CENTRAL BAZAAR. LINDSAY McCABE AND JESSICA DREW.

NOTHIN' LIKE THIS BACK HOME IN SAN FRAN, EH, PARTNER?

HARD TO FIGURE THAT IN A DAY OR SO, WE'LL BE THERE...

...AN' ALL THIS, A MEMORY.

NICE TO HEAR YOU WAX SO ROMANTIC, McCABE...

...ABOUT A JOB THAT NEARLY GOT US BOTH KILLED.

YOU WANT?

Ieuchk-- IT'S WIGGLING!

TASTE GOOD! YOU LIKE!

MAYBE NEXT TIME, OKAY?

YOU HUNGRY, LITTLE LADY? NO PROBLEM!

?!!?

!?!

SMOOCH!

SMOOCH!

STICK WITH ME--

--Y'KNOW, YOU'RE THE SPARKLINGEST CUTIES I'VE LAID EYES ON IN A TROLL'S AGE--

--AN' I'LL SHOW YOU A DINNER...

...AN' A PARTY...

...YOU'LL NEVER FORGET!

ROUGHHOUSE!

MIGHT I REMIND THEE, COMRADE...

...THAT WE ARE HERE FOR REASONS OTHER THAN FLESHLY ENTERTAINMENT.

Sigh! SPOILSPORT, YOU NEVER LET ME HAVE ANY FUN!

Hsssst! DON'T'CHU FRET NONE, CUTIES!

BUSINESS MAY BE BUSINESS, BUT A MAN'S GOTTA HAVE HIMSELF SOME *PLAY* TIME, TOO, KNOW WHAT I'M SAYIN'?

SO YOU GET'CHERSELVES DOLLED UP REAL NICE, AN' WE'LL HOOK UP LATER.

I GUARANTEE A NIGHT THAT'LL *RING* YOUR CHIMES!

WHY WAIT?

YOU WANT "CHIMES" RUNG, CHUM, I'LL BE GLAD TO OBLIGE--

--RIGHT HERE AND NOW!

JESS! *JESSICA!*

RELAX, PARTNER! LET IT RIDE!

LINDSAY-- HOW CAN YOU *SAY* THAT?!

I DON'T KNOW, CALL IT AN INBORN RESPECT--

--FOR A GUY THE SIZE OF A MACK TRUCK!

HIS BUDDY, THOUGH-- HE'S *CREEPY--*

huh?!?

AYAAAA

HELP ME-- --FOR MERCY'S SAKE-- --*DEMONS--*

--MURDER!

SHE'S-- COVERED IN *BLOOD!*

STAY BY HER, LINDSAY--

--DO WHAT YOU CAN!

I'LL SEE WHERE SHE CAME FROM!

TRAIL LEADS TO THIS BUILDING ON THE EDGE OF THE MARKET.

NO IDEA WHAT'S INSIDE--

--BEST NOT TO CHARGE IN THE FRONT DOOR.

NO WINDOWS.

I'LL HAVE TO TRY THE ROOF.

THANK HEAVEN, I STILL *POSSESS...*

...MY ABILITY TO STICK TO WALLS.

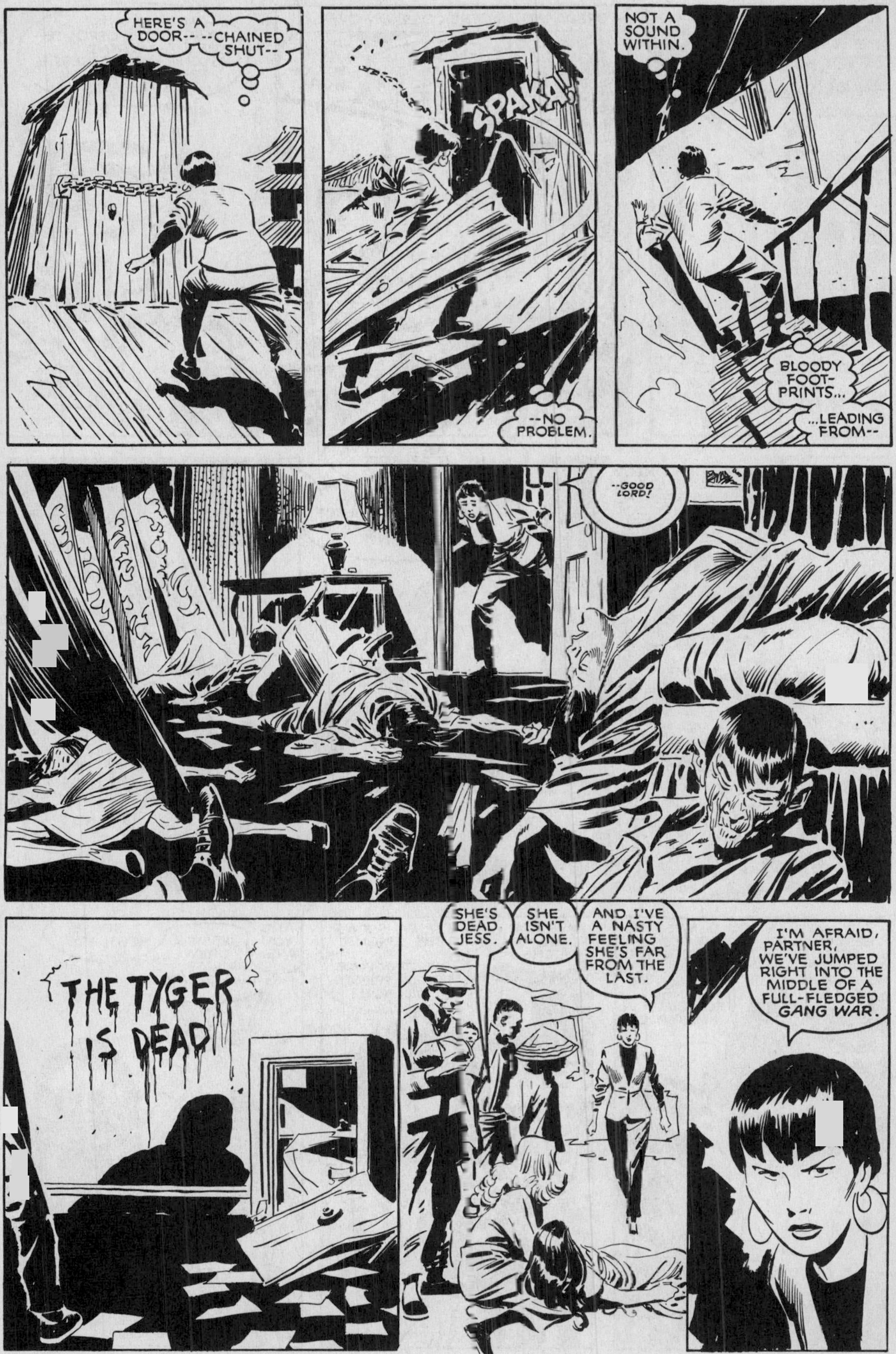
HERE'S A DOOR-- --CHAINED SHUT--
SPAKA!
--NO PROBLEM.
NOT A SOUND WITHIN.
BLOODY FOOT-PRINTS...
...LEADING FROM--
--GOOD LORD!
THE TYGER IS DEAD
SHE'S DEAD JESS.
SHE ISN'T ALONE.
AND I'VE A NASTY FEELING SHE'S FAR FROM THE LAST.
I'M AFRAID, PARTNER, WE'VE JUMPED RIGHT INTO THE MIDDLE OF A FULL-FLEDGED GANG WAR.

YOU WANT INFORMATION IN MADRIPOOR, *PRINCESS BAR'S* THE PLACE TO GO.

THAT'S WHY *I* BOUGHT HALF-INTEREST IN THE PLACE.

THAT'S ALSO WHY-- AFTER A *FRUSTRATIN'* INCONCLUSIVE TALK WITH THE COPS--

--DREW AND McCABE COME ON OVER.

WE KNOW COY FROM SAN FRANCISCO, HE TRIED TO SET HIMSELF UP AS THE LOCAL CRIME CZAR.

JESS WAS INSTRUMENTAL IN DRIVING HIM OUT OF TOWN.

HE'S A NASTY PIECE OF WORK.

HIS NIECE IS EXACTLY THE OPPOSITE-- SHE'S A *MUTANT,* PSYCHICALLY POSSESSES PEOPLE, USES 'EM AS PUPPETS--

--WORKIN' FOR COY GOES AGAINST EVERYTHING SHE BELIEVES IN.

SHE'D ONLY DO IT IF HE HAD SOME HOLD OVER HER. FIND THAT KEY-- BREAK IT-- AN' WE SET HER FREE.

PARAMOUNT NEED, THOUGH, IS TO NAIL COY'S *ENFORCERS* BEFORE THEY DO ANY MORE DAMAGE.

COY'S HIT TYGER'S PROTECTION, HER PEOPLE AN' HER MONEY-- THAT HOUSE THAT WAS RAIDED WAS HER MAJOR "BANK"--

--SHE CAN'T SURVIVE MANY MORE BODY BLOWS LIKE THAT.

I DID NOT CLAW MY WAY TO THE TOP OF THE MOUNTAIN, MY FRIEND...

...SIMPLY FOR THE VIEW.

AND I AM FAR FROM READY TO RELINQUISH MY PLACE TO ANOTHER.

YOUR PREDECESSOR, *ROCHE,* PROBABLY FELT THE SAME.

YOU DUMPED HIM, COY FIGURES TO DO THE SAME TO YOU.

WAY OF THE JUNGLE, ESPECIALLY IN MADRIPOOR.

HAVE YOU FORGOTTEN, PATCH--

--THE *TIGER* IS *KING* OF THE JUNGLE?

INTRODUCE ME TO YOUR FRIENDS, WILL YOU?

I'M LINDSAY McCABE.

AND YOU ARE...

JESSICA DREW. PRIVATE INVESTIGATOR.

I SENSE HOSTILITY.

I DON'T LIKE CRIMINALS.

NO MATTER HOW FANCY THEIR APPEARANCE OR AIRS.

I AM WHAT I AM, MS. DREW.

PATCH, I HAVE BEEN SUMMONED TO THE PALACE.

I SHOULD LIKE YOU TO ACCOMPANY ME.

PRINCE GETTIN' INVOLVED WITH LOWTOWN AFFAIRS, THAT ISN'T LIKE HIM.

THOSE WERE RANJAMARYAN'S RESPONSIBILITIES, REMEMBER? WITH THE CHANCELLOR SLAIN, THE PRINCE MUST ACT FOR HIMSELF.

I SUPPOSE HE WISHES TO SETTLE MATTERS-- HEAD OFF ANOTHER WAR-- BEFORE THEY GET OUT OF HAND.

A PITY HE HASN'T YET REALIZED THEY ALREADY ARE.

ELIMINATE COY AND WE ELIMINATE THE THREAT.

HAD YOU SEIZED HIS NIECE WHEN YOU HAD THE OPPORTUNITY, WE MIGHT HAVE GAINED OURSELVES AN INVALUABLE BARGAINING CHIP.

I DON'T WORK FOR YOU, TYGER.

I'M ESPECIALLY NOT YOUR PET EXECUTIONER.

IF I'M ANYTHING, I'M YOUR CONSCIENCE, AN' RIGHT NOW...

...YOU'RE DANCING ON THE EDGE OF THE ABYSS.

YOU WANT TO PLAY BY COY'S RULES...

...YOU CAN DRIVE YOURSELF THE REST OF THE WH-HEY!

NICE CAR. A REAL CLASSIC!

SHAME I GOTTA BUST IT TO BITS!

SKOOM!

ONLY KNOW A HANDFUL OF FOLKS IN THE WORLD WITH THAT KIND OF MUSCLE. ONE PUNCH AND THERE'S NOTHING LEFT OF TYGER'S ROLLS...

...BUT SCRAP METAL.

BEFORE I KNOW IT...

...IT'S MY TURN.

BYE-BYE, BODYGUARD!

SKRAMM

JOKE'S ON HIM.

HE FIGURES I'M PULPED.

(ALTHOUGH HE'S PRO ENOUGH TO MAKE SURE.)

DOESN'T KNOW MY SKELETON'S LACED WITH ADAMANTIUM, STRONGEST METAL KNOWN, MAKIN' IT VIRTUALLY UNBREAKABLE.

MAKES MY PUNCHES SOMETHIN' FIERCE, TOO.

POW

I TAP AN AVERAGE GUY...

...HE'S OUT FOR THE COUNT.

THIS ONE, I GIVE ALL I'VE GOT.

NOT BAD! NOT BAD!! FIRST DECENT HIT I'VE TAKEN IN AGES!

NICE TRY, SHORTY-- --BUT IT AIN'T ENOUGH!

ASSASSIN! LEARN TO YOUR COST, THAT *TYGER* CAN DEFEND HERSELF!

OWW!

YOU RUINED MY SUIT!

STUPID COW, YOU GOT THE SLIGHTEST NOTION...

...HOW HARD IT IS GETTIN' DECENT OUTFITS IN MY SIZE!

THEN NEXT I SHALL TEAR YOUR *THROAT*...

...INSTEAD OF YOUR CLOTHES...

...AND SPARE YOU FUTURE AGGRIVATI-*OH!*

SPIRIT IS EVER TO BE ADMIRED, MILADY. I REGRET I MUST DENY THEE THE *WARRIOR'S* DEATH THOU HATH MOST MANIFESTLY EARNED.

FOR *BLOODSPORT*, REGRETTABLY...

...THERE IS BUT ONE WAY TO KILL.

AT HIS TOUCH...

...*TYGER BLEEDS!*

I TOSS CAUTION, RATIONALITY, COMMON SENSE TO THE WINDS.

ONLY THE *BERSERKER* IN MY SOUL CAN SAVE US NOW.

SNIKT!

THAT-- AND MY *CLAWS!*

FORGOT ABOUT OL' *ROUGHOUSE*, DIDJA, SHORTY?

THOOM

YUP.

CARELESS.

STUPID.

GONNA COST *TYGER* AN' ME BOTH...

...OUR *LIVES*.

HEY, LI'L GUY, GIVE YOURSELF A *BREAK!*

YOU KEEP GETTIN' UP...

...I'LL KEEP KNOCKIN' YOU *DOWN*.

GUARANTEE YOU'LL *BREAK* BEFORE *I* WILL!

NON!

KARMA! WEARIN' HER OLD UNIFORM AS ONE OF THE *NEW MUTANTS*.

YOU HAVE DONE SUFFICIENT HARM THIS NIGHT.

YOU WILL DO *NO MORE!*

M'SIEU-- GATHER UP THE LADY--

--LEAVE THIS PLACE!

I *TRY*.

BUT NOTHIN' *WORKS*.

QUICKLY, M'SIEU! THEIR WILLS ARE FIERCE, I CANNOT HOLD THEM LONG! IN OUR BLESSED SAVIOR'S NAME-- GO!

TYGER'S PALE--

--FULL MOON HAS MORE COLOR--

--BUT SHE'S STILL BREATHING, FIGHTING AS HARD AS SHE CAN.

COY'S BULLYBOYS ARE HELPLESS. I'LL PROBABLY NEVER HAVE A BETTER SHOT AT THEM.

ASSUMING I SUCCEED.

ASSUMING KARMA LETS ME.

I AM SORRY, I SHOULD HAVE BEEN HERE SOONER.

THAT YOU'RE HERE AT ALL MEANS MORE'N YOU KNOW.

CAN'T TAKE THAT RISK.

I'M OBLIGED, GIRL.

WHAT--?!

BOTH GONE--!

WHERE? HOW?! IT CAN'T BE!?!

SHE FLASHED A SMILE AS I CARRIED TYGER AWAY.

GRATITUDE, I THINK, FOR THIS SMALL CHANCE TO RECAPTURE HOW IT FELT TO BE ON THE SIDE OF THE ANGELS.

HOPE SHE GETS ANOTHER.

BY THE TIME I REACH THE PRINCESS, I'M PRETTY MUCH OKAY-- MY MUTANT HEALING FACTOR (MY PRIMARY POWER) TAKING CARE OF MY WOUNDS.

TYGER ISN'T SO LUCKY.

SHE NEEDS A HOSPITAL, PATCH.

THAT'S THE SECOND PLACE THEY'LL CHECK-- RIGHT AFTER THEY COME HERE.

YOU'LL HAVE TO MOVE HER TO A SAFE HOUSE AN' GO TO GROUND TILL THE DUST SETTLES.

WHAT DO YOU MEAN US?!

WE DON'T KNOW THIS TOWN!

I CAN'T DO IT, McCABE, AND I GOT NO ONE ELSE TO TRUST.

THIS ISN'T OUR FIGHT, PATCH.

LOOK, DREW--TYGER DOESN'T TOUCH DRUGS OR SLAVES. HER PREDECESSOR, ROCHE, DEALT IN BOTH. SO DOES COY.

WHEN TYGER TOOK OVER, SHE STARTED MOVING AGAINST THE MAJOR PLAYERS. NOW, THROUGH COY, THEY'RE PUSHING BACK.

YOU MAY BELIEVE THERE'S NO DIFFERENCE BETWEEN THEM...

...BUT THERE IS.

SO WHERE'LL *YOU* BE, FOR ALL THIS?

COY'S CLOUT COMES FROM THE DRUGS HE SHIPS. HE'S PROBABLY USING THAT PROFIT POTENTIAL TO BUY THE PRINCE'S SUPPORT.

YOU MEAN MADRI-POOR'S *RULER*...

...IS PART OF THIS?!

McCABE, HE'S A *PIRATE*, DESCENDED FROM A HUNDRED GENERATIONS OF PIRATES.

ANYWAY, NO DRUGS, NO PROFIT, NO CLOUT. AN' HOPEFULLY, AN EVEN FIGHT.

WHADAYA SAY, JESS?

I...

...WON'T STAND BY AND LET *ANYONE* BE BUTCHERED...

...THE WAY THOSE POOR PEOPLE WERE THIS AFTER-NOON. EVEN TYGER.

LINDSAY, WHAT'RE YOU DOING?! I CAN CARRY HER MORE EASILY!

AN' SUPPOSE WE RUN INTO TROUBLE, PARTNER, WHAT THEN?

WE'LL NEED YOUR MUSCLE TO BUST HEADS.

COY'S ENFORCERS SHOW, BEST TO CHOOSE DISCRETION OVER VALOR.

HARDER YOU HIT, BETTER ROUGHHOUSE LIKES IT.

THEN I SHOULD PUT HIM IN SEVENTH-HEAVEN.

WISH I COULD BE THERE TO SEE THAT.

GOOD LUCK, PATCH.

LIKEWISE.

WE'LL ALL NEED IT, TO COME THROUGH THIS CAPER.

AN' THE EDGE IN DREW'S VOICE TELLS ME SHE KNOWS EXACTLY HOW THIN OUR CHANCES ARE.

BUT SHE'S HELPING ANYWAY. I LIKE THAT.

THEY'RE ON THEIR WAY. I'VE GOT TO DO THE SAME.

FREEZE!

ONLY ME, ARCHIE. TRIFLE EDGY, AREN'T YOU?

IT WAS A GREAT DREAM, PATCH. I DON'T APPRECIATE BEIN' WOKEN OUT OF IT.

I GOT A JOB FOR YOU.

NOT INTERESTED.

I'M CALLING IN TYGER'S MARKER, CORRIGAN.

I CAN'T TAKE "NO" FOR AN ANSWER.

TWELVE-GAUGE, DOUBLE-BARRELED BUCKSHOT...

...SAYS YOU WILL!

I'D RECONSIDER, ARCH...

..IF I WERE YOU.

SOVEREIGN HOTEL. IMPERIAL PENTHOUSE.

AFTER SOUTH VIETNAM FELL TO THE COMMUNISTS, I CONSIDERED RELOCATING TO MADRIPOOR...

...BUT ROCHE WAS CRIMELORD THEN, AND IN HIS PRIME.

AND I LACKED THE RESOURCES TO PROPERLY CHALLENGE HIM.

TODAY, HOWEVER-- THANKS TO TYGER-- HE IS BUT A MEMORY, HIS CRIMINAL EMPIRE RIPE FOR THE CONQUEST.

POWER, MY DEAR SHAN-- AS I HOPE YOU ARE TO LEARN-- IS THE ULTIMATE ADDICTION.

ONCE TASTED, ALL OTHERS PALE-- ALMOST TO INSIGNIFICANCE-- IN COMPARISON.

ALTHOUGH, OF COURSE, THEY DO HAVE THEIR PROPER PLACE.

MASTER, BLOODSPORT AND ROUGHOUSE AWAIT YOUR PLEASURE.

ADMIT THEM.

MAYBE AFTER, SWEETIE-PIE, YOU AN' ME...?

YOU SHOULD LIVE SO LONG-- humph!

HAWR!

SHE IS OUR LORD'S PROPERTY, MY FRIEND-- HAST THOU LEARNED NOTHING FROM BITTER EXPERIENCE?!

I TRU'ST, GENTLEMEN, YOUR NEWS IS ON A PAR WITH THIS MOST GLORIOUS OF MORNINGS?

REGRETTABLY, LORD, NO.

THE TYGER YET LIVES.

THE AMBUSH WENT AS PLANNED--

--UNTIL THE INTERVENTION OF SOME UNKNOWN PARTY ALLOWED OUR PREY TO ESCAPE.

THE TYGER HAS GONE INTO HIDING.

THUS FAR, SHE IS NOWHERE TO BE FOUND.

GENTLEMEN, THE LONGER THIS DRAGS ON, THE GREATER THE POTENTIAL FOR DISASTER

THE PRINCE CAN WITHDRAW HIS SUPPORT AS EASILY AS HE GAVE IT

UNDERSTAND ME PLAINLY-- I WILL NOT BE FAILED AGAIN!

WE HEAR, LORD.

I HAVE TASTED THE TYGER'S BLOOD, WE ARE BOUND, SHE AND I, SHE CANNOT HIDE FROM ME FOREVER.

HER BUDDY-BODYGUARD, PATCH, HE SKIPPED TOWN.

TOOK OFF FOR PARTS UNKNOWN WITH THE FLYBOY, CORRIGAN.

PERHAPS HE IS BOWING TO THE INEVITABLE, UNCLE...

A TEMPTING NOTION, SHAN...

...AND ABANDONING A LOST CAUSE?

...BUT THE PRUDENT TACTICIAN...

...MUST EVER ASSUME THE WORST.

THE BEST WAY TO COUNTER-ATTACK IS TO STRIKE AT MY OPIUM PLANTATIONS ON THE MAINLAND.

IF PATCH IS SAVING HIS OWN SKIN, FINE, LET HIM GO.

IF, ON THE OTHER HAND, HE'S OFF TO PLAY THE HERO--

--ALONG WITH CORRIGAN, THIS PROVING AN IDEAL OPPORTUNITY TO TEST HIS TRUE LOYALTY--

--I WANT A MOST APPROPRIATE WELCOME PREPARED.

I PROPOSE A *TOAST*, MY FRIENDS-- --TO MY *TRIUMPH*... ...AND THE *DEATHS* OF ALL MY ENEMIES!

WHY-- DEAR SHAN-- --YOU AREN'T *DRINKING!*

COULD IT BE, NIECE... ...YOU DON'T SHARE MY SENTIMENT?

THERE'S MY GIRL, I KNEV I COUL COUNT ON YOU.

COME, GENTLEMEN, LET US PUT OUR HEADS TOGETHER... ...AND SET ABOUT THE FURTHER DISMANTLING OF TYGER'S ORGANIZA- TION.

WHAT HAVE I DONE?

TASH!

MOTHER OF ANGELS-- --WHAT AM I TO DO?!!

NEXT: *HUNTER'S MOON!*

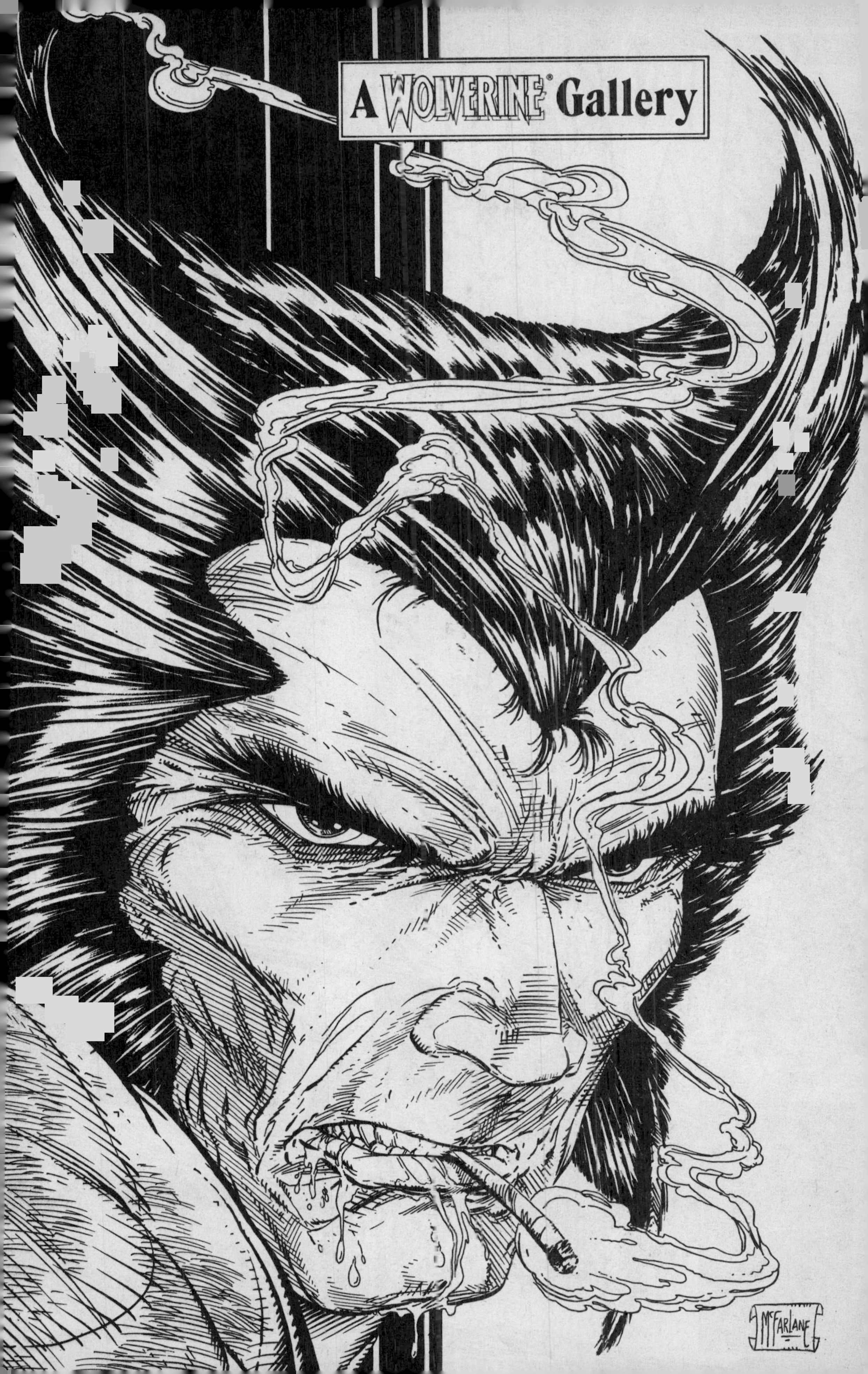
A WOLVERINE® Gallery
McFARLANE

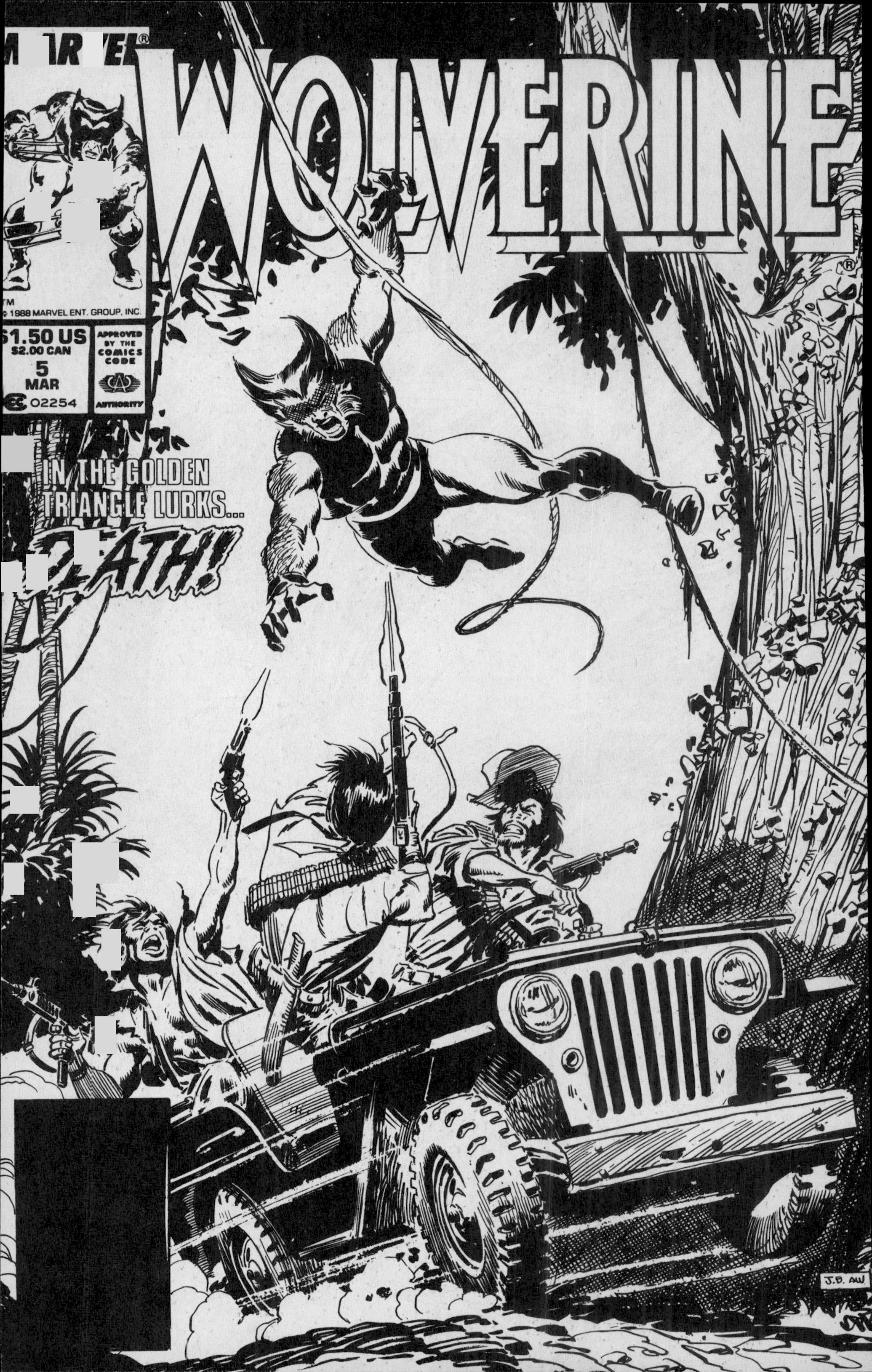
WOLVERINE
© 1988 MARVEL ENT. GROUP, INC.
$1.50 US
$2.00 CAN
5
MAR
02254
APPROVED BY THE COMICS CODE AUTHORITY
IN THE GOLDEN TRIANGLE LURKS...
J.B. AW

THE IMPERIAL PENTHOUSE OF THE SOVEREIGN HOTEL, MADRIPOOR...

WHAT HAVE I DONE?!

I TRIED TO HELP M'SIEU PATCH AND HIS LADY FRIEND, TYGER.

INSTEAD, I HAVE ONLY MADE MATTERS MUCH, MUCH WORSE!

MOTHER OF ANGELS--

--WHAT AM I TO DO?!

MISS MANH?

BLOODSPORT--

--CHIEF AMONG MY UNCLE'S PET ASSASSINS.

ART WELL, LADY?

I THANK YOU FOR YOUR CONCERN, M'SIEU.

I AM QUITE WELL.

FORGIVE ME... ...BUT IT IS MY GIFT--AND CURSE-- TO SENSE THE *TRUTH* THAT OFT LIES BEHIND THE SPOKEN WORD.

THY HEART AND SOUL ARE SORELY TROUBLED.

I AM THY HUMBLE SERVANT...

...AND WOULD HELP--

LADY-- THOU'RT *BLEEDING.*

CE N'EST PAS RIEN!

IT IS *NOTHING,* M'SIEU-- THE SMALLEST OF CUTS.

SAINTS, WHERE IS MY COURAGE?!

HOW IS IT HE CAN TERRIFY ME-- WITH BUT A *LOOK?!!*

THE BLOOD IS THE LIFE, LADY.

FAR TOO PRECIOUS TO BE TAKEN FOR GRANTED...

...OR WASTED.

I HAVE TASTED THINE, *XI'AN COY MANH.*

THE SKEIN OF OUR LIVES HAS THUS BECOME ENTWINED.

WE ARE BOUND, MILADY, TOGETHER.

TILL *DEATH.*

AND MAYHAP, *BEYOND.*

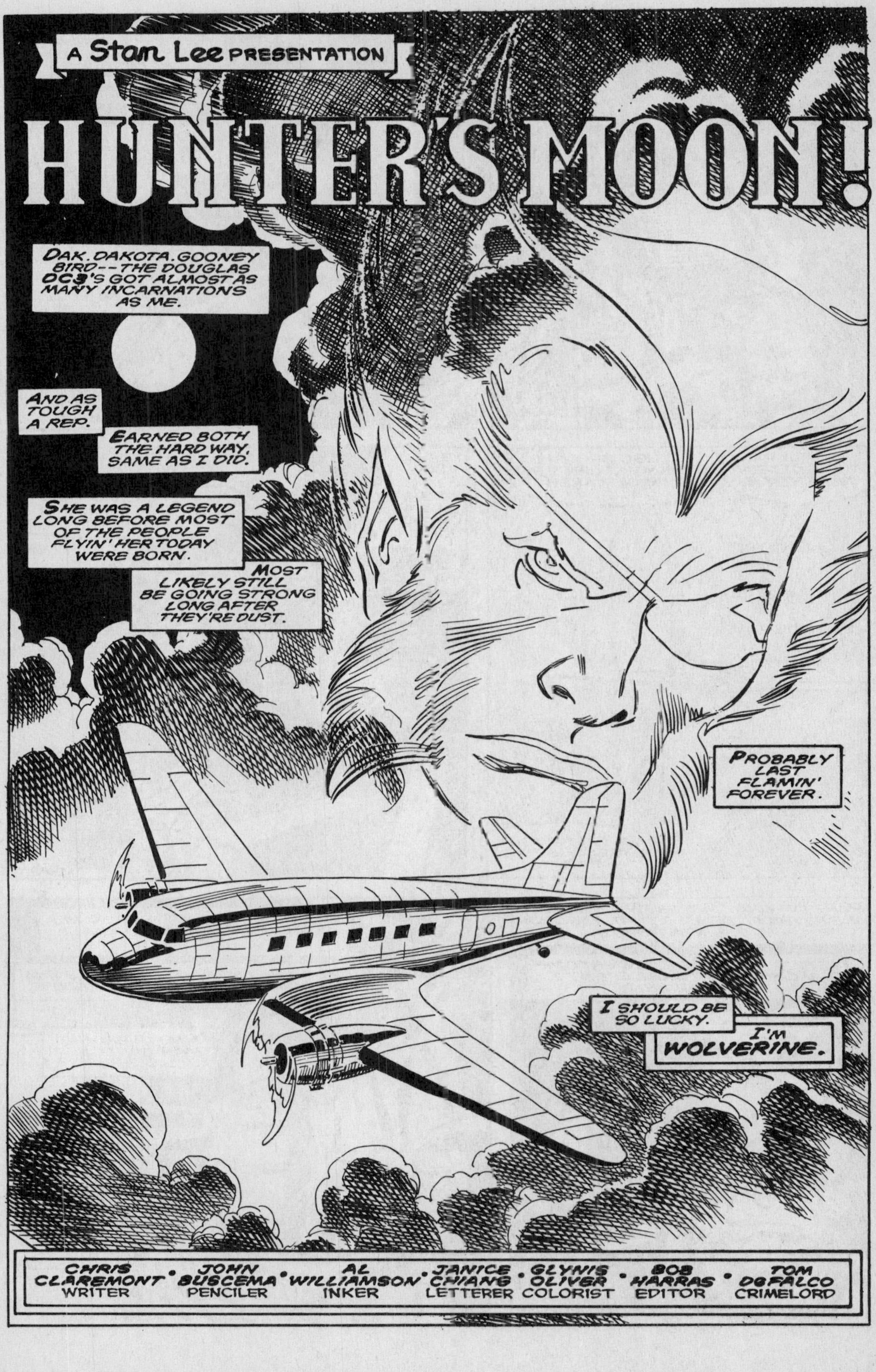
A Stan Lee PRESENTATION
HUNTER'S MOON!
DAK. DAKOTA. GOONEY BIRD--THE DOUGLAS DC3'S GOT ALMOST AS MANY INCARNATIONS AS ME.
AND AS TOUGH A REP.
EARNED BOTH THE HARD WAY, SAME AS I DID.
SHE WAS A LEGEND LONG BEFORE MOST OF THE PEOPLE FLYIN' HER TODAY WERE BORN.
MOST LIKELY STILL BE GOING STRONG LONG AFTER THEY'RE DUST.
PROBABLY LAST FLAMIN' FOREVER.
I SHOULD BE SO LUCKY.
I'M WOLVERINE.
CHRIS CLAREMONT WRITER • JOHN BUSCEMA PENCILER • AL WILLIAMSON INKER • JANICE CHIANG LETTERER • GLYNIS OLIVER COLORIST • BOB HARRAS EDITOR • TOM DEFALCO CRIMELORD

BUT THE WORLD BELIEVES WOLVERINE'S DEAD-- SO IN MADRIPOOR, I GO BY THE NAME, "PATCH".

COULD DO WITH LESS MOON...

...AND A LOT MORE CLOUDS.

FLYBOY'S ARCHIE CORRIGAN. LIKE ME AN' THIS OLD WARHORSE, THE BEST AT WHAT HE DOES.

LIKE US, A BODY WITH A HISTORY.

NOT THE NIGHT I'D CHOOSE...

NO USE GROUSIN' OVER WHAT CAN'T BE CHANGED, ARCH.

--TO FLY INTO THE GOLDEN TRIANGLE.

WE GO TONIGHT BECAUSE WE HAVE TO.

YEAH, I KNOW.

TYGER'S LIFE IS ON THE LINE.

I NEED A STRETCH. TAKE OVER, WILLYA?

THERE'S COFFEE AND SANDWICHES AFT, YOU WANT?

I'LL PASS.

PART OF WHAT MAKES ME A MUTANT ARE PHYSICAL SENSES THAT FUNCTION AT THEIR ULTIMATE.

THERE'S A RESIDUAL UNDERTONE TO ARCHIE'S NATURAL SCENT I RECOGNIZE.

BELONGS TO BLOODSPORT.

SLIGHTEST OF QUAVERS TO HIS VOICE. MORE THAN NORMAL TENSION.

ODDS ARE THE BAD GUYS MADE HIM AN OFFER HE DIDN'T DARE REFUSE.

AND IF ARCHIE HAS SWITCHED SIDES...

...THE LAST THING HE'S GOING FOR IS A SNACK.

TOO BAD.

THAT *SOUND--??*

CHECKED PATCH OUT BEFORE WE TOOK OFF. HE'S CLEAN.

I'VE GOT THE ONLY GUN.

NOW I'VE GOT TO *USE* IT.

PATCH IS AFTER THE OPIUM CROP THAT'S COY'S BANKROLL.

DESTROY THAT, IT BECOMES A FAIR FIGHT BETWEEN COY AND TYGER.

KILL PATCH, SHE'S FINISHED.

PROUD OF YOURSELF, COLONEL?

THIS HOW YOU *REPAY* THEIR FRIENDSHIP?

BUT IF I DON'T--

--THAT *VAMPIRE*--

--THEN *BLOODSPORT*--

--HE'LL COME BACK FOR *ME!*

THAT SOUND AGAIN--

--LIKE SOMETHING METAL...

...RETRACTING INTO ITS HOUSING.

DOES PATCH *KNOW?*

DOES IT *MATTER?*

WHAT CAN HE DO AGAINST A BULLET?

SNAKT!

WHO'M I KIDDING? I'VE FLOWN A STRAIGHT COURSE ALL MY LIFE.

IF THE 'NAM TAUGHT ME ANYTHING...

...IT'S THAT YOU STAND BY YOUR WINGMAN NO MATTER WHAT.

TOO OLD, TOO LATE, TO CHA HEY?!!?

HANG ON, ZOOMIE.

THROTTLE TO THE FIREWALL.

...YOKE ALL THE WAY FORWARD...

...I HEAD US FOR THE GROUND...

...LIKE A DIVE-BOMBER.

ARE YOU CRAZY!!

PATCH! WHAT THE DEVIL-- -:OW:-- ARE YOU DOING?!

FIGHTER ANSWERS FOR ME, AS IT LOOPS AROUND FOR ANOTHER PASS.

IT'S A MUSTANG, SAME VINTAGE AS OUR GOONEY.

PROBABLY THE HOTTEST PISTON COMBAT AIRCRAFT EVER BUILT. A LONG WAY FROM STATE OF THE ART, BUT IT GETS THE JOB DONE.

PILOT AIN'T HOT.

BUT AGAINST AN UNARMED TRANSPORT, HOW GOOD DOES HE HAVE TO BE, RIGHT?

NO MARKINGS.

ISN'T PART OF ANY LOCAL AIR FORCE--'CEPT MAYBE COY'S.

PRC -- MAINLAND CHINESE -- HAD A COUPLE OF P-SI SQUADRONS LEFT OVER FROM THE BIG DEUCE.

BRIBE HERE, HEIST THERE -- EASY AS SIN...

...FOR A DRUGLORD TO GET HIS HANDS ON 'EM.

OUTSTANDING!

MIND TELLING ME HOW COME YOU'RE DOING THAT PILOT'S JOB FOR HIM?!

WE'RE TOO LOW, PATCH --

-- PULL UP!

BLAST! HE CLIPPED OUR PORT FAN!

SHE'S SMOKING -- -- FEATHER THE ENGINE AND HIT THE EXTINGUISHER...

...BEFORE IT STARTS TO BURN!

CAN'T. WE NEED THE POWER.

YOU'RE CRAZY! THIS IS -- ¡UHNF! -- MY AIRPLANE!

HE'S HOLDING THE STICK -- TOO STRONG -- CAN'T FORCE IT BACK!

RELAX, ARCHIE. THERE'S A METHOD TO MY MADNESS, I EVEN HAVE A PLAN.

AT THE PROVERBIAL LAST MINUTE...

...WE HAUL BACK ON OUR YOKES.

GOONEY RESPONDS LIKE A TROOPER...

...LIKE I KNEW SHE WOULD.

NOW IT'S ARCHIE'S TURN.

WAIT FOR MY SIGNAL.

WHEN YOU HEAR IT, YOU COME!

FROM WHERE, CHUMP, THE GRAVE?!

HEY?! WHERE'RE YOU GOING --

-- PATCH, YOU HAVEN'T GOT A 'CHUTE!!

DO TELL.

MUSTANG FOLLOWED US INTO OUR CLIMB.

BEFORE THE DRIVER REALIZES IT...

...I'M ON TOP OF HIM.

ORDINARY MAN, THE IMPACT WOULD BUST HIM TO A PULP.

BUT MY BONES CAN'T BE BROKEN.

AND I HAVE CLAWS--

SNIKT!

--THAT'LL CUT THROUGH ANYTHING!

PILOT NEVER HAS A CHANCE.

DOESN'T BREAK MY HEART. HE HADN'T GIVEN US ANY, EITHER.

SKBOOM!

'COURSE, THAT STILL LEAVES ME...

...A THOUSAND METERS UP...

...AN' FALLIN' FAST.

BUT LIKE I SAID, I'M A MUTANT. WHAT MAKES ME ONE IS A HEALING FACTOR...

...CAPABLE OF HANDLING ALMOST ANY WOUND.

I'M BANKING ON IT TO SAVE ME.

I FIGURE THIS'LL BE NO WORSE...

...THAN BEING HIT BY THE HULK.

SPLASH!

MADRIPOOR LOWTOWN.

PAM PAM PAM

HEY THERE, ANYBODY *HOME?*

THIS IS THE RIGHT ADDRESS.

PATCH SAID WE COULD TURN TO THESE GUYS FOR HELP.

DIDN'T TELL US THE STUPID PLACE'D BE LOCKED TIGHT AS FORT KNOX!

C'MON C'MON C'MON--

--OPEN THE DOOR AND LET US *IN!*

CAN'T KEEP *SHLEPPING* TYGER ALL OVER TOWN, SHE--!

LINDSAY!

WHA--!?

LANDAU, LUCKMAN & LAKE

GEEZ, JESS--IT'S SO WEIRD SEEING YOU COME DOWN WALLS LIKE THAT!

DIDN'T MEAN TO STARTLE YOU, PARTNER.

SCOUTED THE NEIGHBORHOOD. NO SIGN OF THE OPPOSITION.

YET.

OUR LUCK WON'T HOLD FOREVER, Y'KNOW.

Y'ASK ME, WE BETTER BAG THIS JOINT.

NOBODY'S HERE.

YOUR PARDON, YOUNG LADIES--

--BUT IS THERE A REASON FOR RAISING SUCH A COMMOTION...

...AT THIS UNHOLY HOUR?

?!?!?!

PATCH SENT US.

AH.

WELL.

YOU'D BEST COME IN, THEN.

I AM CHANG.

JESSICA DREW.

LINDSAY McCABE.

AND YOUR COMPANION...?

WOULD PREFER TO REMAIN ANONYMOUS.

BETTER FOR ALL CONCERNED.

I UNDERSTAND.

THIS IS NOT THE BEST PLACE TO STAY.

BUT I BELIEVE I CAN PROVIDE SOME APPROPRIATE ALTERNATIVES!

BETTER MAKE IT SNAPPY.

THE GOONS CHASING OUR FRIEND ARE REALLY HOT FOR HER BLOOD.

IN EVERY SENSE OF THE WORD.

YOU DOING OKAY, PARTNER?

NEVER BETTER!

WHO'M I KIDDING, RIGHT?

RIGHT. NO CRIME BEING SCARED. NOR SHAME.

EASY FOR YOU TO SAY, YOU HAVE SUPER-POWERS. YOU CAN DEFEND YOURSELF.

I KEEP REMEMBERING THE LAST TIME WE "BABY-SAT" SOMEONE...

...WHEN I ALMOST GOT KILLED.

IF YOU'LL PERMIT, MISS McCABE--

I BELIEVE I MIGHT OFFER A SOLUTION--

THE GOLDEN TRIANGLE--

--NEAR THE HEADWATERS OF THE MEKONG, AT THE CONFLUENCE OF THE BORDERS OF THAILAND, BURMA AND LAOS.

NOTHIN' TO THE NAKED EYE, BRO.

BIG NADA ON INFRARED.

ANYBODY COME DOWN HERE, HE WENT SPLAT.

WASTE O' TIME, OUR HUMPIN' ALL THIS WAY.

WILD GOOSE CHASE, AXE-- BORRRRING!

ORDERS, SHOTGUN.

PHOOEY.

ROVER TO HOTHOUSE-- BATTLE-AXE HERE, BOSS.

SEARCH COMPLETED. GRID SECTORS KILO, MIKE, NOVEMBER.

RESULTS NEGATIVE. ONE WRECK, OURS. NO SIGN OF THE GOONEY. NO BAGGIES, NO WALKERS, OVER.

REPORT ACKNOWLEDGED.

CONTINUE SEARCH.

AWH, C'MON, HARDCASE--GIVE US A BREAK!

THIS ISN'T A DEMOCRACY, BATTLEAXE.

I SAY, YOU GO, AN' THAT'S THE WAY OF IT.

EYEBALL THE CRASH SITE, I WANT TO KNOW WHAT BROUGHT THE MUSTANG DOWN.

HEY, LIMEY-- DON'CHU WORRY NONE, MAN.

ANYBODY SHOWS, WE'LL NAIL HIS HIDE TO THE WALL, BUT GOOD.

I HEARD THAT, HARDCASE. THOSE LOCAL POGYBAIT JELLY-BELLIES COULDN'T TAKE DOWN A TROOP O' GIRL SCOUTS.

WHICH IS WHY, SERGEANT. COLONEL COY HIRED US TO ASSIST THEM.

SO LET'S DO OUR JOB, EH?

ASK ME, BRO, SOME JOBS AIN'T WORTH THE BREAD, Y'KNOW?

SO WHO ASKED YOU, WHITEBREAD?

LET'S ROLL HARD AN' FAST--

--FINISH OUR SWEEP AN' BOOGIE TO THE BARN.

SOMETHIN'S GOT HARDCASE ON EDGE.

FEEL BETTER ONCE WE'RE BACK WITH HIM.

THEY MAKE THEIR MOVE...

...I MAKE MINE.

BATTLEAXE--

--I HEARD SOMETHING!

SNIKT!

GOOD MAN.

ON THE BALL, KNOWS HIS TRADE.

DOESN'T SAVE HIM.

OR HIS BUDDY.

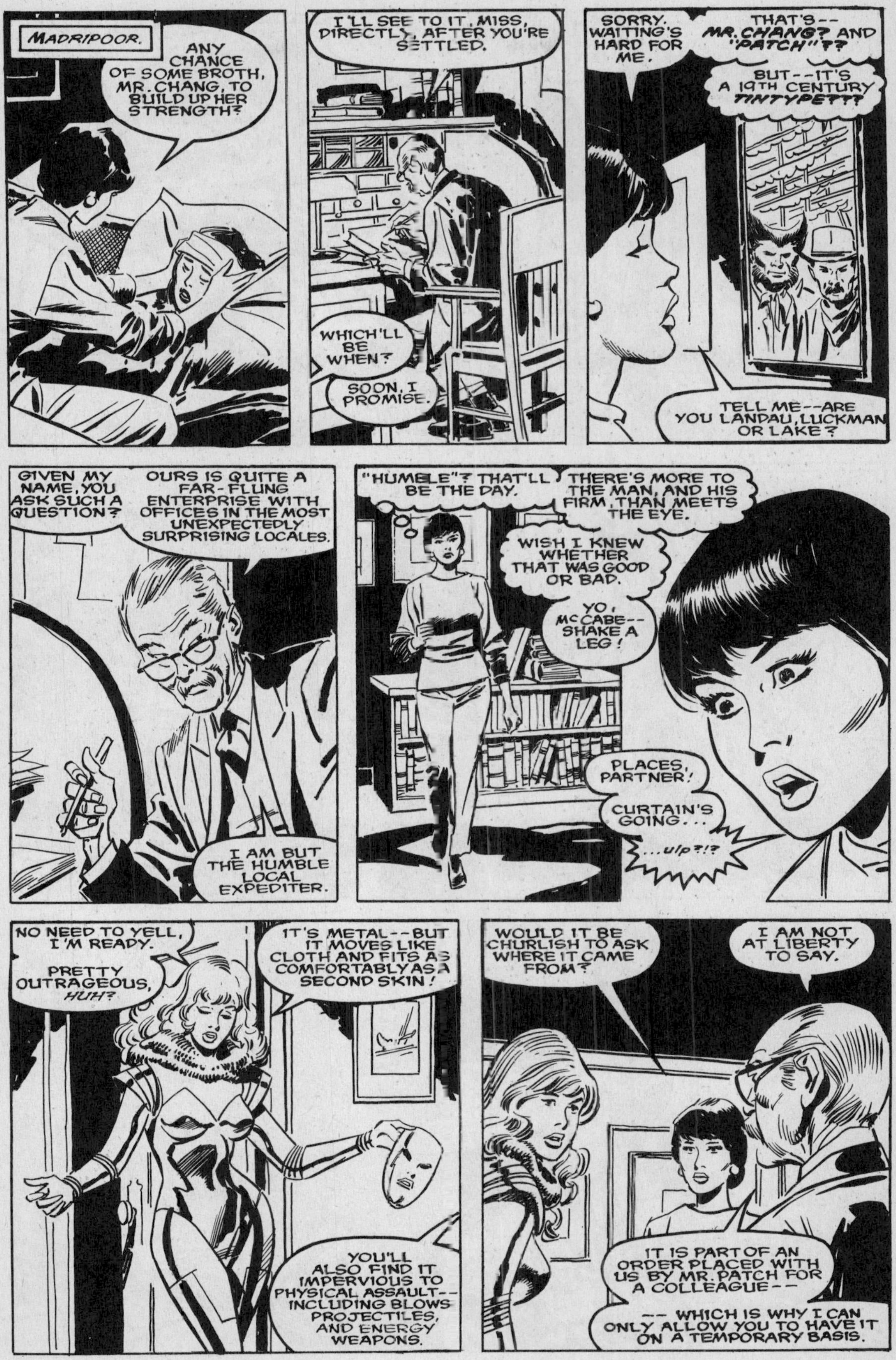
MADRIPOOR.
ANY CHANCE OF SOME BROTH, MR. CHANG, TO BUILD UP HER STRENGTH?
I'LL SEE TO IT, MISS, DIRECTLY, AFTER YOU'RE SETTLED.
WHICH'LL BE WHEN?
SOON, I PROMISE.
SORRY. WAITING'S HARD FOR ME.
THAT'S-- MR. CHANG? AND "PATCH"??
BUT--IT'S A 19TH CENTURY TINTYPE???
TELL ME--ARE YOU LANDAU, LUCKMAN OR LAKE?
GIVEN MY NAME, YOU ASK SUCH A QUESTION?
OURS IS QUITE A FAR-FLUNG ENTERPRISE WITH OFFICES IN THE MOST UNEXPECTEDLY SURPRISING LOCALES.
I AM BUT THE HUMBLE LOCAL EXPEDITER.
"HUMBLE"? THAT'LL BE THE DAY.
THERE'S MORE TO THE MAN, AND HIS FIRM, THAN MEETS THE EYE.
WISH I KNEW WHETHER THAT WAS GOOD OR BAD.
YO, McCABE-- SHAKE A LEG!
PLACES, PARTNER!
CURTAIN'S GOING...
...ulp?!?
NO NEED TO YELL, I'M READY.
PRETTY OUTRAGEOUS, HUH?
IT'S METAL--BUT IT MOVES LIKE CLOTH AND FITS AS COMFORTABLY AS A SECOND SKIN!
YOU'LL ALSO FIND IT IMPERVIOUS TO PHYSICAL ASSAULT-- INCLUDING BLOWS, PROJECTILES, AND ENERGY WEAPONS.
WOULD IT BE CHURLISH TO ASK WHERE IT CAME FROM?
I AM NOT AT LIBERTY TO SAY.
IT IS PART OF AN ORDER PLACED WITH US BY MR. PATCH FOR A COLLEAGUE--
--WHICH IS WHY I CAN ONLY ALLOW YOU TO HAVE IT ON A TEMPORARY BASIS.

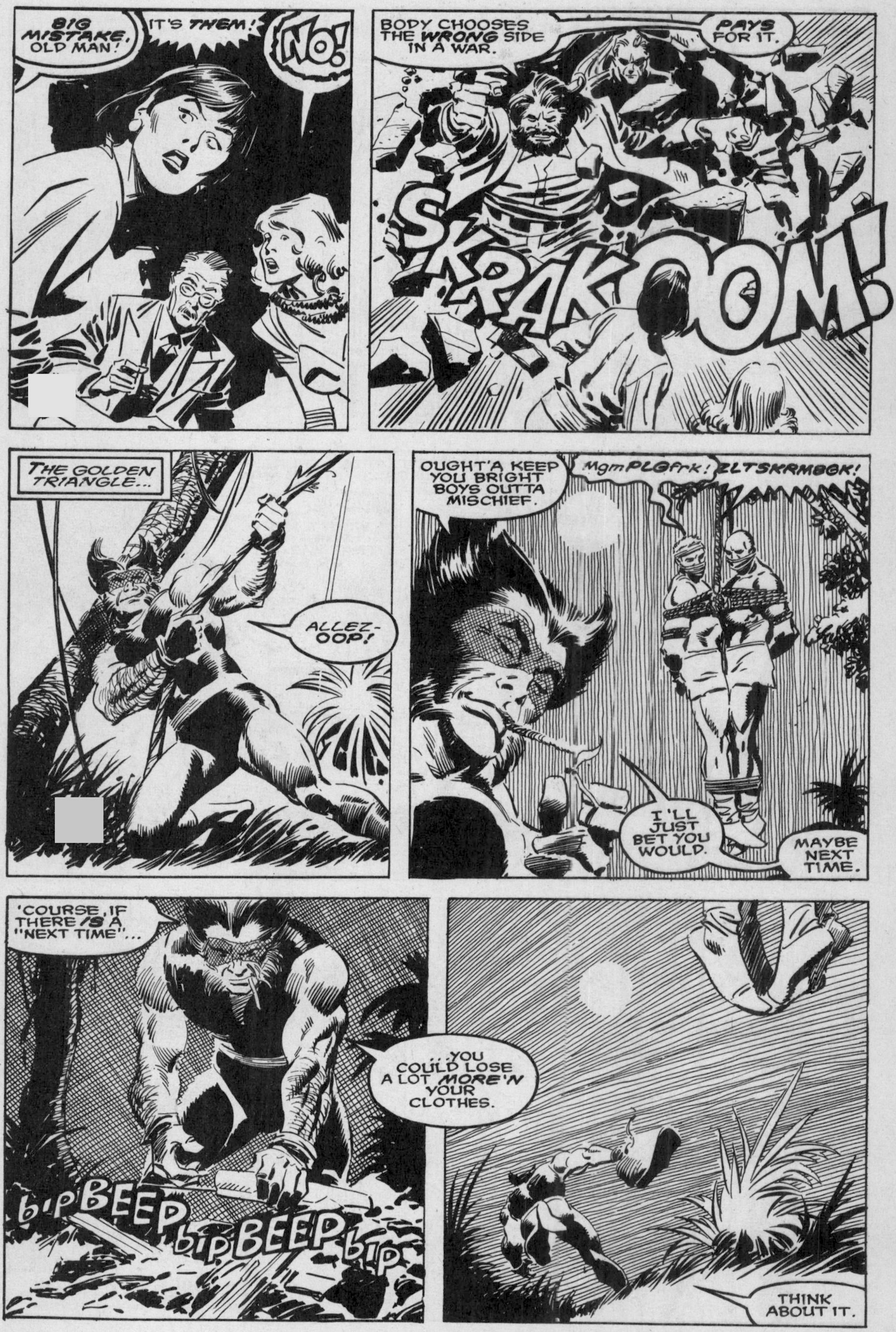
BIG MISTAKE, OLD MAN!
IT'S THEM!
NO!
BODY CHOOSES THE WRONG SIDE IN A WAR.
PAYS FOR IT.
SKRAKOOM!
THE GOLDEN TRIANGLE...
ALLEZ-OOP!
OUGHT'A KEEP YOU BRIGHT BOYS OUTTA MISCHIEF.
MgmPLGfrk!
ZLTSKRMBGK!
I'LL JUST BET YOU WOULD.
MAYBE NEXT TIME.
'COURSE, IF THERE IS A "NEXT TIME"...
...YOU COULD LOSE A LOT MORE'N YOUR CLOTHES.
bip BEEP bip BEEP bip
THINK ABOUT IT.

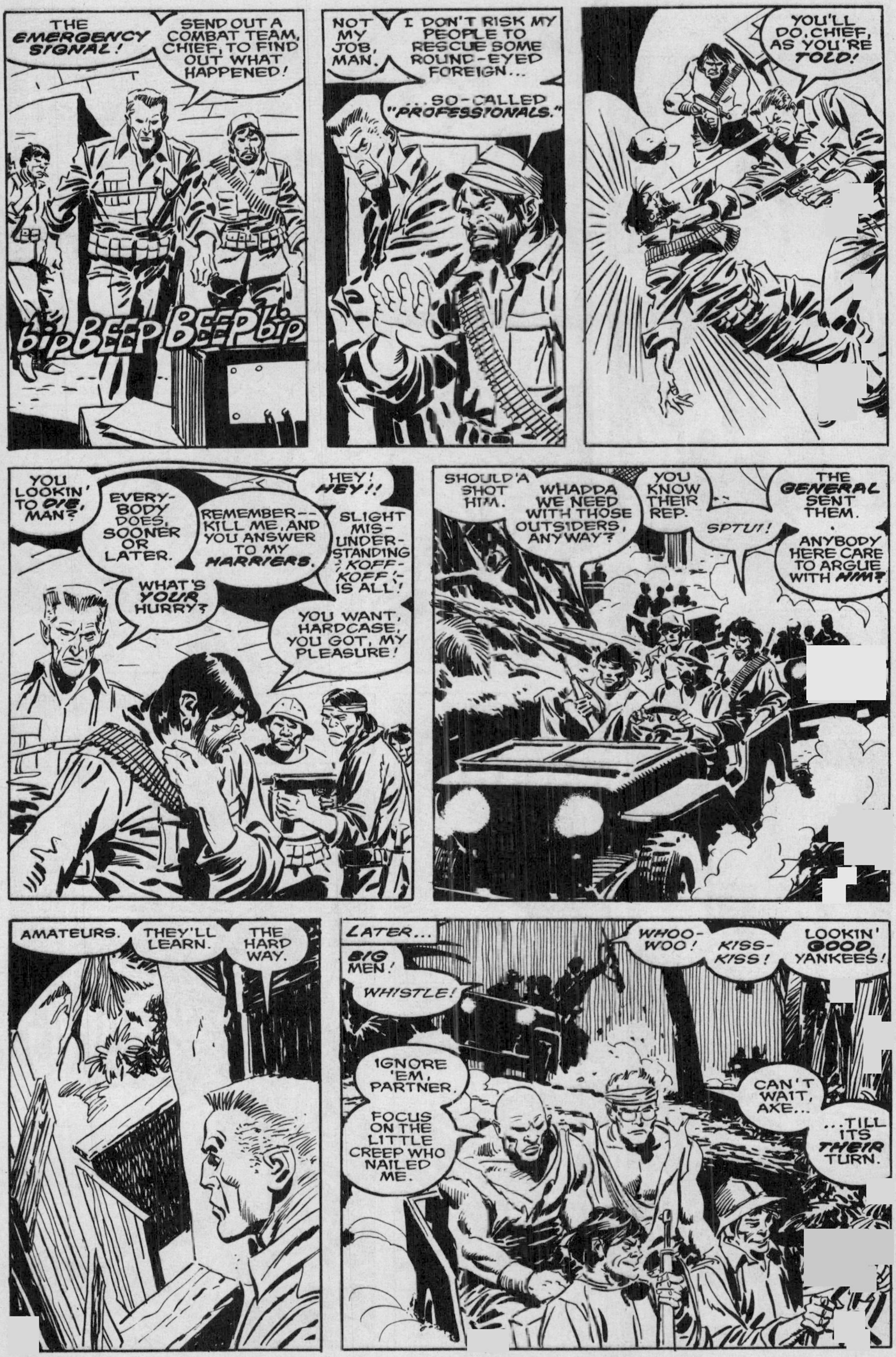
THE EMERGENCY SIGNAL!
SEND OUT A COMBAT TEAM, CHIEF, TO FIND OUT WHAT HAPPENED!
bip BEEP BEEP bip
NOT MY JOB, MAN.
I DON'T RISK MY PEOPLE TO RESCUE SOME ROUND-EYED FOREIGN...
...SO-CALLED "PROFESSIONALS."
YOU'LL DO, CHIEF, AS YOU'RE TOLD!
YOU LOOKIN' TO DIE, MAN?
EVERY-BODY DOES, SOONER OR LATER.
WHAT'S YOUR HURRY?
REMEMBER-- KILL ME, AND YOU ANSWER TO MY HARRIERS.
HEY! HEY!!
SLIGHT MIS-UNDER-STANDING --KOFF-KOFF!-- IS ALL!
YOU WANT, HARDCASE, YOU GOT, MY PLEASURE!
SHOULD'A SHOT HIM.
WHADDA WE NEED WITH THOSE OUTSIDERS, ANYWAY?
YOU KNOW THEIR REP.
SPTUI!
THE GENERAL SENT THEM.
ANYBODY HERE CARE TO ARGUE WITH HIM?
AMATEURS.
THEY'LL LEARN.
THE HARD WAY.
LATER...
BIG MEN!
WHISTLE!
WHOO-WOO!
KISS-KISS!
LOOKIN' GOOD, YANKEES!
IGNORE 'EM, PARTNER.
FOCUS ON THE LITTLE CREEP WHO NAILED ME.
CAN'T WAIT, AXE...
...TILL ITS THEIR TURN.

CLOWNS HAVE BEEN TOP DOGS AROUND THESE PARTS FOR SO LONG...

...THEY'VE GROWN SLOPPY.

ROAD DISCIPLINE'S PATHETIC.

SUITS ME FINE.

JEEP UP AHEAD DOESN'T NOTICE THE SWITCH.

I COMPLETE THE DISGUISE...

...WITH THE UNIFORM I TOOK OFF THE HARRIERS.

NO MINEFIELDS, NO PERIMETER SECURITY...

...NOT EVEN GUARDS ON THE MAIN GATE.

ALMOST TOO EASY.

MY TURN TO REMIND MYSELF...

SNIKT!

...NOT TO GET COCKY.

AS I REACH THE FORT...

...I SLICE MY CLAWS THROUGH THE TRANSMISSION.

QUICKLY...

...NOISILY...

...MESSILY...

...MY JEEP DIES...

GNRRNRRKBANG

...RIGHT WHERE I WANT IT.

GOT A **FIRE** HERE!

WE NEED WATER...

...AN EXTINGUISHER...

...SHOVE IT OUTTA THE WAY!

EVERYBODY'S FOCUS IS ON THE JEEP.

SO NOBODY NOTICES ME BLEND WITH THE CROWD AND SLIP AWAY.

ONE MAN, AXE--I DON'T BELIEVE IT!

NEITHER DID WE.

NEVER SEEN MOVES LIKE HIS.

SHOULD HAVE BROUGHT THE WHOLE TEAM. THEY'RE A MATCH EVEN FOR THE AVENGERS-- **WHAT?!**

HOLY--?!?

TOOK THE CAP OFF THE GAS TANK A' THE SPARE JERRY CANS BEFORE I DROVE IN.

BFCOM!

DIDN'T TAKE THE FIRE LONG TO REACH 'EM.

CHUMPS ARE STILL AS LACKADAISICAL AS CAN BE.

NONE OF 'EM REALIZE...

...THEY'RE UNDER ATTACK.

NOT THAT IT'D HELP 'EM MUCH...

...IF THEY DID.

I DECK 'EM AN' RUN.

LEAVIN' 'EM WITH BUSTED BONES...

...AN' SORE HEADS.

ONE BRIGHT BOY RAISES THE ALARM.

OVER HERE!

THERE'S AN **INTRUDER** IN THE COMPOUND! OVER HERE!

HIS MISTAKE.

CHOLLO, TAKE THE WINDOW! YOU TWO BACK ME UP! I'LL KICK THE DOOR!

WAK!

MERCY--!

THEY DEAD?

BETTER FOR THEM... ...IF THEY ARE.

WHO IS THIS GUY?!

CAN HE WALK THROUGH WALLS, OR WHAT?!

HE'S DROPPIN' US RIGHT AN' LEFT--

--HOWCUM HE AIN'T KILT NOBODY?!

DEAD IS DEAD, YOU LEAVE THE BODIES AN' MOVE ON.

HARDER TO ABANDON A BUDDY...

...WHO'S STILL BREATHIN'.

AN' CARIN' FOR THOSE WOUNDED SHOULD SLOW 'EM DOWN.

TAKE SHOOTERS AWAY FROM THE SEARCH FOR ME.

IN NO TIME AT ALL, THE BANDITS ARE ROYALLY SPOOKED.

WHICH IS MY CUE TO UP THE ANTE.

FIRE!

WHAT'LL WE DO?!

THEY AREN'T MEN ENOUGH LEFT TO FIGHT THE FIRE AND THAT INTRUDER!

DEVIL TAKE 'EM BOTH!

THAT OPIUM'S WHAT MATTERS!

WE'LL GET IT CLEAR...

...THEN COME BACK AFTER OUR "FIREBUG."

ROLL OUT! AND KEEP YOUR GUNS COCKED!

ANYTHING TWITCHES OUTSIDE THE WALL--

--SPLATTER IT!

CHIEF--THE JEEP'S STILL BLOCKIN' THE GATE!

NOT ANY MORE.

YOU WANT I SHOULD RUN HIM DOWN, TOO?

???

JOY RIDE'S OVER, BOYS.

GRAVY TRAIN'S REACHED THE END OF THE LINE.

WATCH THE FLANKS. THIS COULD BE AN AMBUSH!

IT'S AN AMBUSH ALL RIGHT, BUB.

BUT I'M ALONE.

THESE DRUGS ARE DESTINED FOR MADRIPOOR.

THAT'S TYGER'S TURF.

HER FEELINGS ABOUT DOPE ARE COMMON KNOWLEDGE.

YOU SURE YOU WANT TO CROSS HER?

THE WORD IS, SHE'S AS GOOD AS DEAD.

AND SO ARE YOU!!

BUDDA-BUDDA!

SO MUCH FOR *THAT* PROBLEM!

I WONDER. AFTER THE WAY HE TOOK THIS OPERATION APART...

...IT MAKES NO SENSE FOR HIM TO LET HIMSELF BE TAKEN OUT SO STUPIDLY.

I DON'T LIKE THE WAY WE'RE STRUNG OUT ALONG THIS RIDGE-LINE.

NO SIGN OF ANYBODY--

--HOLD IT! ENGINES!

A *PLANE*, HARDCASE, HEADIN' OUR WAY!

I *KNEW* IT!

AWAY FROM THE TRANSPORT, ALL OF YOU!

IF YOU WANT TO LIVE--

--RUN FOR THE TREES.

WHILE THE BANDITS WERE LOADING THEIR TRUCKS....

...I WAS CALLIN' ARCHIE ON THE SHORT-WAVE, SETTIN' UP THIS SURPRISE.

HE'D FIXED THE ENGINE AN' UNLIMBERED THE CRATES IN BACK.

Y'SEE, THIS IS NO ORDINARY "GOONEY BIRD."

IN WILDER DAYS, SHE SERVED AS "PUFF, THE MAGIC DRAGON".

A *GUNSHIP* --WITH THREE VULCAN 20 MM ROTARY BARRELED CANNONS, FIRING 6000 ROUNDS A MINUTE.

WITH THEM, THERE ISN'T THE USUAL BANG-BANG SOUND OF GUNSHOTS.

BZZZZZ

VULCANS MAKE A DEEP, THRUMMING BUZZSAW SOUND THAT RAISES THE HACKLES ON YOUR NECK.

THEY FIRE EXPLOSIVE SHELLS AS LONG AS A MAN'S HAND.

BZZZZZZ

AND MAKE A HECKUVA MESS.

WHROOM!

KBOOM!

GONE! A BILLION-DOLLAR SHIPMENT-- --ALL GONE!

GENERAL COY--HE'LL HAVE MY *HEAD!*

NOPE. THAT'S *MY* PLEASURE.

I-I *SHOT* YOU.

A FULL CLIP! YOU SHOULD BE *DEAD!!!*

CARE TO TRY AGAIN?

SNIKT!

SLUKT!

SOME *MESS*, BRO!

GOTTA HAND IT TO THAT L'IL FELLA... ...HE HAS *STYLE!*

WOULDN'T MIND MEETING HIM AGAIN.

AS FRIEND OR FOE, BRO?

GOOD QUESTION.

EITHER WAY, SURE BE AN EXPERIENCE

WHATEVER THAT GENERAL HAD PLANNED...

...THEY JUST WENT DOWN THE DUMPER.

HECK, IF THIS IS WHAT HE'S UP AGAINST...

...DUDE'LL BE LUCKY TO RABBIT WITH A WHOLE SKIN.

SO WERE WE, SHOTGUN.

HE COULD HAVE CANCELED OUR TICKET ANYTIME. HE *CHOSE* NOT TO.

NEXT TIME--AND MARK MY WORDS...

...THERE WILL BE A NEXT TIME--

--WE WON'T GIVE HIM THE CHANCE.

OUT*STANDING.*

MANOMANOMAN--

--HAVEN'T ENJOYED MYSELF SO MUCH SINCE THE 'NAM!

YOU DID GOOD YOURSELF, ARCHIE, I'M OBLIGED.

SO--THIS MEANS WE'VE BROKEN COY'S BACK?

CRIPPLED HIM, FOR A WHILE,

BUT IT WON'T COUNT FOR SPIT...

...IF TYGER ISN'T STILL ALIVE.

YOU THINK THERE'S A CHANCE, PATCH?

ANYTHING'S POSSIBLE.

LANDAU LUCKMAN & LAK

NEXT: **ROUGHOUSE!**

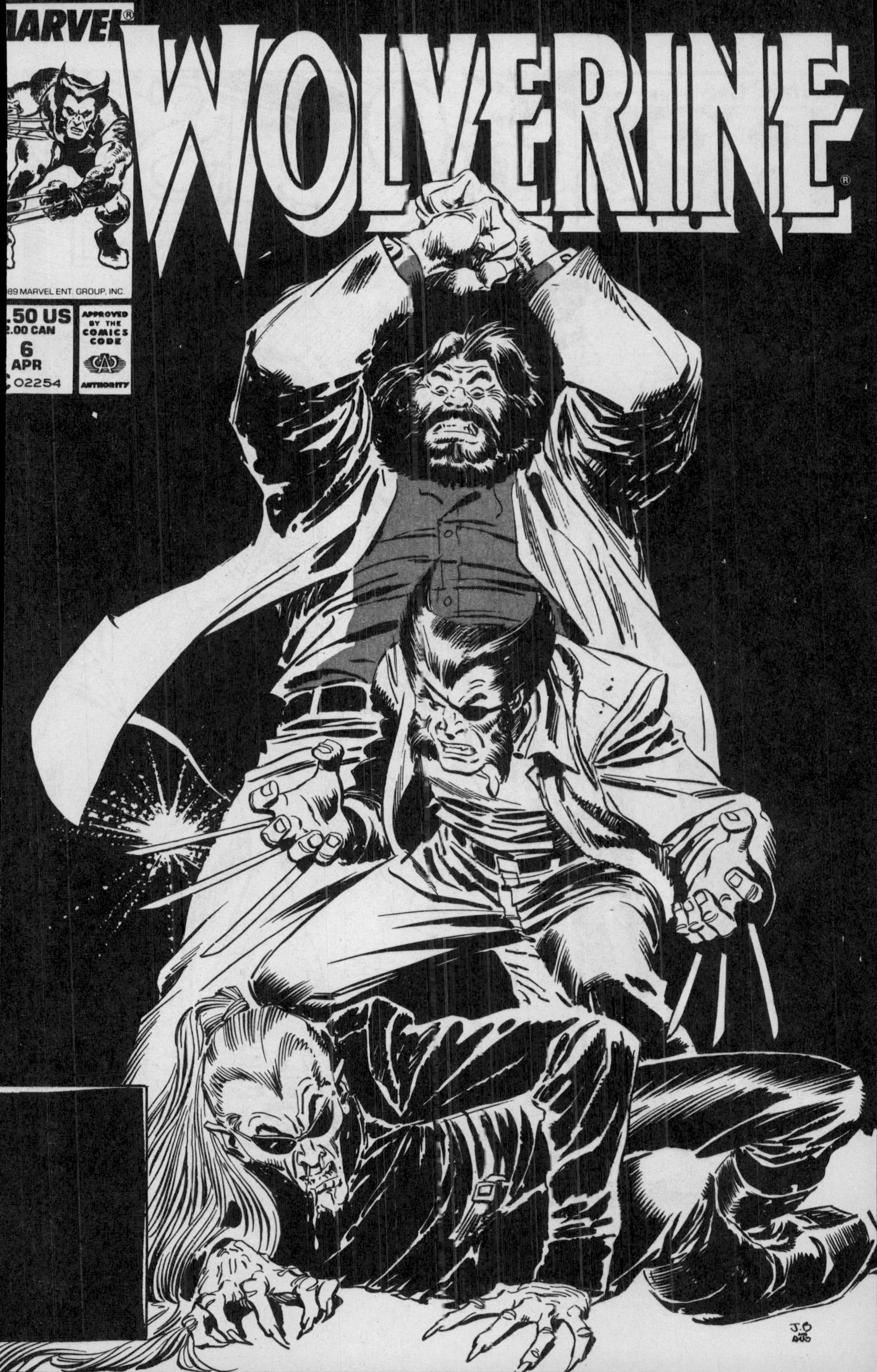
MARVEL
WOLVERINE
89 MARVEL ENT. GROUP, INC.
.50 US
2.00 CAN
6
APR
02254
APPROVED BY THE COMICS CODE AUTHORITY

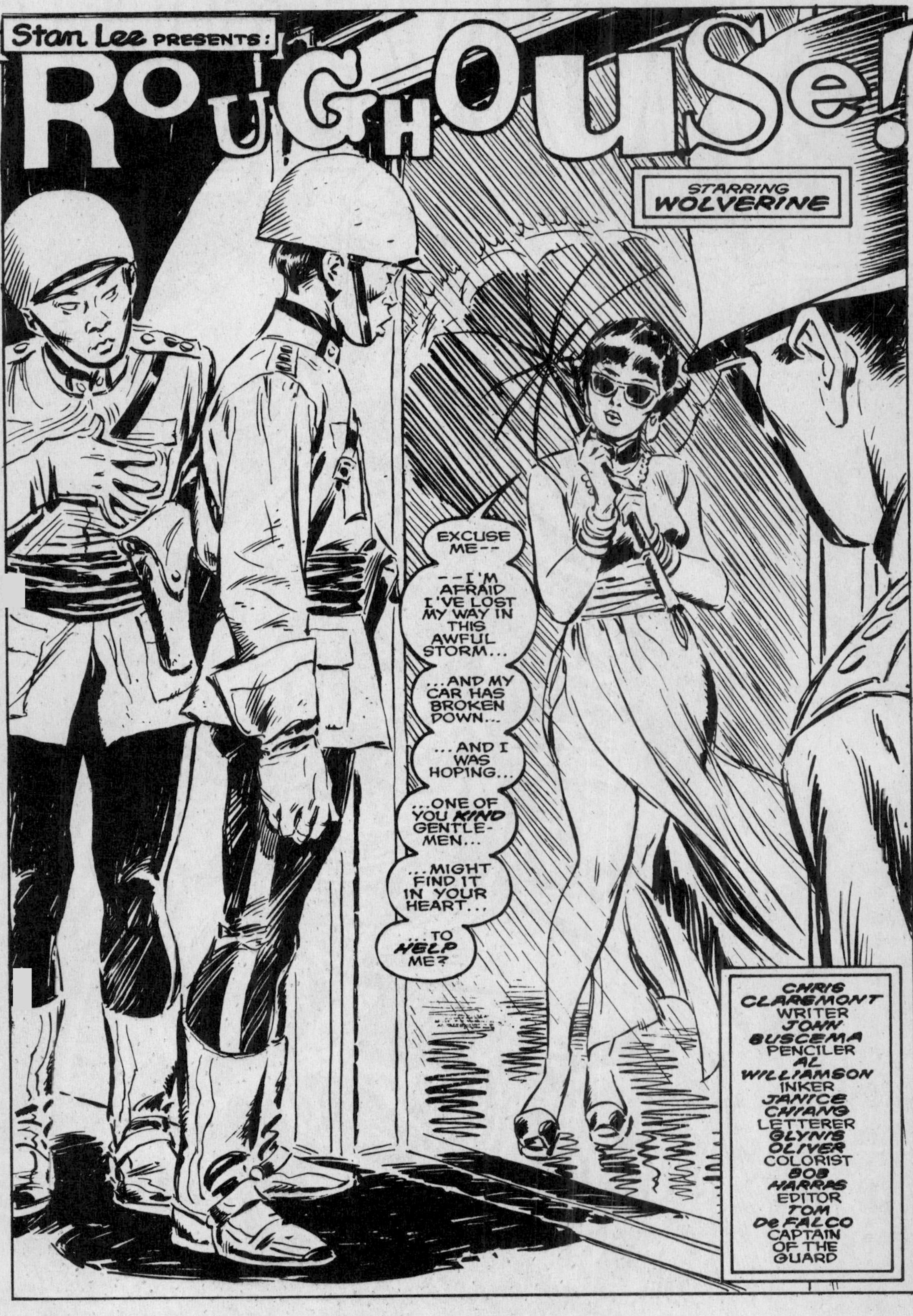

Stan Lee PRESENTS:
ROUGHOUSE!
STARRING WOLVERINE
EXCUSE ME--
--I'M AFRAID I'VE LOST MY WAY IN THIS AWFUL STORM...
...AND MY CAR HAS BROKEN DOWN...
...AND I WAS HOPING...
...ONE OF YOU KIND GENTLEMEN...
...MIGHT FIND IT IN YOUR HEART...
...TO HELP ME?
CHRIS CLAREMONT WRITER
JOHN BUSCEMA PENCILER
AL WILLIAMSON INKER
JANICE CHIANG LETTERER
GLYNIS OLIVER COLORIST
BOB HARRAS EDITOR
TOM DeFALCO CAPTAIN OF THE GUARD

THIS IS THE *PALACE* OF HIS ROYAL HIGHNESS, THE *PRINCE OF MADRIPOOR!*

IT *IS!*

I'M SORRY, IT'S RAINING SO HARD...

...ALL I REGISTERED WAS THE LIGHT AT YOUR GATE...

WE ARE HIS *HOUSEHOLD* GUARD.

THANK *HEAVEN* FOR THAT! AT LEAST, I KNOW I'M IN THE *SAFEST* OF HANDS!

I'M SURE THERE'S NOTHING SERIOUSLY WRONG.

IT'S JUST, I DON'T KNOW WHAT TO *DO!*

STAY BY YOUR POSTS, MEN. I'LL SEE TO THE LADY.

YES, LIEUTENANT. AS YOU COMMAND.

PIG!

TYPICAL OFFICER, HOGGING ALL THE FUN!

WHAT COULD HAVE BROUGHT YOU OUT ON SUCH A DREADFUL NIGHT?

STRANGE AS IT MAY SOUND...

...A MATTER OF LIFE AND DEATH.

WELL--YOU GET BEHIND THE WHEEL, MISS...

...AND WE'LL SEE IF WE CAN'T GET THIS MAGNIFICENT BEAST TO WAKE UP AND ROAR.

ACTUALLY, LIEUTENANT...

...THAT WON'T BE NECESSARY.

I'D MUCH PREFER IT...

...IF YOU TOOK ME INSIDE THE PALACE.

GOT HIM! HE'S *POSSESSED!*

NOTHING WE COULD DO.

AUTO'LL NEED A GARAGE TO PUT IT RIGHT.

THE YOUNG LADY'S DRENCHED. I'M TAKING HER FOR SOME DRY CLOTHES...

...AND TO SUMMON A TOW TRUCK AND A TAXI!

DON'T BE TOO LONG, SIR.

YOU MUST BE JOKING.

SOMEDAY, SOMEHOW, I PRAY THE DEMON LORDS GIVE ALL SUCH OFFICERS...

...THE FATE THEY SO RICHLY DESERVE!

INCROYABLE!

THIS PUTS EVEN THE PALAIS de VERSAILLES TO SHAME!

THE PRINCE MUST HAVE THE WEALTH OF AGES GATHERED HERE!

AND THE SHEER SIZE-- IT BEGGARS THE MIND!

MY OFFICER HAS NO NOTION OF WHERE TO FIND THOSE I SEEK-- HOWEVER WILL I--??!

UHNHHN?

WHUATT??

WHERE?!

HOWT?!T

YOU!

THE LAST I REMEMBER...

...WE WERE OUTSIDE THE WALLS!

SACRE COEUR-- I LET MY CONCENTRATION LAPSE!

--THE OFFICER IS NO LONGER UNDER MY CONTROL!

ANSWER ME, GIRL! HOW DID YOU TRICK--

--WAIOWNGH!

SOK!

??

!!!
OOO

NOT A SOUND, *KARMA!* OR YOU'RE LIABLE TO ATTRACT MORE TROUBLE THAN EVEN *WE* CAN HANDLE.

M'SIEU-- M'SIEU *PATCH!*

BUT MON UNCLE-- HE BOASTED YOU WERE *DEAD!*

HE AIN'T THE FIRST.

I. . I AM HAPPY TO SEE YOU WELL.

LIKEWISE.

BUT WHAT'RE YOU DOIN' HERE?

WHO THE BLAZES IS *SHE*, PATCH?

ARCHIE CORRIGAN, MEET, "SHAN" COY MANH. *GENERAL COY'S* HER UNCLE.

OH, JOY.

MY UNCLE HAS CAPTURED HIS RIVAL CRIMELORD, *MAM'SELLE TYGER*, TOGETHER WITH THE TWO AMERICAN WOMEN WHO WERE PROTECTING HER.

JESSICA DREW AND *LINDSAY McCABE.*

OUI.

COAST IS CLEAR, PATCH.

BEST TO SCRAMBLE...

...WHILE WE GOT THE CHANCE.

ARE THEY DEAD?

I BELIEVE NOT-- ALTHOUGH MY UNCLE'S PET-ASSASSINS *BLOODSPORT* AND *ROUGHOUSE*, EVIDENTLY TRIED THEIR BEST.

BECAUSE MY UNCLE IS IN LEAGUE WITH THIS ISLAND'S RULER...

..MAM'SELLE TYGER AND THE OTHERS WERE BROUGHT HERE.

I FOLLOWED, TO *FREE* THEM.

ONCE, *M'SIEU*, I WAS BETTER THAN I AM.

PROUD TO BE WHAT PEOPLE CALL A "SUPER HERO".

BUT I SACRIFICED THAT LIFE--

--CAST ASIDE THOSE NOBLE IDEALS--

--WHEN I ENTERED MY UNCLE'S SERVICE.

LAST TIME I ASKED WHY...

...YOU SAID IT WAS NONE O' MY BUSINESS.

MONTHS AGO, MY YOUNGER BROTHER AND SISTER WERE KIDNAPED.

MY HOPE--MY *LAST* HOPE, FOR I HAVE TRIED EVERY OTHER MEANS--

--IS THAT MY UNCLE'S UNDERWORLD CONTACTS--

..WOULD ENABLE ME TO LOCATE AND RESCUE THEM.

IN A WORD, I "*POSSESS*" THEM.

DO NOT BE ALARMED, *MESSIEURS*.

I AM A *MUTANT*, WITH THE POWER TO TAKE PSYCHIC CONTROL OF OTHERS' MINDS.

WHEN I RELEASE THIS SERVANT, HE WILL REMEMBER NOTHING OF OUR PRESENCE.

NIFTY TRICK. COULD'A USED IT MYSELF, MORE 'N ONCE.

WHAT MADE YOU CHANGE YOUR MIND?

YOU, M'SIEU.

REMINDING ME OF THE "ME" I'D TRIED SO HARD TO FORGET.

I DISCOVERED I COULD NO LONGER TURN A BLIND EYE TO MY UNCLE'S VILLAINY.

THE TIME HAS COME-- I PRAY, NOT TOO LATE--

--FOR ME TO TRY TO BE TRUE TO MY NAMESAKE, *KARMA*...

...AND BALANCE THE EVIL I HAVE DONE...

...OR DONE BECAUSE OF ME...

...WITH GOOD.

WALK CLEAR O' THAT POOL, YOU TWO.

WHY—YAIKES!?! WHATINNASAMHILL—?!!

HOW'D YOU KNOW IT WAS THERE?!

PRINCE HAS SOME INTERESTING PETS.

—SAME WAY WE'RE FINDING THE LADIES——

—BY FOLLOWING MY NOSE.

I MAKE A JOKE...

...TO DISGUISE THE TRUTH.

IT'S THEIR SCENT THAT'S LED US THERE.

Y'SEE, I'M AS MUCH A MUTANT AS KARMA, ONLY MY POWER'S PHYSICAL.

MAKES ME A TRACKER...

...AN' FLAMIN' HARD TO KILL.

AS GENERAL NGUYEN NGOC COY—— FORMERLY OF THE SOUTH VIETNAMESE NATIONAL POLICE—— IS ABOUT TO LEARN.

IN, WENCH!

HEY—— NOT SO HARD!

LOSING BALANCE——

——FLOOR POLISHED SLICK AS ICE!

WHAT A WAY TO MAKE AN ENTRANCE!

HOW NICE OF YOU, MS. MC CABE, TO SHOW A SLAVE'S PROPER RESPECT...

...BY ABASING HERSELF AT THE FEET OF HER MASTER.

I'M NO SLAVE YOU—— OWHW!

COLLAR SAYS DIFFERENT, CUTIE——

MAYBE LATER, IF YOU BEHAVE——

...YOU AN' ME, WE'LL PLAY.

ALL IN DUE COURSE, ROUGHOUSE.

HER COMPANION, DREAD LORD, MEETS WITH THY APPROVAL?

THE BLOOD I HAVE TAKEN FROM HER WILL DO NO LASTING HARM...

...BUT MERELY RENDER HER MORE TRACTABLE.

I CONFESS LORD, HER ESSENCE IS UNLIKE ANY I HAVE EVER TASTED.

WE ARE EACH OF US CONNOISSEURS, MY FRIEND.

THOUGH MY PREFERENCE IS FOR WINE.

PERHAPS, WHEN OUR BUSINESS IS COMPLETE...

...I SHALL GIVE HER TO YOU

FOOLISH WOMAN, TO *DARE* MATCH YOURSELVES AGAINST ME.

"TRUE, YOU LED MY MEN A MERRY CHASE.

"BUT WHEN BLOODSPORT TASTES OF SOMEONE'S BLOOD...

"...AS HE DID TYGER'S...

"...THEY ARE PSYCHICALLY *BOUND*.

"ONCE HE TRACKED YOU DOWN...

"...IT WAS THE SIMPLEST OF MATTERS...

"...FOR ROUGHHOUSE TO SMASH YOUR HIDING PLACE DOWN ABOUT YOUR EARS.

"THE OLD MAN, CHANG, WAS DRAINED DRY...

"...HIS BLOODLESS CORPSE LEFT AS A WARNING TO ANY OTHERS FOOL ENOUGH TO THINK OF CHALLENGING ME

"IN TRUTH, MY DEARS, YOUR DOOM WAS SEALED FROM THE OUTSET.

"DEFENDING TYGER--FOR YOU AND PATCH BOTH--WAS THE MOST HOPELESS AND *LOST* OF CAUSES."

THEN *WHY,* COY...

...ARE WE STILL *ALIVE?*

PERHAPS, WRETCHED-WOMAN, BECAUSE DEATH IS TOO QUICK AND EASY AN END!

YOU CAUSED ME CONSIDERABLE INCONVENIENCE, MS. DREW, AND I AM A GREAT BELIEVER IN REPAYING HURTS DONE ME A THOUSAND-FOLD!

SLAP

SOME APPROPRIATE DRUGS TO REORIENT YOUR MIND--

--RE-EDUCATION TO TEACH YOU THE "PROPER" SKILLS--

--THE PAIR OF YOU WILL BRING A TIDY SUM ON THE AUCTION BLOCK.

ALTERNATELY, I MIGHT FOREGO PROFIT FOR PLEASURE.

THAT IS WHY I HAVE NOT EMPLOYED MY NIECE, KARMA, TO POSSESS YOU AND FORCE YOU TO DO MY BIDDING.

DEATH IS BUT AN END. *DYING* HOWEVER--THAT IS SOMETHING ALTOGETHER DIFFERENT.

THINK OF THE AGONIES I MIGHT INFLICT--

--TANTALIZING YOU WITH THE PROMISE OF THAT FINAL, BLESSED, YEARNED FOR, *BEGGED* FOR RELEASE...

...EVER TO BE DENIED.

BUT WHY DWELL ON SUCH UNPLEASANTNESS?

I CAN ALSO BE GENEROUS.

YOUR LIVES, FOR ONE THING, FREEDOM, FOR ANOTHER, WEALTH.

YEAH, SURE, RIGHT, SO WHO DO WE HAVE TO KILL?

INTERESTING THAT *YOU* SHOULD POSE THAT QUESTION MS. MCCABE. FOR I SUSPECT YOU MUST ALSO PROVIDE THE ANSWER.

BEHOLD HERE, MY RIVAL, *TYGER TIGER*-- ENCASED IN WHAT APPEARS TO BE A SUIT OF IMPENETRABLE ARMOR.

BULL!

THIS IS *RIDICULOUS!*

THERE'S *NOTHING* IN THIS WORLD I CAN'T SMASH!

GIMME A MINUTE-- *UHNF*--

I'LL PEEL THIS METAL SKIN--*WHUNF*--

--RIGHT *OFFA* HER-- *RAGHUNF!*

YMIR'S. ICY BREATH--IT WON'T BREAK!

REGRETTABLY, LORD I CAN BE OF NO HELP TO THEE, EITHER.

TO DRAIN A PERSON'S BLOOD, AS I DO NOW WITH JESSICA'S...

...MY FLESH MUST TOUCH THEIRS.

SO LONG AS TYGER WEARS YON ARMOR...

...SHE IS SAFE FROM ME.

ENOUGH. MY PATIENCE IS AT END.

I HAVE MADE A MORE THAN REASONABLE OFFER.

WHICH IS GOOD...

...SOLELY, UNTIL YOU GET WHAT YOU WANT...

IT IS THAT, OR *NOTHING.*

THE ARMOR WAS *YOURS*, MS. MCCABE, YET YOU GAVE IT TO TYGER. A NOBLE GESTURE--BUT IS IT WORTH YOUR *LIFE?!*

YOU DRESSED HER. LOGICALLY THEN, YOU SHOULD HAVE THE KEY TO REMOVING IT.

USE IT, WOMAN, WHILE YOU'VE STILL THE CHANCE TO LEAVE HERE... ...ALIVE AND WHOLE.

JESS...?

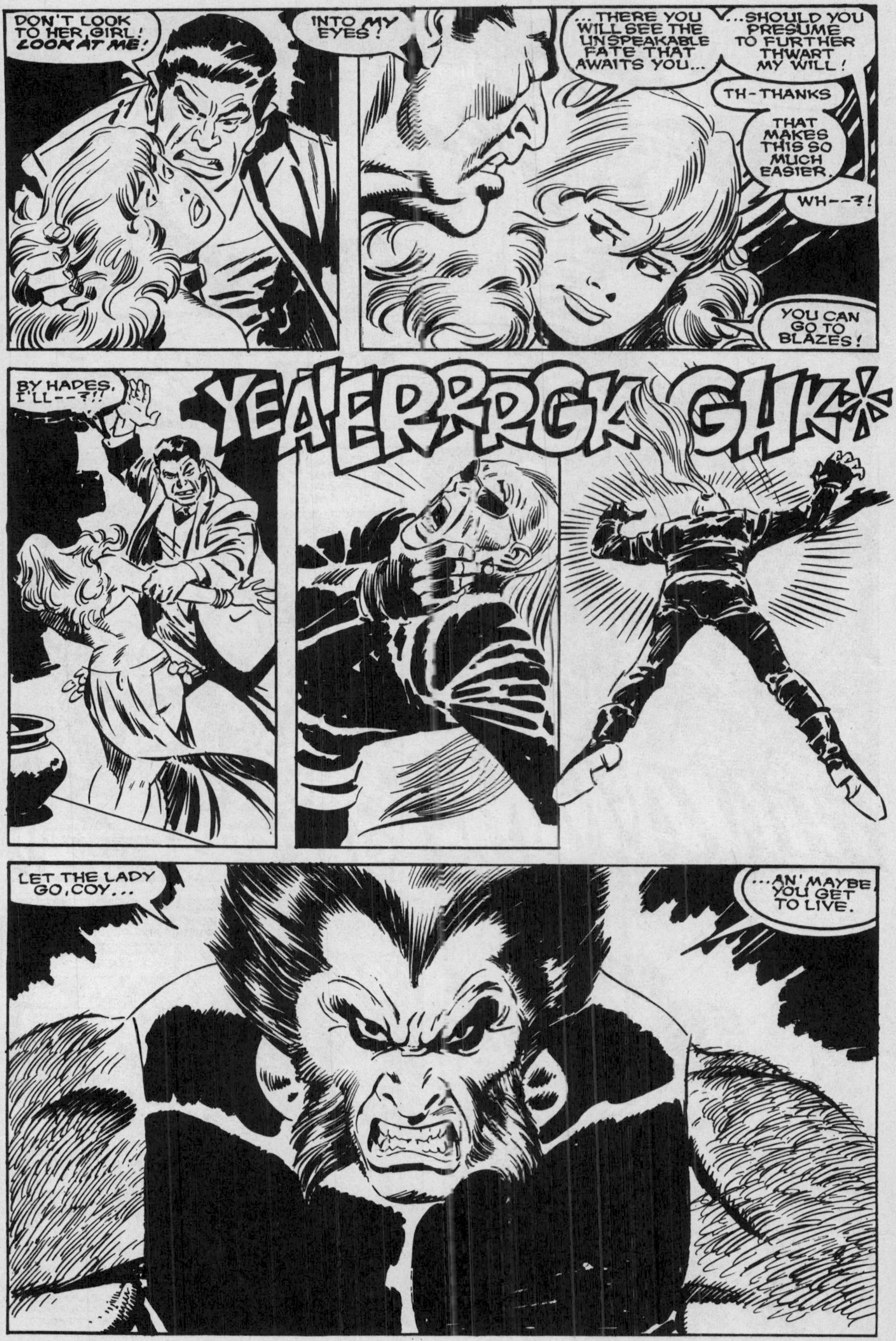
DON'T LOOK TO HER GIRL! LOOK AT ME!
INTO MY EYES!
...THERE YOU WILL SEE THE UNSPEAKABLE FATE THAT AWAITS YOU...
...SHOULD YOU PRESUME TO FURTHER THWART MY WILL!
TH-THANKS
THAT MAKES THIS SO MUCH EASIER.
WH--?!
YOU CAN GO TO BLAZES!
BY HADES, I'LL--?!!
YEAERRRGK GHK!
LET THE LADY GO, COY...
...AN' MAYBE YOU GET TO LIVE.

JUST BY WALKIN' YOUR MISBEGOTTEN CARCASS THROUGH THAT DOOR, LITTLE MAN--

--YOU GET TO DIE!

SHWAMM!

THERE'S PROBABLY AN EASIER WAY TO DO THIS.

SNIKT!

BUT THAT ISN'T MY STYLE.

STILL STANDIN', RUNT?

SUITS ME!

I FIGURE TO BUST YOU A BONE AT A TIME.

AN' GRIND WHAT'S LEFT TO PULP AN' POWDER.

WORDS ARE CHEAP, LUMMOX.

AN' HE DOESN'T LIKE MINE AT ALL. MAKES HIM MAD. MAKES HIM CARELESS.

MY CLAWS ARE OUT.

THEY'RE ADAMANTIUM, FORGED SO RAZOR-SHARP THEY'LL CUT ANYTHING.

ROUGHHOUSE CHARGES RIGHT INTO THEM.

:GWUHH!:

NORMALLY, A MAN FACES ME WITH FISTS, I MEET HIM IN KIND.

BUT ROUGHHOUSE IS NO MORE A "NORMAL" MAN...

...THAN I AM.

LAST TIME WE TANGLED, I BARELY GOT OUT ALIVE.

I'M NOT ABOUT TO GIVE HIM A SHOT AT FINISHING THE JOB.

ALL RIGHT, COY--YOUR TURN.

SMILE ON HIS FACE?

NOT EVEN A TRACE OF FEAR SCENT??

TOO LATE, I REALIZE THE IMPLICATIONS.

BY THEN, BLOODSPORT'S GOT ME COLD.

I'D SLASH HIS THROAT OPEN FROM EAR TO EAR.

BUT THE VAMPIRE MUST HAVE A HEALING FACTOR THAT'S ON PAR WITH MY OWN.

MOMENT HE GRABS ME...

...I START TO BLEED.

THERE'S NO WOUND, NOT EVEN A MARK...

...IT POURS RIGHT THROUGH MY SKIN.

STRENGTH GOES WITH IT.

ZAP HIM, HONEY--

--OR PATCH IS A GONER!

I AM *TRYING,* M'SIEU--

--AS I HAVE BEEN SINCE 'BLOODSPORT' AWOKE.

BUT HIS RESISTANCE IS MUCH STRONGER THAN BEFORE--

--PERHAPS, IS IT BECAUSE HE HAS TASTED *MY* BLOOD?!

SACRE PERE-- I MUST NOT, *DARE* NOT, THINK OF THAT!

FOR PATCH'S LIFE--AND MY OWN SOUL-- --I MUST *PREVAIL!*

AKGH!

KARMA AGAIN, BLESS HER, HAS TO BE!

ALL I NEED IS *TIME* FOR MY BODY TO RESTORE ITSELF!

NO SUCH LUCK.

NICE MOVE, RUNT!

SNEAKY AS I'VE EVER SEEN!

TOO BAD NEITHER ME NOR BLOODSPORT...

...CAN BE SLAIN BY *MORTAL* STEEL.

HAPPY LANDINGS!

ONCE MORE, I AM ATTACKED BY SOME UNSEEN PRESENCE!

A/EOW!

I--COULD NOT HOLD HIM!

CRIPES!

LADY'S REACTIN' LIKE SHE JUST TOOK A LEAD PIPE UPSIDE HER HEAD!

I TASTE BLOOD ABOUT ME--

--MY ASSAILANT IS NEAR!

LATER, BLOODSPORT!

DEAL WITH JESSICA DREW FIRST!

SHE DIES, COY--

--SO DOES YOUR NIECE!

THE REDOUBTABLE COLONEL CORRIGAN, I'VE BEEN EXPECTING YOU.

BUT ARCHIE, ARCHIE-- THAT PLOY IS SO OLD.

WORSE LUCK, I KNOW YOU TOO WELL. YOU'RE MANY THINGS--

--NOT LEAST OF WHICH IS A DISGRACE TO UNIFORM AND COUNTRY--

--BUT COLD-BLOODED KILLER IS NOT ONE OF THEM.

SHAN IS BARELY MORE THAN A CHILD. YOU WON'T SHOOT.

SCORE ONE FOR YOU, GENERAL.

BUT I GOT NO COMPUNCTION ABOUT PUNCHING YOUR TICKET!

AND THOU, AIRMAIN... ...HAST NO HOPE OF SUCCESS.

THOU WERT WARNED, ARCHIBALD.

NOW, THY LIVING HEART IS *MINE* CLAIM.

MAYBE THE LUG CAN'T BE KILLED...

...BUT I THINK HE CAN BE HURT.

HE'S MOVIN' A LOT SLOWER AN' THERE'S LESS FORCE TO HIS PUNCHES.

MIND YOU, WE'RE STILL TALKIN' ABOUT SHOTS THAT'D BE CURTAINS FOR ANYONE BUT ME. OR MAYBE THE HULK.

MY SKELETON'S LACED WITH ADAMANTIUM--SAME METAL MY CLAWS ARE MADE OF--

--MAKES THE BONES VIRTUALLY UNBREAKABLE.

BEEN BIDING MY TIME.

TAKING HITS... ...LETTING MY HEALING FACTOR PULL ME TOGETHER.

WHEN HE FIGURES I'M FINISHED, I COME BACK HARD.

SO MUCH FOR THAT IDEA.

WHAT?!

GET AWAY FROM HIM, MISTER! KEEP YOUR DISTANCE THAT'S YOUR ONLY HOPE!

FOLLOW YOUR OWN ADVICE, PARTNER-- --WHERE HE GRABBED FOR YOU...

...JESS, YOU'RE BLEEDING!

HE'S DRAINED SO MUCH ALREADY...

BUT I'M THE ONLY ONE HERE WITH EVEN A PRAYER OF MATCHING HIM.

SPEED'S THE KEY. HIT AND RUN. GAMBLING I'M AGILE ENOUGH TO STAY OUT OF REACH.

MOST INVENTIVE. BUT THINE AURA BETRAYS THEE, SWEETLING.

STANDING IS AN EFFORT!

I FEAR OUR DUEL WILL BE OVER...

...BEFORE IT'S WELL AND TRULY BEG--UWEH?

BUT OURS, BUTCHER, WILL NO?!

TYGER!

SLAMMO

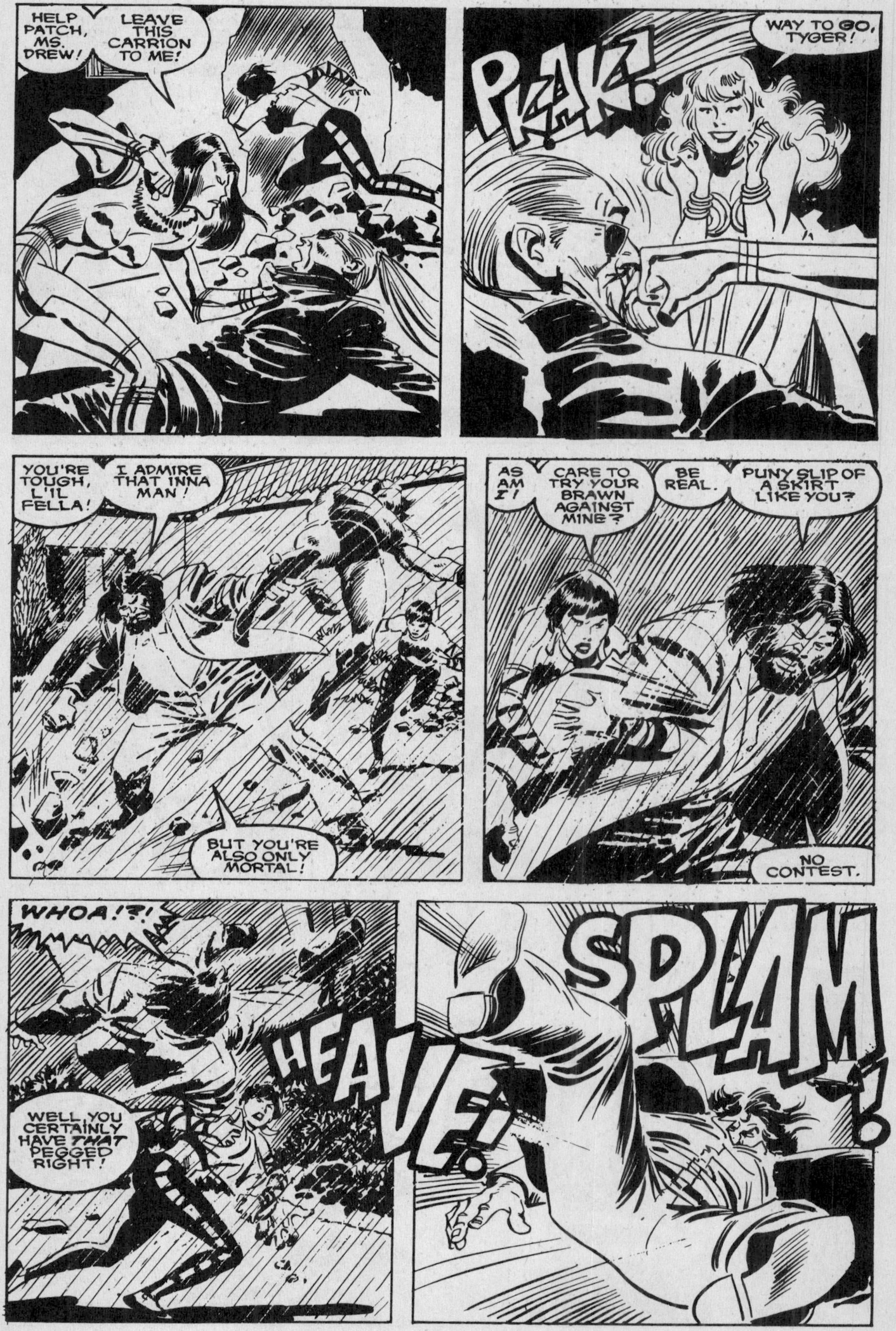
HELP PATCH, MS. DREW!
LEAVE THIS CARRION TO ME!
PKAK!
WAY TO GO, TYGER!
YOU'RE TOUGH, L'IL FELLA!
I ADMIRE THAT INNA MAN!
BUT YOU'RE ALSO ONLY MORTAL!
AS AM I!
CARE TO TRY YOUR BRAWN AGAINST MINE?
BE REAL.
PUNY SLIP OF A SKIRT LIKE YOU?
NO CONTEST.
WHOA!?!
WELL, YOU CERTAINLY HAVE THAT PEGGED RIGHT!
HEAVE!
SPLAM!

SNEAKY, SWEETIE-- --YOU'RE STRONGER'N YOU LOOK! OKEY-DOKE, THEN YOU WANNA PLAY ON MY TERMS...

THOOM

...IT'S YOUR *FUNERAL!*

OH! TENTACLE-- --HUGE-- SOMETHING IN THE POOL--

--IT'S *GRABBED* ME!

END OF FIGHT, CUTIE.

END OF STORY.

END OF LIFE.

NOT HARDLY, LUMMOX. IF THE LADY KICKS...

SHKOW!

...I GUARANTEE IT WON'T BE ALONE!

WATER'S THICK WITH TENTACLES.

NO SIGN OF WHAT THEY'RE ATTACHED TO.

ROUGHHOUSE APPEARS THE JUICIER MEAL, THEY CONCENTRATE ON HIM.

SUITS ME.

WATER'S SO MURKY, EVEN I CAN BARELY SEE. MEANS THERE'S ALMOST NO LIKELIHOOD OF JESS SPOTTIN' MY CLAWS.

GOOD THING, 'CAUSE THEY'RE HER ONLY HOPE.

ME AN' MY FELLOW X-MEN, WORLD BELIEVES US TO BE DEAD.

IT'S IMPORTANT TO KEEP THAT SECRET.

JESS SEES MY CLAWS, OUR COVER'S BLOWN.

BUT SHE'S A FRIEND.

I DON'T HAVE MANY.

I WONDER, IF THE X-MEN'S MISSION IS WORTH HER LIFE?

GLAD I DON'T HAVE TO FIND AN ANSWER TONIGHT.

WHAT WAS THAT THING?

DON'T ASK.

JUST HOPE IT'S ONE OF A KIND.

LIKE US, EH?

I OWE YOU, PATCH.

I DON'T COUNT CHOPS WITH FRIENDS, DREW.

WHAT ABOUT ROUGHOUSE?! D'YOU THINK--?!!

NOPE.

NOTHING LIKE A MOONLIGHT DIP TO REFRESH A BODY.

YOU TWO SEEN THE LIGHT YET...

...AND HAD ENOUGH?

SHAK

CHUMP--

--WE HAVEN'T EVEN STARTED!

WHOOF! SWEETIE, THE GALS BACK HOME, IF THEY'D SCRAPPED GOOD AS YOU...

...I'D A NEVER LEFT!

YOUR TURN, SHORTY.

FREE PUNCH. TAKE YOUR BEST SHOT.

THERE'S A PART O' ME I DON'T MUCH LIKE.

A BERSERKER IN MY SOUL.

PURE CRAZY... BURIED SO DEEP...

I KNOW I'LL NEVER BE RID OF IT.

EVERY SO OFTEN, IT REARS UP AN KICKS LOOSE...

...AN' PEOPLE DIE.

STALEMATE, WARRIOR. I CANNOT HARM THEE.

BUT NEITHER CANST THOU, ME, SINCE I CANNOT BE SLAIN BY ANY MORTAL FORGING.

STILL--THY COMPANIONS HAVE NO SUCH PROTECTION.

YO, VAMPIRE! WHOEVER SAID THAT OUTFIT WAS MADE BY HUMAN BEINGS...

...OR EVEN MORTALS, FOR PETE'S SAKE!

BY THE ETERNAL-- --COULD THAT BE--?!

ONLY ONE WAY TO LEARN, DOG-SON!

KRAK!

BLOODSPORT!

IS HE--?! NO, IMPOSSIBLE!

AND WHAT-- WHAT THAT WRETCHED GIRL SAID--?!

EVEN IF HE ISN'T DEAD... ...HE'LL STILL NEED TIME-- AND BLOOD--TO RECOVER.

WHERE'S CORRIGAN'S GUN?! THAT SHOULD GIVE ME AN EDGE--!

ROUGHHOUSE!

IN HERE, MAN, AT ONCE! YOU'RE NEEDED!

YOU RANG?

:NO!:

SURPRISE, SUCKER!

PLEASE. RESTRAIN YOURSELF.

SO LONG AS IT ENDS WITH YOU AS DUST IN A COFFIN, COY...

...I'M HAPPY.

PERHAPS WE CAN COME TO SOME ACCOMMODATION.

SAY YOUR PRAYERS, GENERAL. HADES AWAITS WITH OPEN ARMS!

NO DOUBT, MY DEAR. UNFORTUNATELY FOR YOU, THE ONLY SOUL ON MADRIPOOR--AND ESPECIALLY WITHIN THE WALLS OF THE ROYAL PALACE-- POSSESSING THE RIGHT AND POWER TO ORDER SUMMARY EXECUTIONS--

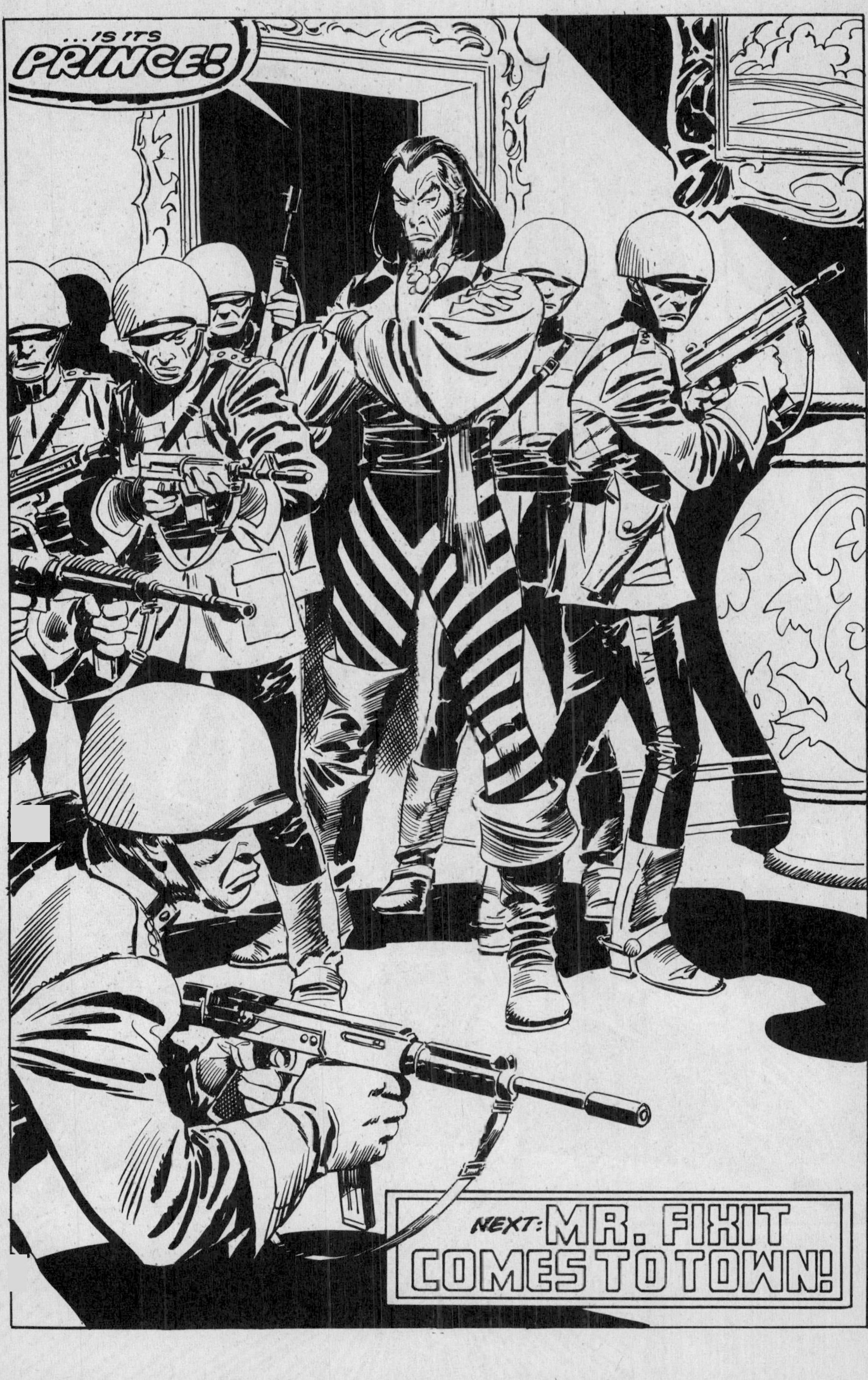
...IS ITS PRINCE!
NEXT: MR. FIXIT COMES TO TOWN!

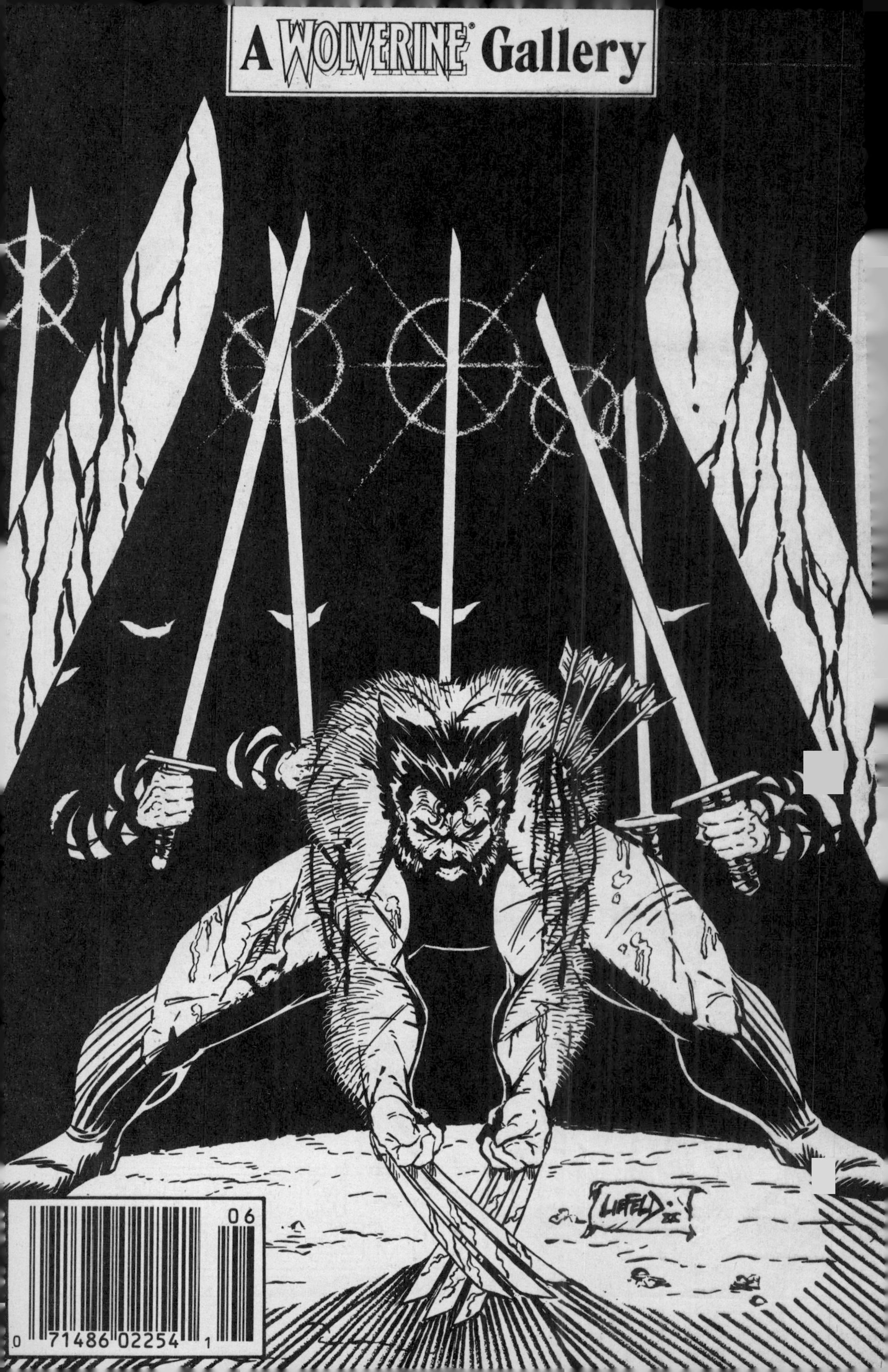
A WOLVERINE Gallery
LIEFELD
06
0 71486 02254 1

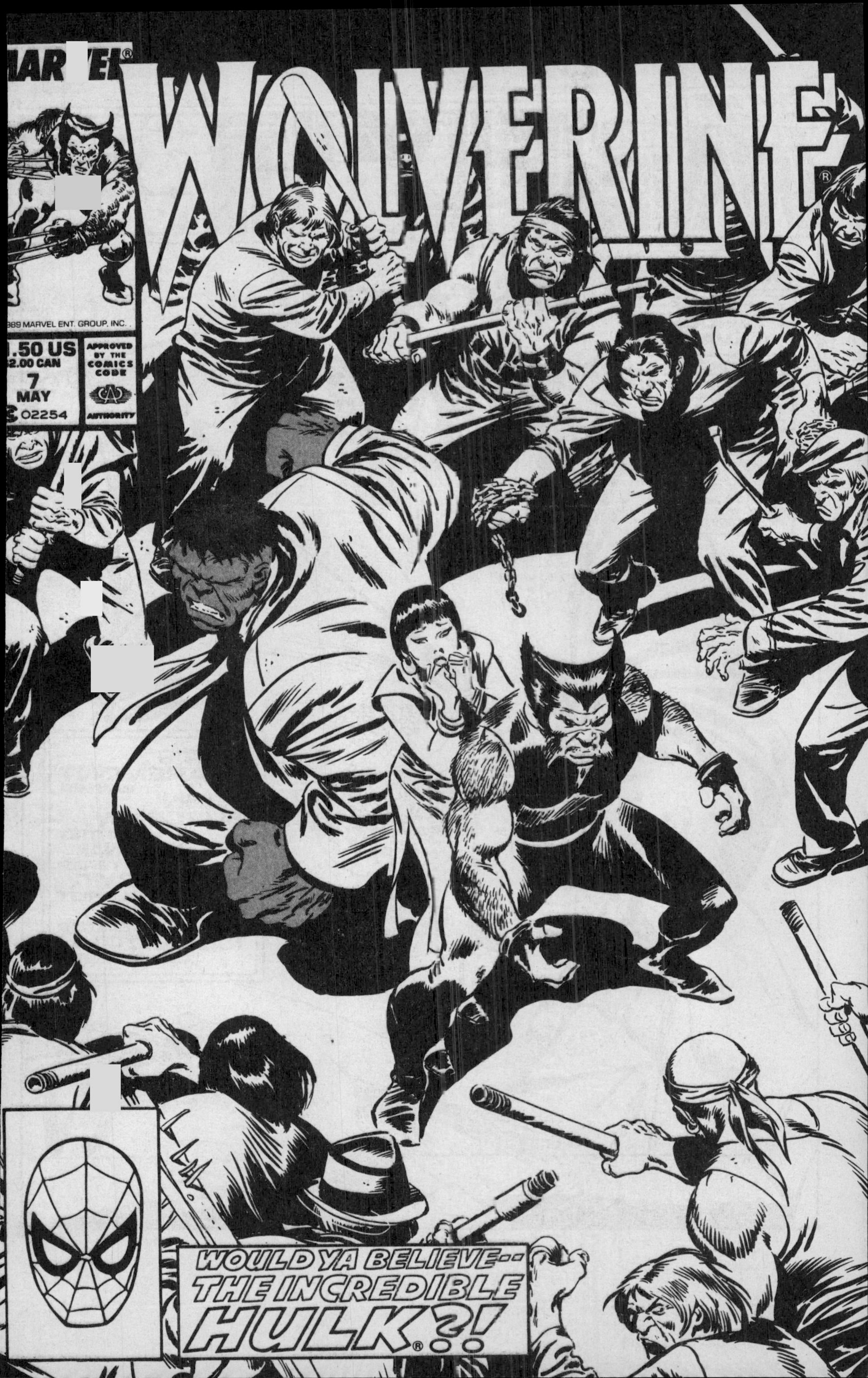
WOLVERINE
1989 MARVEL ENT. GROUP, INC.
1.50 US
2.00 CAN
7
MAY
02254
APPROVED BY THE COMICS CODE AUTHORITY
WOULD YA BELIEVE--
THE INCREDIBLE
HULK?!

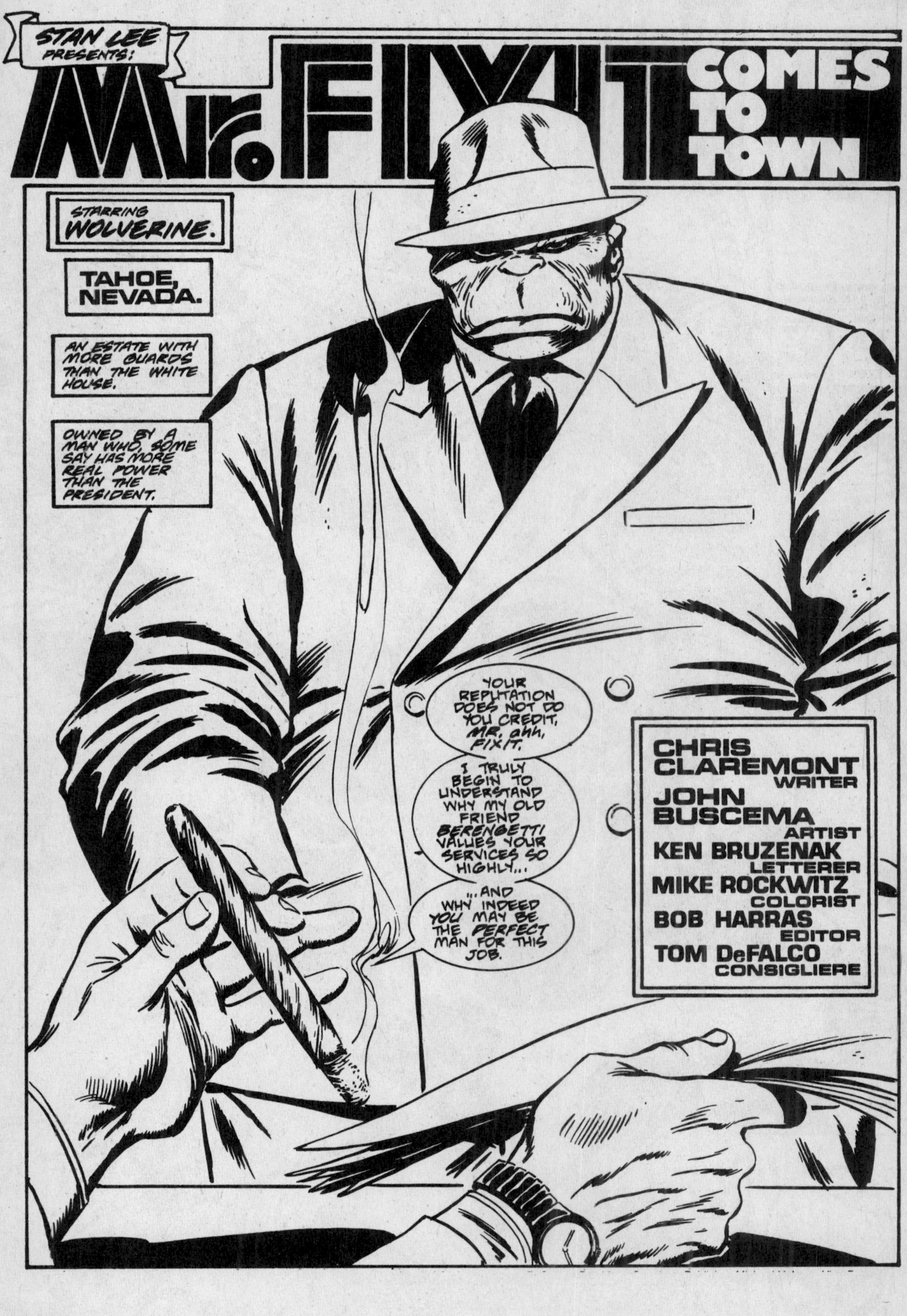
STAN LEE PRESENTS:
Mr. FIXIT COMES TO TOWN
STARRING WOLVERINE.
TAHOE, NEVADA.
AN ESTATE WITH MORE GUARDS THAN THE WHITE HOUSE.
OWNED BY A MAN WHO, SOME SAY HAS MORE REAL POWER THAN THE PRESIDENT.
YOUR REPUTATION DOES NOT DO YOU CREDIT, MR. ahh, FIXIT.
I TRULY BEGIN TO UNDERSTAND WHY MY OLD FRIEND BERENGETTI VALUES YOUR SERVICES SO HIGHLY...
...AND WHY INDEED YOU MAY BE THE PERFECT MAN FOR THIS JOB.
CHRIS CLAREMONT WRITER
JOHN BUSCEMA ARTIST
KEN BRUZENAK LETTERER
MIKE ROCKWITZ COLORIST
BOB HARRAS EDITOR
TOM DeFALCO CONSIGLIERE

MANY YEARS AGO, I DID HIM A SERVICE.

NOW, I AM NOT THE KIND OF MAN WHO KEEPS BOOK ON FRIENDSHIP...

...BUT HEARING OF MY SITUATION...

...MICHAEL, IN HONOR OF THAT DEBT, WAS KIND AND GENEROUS ENOUGH TO ASK YOU TO HEAR MY PROPOSAL.

AS WERE YOU, JOSEPH, TO ACCEDE TO MY INVITATION.

BERENGETTI'S A KINDA STAND-UP GUY.

TOO TRUE. SALT OF THE PROVERBIAL EARTH. OCCASIONALLY TO HIS COST.

HOWEVER--TO BUSINESS-- TO FURTHER MY, AH, INTERESTS IN THE FAR EAST, I ENGAGED IN A PARTNERSHIP WITH A MAN WHOSE BONAFIDES WERE, IN THEIR OWN WAY, AS IMPECCABLE AS MICHAEL'S.

SO OR I WAS LED TO BELIEVE.

"RECENT EVENTS HAVE BEGUN TO SUGGEST OTHERWISE."

CUTE.

YUM!

DATE?

BORRRING!

LEMME GUESS.

YOU WANT ME TO FIND OUT THE SCORE?

PRECISELY.

I'M A BUSINESSMAN. I SEE NO GOOD PURPOSE IN SUBSIDIZING A LOSING OPERATION.

I LIKE EVEN LESS BEING PLAYED FOR A FOOL.

NO PROBLEM.

THAT'S WHY THEY CALL ME "MR. FIXIT."

SPLENDID. AND CONTINGENT UPON A SUCCESSFUL OUTCOME...

...WE MIGHT LATER DISCUSS A MORE... PERMANENT ASSOCIA- TION.

I'M ALREADY SPOKEN FOR.

I QUITE UNDER- STAND.

BUT A MAN SHOULD ALWAYS KEEP HIS OPTIONS OPEN.

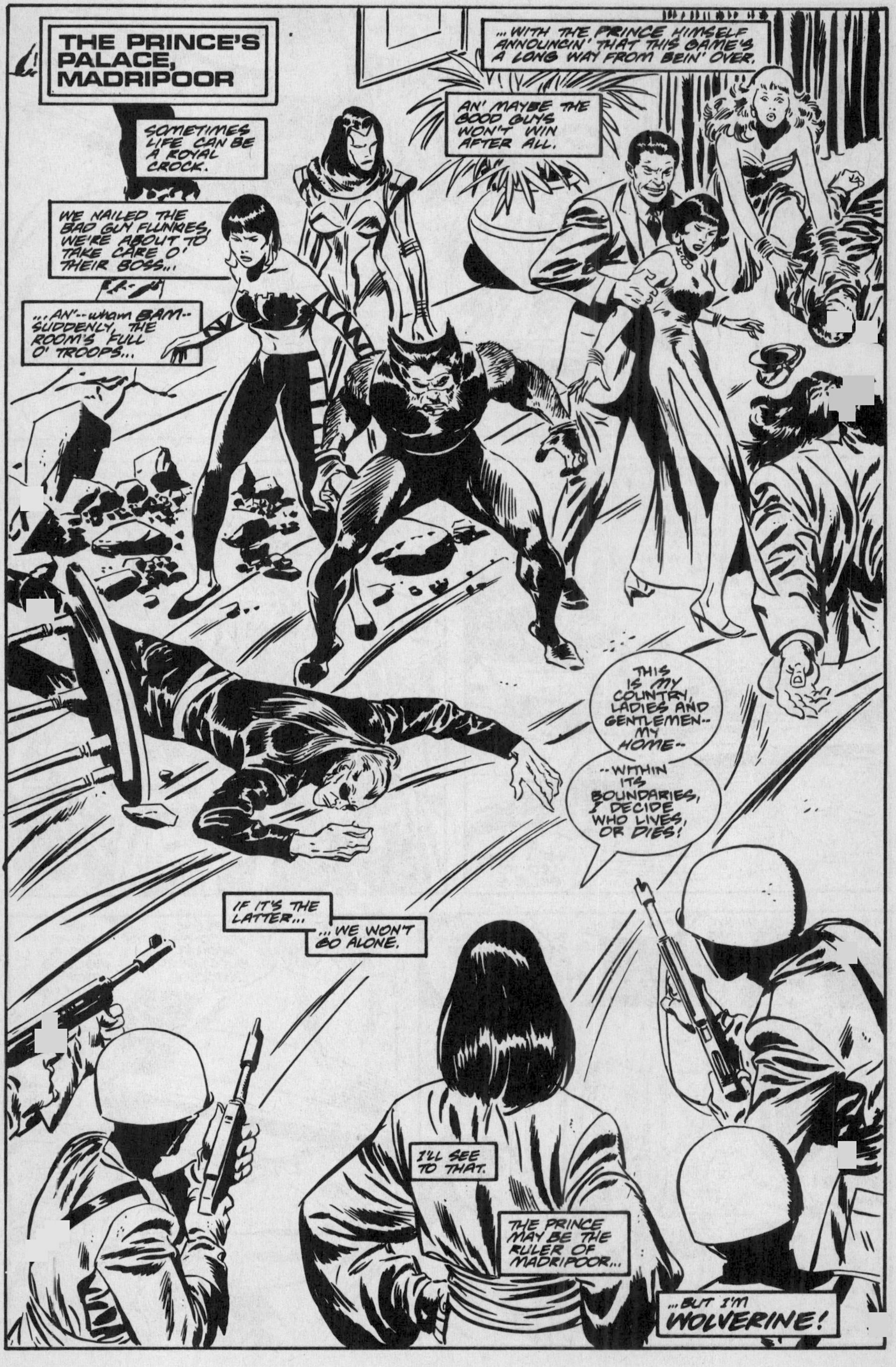
THE PRINCE'S PALACE, MADRIPOOR
SOMETIMES LIFE CAN BE A ROYAL CROCK.
WE NAILED THE BAD GUY FLUNKIES, WE'RE ABOUT TO TAKE CARE O' THEIR BOSS...
...AN'--WHAM BAM--SUDDENLY, THE ROOM'S FULL O' TROOPS...
...WITH THE PRINCE HIMSELF ANNOUNCIN' THAT THIS GAME'S A LONG WAY FROM BEIN' OVER.
AN' MAYBE THE GOOD GUYS WON'T WIN AFTER ALL.
THIS IS MY COUNTRY, LADIES AND GENTLEMEN-- MY HOME--
--WITHIN ITS BOUNDARIES, I DECIDE WHO LIVES, OR DIES!
IF IT'S THE LATTER...
...WE WON'T GO ALONE.
I'LL SEE TO THAT.
THE PRINCE MAY BE THE RULER OF MADRIPOOR...
...BUT I'M WOLVERINE!

DISGRACEFUL! YOUR DEPREDATIONS HAVE LAID WASTE TO THIS WING OF THE PALACE...

...SLAIN A RARE AND TREASURED PET...

...I'M OF HALF A MIND TO THROW THE LOT OF YOU--

--FOES AND SUPPOSED FRIENDS ALIKE--

--INTO MY DEEPEST-- EH?!

CAN IT BE?

PARDON MY BOORISHNESS, MISS...

...BUT HAVE I THE HONOR OF ADDRESSING THE AMERICAN ACTRESS, LINDSAY McCABE?

U-- YEAH...YES...I AM...THAT'S ME!

BY HEAVEN...

...I AM BLESSED.

I HAVE LONG BEEN AN ADMIRER OF YOUR WORK.

WHAT YOU MIGHT CALL...

...A FAN!

ARE YOU MAD?

YOU'VE YOUR ENEMIES HERE IN THIS ROOM, AT YOUR MERCY!

WHY ARE YOU SOCIALIZING WITH PEOPLE YOU SHOULD KILL?

HAVE A CARE, GENERAL COY...

...LEST YOU FIND YOURSELF NUMBERED AMONG THEM.

CAPTAIN, CONSIDER THESE MY GUESTS.

SEE TO THEIR NEEDS, WHEN THEY'RE PRESENTABLE...

...BRING THEM TO ME.

THIS WAY, SIR.

PATCH-- HE'S GOT MY PARTNER!

YOU WANT TO RESCUE HER, DREW...

...IT'LL BE MESSY.

COY LOOKS NERVOUS, SMALL WONDER. WITH THE PRINCE'S COVERT SUPPORT, HE PULLED AN ALL-OR-NOTHING SNEAK ATTACK...

...ON HIS CHIEF RIVAL FOR THE TOP SPOT IN MADRIPOOR'S UNDERWORLD...

--LADY NAMED TYGER TIGER.

ONLY IT DIDN'T WORK.

TYGER'S STILL ALIVE--

--THANKS, IN PART, TO ME, FLIER ARCHIE CORRIGAN AN' JESSICA DREW.

AN' THE PRINCE IS TURNIN' OUT TO MAYBE BE THE FRIEND AN' ALLY COY COUNTED ON.

LIKE I SAID, LIFE CAN BE A CROCK.

YOU HEARD THE MAN, FOR NOW, WE'LL TAKE HIM AT HIS WORD.

U.S. 395--hard by the **CHINA LAKE NAVAL WEAPONS TEST CENTER**

VROOM VROOM

VROOM VROOM

WHOA!

BE STILL MY HEART!

HEY, CHAZ-- IS SHE A LOOKER, OR WHAT?

DON'T BE CRUDE LAURENCE. IT'S SO COMMON.

SAY, INSTEAD, THIS IS A PERFECT NIGHT FOR ROMANCE...

...AND YOU, DARLING, ARE THE PERFECT GIRL TO SHARE IT WITH.

AND POLITE, TOO.

EXCUSE ME, I'M WORKING.

YOU KNOW WHAT THEY SAY, DON'T YOU...

..."ABOUT "ALL WORK AND NO PLAY?"

I DON'T PLAY... ...WITH CHILDREN!

SWAK!

WHY, CHAZ, THE NERVE OF THE GUTTER-SNIPE!

NEXT SHE'LL BE CALLING US...

...SPOILED ROTTEN LITTLE PREPPY BRATS!

HARDLY, MUFFY--

--THROUGH BUSTED TEETH!

POW!

TELL ME, DRIVER-GIRL...

FLIKT!

...YOU CARRYING ANY PASSENGERS?

BRIDE AND GROOM, PERHAPS? TEENER-BEENERS OUT ON A PROM NIGHT PROWL??

SOME FAT OLD CORPORATE CROCK, SPARKING WITH HIS SECRETARY???

SKREEEE

A KNIGHT IN SHINING ARMOR, WHO'D CARE TO STEP OUT...

...TO DEFEND YOUR HONOR?

KLATCH

AIN'T NOBODY EVER TAUGHT YOU, KIDDO...

...TO BE CAREFUL WHAT YOU WISH FOR?

YOU OKAY, CONNIE?

I'M SORRY, JOE.

I DIDN'T WANT TO BOTHER YOU. I THOUGHT I COULD HANDLE IT.

THE CAR'LL COST YOU.

THE BLACK EYE'LL COST YOU MORE.

THAT SOUNDS LIKE A THREAT!

AU CONTRAIRE, MON BRAVE-- OUR FEELING IS THAT YOU SHOULD PAY.

LEAVE US YOUR DRIVER...

...AND YOU GET TO WALK AWAY UNTOUCHED.

IS THAT A FAIR DEAL, OR WHAT?

SPORT...

YOU REALLY SHOULD'A QUIT...

...WHILE YOU WERE AHEAD.

TRASH!

BASH!

CRASH!

OUR BIKES... HE'S WRECKING THEM!

BETTER THEM THAN US, CHAZ!

I'M OUTTA HERE!

YOU MAY BE A COWARD, DEX--

...BUT I'M NOT!

SKAK!

NOPE.

YOU'RE A JERK!

OHO--

...NOW THE BIG BAD BOY KAHUNA...

...TURNS INTA A BIG FAT CHICKEN.

NICE SET O' WHEELS.

PROB'LY COST DADDY A BUNDLE.

BET THERE'S NOTHIN' ON THE ROAD CAN CATCH 'EM.

TOO BAD FOR YOU...

...I DON'T USE ROADS.

GOING MY WAY, SUCKER?

THOOM!

SPLAMM!

Y'KNOW, CHAZ, YOU'RE WHAT WE IN VEGAS CALL A PIMPLE ON THE BUTT OF THE UNIVERSE.

BET YOU KNOW ALL ABOUT WHAT TO DO WITH ZITS, RIGHT?

SMART-MOUTH UPPER CLASS PIECE O' WORK LIKE YOU...

...SURE YOU DO!

GUH-GWUH-GWUH-GWUH!

YOU POP 'EM!

CHAZ SAW THE LIGHT.

THAT'S WHY HE'S STILL BREATHIN'.

REST O' YOU ZITS BETTER PROFIT FROM HIS EXAMPLE.

I GOTTA GO NOW.

BUT I EXPECT YOU TO HELP CONNIE FIX MY CAR, AN' PAY FOR ALL THE REPAIRS.

AN' THEN TURN YOURSELVES IN TO THE COPS, FULL CONFESSIONS ALL 'ROUND.

I HEAR ANYTHING DIFFERENT.

I'LL BE BACK.

YOU HEARD MR. FIXIT RATBAGS-- MOVE!

YES, MA'AM!

YES, MA'AM!

YES, MA'AM!

YES, MA'AM!

MADRIPOOR...

I AM IN THE HEART OF THE PALACE GROUNDS--

...WITH GUARDS AT EVERY DOOR...

...AND A HALF-DOZEN KILOMETERS BETWEEN ME AND THE PERIMETER WALL.

THIS IS THE MOST GILDED OF CAGES...

"--BUT A CAGE NONETHE-LESS.

AND YET, THOUGH I'M A PRISONER...

...I'M FAR FROM HELPLESS.

THIS ARMOR IS IMPERVIOUS TO ANY WEAPON OR FORCE OR POWER.

WEARING IT MAKES ME...

...THE NEXT BEST THING TO INVULNER-ABLE.

WHO COULD STOP ME TAKING MY REVENGE AGAINST MY ENEMIES?

THE PROBLEM IS...

I CAN'T TAKE THE CURSED THING OFF!

IT WAS ORIGINALLY GIVEN TO LINDSAY McCABE. ONLY LINDSAY CAN REMOVE IT.

AND SHE IS IN THE HANDS OF THE PRINCE...

...WHO IS COY'S ALLY.

IF ANYTHING HAPPENS TO HER, I AM TRAPPED--

--TO DIE EITHER OF STARVATION OR THIRST-- EH?!!!?

NOT TO WORRY, DARLIN'!

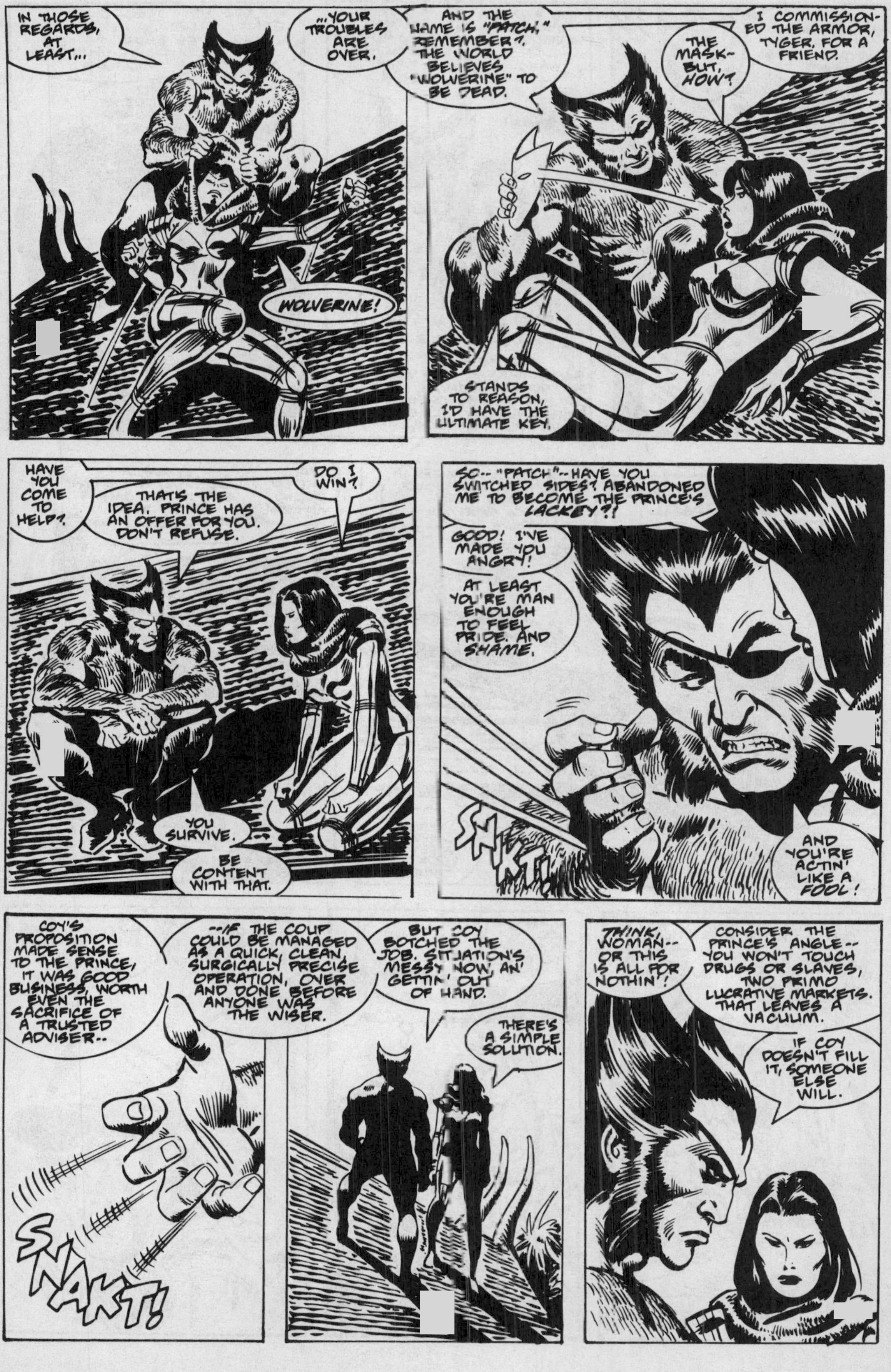
IN THOSE REGARDS, AT LEAST...
...YOUR TROUBLES ARE OVER.
WOLVERINE!
AND THE NAME IS "PATCH," REMEMBER? THE WORLD BELIEVES "WOLVERINE" TO BE DEAD.
THE MASK-- BUT, HOW?
I COMMISSIONED THE ARMOR, TYGER, FOR A FRIEND.
STANDS TO REASON, I'D HAVE THE ULTIMATE KEY.
HAVE YOU COME TO HELP?
THAT'S THE IDEA. PRINCE HAS AN OFFER FOR YOU. DON'T REFUSE.
DO I WIN?
YOU SURVIVE.
BE CONTENT WITH THAT.
SO-- "PATCH"-- HAVE YOU SWITCHED SIDES? ABANDONED ME TO BECOME THE PRINCE'S LACKEY?!
GOOD! I'VE MADE YOU ANGRY!
AT LEAST YOU'RE MAN ENOUGH TO FEEL PRIDE. AND SHAME.
SNIKT!
AND YOU'RE ACTIN' LIKE A FOOL!
COY'S PROPOSITION MADE SENSE TO THE PRINCE, IT WAS GOOD BUSINESS, WORTH EVEN THE SACRIFICE OF A TRUSTED ADVISER--
--IF THE COUP COULD BE MANAGED AS A QUICK, CLEAN, SURGICALLY PRECISE OPERATION, OVER AND DONE BEFORE ANYONE WAS THE WISER.
SNAKT!
BUT COY BOTCHED THE JOB. SITUATION'S MESSY NOW, AN' GETTIN' OUT OF HAND.
THERE'S A SIMPLE SOLUTION.
THINK, WOMAN-- OR THIS IS ALL FOR NOTHIN'!
CONSIDER THE PRINCE'S ANGLE-- YOU WON'T TOUCH DRUGS OR SLAVES, TWO PRIMO LUCRATIVE MARKETS. THAT LEAVES A VACUUM.
IF COY DOESN'T FILL IT, SOMEONE ELSE WILL.

ON THE OTHER HAND, YOU DO FINE WITH WHAT'S LEFT.

YOU'RE MORE A CRIMELORD AFTER HIS OWN HEART.

COY ALONE IS TOO DANGEROUS A THREAT TO HIS THRONE.

YOU ALONE MEANS NEVER-ENDING TURF WARS.

THE PAIR OF YOU, BALANCING AND CHECKING EACH OTHER...

...TO HIM THAT'S THE BEST OF ALL WORLDS.

CHANCELLOR RANJAMARYAN WAS YOUR FRIEND AS MUCH AS MINE. COY HAD HIM BUTCHERED--THE PRINCE SANCTIONED IT-- DOES THAT MEAN NOTHING?!

RANJA'S DEAD. YOU'RE NOT.

TRUST ME, DARLIN', I WANT COY AS BADLY AS YOU, BUT THIS ISN'T THE MOMENT.

YOU GOT THE INSTINCTS, BABY TIGER,

I GOT THE YEARS.

AND I THOUGHT I WAS HARD-HEADED.

LAX--LOS ANGELES INTERNATIONAL AIRPORT...

SOVEREIGN AIRWAYS ANNOUNCES BOARDING FOR FLIGHT 001, IMPERIAL SERVICE TO MADRIPOOR...

AHWH, CRIPES, WILLYA LOOK AT THIS?!

HARD-SIDED LOUIS VUITTON.

COSTS A BUNDLE, AN' EVEN EMPTY, WEIGHS A LOUSY TON!

AN' THESE'RE STUFFED FULL!

LOTTA PIECES, TOO. THIS FELLA TRAVELS IN STYLE.

LESSEE WHO IT IS, TRYIN' SO HARD TO GIVE DECENT WORKIN' STIFFS A RUPTURE.

HECK, CALL THIS A NAME: "...JOE FIXIT?"

WHASSAMATTA, LOU, YOU GOT A SUICIDE COMPLEX OR WHAT???

MMMPLGFH!

THAT'S A NAME YOU DON'T WANNA MENTION, ANYWHERE, EVER!

AN' A GUY YOU DON'T EVER WANNA GET MAD AT YOU.

GIMME A BREAK, ARNIE. WHAT MAKES HIM SO SPECIAL?

CRRRREEEK!

GEEZ!

CREEK CREACK

CREEK CREEK

THAT MUST BE HIM!

SPRUN NNG!

I'LL :AHEM:... ...LOAD HIS STUFF... ...REAL CAREFUL... ...WHERE IT WON'T GET BUMPED OR SCRATCHED.

MADRIPOOR...

I AM DELIGHTED TO SEE YOU BOTH REACH THIS ACCOMMODATION.

AS I AM SURE IT WILL PROVE BENEFICIAL TO ALL CONCERNED.

CAPTAIN, ESCORT THESE WORTHIES TO THEIR RESPECTIVE DOMICILES.

USE SEPARATE GATES TO LEAVE...

...AT OPPOSITE SIDES OF THE PALACE GROUNDS.

NO SENSE TEMPTING FATE...

...ANY MORE THAN WE'VE ALREADY DONE THIS NIGHT.

AS SHE LEAVES, KARMA TOSSES THE QUICKEST OF GLANCES MY WAY.

I'M NOT THE ONLY ONE TO CATCH IT.

SHE'S A GOOD KID.

SHE DESERVES BETTER THAN COY AS HER UNCLE.

FATE DEALS THE CARDS, DREW. WE JUST PLAY 'EM BEST WE CAN.

BUT SHE'S RIGHT. I OWE THE GIRL MY LIFE, MORE'N ONCE. I CAN'T ABANDON HER.

NOW THAT BUSINESS IS OUT OF THE WAY...

...ON TO MORE ENJOYABLE PURSUITS.

THE ROYAL COUTURIER HAS DONE YOU PROUD, LINDSAY--

--I MAY CALL YOU "LINDSAY," MAY I NOT?

TO MY MOST... INTIMATE COMPANIONS...

QUIT LOOKIN' GRUMPED, DREW.

THERE ARE WORSE FATES THAN BEIN' THE PRINCE'S PAL.

...I AM BARAN.

TRUE-- YOU CAN BE HIS CHANCELLOR.

SCORE ONE FOR THE LADY. SHE'S SHARP AS MY CLAWS, WITH A SUPER-STRENGTH THAT MAKES HER A MATCH FOR ROUGHHOUSE. MY KINDA GAL.

LUCKY FOR US BOTH...

...SHE FEELS DIFFERENT.

I HAVE LONG ADMIRED YOUR WORK, LINDSAY...

...AS YOU CAN PLAINLY SEE.

WOW!

JESS-- PATCH--THIS WHOLE ROOM-- THOSE STATUES-- THEY'RE ME!

I HAVE MASTER PRINTS OF ALL YOUR FILMS AND TELEVISION APPEARANCES. AND I CONFESS, VIDEO TAPES OF YOUR THEATRICAL PERFORMANCES, AS WELL.

OH LORD, MOST OF IT WAS SO BAD...

...I THINK I WANT TO DIE!

PROTESTS WOULD CARRY MORE WEIGHT, PARTNER...

...IF YOU WEREN'T GRINNING EAR TO EAR.

HEY, JESS, GIMME A BREAK--

--CAN I HELP IT IF THIS IS A GAS!

WEIRD, BUT A DEFINITE GAS!

THAT'S MY FIRST MAJOR ROLE IN "DEMON DEBS," AND ITS SEQUEL, "DEMON BLUES," I WAS A SORORITY SUCCUBUS AT YALE!

My first "A"-picture, "Last Train from Moscow."

The hero-spy's gal-friday.

I got killed in the first reel.

This was "Cyber Witch." High-tech punkette bad girl sorceress of the future.

Demon script.

The studio butchered it.

Oh, golly--another pair of "classics" come back to haunt me.

Over there, that's "Lethal Latex Lovelies," not too proud of that, but I had to pay the rent.

And last, a character whose name says it all--

..."Ms. Merc!"

That's when I decided the time had come to hit the boards again and do some serious theater.

I joined the San Francisco Rep.

But you never appeared in any productions.

Uh, no. I, ah, sort of ran into trouble--

...I got tossed off a roof-top by a super-villainess named Viper.

After I got out of the hospital, I sort of hooked up with Jess as her assistant, to fill the time till I was ready to go back on stage.

Haven't had a dull moment since.

If you don't mind...

Your pen-- ...it's solid gold!

...May I trouble you for your autograph?

Quelle surprise!

Here's hoping your autograph is all he asks for.

Because an absolute monarch descended from pirate freebooters...

...might not be inclined to take "no" for an answer.

I wonder how Patch reads this--

--he's gone!?!

THE SOVEREIGN HOTEL"

--BEST IN MADRIPOOR, POSSIBLY THE WHOLE WORLD--

--COY LIVES IN THE PENTHOUSE TRIPLEX.

FROM THE SOUND OF THINGS...

...HE DOESN'T HOLD MUCH...

HOW DARE HE BETRAY ME?!!

...WITH THE CONCEPT OF GRACE UNDER ADVERSITY.

MAYBE WE'LL GET LUCKY AN' HE'LL BUST A BLOOD VESSEL.

FAT CHANCE.

HIS KIND TEND TO LIVE FOREVER.

IT'S THE INNOCENTS--AN' HEROES, LIKE KARMA--WHO DIE YOUNG. AN' HARD.

MY UNCLE IS SO OBSESSED WITH HIMSELF...

...HE HASN'T THOUGHT TO QUESTION MY PRESENCE AT THE PALACE.

OR WHY I WAS DRESSED SO SCANDALOUSLY.

IF HE SHOULD EVER SUSPECT THAT I WAS WORKING AGAINST--OH!!

WELL, NOW-- AIN'T THIS A SIGHT FOR SORE EYES.

THESE ARE MY ROOMS, M'SIEU! YOU HAVE NO BUSINESS HERE.

AIN'T COME ON "BUSINESS," SWEETNESS.

YOU HAVE BEEN DRINKING.

THA'S A FACT. BUT I HATE TO PARTY ALONE.

YOU'RE A FINE FIGURE OF A GAL SHAN COY MANH.

ALL YOU NEED TO MAKE YOUR LIFE COMPLETE... ...IS A MAN.

MAYBE SO, LUMMOX--

TAP TAP TAP

SLAMMO

...BUT YOU AIN'T HIM!

ALL YOURS, DARLIN'!

MERCI, M'SIEU PATCH.

I HAVE HIS MIND--

HE IS POSSESSED! NOW, ROUGHHOUSE-- SLEEP!

FELLA CAN TAKE A PUNCH.

THANKS FOR THE ASSIST.

I AM GLAD YOU CAME...

..."FOR... OTHER REASONS.

MY UNCLE IS IN DANGER.

HE HAS AN "ARRANGEMENT" WITH AN AMERICAN CRIMELORD. BUT YOUR DESTROYING HIS OPIUM CROP IS PREVENTING HIS FULFILLING HIS OBLIGATIONS.

AN-- HOW YOU SAY-- "ENFORCER" KNOWN AS "MR. FIXIT" IS BEING SENT TO DEAL WITH HIM.

SO LET HIM!

PATCH-- NO!

MY UNCLE IS STILL MY BEST AND ONLY HOPE TO FIND MY KIDNAPED BROTHER AND SISTER!

FOR THEIR SAKE, I MUST STAND BY HIM!

NO MATTER THE COST.

NO MATTER THE COST. M'SIEU-- ROUGHOUSE!

Uhrhrr

NO PROBLEM.

Buh... ...buh... ...buh...

BHAM

MADRIPOOR INTERNATIONAL AIRPORT...

A BRUTE WHO MAKES THE "TERMINATOR" LOOK LIKE A PANSY.

ACCORDING TO MY SOURCES, WHAT YOU SEE WITH FIXIT IS WHAT YOU GET.

ONE THING DOESN'T FIT, THOUGH.

IN ALL HIS TIME IN VEGAS, NEITHER FIXIT NOR HIS BOSS, BERENGETTI, HAD EVER BEEN PART OF ANY MOB OPERATION.

IN THEIR OWN WAY, BOTH WERE STRAIGHT ARROW GUYS.

SO WHY THE TOTAL CHANGE OF HEART?

STILL NOT SURE WHY I'M HERE.

WHO'M I KIDDING?

KARMA ASKED.

THIS IS FOR HER.

CLUMP

BABUMP

TROUBLE?

CASES-- SO MANY-- SO HEAVY!

LIKE THE MAN SAYS...

...YOU WANT A JOB DONE RIGHT...

..."YOU GOTTA DO IT YOURSELF!"

BINGO! AN' THEN SOME.

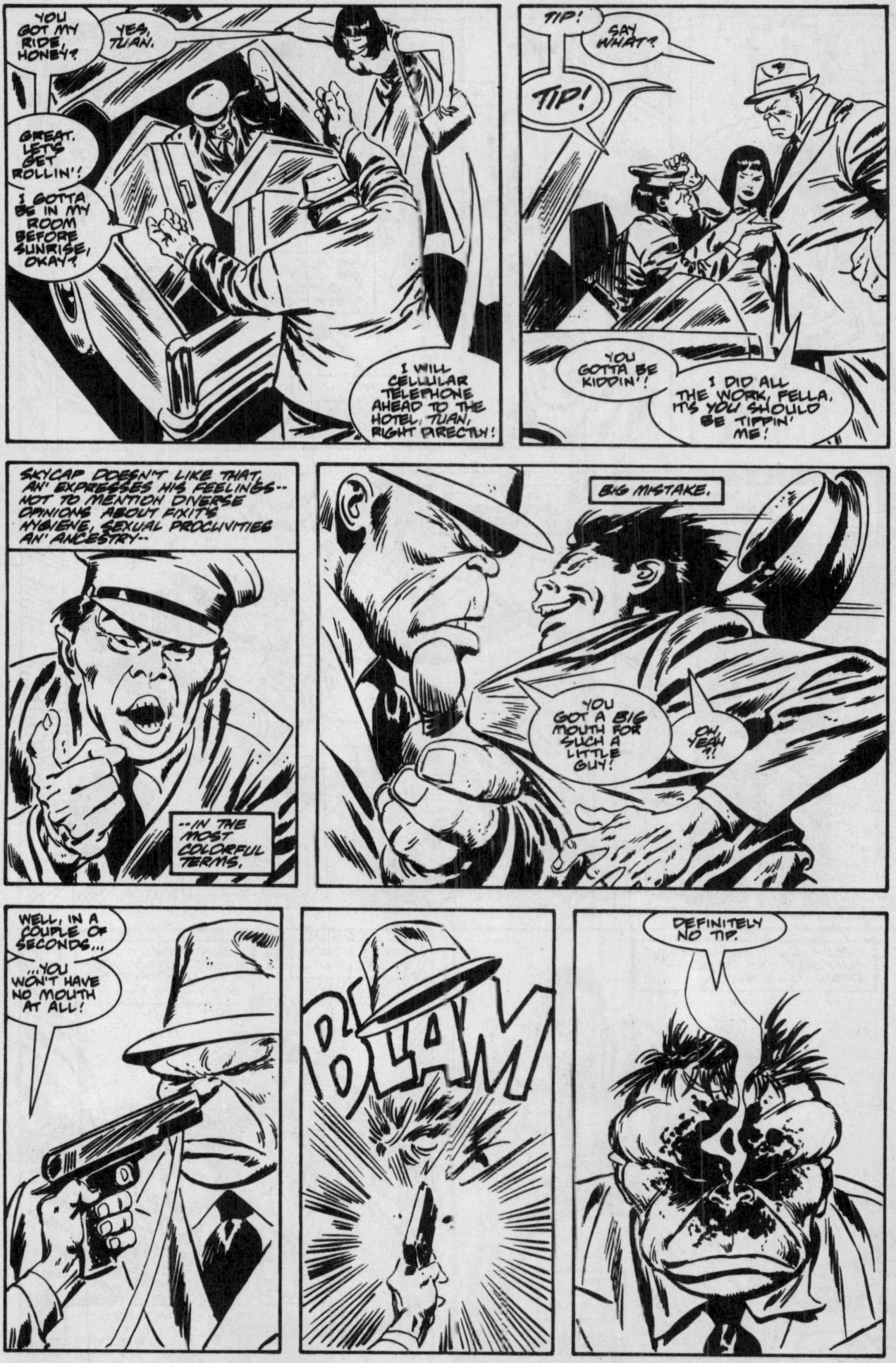
YOU GOT MY RIDE, HONEY?
YES, TUAN.
GREAT. LET'S GET ROLLIN'!
I GOTTA BE IN MY ROOM BEFORE SUNRISE, OKAY?
I WILL CELLULAR TELEPHONE AHEAD TO THE HOTEL, TUAN, RIGHT DIRECTLY!
TIP!
SAY WHAT?
TIP!
YOU GOTTA BE KIDDIN'!
I DID ALL THE WORK, FELLA. IT'S YOU SHOULD BE TIPPIN' ME!
SKYCAP DOESN'T LIKE THAT, AN' EXPRESSES HIS FEELINGS-- NOT TO MENTION DIVERSE OPINIONS ABOUT FIXIT'S HYGIENE, SEXUAL PROCLIVITIES AN' ANCESTRY--
--IN THE MOST COLORFUL TERMS.
BIG MISTAKE.
YOU GOT A BIG MOUTH FOR SUCH A LITTLE GUY!
OH, YEAH ?!
WELL, IN A COUPLE OF SECONDS...
...YOU WON'T HAVE NO MOUTH AT ALL!
BLAM
DEFINITELY NO TIP.

INTERESTING.

I'M NOT THE ONLY RECEPTION COMMITTEE.

DON'T LOOK LIKE TYGER'S MUSCLE.

COY, MAYBE? TRYING TO NAIL FIXIT BEFORE FIXIT DOES HIM?

NO MATTER. I NEVER FORGET A SCENT...

...OR A FACE...

...EVEN IF IT'S GREY INSTEAD O' GREEN.

FIGHTING STYLE CONFIRMS IT.

TYPICALLY, THOUGH, SOME BUFFOON HAS TO GO AN' SPOIL THINGS...

...BY PULLIN' A GUN.

THEY WON'T HURT FIXIT...

...BUT THERE'S A WHOLE CONCOURSE FULL O' TRAVELERS BEHIND HIM...

BKOP!

...WHO AREN'T QUITE SO BULLET-PROOF.

FIXIT HAS A STYLE ALL HIS OWN. SOMETIMES-- ESPECIALLY IF YOU'RE NOT ON THE RECEIVING END--

--WATCHING HIM IN ACTION CAN BE A REAL TREAT.

OW! OW! OW! OW! OW! OW! OW! OW! OW! OW! OW! OW! OW! OW!

HIS DRIVER'S NO HARDCASE, THOUGH. SHE PLAYS SMART--KEEPING HERSELF AS LOW AN' INCONSPICUOUS AS POSSIBLE...

...AN' PRAYIN' SHE DOESN'T GET NOTICED.

NO SUCH LUCK. AIEEEEE!

KEEP YOUR DISTANCE, YANKEE DOG...

...OR THIS TRAIN JOINS HER ANCESTORS.

HE DRAGS HER FOR THE ALLEY...

...WHERE HIS OUTFIT STASHED THEIR GETAWAY BIKES.

SO MUCH SCRAP METAL NOW, THANKS TO ME.

KRUNTCH!

NO LIGHTS, EITHER. I SMASHED 'EM.

JOYBOY DOESN'T SO MUCH SEE MY CLAWS, AS FEEL 'EM.

HE DROPS HIS HOSTAGE.

I DROP HIM.

WHUMPGHF!

NO SIGN OF FIXIT. I EXPECTED HIM TO FOLLOW.

CHUMP!

TURNS OUT HE HAD OTHER THINGS TO WORRY ABOUT.

HAND GRENADE!

PLAYTIME'S OVER, LUMPS.

YOU BETTER SCAT...

...WHILE YOU'RE STILL ABLE--

--BEFORE YOU MAKE ME MAD!

FA-BOOM!

AND ON CUE, THE GOONS PROVE BEYOND ALL SHADOW OF A DOUBT...

...PRECISELY WHAT THEY'RE MADE OF.

NICE TOWN.

REALLY KNOWS HOW TO MAKE A FELLA FEEL WELCOME.

WHO'S SIDE YOU ON?

THE ANGELS, CAN'T YOU TELL?

THE LADY LOOKS PRETTY ROCKY.

SHE SHOULD SEE A DOC.

THAT'LL TAKE TOO LONG.

SHE LOOKS OKAY, SHE'LL BE FINE, WE'LL GO TO MY HOTEL FIRST...

CHAUFFEUR'S IN NO FIT STATE TO DRIVE.

THEN YOU DO IT.

I'LL MAKE IT WORTH YOUR WHILE...

...YOU GET ME TO THE HOTEL BEFORE DAWN.

BUB, YOU JUST MADE AN OFFER I WON'T REFUSE.

COPS WON'T LIKE US BUGGING OUT LIKE THIS...

...BUT THAT'S FIXIT'S PROBLEM.

BESIDES, I WANT TO FIND OUT...

...WHAT'S SO SPECIAL ABOUT THE SUNRISE.

WE MAKE THE SOVEREIGN WITH TIME TO SPARE...

...AND FIXIT PROVES AS GENEROUS AS HIS WORD. I GIVE THE MONEY TO HIS DRIVER.

I WAIT FOR FULL MORNING BEFORE I MAKE MY MOVE.

DOOR WEARS A "DO NOT DISTURB" SIGN.

SO I BUST IN SILENT AS A GHOST.

ALMOST BLOW THE CAPER BY LAUGHING ALOUD WHEN I SEE WHO'S ON THE BED--

--NOT THAT WOLVERINE HAS ANYTHING TO FEAR FROM...

...ROBERT BRUCE BANNER.

BRUCIE BY DAY, HULK BY NIGHT--NO WONDER HE WAS SO PARANOID ABOUT GETTING UNDER COVER.

SUNLIGHT MAKES BANNER BOSS, AND HULK'S NEVER LIKED THAT. MUST USE SEDATIVES TO KEEP HIM ASLEEP TILL NIGHT.

HE'LL LIKE IT LESS, BEFORE I'M THROUGH.

IN FACT, MR. FIXIT'LL REGRET THE MOMENT HE SET FOOT IN MY TOWN.

NOW--I LAUGH, BECAUSE THIS IS GONNA BE FUN.

NEXT: **IF IT AIN'T BROKE--!**

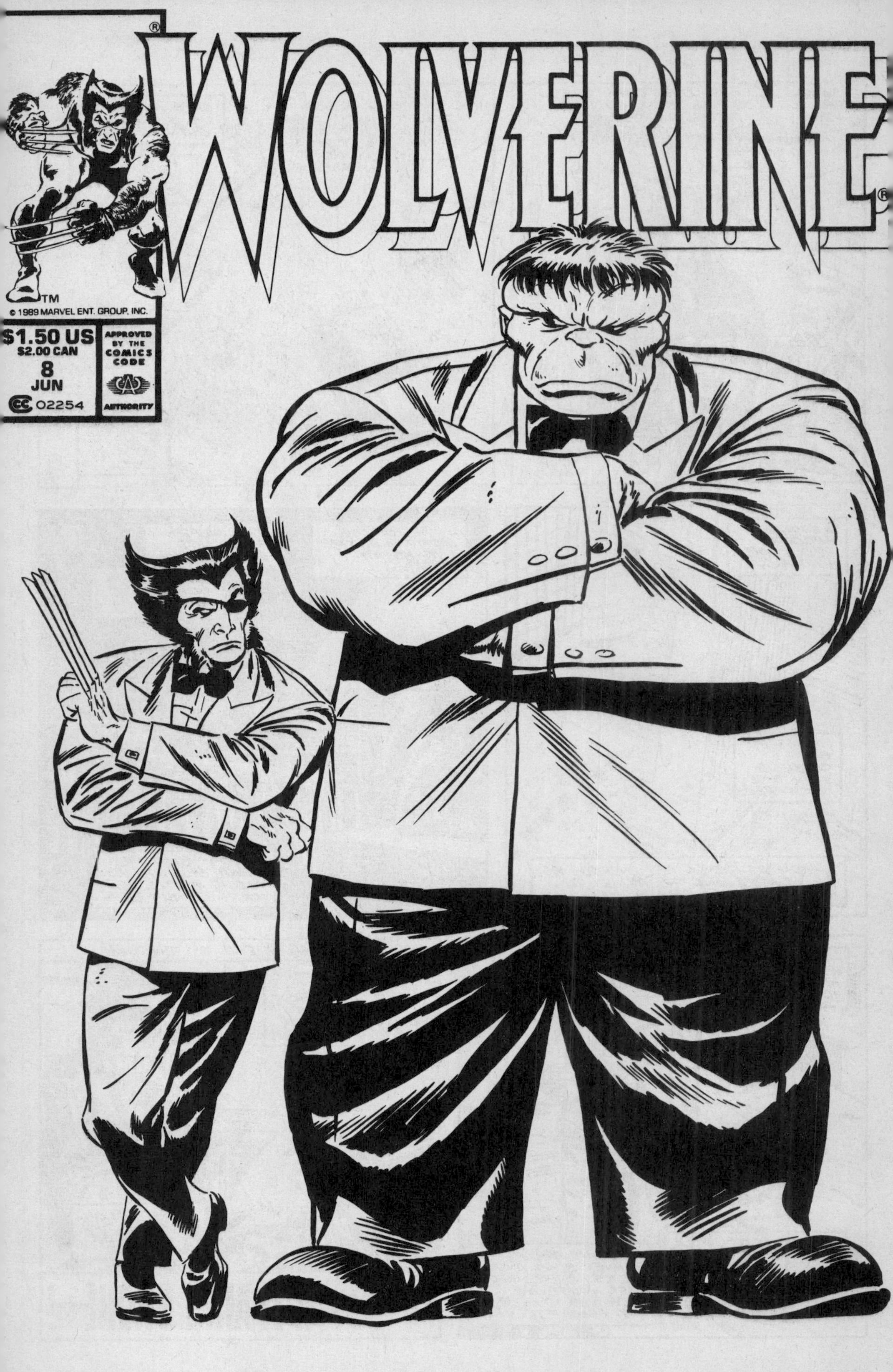
WOLVERINE
TM
© 1989 MARVEL ENT. GROUP, INC.
$1.50 US
$2.00 CAN
8
JUN
02254
APPROVED BY THE COMICS CODE AUTHORITY

IF IT AIN'T BROKE--!

STAN LEE PRESENTS:

THE SOVEREIGN HOTEL-- MADRIPOOR.

HE LEFT A WAKE-UP CALL FOR SUNSET.

I FIGURE A HALF-HOUR TO SHOWER AN' SHAVE--AN WHATEVER--BEFORE HE OPENS HIS DRAWERS AN' SUITCASES FOR A NEW SET OF CLOTHES.

THAT'S WHEN THE FUN BEGINS.

CHRIS CLAREMONT: writer ✧ **JOHN BUSCEMA:** artist
KEN BRUZENAK: letterer ✧ **GLYNIS OLIVER:** colorist ✧ **BOB HARRAS:** editor ✧ **TOM DeFALCO:** your tour guide

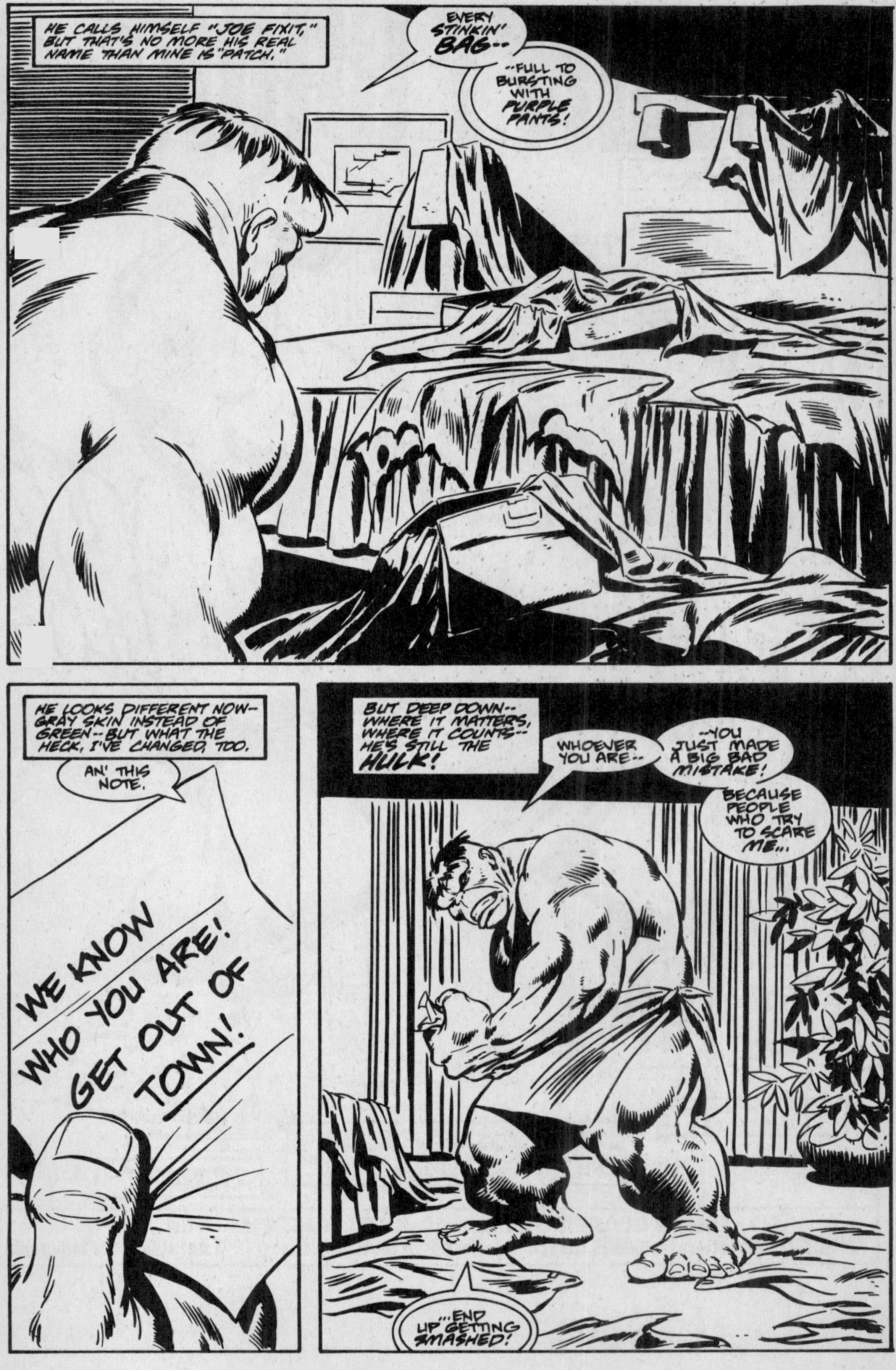
HE CALLS HIMSELF "JOE FIXIT," BUT THAT'S NO MORE HIS REAL NAME THAN MINE IS "PATCH."
EVERY STINKIN' BAG--
--FULL TO BURSTING WITH PURPLE PANTS!
HE LOOKS DIFFERENT NOW-- GRAY SKIN INSTEAD OF GREEN--BUT WHAT THE HECK, I'VE CHANGED, TOO.
AN' THIS NOTE.
WE KNOW WHO YOU ARE! GET OUT OF TOWN!
BUT DEEP DOWN-- WHERE IT MATTERS, WHERE IT COUNTS-- HE'S STILL THE HULK!
WHOEVER YOU ARE--
--YOU JUST MADE A BIG BAD MISTAKE!
BECAUSE PEOPLE WHO TRY TO SCARE ME...
...END UP GETTING SMASHED!

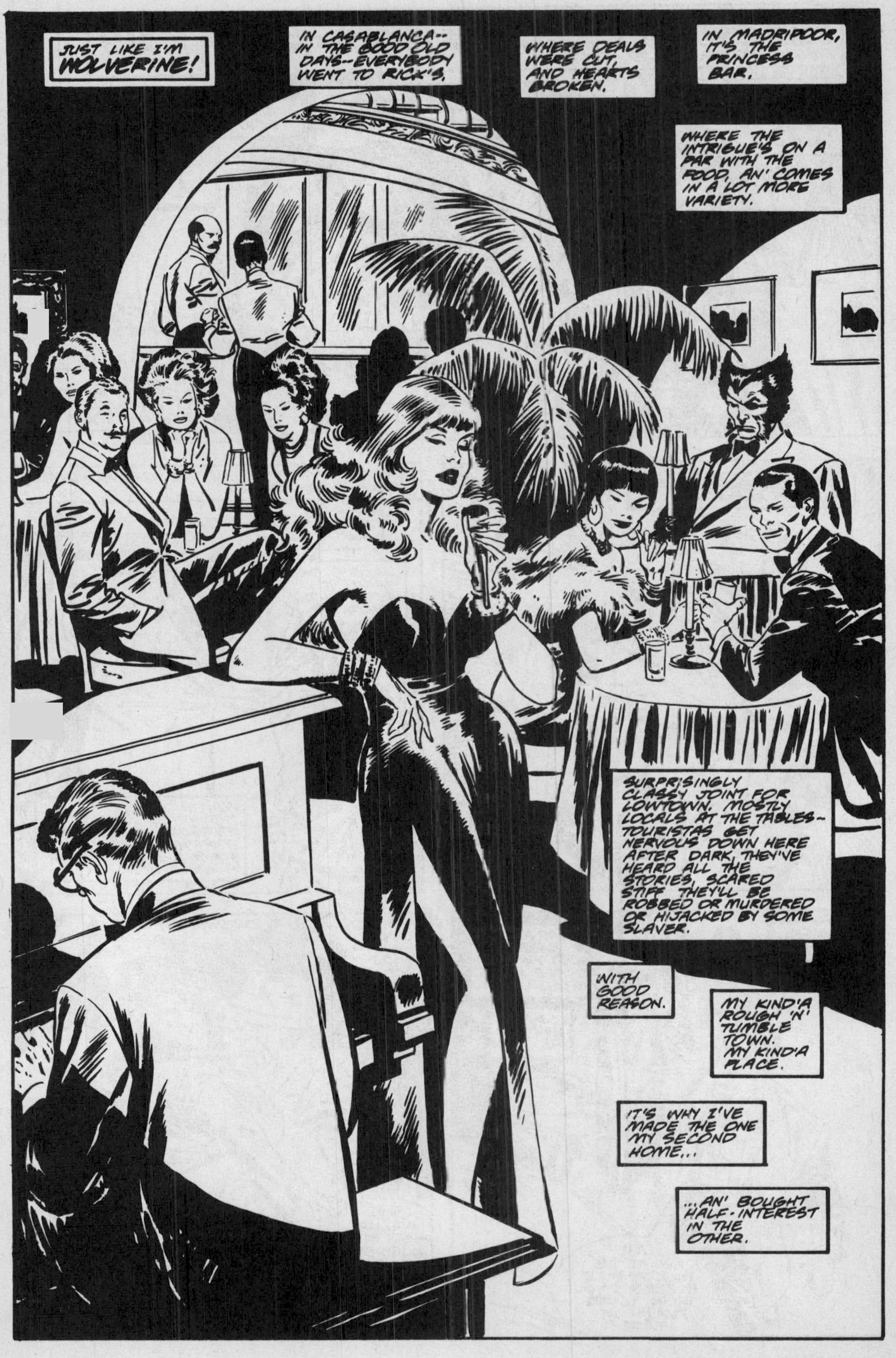
JUST LIKE I'M WOLVERINE!
IN CASABLANCA-- IN THE GOOD OLD DAYS--EVERYBODY WENT TO RICK'S.
WHERE DEALS WERE CUT, AND HEARTS BROKEN.
IN MADRIPOOR, IT'S THE PRINCESS BAR.
WHERE THE INTRIGUE'S ON A PAR WITH THE FOOD, AN' COMES IN A LOT MORE VARIETY.
SURPRISINGLY CLASSY JOINT FOR LOWTOWN. MOSTLY LOCALS AT THE TABLES-- TOURISTAS GET NERVOUS DOWN HERE AFTER DARK. THEY'VE HEARD ALL THE STORIES, SCARED STIFF THEY'LL BE ROBBED OR MURDERED OR HIJACKED BY SOME SLAVER.
WITH GOOD REASON.
MY KIND'A ROUGH 'N' TUMBLE TOWN. MY KIND'A PLACE.
IT'S WHY I'VE MADE THE ONE MY SECOND HOME...
...AN' BOUGHT HALF-INTEREST IN THE OTHER.

LINDSAY McCABE'S FILLIN' IN FOR OUR USUAL CHANTEUSE, DOIN' A FAIR JOB OF IT, TOO. SO GOOD, IN FACT, MY PARTNER, ODONNELL, FIGURES TO ASK HER TO STAY ON.

ME, I'M MORE INTERESTED IN THE AUDIENCE.

TIGER TIGER SITS ALONE, SHE'S CO-CRIMELORD OF THE ISLAND...

...SHARING THAT THRONE, UNDER DURESS, WITH GENERAL NGUYEN NGOC COY, WHO IS THE BADDEST OF BAD NEWS.

UNLIKE HIS NIECE, SWAN.

THEN THERE'S TAI, CHIEF OF POLICE, WHO DOES A BETTER JOB THAN MOST SUSPECT.

AND LASTLY, McCABE'S PRIVATE EYE PARTNER, JESSICA DREW.

THAT'S THE SCOREBOARD. AND THE PLAYERS.

NOW FOR SOME ACTION.

SAY THIS FOR FIXIT, THE LUG KNOWS HOW TO MAKE AN ENTRANCE.

NICE SUIT.

HENG'S ON JASMINE ROW, BY THE TAILORING.

WAITIN' WHILE THEY MADE IT TO MEASURE IS PROBABLY WHAT HELD HIM UP SO LONG. I EXPECTED HIM A WHILE AGO.

'COURSE...

...I WAS HOPIN' FOR BARE CHEST AN' PURPLE PANTS INSTEAD.

CAN'T WIN 'EM ALL.

AN' WHAT THE BLOODY BLUE BLAZES D'YOU THINK YOU'RE PLAYIN' AT, MATE ?!

I'M JOE FIXIT.

YOU GOT A NAME, CHUMP?

O'DONNELL. THIS IS MY PLACE.

YOU WANNA STAY IN BUSINESS, LIMEY...

...YOU TALK STRAIGHT AN' MAKE NICE, CAPEESH?

DOLLAR AIN'T WHAT IT SHOULD BE--

--BUT THIS OUGHT'A COVER THE DAMAGE TO YOUR DOOR.

PLAY SMART, O'DONNELL, AN' THAT'LL BE THE *ONLY* THING DAMAGED.

I WANT A MAN.

SORRY CAN'T HELP YOU.

HARDY-HAR-HAWR!

NICE JOKE, I LAUGHED. DON'T PUSH YOUR LUCK.

I'M LOOKIN' FOR A GUY NAMED *PATCH*.

I'M PATCH.

AMAZING HOW TWO LITTLE WORDS...

...CAN EMPTY A PLACE.

NOBODY WANTS TO BE ANY-WHERE NEAR ME AN' FIXIT.

CAN'T SAY I BLAME 'EM.

I NEED INFORMATION, I'M TOLD YOU'RE THE MAN TO SEE.

OH? SUPPOSE I'M NOT IN THE MOOD TO HELP?

FORTY SAYS THERE'S A FIGHT!

A HUNDRED ON PATCH!

ON FIXIT!

DISMEMBER-MENT!

DEATH!

TWO-TO-ONE!

FIVE-TO-THREE!

IT'LL BE SLAUGHTER!

HOW MUCH YOU WANNA BET?

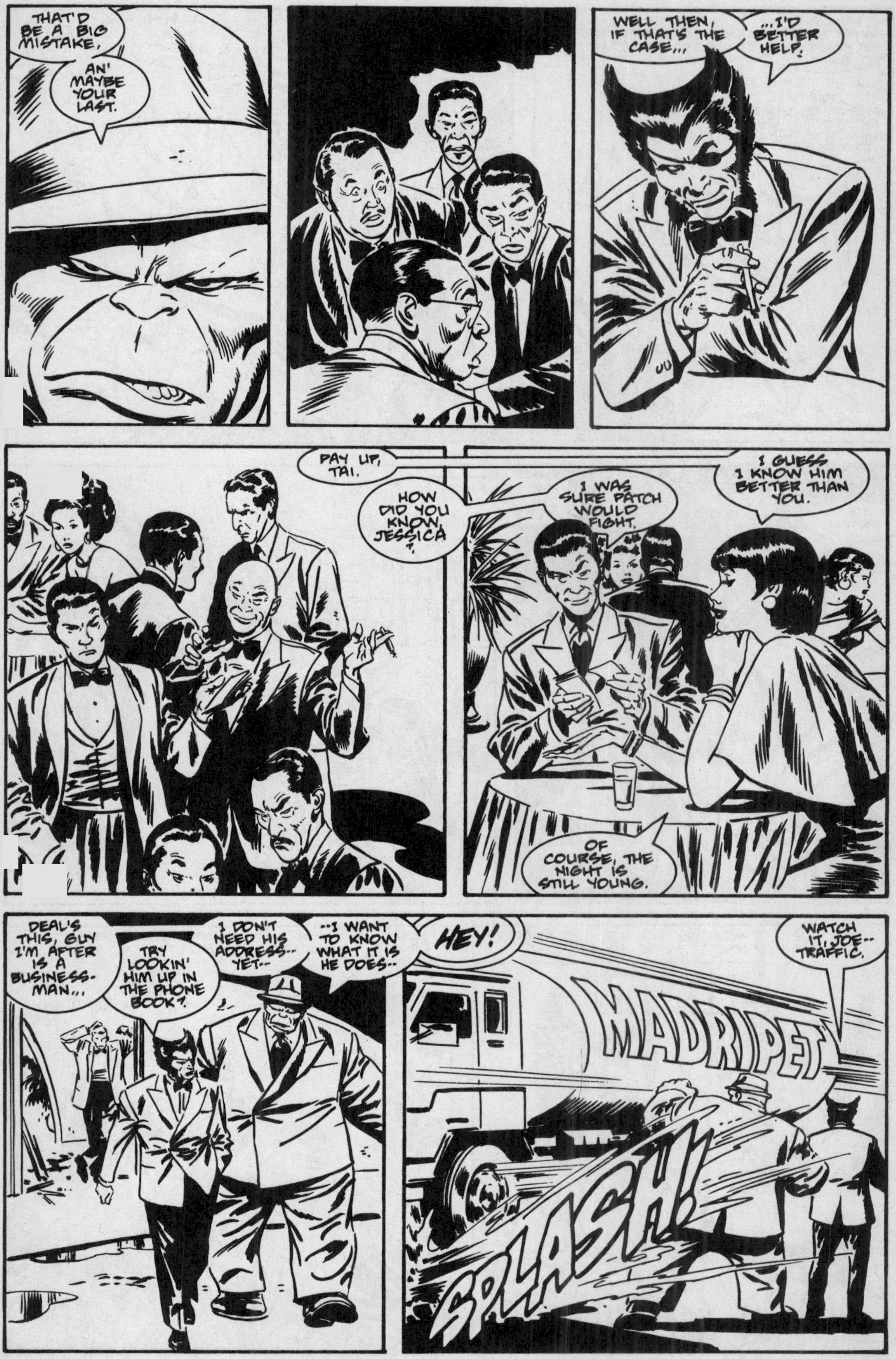
THAT'D BE A BIG MISTAKE,
AN' MAYBE YOUR LAST.
WELL THEN, IF THAT'S THE CASE...
...I'D BETTER HELP.
PAY UP, TAI.
HOW DID YOU KNOW, JESSICA?
I WAS SURE PATCH WOULD FIGHT.
I GUESS I KNOW HIM BETTER THAN YOU.
OF COURSE, THE NIGHT IS STILL YOUNG.
DEAL'S THIS, GUY I'M AFTER IS A BUSINESS-MAN...
TRY LOOKIN' HIM UP IN THE PHONE BOOK?
I DON'T NEED HIS ADDRESS.. YET--
--I WANT TO KNOW WHAT IT IS HE DOES--
HEY!
WATCH IT, JOE-- TRAFFIC.
MADRIPET
SPLASH!

HULK'S BIG AS A HOUSE—ESPECIALLY COMPARED TO ME. SPRAY THAT DRENCHED HIM, LEAVES ME DRY.

SUIT'S RUINED

ARRRGH!

KNOWING HENG, IT PROBABLY COST A BUNDLE.

LIFE IS TOUGH.

FOR HULK... ...IT'S ONLY THE BEGINNING.

HE RESPONDS IN CHARACTER.

LOUSY STINKIN' ROTTEN SCUMMY SLIMEBALL, WHEN I GET MY HANDS ON THAT DRIVER--!

SMASH!!

BAD MOVE.

NOT A WORD, PATCH, HEAR ME?

I SEE EVEN A HINT OF A SMILE... ...OR A LAUGH... ...YOU'RE HISTORY!

INDUSTRIAL SLUDGE. SMELLS WORSE'N IT LOOKS.

BEFORE WE DO ANYTHING ELSE, WE BETTER GET YOU CLEANED OFF.

TRUST ME, YOU'LL FEEL BETTER.

PURPLE PANTS!

AH... YOU COULD FIND FOR ME WAS PURPLE PANTS?

IT AIN'T MY COLOR.

THAT A PROBLEM?

IN CASE YOU HADN'T NOTICED... ...MOST PEOPLE-- ESPECIALLY OUT EAST-- DON'T COME IN YOUR SIZE.

IT'S THE BEST I COULD DO.

A SESSION HERE SHOULD PUT YOU RIGHT.

"MR. MAX'S SPA?" YOU GOTTA BE KIDDING!

RATHOLE'S MORE LIKE IT. WHAT A DUMP!

IF YOU LEARN NOTHIN' ABOUT MADRIPOOR, BUB... ...IT'S THAT NOTHIN' ON THIS ISLAND IS EVER WHAT IT SEEMS.

NOK NOK

YOU!

ME.

GET LOST! AN' TAKE YOUR PET GORILLA WIT'CHU!

YOU WANNA INSULT ME, BUSTER...

...YOU DO IT TO MY FACE!

BRAM

YOU GOT A RIGHTEOUS WAY WITH PEOPLE, JOE.

DON'T HURT ANY TO BE POLITE TO STRANGERS. NICE PLACE. NOW WHAT?

WE WAIT FOR THE RECEPTIONIST.

THEY BUSTED IN THE DOOR.

NAIL 'EM!

WHOMP

WHAT IS THIS?

EVERYWHERE I GO, SOMEBODY WANTS TO GIVE ME GRIEF!

I'M NOT WORRIED.

HULK'S ALWAYS BEEN GOOD AT GIVING BETTER THAN HE GETS.

AND WHILE HE KEEPS THE BULLY-BOYS BUSY...

...I'M FREE TO PROWL.

SCORES OF FRESH SCENTS--ALL FEMALE--LEADING TO A LOCKED DOOR.

KRAK ABB RASS HOW

MAX'S IS OSTENSIBLY A BAWDY HOUSE.

THAT'S LEGAL IN MADRIPOOR.

BUT THAT FALSE FRONT MASKS ITS REAL PURPOSE AS THE CENTRAL CLEARING HOUSE FOR THE LOCAL SLAVE TRADE-- WHICH ISN'T LEGAL.

THE OWNERS, THOUGH, ALWAYS HAD ENOUGH "JUICE"--BASICALLY INFLUENCE AND RAW MUSCLE--TO STOP ANY INVESTIGATION.

THAT IS, UNTIL TONIGHT.

Whuzzat?

INTRUDER INNA CELL BLOCK!

PATCH!
YOU WERE WARNED, SHRIMP!

I COULD USE MY CLAWS, END THIS SCRAP REAL QUICK.

BUT THAT'D BLOW MY COVER, SINCE NO ONE'S SUPPOSED TO KNOW WOLVERINE'S ALIVE.

OR JUST HIT 'EM HARD. MY BONES ARE UNBREAKABLE, Y'SEE, STRONGER IN THEIR OWN WAY THAN FORGED STEEL -- THAT'S WHY SMASHING THE DOOR WAS SO EASY--

--BUT I'VE A BETTER IDEA.

MY PHYSICAL SENSES OPERATE AT THEIR ULTIMATE EFFICIENCY.

HULK'S BREATHING-- AND HIS SCENT--

THUMP!

--GAVE HIS PRESENCE AWAY.

SINCE I KNEW HE WAS THERE, I FIGURED I'D LET HIM DO THE WORK.

WHAT'S THIS-- GALS IN CAGES?!!

I'M REALLY STARTIN' NOT TO LIKE THIS PLACE.

BREAKS OUR HEART, BIG BOY!

PUNCH!

JUST LIKE WE'RE GONNA BREAK YOUR FACE!

OW!

MY HAND!

CRIPES, I THINK I BROKE IT!

I KNOW THE FEELING.

DIFFERENCE IS, MY BODY HAS A HEALING FACTOR-- THE GENETIC QUIRK THAT MAKES ME A MUTANT--

--THAT TAKES CARE OF ANY WOUND.

THESE BRUISERS AREN'T SO LUCKY.

THWUD

WHAT'S THIS ALL ABOUT?

WE'VE BEEN KIDNAPED!

HELP US, PLEASE!

THOSE SWINE MEAN TO SELL US INTO SLAVERY!

NOT ANYMORE.

NOT WHILE I'M AROUND.

HULK DID ALL THE WORK.

SEEMS ONLY FAIR TO LET HIM HAVE A TASTE OF GLORY.

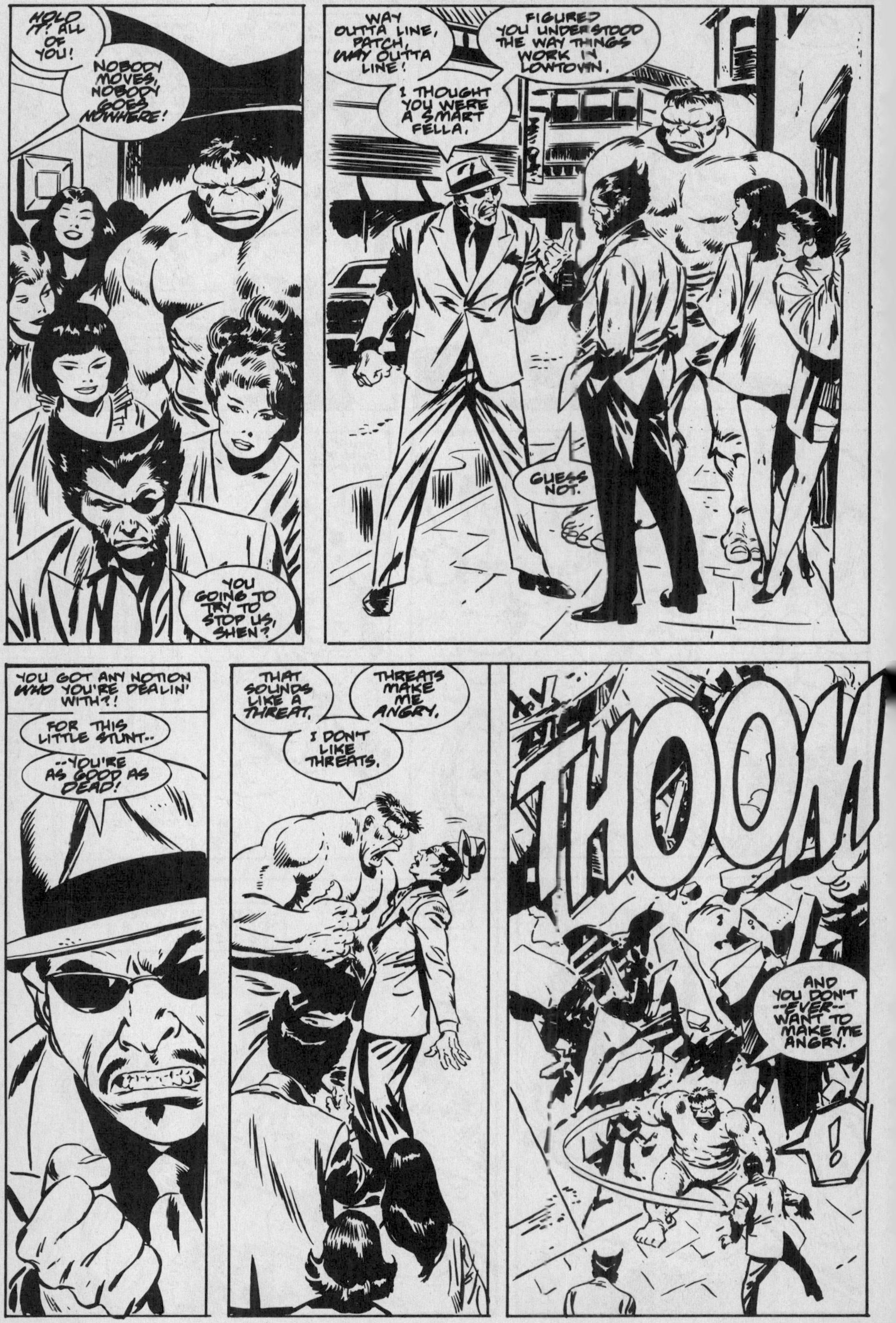
HOLD IT! ALL OF YOU!
NOBODY MOVES, NOBODY GOES NOWHERE!
YOU GOING TO TRY TO STOP US, SHEN?
WAY OUTTA LINE, PATCH, WAY OUTTA LINE!
FIGURED YOU UNDERSTOOD THE WAY THINGS WORK IN LOWTOWN.
I THOUGHT YOU WERE A SMART FELLA.
GUESS NOT.
YOU GOT ANY NOTION WHO YOU'RE DEALIN' WITH?!
FOR THIS LITTLE STUNT..
--YOU'RE AS GOOD AS DEAD!
THAT SOUNDS LIKE A THREAT.
THREATS MAKE ME ANGRY.
I DON'T LIKE THREATS.
THOOM
AND YOU DON'T --EVER-- WANT TO MAKE ME ANGRY.
!

"NOW THIS IS THE LIFE!"

"MAYBE I MISJUDGED THAT LITTLE TWERP, PATCH. HE'S TURNIN' OUT TO BE AN OKAY GUY.

"BEST O' THE BEST-- WINE, WOMEN, YOU NAME IT.

"MY WISH IS THEIR COMMAND.

"AN THEY LOVE IT.

"WAITAMINNIT-- HOW COME MY ARM GOT SO SMALL??

"COLOR'S WRONG, TOO.

I'M GRAY, NOT WHITE!

"THAT REFLECTION--

"--THAT FACE--

BANNER!

"...OR SOMETHIN' THAT REALLY HAPPENED?!

I HATE THIS, NOT KNOWIN' WHAT HAPPENS WHEN I'M HIM!

WAS IT BANNER HAVIN' ALL THAT FUN, ?!

PJ'S ALL TORN--'CAUSE THEY'RE WAY TOO SMALL FOR ME!

MEM'RIES GOIN' HAZY-- WAS THAT A DREAM NIGHTMARE'S MORE LIKE IT...

TUAN, THE SUN HAS SET.

WE HAVE BROUGHT FRESH CLOTHES, AS YOU REQUESTED...

...AND A MODEST REPAST--

--OH!!?

WHO ARE YOU!

WHERE IS ROBERT!!

WHAT HAVE YOU DONE WITH HIM?!?

FORGET HIM.

HE'S GONE.

GOT SOMEONE BETTER TO PLAY WITH.

ALARME!

AU SECOURS, MES AMIS!

PATCH, COME AT ONCE-- PATCH!

HEY, GALS! WAIT--

--WHUNGFF!

THUMPT!

SLEEP WELL?

GRRRR

WHY SO CRANKY?

I TOLD JASMINE TO TAKE CARE OF YOU.

WAY I HEAR, HER LADIES DID A SUPERLATIVE AND MUCH-APPRECIATED JOB...

...ALL DAY LONG.

DAY?

I KNOW WHAT HE'S THINKING. DURING DAYLIGHT HE'S HIS ALTER-EGO, BRUCE BANNER. HULK ONLY COMES OUT AT NIGHT.

SO HE'S WONDERING IF BANNER GOT THE GOOD TIMES, WHICH IS SURE TO MAKE HIM CRAZY.

HE WANTS EQUAL TIME.

NOT A HOPE.

IT'S YOUR TAB, BUB, YOU CAN DO AS YOU PLEASE.

DOESN'T LIKE THAT, THE THOUGHT OF PAYIN' FOR BANNER'S PARTY.

BUT YOU'RE SUPPOSED TO BE ON A JOB, RIGHT?

YOU MY CONSCIENCE, OR WHAT?

IT'S YOUR CHOICE.

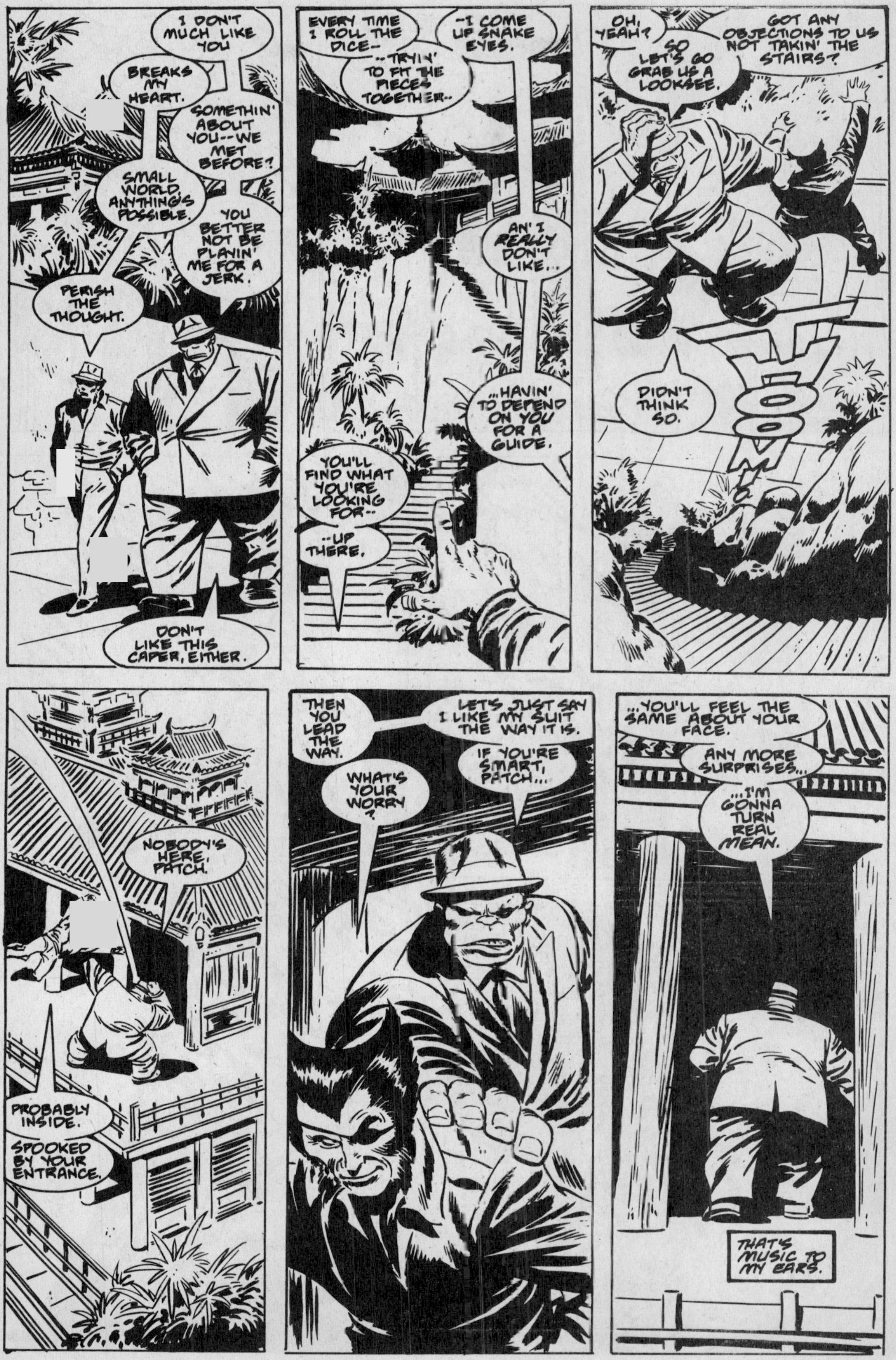
I DON'T MUCH LIKE YOU
BREAKS MY HEART.
SOMETHIN' ABOUT YOU--WE MET BEFORE?
SMALL WORLD. ANYTHING'S POSSIBLE.
YOU BETTER NOT BE PLAYIN' ME FOR A JERK.
PERISH THE THOUGHT.
DON'T LIKE THIS CAPER, EITHER.
EVERY TIME I ROLL THE DICE--
--I COME UP SNAKE EYES.
--TRYIN' TO FIT THE PIECES TOGETHER..
AN' I REALLY DON'T LIKE...
...HAVIN' TO DEPEND ON YOU FOR A GUIDE.
YOU'LL FIND WHAT YOU'RE LOOKING FOR--
--UP THERE.
OH, YEAH?
SO LET'S GO GRAB US A LOOKSEE.
GOT ANY OBJECTIONS TO US NOT TAKIN' THE STAIRS?
DIDN'T THINK SO.
THOOM
NOBODY'S HERE, PATCH.
PROBABLY INSIDE.
SPOOKED BY YOUR ENTRANCE.
THEN YOU LEAD THE WAY.
LET'S JUST SAY I LIKE MY SUIT THE WAY IT IS.
WHAT'S YOUR WORRY?
IF YOU'RE SMART, PATCH...
...YOU'LL FEEL THE SAME ABOUT YOUR FACE.
ANY MORE SURPRISES...
...I'M GONNA TURN REAL MEAN.
THAT'S MUSIC TO MY EARS.

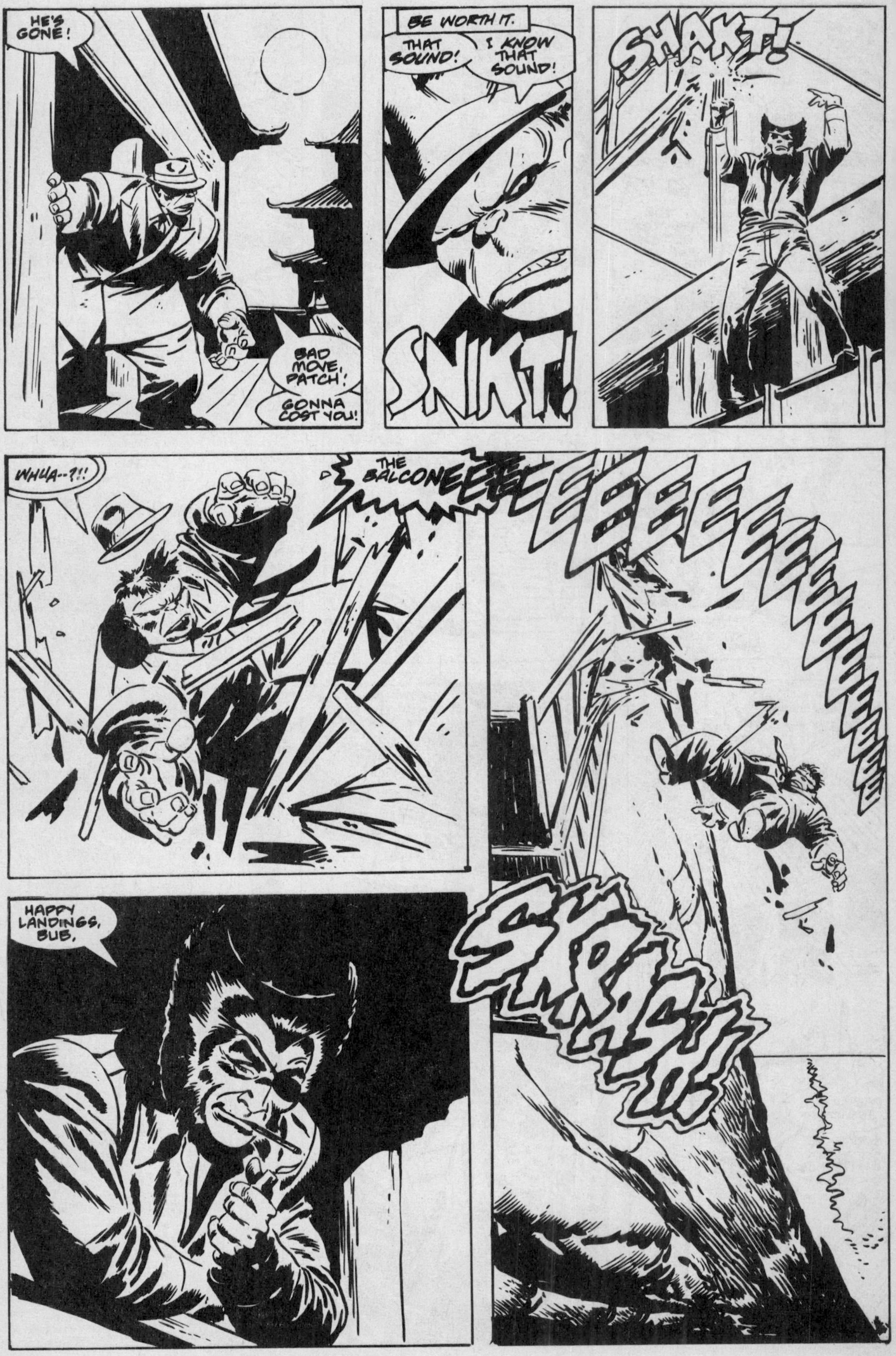
HE'S GONE!
BAD MOVE, PATCH!
GONNA COST YOU!
BE WORTH IT.
THAT SOUND!
I KNOW THAT SOUND!
SNIKT!
SHAKT!
WHUA--?!!
THE BALCONEEEEEEEEEEEEEEEE
HAPPY LANDINGS, BUB.
SPLASH!!

AS YOU CAN PLAINLY SEE, MR. LIU, OURS IS A STATE-OF-THE-ART COCAINE REFINING AND PROCESSING FACILITY...

...THE LARGEST AND MOST MODERN IN THE WORLD.

AND THE PRINCE TOLERATES YOUR OPERATION?

CONSIDERING THE MONEY WE PAY IN BRIBES, HE'D BETTER!

AND EVEN IF HIS CHIEF OF POLICE WANTED TO CLOSE US DOWN...

...I HAVE ENOUGH MAN-AND FIRE-POWER...

...TO TURN ANY SUCH RAID INTO A SMALL WAR.

A WAR I'LL WIN.

THESE MANBOT ANDROIDS ARE EACH THE EQUIVALENT OF A COMPANY OF SOLDIERS.

THEY CAN DEAL WITH ANY THREAT...

...EVEN THAT HULKING, OVERPRESSED MAN-O'-MUSCLE FOREIGNER...

I'M GONNA KILL HIM I'M GONNA KILL HIM I'M GONNA

...WHO'S BEEN MAKING SO MUCH TROUBLE --!

B BOOM

I FIGURE, ANYBODY WHO'S JUST BELLY-FLOPPED A THOUSAND FEET ONTO STEEL AND CONCRETE...

...HE ISN'T LIKELY TO BE IN THE BEST O' MOODS.

LIKEWISE, GUYS WATCHIN' A MEGABUCK DRUG OPERATION-- AN' MAYBE THEIR LIVES--

IH--IT'S THE STRANGER!

--GO UP THE SPOUT.

SPARK AN' TINDER, A CONFLAGRATION JUST ACHIN' TO HAPPEN.

KOBE STARTS IT OFF.

GUN HIM!!

TO PARAPHRASE AN' OLD ARMY BUDDY:

..."I DO SO LOVE IT WHEN A PLAN COMES TOGETHER."

NOBODY MAKES BOOK ON THIS SCRAP.

THEY'RE TOO BUSY RUNNIN'.

POW WHAM BAM BASH SMASH HIT BNOP RDAM

GO-BE-R!

OR FLYIN'.

AS WARS GO...

...THIS ONE TURNS OUT AS SHORT...

...AS IT IS OH-SO-VERY SWEET.

WE'RE DEAD MEN.

WE CAN EXPLAIN!

THIS ISN'T OUR FAULT!

IDIOT! LAST MONTH, THE GENERAL'S CROP OF RAW OPIUM WAS DESTROYED.

NOW, HE'S LOSING HIS ENTIRE STOREHOUSE OF REFINED PRODUCT.

YOU THINK HE'LL LISTEN!

TALK WON'T SATISFY HIM, KOBE.

ONLY BLOOD!

I KNOW THAT FEELING.

NO, PLEASE-- MERCY!

I BEG YOU-- I HAVE A WIFE, A FAMILY-- MY AGED MOTHER--

SHADDAP!

SORRY ABOUT THE SUIT.

DARN STRAIGHT.

YOU **SUCKERED** ME, SHRIMP!

AND I'M GONNA TAKE IT OUTTA YOUR HIDE!

SMALL PRICE, JOE, FOR THE "FIXIT" JOB YOU JUST DID.

WHUZZAT MEAN??

YOU JUST **WRECKED** THE BIGGEST **DRUG FACTORY** IN THIS PART O' THE WORLD.

NOT TO MENTION THAT **SLAVER RING.**

NOT A BAD **TWO DAYS** WORK.

YOU SET ME UP!

I WASN'T THE FIRST ONE, CHUMP, YOU'VE BEEN CONNED FROM THE START.

DON'T BELIEVE ME, JUST ASK...

...YOUR LOCAL CLIENT-- JOE FIXIT, MEET **GENERAL NGUYEN NGOC COY,** AND BODYGUARDS.

MADMAN! WHAT HAVE YOU **DONE** ?!

THE **DON** SENT YOU TO **HELP** ME, NOT **CRIPPLE** MY OPERA-TION!

SAY **WHAT** ??

I HAVE A **RIVAL CRIME-LORD,** WHO YOU WERE SUPPOSED TO ELIMIN-ATE.

INSTEAD, CRETIN, YOU'VE DONE HER **WORK** FOR HER!

THANKS FOR TELLING ME.

MAKES ME FEEL A WHOLE LOT **BETTER** ABOUT WHAT'S HAPPENED.

I'M NO **HITTER.**

AND ESPECIALLY NOT A WISEGUY. I DON'T DO MOB JOBS.

MY BOSS, **BERENGETTI,** IS A STRAIGHT-ARROW.

FROM WHAT YOU'RE TELLIN' ME, THE **DON** LIED-- TO ME AN BERENGETTI **BOTH** !

I DON'T LIKE THAT, OR THIS **CAPER,** OR **YOU.**

AS OF NOW, I'M DEALING MYSELF **OUT,** AN' I REALLY HOPE YOU TRY TO STOP ME.

NO TAKERS? TOO BAD.

YOU'RE **SMARTER'N** YOU **LOOK.**

THE DON I'LL DEAL WITH WHEN I GET BACK STATESIDE--

--BUT YOU, PATCH!

WHAT ABOUT ME?

YOU COULDA TRUSTED ME!

BE REAL. WE HEARD YOU HAD SCRUPLES. BEST TO BE SURE.

ALSO-- THIS IS MY TURF, FIXIT.

PLAY IN YOUR OWN BACK YARD. LEAVE ME AN' MINE BE.

AN IF I DON'T?

WHAT'S TO STOP ME DUMPIN' YOU, THIS COY BOY, ALL'A YOU-- AN' TAKIN' OVER?

YOURSELF, JOE, AND NATURE.

HALF THE DAY IS SUNLIGHT, BRIGHT EYES.

AND IN EVERY WAY, MR. FIXIT IS INVULNERABLE...

ROBERT BRUCE BANNER ISN'T.

THINK ABOUT THAT.

HE DOES, LONG AND HARD.

AN' THEN HE GIVES HIS ANSWER.

K-R-C-V!!

OKAY, I'M GOIN'.

BUT THAT WAS FOR TREATIN ME LIKE SOME JERK.

WHATEVER YOU FIGURE, SHORT-STUFF, I'M NO BUFFOON.

YOU TREAT ME WITH RESPECT!

I GET THE MESSAGE.

BOTH OF 'EM.

HE DIDN'T PULL THAT PUNCH LIKE MAYBE HE KNEW MY BONES COULDN'T BE BROKEN.

AND THE WAY HE SMILES AS HE DUSTS HIMSELF OFF MAKES ME WONDER...

...IF PERHAPS THE HULK HAS GROWN A LOT SMARTER THAN I EVER GAVE HIM CREDIT FOR.

THIS IS A WEST-BOUND FLIGHT, RIGHT?

NIGHT-TIME ALL THE WAY, RIGHT?

AS PER INSTRUCTIONS.

RELAX, JOE, EVERYTHING'S BEEN TAKEN CARE OF.

YOU'RE A GOOD SPORT, PATCH, YOU TOOK THAT HIT LIKE A MAN.

GATE 3

GATE 4

AND I ALWAYS GIVE BETTER THAN I GET.

YOU TOOK A FEW YOURSELF, JOE.

NEVER THOUGHT I'D SAY THIS, BUT IT'S BEEN A TREAT.

HOPE THE DON FEELS THE SAME...

...AFTER I TELL HIM HOW I FEEL

...ABOUT BEIN' CONNED.

ALMOST WISH I COULD BE THERE TO SEE IT.

HAVE A GOOD FLIGHT.

FIRST CLASS ALL THE WAY!

CABIN CREW'S BEEN TOLD TO TAKE SPECIAL CARE OF YOU.

FANTASTIC!

TIME TO PARTY, LADIES!

EXCUSE ME, SIR, IS THIS WHERE WE CHECK IN...

...FOR THE WEST-BOUND FLIGHT TO LONDON?

ME, DEAR ME, SOMEONE MUST HAVE SWITCHED THE SIGNS.

THIS IS THE EAST-BOUND TO LOS ANGELES.

WEATHER'S CLEAR AS CAN BE, THE WHOLE ROUTE.

RIGHT ABOUT NOW...

...THE PLANE OUGHT TO BE CLIMBING...

...INTO THE MOST BEAUTIFUL SUNRISE.

PATCH!?!

ARRRGHH!

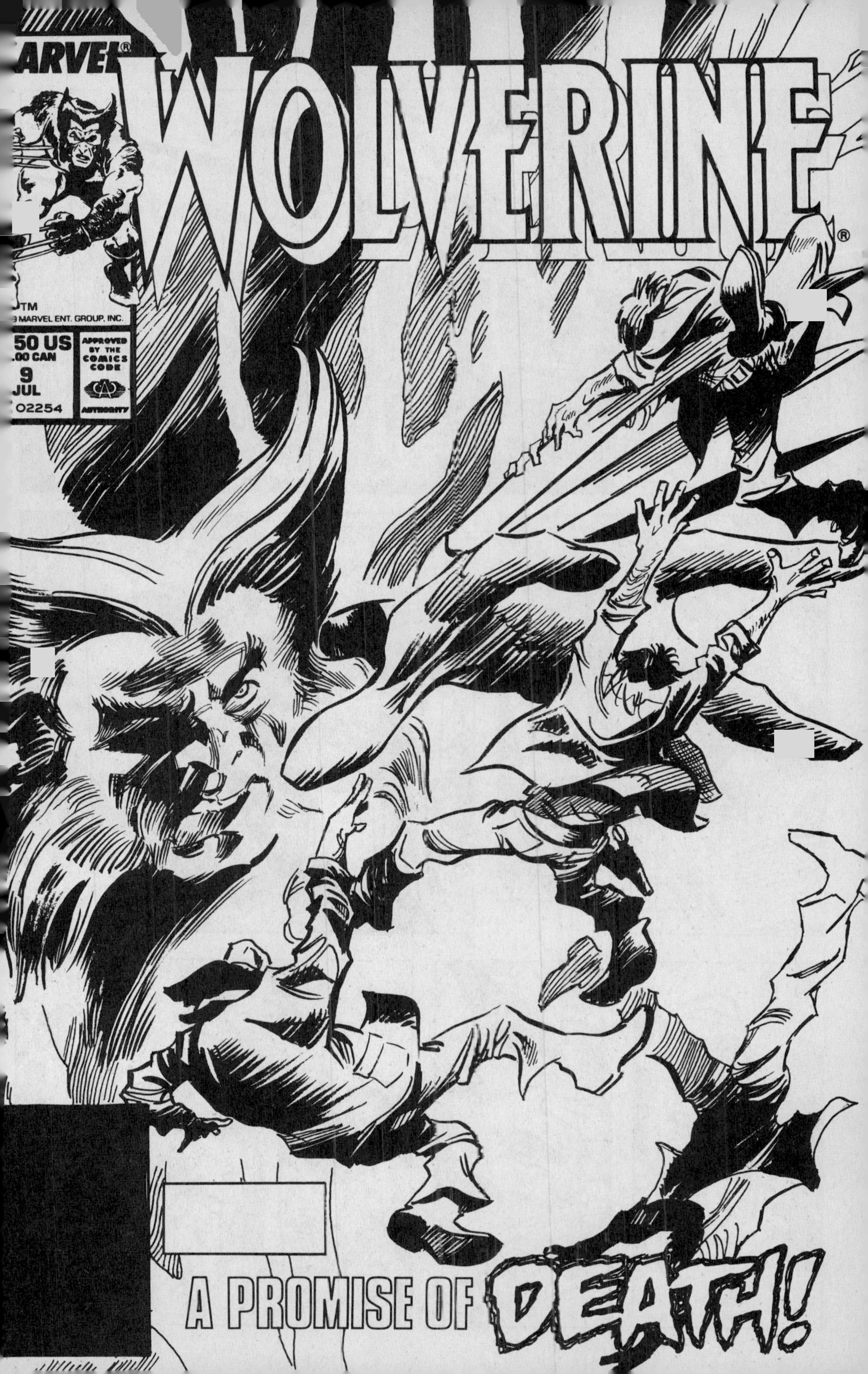
ARVEL
WOLVERINE
TM
MARVEL ENT. GROUP, INC.
50 US
.00 CAN
9
JUL
02254
APPROVED BY THE COMICS CODE AUTHORITY
A PROMISE OF DEATH!

EXCUSE ME.

WE'D LIKE A CABIN.

JUS' HOLD YER WATER. I'LL BE WITH YA INNA MINNIT, SOON'S I FINISH LOOKIN' AT THIS... *INTERVIEW.*

I SAID...

SNIKT

PLAFF

...WE'D LIKE A CABIN. NOW.

BEFORE MY FRIEND *ROLLINS* HERE GETS TESTY.

OH, I'M AS TESTY AS *SPIT,* MALONE.

SURE. FINE.

YOU CAN HAVE THE SCENIC *"NORMAN BATES"* CABIN.

YOU'RE A PANIC.

RIIIP

WHAT WAS *THAT?!*

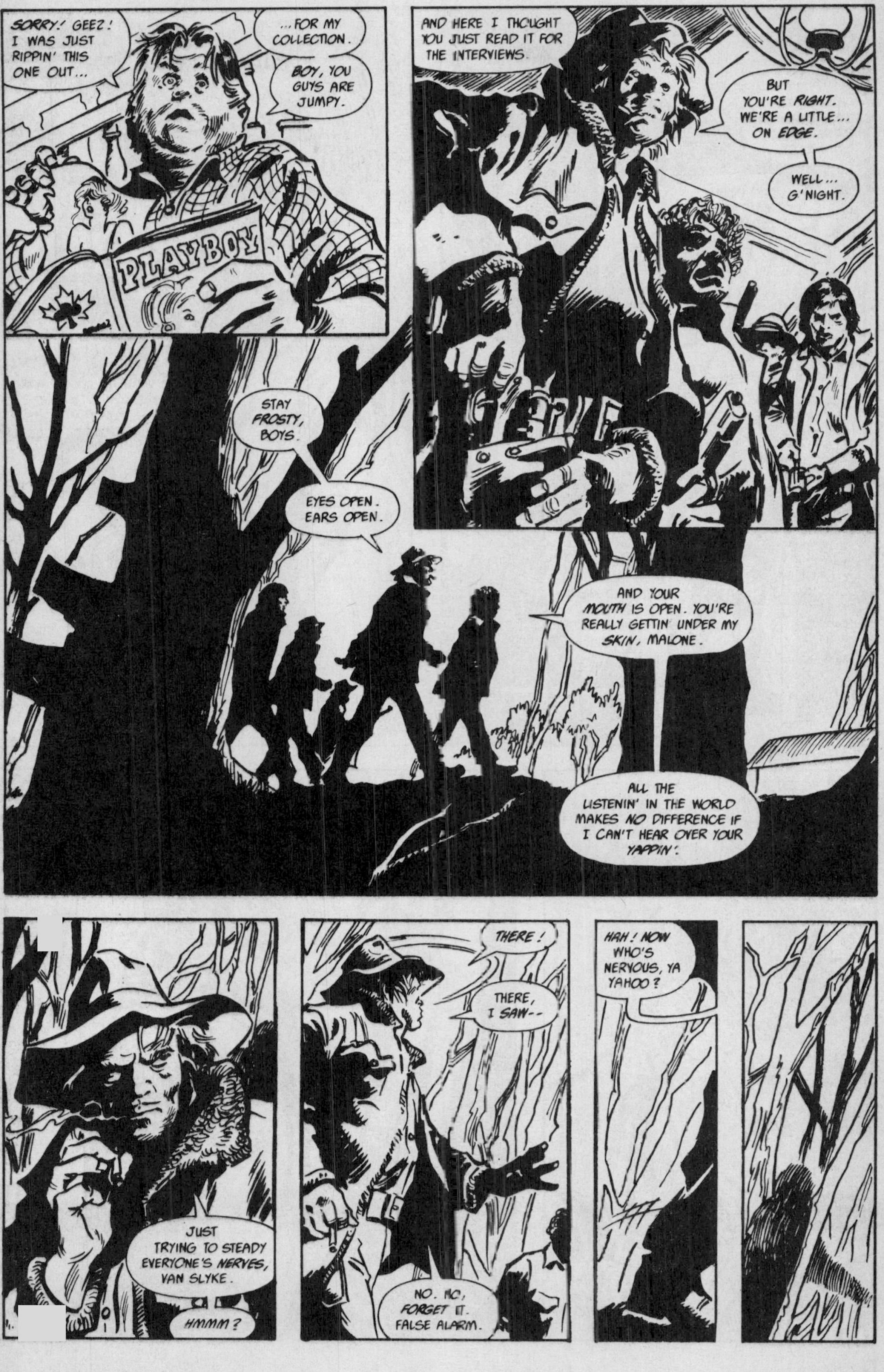
SORRY! GEEZ! I WAS JUST RIPPIN' THIS ONE OUT...
...FOR MY COLLECTION.
BOY, YOU GUYS ARE JUMPY.
PLAYBOY
AND HERE I THOUGHT YOU JUST READ IT FOR THE INTERVIEWS.
BUT YOU'RE RIGHT. WE'RE A LITTLE... ON EDGE.
WELL... G'NIGHT.
STAY FROSTY, BOYS.
EYES OPEN. EARS OPEN.
AND YOUR MOUTH IS OPEN. YOU'RE REALLY GETTIN' UNDER MY SKIN, MALONE.
ALL THE LISTENIN' IN THE WORLD MAKES NO DIFFERENCE IF I CAN'T HEAR OVER YOUR YAPPIN'.
JUST TRYING TO STEADY EVERYONE'S NERVES, VAN SLYKE.
HMMM?
THERE!
THERE, I SAW--
NO. NO, FORGET IT. FALSE ALARM.
HAH! NOW WHO'S NERVOUS, YA YAHOO?

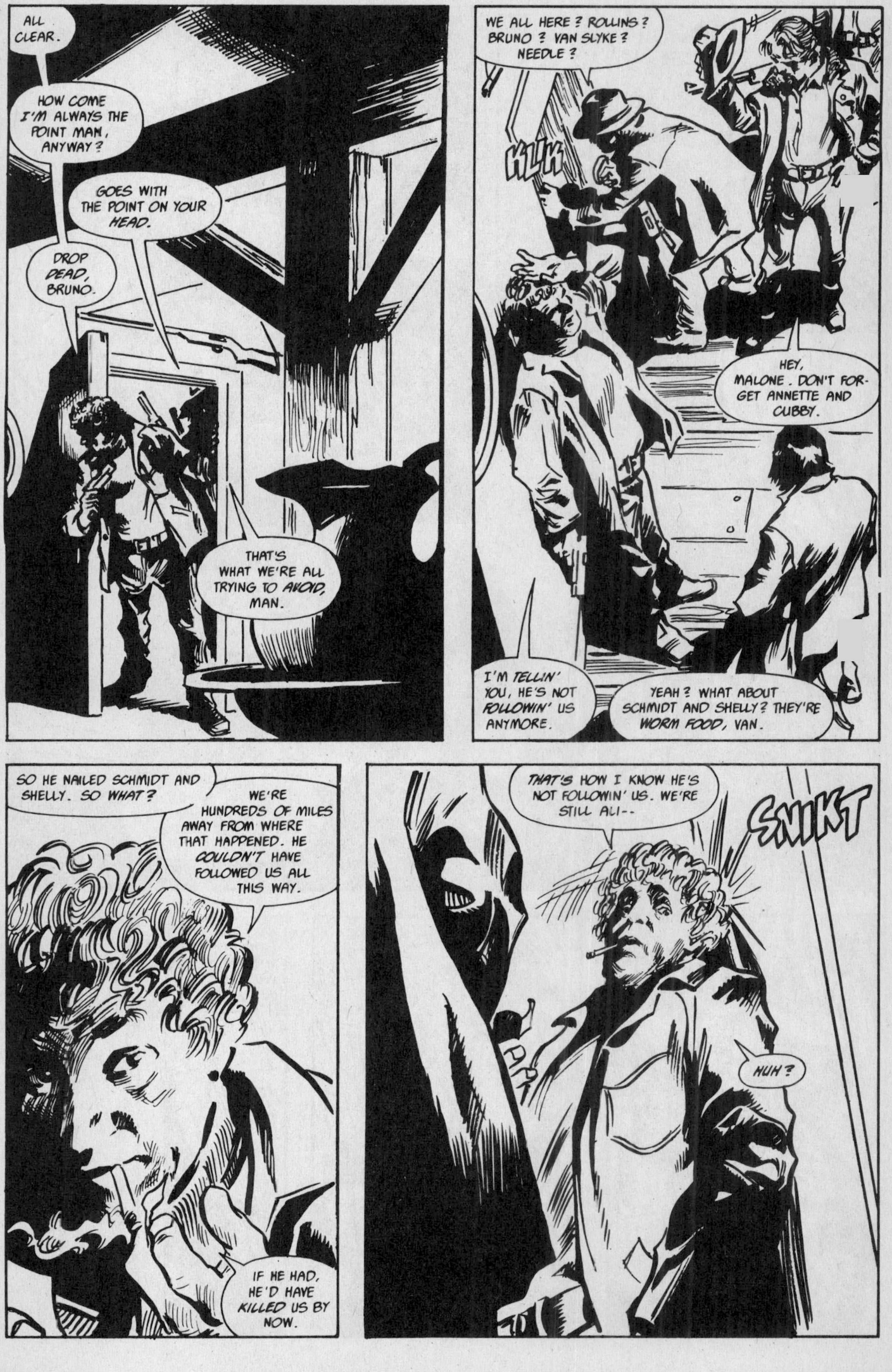
ALL CLEAR.
HOW COME I'M ALWAYS THE POINT MAN, ANYWAY?
GOES WITH THE POINT ON YOUR HEAD.
DROP DEAD, BRUNO.
THAT'S WHAT WE'RE ALL TRYING TO AVOID, MAN.
WE ALL HERE? ROLLINS? BRUNO? VAN SLYKE? NEEDLE?
KLIK
HEY, MALONE. DON'T FORGET ANNETTE AND CUBBY.
I'M TELLIN' YOU, HE'S NOT FOLLOWIN' US ANYMORE.
YEAH? WHAT ABOUT SCHMIDT AND SHELLY? THEY'RE WORM FOOD, VAN.
SO HE NAILED SCHMIDT AND SHELLY. SO WHAT?
WE'RE HUNDREDS OF MILES AWAY FROM WHERE THAT HAPPENED. HE COULDN'T HAVE FOLLOWED US ALL THIS WAY.
IF HE HAD, HE'D HAVE KILLED US BY NOW.
THAT'S HOW I KNOW HE'S NOT FOLLOWIN' US. WE'RE STILL ALI--
SNIKT
HUH?

STAN LEE PRESENTS:
PROMISES TO KEEP
WRITTEN BY PETER DAVID
ART BY GENE COLAN
LETTERS BY BILL OAKLEY • COLORS BY MARK CHIARELLO
EDITED BY BOB HARRAS
EDITOR IN CHIEF: TOM DEFALCO
KRRAASH

HOLY--

VAN SLYKE!!

NOOOOO

THOUGHT I CAME FOR YOU, MALONE?

NOT YET. NOT YET.

HIS VOICE CAME FROM OVER THERE!

BAM BAM BAM BAM

WE GOT HIM!

SOK

IDIOT! WE DIDN'T GET HIM THE LAST TIME!

OR THE TIME BEFORE THAT!

WE MUST'VE GOTTEN HIM!

BUT SINCE YOU'RE SO SURE, ROLLINS, YOU TAKE FIRST WATCH.

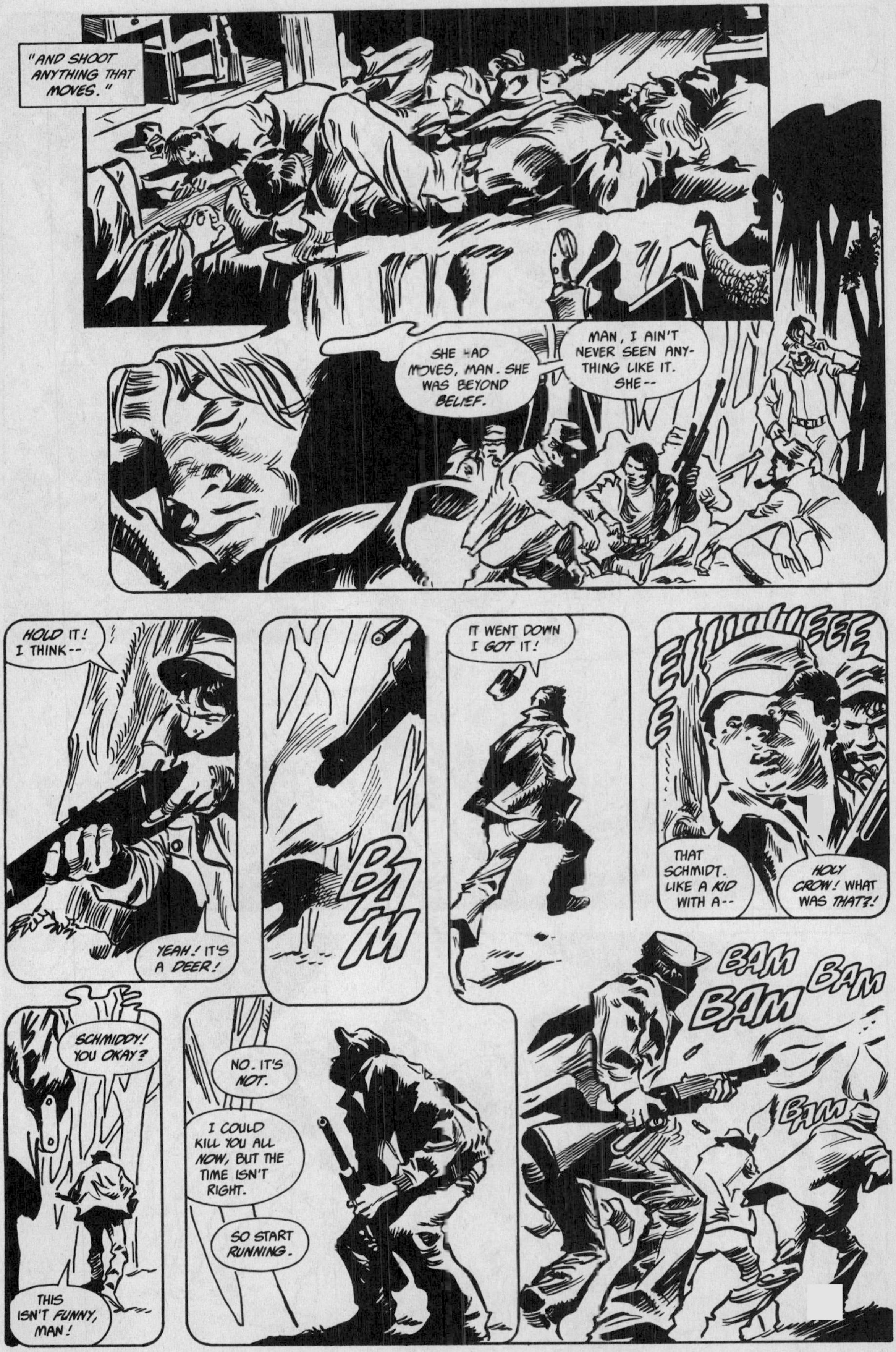
"AND SHOOT ANYTHING THAT MOVES."
SHE HAD MOVES, MAN. SHE WAS BEYOND BELIEF.
MAN, I AIN'T NEVER SEEN ANYTHING LIKE IT. SHE--
HOLD IT! I THINK--
YEAH! IT'S A DEER!
BAM
IT WENT DOWN I GOT IT!
EEEEEEEE
THAT SCHMIDT. LIKE A KID WITH A--
HOLY CROW! WHAT WAS THAT?!
SCHMIDDY! YOU OKAY?
THIS ISN'T FUNNY, MAN!
NO. IT'S NOT.
I COULD KILL YOU ALL NOW, BUT THE TIME ISN'T RIGHT.
SO START RUNNING.
BAM BAM BAM
BAM

NICE TRY.

WHAT HAVE YOU DONE WITH SCHMIDT?

HERE HE IS.

YOU'RE THE NEXT BODY.

KLUMP

OF COURSE, YOU DON'T DARE GO TO THE AUTHORITIES. AFTER ALL...

...THEY'D LOVE TO GET THEIR HANDS ON YOU GUYS.

NO, YOU'RE ON YOUR OWN. JUST YOU--

--AND ME.

AAAAAAA

MALONE! WHAT *IS* IT?!

I WAS... I WAS DREAMING ABOUT WHEN THIS WHOLE THING *STARTED*. SORRY.

ROLLINS. YOU'RE SUPPOSED TO BE ON *WATCH*. WHY ARE YOU *LYING* THERE?

OH, CRIPES, HE'S DEAD. I *KNOW* IT.

OH, NOW WE'RE A *GHOST*. VERY FUNNY, ROLLINS.

SNIKT

REMEMBER IRAQ?

KLEEECH

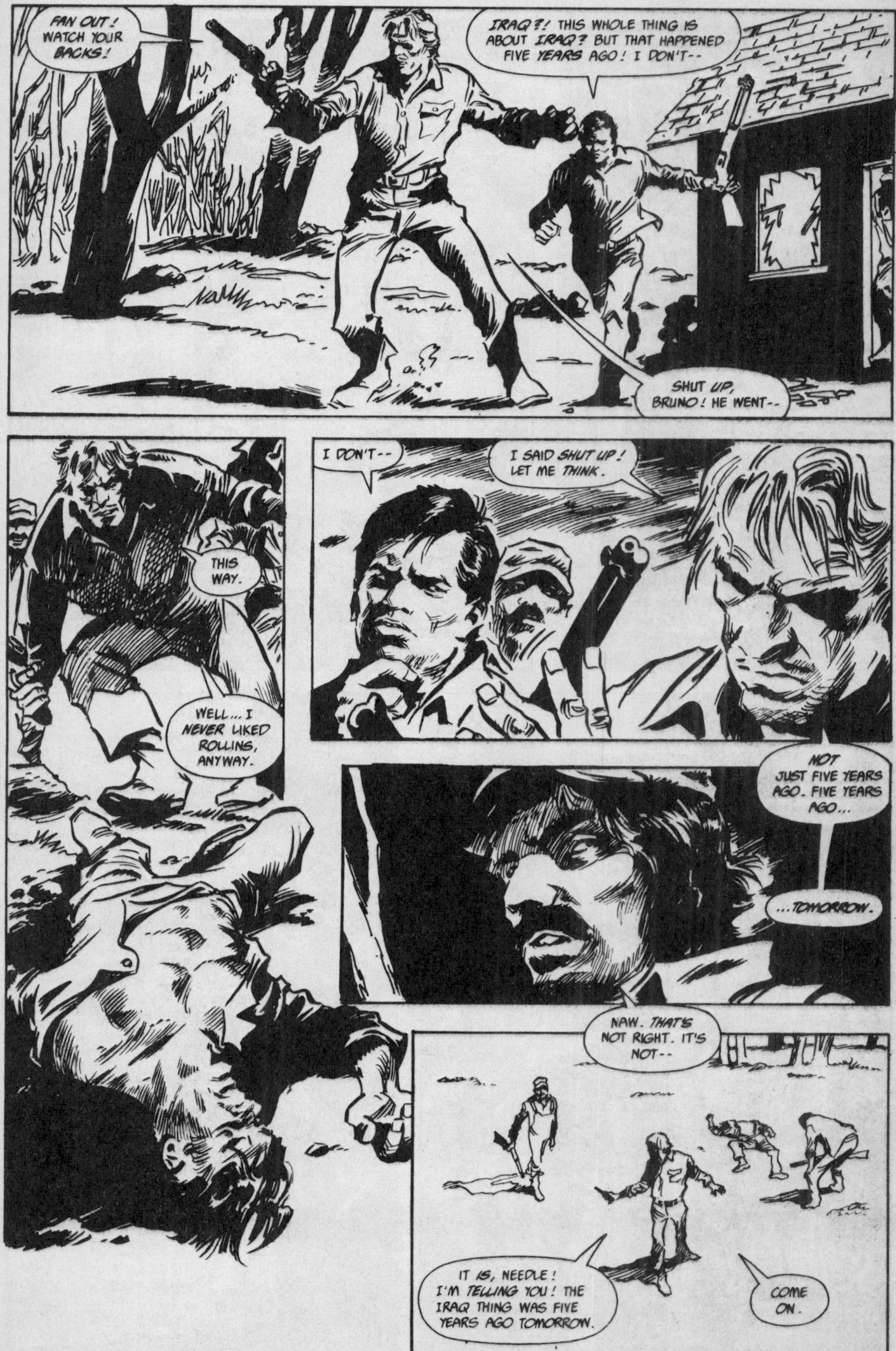
FAN OUT! WATCH YOUR BACKS!
IRAQ?! THIS WHOLE THING IS ABOUT IRAQ? BUT THAT HAPPENED FIVE YEARS AGO! I DON'T--
SHUT UP, BRUNO! HE WENT--
THIS WAY.
WELL... I NEVER LIKED ROLLINS, ANYWAY.
I DON'T--
I SAID SHUT UP! LET ME THINK.
NOT JUST FIVE YEARS AGO. FIVE YEARS AGO...
...TOMORROW.
NAW. THAT'S NOT RIGHT. IT'S NOT--
IT IS, NEEDLE! I'M TELLING YOU! THE IRAQ THING WAS FIVE YEARS AGO TOMORROW.
COME ON.

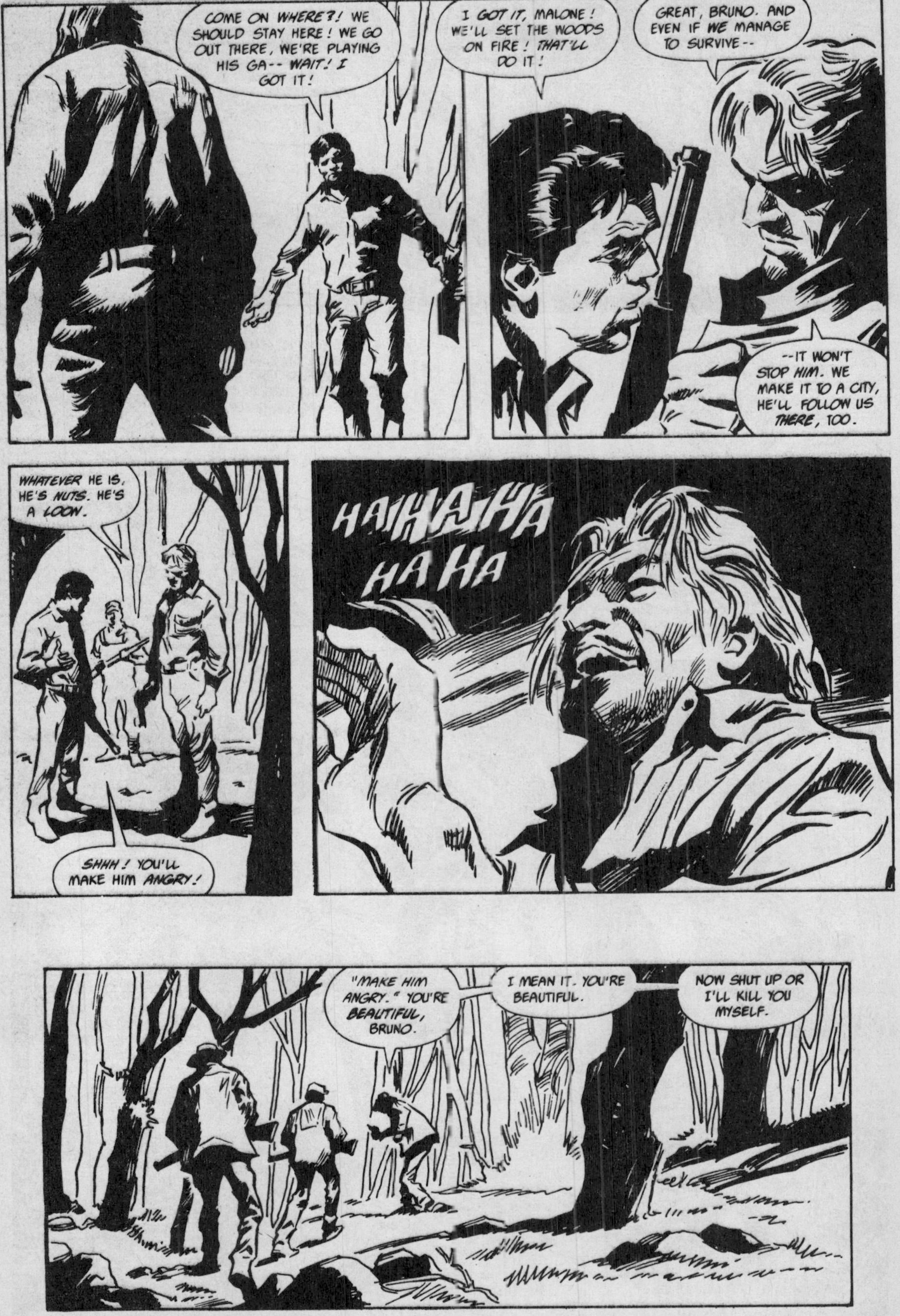
COME ON WHERE?! WE SHOULD STAY HERE! WE GO OUT THERE, WE'RE PLAYING HIS GA-- WAIT! I GOT IT!
I GOT IT, MALONE! WE'LL SET THE WOODS ON FIRE! THAT'LL DO IT!
GREAT, BRUNO. AND EVEN IF WE MANAGE TO SURVIVE--
--IT WON'T STOP HIM. WE MAKE IT TO A CITY, HE'LL FOLLOW US THERE, TOO.
WHATEVER HE IS, HE'S NUTS. HE'S A LOON.
SHHH! YOU'LL MAKE HIM ANGRY!
HAHAHAHA
HAHA
"MAKE HIM ANGRY." YOU'RE BEAUTIFUL, BRUNO.
I MEAN IT. YOU'RE BEAUTIFUL.
NOW SHUT UP OR I'LL KILL YOU MYSELF.

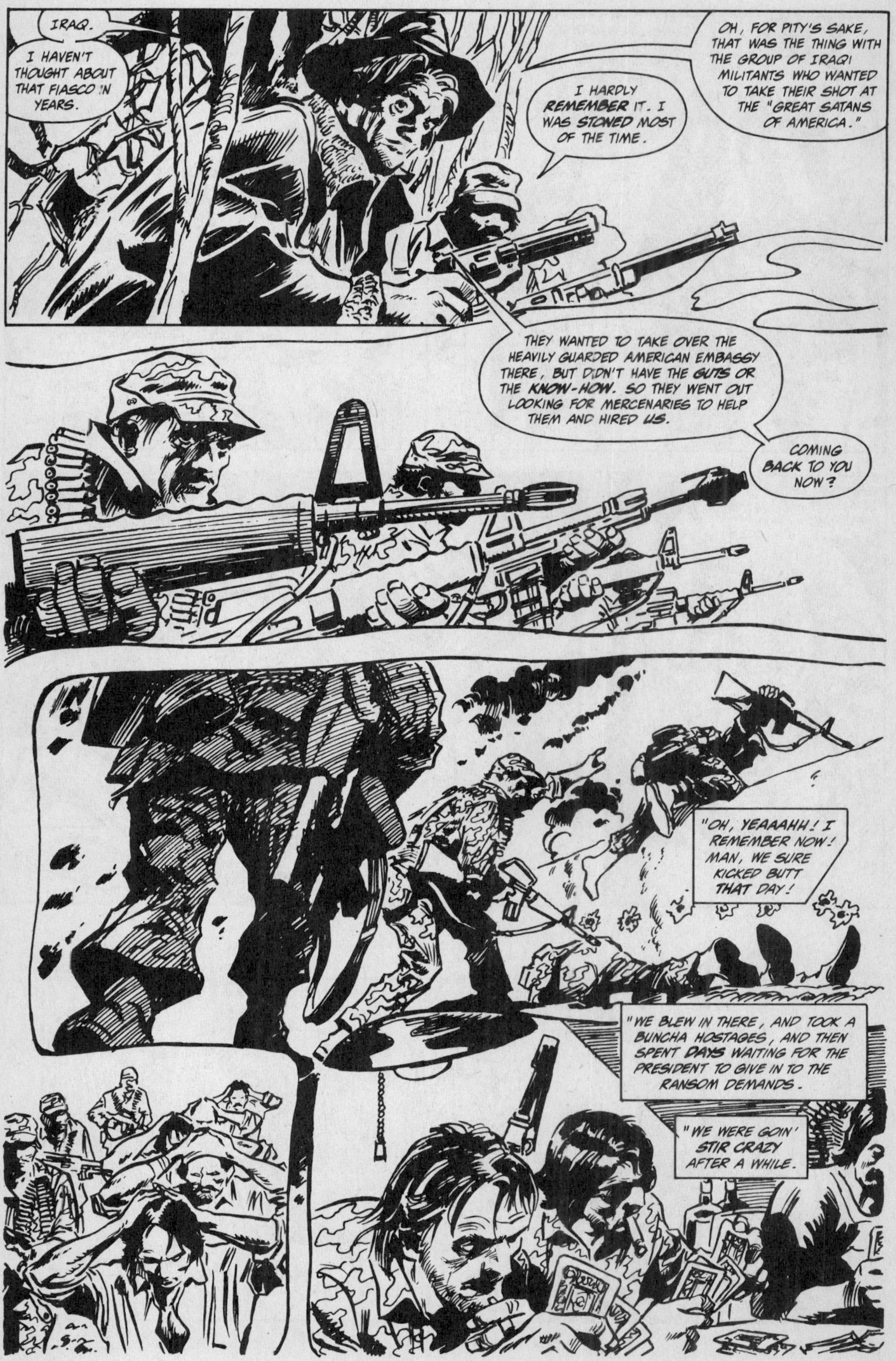
IRAQ.
I HAVEN'T THOUGHT ABOUT THAT FIASCO IN YEARS.
I HARDLY REMEMBER IT. I WAS STONED MOST OF THE TIME.
OH, FOR PITY'S SAKE, THAT WAS THE THING WITH THE GROUP OF IRAQI MILITANTS WHO WANTED TO TAKE THEIR SHOT AT THE "GREAT SATANS OF AMERICA."
THEY WANTED TO TAKE OVER THE HEAVILY GUARDED AMERICAN EMBASSY THERE, BUT DIDN'T HAVE THE GUTS OR THE KNOW-HOW. SO THEY WENT OUT LOOKING FOR MERCENARIES TO HELP THEM AND HIRED US.
COMING BACK TO YOU NOW?
"OH, YEAAAHH! I REMEMBER NOW! MAN, WE SURE KICKED BUTT THAT DAY!
"WE BLEW IN THERE, AND TOOK A BUNCHA HOSTAGES, AND THEN SPENT DAYS WAITING FOR THE PRESIDENT TO GIVE IN TO THE RANSOM DEMANDS.
"WE WERE GOIN' STIR CRAZY AFTER A WHILE.

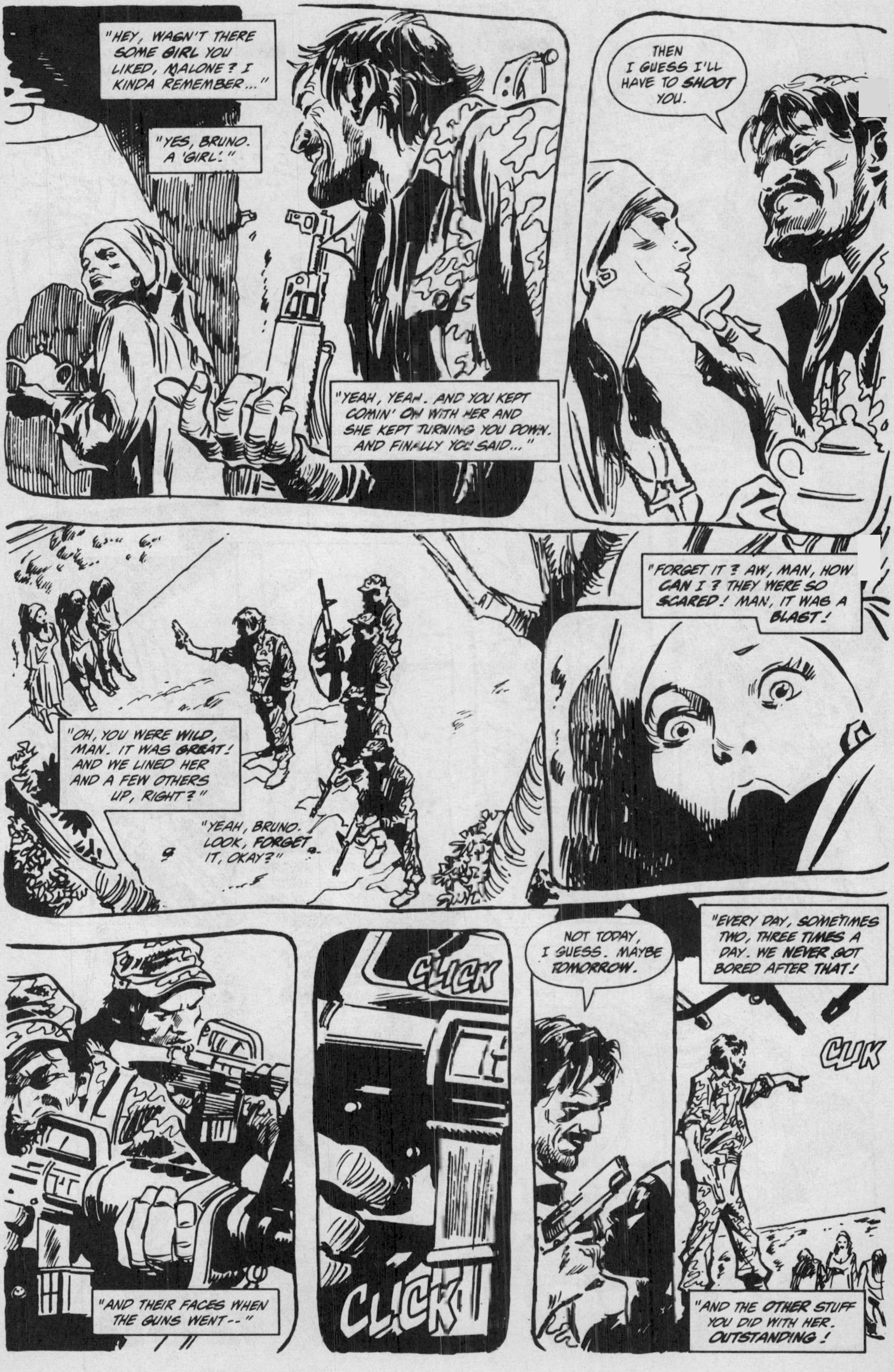

"HEY, WASN'T THERE SOME GIRL YOU LIKED, MALONE? I KINDA REMEMBER..."
"YES, BRUNO. A 'GIRL.'"
"YEAH, YEAH. AND YOU KEPT COMIN' ON WITH HER AND SHE KEPT TURNING YOU DOWN. AND FINALLY YOU SAID..."
THEN I GUESS I'LL HAVE TO SHOOT YOU.
"OH, YOU WERE WILD, MAN. IT WAS GREAT! AND WE LINED HER AND A FEW OTHERS UP, RIGHT?"
"YEAH, BRUNO. LOOK, FORGET IT, OKAY?"
"FORGET IT? AW, MAN, HOW CAN I? THEY WERE SO SCARED! MAN, IT WAS A BLAST!"
"AND THEIR FACES WHEN THE GUNS WENT--"
CLICK
CLICK
NOT TODAY, I GUESS. MAYBE TOMORROW.
"EVERY DAY, SOMETIMES TWO, THREE TIMES A DAY. WE NEVER GOT BORED AFTER THAT!"
CLIK
"AND THE OTHER STUFF YOU DID WITH HER. OUTSTANDING!"

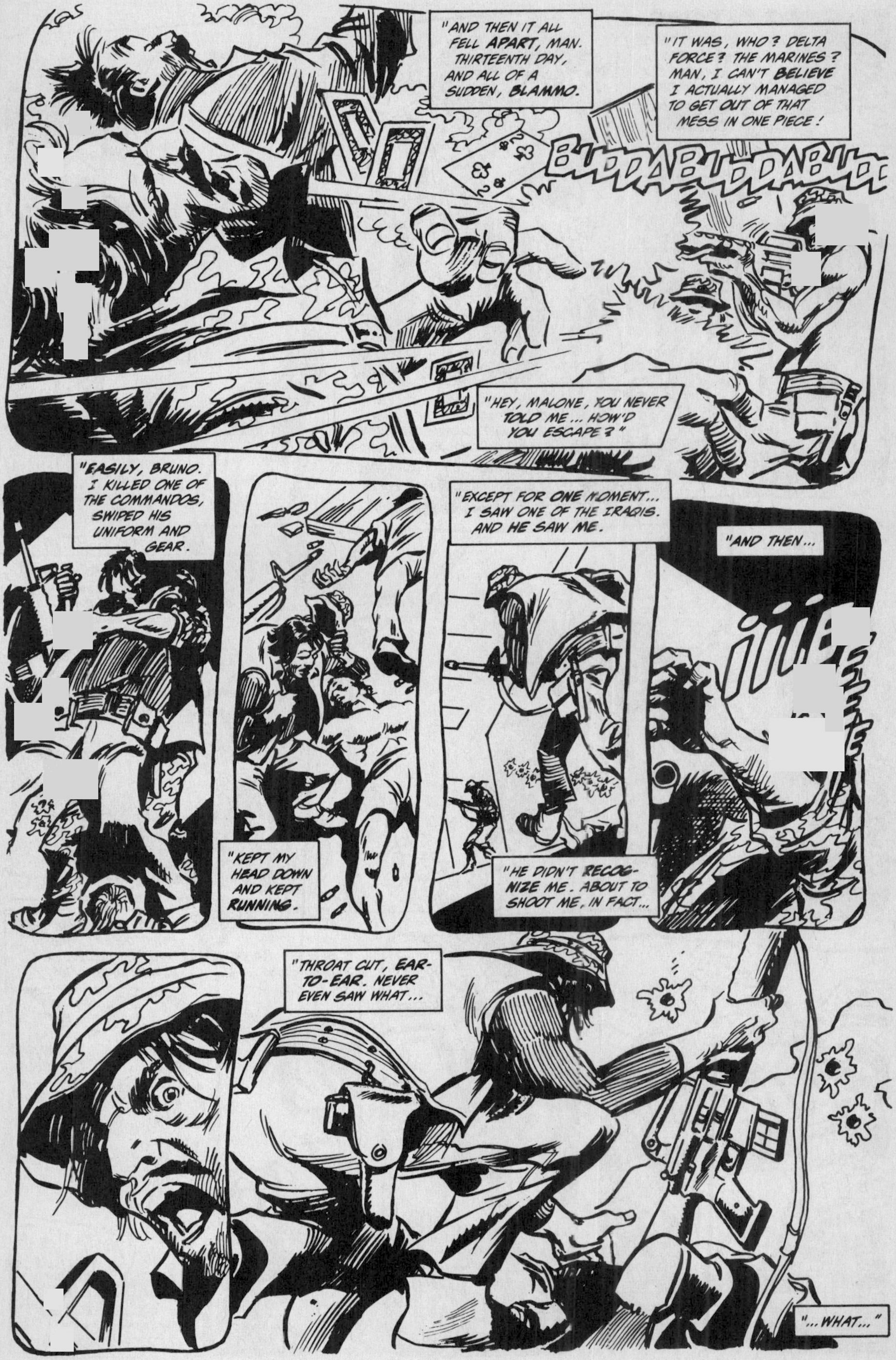
"AND THEN IT ALL FELL APART, MAN. THIRTEENTH DAY, AND ALL OF A SUDDEN, BLAMMO.
"IT WAS, WHO? DELTA FORCE? THE MARINES? MAN, I CAN'T BELIEVE I ACTUALLY MANAGED TO GET OUT OF THAT MESS IN ONE PIECE!
BUDDABUDDABUDD
"HEY, MALONE, YOU NEVER TOLD ME... HOW'D YOU ESCAPE?"
"EASILY, BRUNO. I KILLED ONE OF THE COMMANDOS, SWIPED HIS UNIFORM AND GEAR.
"KEPT MY HEAD DOWN AND KEPT RUNNING.
"EXCEPT FOR ONE MOMENT... I SAW ONE OF THE IRAQIS. AND HE SAW ME.
"HE DIDN'T RECOGNIZE ME. ABOUT TO SHOOT ME, IN FACT...
"AND THEN...
"THROAT CUT, EAR-TO-EAR. NEVER EVEN SAW WHAT...
"...WHAT..."

HOLY GEEZ! HE WAS *THERE*!

WHATEVER HE WAS...*IS*...HE WAS THERE AT THE OPERATION THAT FELL APART. FIVE YEARS AGO...

...TOMORROW.

HEY, THERE! HOW YOU GUYS DOING?

EVERYTHING OKAY? YOU LOOK LIKE YOU SAW A--

SHUT UP.

YESSIR.

HAVE A NICE DAY.

YESSIR.

CHECK *THIS*! WE'RE GOING TO MAKE IT!

WE GOTTA BE DOIN' AT LEAST THIRTY MILES PER, MAN!

HAVEN'T SHOT THE RAPIDS SINCE I WAS A *KID*.

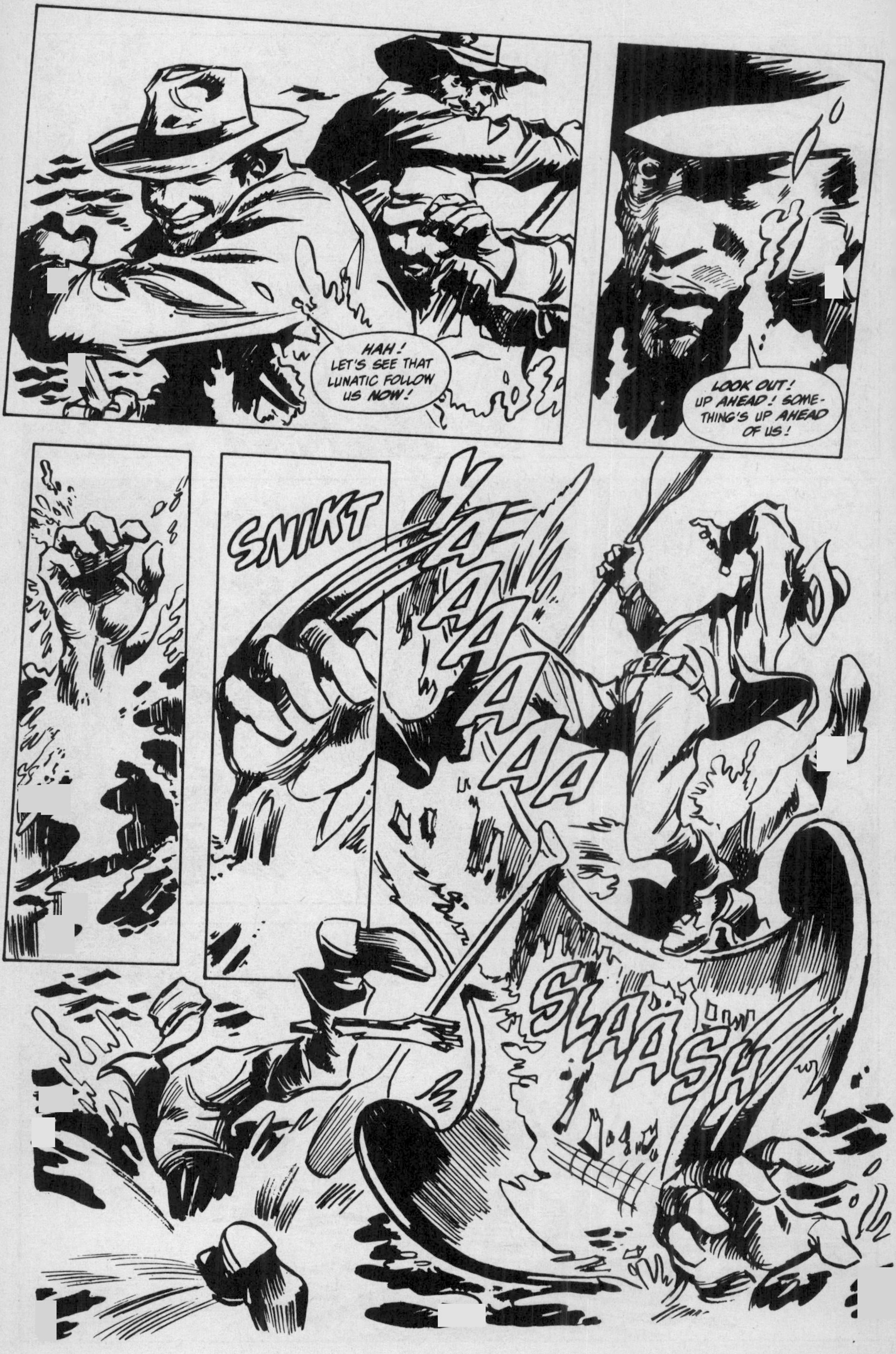

HAH! LET'S SEE THAT LUNATIC FOLLOW US NOW!
LOOK OUT! UP AHEAD! SOME-THING'S UP AHEAD OF US!
SNIKT
YAAAAAAA
SLAASH

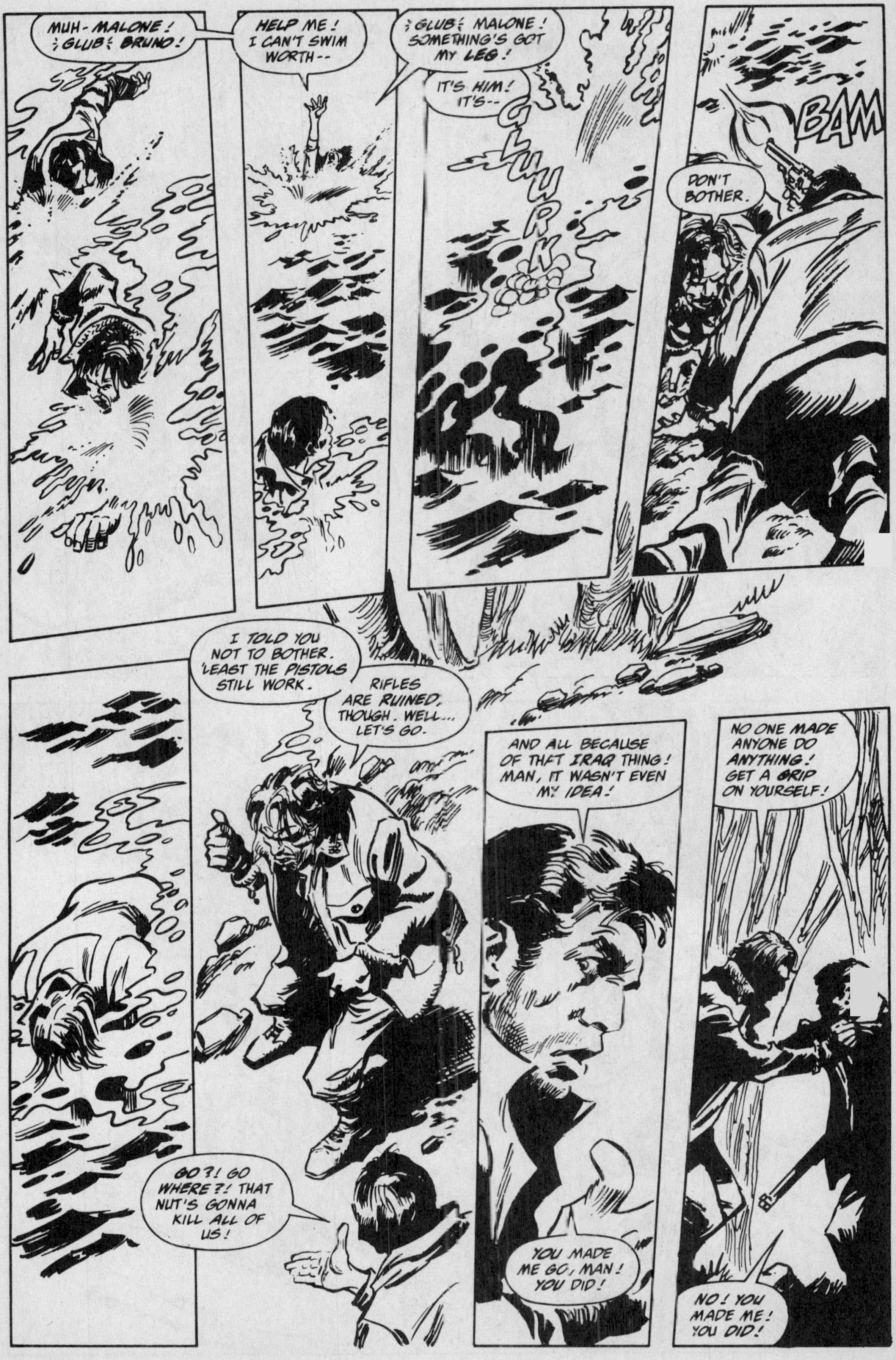

MUH-MALONE! ;GLUB; BRUNO!
HELP ME! I CAN'T SWIM WORTH--
;GLUB; MALONE! SOMETHING'S GOT MY LEG!
IT'S HIM! IT'S--
GLUURRK
BAM
DON'T BOTHER.
I TOLD YOU NOT TO BOTHER. 'LEAST THE PISTOLS STILL WORK.
RIFLES ARE RUINED, THOUGH. WELL... LET'S GO.
GO?! GO WHERE?! THAT NUT'S GONNA KILL ALL OF US!
AND ALL BECAUSE OF THAT IRAQ THING! MAN, IT WASN'T EVEN MY IDEA!
YOU MADE ME GO, MAN! YOU DID!
NO ONE MADE ANYONE DO ANYTHING! GET A GRIP ON YOURSELF!
NO! YOU MADE ME! YOU DID!

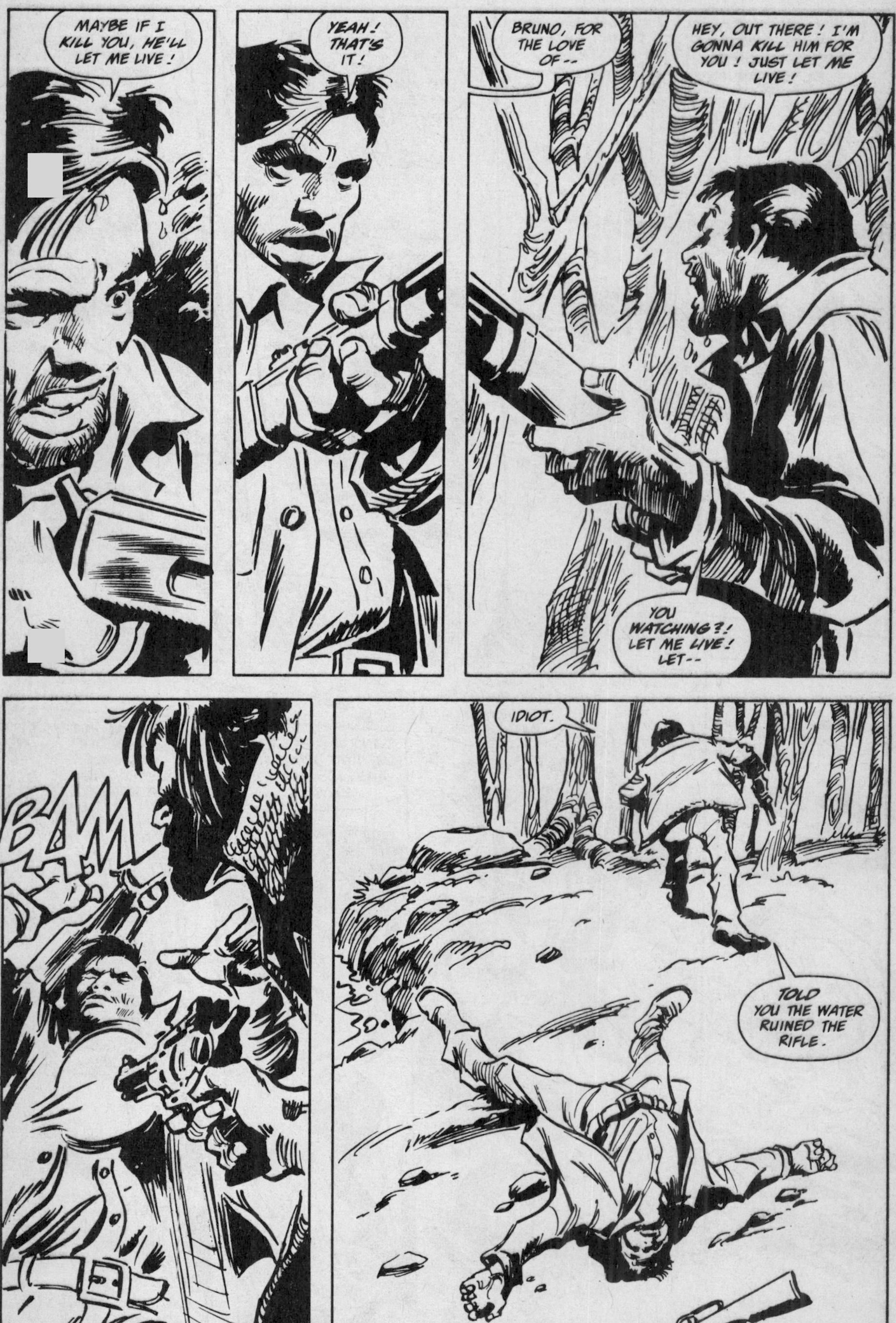
MAYBE IF I KILL YOU, HE'LL LET ME LIVE!
YEAH! THAT'S IT!
BRUNO, FOR THE LOVE OF--
HEY, OUT THERE! I'M GONNA KILL HIM FOR YOU! JUST LET ME LIVE!
YOU WATCHING?! LET ME LIVE! LET--
BAM
IDIOT.
TOLD YOU THE WATER RUINED THE RIFLE.

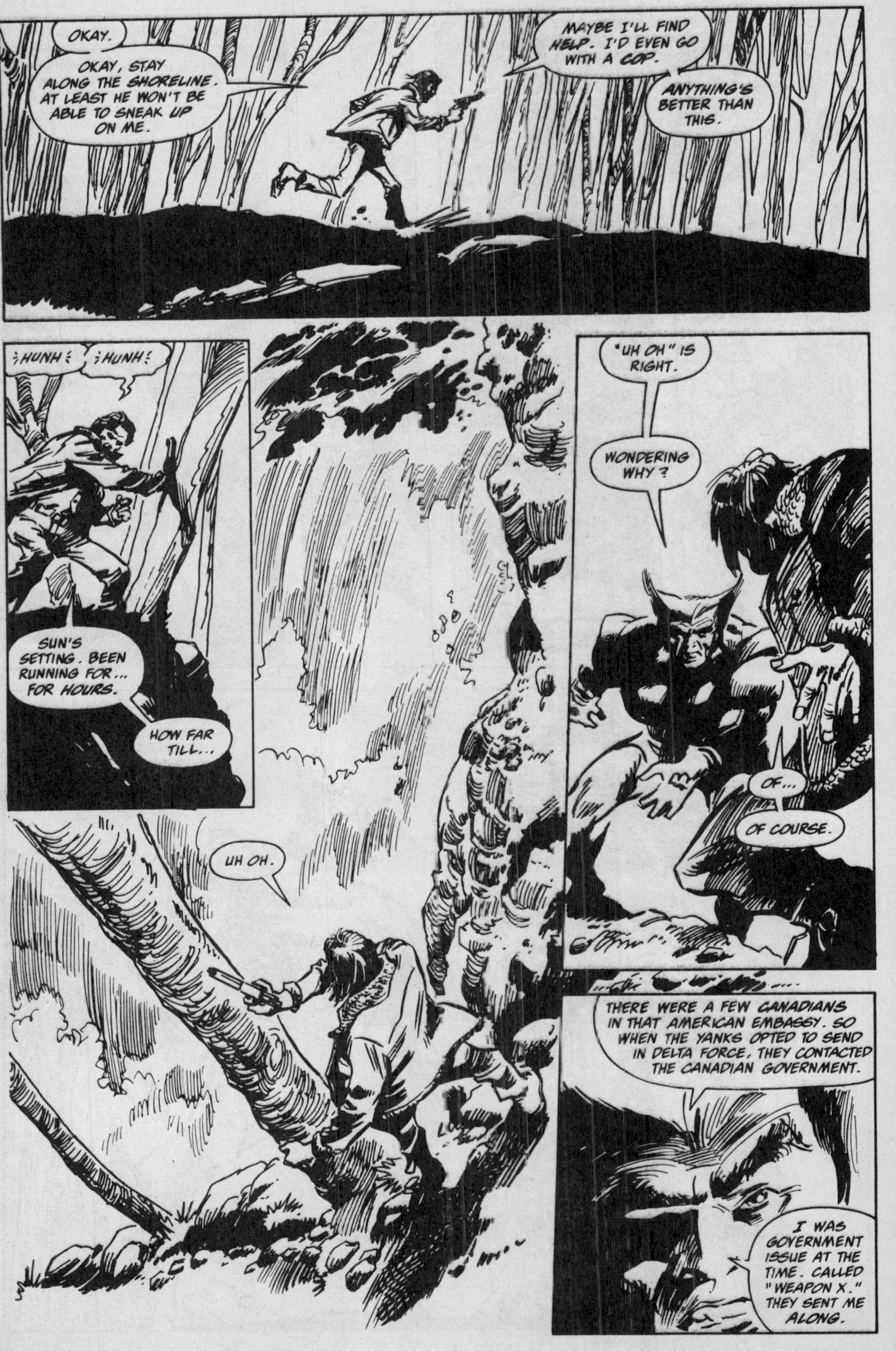
OKAY.
OKAY, STAY ALONG THE SHORELINE. AT LEAST HE WON'T BE ABLE TO SNEAK UP ON ME.
MAYBE I'LL FIND HELP. I'D EVEN GO WITH A COP.
ANYTHING'S BETTER THAN THIS.
HUNH
HUNH
SUN'S SETTING. BEEN RUNNING FOR... FOR HOURS.
HOW FAR TILL...
UH OH.
"UH OH" IS RIGHT.
WONDERING WHY?
OF...
OF COURSE.
THERE WERE A FEW CANADIANS IN THAT AMERICAN EMBASSY. SO WHEN THE YANKS OPTED TO SEND IN DELTA FORCE, THEY CONTACTED THE CANADIAN GOVERNMENT.
I WAS GOVERNMENT ISSUE AT THE TIME. CALLED "WEAPON X." THEY SENT ME ALONG.

CANADIANS IN THE EMBASSY?

YEAH. INCLUDING A CANADIAN NUN.

AH.

YEAH. MARCHED HER OUT EVERY DAY. PRETENDED YOU'D KILL HER.

"NOT YET," YOU'D SAY. AND THEN YOU'D USE HER.

WHEN I FOUND HER, SHE WAS DYING. CAUGHT A BULLET IN THE CROSSFIRE.

ONE CIVILIAN CASUALTY. WHAT THE MILITARY CALLS "ACCEPTABLE LOSSES."

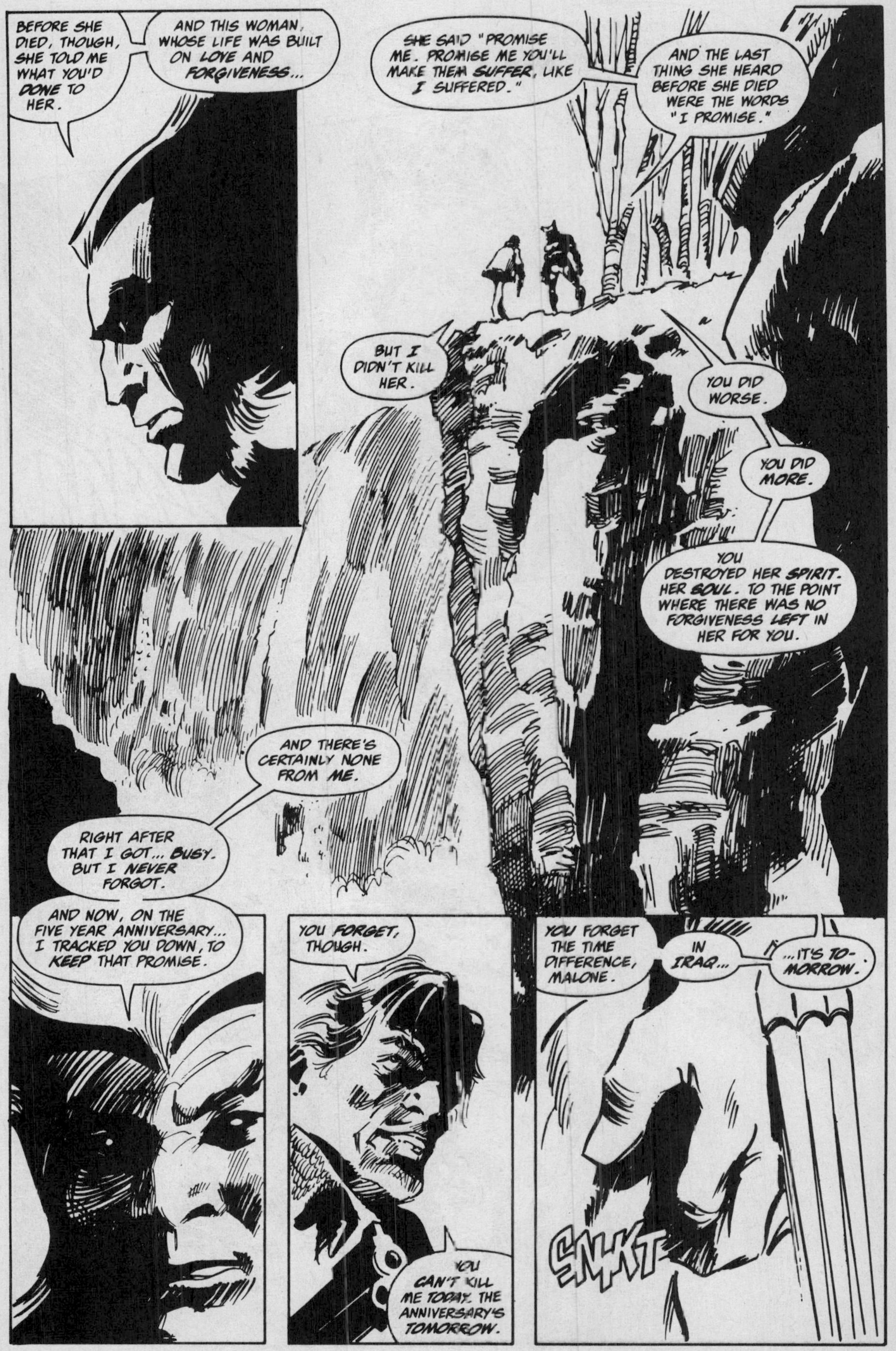

BEFORE SHE DIED, THOUGH, SHE TOLD ME WHAT YOU'D DONE TO HER.
AND THIS WOMAN, WHOSE LIFE WAS BUILT ON LOVE AND FORGIVENESS...
SHE SAID "PROMISE ME. PROMISE ME YOU'LL MAKE THEM SUFFER, LIKE I SUFFERED."
AND THE LAST THING SHE HEARD BEFORE SHE DIED WERE THE WORDS "I PROMISE."
BUT I DIDN'T KILL HER.
YOU DID WORSE.
YOU DID MORE.
YOU DESTROYED HER SPIRIT. HER SOUL. TO THE POINT WHERE THERE WAS NO FORGIVENESS LEFT IN HER FOR YOU.
AND THERE'S CERTAINLY NONE FROM ME.
RIGHT AFTER THAT I GOT... BUSY. BUT I NEVER FORGOT.
AND NOW, ON THE FIVE YEAR ANNIVERSARY... I TRACKED YOU DOWN, TO KEEP THAT PROMISE.
YOU FORGET, THOUGH.
YOU CAN'T KILL ME TODAY. THE ANNIVERSARY'S TOMORROW.
YOU FORGET THE TIME DIFFERENCE, MALONE.
IN IRAQ...
...IT'S TO-MORROW.
SNIKT

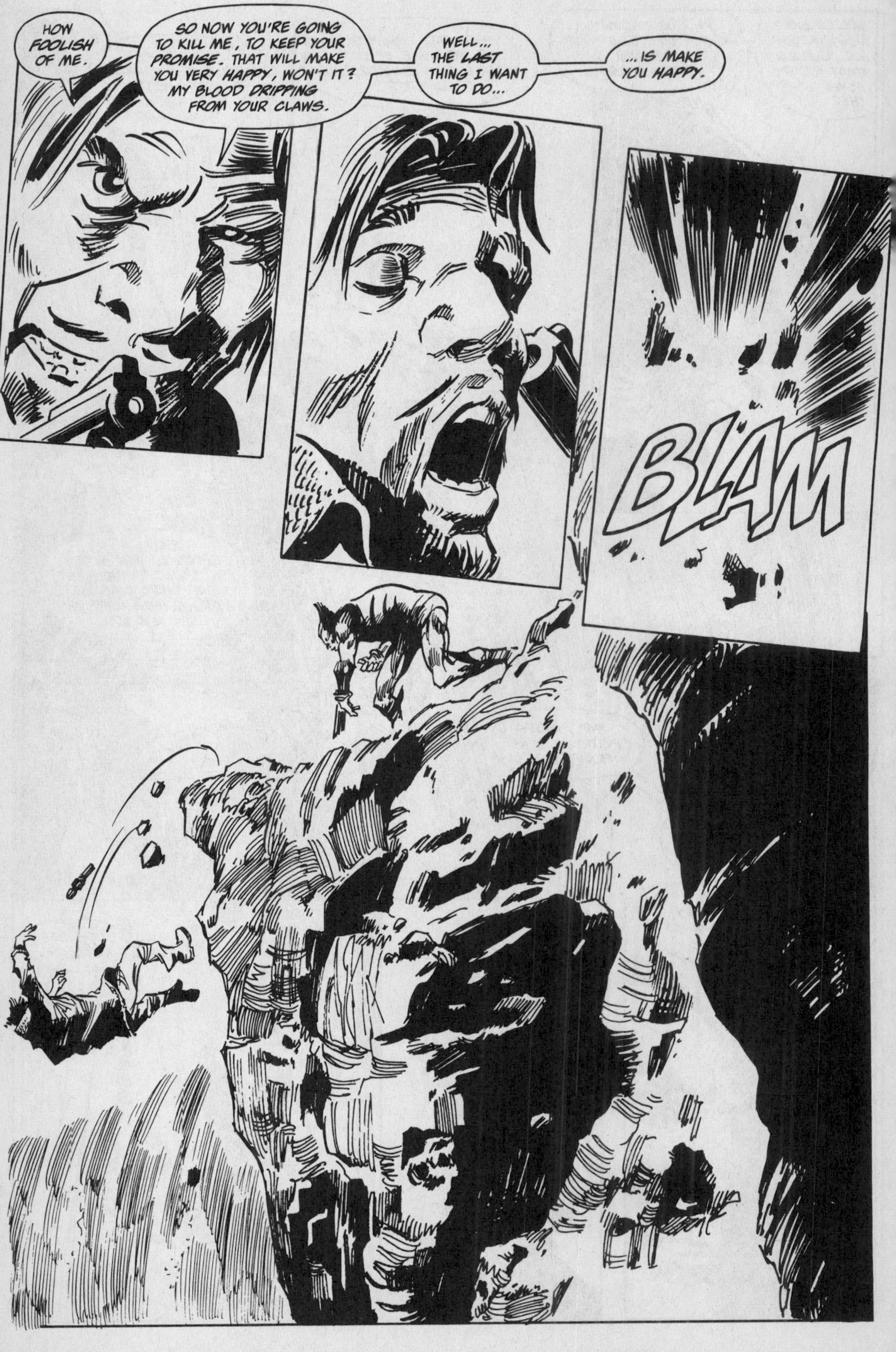
HOW FOOLISH OF ME.
SO NOW YOU'RE GOING TO KILL ME, TO KEEP YOUR PROMISE. THAT WILL MAKE YOU VERY HAPPY, WON'T IT? MY BLOOD DRIPPING FROM YOUR CLAWS.
WELL... THE LAST THING I WANT TO DO...
...IS MAKE YOU HAPPY.
BLAM

NOPE.

KILLING YOU WOULDN'T HAVE MADE ME HAPPY.

MAYBE YOU THINK YOU WON. FINE. MAKES NO DIFFERENCE TO ME.

BECAUSE TAKING A LIFE *DOESN'T* BRING ME ANY JOY.

HARDLY ANYTHING DOES... EXCEPT INNOCENCE.

BECAUSE I SEE IT SO LITTLE, I'VE LEARNED TO CHERISH IT.

AND ALL YOU KNEW HOW TO DO...

...WAS DESTROY IT.

HEY, PATCH?

PATCH? I ASKED IF YOU WANT ANOTHER?

YOU OKAY, PATCH? IT'S LIKE YOU'RE A MILLION MILES AWAY.

I WAS, DARLIN'. I WAS THINKING ABOUT A LONG TIME AGO...

...BACK BEFORE I HAD ANY FRIENDS... OR X-FRIENDS.

THAT'S WHAT YOU'RE THINKING ABOUT? EX-FRIENDS?

ABOUT AN EX-NUN, ACTUALLY. SHE DIED, YEARS AGO. YEARS AGO TODAY, IN FACT. AND I WAS THINKING ABOUT THE MAN WHO AVENGED HER A COUPLE YEARS BACK.

WAS IT YOU?

A MAN LIKE ME.

MORE OF A LONER. MORE VICIOUS. MORE LOTS OF THINGS.

BUT LESS OF A MAN.

YEAH, BRING ANOTHER, DARLIN'. LOOKS TO BE A LONG NIGHT.

END

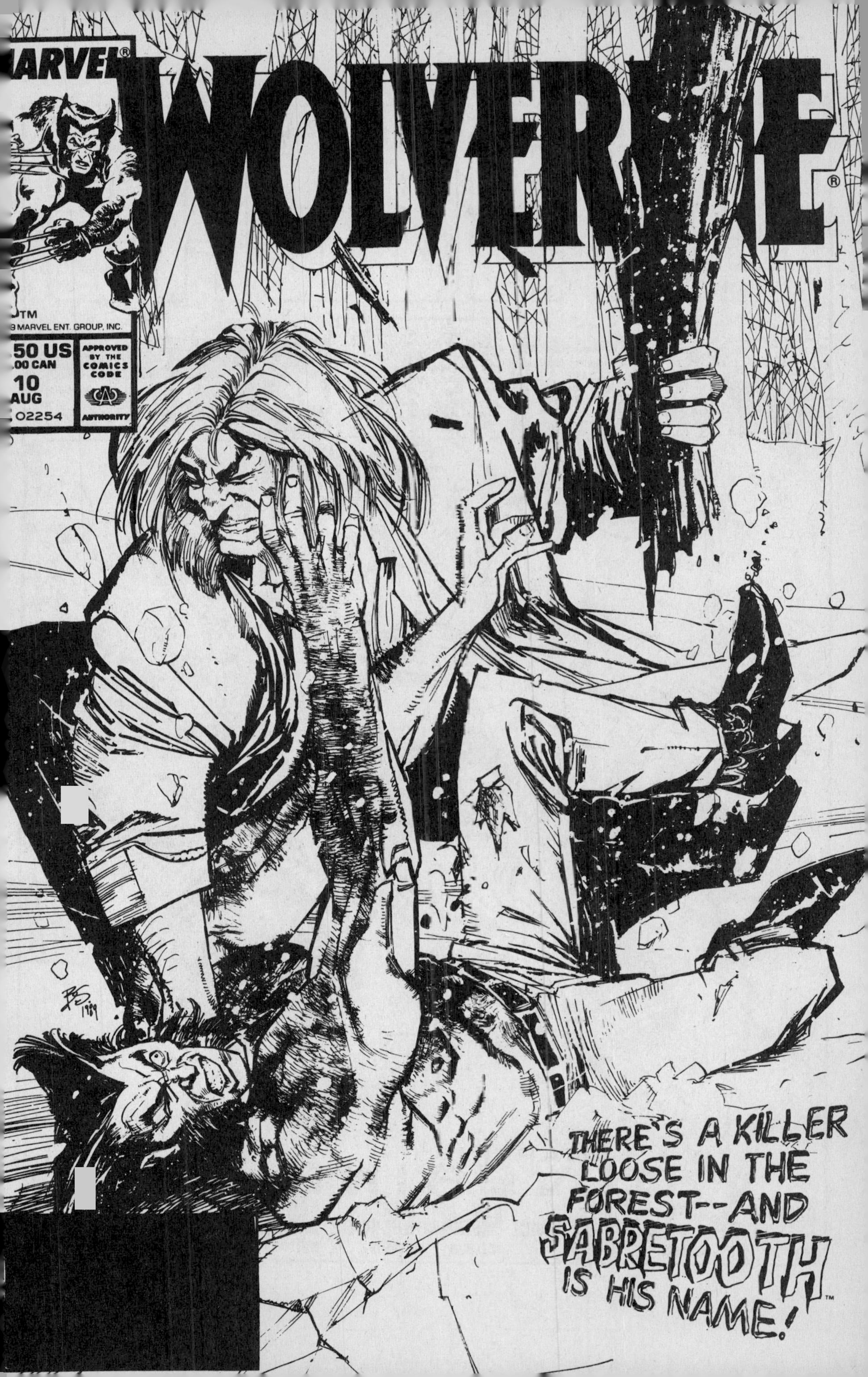

MARVEL
APPROVED BY THE COMICS CODE AUTHORITY
AUG
THERE'S A KILLER LOOSE IN THE FOREST--AND SABRETOOTH IS HIS NAME!

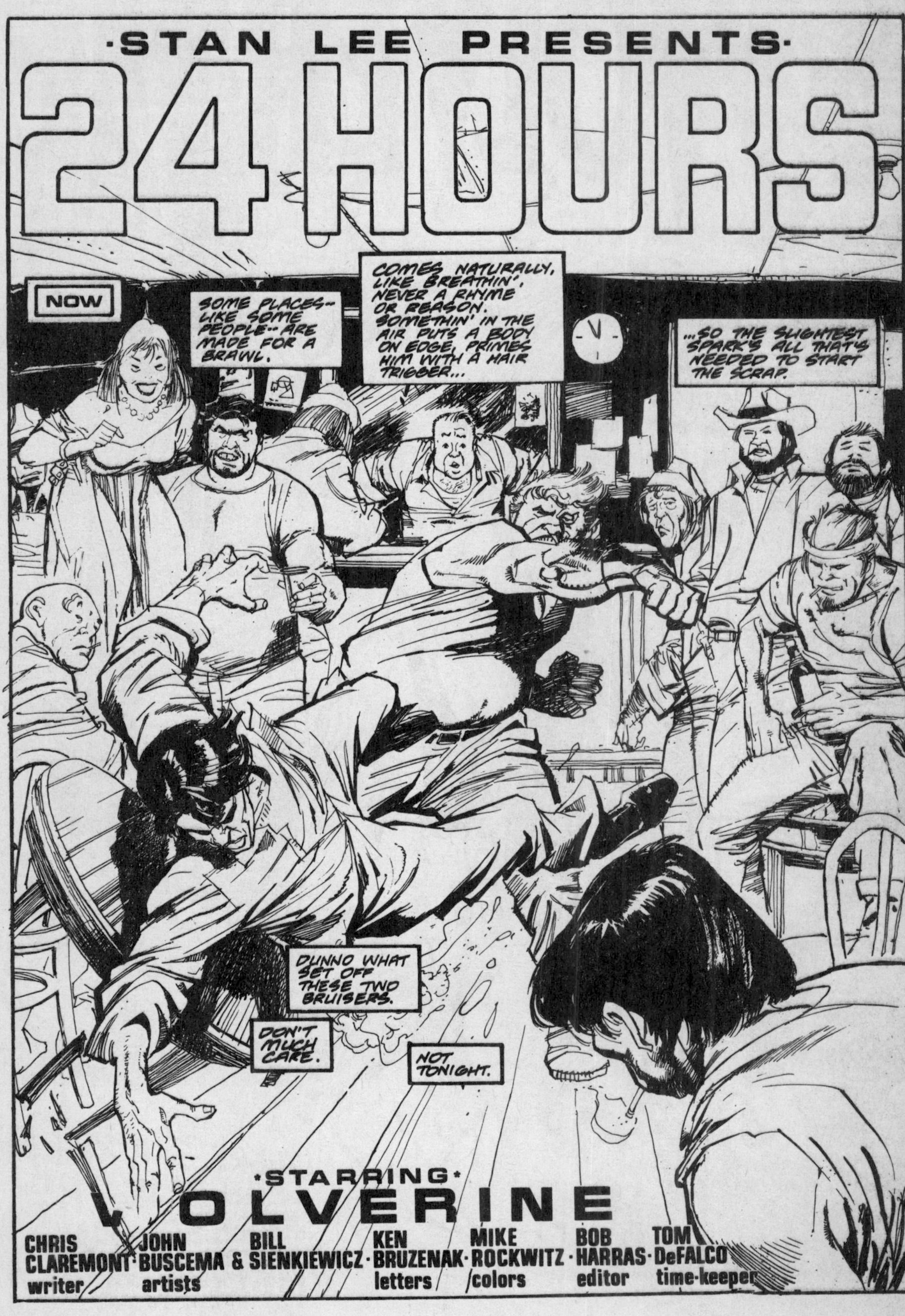
·STAN LEE PRESENTS·
24 HOURS
NOW
SOME PLACES-- LIKE SOME PEOPLE-- ARE MADE FOR A BRAWL.
COMES NATURALLY, LIKE BREATHIN', NEVER A RHYME OR REASON. SOMETHIN' IN THE AIR PUTS A BODY ON EDGE, PRIMES HIM WITH A HAIR TRIGGER...
...SO THE SLIGHTEST SPARK'S ALL THAT'S NEEDED TO START THE SCRAP.
DUNNO WHAT SET OFF THESE TWO BRUISERS.
DON'T MUCH CARE.
NOT TONIGHT.
·STARRING·
WOLVERINE
CHRIS CLAREMONT · writer
JOHN BUSCEMA & BILL SIENKIEWICZ · artists
KEN BRUZENAK · letters
MIKE ROCKWITZ · colors
BOB HARRAS · editor
TOM DeFALCO · time-keeper

NOT MY USUAL STOMPING GROUND. PRETTY DOWN-MARKET, EVEN FOR MADRIPOOR LOWTOWN.

BUT TONIGHT, I'M STEERIN' CLEAR OF PEOPLE I KNOW, PLACES I CARE FOR.

ONLY HIDE I WANT TO PUT AT RISK...

...IS MY OWN.

FUNNY HOW, WHEN MY WORLD TWISTS NASTY, FIRST PLACE I THINK TO GO IS A SALOON.

ALWAYS FELT COMFORTABLE IN ONE.

CELEBRATED THE BEST-- AND WORST--OF TIMES.

THEN

THAT'S WHERE THIS STARTED.

QUALITY PLACE, MADE MORESO BY MEMORY FOR ALL OF ITS BEING DUMPED IN THE MIDDLE OF FLAMIN' FRONTIER NOWHERE.

AND, IN THEIR OWN, ROUGH-HEWN WAY, QUALITY FOLK.

MOST OF 'EM, ANYWAY.

GLORY!?!

SHE'S DEAD!

SILVER FOX IS DEAD!

HAPPENS, BOY. SPECIALLY TO SQUAWS... ...UPPITY ENOUGH TO SAY "NO."

SABRE-TOOTH-- --YOU KILLED HER!

WHAT OF IT?

SHOULD WARN YOU, THOUGH, BOY-- --THESE OTHERS, CROSS 'EM AN' YOU TRADE PUNCHES 'TIL SOMEBODY DROPS, AN' THERE'S USUALLY THE END OF IT.

TIME, THAT AIN'T FIGHTING, THAT'S PLAY.

I DON'T PLAY.

TAKE ME ON, IT ENDS WHEN ONE OF US IS DEAD.

NO MATTER WHAT IT TAKES, OR HOW LONG!

HE ISN'T FOOLING!

FOR PITY'S SAKE, LOGAN-- SHE'S JUST AN INDIAN!

NOW

SHOULD'VE EXPECTED THIS, SOONER OR LATER.

BAD JOSS FOR THE BRUISERS.

I'M IN A MOOD.

FIGHT'S DONE, BUB, CALL IT QUITS.

THE HECK YOU SAY SHORTY!

HOW 'BOUT WE START ON YOU!

THAT'D BE A MISTAKE.

ZUMPF!

YOU WANT TO GIVE ME GRIEF, LIKE YOUR BUDDY?

I MEAN WHAT'S A MAN HAVE TO DO TO ENJOY A QUIET BEER.

BONG BONG BONG

BONG BONG BONG

MIDNIGHT.

PERSONAL CLOCK'S RUNNING.

AHCH-- THE DEVIL WITH THIS.

YOU BUFFOONS AREN'T WORTH THE EFFORT.

LOTS O' BETS RIDIN' ON THE PUNCH-UP.

LOTS O' PLAYERS UNHAPPY WITH ME FOR BUTTIN' IN.

FIGURE I WON'T BE WELCOME BACK HERE-- EVER.

BREAKS MY HEART.

PRETTY IMPRESSED, ACTUALLY. BOOZE THEY SERVE, WOULD'VE FIGURED IT KINDER TO THE INSIDES TO GUZZLE STRAIGHT SULFURIC ACID. PROBABLY TASTE BETTER.

AT LEAST MY MUTANT HEALING FACTOR REPAIRS ANY DAMAGE TO MY BODY. WHAT'S THEIR EXCUSE?

MADRIPOOR'S A BIG CITY-- POPULATION IN SEVEN FIGURES, EASY..

--ITS HIGHTOWN AS 21st CENTURY COSMOPOLITAN AS LOWTOWN IS MEDIEVAL.

AND YET, IN ITS WAY, AS FIERCE AND UNTAMED A JUNGLE AS THE REAL, NATURAL ONE THAT COVERS MOST OF THIS ISLAND.

MY TURF.

ROOFS ARE BETTER THAN THE STREET. EASIER TO SEE ANY OPPOSITION COMING, MORE PLACES TO SCOOT, IF NEEDFUL.

DID I LOVE SILVER FOX? THOUGHT SO, AT THE TIME. NOT SO 'CERTAIN ANYMORE, IT WAS TOO LONG AGO.

DID IT MATTER IN THE END? PROBABLY NOT.

SABRE AN' ME, WE'D BEEN SPOILING FOR A FIGHT. HE'D ALWAYS HELPED HIMSELF TO WHATEVER WAS MINE, CHALLENGING ME TO STOP HIM. SOMETHING ALWAYS HELD ME BACK. KNEW HE HATED ME, HADN'T A CLUE WHY. MAYBE IT WAS SIMPLY WHAT HE SAID-- THAT THE WHOLE WORLD WASN'T BIG ENOUGH FOR THE PAIR OF US.

THEN

I WAS COVERED WITH FOX'S BLOOD.

SABRE STUNK OF IT.

SHE'D DIED HARD, AND HE'D ENJOYED EVERY MINUTE.

I MEANT TO PAY HIM BACK IN KIND.

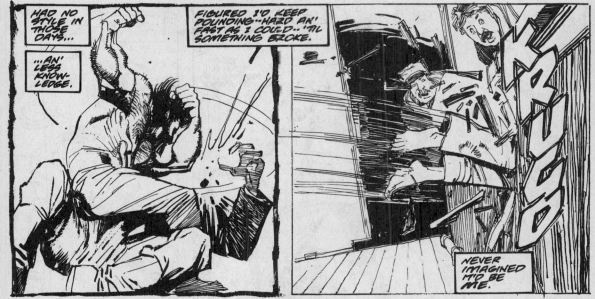

HAD NO STYLE IN THOSE DAYS...

...AN' LESS KNOWLEDGE.

FIGURED I'D KEEP POUNDING--HARD AN' FAST AS I COULD--'TIL SOMETHING BROKE.

NEVER IMAGINED IT'D BE ME.

NO UNBREAKABLE ADAMANTIUM REINFORCED BONES, THEN...

...NO CLAWS.

I WAS AS CLOSE TO HUMAN AS I EVER CAME.

BUT I WAS TOUGH.

MADE SABRE-TOOTH'S DAY...

AS WELL AS TOO FLAMIN' DUMB TO REALIZE HOW MUCH TROUBLE I WAS IN.

ARRRRGH!

...TO TEACH ME.

NOW

MEMORY HURTS MORE'N THE ORIGINAL WOUNDS.

NIGHT'S QUIET...

...AS THOUGH THE CITY'S HOLDIN' ITS BREATH.

WE'RE ALL OF US WAITIN'!

YAHGHN!

THIS IS THE PART I HATE.

TOO MUCH IMAGINATION.

TOO MUCH EXPERIENCE.

SCREAM...!

CUTE.

CLEAN, TOO.

KEEP AWAY FROM ME!

SPUNKY, TOO. I LIKE THAT.

HEY, SWEETNESS, YOU SASHAY THROUGH LOWTOWN...

...BEST YOU BE PREPARED TO PAY!

U.S. NAVY.. SWABBIES ON LIBERTY, FROM THE SUB IN PORT--

..MAN'S DOWN...

...BUT HE GAVE A FAIR ACCOUNT OF HIMSELF BEFORE HE GOT KNIFED.

I PICK UP WHERE HE LEFT OFF.

THESE ARE GUESTS IN OUR TOWN.

AS SUCH, THEY SHOULD BE TREATED WITH COURTESY AND RESPECT.

SEZ YOU, FELLA.

MY MATES.. AN' MY GUN GOT A DIFFERENT NOTION.

HEARD THAT LINE BEFORE, BUB--

..FROM LOTS BETTER'N YOU.

BAM BAM

BAM BAM

"DIDN'T WORK FOR THEM, EITHER."

BRRR

HE ISN'T WORTH USING MY CLAWS.

ONE GOOD PUNCH IS ALL IT TAKES.

HIS PAL...

...DOESN'T TAKE THE HINT.

KRAK!!

FINALLY, MY MESSAGE SINKS IN...

...AND THE REST OF THE GANG HEADS OFF...

...IN SEARCH OF EASIER PICKINGS.

IS HE--?!

BREATHING. BARELY.

LOST A LOT OF BLOOD.

THIS IS MY FAULT.

WE WERE LOOKING FOR SOME ADVENTURE.

THEN YOU GOT WHAT YOU WANTED.

IS THERE A HOSPITAL?

IN LOWTOWN?

WON'T GET AN AMBULANCE DOWN THESE PARTS, EITHER.

BUT I KNOW A PLACE...

...THAT'S ALMOST AS GOOD.

STAY CLOSE. STAY WARY. LET'S GO.

THEN

AFTER WRECKING MOST O' THE SALOON...

SKWASH!

...WE TOOK OUR FIGHT OUTSIDE.

FAIR DAY, FOR HIGH-COUNTRY WINTER.

PLENTY COLD.

BUT MY BLOOD WAS BLAZIN' SO HOT...

...I DIDN'T NOTICE.

I'D NEVER MET MY MATCH, 'TIL THAT DAY.

KLUDD!

WHOLE SIDE SEEMED TO CAVE IN.

AN' WHEN THE IMPACT SLAMMED ME INTO THE WOODPILE...

...SO DID IT.

TIMBER CAME CAME IN ALL SIZES--LOGS TO FULL-WIDTH UNSPLIT TRUNKS--

--PILED HIGH AS A HOUSE.

MADE A PRETTY IMPRESSIVE MESS.

NOW

IT'S PATCH, JOY! I GOT TROUBLE!

"MADAME JOY'S"? IS THIS...?!

EXACTLY WHAT IT LOOKS LIKE, GIRL.

TRUST YOU, OLD FRIEND, TO DROP IT ON MY DOOR-STEP.

SLASHES ARE SUPERFICIAL-- MOSTLY MESSY--

--BUT HE TOOK ONE BLADE TO THE HILT.

NO TIME TO GET HIM TO HIGHTOWN OR HIS SHIP.

YOU DID RIGHT THEN, PATCH, BRINGING HIM HERE.

INGA, SUMMON DR. FONG.

GET MAVIS, READY THE DISPENSARY.

SNAP TO, LADIES--

--WE'VE A LIFE TO SAVE!

HOLD ON, SAILOR. YOU'RE IN GOOD HANDS.

IF I GOTTA GO, MAN...

...HECKUVA PLACE TO GO FROM.

AIN'T THAT THE TRUTH.

AS FOR YOU, YOUNG LASS...

...LET'S GET YOU OUT OF THESE BLOODY CLOTHES AND INTO A HOT TUB.

PLEASE, I'D LIKE TO--!

YOU'LL JUST BE IN THE WAY.

INZA, LOOK AFTER HER, WILL YOU, THERE'S A DEAR?

GIRL HAS BRASS, HOLDIN' HERSELF TOGETHER-- FIGHTIN' OFF FEAR AN' SHOCK-- THROUGH SHEER WILL POWER.

NEVER A DULL MOMENT, PATCH...

"...WHERE YOU'RE CONCERNED.

MUST HAVE A KNACK.

SAME AS YOU, DREW.

TOUCHÉ. ANYTHING SERIOUS?

IT WILL BE IF YOU DON'T LET ME DO SOME PROPER WORK!

SCOOT THE PAIR OF YOU!

I'LL CALL WHEN THERE'S NEWS.

LOVELY LADY-- THOSE SAILORS ARE IN THE BEST OF HANDS.

YUP.

LOVELY PLACE, AS WELL.

HARDLY WHAT YOU'D EXPECT.

ESPECIALLY IN LOWTOWN.

THAT'S MADRIPOOR FOR YOU--

--WHERE NOTHING'S WHAT IT SEEMS.

THAT YOUR PARTNER WAVING?

YOU ON A CASE?

HARDLY. WE LIVE HERE.

THAT A FACT?

CARE TO SEE OUR PLACE?

LEAD THE WAY, DARLIN'

DREW, THIS ISN'T EXACTLY WHAT I HAD IN MIND.

MORE FUN THAN TAKING THE STAIRS.

AND LOTS QUICKER.

EASY FOR HER TO SAY. JESSICA DREW'S SUPER-POWERS ENABLE HER TO STICK TO WALLS.

I HAVE TO CLIMB THE OLD-FASHIONED WAY.

SHE WINS...

BUT I GIVE HER A RACE.

NOT TOO SHABBY

INDEED...THERE AREN'T MANY PEOPLE IN THE WORLD WHO'RE A MATCH FOR ME, PATCH.

DO TELL.

FLAMIN' MEMORIES.

THEN

ALWAYS FLASHIN' BACK STRONGEST WHEN YOU NEED 'EM LEAST.

GONE!

BUT NOT UNSCATHED.

EVEN WITHOUT YOUR BLOOD-TRAIL, BOY, THERE'S NOWHERE YOU CAN HIDE FROM ME--

"--NOT WHEN I KNOW YOUR SCENT."

I RAN

NO RHYME

NO REASON

NO SENSE

'TIL I DROPPED

AND THERE I KNEW I'D DIE.

SIMPLEST BINARY EQUATION--

--I WAS BEAT AND BEATEN...

...SO WHY PROLONG THE AGONY?

I'D NEVER KNOWN FEAR BEFORE.

NOW I KNEW NOTHING BUT.

SURPRISED MYSELF, THOUGH.

PUSHED OFF MY FACE.

ALL THE WAY TO MY FEET.

COULDN'T QUIT.

WOULDN'T!

MAYBE I WAS BEATEN.

PROBABLY GOING TO DIE.

BUT I WASN'T ABOUT TO QUIT!

NOW

...ANBODY HOME IN THERE?

EARTH TO PATCH LINDSAY TO PATCH YOO HOO...

PUT A LOCK ON IT McCABE

SORRY. IT'S JUST YOU ZONED OUT TOTALLY

LOST IN MY THOUGHTS.

MUST'VE BEEN PRETTY INTENSE.

PRIVATE BUSINESS.

WE'RE "PRIVATE EYES." MAYBE WE CAN HELP?

VERY NICE.

THIS PLACE? IF YOU ASK ME AS IN...

..."TOO GOOD TO BE TRUE."

JESS, YOU'RE SUSPICIOUS OF EVERYONE AND EVERYTHING.

SMART LADY.

ATTITUDE'S KEPT ME HEALTHY MOST OF MY LIFE.

DREW & McCABE Resolutions

VERY IMPRESSIVE.

IF YOU LIKE LIVING IN A BAWDY HOUSE.

WORSE PLACES, WORSE PEOPLE.

BE AMAZED WHAT A BODY CAN HEAR.. AND LEARN--IN A JOINT LIKE THIS.

ALSO, JOY'S IN THE PRINCE'S HOUSE, RUN UNDER HIS IMPRIMATUR.

PROBABLY BARAN'S WAY OF SAYING, SO ARE YOU.

MAYBE WE DON'T LIKE THAT.

SO WHY DO I FEEL LIKE A NUT...

BARAN NEEDS EYES AND EARS IN LOWTOWN, EVIDENTLY, YOU'RE IT.

...CLAMPED TIGHT BETWEEN THE JAWS OF A NUT-CRACKER?

LOOK--ONE SIDE YOU GOT COY. OPPOSING HIM, TYGER.

RIVAL CRIMELORDS, ROUGHLY EQUAL FORCES, BALANCING EACH OTHER.

BUT ALWAYS HUSTLING FOR THE EDGE THAT'LL ENABLE THEM TO GRAB TOTAL CONTROL.

PRINCE HAS TO KNOW THE GAME AND SCORE-- WHO TO MOVE AGAINST WHEN NECESSARY, AND HOW HARD. USED TO BE THE ROLE HIS CHANCELLOR PLAYED.

TOO BAD THE PRINCE ALLOWED GENERAL COY TO MURDER HIM.

RANJAMARYAN BROKE THE RULES, SIDED WITH TYGER.

IN BARAN'S EYES THAT WAS TREASON.

HE WANTS SOMEBODY NEUTRAL, WHOSE LOYALTY IS TO HIM.

IN THAT CASE, HE MADE A BIG MISTAKE CHOOSING US.

YOU WANT OUT, DARLIN', SAY THE WORD.

BUT IF YOU STAY IT'S ON MADRIPOOR RULES.

WHICH MEANS, NO RULES.

PATCH, WHAT ABOUT YOUR IF SOMETHING'S WRONG...

OBLIGED, DREW, BUT LIKE I SAID:

"PRIVATE BUSINESS."

BE SEEING YOU, LADIES.

THEN

USED TO DO THIS FOR FUN.

NO MAN NOR BEAST WAS MY EQUAL...

...SO I SET MYSELF AGAINST NATURE.

ALWAYS PUSHING LIMITS--

--BECAUSE IT NEVER ENTERED MY FOOL HEAD...

...THAT I HAD ANY.

LIVE AND LEARN.

:pant:

:pant: PANT: :pant:

SOUND LIKE A DOG, BOY.

YOU WANT TO DIE LIKE ONE--

--ON YOUR BELLY--

--OR ON YOUR FEET...

...LIKE A MAN?

...AND HIGHTOWN.

DAY...

POLICE HEAD-QUARTERS.

AND TO WHAT, PRAY TELL...

...DO I OWE THE HONOR OF THIS VISIT, PATCH?

HOW 'BOUT ONE OLD PAL, TAI, LOOKIN' UP ANOTHER?

IF SO, THEN I AM MOST PLEASED TO SEE YOU.

EVEN IF YOU ARE SITTING IN MY CHAIR.

BEEN A LONG NIGHT AN' IT'S A COMFY SEAT.

BY ALL MEANS THEN, INDULGE.

CONSIDER IT MY "THANKS" FOR YOUR TIMELY INTERVENTION WITH THE AMERICAN SAILORS.

REGRETTABLY, HOWEVER, THOSE BRAVOS YOU TROUNCED ARE IN A LESS CHARITABLE FRAME OF MIND.

YOU'VE BEEN STIRRING UP A VERITABLE HORNET'S NEST IN LOWTOWN, PATCH.

IS THIS TO BE A REGULAR OCCURANCE?

HADN'T GIVEN IT A THOUGHT.

PERHAPS YOU SHOULD. YOU'RE DEALING WITH...

...SOME VERY UGLY CUSTOMERS.

REGARDING THIS OTHER MATTER...

...MY BEST DETERMINATION, BOTH THROUGH OFFICIAL CHANNELS AND THE "OLD BOY NETWORK," IS THAT THE MAN YOU ASKED ABOUT IS DEAD.

THANKS, TAI, I'M OBLIGED.

DOESN'T MEAN MUCH. AS WOLVERINE...

...I'M SUPPOSED TO BE DEAD, TOO. BUT IT DIDN'T HURT TO CHECK.

MY PLEASURE. BY THE WAY, PATCH-- HAPPY BIRTHDAY.

WHAT--?! BUT HOW--??!

AS CHIEF OF POLICE, MY FRIEND...

...IT IS MY JOB TO KNOW.

TAKE CARE.

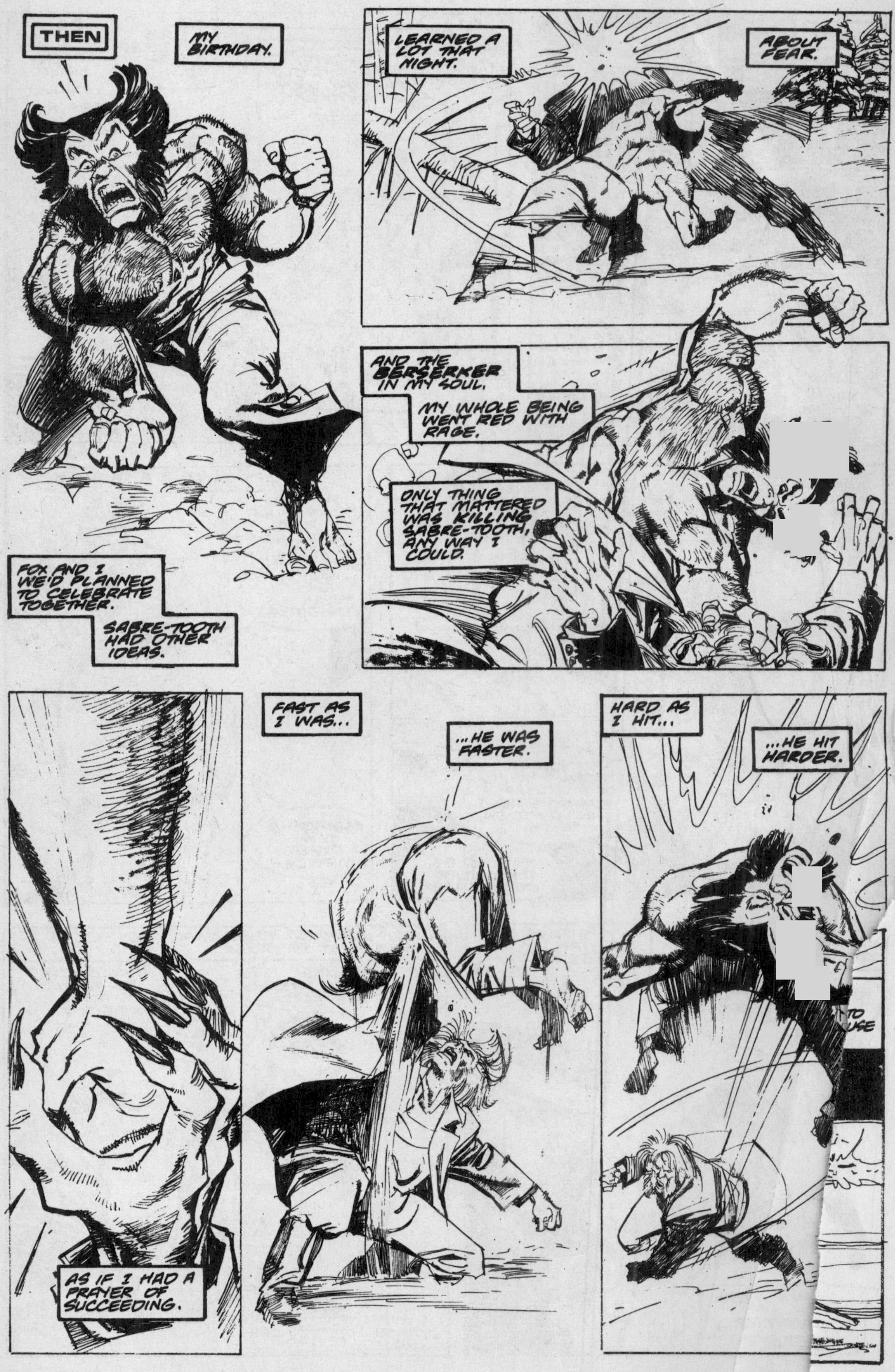
THEN
MY BIRTHDAY.
FOX AND I WE'D PLANNED TO CELEBRATE TOGETHER.
SABRE-TOOTH HAD OTHER IDEAS.
LEARNED A LOT THAT NIGHT.
ABOUT FEAR.
AND THE BERSERKER IN MY SOUL.
MY WHOLE BEING WENT RED WITH RAGE.
ONLY THING THAT MATTERED WAS KILLING SABRE-TOOTH, ANY WAY I COULD.
AS IF I HAD A PRAYER OF SUCCEEDING.
FAST AS I WAS...
...HE WAS FASTER.
HARD AS I HIT...
...HE HIT HARDER.

TOO STUBBORN...

...TOO STUPID...

...I KEPT COMING.

THAT MADE HIM LAUGH.

I LEARNED FEAR...

...AND RAGE-- --NOW, FINALLY...

AT THE HANDS OF THE CONSUMMATE MASTER...

...I LEARNED WHAT IT TRULY MEANT...

...TO BE HURT.

NOW

SLOW, MEASURED PACE. EASY STRIDE.

NATURAL ATHLETE...

shup-shep *shup shep shup* *shep shup shu*

...SNEAKS MAKING HARDLY ANY SOUND AT ALL ON THE DOCK.

HEARD 'EM FINE, AGES AGO...

UMPFF!

...WHEN THEY STARTED FOLLOWING ME.

SAME AS I SMELLED THE SCENT THAT TOLD ME WHO IT WAS.

EXPLAIN, DREW.

I'M **WORRIED** ABOUT YOU, PATCH-- EVERYBODY'S WORRIED!

TEARING THROUGH LOWTOWN LIKE A ONE-MAN TYPHOON.

YOUR FRIENDS DECIDED, THE BLAZES WITH YOUR FEELINGS...

...WE'D BEST KEEP TABS ON YOU.

AND IF YOU'VE A PROBLEM WITH THAT, CHUM--

--TOUGH!

YES MA'AM!

WON'T HAVE TO WORRY MUCH LONGER, THOUGH.

MIDNIGHT, YOU MEAN?

PATCH-- HAS IT SOMETHING TO DO WITH THIS BEING YOUR BIRTHDAY?

FLAMIN' BLABBERMOUTH BUSYBODY, TAI, I SWEAR--!

THERE HE IS!

GUN 'IM, DARYL!

BE A PLEASURE, DARYL!

NO BRUISERS FROM THE BAR LOOKIN' TO EVEN YOUR SCORE.

TAI WAS RIGHT--

--GUYS BEAR A SERIOUS GRUDGE.

JESS GOES HIGH, LEAP TAKES HER THE WAREHO' ROOF.

DON'T HAVE HER LEGS.

I GO LOW.

DARYLS COME LOADED FOR BEAR.

POOM!

TRADE IN THEIR SUB-MACHINE GUN FOR A GRENADE LAUNCHER.

SO MUCH FOR THE WAREHOUSE.

SKBLAMM!

EVEN NASTIER TREATS IN STORE FOR ME.

FLAME-THROWER!

FIRE PINS ME DOWN,

POOM!

BUT I'VE GOT GOOD COVER.

FORGOT ABOUT THE GRENADES.

KRAKOW!

I GOT HIM! I GOT HIM!

FWOOSH!

LOOKIT THAT SUCKER BURN!

TEACH HIM TO MESS WITH US!

CRYIN' SHAME, THOUGH IT WAS OVER SO QUICK.

ABSOLOOTLY!

POP ANOTHER BREWSKI, BRO!

THEN WE'LL WHEEL HOME TO START...

...SOME RIGHTEOUS CELEBRATING!

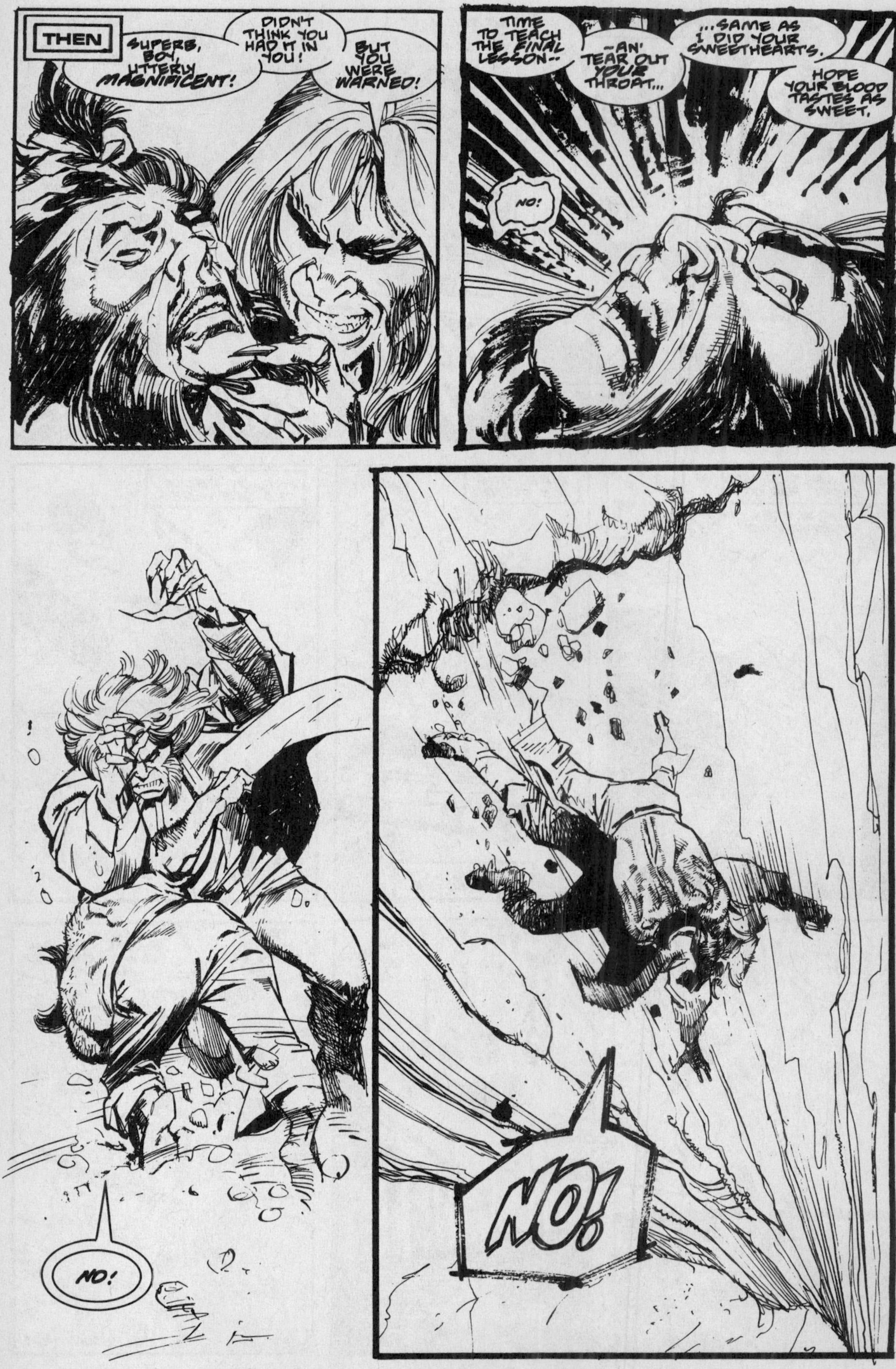
THEN
SUPERB, BOY, UTTERLY MAGNIFICENT!
DIDN'T THINK YOU HAD IT IN YOU!
BUT YOU WERE WARNED!
TIME TO TEACH THE FINAL LESSON--
--AN' TEAR OUT YOUR THROAT...
...SAME AS I DID YOUR SWEETHEARTS.
HOPE YOUR BLOOD TASTES AS SWEET.
NO!
NO!
NO!

NOW

THERE YOU ARE! HURT AT ALL, PATCH?

BEEN WORSE.

THANKS FOR ACING THE BROTHERS, DREW.

WHAT'RE YOU TALKING ABOUT?

I DIDN'T DO ANYTHING. I JUST DUG MYSELF OUT OF THE WAREHOUSE.

I THOUGHT YOU NAILED THEM.

NOPE.

SOMEONE MUST HAVE. THERE ISN'T A SIGN OF THEM OR THEIR CADILLAC, AND I DOUBT THEY'D QUIT ON THEIR OWN.

GUESS WE OWE SOMEBODY A FAVOR, THEN. WONDER WHO?

WONDER MORE WHY?

THEN

Uhmmmm

VERY GOOD, BOY.

FIGURED TO TAKE ME WITH YOU, EH?

NICE TRY.

BUT YOU MISSED.

SHAME IT HAD TO END LIKE THIS.

BUT THEN, GIVEN WHO WE ARE...

...WHAT OTHER ENDING COULD THERE BE?

THE JOKE, THOUGH, WAS ON HIM-- BECAUSE I SURVIVED, TOO.

"PRINCESS BAR" IS MY PLACE.

"DARYLS' CADDY PARKED OUT FRONT.

SALOON'S CLOSED FOR THE NIGHT

PLACE SHOULD BE EMPTY. STAFF ALL GONE HOME.

I GO IN HARD.

I NEEDN'T HAVE BOTHERED.

DEAD AND COLD, THE BOTH OF THEM.

WASN'T A GENTLE PASSING, EITHER.

WOUNDS LOOK PAINFULLY FAMILIAR.

THERE'S A BIRTHDAY CARD...

...TO GO WITH THEIR RIBBONS.

SIGNATURE, IN BLOOD, MATCHES THE SLASHES ON THEIR BODIES AND ON MINE.

NOBODY KILLS YOU BUT ME-- ESPECIALLY TODAY!

NOT, BUB...

...IF I GET YOU FIRST!

NEXT-- BE HERE FOR THE **GEHENNA STONE** A SIX-PART **WOLVERINE** EPIC

A WOLVERINE® Gallery

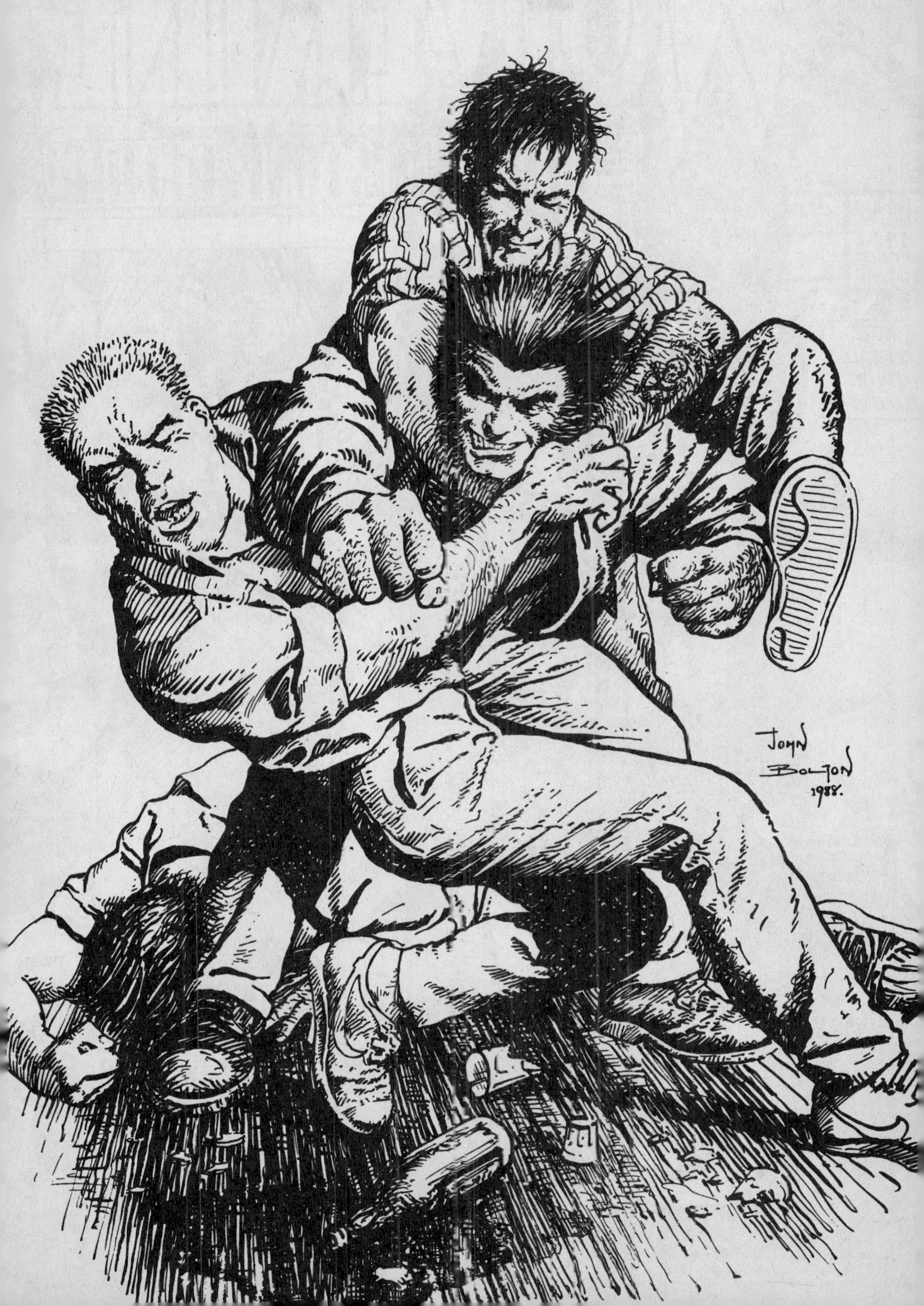
JOHN BOLTON 1988.

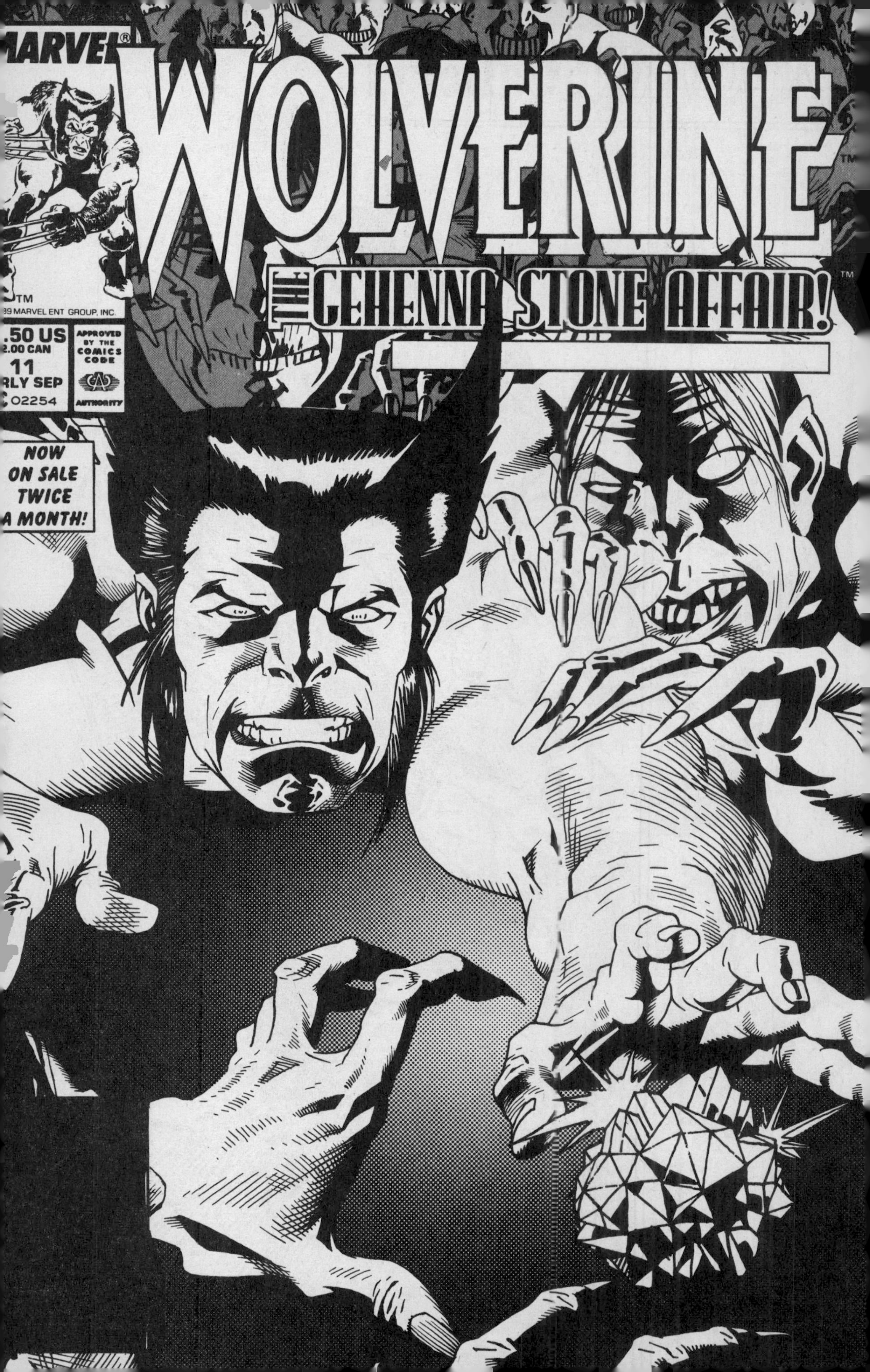
MARVEL®
WOLVERINE™
THE GEHENNA STONE AFFAIR!™
TM
©1989 MARVEL ENT. GROUP, INC.
.50 US
2.00 CAN
11
RLY SEP
C 02254
APPROVED BY THE COMICS CODE AUTHORITY
NOW ON SALE TWICE A MONTH!

"Down to Gehenna or up to the Throne He travels the fastest who travels alone."
-- Kipling

"What do you think of Kipling?"

"I don't know. I've never kippled."
..Old Joke

SAN FRANCISCO
MUSEUM
of
ANTIQUITIES

klip   klip   klip

klip   klip

IS HE GONE JAROCHA?

YEAH, ERNST. HE'S GONE. I TOLD YOU HE'D BE GONE.

AAAHHHH...

COME ON, COME ON, WE HAVEN'T GOT ALL NIGHT.

YOU BETTER HAVE PACKED THE SUCTION CU-- AH. HERE IT IS.

TOLD YOU I DID.

SHHHH.

SHHHH YOURSELF.

SCREEEK

ARE YOU CERTAIN YOU CUT THE RIGHT WIRE DOWN IN THE ALARM BOX?

I TOLD YOU I DID.

RRRRRINNNNNNNNNNNG

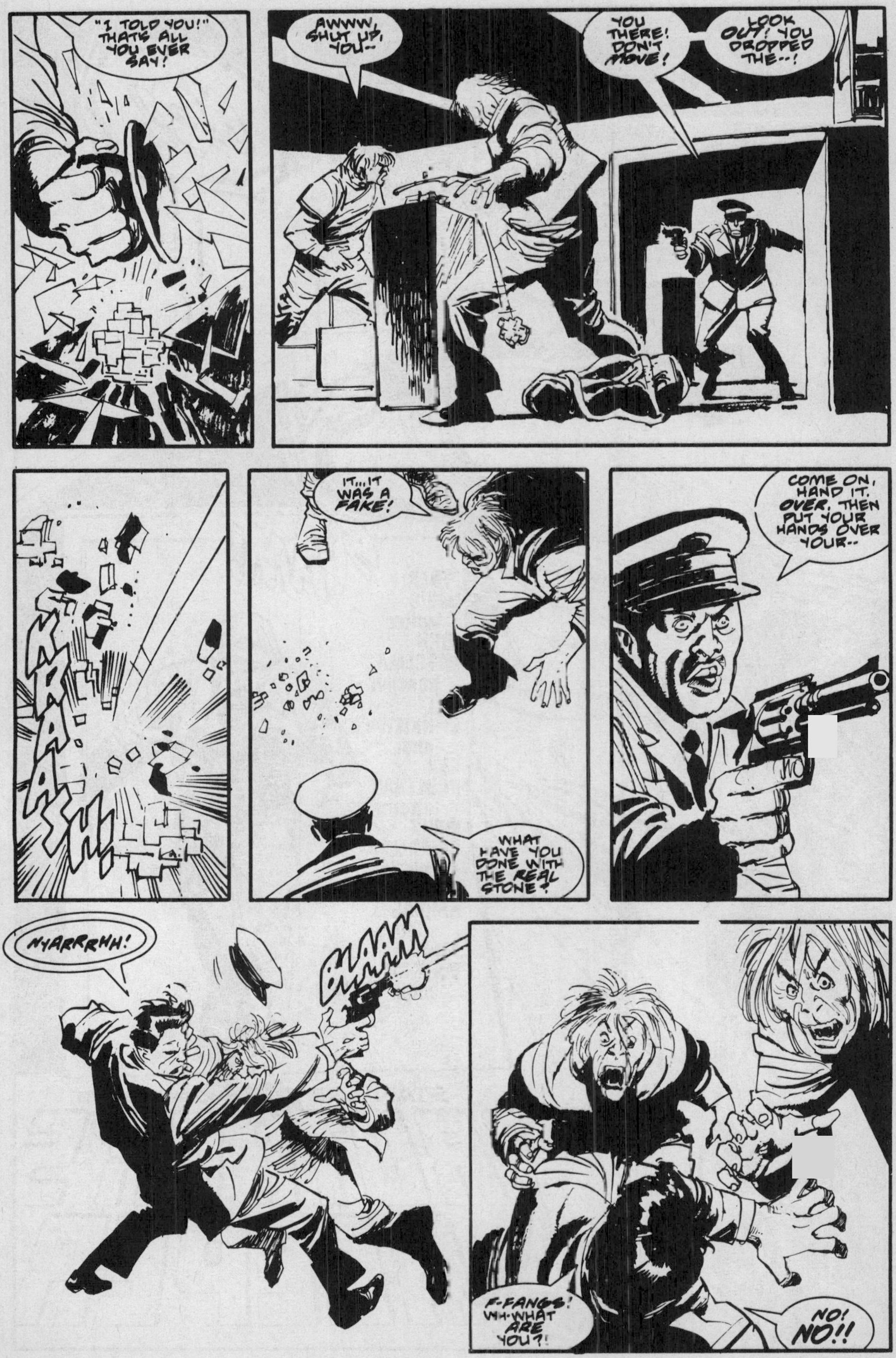
"I TOLD YOU!" THAT'S ALL YOU EVER SAY!
AWWW, SHUT UP, YOU--
YOU THERE! DON'T MOVE!
LOOK OUT! YOU DROPPED THE--!
KRAASH!
IT...IT WAS A FAKE!
WHAT HAVE YOU DONE WITH THE REAL STONE?
COME ON, HAND IT OVER, THEN PUT YOUR HANDS OVER YOUR--
NYARRRHH!
BLAAM
F-FANGS! WH-WHAT ARE YOU?!
NO! NO!!

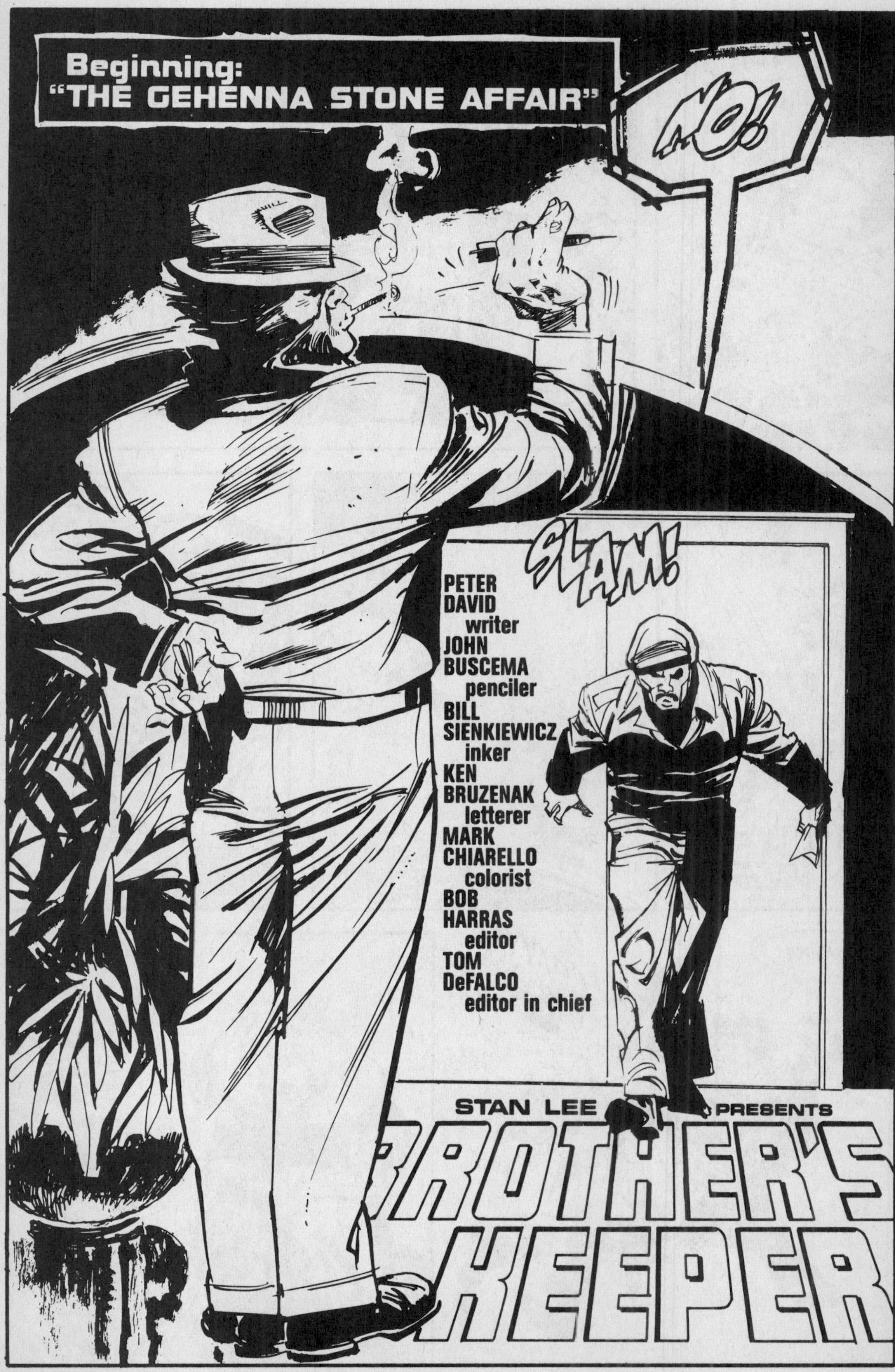
Beginning:
"THE GEHENNA STONE AFFAIR"
NO!
SLAM!
PETER DAVID writer
JOHN BUSCEMA penciler
BILL SIENKIEWICZ inker
KEN BRUZENAK letterer
MARK CHIARELLO colorist
BOB HARRAS editor
TOM DeFALCO editor in chief
STAN LEE PRESENTS
BROTHER'S KEEPER

THE USUAL, TRISH.

YOU DON'T HAVE A USUAL, ARCHIE!

FIND ME ONE.

I'M CALLED WOLVERINE.

OR LOGAN.

OR PATCH.

OR MOTHERLESS SCUM.

PRINCESS BAR.

DEPENDS WHO I'M WITH AND WHETHER WE'RE TRYING TO KILL EACH OTHER.

NOW ARCHIE CORRIGAN, OVER THERE... HE CALLS ME "FRIEND."

IN MADRIPOOR, FRIENDS AREN'T NUMEROUS. I SHOULD SEE WHAT'S BOTHERING HIM.

WHAT DO YOU WANT, PATCH?

THOUGHT IT MIGHT BE MORE WHAT YOU WANT.

FOR INSTANCE, SOMEONE TO CRAB TO.

WHAT WOULD YOU CARE?

MIGHT BE GOOD FOR A LAUGH.

OH, YOU ARE ALL HEART.

OKAY, IT'S MY BROTHER. THEY WANT TO HAVE HIM DECLARED INCOMPETENT, AND I'M THE ONLY ONE WHO CAN STOP THEM...

...AND I'M NOT SURE I WANT TO.

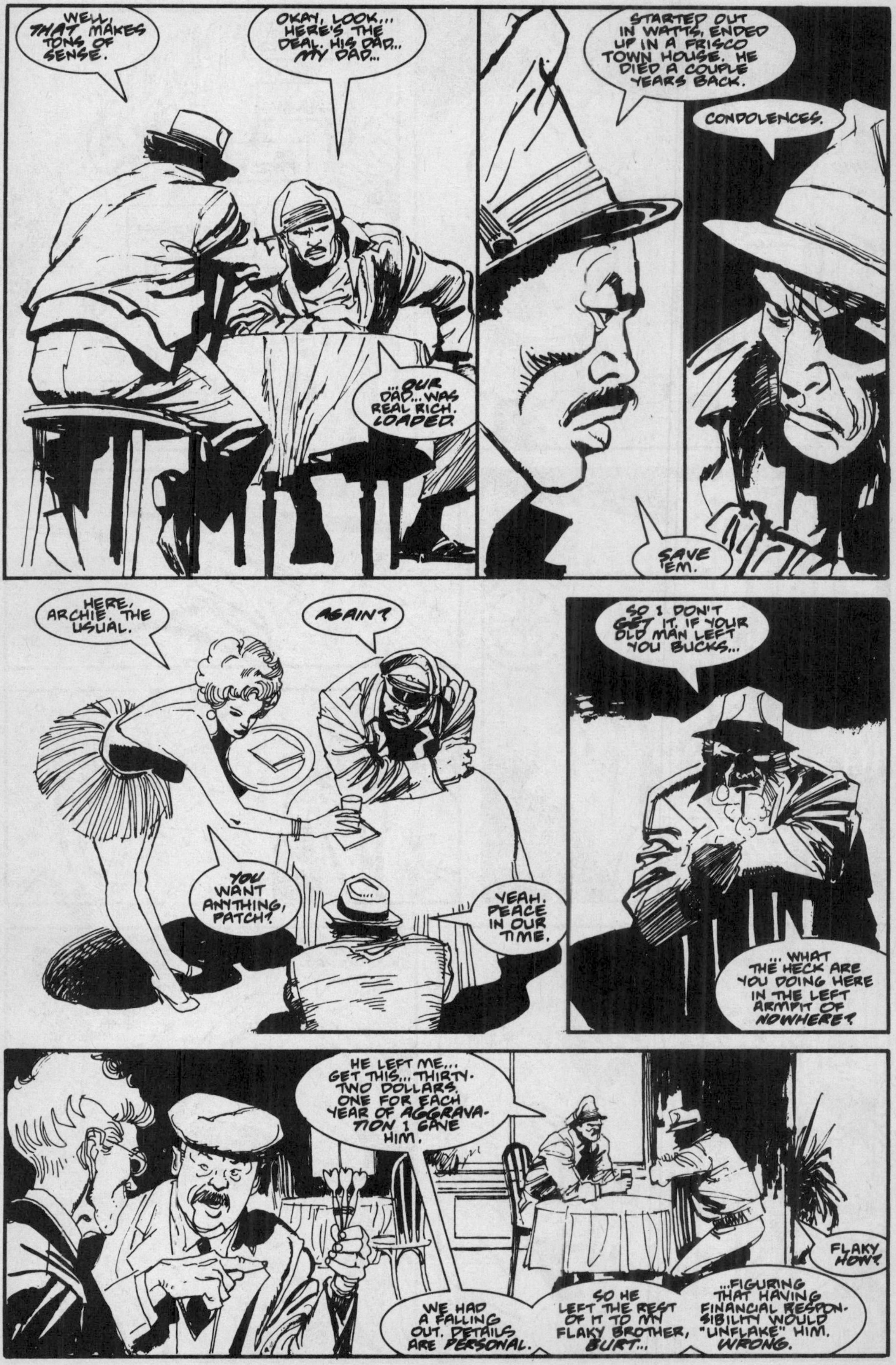
WELL, THAT MAKES TONS OF SENSE.
OKAY, LOOK... HERE'S THE DEAL. HIS DAD... MY DAD...
...OUR DAD... WAS REAL RICH. LOADED.
STARTED OUT IN WATTS, ENDED UP IN A FRISCO TOWN HOUSE. HE DIED A COUPLE YEARS BACK.
CONDOLENCES.
SAVE 'EM.
HERE, ARCHIE. THE USUAL.
AGAIN?
YOU WANT ANYTHING, PATCH?
YEAH. PEACE IN OUR TIME.
SO I DON'T GET IT. IF YOUR OLD MAN LEFT YOU BUCKS...
... WHAT THE HECK ARE YOU DOING HERE IN THE LEFT ARMPIT OF NOWHERE?
HE LEFT ME... GET THIS... THIRTY-TWO DOLLARS. ONE FOR EACH YEAR OF AGGRAVATION I GAVE HIM.
WE HAD A FALLING OUT. DETAILS ARE PERSONAL.
SO HE LEFT THE REST OF IT TO MY FLAKY BROTHER, BURT...
...FIGURING THAT HAVING FINANCIAL RESPONSIBILITY WOULD "UNFLAKE" HIM. WRONG.
FLAKY HOW?

I WANT A *REMATCH!* DOUBLE OR NOTHING.

WE WEREN'T *BETTING.*

TRIPLE THEN.

CAN'T PASS *THAT* UP.

SO HOW'S HE FLAKY?

HE'S A HUGE MOVIE FAN, AND HE CAN'T KEEP *REALITY* STRAIGHT.

shk

HE GETS OBSESSED WITH A *FILM* AND STARTS *LIVING* IT.

shk

HE'S BEEN SAM SPADE, SHERLOCK HOLMES, TARZAN...

shk

...WORST WAS DOROTHY FROM "WIZARD OF OZ."

ANYWAY, MY LATE MOM'S SISTER...RUTHIE...ALSO GOT STIFFED BY MY DAD.

SO NOW SHE'S TRYING TO ESTABLISH CONSERVATORSHIP OVER BURT'S MONEY. ONCE SHE HAS HER HOOKS IN IT...

...ANYWAY, BURT WROTE ME, ASKING FOR HELP. HEARINGS IN LESS THAN A WEEK.

"THIS ENTIRE BUSINESS IS ILL-TIMED, BROTHER. I AM CURRENTLY OCCUPIED WITH A GREAT STRUGGLE AGAINST THE FORCES OF EVIL."

WELL, AT LEAST *SOMEBODY* IS.

IT'S NOT FUNNY, PATCH.

SO WHAT'RE YOU GOING TO *DO*, ARCH?

WHAT ELSE CAN I DO? KNOWING RUTH, SHE MIGHT EVEN TRY TO HAVE HIM COMMITTED. HE'S SCREWY, BUT HE'S NO *DANGER* TO ANYONE. IT'S NOT *FAIR*.

SAY, PATCH... WHY NOT COME *WITH* ME?

'CAUSE IT'S NONE OF MY *FLAMIN'* BUSINESS, THAT'S WHY.

WHY SHOULD I GO TO SAN FRANCISCO? IT'S NOT LIKE I LEFT MY *HEART* THERE.

BUT YOU HAVE A *WAY* WITH PEOPLE.

SO DOES A LOWTOWN STREET-WALKER.

OH, COME ON. WHAT'RE YOU *AFRAID* OF? YOU'LL MISS THE MADRIPOOR TOURIST SEASON?

OOOOOFFF!

KUD

AND STAY *OUTTA* THIS BAR!

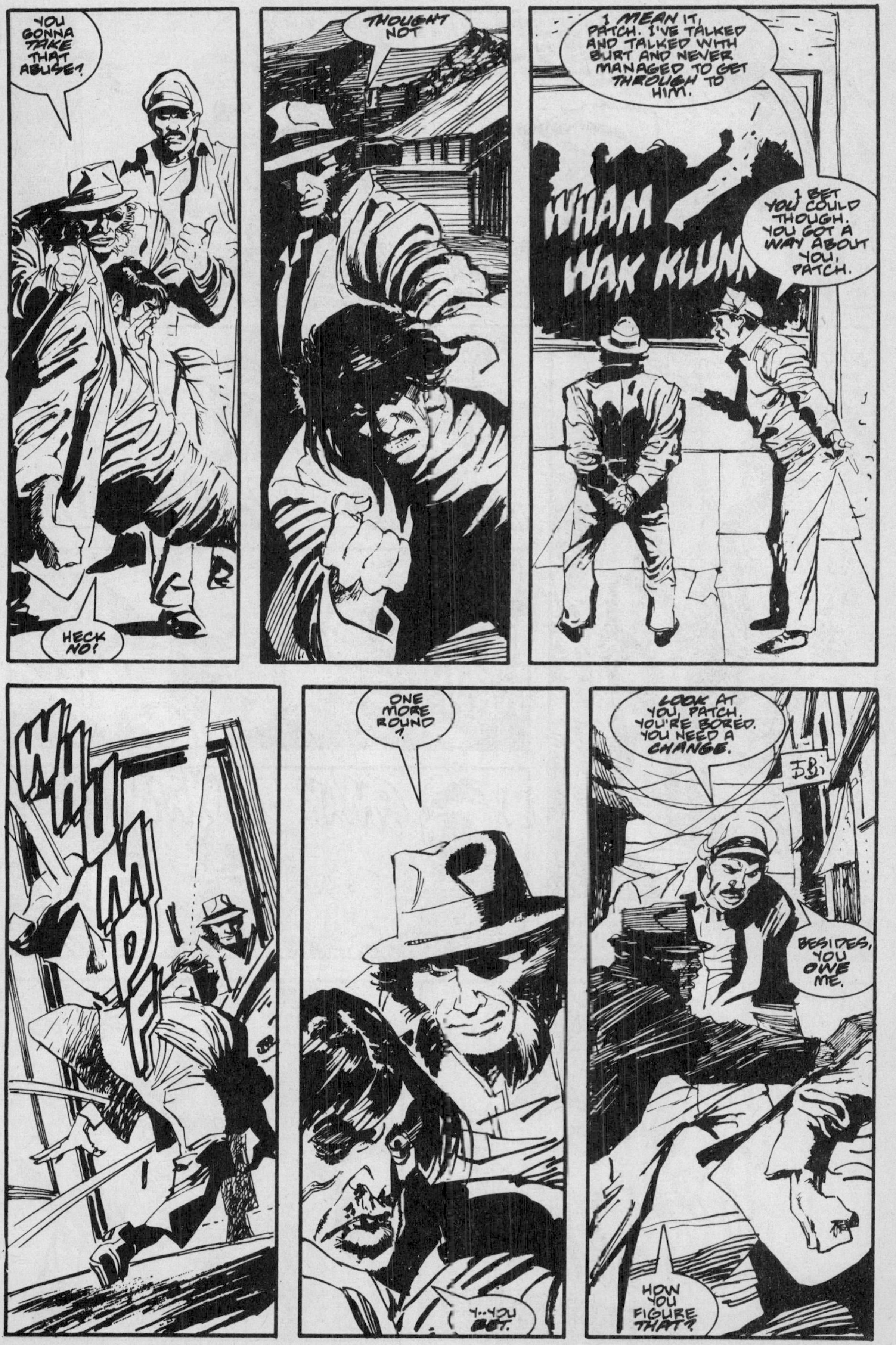
YOU GONNA TAKE THAT ABUSE?
HECK NO!
THOUGHT NOT
I MEAN IT, PATCH. I'VE TALKED AND TALKED WITH BURT AND NEVER MANAGED TO GET THROUGH TO HIM.
WHAM
WAK KLUN
I BET YOU COULD THOUGH. YOU GOT A WAY ABOUT YOU, PATCH.
WHUMPF
ONE MORE ROUND?
Y..YOU BET.
LOOK AT YOU, PATCH. YOU'RE BORED. YOU NEED A CHANGE.
BESIDES, YOU OWE ME.
HOW YOU FIGURE THAT?

WELL, WHEN WE WERE INVOLVED WITH ROUGHHOUSE AND...THAT OTHER GUY...I DIDN'T TRY TO KILL YOU ON THE PLANE, EVEN THOUGH THEY WANTED ME TO.

NOW THAT'S LAME.

I KNOW, BUT ITS ALL I COULD COME UP WITH. PLEASE, PATCH.

I DUNNO. WHAT DO YOU THINK, DREW?

HOW LONG DID YOU KNOW I WAS THERE?

SINCE YOU STARTED FOLLOWING US.

HEY, JESSICA.

HEY, ARCH. SORRY... WHEN I HEARD SAN FRANCISCO MENTIONED, I COULDN'T HELP MYSELF. THAT'S MY OLD STOMPING GROUNDS, AND I'D LOVE TO TAG ALONG. IF PATCH GOES, THAT IS.

TELL YOU WHAT. WE'LL LEAVE IT TO FATE.

GUY FLIES OUT THE DOOR, I STAY. WINDOW, I GO.

WUNK POW KRUNCH!

SMAK WAM

KRAK SHH SHOO

HERE I THOUGHT YOU HAD WHAT IT TOOK.

CONSIDER OUR PARTNERSHIP DISSOLVED.

NOW DON'T WORRY ABOUT A THING. I'VE BEEN DOING THIS LONG ENOUGH, SO I KNOW JUST WHERE TO FLY...

...SO WE CAN AVOID LITTLE THINGS LIKE NORMAL AIRPORTS AND CUSTOMS.

GOOD. THEY ALWAYS LOSE MY LUGGAGE, ANYWAY.

OF COURSE, EVEN IF HE COULDN'T, I GOT MY FAKE PASSPORT. BUT THAT'S NOT WHAT CONCERNS ME.

I SET UP THE WHOLE MADRIPOOR LIFE AND RATIONALIZED THAT IT WAS A WAY TO GIVE ME SOME TIME OFF FROM THE X-MEN. SOME DISTANCE.

BUT NOW I'M STARTING TO GET INVOLVED WITH THE PEOPLE I'M MEETING HERE.

THE X-MEN ARE MY FAMILY, AND I WAS NEVER EVEN REALLY SURE IF I NEEDED ONE. I SURE DON'T NEED TWO.

SOONER OR LATER, I MIGHT HAVE TO MAKE A CHOICE...

...AND I'M NOT SURE WHICH WAY IT'LL FALL.

MR. CORRIGAN! HOW PLEASANT!

HI, JAKES! WHERE'S BURT?

THE STUDY, SIR. AS ALWAYS.

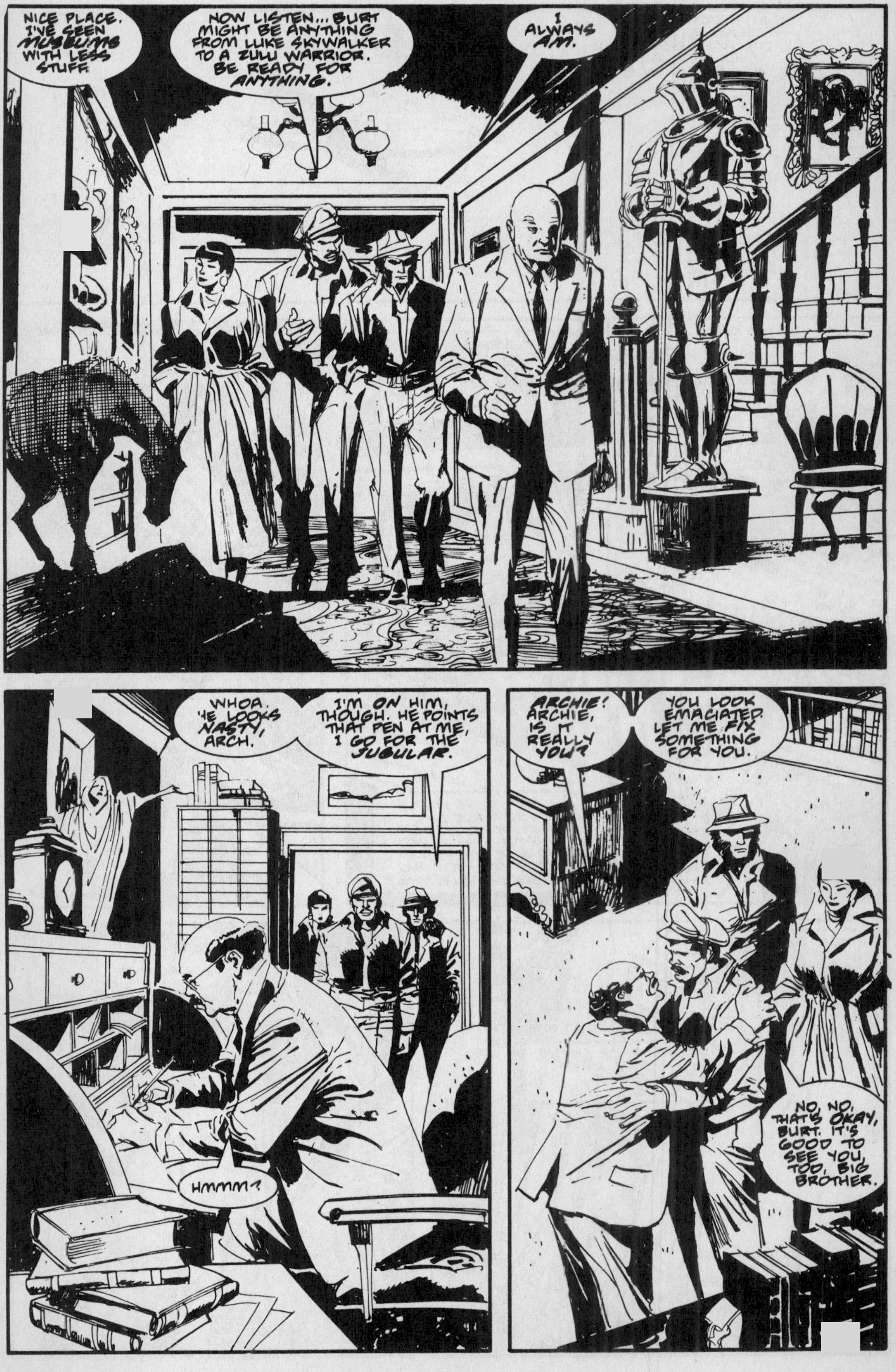
NICE PLACE. I'VE SEEN MUSEUMS WITH LESS STUFF.
NOW LISTEN... BURT MIGHT BE ANYTHING FROM LUKE SKYWALKER TO A ZULU WARRIOR. BE READY FOR ANYTHING.
I ALWAYS AM.
WHOA. HE LOOKS NASTY, ARCH.
I'M ON HIM, THOUGH. HE POINTS THAT PEN AT ME, I GO FOR THE JUGULAR.
HMMM?
ARCHIE! ARCHIE, IS IT REALLY YOU?
YOU LOOK EMACIATED. LET ME FIX SOMETHING FOR YOU.
NO, NO, THAT'S OKAY, BURT. IT'S GOOD TO SEE YOU, TOO, BIG BROTHER.

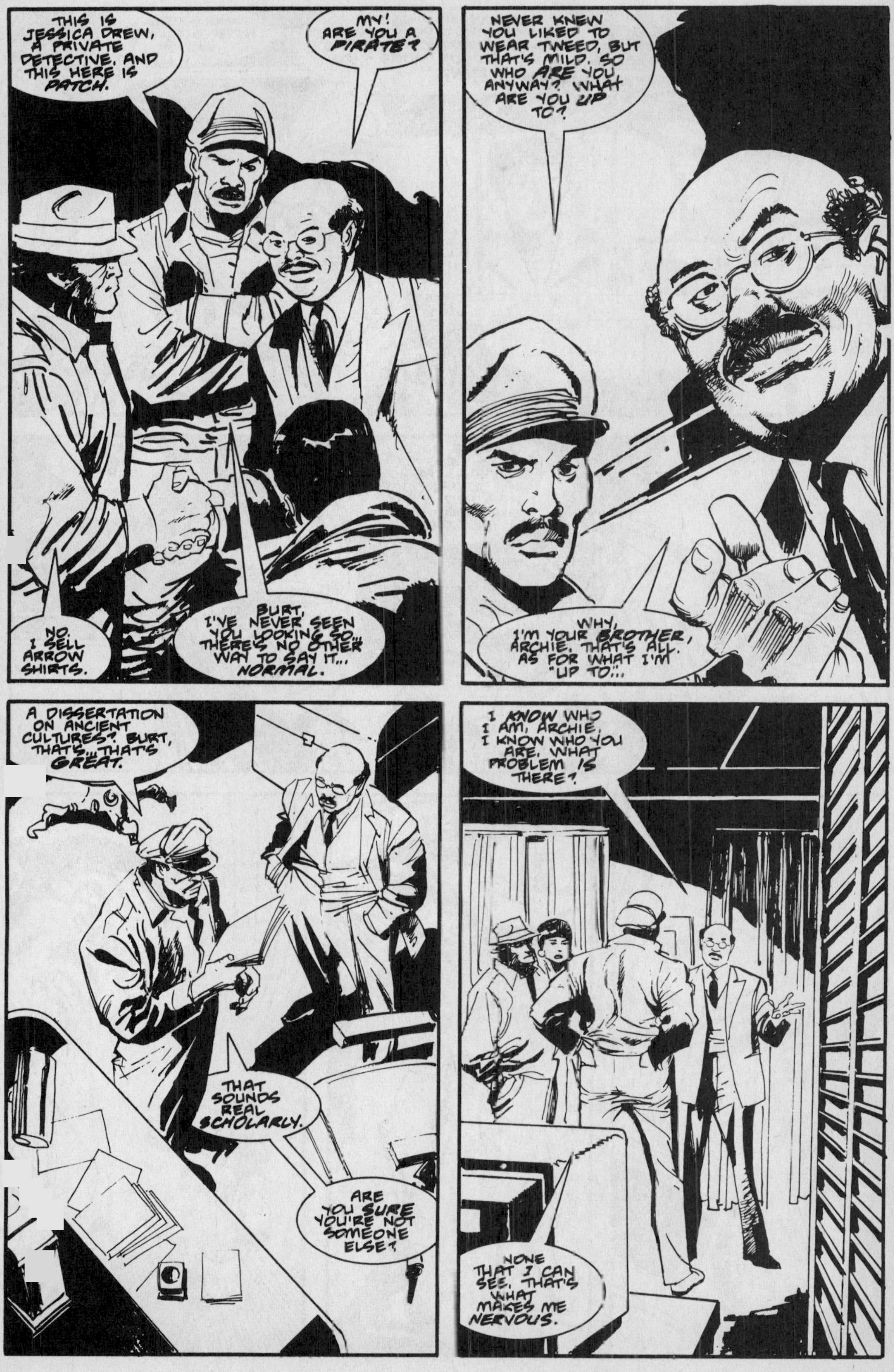
THIS IS JESSICA DREW, A PRIVATE DETECTIVE. AND THIS HERE IS PATCH.
MY! ARE YOU A PIRATE?
NO. I SELL ARROW SHIRTS.
BURT, I'VE NEVER SEEN YOU LOOKING SO... THERE'S NO OTHER WAY TO SAY IT... NORMAL.
NEVER KNEW YOU LIKED TO WEAR TWEED, BUT THAT'S MILD. SO WHO ARE YOU ANYWAY? WHAT ARE YOU UP TO?
WHY, I'M YOUR BROTHER, ARCHIE. THAT'S ALL. AS FOR WHAT I'M "UP TO"...
A DISSERTATION ON ANCIENT CULTURES? BURT, THAT'S... THAT'S GREAT.
THAT SOUNDS REAL SCHOLARLY.
ARE YOU SURE YOU'RE NOT SOMEONE ELSE?
I KNOW WHO I AM, ARCHIE. I KNOW WHO YOU ARE. WHAT PROBLEM IS THERE?
NONE THAT I CAN SEE. THAT'S WHAT MAKES ME NERVOUS.

LATER...

HE SEEMS PRETTY NORMAL TO ME.

I KNOW, AND HE PROMISED HE'D BE AT THE HEARING TOMORROW MORNING. CAN'T ASK FOR MORE THAN *THAT.*

WELL, THE HOTEL'S ON ME, GUNS.

I STILL THINK WE SHOULD'VE STAYED WITH HIM. MADE SURE THAT--

JAKES WILL SEE HE GETS TO THE HEARING. BESIDES, THAT TOWN HOUSE HAS TOO MANY UNPLEASANT MEMORIES.

TRUST ME ON THIS.

AND... I'M GLAD I HAD THE CAB DROP ME OFF HERE AT MY OFFICE. IT'S BEEN AGES SINCE I TOUCHED BASE.

I SHOULD REALLY DECIDE WHETHER TO RE-OPEN PERMANENTLY OR JUST CLOSE UP AND MOVE TO MADRIPOOR FOR GOOD.

THE PRINCE'S SUPPORT HAS BEEN VERY LUCRATIVE, AND THE PRINCE HIMSELF HAS BEEN...

...WELL, BETTER NOT GO OFF ON THAT TANGENT.

"DEAR MS. DREW, YOU ARE A MONTH BEHIND ON RENT, IF YOU DO NOT..."

KILL MAH LANDLORD. KILL MAH LANDLORD.

EXCUSE ME, MISS DREW? MY NAME IS TUTTLE. I'M CURATOR FOR THE MUSEUM OF ANTIQUITIES?

WE HAVE A PROBLEM.

WELL YOUR TIMING IS EXCELLENT, MR. TUTTLE, BUT I'M NOT SURE HOW LONG I'LL BE IN TOWN.

IF YOU COULD SPARE THE TIME, WE'VE HAD A MAJOR SCANDAL.

BEST KIND.

SEVERAL DAYS AGO, INTRUDERS BROKE IN AND TRIED TO STEAL A PARTICULAR, VERY VALUABLE DIAMOND. BUT ALL THEY GOT WAS A PASTEBOARD REPLICA, WHICH BROKE.

YOU HAD A FAKE WAITING FOR THEM? SHARP.

BUT WE DIDN'T KNOW IT! SOMEONE ELSE SUBSTITUTED A FAKE DIAMOND FOR OUR REAL ONE, WITHOUT OUR KNOWLEDGE!

NOT ONLY THAT, BUT THE GUARD, WHO STUMBLED UPON THE INTRUDERS *SWEARS* THEY WERE...

...*VAMPIRES.* I...I KNOW IT SOUNDS INSANE, BUT--

YOU'D BE *AMAZED* WHAT DOESN'T SOUND INSANE TO ME, MR TUTTLE, BUT VAMPIRES WOULDN'T LEAVE YOUR GUARD ALIVE.

WELL, THEY ATTACKED HIM AND HE FAINTED, WHEN HE WAS FOUND, SURE ENOUGH, THERE WERE WOUNDS ON HIS NECK...

...AND THERE WAS BLOOD ALL OVER, BUT HE HADN'T BEEN DRAINED, LIKE YOU READ IN STORIES.

MISS DREW, WILL YOU HELP ME LOCATE THE DIAMOND? I'LL GIVE YOU ALL THE PHOTOS YOU NEED OF IT, AND OUT OF MY OWN *POCKET,* IF NECESSARY.

LOOK, I'LL DO SOME POKING AROUND.

BUT SAVE YOUR MONEY UNTIL I GET A CLEARER IDEA OF WHAT'S *HAPPENING,* OKAY?

THANK YOU, I'LL BE IN TOUCH.

WHAT A HEALTHY YOUNG WOMAN.

DREW DIDN'T STUMBLE IN UNTIL LATE LAST NIGHT. MUTTERED SOMETHING ABOUT A CASE, AND, WHEN WE LEFT FOR THE COURTHOUSE THIS MORNING, WAS STILL SNORING.

TIME CHANGE FROM MADRIPOOR MIGHT BE THROWING HER, TOO. DOESN'T BOTHER ME, OF COURSE, WITH MY CONSTITUTION...

AND A VETERAN PILOT LIKE ARCHIE RESETS HIS INTERNAL CLOCK WITH NO SWEAT.

HE'S SWEATING NOW, THOUGH. I CAN SMELL IT.

AND IT'S PRETTY OBVIOUS WHY.

IT'S GOING ON 10:15, MR. SCHOENFELD, AND COURT WAS CONVENED AT TEN.

THIS IS NOT THE WAY I LIKE TO START OFF MY DAY, AND IT CERTAINLY ISN'T THE WAY YOUR CLIENT WANTS TO START OFF A HEARING ON HIS COMPETENCY.

WHERE IS BURT CORRIGAN, MR. SCHOENFELD?

YOU SHOULD HAVE BEEN THERE *WITH* HIM, CORRIGAN.

HE'S A *GROWN MAN.* I'M *NOT GONNA* HOLD HIS HAND.

SAID JAKES WHEN HE GOT UP THIS MORNING, BURT WAS *GONE.* WHAT DO YOU WANT FROM *ME?*

ADMIT IT, ARCHIE! NOT ONLY IS BURT UNDEPENDABLE, HE'S *CRAZY!* HE SHOULDN'T JUST BE JUDGED INCOMPETENT, HE SHOULD BE PUT *AWAY!*

COUNSELOR, *PLEASE,* INSTRUCT YOUR CLIENT TO--

OH, YOU'D *LIKE* THAT, WOULDN'T YOU, RUTH! JUST SO YOU COULD GET YOUR CLAWS INTO HIS INHERITANCE!

WELL, BEING *LATE* ISN'T A FEDERAL OFFENSE, AND I'M TELLING YOU HE'LL *BE* HERE!

KA'KLOP

KA'KLOP

KA'KLOP

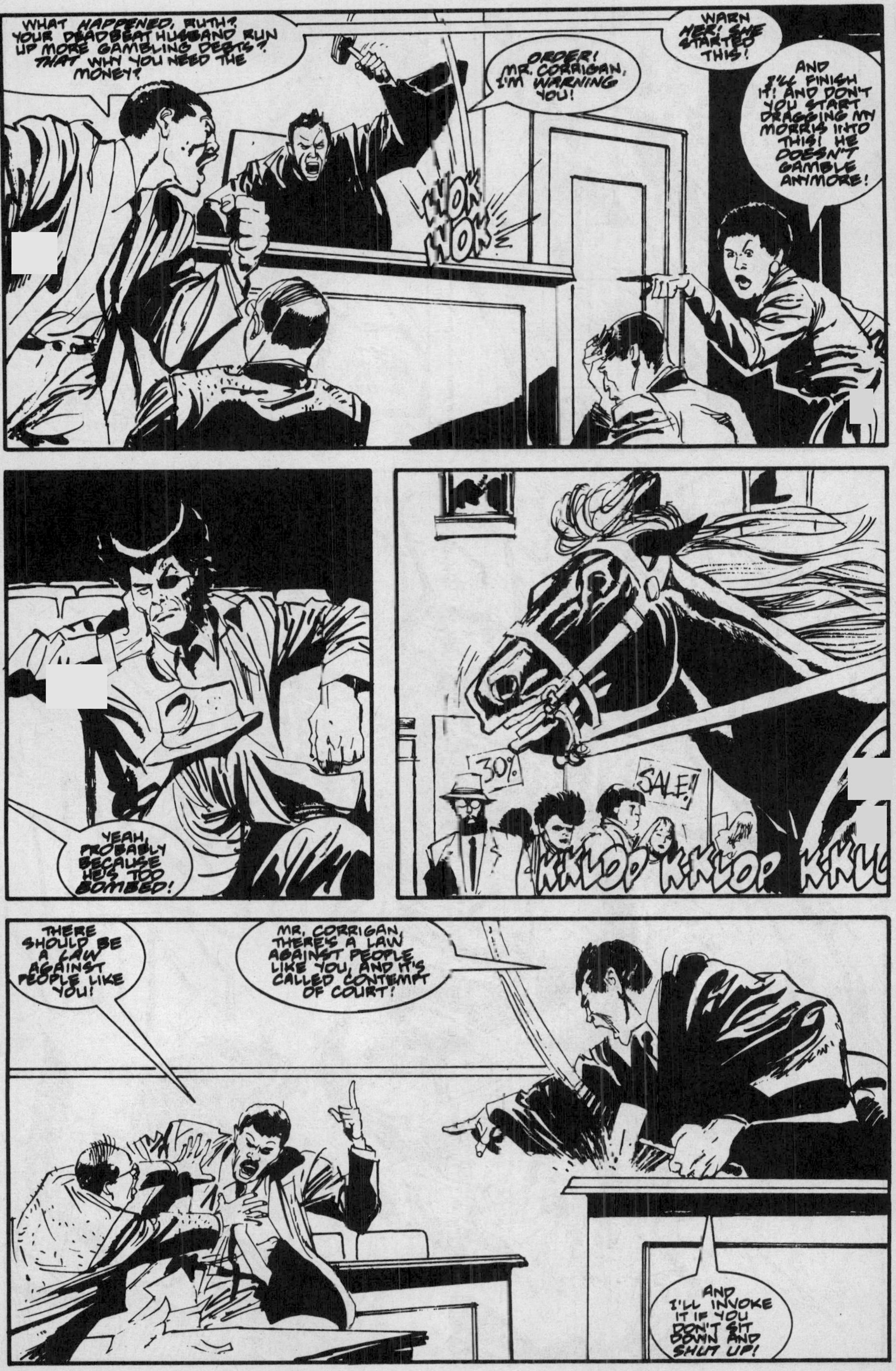
WHAT HAPPENED, RUTH? YOUR DEADBEAT HUSBAND RUN UP MORE GAMBLING DEBTS? THAT WHY YOU NEED THE MONEY?
ORDER! MR. CORRIGAN, I'M WARNING YOU!
WHOK WHOK
WARN HER! SHE STARTED THIS!
AND I'LL FINISH IT! AND DON'T YOU START DRAGGING MY MORRIS INTO THIS! HE DOESN'T GAMBLE ANYMORE!
YEAH, PROBABLY BECAUSE HE'S TOO BOMBED!
30%
SALE!!
K-KLOP K-KLOP K-KLO
THERE SHOULD BE A LAW AGAINST PEOPLE LIKE YOU!
MR. CORRIGAN, THERE'S A LAW AGAINST PEOPLE LIKE YOU, AND IT'S CALLED CONTEMPT OF COURT!
AND I'LL INVOKE IT IF YOU DON'T SIT DOWN AND SHUT UP!

THEY'RE ALL SHOUTING SO MUCH THEY DON'T HEAR IT.

BUT I DO. HEAR IT. SMELL IT. SENSE IT.

COMING THIS WAY, FAST.

GET DOWN! EVERYBODY!

SIR! GET BACK IN YOUR SEAT THIS INST—

AW NO! IT CAN'T BE!

HE THINKS HE'S HARRISON FORD!

BURT, WHERE IN THE BLUE BLAZES DID YOU GET A HORSE?!

I DON'T KNOW, I'M MAKING THIS UP AS I GO!

MR. CORRIGAN, I NEVER THOUGHT I'D SAY THIS IN A COURT-ROOM, BUT GET OFF THAT HORSE!

YOU DON'T UNDERSTAND! THERE'S EVIL IN THE WORLD! THE FORCES OF BA'AL WANT TO CREATE A NEW RACE OF UNDEAD, AND I HAVE TO STOP THEM!

ARCHIE! GET OVER HERE! THERE'S A--

NOT NOW, PATCH!

BURT, THIS IS IT. I CAN'T BELIEVE I WAS ARGUING ON YOUR BEHALF A MINUTE AGO.

IT WAS BAD ENOUGH WHEN YOU WERE HOLMES AND YOU SAID MORIARTY WAS AFTER YOU WITH AIR GUNS BUT THIS... THIS! YOU NEED HELP!

RIGHT! HELP AGAINST THE--

BURT, THERE'S NO FORCES OF EVIL! GOT THAT? NONE!

NEXT: STRAITS OF SAN FRANCISCO IN TWO WEEKS

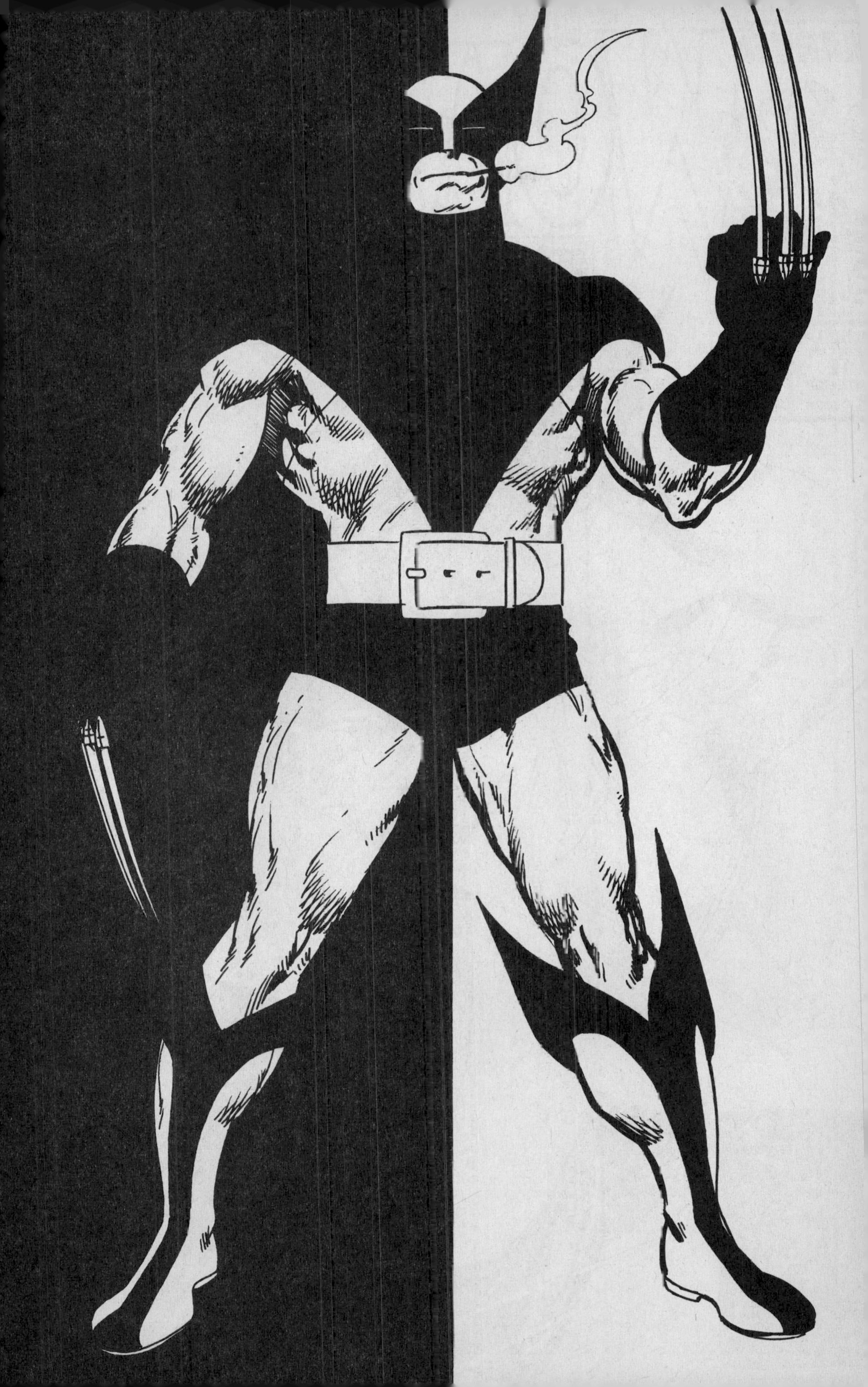

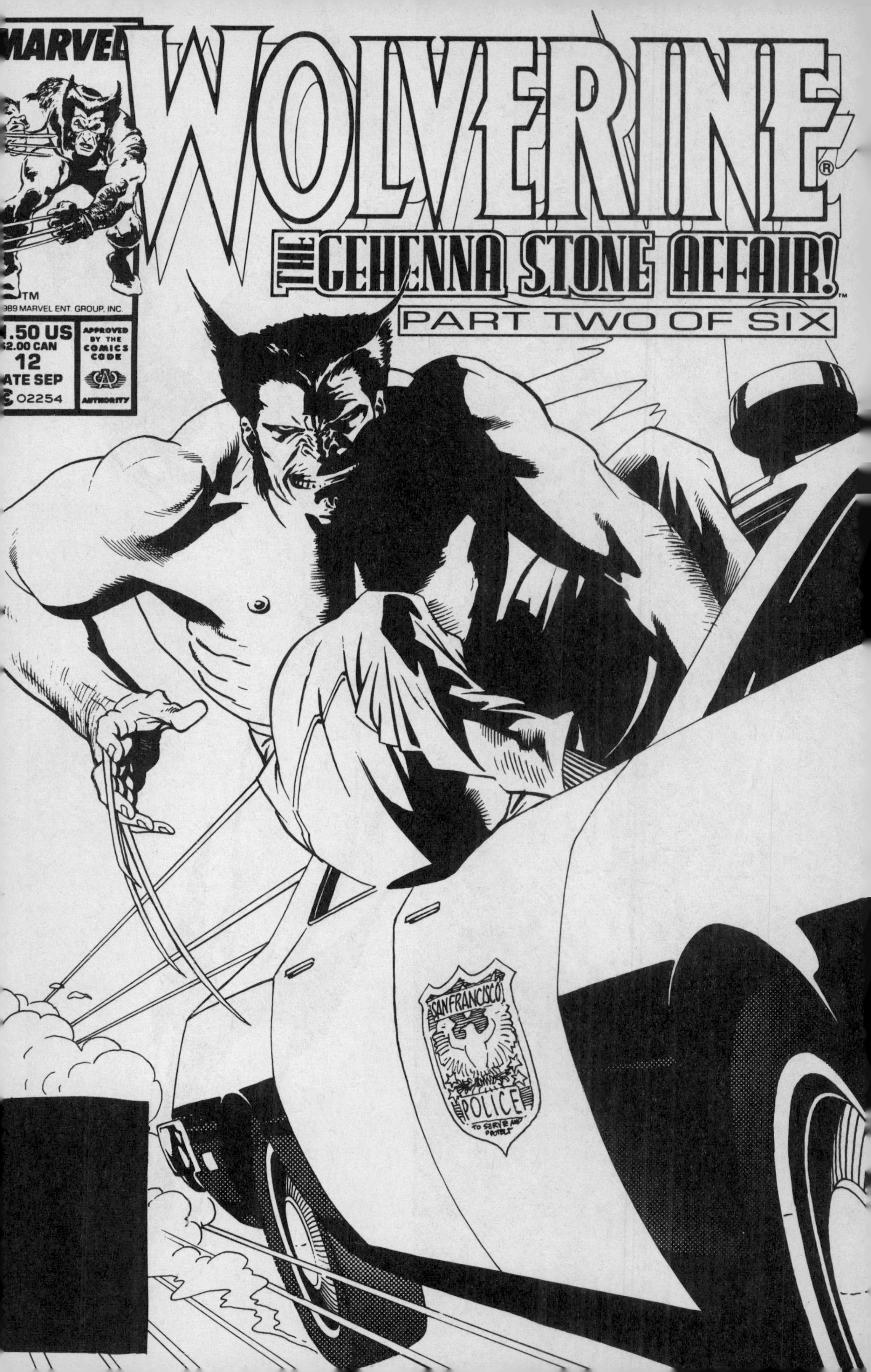
MARVEL
WOLVERINE®
THE GEHENNA STONE AFFAIR!™
PART TWO OF SIX
TM
1989 MARVEL ENT. GROUP, INC.
.50 US
$2.00 CAN
12
ATE SEP
C 02254
APPROVED BY THE COMICS CODE AUTHORITY
SAN FRANCISCO
POLICE

K-WHAM
KRASH
THUD
WUMPF

WOAK
BCHOW

PLEASE, DEAR LORD... ...LET ME LIVE TO RETIREMENT.

THE PHONE! LET THEM NOT HAVE CUT THE LINES!

HELLO! THIS IS JUDGE FENSTER AT THE COURT HOUSE!

GET YOUR PEOPLE OVER HERE!

YOUR HONOR, I CAN BARELY UNDERSTAND YOU. SLOW DOWN. WHAT'S WRONG.

WRONG? WHAT'S WRONG IS, WE WERE HAVING A NICE, SIMPLE SANITY HEARING...

...WHEN THE DEFENDANT SMASHED THROUGH MY WINDOW, RIDING A HORSE, DRESSED LIKE HARRISON FORD...

...PURSUED BY A HORDE OF VAMPIRES!

UH HUH.

SO, TELL ME, "JUDGE"...

...WHY WAS THE HORSE DRESSED LIKE HARRISON FORD?

GET YOUR BUTTS OVER HERE!

SCRIPT
PETER
DAVID

PENCILS
JOHN
BUSCEMA

INKS
BILL
SIENKIEWICZ

LETTERS
KEN
BRUZENAK

COLORS
GLYNIS
OLIVER

EDITOR
BOB
HARRAS

CHIEF
TOM
DeFALCO

THERE'S ONE SNEAKING UP BEHIND ME. THINKS I DON'T SEE HIM.

I DON'T. BUT I SMELL HIM A MILE OFF.

BROKE HIS FANGS? WELL, NO GREAT SURPRISE.

REAL VAMPIRES DON'T WALTZ AROUND IN BROAD DAYLIGHT. BUT WHY THE MASQUERADE?

I BEEN KEEPING MY CLAWS UNDER WRAPS, SINCE CLAWS EQUAL WOLVERINE, AND WOLVERINE IS SUPPOSEDLY DEAD.

BUT IF I DON'T STOP PUSSYFOOTING AROUND, WE'LL WIND UP WITH GENUINE DEAD PEOPLE.

LIKE MAYBE ARCHIE, HIS BROTHER BURT, JESSICA...

OH, RIGHT. JESSICA DREW ISN'T HERE. ONE LESS TO WORRY ABOUT.

DOWN THIS HALL, TO THE RIGHT, RIGHT AGAIN, AND THEN I'M--

W-THUMP!

--THERE?

HOLY JEEZ! THAT'S SOME WILD SANITY HEARING.

THERE'S ANOTHER ONE! GET HER!!

URRKKH! BURT!

I'M GONNA GET YOU FOR THIS!

HELP!

PATCH!!

WHEN I'M IN MADRIPOOR, I GO BY "PATCH."

AND WHEN I'M FLYING TO AND FROM MADRIPOOR, I GO BY ARCHIE CORRIGAN, THE BEST PILOT I'VE EVER KNOWN.

AND GOOD HELP IS SO HARD TO FIND.

LUCKILY FOR ARCHIE, HE FOUND THE BEST.

HIS BROTHER BURT IS IN TROUBLE, TOO. BUT EVEN I CAN'T BE EVERYWHERE.

THIS WAS SUPPOSED TO BE SIMPLE. ARCHIE WANTED ME ALONG FOR HIS BROTHER'S SANITY HEARING. AND I, LIKE A DOPE, AGREED TO IT.

SANITY HEARING IS RIGHT.

THIS WHOLE THING IS INSANE.

THEN AGAIN, I'M THE ONE WITH THE CLAWS AND THE ADAMANTIUM-LACED SKELETON AND THE HEALING FACTOR...

...SO WHAT DO I KNOW ABOUT SANITY?

YOU! ON THE HORSE!

HOLD IT!

WHAMM!

I SAID HOLD IT!

BURT! IT IS YOU!

MARION!

JESSICA! JESSICA DREW! WE MET YESTERDAY.

OH, RIGHT.

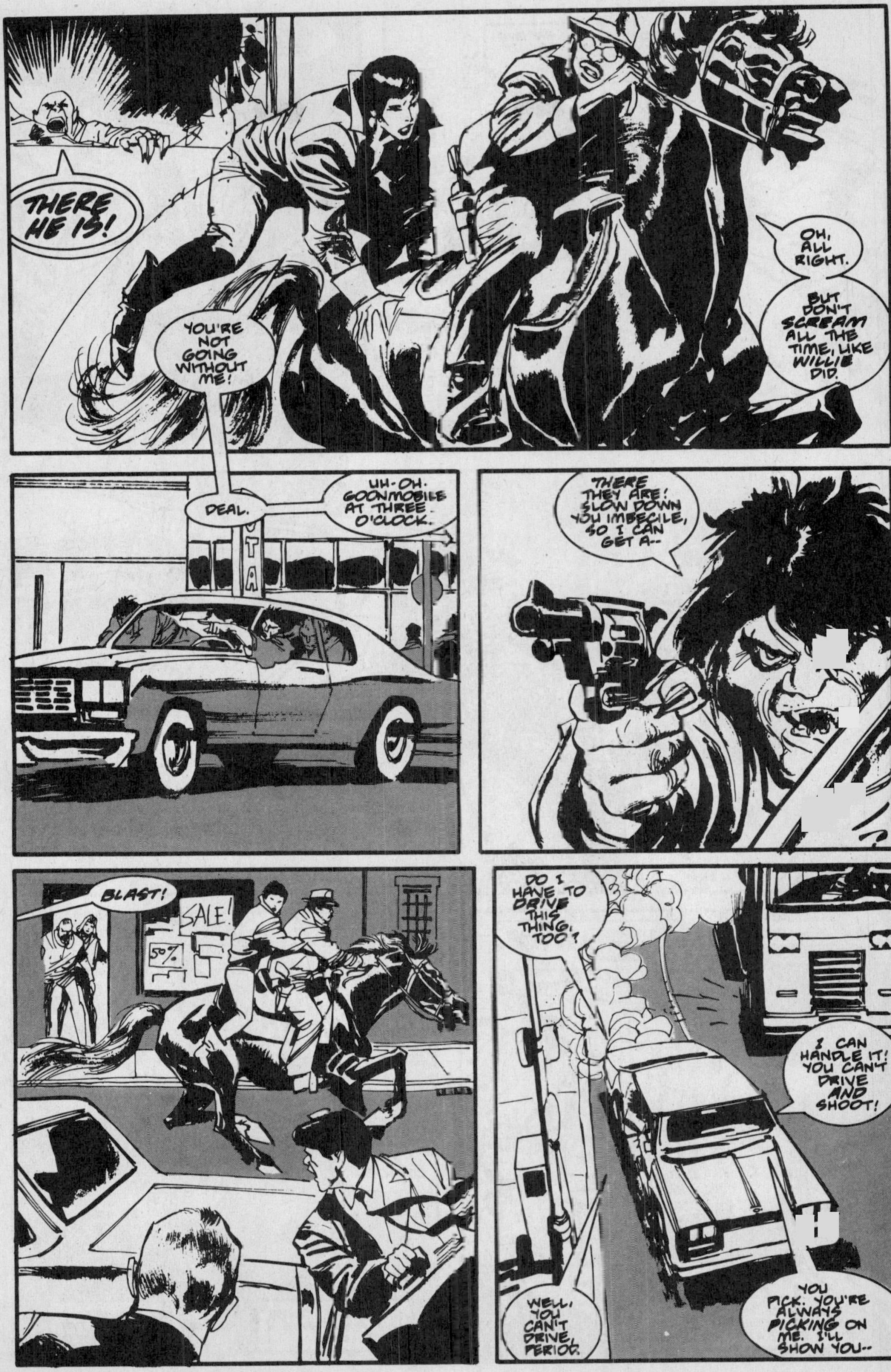
THERE HE IS!
YOU'RE NOT GOING WITHOUT ME!
OH, ALL RIGHT.
BUT DON'T SCREAM ALL THE TIME, LIKE WILLIE DID.
DEAL.
UH-OH. GOONMOBILE AT THREE O'CLOCK.
THERE THEY ARE! SLOW DOWN YOU IMBECILE, SO I CAN GET A--
BLAST!
SALE!
50%
DO I HAVE TO DRIVE THIS THING, TOO?
I CAN HANDLE IT! YOU CAN'T DRIVE AND SHOOT!
WELL, YOU CAN'T DRIVE, PERIOD.
YOU PICK. YOU'RE ALWAYS PICKING ON ME. I'LL SHOW YOU--

UH OH, SIRENS. WE'RE ABOUT TO HAVE COMPANY.

THE KIND I DON'T WANT TO HAVE TO GIVE LONG EXPLANATIONS TO.

C'MON! COURT'S ADJOURNED.

PERFECT.

THEY ONLY LEFT ONE MAN TO COVER THE WINDOW.

NOT THAT IF THEY'D LEFT MORE, IT WOULD'VE MADE MUCH DIFFERENCE.

OH, OFFICER...

ONE MAN. TAKES ONE-POINT-FIVE SECONDS.

NO DOUBT ABOUT IT, I'M GETTING OLD.

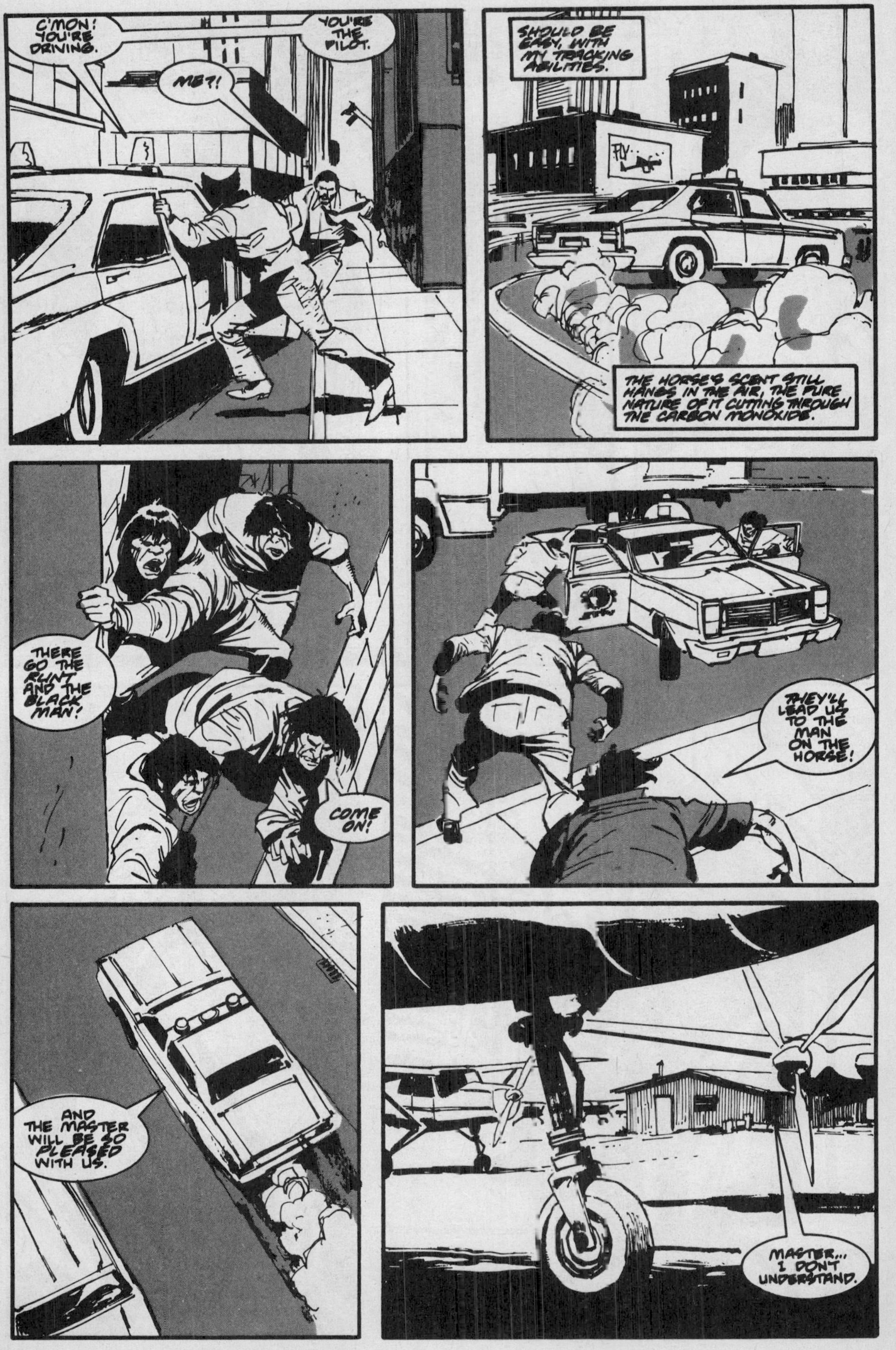
C'MON! YOU'RE DRIVING.
ME?!
YOU'RE THE PILOT.
SHOULD BE EASY, WITH MY TRACKING ABILITIES.
THE HORSE'S SCENT STILL HANGS IN THE AIR, THE PURE NATURE OF IT CUTTING THROUGH THE CARBON MONOXIDE.
THERE GO THE RUNT AND THE BLACK MAN!
COME ON!
THEY'LL LEAD US TO THE MAN ON THE HORSE!
AND THE MASTER WILL BE SO PLEASED WITH US.
MASTER... I DON'T UNDERSTAND.

WHY ARE WE HIDING HERE?

WHEN WE COULD BE OUT PURSUING THE POSSESSOR OF THE STONE FRAGMENT?

NOT...NOT THAT I'M DOUBTING YOU, YOU UNDERSTAND. BUT...

BECAUSE, LITTLE ONE, IT IS THE JOB OF MY MINIONS TO PURSUE...

...AND DRIVE THE ONES WE SEEK TO ME.

AND THEY SHALL, I HAVE FORESEEN IT...

...IN THE GEHENNA STONE.

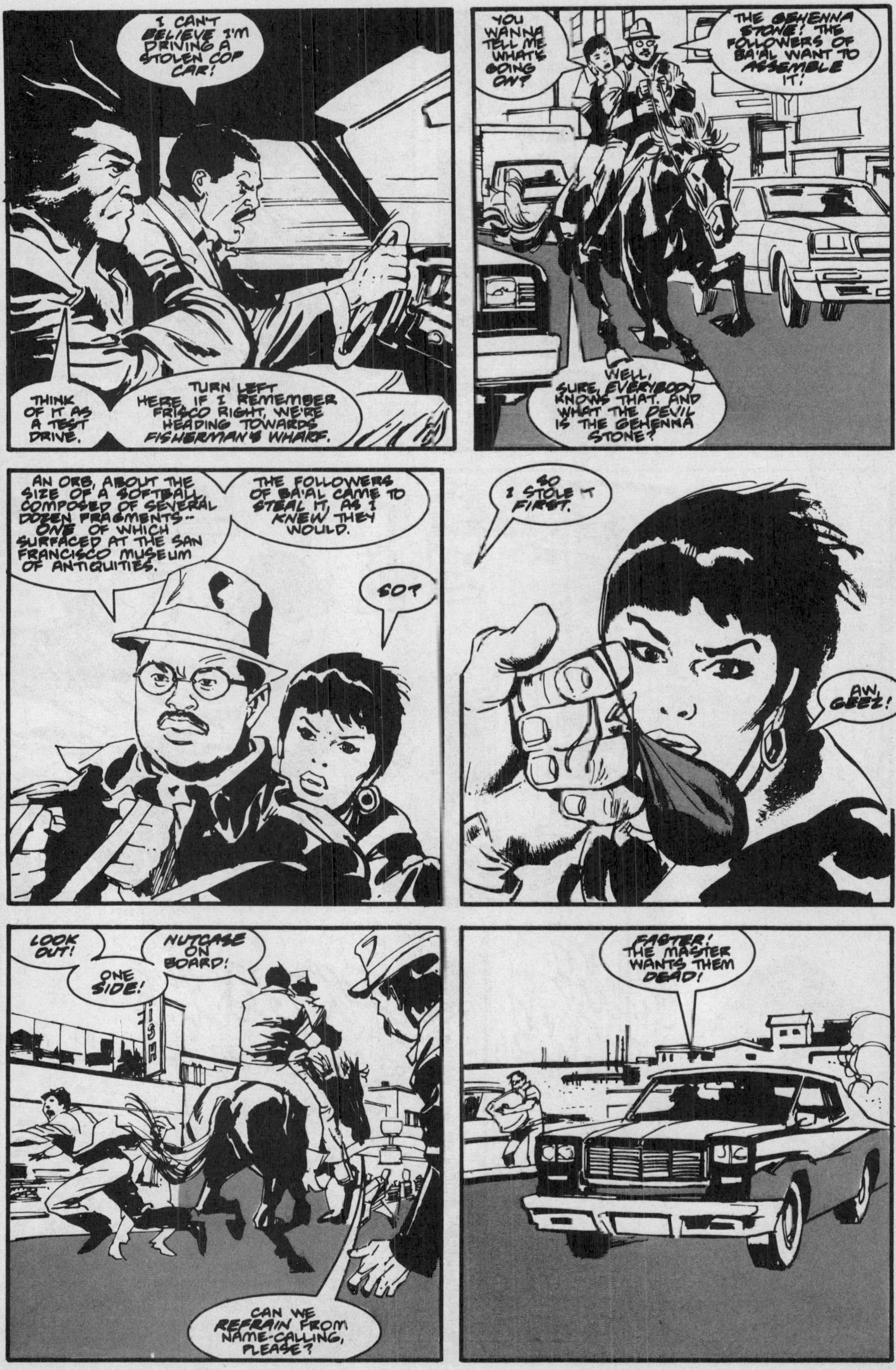

I CAN'T BELIEVE I'M DRIVING A STOLEN COP CAR!
THINK OF IT AS A TEST DRIVE.
TURN LEFT HERE, IF I REMEMBER FRISCO RIGHT, WE'RE HEADING TOWARDS FISHERMAN'S WHARF.
YOU WANNA TELL ME WHAT'S GOING ON?
THE GEHENNA STONE! THE FOLLOWERS OF BA'AL WANT TO ASSEMBLE IT!
WELL, SURE, EVERYBODY KNOWS THAT. AND WHAT THE DEVIL IS THE GEHENNA STONE?
AN ORB, ABOUT THE SIZE OF A SOFTBALL, COMPOSED OF SEVERAL DOZEN FRAGMENTS-- ONE OF WHICH SURFACED AT THE SAN FRANCISCO MUSEUM OF ANTIQUITIES.
THE FOLLOWERS OF BA'AL CAME TO STEAL IT, AS I KNEW THEY WOULD.
SO?
SO I STOLE IT FIRST.
AW, GEEZ!
LOOK OUT!
ONE SIDE!
NUTCASE ON BOARD!
CAN WE REFRAIN FROM NAME-CALLING, PLEASE?
FASTER! THE MASTER WANTS THEM DEAD!

THERE THEY ARE! AND THE VAMPIRES ARE RIGHT *BEHIND* THEM!

I GOT EYES...

...EYE...

SKIP IT. JUST *STEP* ON IT.

PERSISTENT, AREN'T THEY?

THE *NAZIS* WERE PERSISTENT, TOO.

YEAH? AND HOW DID YOU BEAT THE NAZIS?

WELL, ACTUALLY, THROUGH *DIVINE* INTERVENTION.

WELL, THE LORD HELPS *THOSE* WHO HELP THEMSELVES.

BAM! BAM!

BAM! BAM!

P-KRASH!

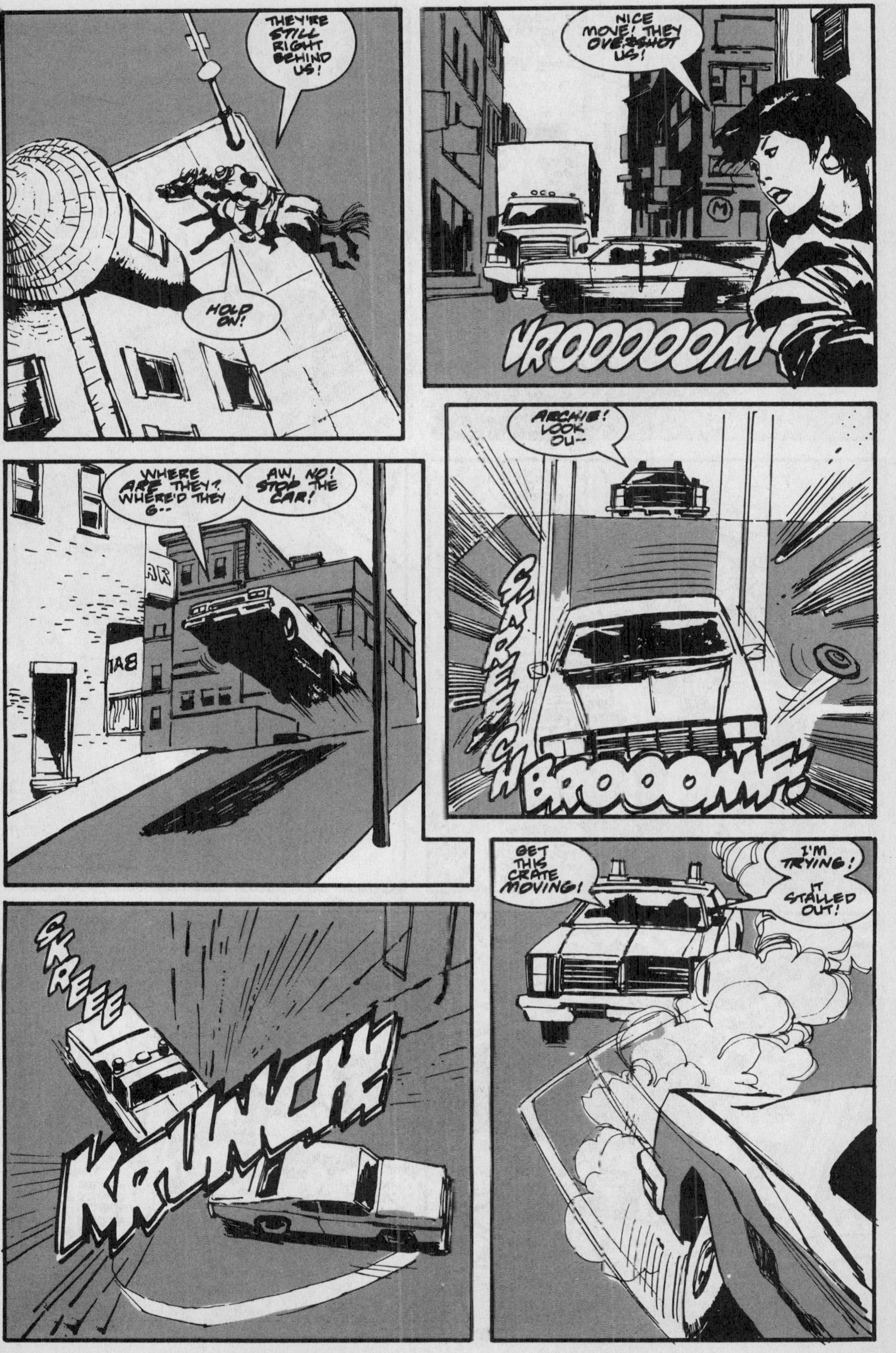
THEY'RE STILL RIGHT BEHIND US!
HOLD ON!
NICE MOVE! THEY OVERSHOT US!
VROOOOOM!
ARCHIE! LOOK OU--
WHERE ARE THEY? WHERE'D THEY G--
AW, NO! STOP THE CAR!
BROOOOMF!
GET THIS CRATE MOVING!
I'M TRYING! IT STALLED OUT!
SKREEE
KRUNCH

WE LOST THEM.

NO NEED TO WORRY NOW.

SKREEEE

SPOKE TOO SOON.

IT WOULD SEEM SO.

THERE'S NEVER A POLICE CAR WHEN YOU NEED IT.

THERE THEY GO!

MOVE IT, ARCHIE.

SHOW 'EM LIFE IN THE FAST LANE.

GRAND OPEN

WHAT STORE IS THIS, MISTER?

"PAGE AFTER PAGE," I CARRY COMICS, MOSTLY. HAD A STORE IN LAS VEGAS....

GOT WRECKED. MY FRIEND, BILL LIEBOWITZ, SUGGESTED I MOVE OUT HERE. IT'S QUIETER.

VROOOOMM

PULL ALONGSIDE 'EM.

PATCH, WHAT'RE YOU DOING?!

AEROBICS! NOW CLAM UP AND DRIVE!

THEY'RE CATCHING UP! YOU'D BETTER JUMP OFF! THIS COULD GET UGLY!

AND MISS ALL THE FUN?! NO WAY?!

SNIKT

SHRUKKT

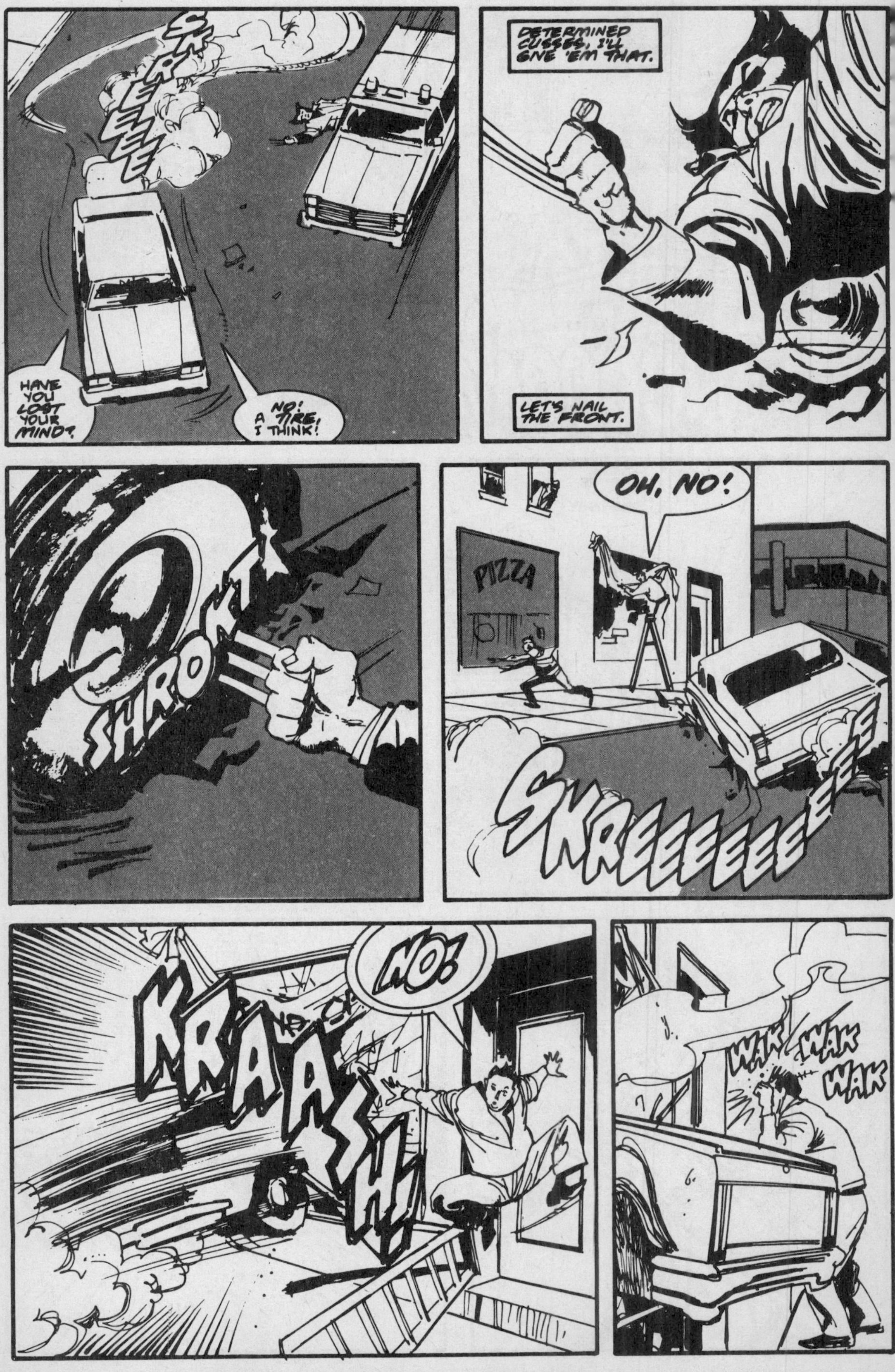
SKREEEEE
HAVE YOU LOST YOUR MIND?
NO! A TIRE, I THINK!
DETERMINED CUSSES, I'LL GIVE 'EM THAT.
LET'S NAIL THE FRONT.
SHROKT
PIZZA
OH, NO!
SKREEEEEEEEE
KRAASH!
NO!
WAK WAK WAK

WELL, THAT WAS FU--

KRAK

ARRHH!

GOT HIM!

IGNORE HIM! SHOOT OUT THE TIRES!

BLAM! BLAM!

IT'S MY GUN! I'LL SHOOT WHAT I WANT TO SHOOT!

SECOND ONE...

...BARELY FEEL IT...

...ADAMANTIUM SKULL'S STILL RINGING...

...CAN'T THINK...

...ARCHIE... YELLING SOMETHING...

...CAN'T HEAR HER...

...HEAD'S POUNDING... OR IS THAT HOOVES?

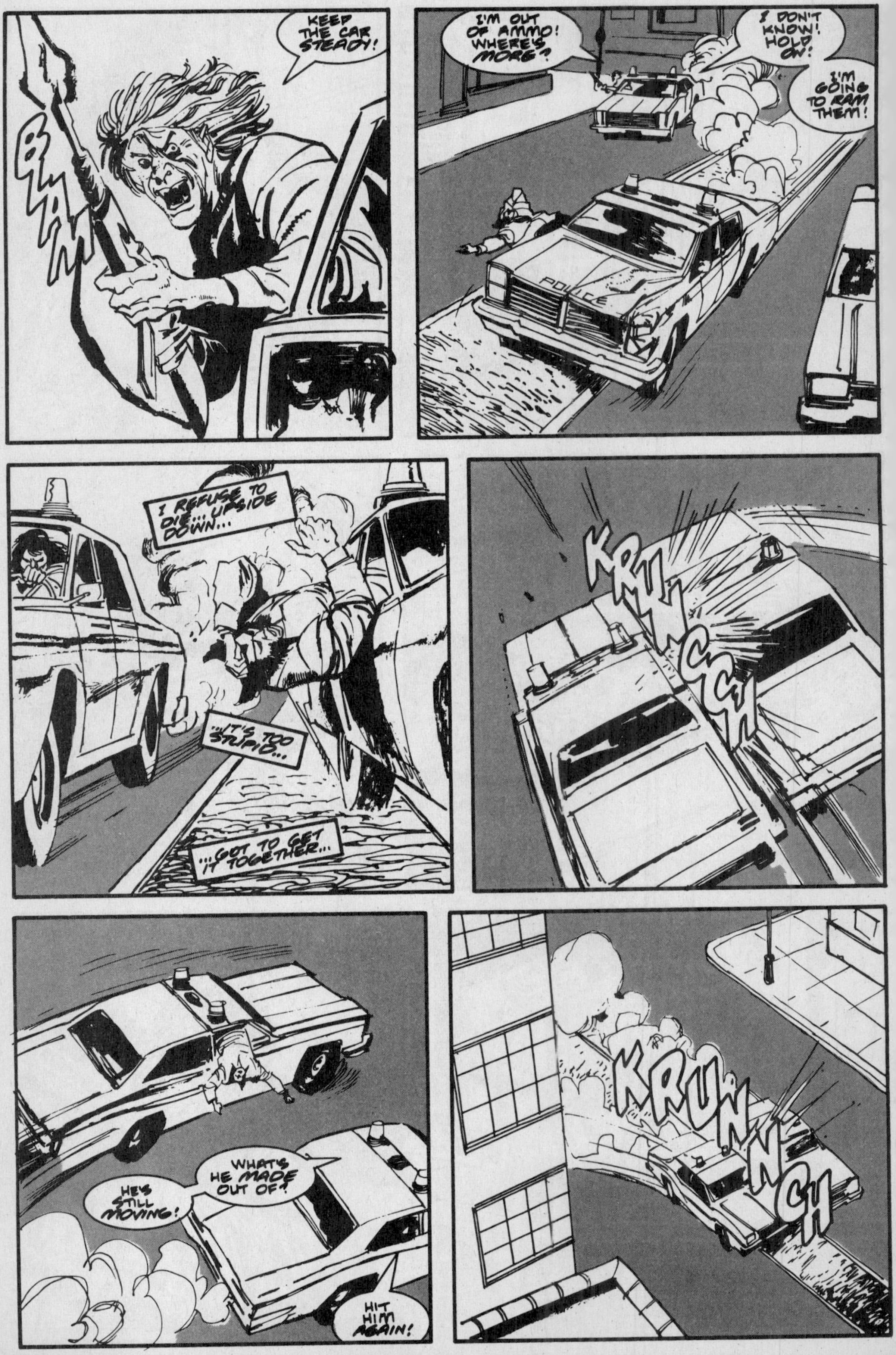
KEEP THE CAR STEADY!
BLAM
I'M OUT OF AMMO! WHERE'S MORE?
I DON'T KNOW! HOLD ON!
I'M GOING TO RAM THEM!
POLICE
I REFUSE TO DIE... UPSIDE DOWN...
...IT'S TOO STUPID...
...GOT TO GET IT TOGETHER...
KRUNCCH
WHAT'S HE MADE OUT OF?
HE'S STILL MOVING!
HIT HIM AGAIN!
KRUNNCH

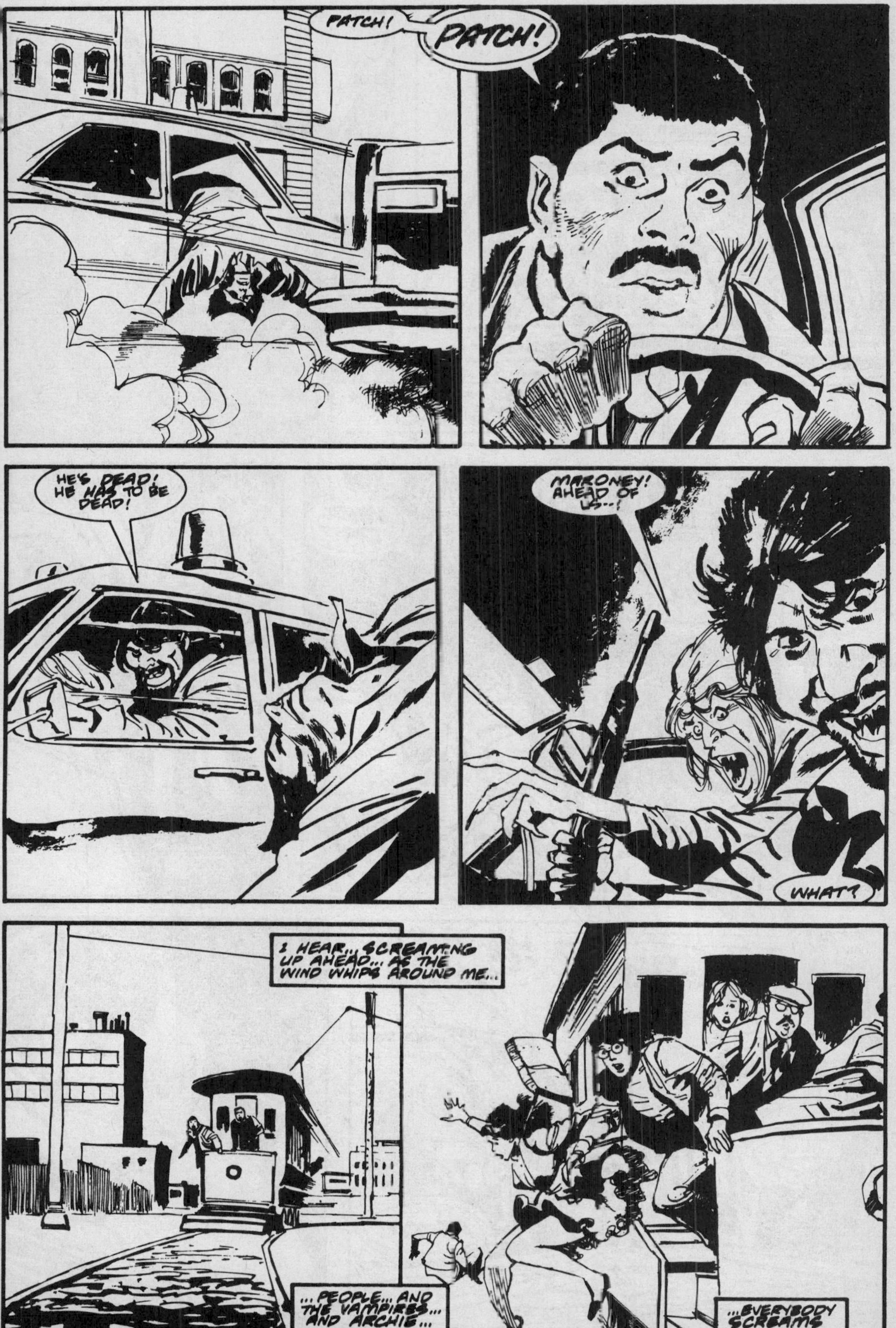

PATCH!
PATCH!
HE'S DEAD! HE HAS TO BE DEAD!
MARONEY! AHEAD OF US--!
WHAT?
I HEAR... SCREAMING UP AHEAD... AS THE WIND WHIPS AROUND ME...
...PEOPLE... AND THE VAMPIRES... AND ARCHIE...
...EVERYBODY SCREAMS NOWADAYS...

SIMPLE CONVERSATION—
THAT'S A DYING ART.

WELL, IF THERE'S ONE
THING I'M AN ARTIST
OF... IT'S DYING...

...THINK I'LL USE
MY CLAWS TO
PAINT A CANVAS

SHUNK

SKRITT

VEER
OFF!

VEER
OFF!

I'M
TRYING!

WHAT
THE
DEVIL?

PATCH!
WHAT'S
GOING
ON?!

KEEP
GOING STRAIGHT
UNTIL I SAY
SO!

I CAN
BARELY
HEAR
YOU!

PATCH!

PATCH!

TRUST
ME

TRUST
ME! I KNOW
WHAT I'M
DOING!

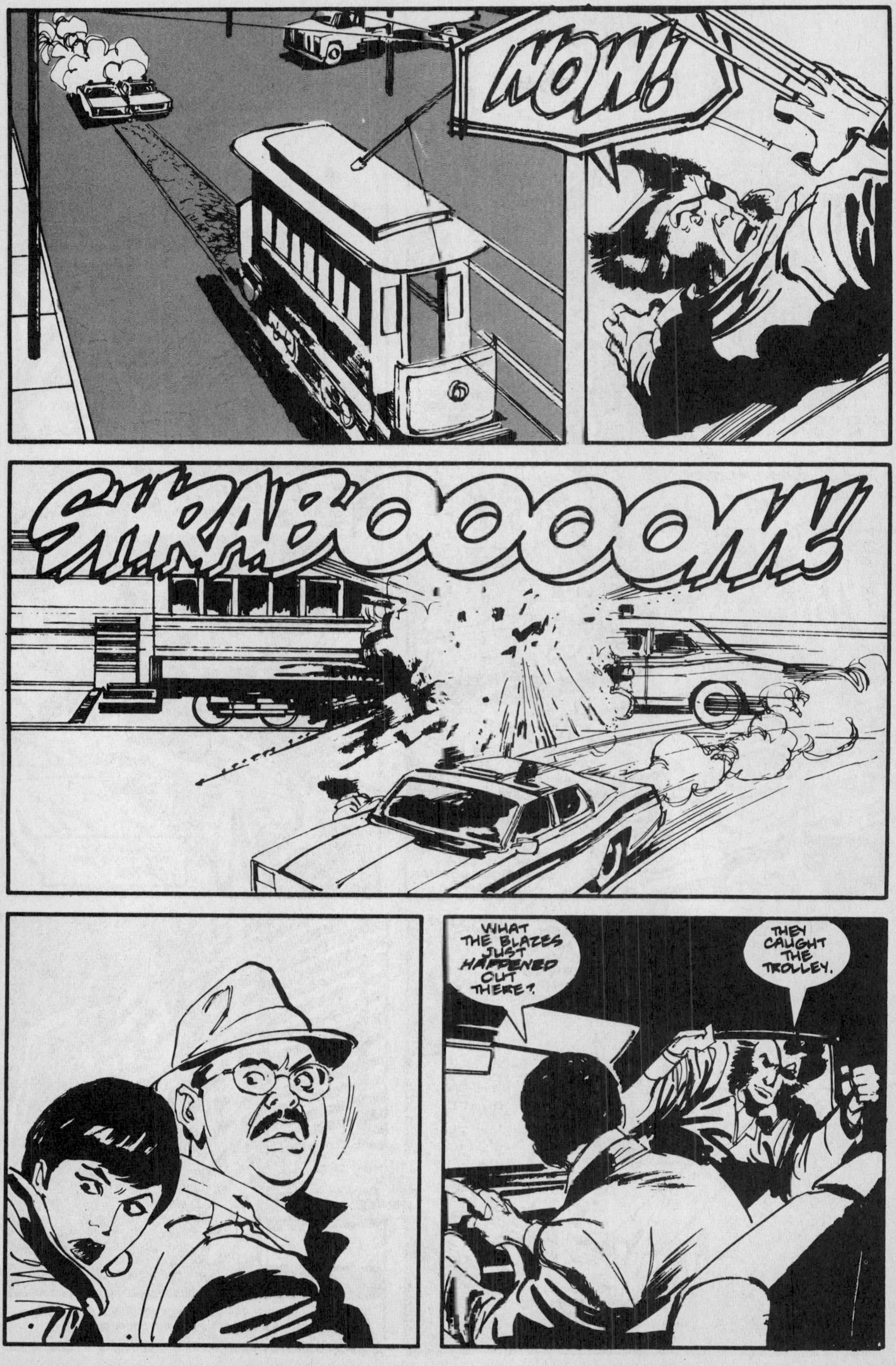
NON!
SKRABOOOOM!
WHAT THE BLAZES JUST HAPPENED OUT THERE?
THEY CAUGHT THE TROLLEY.

I THOUGHT I SAW YOU BEHIND THE WHEEL, ARCHIE.

LIKE I'D LIKE TO SEE YOU UNDER A WHEEL! LIKE UNDER MY FRONT TIRE YOU CRAZY SON OF A—!

TEMPER! LADIES ARE PRESENT.

WE HAVEN'T GOT TIME FOR THIS. FRISCO'S GOING TO GET HOTTER THAN THOSE VAMPIRES OVER THERE.

WE'VE GOT TO GET BACK TO MADRIPOOR!

MADRIPOOR? WITH HIM?

YEAH, WITH HIM. OR HE SPENDS THE NEXT COUPLE CENTURIES IN JAIL.

FINE BY ME!

GOOD. YOU EXPLAIN IT TO HIM WHILE I GET US SOMETHING LESS CONSPICUOUS THAN A COP CAR.

A LOCKBAR. CLAWS MAKE SHORT WORK OF THAT. NOW TO HOTWIRE THIS THING.

KIDS... DON'T TRY THIS AT HOME.

THOUGHT YOU WERE LEAVING INDY THERE BEHIND.

CLAM UP, PATCH. WAY I FIGURE IT, WHETHER HE'S ALONG OR NOT...

...THINGS CAN'T GET ANY WORSE.

NEXT: IT COULD BE AVOIDED NO LONGER: EXPOSITION!!

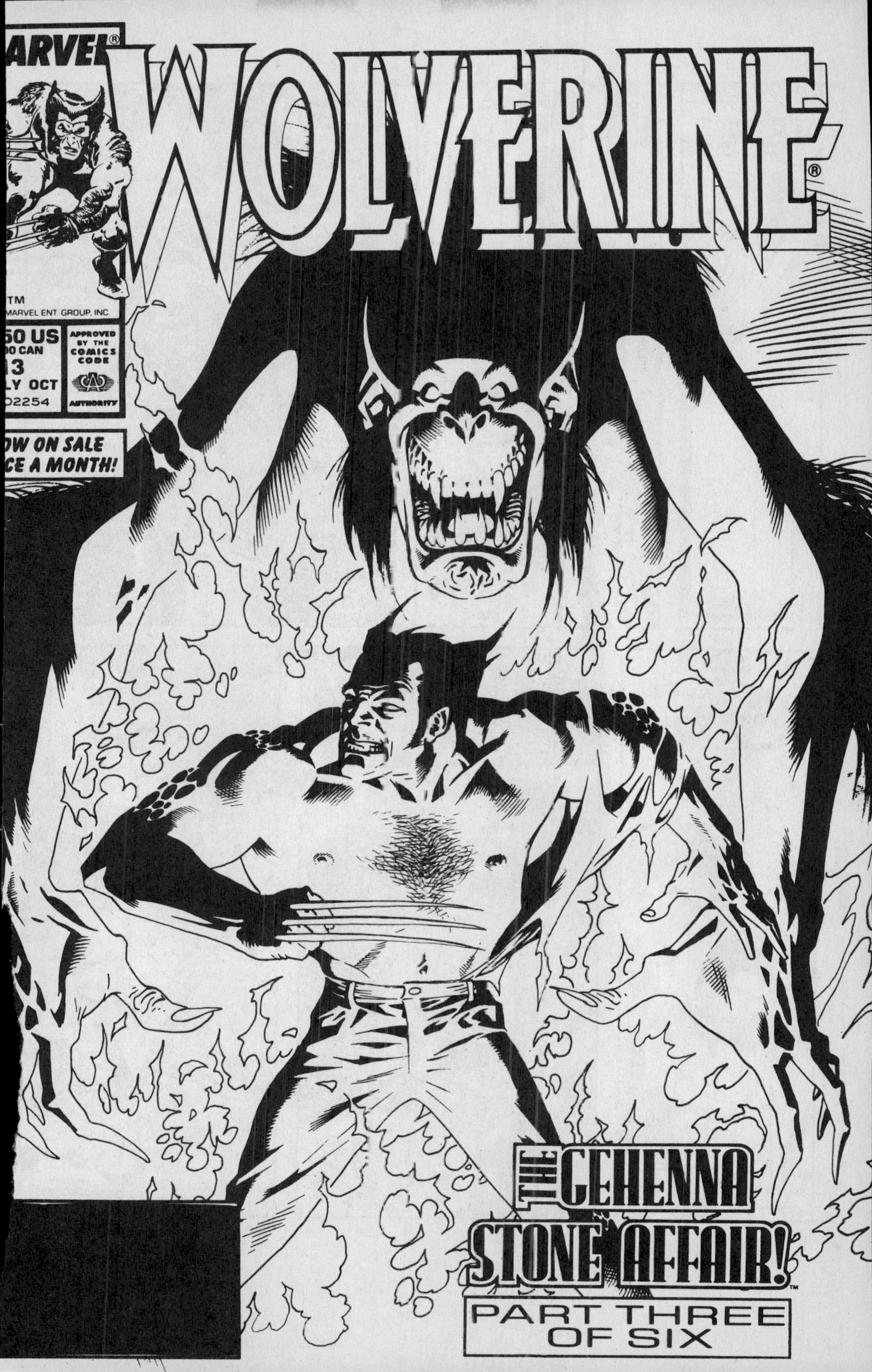
MARVEL
WOLVERINE
APPROVED BY THE COMICS CODE AUTHORITY
THE GEHENNA STONE AFFAIR!
PART THREE OF SIX

MADRIPOOR.

PRINCESS BAR

OR AM I *REALLY* SEEING *DOUBLE?*

SOMEONE *ELSE* WHO THINKS HE'S FUNNY.

MY *BROTHER* AND I *KILLED* THE *LAST* FUNNY MAN.

YEAH I *THOUGHT* THAT WOULD SHUT HIM UP.

WE DO *EVERYTHING* UP AND UP HERE, GENTS... INCLUDING *ASKING* CUSTOMERS FOR SOME *GUARANTEE* OF *PAYMENT?*

TWO *SCOTCH,* STRAIGHT UP, AND *DON'T* WATER IT *DOWN,* OR I'LL *WATER YOU DOWN.*

CHOKE ON *THIS* FOR COLLATERAL, BLONDIE.

LARRY!

STOP *WAVING* THAT *AROUND,* Y'MORON. USE YOUR *BRAINS!*

LISTEN... YOU THE *MAITRE D'* BLONDIE?

I'M THE *OWNER,* MATE O'DONNELL.

FINE, "*MATE.*" WE GOT PLENTY O' *CASH,* AND *MORE* ONCE WE SELL THE *ROCK* MY *IDIOT* BROTHER JUST *SHOWED* YOU. S'*OKAY?*

PARTY *HEARTY,* GENTS.

HEY, O'DONNELL? HAVE I BEEN *DRINKIN'* THAT MUCH?

"COME WITH ME TO SAN FRANCISCO, PATCH. MEET MY BROTHER, PATCH."

"IT'LL BE FUN, PATCH."

"YOU HAVE A WAY WITH PEOPLE, PATCH."

ALL RIGHT ALREADY! HOW MANY TIMES DO I HAVE TO APOLO..

VREEEEEEEEEEEEEE

AW, NUTS!

PULL OVER! THIS IS AN ORDER FROM THE SAN FRACISCO POLICE DEPARTMENT!

VREEEEEEEEEEEEE

YOU ARE DRIVING A STOLEN VEHICLE! PULL TO THE SIDE OF THE ROAD IMMEDIATELY!

VERY SOUND ADVICE.

YOU MEAN I SHOULD PULL OVER?

OF COURSE NOT. WHAT'RE YOU GOING TO DO?

SHOW WHAT A WAY I HAVE WITH PEOPLE.

BLOODTIES

LOTS OF CRAZY THINGS GOING DOWN LATELY.

I WAS CRAZY ENOUGH TO LET ARCHIE DRAG ME HERE TO FRISCO...

...TO HELP ARCHIE'S CRAZY BROTHER, BURT...

...WHO HAD A CRAZY STORY ABOUT VAMPIRES CHASING HIM...

...WHICH TURNED OUT TO BE TRUE, WHICH WAS EVEN CRAZIER.

SO NOW I'M LEAPING OUT OF A STOLEN CAR, WHICH IS GOING TO--PLUS, TO STOP A PURSUING POLICE CAR. CRAZY?

COMPARATIVELY SPEAKING, THAT'S SANE.

Rt. 71 DEM

NEW CALIF
7123L
CLASSIC CAR

PETER DAVID · writer **JOHN BUSCEMA** · penciler **BILL SIENKIEWICZ** · inker **KEN BRUZENAK** · letterer **GLYNIS OLIVER** · colorist **BOB HARRAS** · editor **TOM DeFALCO** · chief

WHAT DO YOU THINK YOU'RE DOING?!

IS THAT A TRICK QUESTION?

HMMM. DIDN'T THINK HE'D SHOOT AT ME IF I DIDN'T PULL A GUN.

THOUGHT THAT WAS PROCEDURE.

WELL, MY MUTANT HEALING FACTOR DEALS WITH THE WOUND...

...AND MY ADAMANTIUM CLAWS SHOULD DEAL WITH PROCEDURES.

I KNOW DIDDLY ABOUT CAR ENGINES...

SHPLUNK!

...SO I'M FORCED TO TAKE A CRASH COURSE.

SSSSSS SSSSS

SLOW DOWN, ARCHIE!

THANKS!

NOW *FLOOR* IT. BUT WATCH THE *SPEED LIMIT.* I HATE TO ATTRACT ATTENTION.

WH... WHAT DID YOU DO TO THE *COPS?*

I PERSUADED THEM TO PULL OVER.

ALL RIGHT, BROTHER-MINE... YOU WANT TO FILL US IN ON WHAT THE DEVIL'S GOING ON?

YEAH. YOU TOLD ME SOMETHING ABOUT SOME KIND OF STONE... THE *GEHENNA STONE,* I THINK YOU CALLED IT.

BUT I CAN'T SAY AS I FOLLOWED WHAT YOU WERE *TALKING* ABOUT.

ALL RIGHT, MS. DREW.

NO REASON YOU *SHOULDN'T* KNOW WHAT YOU'RE INVOLVED WITH.

MADRIPOOR.

HEY, BLONDIE...

O'DONNELL.

YEAH, RIGHT. Y'KNOW WHERE THERE'S A *ROOM* TO BE HAD?

JUST FOR *TONIGHT.* TOMORROW IT'S ON TO SINGAPORE, TO UNLOAD THAT *GEM* FOR *MUCHO BUCKS...*

WILL YOU STOP TALKING ABOUT THE *BLOOD STONE,* LARRY!

WHY DON'T YOU JUST WAVE A BANNER THAT SAYS "ROB US." ARE YOU *COMPLETELY STUPID?*

WAP

NO! I'M *COMPLETELY FED UP!*

KLUD!

I'LL TALK ABOUT WHATEVER I *WANNA* TALK ABOUT!

I'LL... I'LL...

OH... ...OH, GEEZ, GAR...I DON'T KNOW WHAT CAME OVER ME.

I'M *SORRY,* MAN.

YEAH, WELL... I HAVEN'T BEEN MR. CHARM MYSELF LATELY.

IF YOU GENTS STILL NEED A PLACE...WE HAVE A ROOM UPSTAIRS. TWENTY A NIGHT... IF YOU'LL *BEHAVE.*

YEAH, SURE. HERE, O'DONNELL.

WE BEEN THROUGH TOO *MUCH* TOGETHER FOR THIS KIND OF GAR-BARGE, GAR.

'SIDES, HITTIN' YOU IS LIKE HITTIN' *MYSELF.*

NAH. YOUR HEAD'S *THICKER.*

BLOOD IS *THICKER,* MAN. 'SPECIALLY WITH TWINS. LET'S REMEM-BER THAT.

CALIFORNIA.

REMEMBER *THIS*... WHAT I'M ABOUT TO TELL YOU IS *LEGEND.*

TAKE NO CONSOLATION IN THAT. IT'S ALSO *TRUE.*

"IN ANCIENT TIMES, THE FOULEST PLACE ON EARTH WAS GEHENNA.

"SITUATED JUST OUTSIDE OF *JERUSALEM,* GEHENNA WAS THE *CHARNAL PIT,* WHERE THE *REFUSE* WAS BURNED.

"A PLACE OF *UNSPEAKABLE* EVIL....

"...WHERE, IN VIEW OF THE *HOLIEST OF CITIES,* PEOPLE WITH *BLACKENED, CONDEMNED* SOULS...

...COMMITTED HIDEOUS, UNHOLY ATROCITIES.

"THEIR LEADER WAS A *MAN/DEMON* CALLED *BA'AL.*

"HIS *NAME...* IT'S NAME... MEANT *'MASTER'*...

"...AND BA'AL LED THOSE *LOATHSOME* BEINGS IN *PERVERSE* RITUALS...

"...NOT THE *LEAST* OF WHICH WAS THE *CONSUMPTION* OF *HUMAN BLOOD.*

"AND THE LORD WAS SO *DISGUSTED* BY WHAT HE *BEHELD*, THAT HE SENT A FIERCE WARRIOR...

"...HE WAS KNOWN ONLY AS THE *HAND OF GOD*, AND ARMED WITH *UNBREAKABLE STEEL* AND *DIVINE RIGHT*...

"...HE *SMOTE* THE DEMON *BA'AL.*"

I'VE HEARD *SMOKING* CAN BE HAZARDOUS TO YOUR *HEALTH.*

NICE TO KNOW YOU'RE TAKING THIS *SERIOUSLY,* DARLIN'.

RTION RD. EXIT

"BUT, EVEN IN HIS *DEATH THROES,* BA'AL PERPETUATED HIS *EVIL.*

"WHAT PASSED AS HIS *SOUL,* COALESCED OVER HIM...

"...AND ENTERED A GLITTERING, MULTI-FACETED *GEM* THAT HIS FOLLOWERS HAD *PREPARED* FOR HIM.

" WHAT THEY HAD *NOT* PREPARED FOR WAS THE *RIGHTEOUS WRATH* OF THE HAND OF GOD.

"THEY *FOUGHT* THAT MIGHTY *WARRIOR,* BUT IN *VAIN*...

"AND *FINALLY*, ON A FIELD BLOODY WITH CORPSES, THE HAND OF GOD STOOD BEFORE THE *LAST* INCARNATION OF BA'AL...

"...AND SMASHED IT *ASUNDER*.

"THE EVIL OF BA'AL WAS *TRAPPED* IN A HUNDRED FRAGMENTS, AND NOT *CONTENT* WITH THAT...

"...THE HAND OF GOD HURLED THE PIECES TO THE FOUR WINDS, NEVER TO BE REASSEMBLED, UNTIL DOOMSDAY.

"OR SO THE LEGEND GOES.

" IN *RECENT* DAY, HOWEVER, PIECES HAVE BEEN UNEARTHED IN ARCHAEOLOGICAL DIGS...

"...AND WOUND UP IN VARIOUS MUSEUMS AND PRIVATE COLLECTIONS.

"OF COURSE, THE LEGEND IS KNOWN IN ARCHAEOLOGICAL CIRCLES, BUT NO ONE GENUINELY BELIEVES IT."

AND PIECES HAVE BEEN *VANISHING*, IS THAT IT?

SLOWLY, OVER A PERIOD OF TWO YEARS.

SOMEONE DOESN'T WANT TO BE NOTICED...

BUT THEY COULDN'T HIDE THEIR EVIL FROM ME.

THE MOMENT I SAW THE STONE FRAGMENT IN THE MUSEUM, I KNEW I HAD TO... PROTECT IT. SO I GOT ONTO THE BOARD OF DIRECTORS...

...IT'S EASY WHEN YOU HAVE MONEY--

...AND ONCE THERE, MAKING THE SWITCH WAS SIMPLE.

BURT... HOW DO YOU KNOW THE PIECES OF THE STONE HAVE BEEN DISAPPEARING? THAT BEEN GETTING A LOT OF PRESS?

WELL... NO. I JUST KNOW, THAT'S ALL.

SEVERAL MILES AWAY...

HOW DO YOU KNOW THEY WILL BE HERE SHORTLY, MASTER?

BECAUSE IT IS MY JOB TO KNOW.

PREPARE YOURSELF

NOW SOMEONE CLAIMING TO BE DESCENDED FROM BA'AL HIMSELF HAS ARISEN, AND HAS GATHERED NEW FOLLOWERS.

HE INTENDS TO CREATE A NEW RACE OF BLOOD-SUCKING CREATURES ON EARTH, BUT HE NEEDS THE FULL POWER OF THE GEHENNA STONE TO DO IT.

LET ME SEE THAT PIECE A MOMENT, WILL YOU?

NO! IT'S MINE!

MY STONE! YOU CAN'T HAVE IT!

FINE! FINE! YOU CAN KEEP IT!

CAN'T HE, PATCH?

NO SKIN OFF MY NOSE, DREW.

I KNOW OLD BURT IS A FEW BRICKS SHY OF A LOAD...

...BUT EVEN SO, THAT LITTLE OUTBURST WASN'T NORMAL.

AND...

LARRY! YOU ASLEEP?

OH, YOU'D LIKE THAT, WOULDN'T YOU?

LAR, 34 YEARS, WE'VE HARDLY HAD A CROSS WORD. WE'VE WATCHED EACH OTHER'S BACKS, BEEN THERE FOR EACH OTHER.

NOW WE GET OUR HANDS ON THAT STONE FOR THE BUYER IN SINGAPORE, AND IT'S--

YOU'RE JUST JEALOUS, THAT'S ALL! BECAUSE I'M SMARTER! AND BECAUSE I'M OLDER!

JEALOUS! YOU'RE TWO MINUTES OLDER!

AND 28 SECONDS! AND COME TO THINK ABOUT IT, YOU'VE BEEN HARPING ABOUT THAT FOR YEARS! AND IT'S REALLY STARTING TO TEE ME--

OH, FORGET IT. GO TO SLEEP

YOU'D LIKE THAT WOULDN'T YOU?

OH, SHUT UP.

CALIFORNIA.

YOU WERE RIGHT, MASTER! THEY'RE HERE!

OF COURSE.

KILL THEM, AND GET ME THAT FRAGMENT.

WAIT A MINUTE! THIS ISN'T SAN FRANCISCO INTERNATIONAL AIRPORT.

YOUR BROTHER'S QUICK, ARCH. NOW ME...

...I'VE ALWAYS PREFERRED LOGAN AIRPORT.

THANKS FOR SHARING THAT, PATCH.

THIS IS WHERE I LANDED, BURT. LITTLE AIRFIELDS LIKE THIS WITH THE RIGHT PALMS GREASED...

...YOU DON'T HAVE TO DEAL WITH LOTS OF STICKY QUESTIONS.

GOING THROUGH OFFICIAL CHANNELS CAN BE DEADLY SOMETIMES.

ZZZZZ

ZZZZZ

GET BACK!

I...I JUST WANTED TO TAKE A LOOK AT IT!

IT'S MINE!

IT'S OURS! YOU OWE ME THAT!

I OWE YOU SQUAT! I..

I KNEW IT! I KNEW YOU WANTED TO KILL ME!

DROP THAT KNIFE!

UNNHHH!

NYARRHHH!

"DEATH!"

WHAT? WHADDAYOU MEAN, "DEATH"? THIS IS THE OFFICE FOR--

THERE'S DEATH BEHIND THAT DOOR! DON'T OPEN IT!

BUT--

SHUT UP!

BACK AWAY, FAST!

SLAM!

RUN FOR THE HANGAR! MOVE IT!

LATELY, I'VE BEEN TRYING TO KEEP MY CLAWS HIDDEN, SO THE WORLD DOESN'T KNOW "WOLVERINE" IS STILL ALIVE.

BUT I'VE STARTED TO REALIZE THAT BEIN' UNDERCOVER MEANS DIDDLY IF YOU WIND UP SIX FEET UNDERGROUND

I TOSS A QUICK GLANCE AT THE OTHERS. THEY'RE DOING FINE...

...UNTIL THEY STOP DOING FINE.

JESSICA DREW USED TO BE SPIDER-WOMAN. SHE'S NO LONGER WHAT SHE WAS...

...BUT SHE'S STILL A LOT MORE THAN A LOT OF PEOPLE WILL EVER BE.

NOT THAT ARCHIE ISN'T ACQUITTING HIMSELF WELL.

STILL, MASS SLAUGHTER IS BEST LEFT TO EXPERTS, SOMETHING NEITHER ARCHIE NOR JESSICA IS FORTUN- ATELY. NEITHER ARE THESE PSEUDO-VAMPIRES.

UNFORTUNATELY... ...THE VAMPS ARE LEARNING FAST.

BLAM! BLAM!

WHAT A RELIEF. I HARDLY GOT TO SHOOT IT AT ALL IN "TEMPLE OF"--

KRAK!

WE'VE GOT IT! WE'VE GOT IT MASTER!

WATHWAK!

IT'S HIM.

I'VE NEVER SEEN HIM BEFORE...

...BUT IT'S HIM.

THE DEATH I SENSED ON THE OTHER SIDE OF THE DOOR.

ALL RIGHT, THEN.

LET'S SEE IF I CAN DEAL DEATH A DEATH-BLOW.

SHAAK!

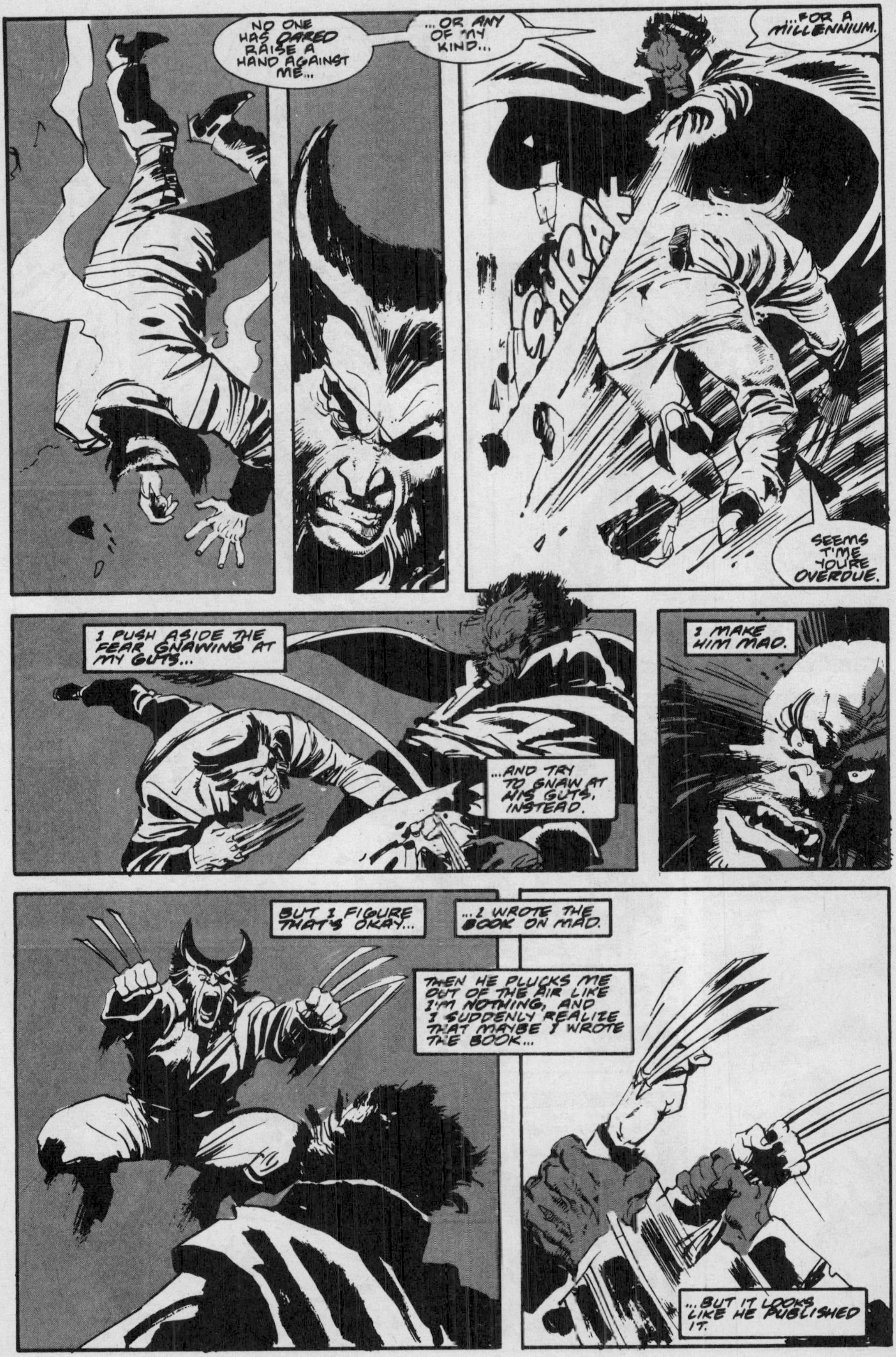
NO ONE HAS DARED RAISE A HAND AGAINST ME...
...OR ANY OF MY KIND...
...FOR A MILLENNIUM.
SEEMS TIME YOU'RE OVERDUE.
I PUSH ASIDE THE FEAR GNAWING AT MY GUTS...
...AND TRY TO GNAW AT HIS GUTS, INSTEAD.
I MAKE HIM MAD.
BUT I FIGURE THAT'S OKAY...
...I WROTE THE BOOK ON MAD.
THEN HE PLUCKS ME OUT OF THE AIR LIKE I'M NOTHING, AND I SUDDENLY REALIZE THAT MAYBE I WROTE THE BOOK...
...BUT IT LOOKS LIKE HE PUBLISHED IT.

WHY CAN'T I... UNH! RIP YOU APART?

ADAMANTIUM BONES... BUT HE DOESN'T HAVE TO KNOW THAT.

THW ACK!

UH, BOY. HE HAS FANGS.

AND, UNLIKE HIS FOLLOWERS, THEY'RE REAL FANGS.

AS REAL... AS THE TROUBLE I'M IN.

I SMELL MEAT COOKIN', AND I HEAR SCREAMING, AND THEN MY MIND GETS AROUND TO INFORMING ME...

...THAT I'M THE SOURCE OF BOTH.

WITH MY SKIN BUBBLING, I JUST HACK AND SLASH, SLAMMING SHUT THE DOOR TO THE PAIN...

...THAT COMES LATER IF THERE IS A LATER.

COME, MY FOLLOWERS!

WE WASTE NO MORE TIME WITH THEM.

PATCH!

PATCH! ARE YOU OKAY?

GEEZ, HE CAN BARELY STAND!

S'OKAY... M' ALWAYS LIKE THIS...

...B'FORE I'VE HAD... M'... M'FIRST CUP OF COFFEE...

ARCHIE, LOOK! THEY'RE GETTING AWAY!

GOOD RIDDANCE! IT'S NOT OUR PROBLEM ANYMORE.

NO! WE'VE GOT TO GO AFTER THEM!

AND WE WILL, ARCHIE! EVEN IF IT'S OVER YOUR DEAD BODY!

WHAT IN THE BLAZES HAS GOTTEN INTO YOU?

WA!

I'VE HAD A BELLYFUL OF YOUR CRAZINESS, BURT!

ENOUGH TO LAST ME A LIFETIME!

BURT'S RIGHT. WE GO AFTER THEM.

BUT...

SAVE YOUR "BUTS," OR I'LL KICK YOURS.

NOBODY FLASH FRIES ME AND GETS AWAY WITH IT. CLEAR

OKAY, OKAY. BUT LET'S HOPE THEY DIDN'T FIND MY PLANE AND TRASH IT.

WHAT WORRIES ME IS HOW THEY KNEW WE'D BE HERE IN THE FIRST PLACE.

I DON'T LIKE THE ENEMY HAVING A LEG UP.

"AND WHEN THEY DO, I WANT TO HACK IT OFF AT THE *KNEE*."

WHAT IN THE *BLOODY*..!

Poit

UH-OH.

BLOODY IS RIGHT.

NO NEED TO ALARM THE CUSTOMERS YET...

...NOT THAT THIS WOULD BE AN *EASY* CROWD TO ALARM.

THEY'VE SEEN JUST *ABOUT* EVERYTH..

HOLY MOSES !!!!

NEXT: *FLYING WOLVES*

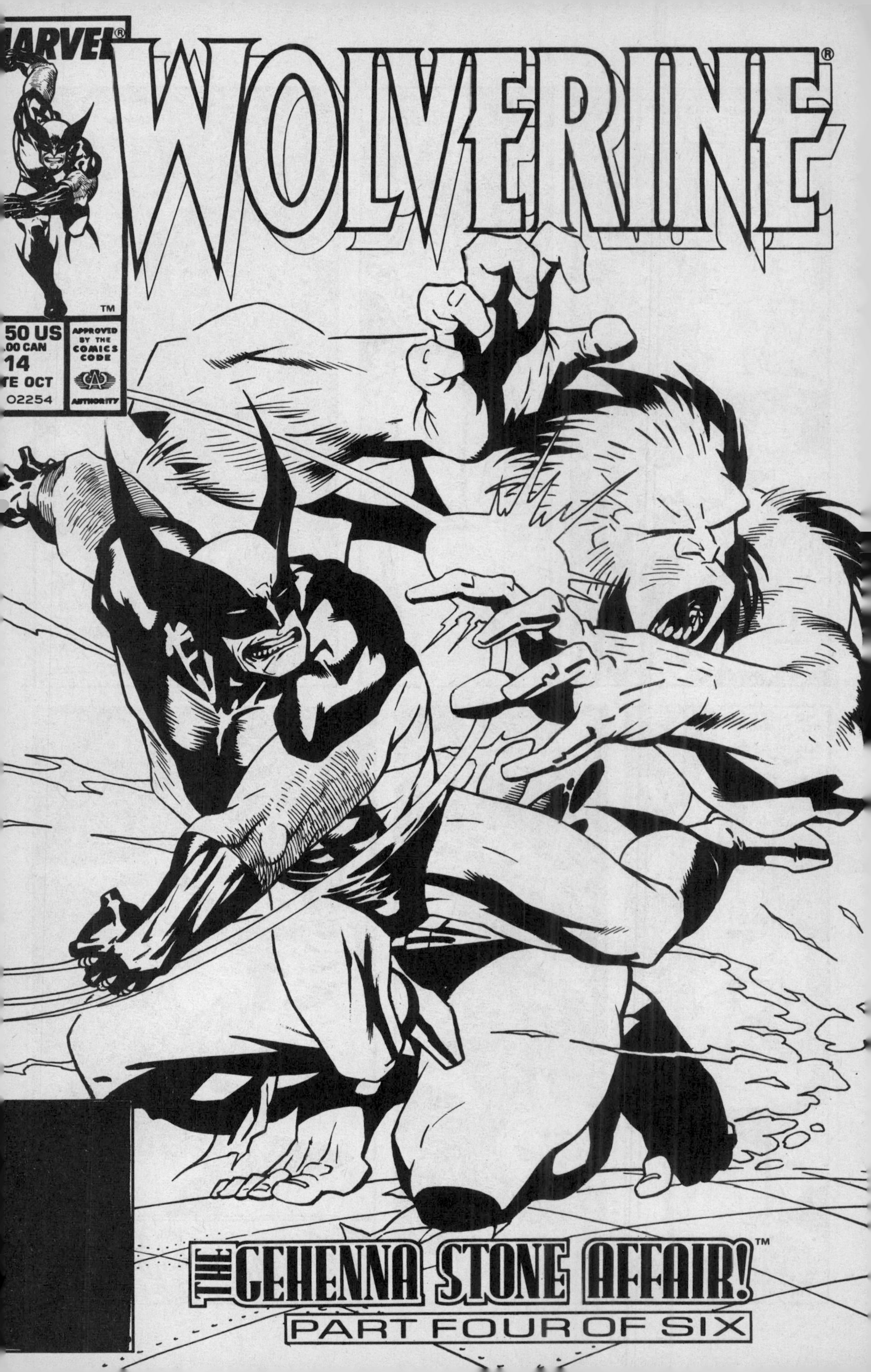
MARVEL®
WOLVERINE®
APPROVED BY THE COMICS CODE AUTHORITY
THE GEHENNA STONE AFFAIR!™
PART FOUR OF SIX

WORDS PETER DAVID · PENCILS JOHN BUSCEMA · INKS BILL SIENKIEWICZ · LETTERS KEN BRUZENAK · COLORS GREG WRIGHT · EDITS BOB HARRAS · CHIEF TOM DeFALCO

THINK THEY SPOTTED US YET?

WE ASSUME THEY HAVE. THAT WAY, THEY CAN'T SURPRISE US.

HEY, BACK THERE, WE'VE SIGHTED THE VAMPS.

YOU HEAR ME, BURT?

JESSICA?

LOUD AND CLEAR.

UH-HUH.

THIS HAS BEEN ONE WEIRD CAPER FROM THE GET GO.

IT WAS BAD ENOUGH WHEN BURT CORRIGAN, DECKED OUT LIKE HARRISON FORD, CRASHES INTO HIS SANITY HEARING YELLING ABOUT VAMPIRES.

SECONDS LATER, VAMPIRES REALLY SHOW UP, OR FAKE VAMPS...

...AND WE'RE BARRELING ALL OVER FRISCO.

ONLY TO WIND UP MEETING THEIR LEADER, A NUTCASE CALLED BA'AL...

...WHO WANTS TO ASSEMBLE SOMETHING CALLED THE GEHENNA STONE AND ACQUIRE ULTIMATE POWER. NOT THAT HE WAS ANY SLOUCH IN THE POWER DEPARTMENT, THEN AGAIN...

...NEITHER 'AM I.

CLOSE ON 'EM.

WHERE YOU OFF TO?

THE LITTLE MUTANTS' ROOM.

WHAT?

NOTHING. I JUST WANT TO CHANGE INTO SOMETHING...

...APROPOS.

DIDN'T THINK I'D NEED IT, EVEN THOUGH I AUTOMATICALLY PACKED IT WHEN WE LEFT ON THE TRIP.

GOOD THING I DID. AND GOOD THING I LEFT IT IN THE PLANE...

...SINCE WE DIDN'T HAVE TIME TO GO BACK TO THE HOTEL.

ALL THIS BECAUSE I WANTED TO HELP ARCHIE'S CRAZY BROTHER BACK IN MADRIPOOR, O'DONNELL'D BE LAUGHING HIMSELF SICK.

MADRIPOOR.

O'DONNELL STILL TALKING WITH CAPTAIN TAI?

YUP. PROMISES TO BE A WHILE, TOO.

PRINCE BAR

SO LET'S SEE IF I HAVE THIS. A PAIR OF TWINS YOU'VE *NEVER* SEEN BEFORE...

...TAKE A ROOM, GO UP-STAIRS...

...AND *KILL* EACH OTHER.

THAT'S IT.

THINK THEY WERE *FIGHTING* ABOUT SOMETHING?

KNIFING EACH OTHER ISN'T THE USUAL WAY OF EXPRESSING *AGREEMENT*, SO PROBABLY, YEAH.

ANY CLUE AS TO WHAT *ABOUT*?

COULDN'T HAZARD A GUESS.

I SEE.

BY THE WAY, O'DONNELL...

YEAH?

...YOUR POCKET IS BLEEDING.

CARE TO SHOW US *WHY*? OR MAYBE YOU COULDN'T HAZARD A GUESS.

HOOLEEE...

IT WAS... UP IN THEIR ROOM. LYING IN THEIR *BLOOD* I JUST THOUGHT THAT--

I KNOW WHAT YOU THOUGHT. FINDERS KEEPERS, EH?

GIVE IT *HERE* O'DONNELL.

NO! IT'S *MINE!*

HMMM...

IF IT'S ALL THAT *IMPORTANT* TO YOU...

...KEEP IT.

FOR THE TIME BEING. AS LONG AS I KNOW WHERE TO FIND IT, SHOULD IT BECOME *NECESSARY.*

O'DONNELL, CAN I TAKE A LOOK AT IT? THERE'S... SOMETHING ABOUT IT...

...IT'S LIKE IT'S... *PULSING* OR SOMETHING. CAN I...?

LATER, LINDSAY.

MUCH *LATER.*

OVER THE PACIFIC...

WONDER HOW *LINDSAY* IS DOING. WISH I'D HAD A CHANCE TO TELL HER I WAS RUNNING OFF.

EVER SINCE I SECRETLY STARTED WORKING FOR THE *PRINCE OF MADRIPOOR,* THERE'S CERTAIN PEOPLE HE'S WANTED ME TO STAY CLOSE TO...AND "PATCH" IS *HIGH* ON THE LIST.

BUT WHEN I FOUND OUT THAT "PATCH" WAS WALTZING OFF, I JUST *HAD* TO COME ALONG TO KEEP AN *EYE* ON HIM.

AND THAT STONE... THERE'S SOMETHING *ABOUT* IT. BURT WAS SO CALM WHEN THOSE PSEUDO-VAMPIRES WERE *CHASING* US...

AND NOW HE CAN BARELY SIT *STILL* EVER SINCE BA'AL CAPTURED THAT FRAGMENT.

WHATEVER THAT STONE'S *GOT,* THE PRINCE WILL *WANT* IT. WHICH MEANS I HAVE TO GET MY HANDS ON IT, WITHOUT LETTING THE *OTHERS* KNOW.

PATCH! WHATEVER YOU'RE UP TO, YOU BETTER BE *DONE* WITH IT, BECAUSE WE'RE RIGHT *ABOVE* THEM.

THEY'RE RIGHT ABOVE US!

YOU SURE I'M BELTED ON?

YOU'RE SECURED. DON'T WORRY.

¡AWRIGHT!

DON'T WORRY! BE HAPPY!

BUDDA BUDDA BUDDA BUDDA BUDDA

CRIMINEY!

THEY'RE SHOOTING AT US!

JESS! GET AWAY FROM THERE!

JESSICA!

DON'T WORRY... ...BE HAP...

HUH?

BUDDA BUDDA BUDDA

SHE'S... SHE'S CLINGING TO THAT PLANE! AND NOW SHE'S SCUTTLING AROUND THE OTHER SIDE, LIKE A SPIDER?!

THIS IS GETTING WEIRDER BY THE MINUTE.

YEAH? ONE THING MAKES ME EDGY...

...IS WEIRDNESS.

WHAT'S HAPPENED?

J-J-JESSICA JUMPED DOWN TO THE PLANE.

YEAH? WELL WE CAN'T LET HER HAVE ALL THE FUN.

HE'S SO BUSY TRYING TO SPOT DREW, HE DOESN'T SEE ME UNTIL IT'S TOO LATE FOR HIM.

THEN AGAIN, THE MOMENT I WOKE UP THIS MORNING...

...IT WAS TOO LATE FOR HIM.

NAILED HIS POPGUN, BUT THE GUNMAN HIMSELF IS INCHES BEYOND MY REACH.

AND BULLETS HAVE A LONGER REACH THAN I DO.

SOME DAY I'LL LEARN TO PACK AN UZI.

UNTIL THEN...

I'LL JUST HAVE TO KEEP IMPROVISING.

WAK!

LIKE SEVERING HALF THE STRAP THAT'S KEEPING HIM ANCHORED TO THE PLANE...

NOW THAT'S A GOOD IMPROV.

WOLVERINE! IT'S ABOUT TIME YOU DITCHED THE PATCH NONSENSE!

CAN BARELY HEAR HER ABOVE THE ROAR OF THE WIND AND PROPS, BUT I THINK SHE'S SAYING...

...SHE'S KNOWN I WAS PATCH ALL ALONG?

WELL, THAT STINKS.

GREAT. MORE COMPANY.

SAYONARA, SUCKER.

HELP ME! HELP!

BA'AL! MASTER! HELLLLP!

HOW ABOUT THAT? THE SHARK BROKE HIS FALL.

THE WIND, THE NOISE, IS WREAKING HAVOC WITH MY SENSES. I DON'T KNOW WHAT IS WAITING FOR ME INSIDE.

WELL, YOU PAYS YOUR MONEY AND YOU TAKES YOUR...

...CHANCES?

BUDDA BUDDA BUDDA

BUDDA

OKAY, GUYS, I CAN TAKE IT...

CAN YOU?

WELL, WHETHER THEY CAN TAKE IT OR NOT...

...THEY CERTAINLY SEEM CAPABLE OF DISHING IT OUT IN LARGE QUANTITIES.

MY HEALING FACTOR'S ALREADY DEALT WITH THE BULLETS...

...AND MY CLAWS WILL DEAL WITH THE REST.

GREAT! WHILE HE'S BUSY, I'LL FIND THE...

SSSHHIIIIIIK

OH, CRUD.

CHNG

THUBONK

WHUUMP

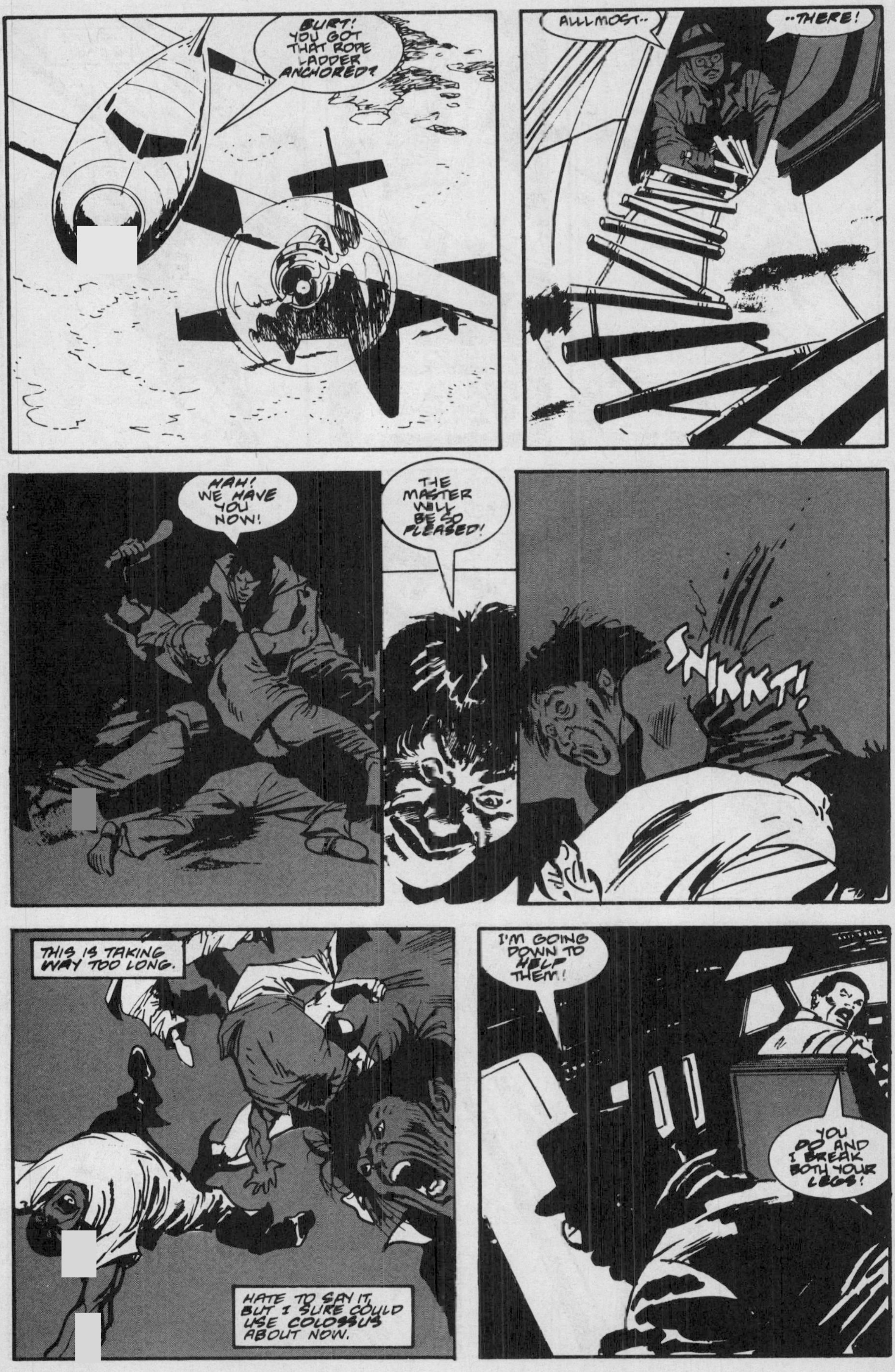
BURT! YOU GOT THAT ROPE LADDER ANCHORED?
ALLLMOST..
..THERE!
HAH! WE HAVE YOU NOW!
THE MASTER WILL BE SO PLEASED!
SNIKKT!
THIS IS TAKING WAY TOO LONG.
HATE TO SAY IT, BUT I SURE COULD USE COLOSSUS ABOUT NOW.
I'M GOING DOWN TO HELP THEM!
YOU DO AND I BREAK BOTH YOUR LEGS!

ARCHIE MUST BE NEARBY, BECAUSE THEY'RE BANKING SHARPLY DOWN TO GET AWAY.

I'M FAR ENOUGH FROM THE DOOR THAT IT'S NO PROBLEM...

DREW ISN'T AS LUCKY. BEFORE SHE CAN ADHERE TO ANYTHING--

...SHE'S GONE.

DIE! DIE!

I'LL PASS.

DOWN, ARCHIE! BRING IT DOWN!

NNYYAUUHHH!

HAH!

ARCHIE! I HAVE TO CUT THE LADDER LOOSE!

YOU CAN'T!

THEN WE HAVE A BIG PROBLEM!

MADRIPOOR...

KNOK KNOK

WHO'S THERE?

LINDSAY.

WHAT ARE YOU DOING HERE AT 5 AM?

I JUST--I WANTED TO SEE THE STONE. IT'S THE MOST BEAUTIFUL THING I'VE EVER--

YEAH, LOOK, MAYBE TOMORROW, BUT--

I WAS LYING THERE IN BED, STARING AT THE CEILING, AND I KEPT THINKING ABOUT IT AND THINKING ABOUT IT...

...AND I THOUGHT IF I CAME STRAIGHT HERE AND ASKED VERY, VERY NICELY YOU'D LET ME HOLD IT FOR A FEW MINUTES.

THAT'S NOT SO MUCH, IS IT? IF I ASK NICELY, THAT IS.

WELL... DEPENDS HOW NICELY YOU ASK.

WHILE...

AH! THAT FITS VERY NICELY INDEED. ONLY ONE FRAGMENT LEFT TO--

LORD BA'AL! A MADMAN WITH KNIVES IN HIS HANDS IS CUTTING US TO PIECES!

WE CAN'T STOP HIM, MASTER!

YES, YOU CAN. YOU CAN DO ANYTHING.

I HEAR A SCREAM FROM THE FRONT CABIN, AND I SMELL THAT SAME STINK OF BLACK ENERGY AS I DID BEFORE...

...AND THEN SOME-THING FROM THE PITS LURCHES OUT AT ME.

BA'AL'S BEEN BUSY.

RRRRRAAARR!

HE'S STRONG ENOUGH TO CRACK CONCRETE....

...AND THAT'S JUST WITH HIS BREATH.

BUT MY BONES, MY CLAWS ARE ADAMANTIUM.

TOO BAD MY NECK ISN'T.

YOU MAY NOT ENTER HERE, VAMPIRE! YOU'RE NOT INVITED!

WHAT THE BLAZES ARE YOU TALKING ABOUT?

SKIP IT!

THK THUNK

AND THERE'S MORE WHERE THAT CAME FROM.

UH OH.

BURT! FOR THE LUVVA MIKE, STOP SCREWIN' AROUND! I TOLD YOU TO GET AWAY FROM THERE!

I'M WORKING ON IT! I'M WORKING ON IT!

CHUD

BURT, ARE YOU THROUGH FOOLING WITH THE DOOR?

KRUNCH

YES.

A DIRECT SHOT FROM AN ADAMANTIUM SKULL WOULD CAVE IN THE FACE OF A NORMAL MAN.

I'LL SETTLE FOR SLOWING THIS JOKER DOWN.

KRUNK

I DON'T EVEN GET THAT.

THAT SHOT SHOULD HAVE LAID HIM OPEN FROM CROTCH TO STERNUM.

IF IT DID...

...HE'S PUTTING UP AN EXCELLENT FRONT.

RRRRRRRR

NOT MUCH FOR CONVERSATION, IS HE?

WELL, YOU'RE A FEISTY LITTLE MAN.

AND YOU'RE... A DEAD BIG MAN.

NOT TODAY. AND NOT AT YOUR HANDS.

GRRRRRRRR

BAD MOVE. HE JUST CRUSHED THE PILOT'S SKULL.

KRAK

I LEAP TO MY FEET AND FACE BA'AL, AND SUDDENLY...

I'M FACED WITH A FEELING I HAD A GHOST OF BACK AT THE AIRPORT.

A FEELING OF DEJA VU, WHICH IS FRENCH FOR "RERUN."

AND THEN LAUGHING BOY IS BACK.

HE SLAMS MY CLAWS INTO THE PANEL, AND ELECTRICITY JOLTS THROUGH ME.

SO I SHARE THE JOY JUICE.

THE WHOLE COCKPIT'S FILLING WITH SMOKE. THE PLANE'S GOING DOWN.

BA'AL'S LAUGHING, AND I'M READY TO CUT HIS THROAT.

THEN I REMEMBER.. JESSICA.

IF SHE'S STILL ALIVE, SHE WON'T BE WHEN THIS PLANE GOES UP.

:COUGH: :ACK:

DREW! HEY, DREW!

IT'S ABOUT :UNH: TIME!

MISS ME?

BEHIND YOU!

GREAT.

LET'S GO!

GO? WHERE?!?

DOWN!

I HEAR ARCHIE'S PLANE ZOOMING TOWARDS US AS WE SKYDIVE...

A LESSER PILOT WOULD NEVER BE ABLE TO PULL THIS OFF.

BUT ARCHIE IS THE BEST THERE IS AT WHAT HE DOES.

HE GETS IT FROM ME.

HE'S GOT IT!

PULL UP! PULL UP!

IT'S INSANE. AS THE PLANE EXPLODES, THE AIR FRYING AROUND US...

I KNOW BA'AL MUST BE DEAD. AND YET--

THE FLAMES SEEM TO CONGEAL INTO HIS FACE, AND IN MY HEAD, I HEAR HIM SNARLING--

"I DON'T HAVE THE ULTIMATE POWER YET, LITTLE MAN, BUT I WILL. AND THEN..."

"...NOT EVEN THE HAND OF GOD WILL STOP ME."

OOOOOHHH...

O'DONNELL. YOU CAN SAY IT. OOOHH D'...

O'DONNELL!

KRACSH

WHAT THE BLOODY BLAZES?

MR. O'DONNELL? I AM JOHANN, THE PRINCE'S AIDE.

THE PRINCE UNDERSTANDS THAT YOU POSSESS SOMETHING THAT MIGHT INTEREST H.M.

HE WANTS IT.

NOW.

Next: *Homecoming*

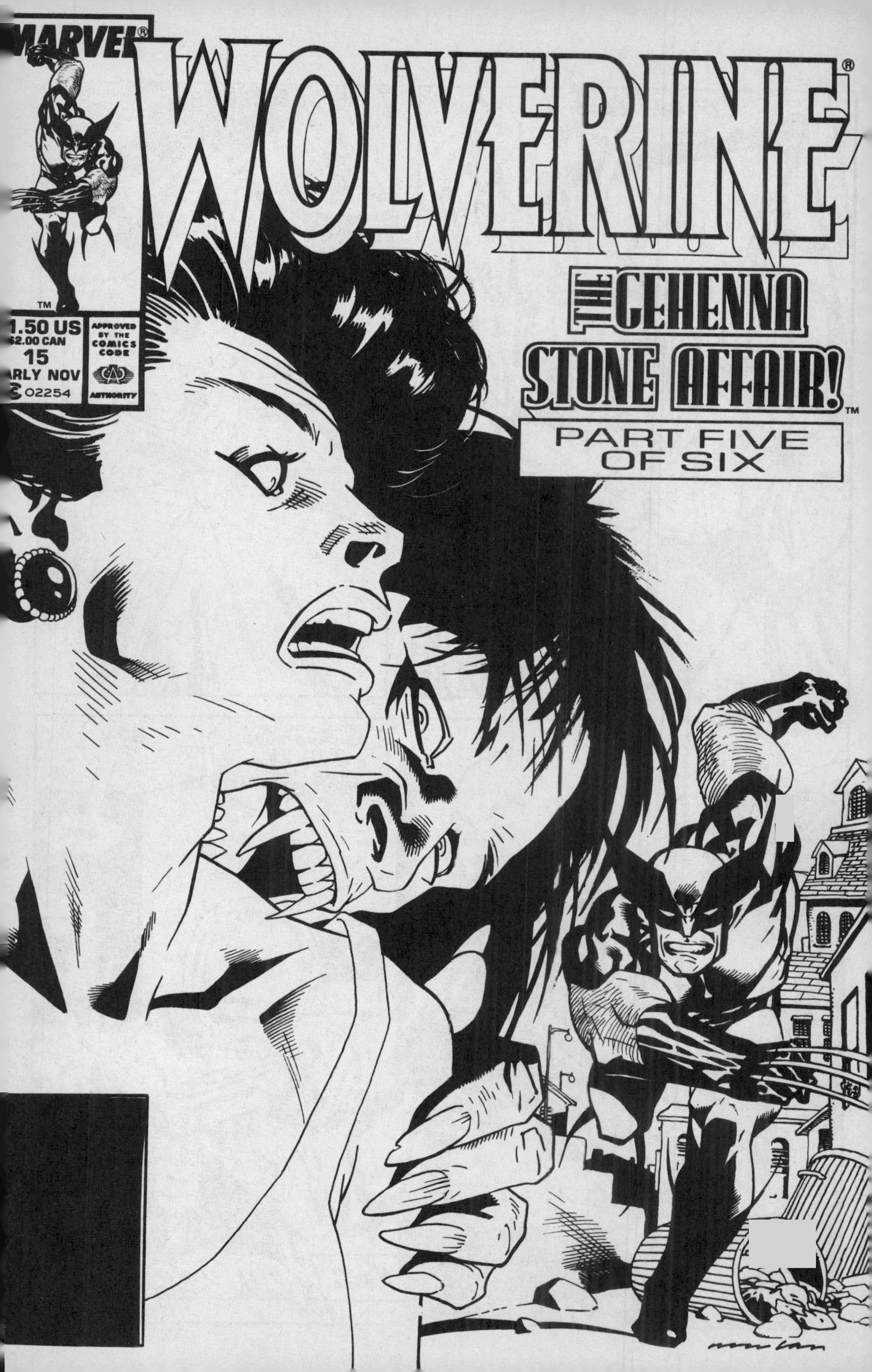

MARVEL®
WOLVERINE®
TM
$1.50 US
$2.00 CAN
15
EARLY NOV
02254
APPROVED BY THE COMICS CODE AUTHORITY
THE GEHENNA STONE AFFAIR!™
PART FIVE OF SIX

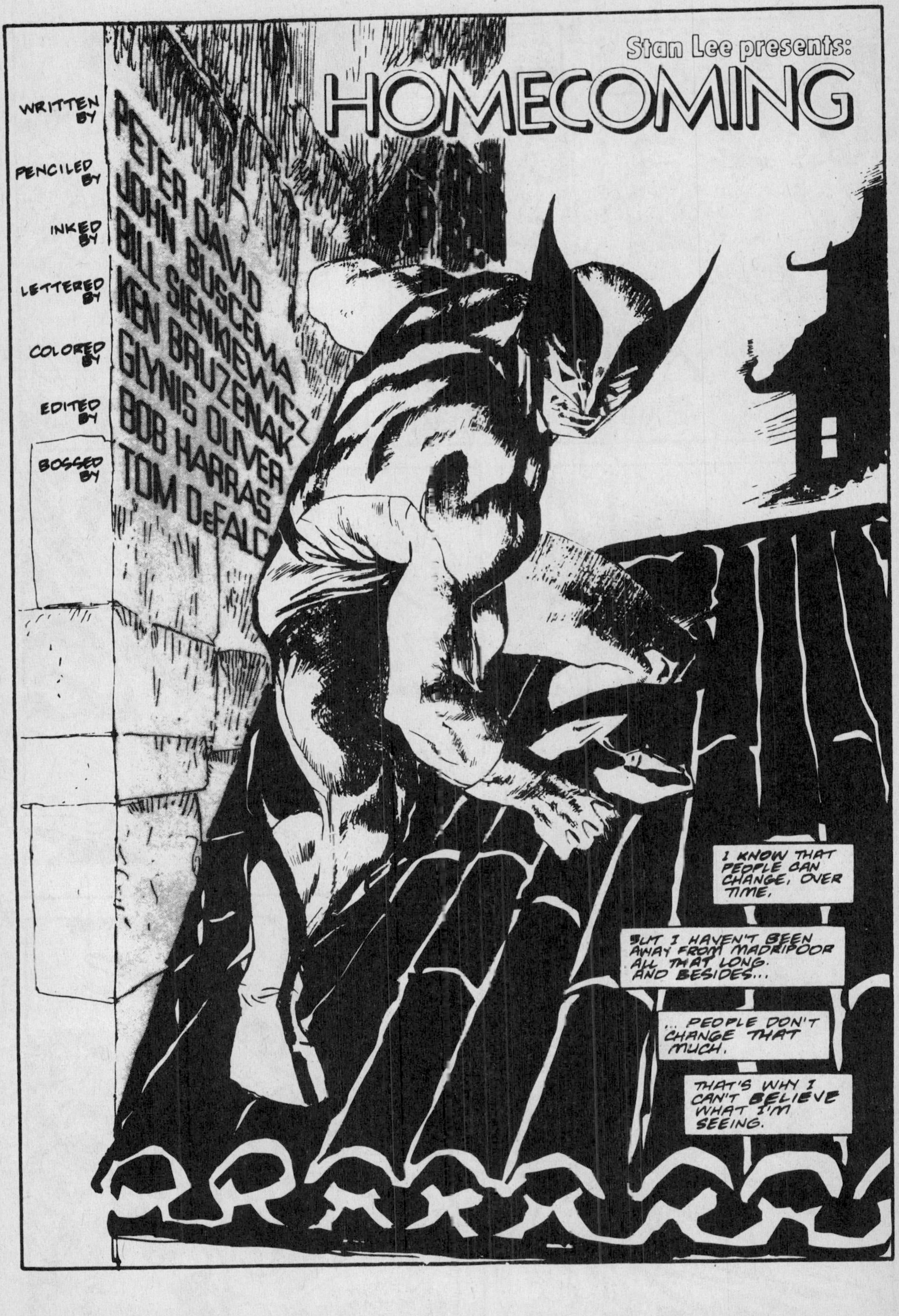
Stan Lee presents:
HOMECOMING
WRITTEN BY PETER DAVID
PENCILED BY JOHN BUSCEMA
INKED BY BILL SIENKIEWICZ
LETTERED BY KEN BRUZENAK
COLORED BY GLYNIS OLIVER
EDITED BY BOB HARRAS
BOSSED BY TOM DeFALCO
I KNOW THAT PEOPLE CAN CHANGE, OVER TIME.
BUT I HAVEN'T BEEN AWAY FROM MADRIPOOR ALL THAT LONG. AND BESIDES...
... PEOPLE DON'T CHANGE THAT MUCH.
THAT'S WHY I CAN'T BELIEVE WHAT I'M SEEING.

HERE IN MADRIPOOR, TAI HAS ALWAYS DONE HIS JOB AS TOP COP WITH TOTAL CALM.

SO WHY IS HE POPPING HIS CORK? AT LINDSAY McCABE, NO LESS?

WHERE IS IT. TELL ME.

I DON'T HAVE IT! I NEVER DID! O'DONNELL DID AND EVEN HE DOESN'T ANYMORE!

YOU'RE LYING!

BUT WE'LL CONVINCE YOU TO TELL THE TRUTH.

AND I'LL HAVE TO CONVINCE YOU...

...TO BACK OFF FROM HER.

KWAN... ...DISPATCH THIS COSTUMED IMBECILE.

NOT NICE.

YOU DON'T HEAR ME MAKING FUN O' YOUR DUDS.

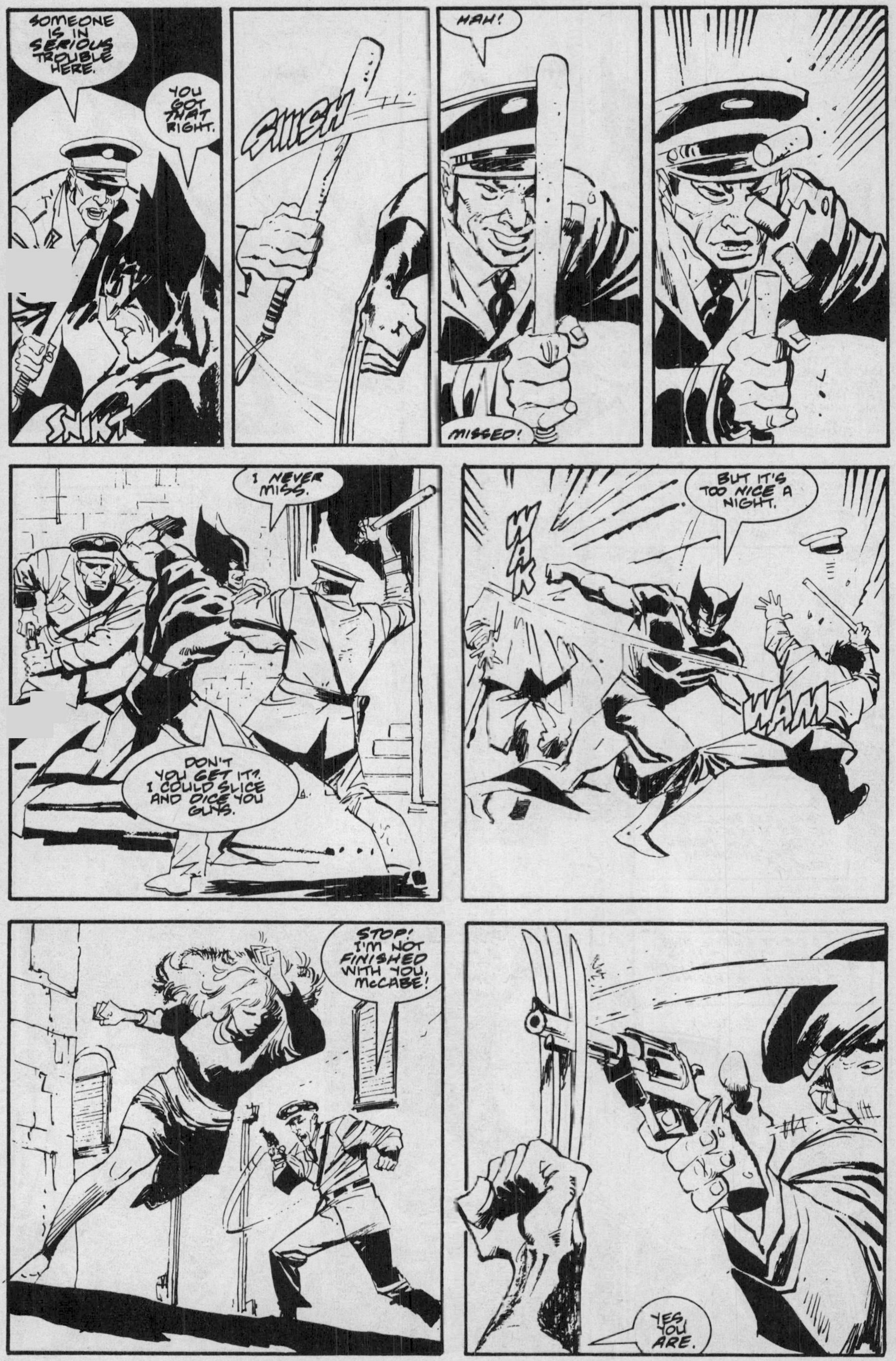
SOMEONE IS IN SERIOUS TROUBLE HERE.
YOU GOT THAT RIGHT.
SNIKT
SHISH
HAH!
MISSED!
I NEVER MISS.
DON'T YOU GET IT?! I COULD SLICE AND DICE YOU GUYS.
BUT IT'S TOO NICE A NIGHT.
WAK
WAM
STOP! I'M NOT FINISHED WITH YOU, McCABE!
YES YOU ARE.

WHAT'S WITH YOU, TAI? THIS ISN'T LIKE YOU.

I DON'T KNOW WHO YOU ARE, AND YOU CERTAINLY KNOW NOTHING OF HOW I DO THINGS.

BUT KNOW THIS...

...YOU'RE A DEAD MAN!

DO YOU HEAR? A DEAD MAN!

WITH THAT LITTLE WARNING FOLLOWING ME, I SWING BACK TO MY PLACE, SWITCH TO LESS CONSPICUOUS CLOTHES, AND HIT THE STREETS.

IT SHOULD FEEL GOOD TO BE BACK IN MADRIPOOR AFTER THE BROUHAHA IN FRISCO.

IT SHOULD...

...BUT INSTEAD... IT FEELS WRONG SOMEHOW.

AND I CAN'T SHAKE THE FEELING THAT IT HAS SOMETHING TO DO WITH THE WHOLE GEHENNA STONE AFFAIR.

BUT THAT'S IMPOSSIBLE... ISN'T IT?

NOT AS MUCH CHATTER IN THE PRINCESS BAR AS USUAL, AND THEN I HEAR WHY.

THEY'RE LISTENING TO THE SHOUTING FROM THE BACK ROOM SOUNDS LIKE O'DONNELL AND...

SONUVAGUN. LINDSAY, SHE'S POPULAR TONIGHT.

SEEMS LIKE, IN HER BOOK, O'DONNELL ISN'T SO POPULAR.

AND YOU'RE GUTLESS, TOO!

I'LL SHOW YOU GUTS, YOU LITTLE...

WHOA SIMMER DOWN.

HAS THE WHOLE TOWN GONE NUTS!

RIGHT! NUTS!

UHHHHHH...

AND NUTS TO YOU! THAT'S TWICE TONIGHT YOU "SAVED" ME, WOLVERINE! BUTT OUT!

YOU KNEW?

I'M GONNA PUKE...

OF COURSE I KNEW. JESSICA TOLD ME.

AND YOU CAN ALL ROT.

THANKS... A BLOODY *LOT* PATCH.

YOU'LL RECOVER. BUT IF YOU HAVE KIDS, THEY'LL BE STUPID.

WHAT THE HECK WAS *THAT* ALL ABOUT?

I DON'T KNOW. I...HEY. NOW CAN I STOP PRETENDING I DON'T KNOW YOU'RE WOLVERINE.

HOW DID *YOU* KNOW?

LINDSAY TOLD ME WEEKS AGO.

OH, *GREAT.* WHEN IT HAPPENED WITH *DREW,* I THOUGHT SHE WAS YANKING ME.

"IT WAS WHEN WE WERE CHASING THIS PLANE FILLED WITH...WELL, YOU DON'T *WANT* TO KNOW WHAT WITH...

"SHE HAD ALREADY JUMPED DOWN ONTO IT. I PUT ON MY COSTUME, LEAPED AFTER HER, AND WHEN I *GOT* THERE, SHE SAID--"

WOLVERINE! IT'S ABOUT *TIME!*

"AND AFTER WE TOOK CARE OF BUSINESS AND GOT BACK INTO THE PLANE--"

OF COURSE I KNEW.

BULL! SOMEBODY WOULD'VE SAID SOMETHING TO ME!

NO *WAY!* WHEN SOMEBODY WITH CLAWS AND A TEMPER WANTS TO BELIEVE HE'S FOOLING PEOPLE, WELL...

NO ONE WANTS TO BE THE ONE TO SAY "HEY, WOLVIE, WHAT'S WITH THE STUPID EYEPATCH?"

SO THE JOKES ON ME. HAR-FLAMIN'-HAR. EVERYONE MUST THINK I'M A CLASS-A LOON.

WELL, YOU ARE A CLASS-A LOON.

MOST FOLKS IN MADRIPOOR HAVE ALIASES. YOU THINK TIGER TYGER IS HER REAL NAME? YOU THINK O'DONNELL IS MINE?

PATCH. LOOK. THE FRENCH FOREIGN LEGION IS WHERE GUYS GO TO FORGET. MADRIPOOR IS WHERE THEY GO TO REMEMBER, EVEN IF WHAT THEY REMEMBER DIDN'T HAPPEN.

OKAY, ENOUGH ABOUT THIS. WHAT'S WITH YOU AND LINDSAY?

YOU! IT'S ALL YOUR FAULT!

I WANTED TO PUSH BURT OUT OF THE PLANE, BUT NO, YOU SAID! HE'S MY BROTHER, YOU SAID!

HI, ARCHIE. HAVING A GOOD DAY, ARE YOU?

CLAM UP, O'DONNELL!

BURT'S ACTING WEIRD, EVEN FOR HIM. IF YOU'D ONLY...

ARCHIE...

SWAT

...WAIT YOUR TURN.

NOW SIT DOWN. WE'LL ORDER YOU A DRINK. THEN WE'LL LISTEN TO O'DONNELL. AND THEN YOU.

AND THEN...

"...WE'RE GOING TO FIGURE OUT WHAT'S GOING ON IN MADRIPOOR."

I FEEL BADLY WALKING OUT ON ARCHIE LIKE THAT.

BUT, BLAST IT, HE HAS TO START TAKING ME SERIOUSLY.

LOVELY YOUNG WOMAN. I WONDER WHAT SHE'S DOING OUT ON A NIGHT LIKE THIS?

HI, SAILOR. LOOKING FOR GOBS OF FUN?

OH.

EEEEEEEEEEK

YOUNG WOMAN?

I'M WARNING YOU, IF THIS IS SOME SORT OF COME-ON, I...

LOOK!

WE'VE BEEN SPOTTED!

TAKE CARE OF HIM... WHILE I PREPARE THIS ONE FOR A BLOOD SACRIFICE... FOR THE MASTER!

BACK AT THE PRINCESS BAR...

SO, ANYWAY, AFTER THE COPS TAKE AWAY THESE TWO STIFFS, LINDSAY STARTED ACTING FUNNY.

REAL FUNNY, LIKE COMING BY MY PLACE AT 4 AM FUNNY.

"SO SHE'S ALL OVER ME, AND I'M FIGURING, I CAN LIVE WITH THAT...

"AND THEN THE ROOF CAVES IN.

"THIS GOON SQUAD, SENT BY THE PRINCE OF MADRIPOOR, BURSTS IN, AND THIS WEIRD DUCK NAMED JOHANN IS LEADING THEM."

YOU HAVE SOMETHING THE PRINCE WANTS.

I SUGGEST YOU TURN IT OVER... NOW.

DON'T DO IT, O'DONNELL! IT'S OURS!

WHAT'S THIS "OURS" STUFF?

MR. O'DONNELL, RETICENCE IS NOT A GOOD IDEA, HEALTH-WISE, OR OTHERWISE.

SO... YOUR CHOICE. WHAT PART OF MY MEN BREAK FIRST? UNLESS YOU'D CARE TO--

COOPERATE?
JUST WHAT
I HAD IN
MIND.

ZIP IT,
LINDSAY.

DON'T
DO IT!
DON'T
TELL
THEM!

HOLD ON,
JOHANN, IT'S
IN HERE
SOMEWH--

KLAKLAK

DON'T...   ...EVEN...

...THINK
IT.

THE
PRINCE
THANKS
YOU, MR.
O'DONNELL.

HOLD
IT!

PUT IT DOWN,
OR I'LL BLOW WHAT
LITTLE BRAINS SHE
HAS FROM HERE
TO SINGA-
PORE!

AT LEAST
WAIT
UNTIL WE
LEAVE.

IT'S SO DIFFICULT
GETTING BRAIN
MATTER STAINS
OUT OF A
SUIT.

THAT WAS SOME BLUFF.

IT WASN'T A BLUFF. I MEAN, I DIDN'T GO THROUGH WITH IT. BUT WHEN I SAID IT, I MEANT IT.

AND LINDSAY KNEW IT. SHE STORMED OUT RIGHT AFTER, AND JUST NOW WAS THE FIRST TIME I'D SEEN HER SINCE.

O'DONNELL... DOESN'T YOUR BEHAVIOR STRIKE YOU AS STRANGE? YOURS AND LINDSAY'S?

STRANGE HOW?

WELL, LINDSAY'S COMIN' ON TO YOU AND YOU'RE NOT QUESTIONING IT, AND THE THREATS, IT'S ALL UNLIKE YOU.

THIS TOWN STINKS SO MUCH IT'S HARD TO SEPARATE THE AROMAS...

...BUT SOMETHING IS DEFINITELY FISHY.

UH-OH. COMPANY.

WHERE IS IT?

AND, BACK WITH BROTHER BURT...

DIDN'T YOU HEAR ME? GET HIM!

NO ONE CAN INTERFERE WITH THE MASTER'S BLOOD SACRIFICE!

WHERE IS HE? WHERE'S BA'AL?

HE SPOKE THE MASTER'S NAME!

HE DIES FOR THAT!

YOU CAN MAKE ALL THE EXCUSES TO KILL ME YOU WANT.

...BUT NOTHING'S HAPPENING TO M--

UNNNHKKK!

I THINK HE'S UNCONSCIOUS.

A PITY. HE WON'T FEEL MY FANGS RIPPING OUT HIS--

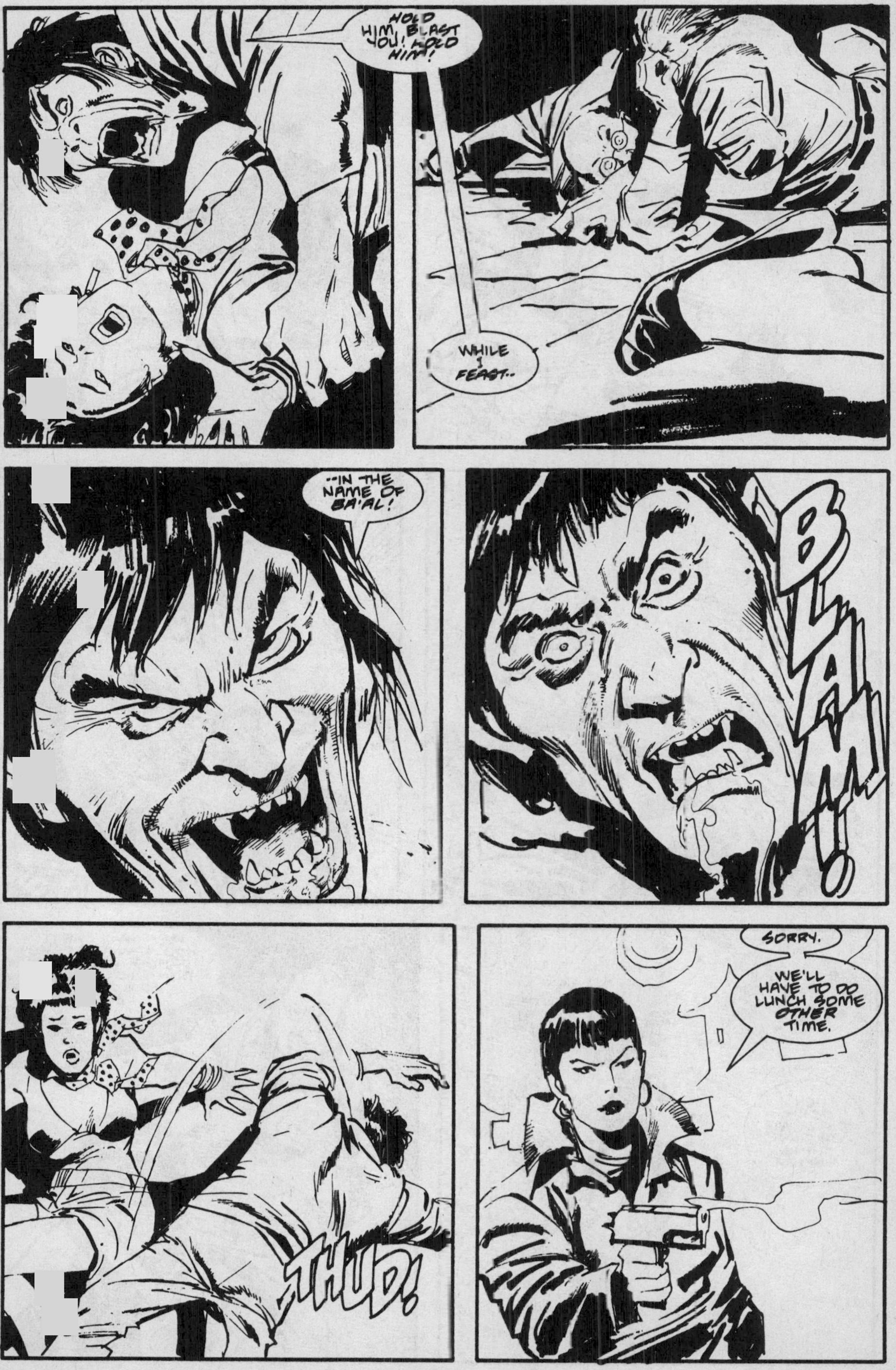
HOLD HIM, BLAST YOU! HOLD HIM!
WHILE I FEAST..
--IN THE NAME OF BA'AL!
BLAM!
THUD!
SORRY.
WE'LL HAVE TO DO LUNCH SOME OTHER TIME.

JESSICA! JESSICA DREW!

I CERTAINLY CAN'T FAULT YOUR TIMING.

STAY BACK! OR BALDY GETS IT!

YOUR PLAY, BURT.

BALDY, HUH?

BLAM BLAM

HEY, DON'T THANK ME OR ANYTHING, SISTER.

YOU SAW THEM! YOU SAW THE FAKE FANGS, HEARD WHAT THEY SAID! THEY'RE FOLLOWERS OF BA'AL.

UH-HUH.

AND NOW WE FOLLOW THE FOLLOWER. BECAUSE IF THEY'RE STILL FOLLOWING...

...THAT MEANS THAT SOMEWHERE, BA'AL IS STILL LEADING.

IT'S GETTING SO YOU CAN'T SIT AROUND WITH FRIENDS AND KNOCK BACK A FEW BREWS...

...WITHOUT SOMEONE SHOWING UP TO WRECK YOUR GOOD TIME.

"CURIOUSER AND CURIOUSER." THAT'S WHAT THEY SAID IN ALICE IN WONDERLAND.

THAT'S HOW I FEEL. LIKE I WENT THROUGH A LOOKING GLASS.

EVERYONE IS ACTING LIKE DISTORTED REFLECTIONS OF THEMSELVES.

AND IF I HAD ANY PATIENCE...

...I'D BE LOSING IT ABOUT NOW.

NOW, I LIKE A FRACAS AS WELL AS THE NEXT GUY, UNLESS THE NEXT GUY IS GANDHI.

BUT ENOUGH'S ENOUGH.

ALL RIGHT! EVERYBODY FREEZE!

ONE MOVE AND WE'VE GOT TAI DIED!

YOU! SOLDIER BOY. WHAT'S GOING ON!

IT'S TAI'S ORDERS! WE HAVE NO IDEA.

I WANT THE GEM! THE FRAGMENTED GEM! I...I CAN'T STOP THINKING ABOUT IT...

HOLD IT.

FRAGMENTED GEM? AND YOU WERE IT?

YES, O'DONNELL HAS IT. AND YOU'RE UNDER ARREST.

SAVE IT FOR HAWAII FIVE-O.

O'DONNELL, THIS GEM TAI MENTIONED...

...WAS IT THE THING THIS JOHANN WAS AFTER? YOU NEVER SAID...

YES. IT WAS.

AND WAS LINDSAY NEAR IT, TOO?

UH-HUH.

DID IT LOOK LIKE THIS SKETCH I JUST MADE?

KIND OF. DIFFERENT FRAGMENTATIONS, BUT THAT'S BASICALLY IT.

YOU DREW THE GEM BURT HAD BACK IN FRISCO?

UH-HUH. THE ONE THAT WAS MAKING HIM SO CRAZED.

AND THE GEM O'DONNELL HAS IS SIMILAR. PERHAPS THEY'RE BOTH PIECES OF THE GEHENNA STONE.

I NEVER HEARD OF ANY GEHENNA STONE. BESIDES, THE PRINCE HAS IT NOW. REMEMBER.

THE MOST POWERFUL MAN IN MADRIPOOR HAS A GEM THAT... PUTS PEOPLE AT EACH OTHER'S THROATS?

PATCH! HOLD IT!

NO TIME, O'DONNELL...

"NO TIME AT ALL."

EH?

THOUGHT SURE THAT SOMEONE WAS...

OH. WELL.

GETTING SLOPPY IN MY OLD AGE. WONDER WHERE BURT GOT OFF TO.

HOLD IT. I KNOW THIS ROAD IF HE STAYS ON IT...

...HE'S GOING TO BE HEADING STRAIGHT TO...

...THE CASTLE OF THE PRINCE OF MADRIPOOR.

WHERE'S YOUR *BROTHER*, ARCHIE, WHERE'S *BURT*?

WE HAD AN *ARGUMENT*. HE WAS BECOMING *OBSESSIVE* ABOUT THAT STONE, SAYING WE HAD TO FIND THE *WHOLE* THING. HE--

DON'T YOU *GET* IT? HE WAS *RIGHT* ABOUT EVERYTHING.

THE GEHENNA STONE *DOES* EXIST, AND AS IT GETS REASSEMBLED, EVERY INDIVIDUAL OUTSTANDING PIECE GETS *STRONGER*.

AND IT BRINGS OUT THE *WORST* IN WHOEVERS BEEN *NEAR* IT. 'CEPT ME, CAUSE I'M *ALWAYS* NASTY.

I GOT A SICK FEELING THAT THAT PIECE IS THE *LAST* ONE.

WHICH GOES WITH MY *OTHER* SICK FEELING...

THAT *BA'AL* AIN'T *DEAD*.

"THE MORE PIECES THAT WERE ASSEMBLED THE STRONGER THE GEHENNA STONE BECOMES. AND IF THE PRINCE HAS THE SINGLE OUTSTANDING PIECE..."

"HE'S IN MORTAL DANGER."

GOOD EVENING, MISS DREW.

GOOD EVENING, SALOMAN.

I'LL SUMMON JOHANN FOR YOU.

EVENING, JOHANN. I'D LIKE TO SEE THE PRINCE. IT'S URGENT.

BUT OF COURSE, MISS DREW! RIGHT THIS WAY.

THE PRINCE ALWAYS HAS TIME FOR HIS FAVORITE AGENT. DO YOU BRING SOME INTERESTING TIDBIT?

INTERESTING ISN'T THE WORD FOR IT.

HIGHNESS. THANK YOU FOR SEEING ME SO QUICKLY.

I HAVE TO TELL YOU THAT YOU MAY HAVE AN INTRUDER IN THE...

...THE...

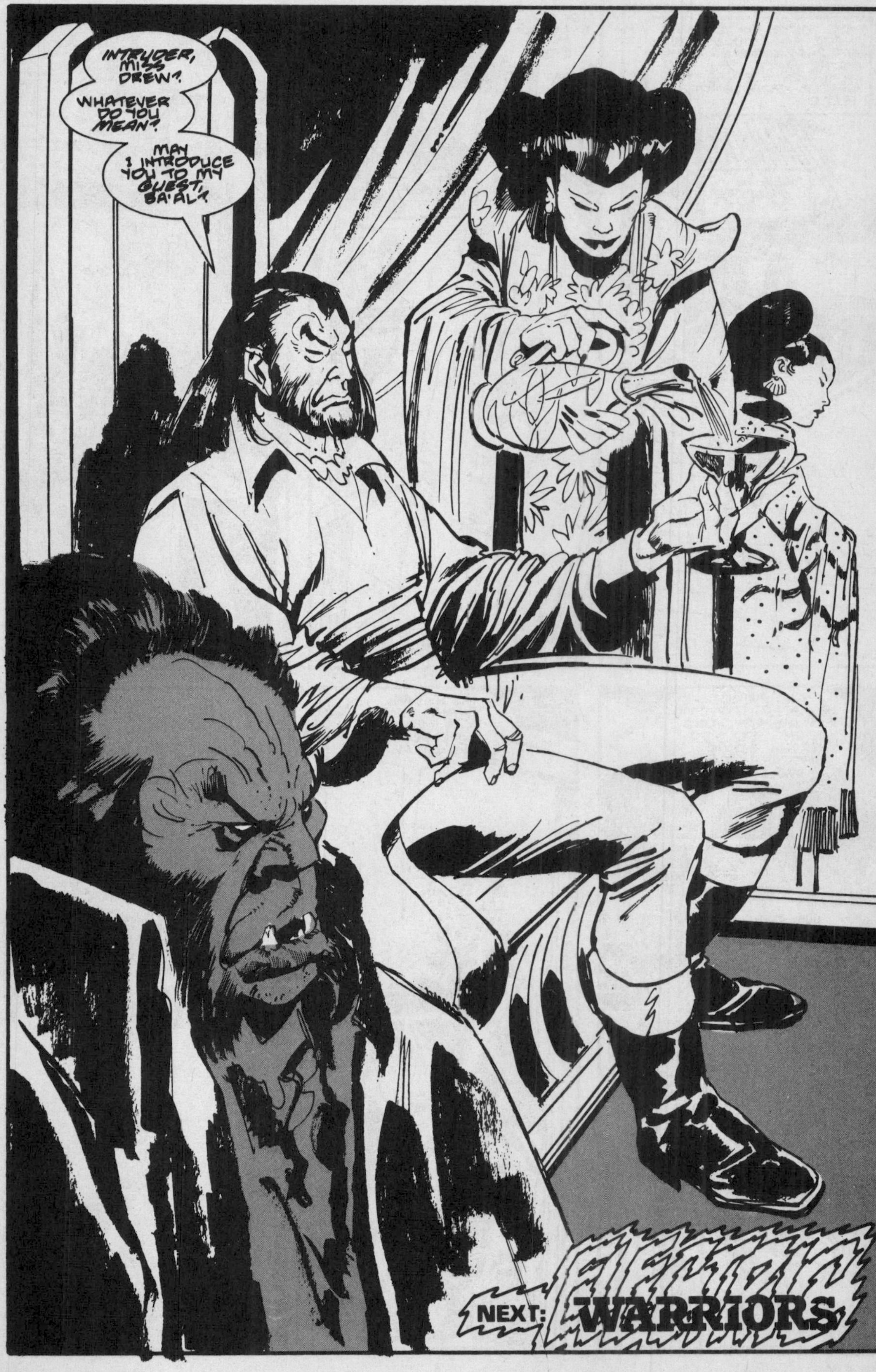

INTRUDER, MISS DREW?
WHATEVER DO YOU MEAN?
MAY I INTRODUCE YOU TO MY GUEST, BA'AL?
NEXT: WARRIORS

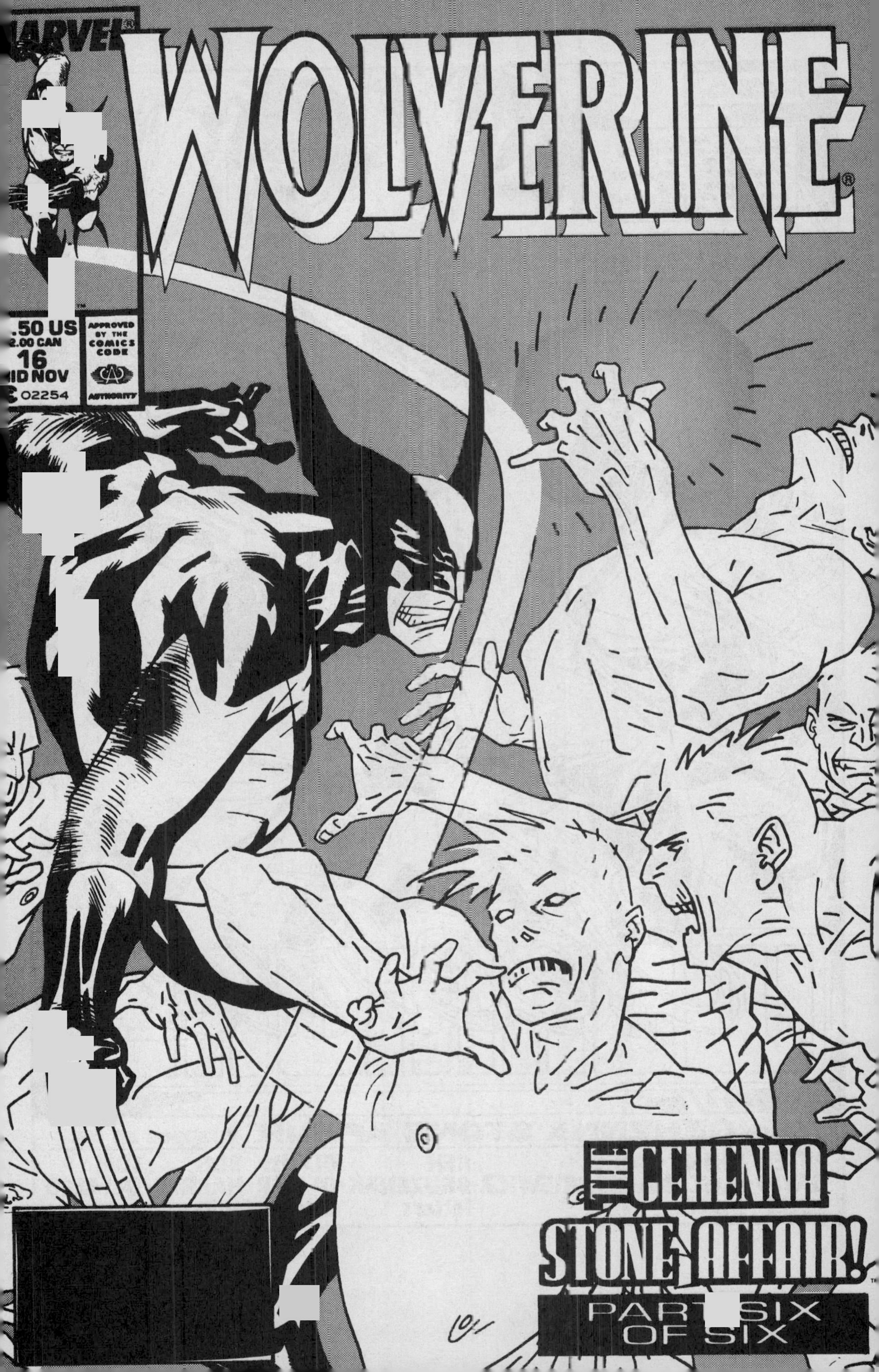
MARVEL
WOLVERINE
.50 US
2.00 CAN
16
ID NOV
02254
APPROVED BY THE COMICS CODE AUTHORITY
THE GEHENNA STONE AFFAIR!
PART SIX OF SIX

MY NAME IS WOLVERINE...

AND I'M HEADING TOWARDS THE PALACE OF THE PRINCE OF MADRIPOOR TO WARN HIM ABOUT THE DANGER OF THE DEADLY GEHENNA STONE...

...WHEN, SUDDENLY, I'M JUMPED BY RAVENOUS PSUEDO-VAMPIRES.

I HATE WHEN THAT HAPPENS.

Electric Warriors

"The GEHENNA STONE AFFAIR" wrapped up by:

PETER DAVID	JOHN BUSCEMA	BILL SIENKIEWICZ	KEN BRUZENAK	GLYNIS OLIVER	BOB HARRAS	TOM DeFALCO
script	pencils	inks	letters	colors	edits	chief

STILL, PERHAPS I CAN TURN THIS TO MY ADVANTAGE.

MY COMPANIONS, TAI, O'DONNELL AND ARCHIE CORRIGAN ARE CAPABLE OF HANDLING THEMSELVES.

THEY WOULDN'T HAVE LIVED THIS LONG IF THEY WEREN'T.

SO I ALLOW THE STRUGGLE TO "DRAG" ME INTO THE WOODS.

MY MIND'S ONLY PARTIALLY ON THE FIGHT. THE REST OF IT IS REALIZING...

...THAT IF I'M WALTZING AROUND WITH THESE GUYS, THEN BA'AL IS STILL ALIVE, MAYBE EVEN WITH THE PRINCE, GETTING THE LAST FRAGMENT OF THE STONE.

THAT BEING THE CASE, IT'S TIME TO GET IT IN GEAR.

URKH!

BAM

GOT REAL QUIET OUT THERE. WHICH MEANS IT'S OVER, ONE WAY OR THE OTHER.

YEAH, I FIGURED IT WOULD BE THE OTHER.

PATCH! YO, PATCH!

WE HAVE NO TIME TO STAND ABOUT WAITING FOR THAT SURLY RUNT.

LOOK WHO'S TALKING.

WE MUST GET TO THE PRINCE. PATCH CAN ATTEND TO HIMSELF.

YEAH, PROBABLY. THOUGH HE IS STILL HUMAN, 'KNOW.

PUTS HIS PANTS ON ONE LEG AT A TIME, JUST LIKE US.

YOUR HIGHNESS, THIS... *CREATURE*... IS PURE *EVIL!* JUST *LOOK* AT HIM! CAN'T YOU *SEE* THAT?

I'M SORRY YOU FIND MY BIRTH DEFORMITIES SO APPALLING MISS. THE GOOD LORD DID NOT BLESS ALL OF US WITH NATURAL BEAUTY SUCH AS YOURS.

THE "GOOD LORD" HAD NOTHING TO DO WITH *YOU*, I'LL BET ON THAT.

HIGHNESS, YOU CAN'T LET HIM HAVE THE FRAGMENT YOU POSSESS. THIS *MONSTER* WANTS TO RECONSTRUCT THE GEHENNA STONE AND ACHIEVE WORLD DOMINATION.

OH, HONESTLY, JESSICA, WHAT AN *ABSURD* FAIRY TALE.

IT'S *NOT* ABSURD! IT'S...

OKAY IT'S ABSURD! BUT IT'S *TRUE!*

BESIDES, IF BA'AL WERE THE MONSTER YOU SAY, HE WOULD BE TRYING TO JUST *TAKE* THE FRAGMENT, INSTEAD OF DISCUSSING *PRICE*, AS WOULD ANY REASONABLE MAN.

ACTUALLY, HIGHNESS, ALTHOUGH THE PRICE YOU'VE QUOTED FOR SUCH A VALUABLE ARCHAEOLOGICAL RELIC IS *FAIR*...

I WAS THINKING OF SOMETHING IN THE WAY OF *BARTER.*

AND WHAT COULD YOU OFFER THAT WOULD INTEREST *ME*, SIR?

HOW DOES *IMMORTALITY* STRIKE YOU?

O'DONNELL AND THE OTHERS ARE LONG BEHIND ME NOW.

SOON, BA'AL. VERY SOON.

HAVEN'T SEEN HER.

JESSICA DREW? LAST WEEK, I THINK...

BLONDE, RIGHT?

CAN'S SAY AS I HAVE. YOU A FRIEND

WE WERE FOLLOWING A VAMPIRE AND I LOST HER.

UH HUH.

WOULDN'T ANYBODY KNOW WHERE SHE IS?

HEH. TRY THE PRINCE. HE KNOWS EVERYTHING ABOUT EVERYTHING.

CASTLE'S RIGHT UP THERE.

THANK YOU.

WAIT! I WAS KIDDING! YOU WON'T GET IN TO SEE THE...

OH, FORGET IT.

IMMORTALITY? FASCINATING. I SHALL HAVE TO *CONSIDER* IT...AS I CONSIDER *JESSICA'S* WORDS AS WELL.

RETURN TOMORROW.

YOU WILL DECIDE NOW... OR NEVER.

I DISLIKE YOUR *TONE*, SIR.

DISLIKE IT ALL YOU *WISH*. I'LL HAVE YOUR DECISION, AND THE *FRAGMENT*.

I THINK NOT. IT'S WELL HIDDEN.

JOHANN, PLEASE ESCORT OUR ARROGANT GUEST OUT.

I'VE BEEN *PATIENT* WITH YOU, PRINCE, BECAUSE IN MANY WAYS, YOU REMIND ME OF *MYSELF*.

BUT I, UNLIKE *YOU*, HAVE *NEVER* BEEN A FOOL!

SILENCE!

THE *PRINCE* WANTS YOU TO LEAVE.

WHAT THE PRINCE WANTS IS AS OF *LITTLE* CONSEQUENCE...

...AS *WHAT YOU WANT*.

YOU HAVE NO IDEA WHAT YOU'RE DEALING WITH! I WILL HAVE THAT FRAGMENT, AND THE BLOOD SACRIFICE NEEDED BEFORE THE FINAL JOINING.

AND FORTUNATELY, I WILL BE ABLE TO HAVE BOTH AT ONE AND THE SAME TIME!

JOHANN!

HIGHNESS! HELP ME!

YOU THOUGHT YOUR HAVING SWALLOWED THE FRAGMENT WOULD HIDE IT FROM ME.

BLAM!

NOTHING COULD HIDE IT FROM ME.

NOT THE ARROGANCE OF A PRINCE.

NOR THE DEVIOUSNESS OF HIS UNDERLING.

YOU... ...ANIMAL!!

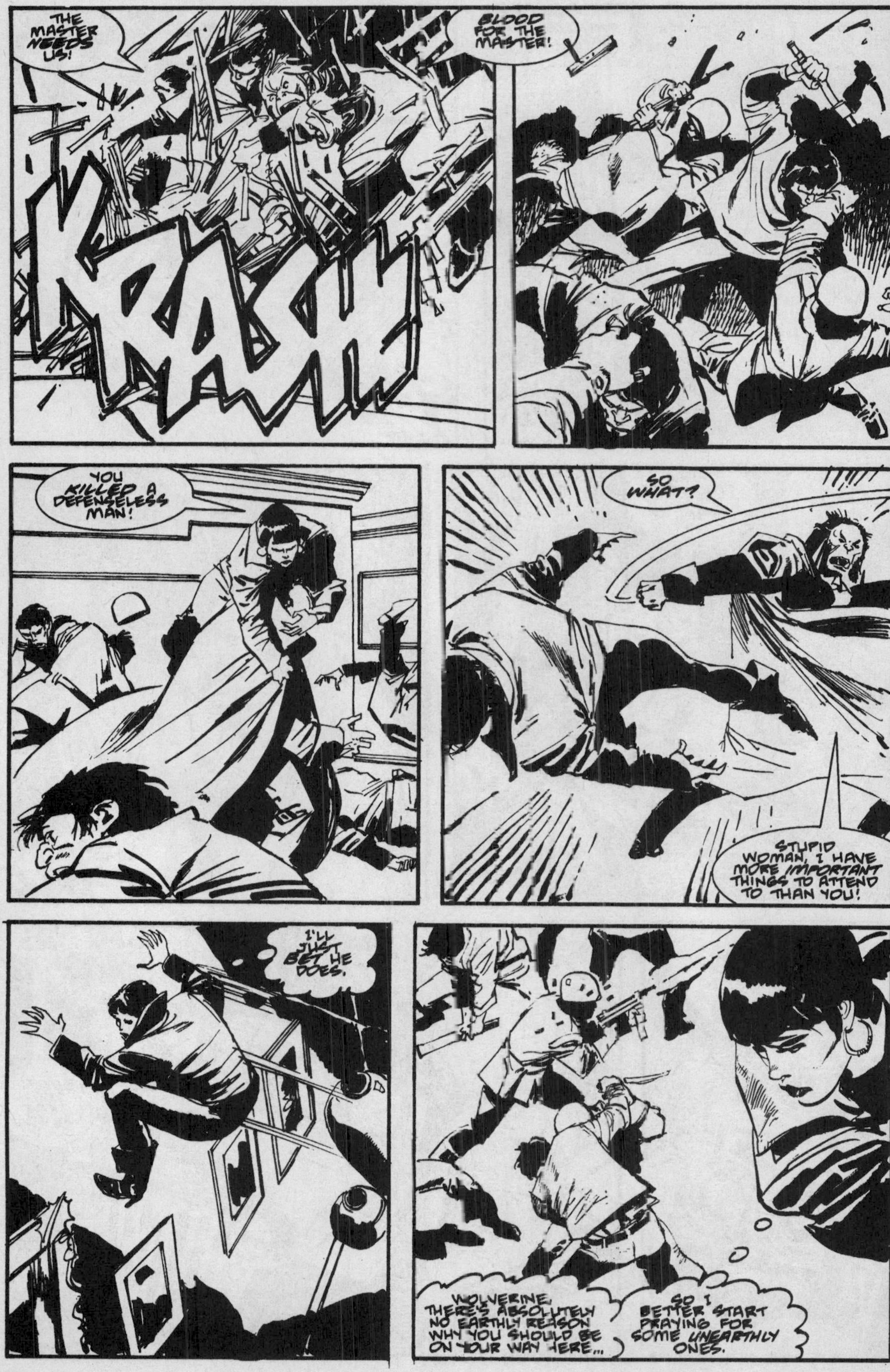
THE MASTER NEEDS US!
KRASH
BLOOD FOR THE MASTER!
YOU KILLED A DEFENSELESS MAN!
SO WHAT?
STUPID WOMAN, I HAVE MORE IMPORTANT THINGS TO ATTEND TO THAN YOU!
I'LL JUST BET HE DOES.
WOLVERINE, THERE'S ABSOLUTELY NO EARTHLY REASON WHY YOU SHOULD BE ON YOUR WAY HERE...
SO I BETTER START PRAYING FOR SOME UNEARTHLY ONES.

SOUNDS LIKE A FIGHT.

SMELLS LIKE BA'AL.

THERE'S DEATH HERE.

IT'S NOT MUCH FURTHER NOW.

THINK PATCH GOT THERE AHEAD OF US?

SOMETHING TELLS ME TO HOPE SO.

VROOM

AH!

STOP! POLICE EMERGENCY!

HEY!

HOLY JEEZ!

BURT! GET BACK HERE!

NO TIME! CLIMACTIC SEQUENCE COMING UP!

WHY ISN'T ANYONE EVER GLAD TO SEE ME?

KILL HIM!

I TOLD YOU.

TROUBLE IS, THERE'S NO APPRECIATION FOR STYLISTS ANYMORE.

SO MUCH SLAUGHTER, WITH SUCH GRACE AND ECONOMY OF MOVEMENT.

I'M AN ARTIST, BUT ARTISTS ARE ONLY LOVED AFTER THEY'RE DEAD.

MAYBE THAT'S WHY PEOPLE ARE ALWAYS TRYING TO KILL ME.

BEAUTIFUL.

THE CULMINATION OF TWO INCARNATIONS OF STRIVING.

COME IN, HIGHNESS. THROW YOUR DREARY KNIFE IF YOU WISH.

IT DOES YOU NO GOOD.

YOU, SEE CENTURIES AGO IT TOOK NOTHING LESS THAN THE HAND OF GOD TO STOP ME.

BUT THAT WAS IN THE DAYS OF MIRACLES.

AND THOSE DAYS ARE AS DEAD AS THE CREATOR WHO WAS RESPONSIBLE FOR THEM.

YOUR LUCK HAS RUN OUT!

WELL, SOMEBODY'S HAS.

WHERE'S THE PRINCE?

WITH BA'AL.

WHERE'S BA'AL?

DON'T KNOW.

SOME DETECTIVE.

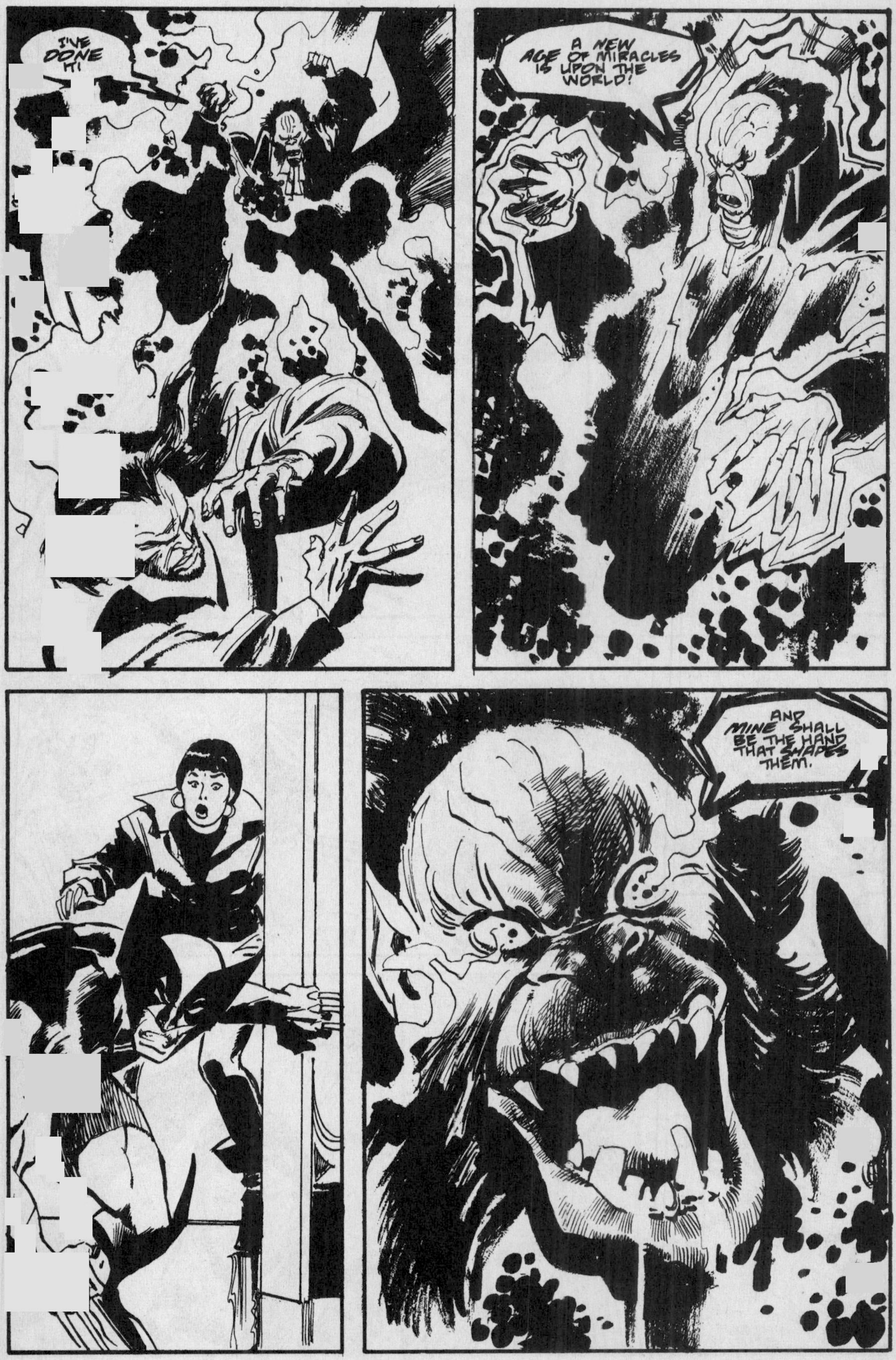
I'VE DONE IT!
A NEW AGE OF MIRACLES IS UPON THE WORLD!
AND MINE SHALL BE THE HAND THAT SHAPES THEM.

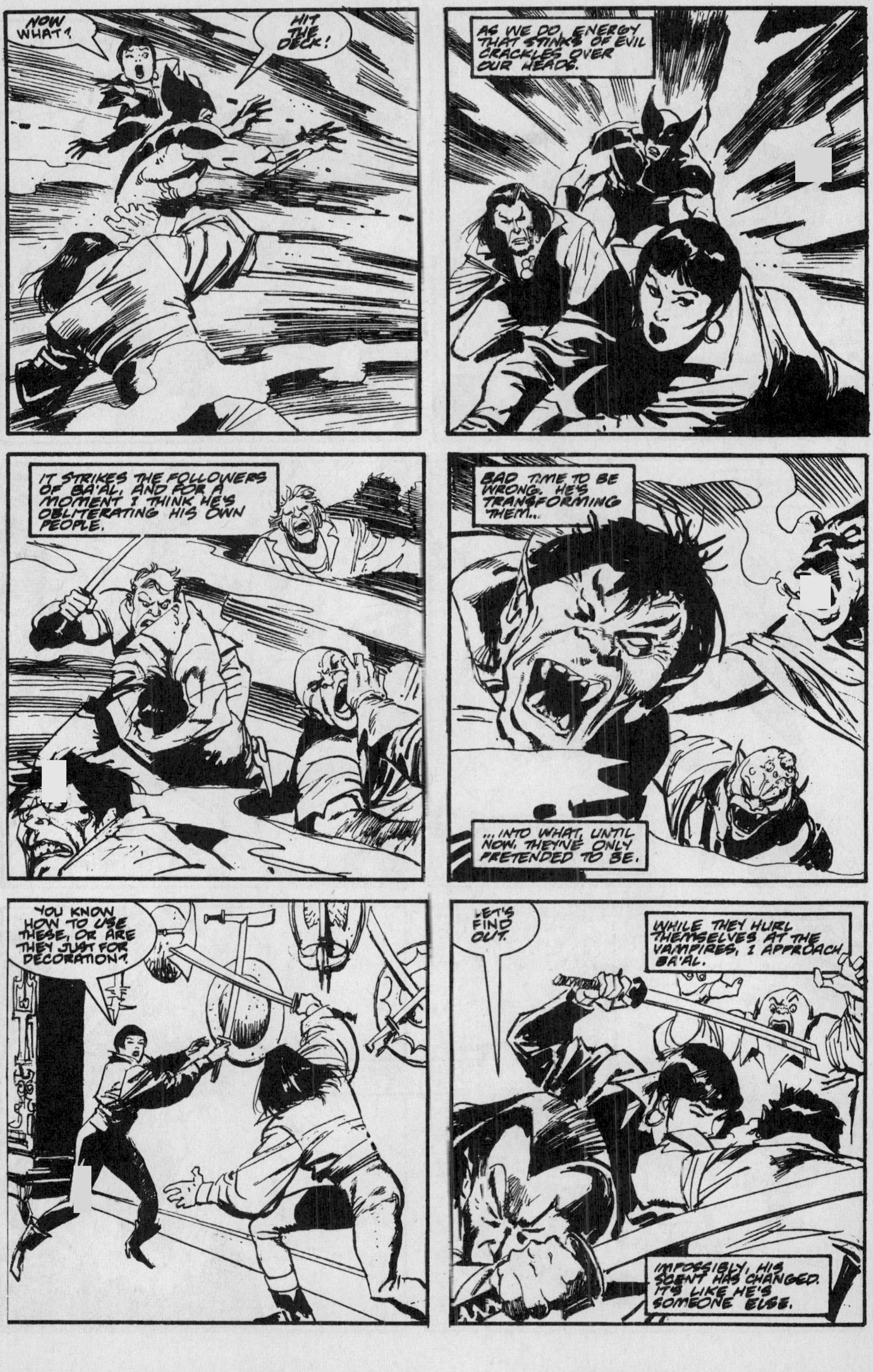
NOW WHAT?
HIT THE DECK!
AS WE DO, ENERGY THAT STINKS OF EVIL CRACKLES OVER OUR HEADS.
IT STRIKES THE FOLLOWERS OF BA'AL, AND FOR A MOMENT I THINK HE'S OBLITERATING HIS OWN PEOPLE.
BAD TIME TO BE WRONG. HE'S TRANSFORMING THEM...
...INTO WHAT, UNTIL NOW, THEY'VE ONLY PRETENDED TO BE.
YOU KNOW HOW TO USE THESE, OR ARE THEY JUST FOR DECORATION?
LET'S FIND OUT.
WHILE THEY HURL THEMSELVES AT THE VAMPIRES, I APPROACH BA'AL.
IMPOSSIBLY, HIS SCENT HAS CHANGED. IT'S LIKE HE'S SOMEONE ELSE.

AND THOUGH WE'VE MET TWICE BEFORE, HE LOOKS AT ME AS IF TRULY SEEING ME FOR THE FIRST TIME. AND...

...HE LOOKS SCARED.

KILL HIM, MY FOLLOWERS! KILL HIM!

HE SOUNDS SCARED, TOO.

I DON'T UNDERSTAND. HE'S GOT THE FOLLOWERS, THE POWER, ALL THE CARDS.

WHY BE SCARED OF ME? IT'S CRAZY!

THEN AGAIN, SO IS HE.

THEN AGAIN, SO AM I.

NICE TRICK, HE GREW HIMSELF CLAWS.

YOU WON'T DEFEAT ME AGAIN, DO YOU HEAR?

THIS IS MY TIME!

MY PLACE!

I HAVE THE POWER...

...AND YOUR TIME IS PAST!

WE HACK AND SLASH, THRUST AND PARRY...

...TRYING TO GET IN TIGHT, THEN DANCING BACK, JUST OUT OF REACH!

AND ALL THE TIME THIS FENCING MATCH IS GOING ON, HE SCREAMS AT ME AS IF I'M SOMEBODY ELSE...

AND I WISH I KNEW WHAT IN BLAZES HE WAS TALKING ABOUT.

HAH!

SSSAAAASSS

THIS TIME, ANCIENT ENEMY... ...THE DAY IS MINE!

KRAK

AM I TOO LATE?

FWOOOOM

KHAAAM

HE'S BROKEN CONTACT WITH THE STONE. I SENSE HIS POWER EBBING, AND EVEN THOUGH MY CHEST IS BURNING, I LUNGE FOR IT.

I GIVE IT ALL I'VE GOT.

NOT ENOUGH.

WHY DID I CONCERN MYSELF WITH YOU?

WHY DID I, EVEN FOR A MOMENT, ALLOW YOU TO CAUSE ME DOUBT?

HE FRIES ME FASTER THAN MY HEALING POWER CAN HANDLE.

IN A COUPLE OF SECONDS, I'M GOING TO BE A WALKING ADAMANTIUM SKELETON AND A FEW SHREDS OF SKIN.

I'M COMPLETELY BLIND, AND I DO SOMETHING I HAVEN'T DONE IN AGES.

I PRAY. NOT THE LIGHT, EASY, "HOPE-TO-GOD THIS WORKS" PRAYING.

BUT AN EARNEST, SINCERE PLEA FOR A HIGHER BEING TO GUIDE MY HAND.

AND I STRIKE.

AND EVEN AS I HEAR THE STONE SHATTER, I SLAM DOWN MY FOOT, PIVOT OFF IT. SPIN...

AND STAB HIM, AIMING FOR THE KILL.

HIS SCREAMS ARE WASHED AWAY BY WHAT I'M FEELING.

IT'S LIKE A CIRCUIT HAS BEEN COMPLETED.

HIS LIFE, HIS DARK ENERGY, FLOWS INTO ONE CLAW THROUGH MY BODY AND OUT, AS IF I'M A CONDUIT...

...A CONDUIT TO SOMETHING GREATER, SOMETHING BEYOND OUR UNDERSTANDING.

IT SOUNDS AS IF THE WHOLE PALACE IS ABOUT TO EXPLODE?!

THEN WHY IN HEAVEN'S NAME ARE WE RUNNING TOWARDS IT?!

LOOK!

NO! IT WAS MY TIME!

MINE!

BOY, THE CLEANING WOMAN'S GOING TO BE BUSY FOR WEEKS.

I DON'T UNDERSTAND, WHERE'S THE MASTER?

WHY AREN'T WE VAMPIRES ANYMORE?

SHUT UP!

JESS! HAVE YOU SEEN BURT? HE WENT DRIVING BY US LIKE--

HE WAS HERE, ALL RIGHT, HELPED STOP BA'AL. THEN I DON'T KNOW... HE VANISHED IN THE CONFUSION.

WHERE IS HE?

SHE DOESN'T KNOW, MATE. LOOK, MAYBE HE'S WITH PATCH.

I KILLED BA'AL.

SHATTERED THE GEHENNA STONE, MAYBE SAVED THE WORLD...

NOW WHAT?

I'm goin' t'Disneyworld.

FWOOOOSH!

THUD

DEAD.

GOOD.

HE WAS UGLY AND HAD BAD BREATH.

SO HOW DO WE KNOW THEY WON'T JUST *REASSEMBLE* THE BLASTED STONE?

BECAUSE WHAT GAVE IT POWER WAS THE LIVING ESSENCE OF BA'AL, JUST LIKE BURT SAID. THAT ESSENCE WAS PLACED IN THE STONE UNTIL IT TOOK OVER THE HOST BODY.

WHEN WOLVIE HERE SHATTERED THE STONE AND *KILLED* THE BODY, THE SPIRIT OF THE ORIGINAL BA'AL HAD NOWHERE TO GO.

NOWHERE BUT *DOWN*, I HOPE.

NICE TO KNOW THOSE TWO MADE UP. WITHOUT STONE FRAGMENTS MUCKING WITH THEIR MINDS MAYBE THEY GET A CLEAR SHOT.

Y'KNOW, PATCH, THE STONE NEVER MADE YOU ACT ANY DIFFERENT THAN YOU USUALLY DO.

DON'T YOU REMEMBER? I'M ALWAYS NASTY. JUST BUSINESS AS USUAL FOR ME.

HOW ABOUT *THIS* THEN? BURT SAID THE ORIGINAL BA'AL WAS SLAIN BY A DIVINE WARRIOR NAMED THE HAND OF GOD.

SO IF THE BA'AL WE FACED WAS REALLY A DIRECT DESCENDANT, OR EVEN A REINCARNATION OF THE ORIGINAL...

WHAT DOES THAT MAKE *YOU*, PATCH?

THIRSTY.

SPEAKING OF BURT, I'M REALLY GETTING WORRIED ABOUT HIM. WHAT IF HE NEVER TURNS UP?

ME, BELIEVE ME, ARCH, IF YOUR CRAZY BROTHER COULD HANDLE VAMPIRE HORDES AND DEMON MONSTERS, HE CAN HANDLE ANYTHING.

HERE'S TO BURT CORRIGAN, WHEREVER... AND *WHOEVER...* HE MAY BE.

DEALER DRAWS A TEN. HOUSE PAYS 20, 21.

TWENTY-ONE IT IS.

ALL RIGHT!

HE DID IT!

SIR, I AM THE OWNER HERE AT THE MONTE CARLO GRANDE, AND I HAVE TO TELL YOU THAT YOU'VE JUST BROKEN THE BANK.

NOT AGAIN

YOU'RE QUITE A RICH AND LUCKY MAN, MR...

BOND... ....JAMES BOND.

NEXT: ARCHIE GOODWIN JOHN BYRNE & KLAUS JANSON INTRODUCE **GEIST!**

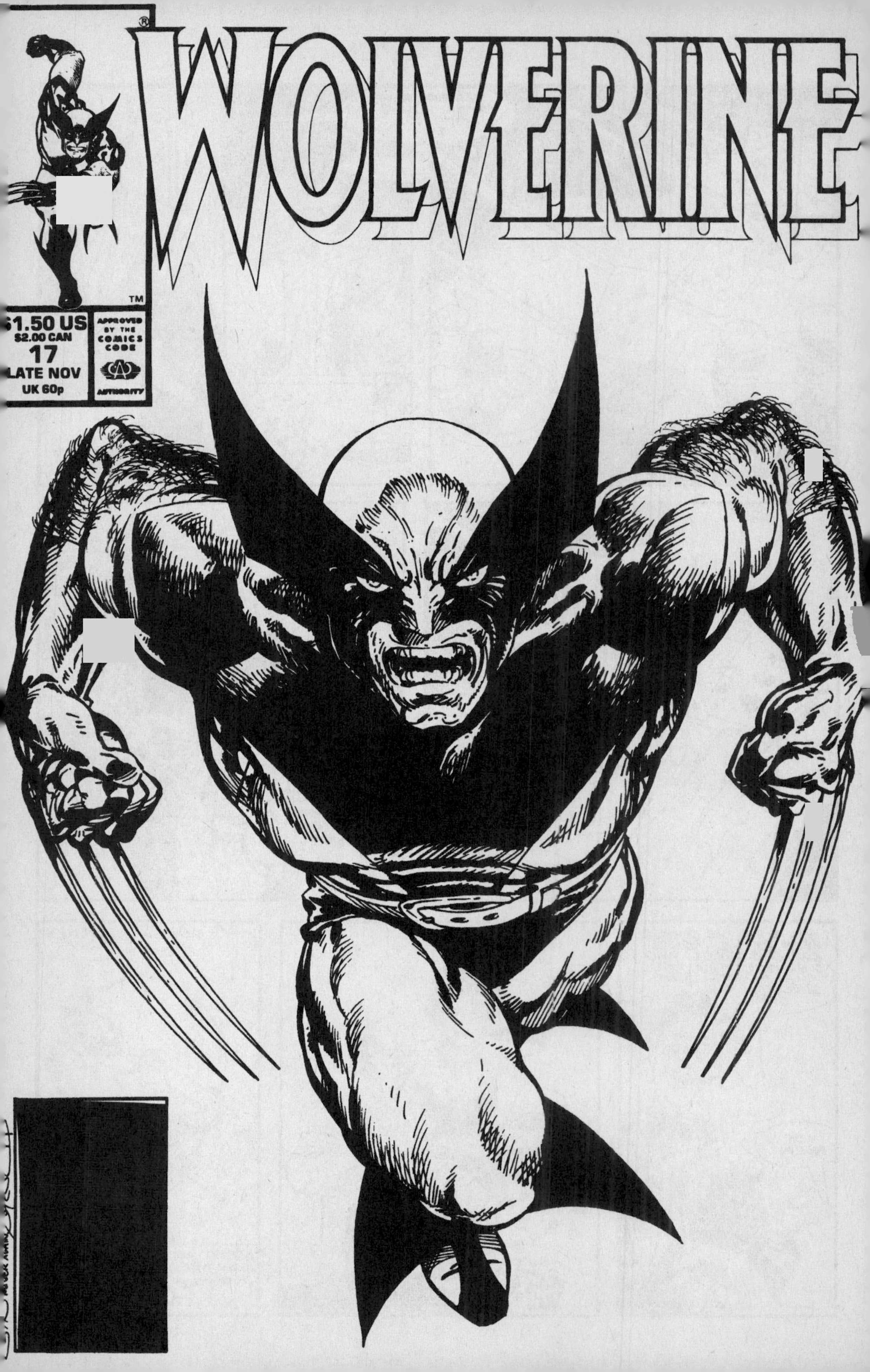

WOLVERINE
$1.50 US
$2.00 CAN
17
LATE NOV
UK 60p
APPROVED BY THE COMICS CODE AUTHORITY

PROLOGUE: THE NOT SO DISTANT PAST ...

LONG BEFORE I HEAR HIS APPROACH, THE WIND CARRIES THE SMELL OF HIM.

HIM... AND THE BLOOD OF HIS PREY.

HE'S A ROGUE.

A KILLER.

SO AM I.

AND TONIGHT...

...THE NEED IS ON US BOTH.

BASICS!

ARCHIE GOODWIN, WRITER
JOHN BYRNE, BREAKDOWNS
KLAUS JANSON, FINISHES
JIM NOVAK, LETTERER
GLYNIS OLIVER, COLORIST
BOB HARRAS, EDITOR
TOM DEFALCO, EDITOR-IN-CHIEF

SQUEEEEEEEE

AND TONIGHT...

...MY NEED, LIKE MY HUNGER, IS STRONGER.

BUT EVEN AS I FEED...

...A *GHOST* IS LAUGHING.

LORD SHINGEN. HEAD OF THE CLAN YASHIDA. FATHER OF THE WOMAN I LOVE.

IT TOOK *TWO* BATTLES TO PROVE MYSELF AGAINST HIM.

...HE DIDN'T SURVIVE THE *SECOND.*.

...YET STILL I CAN LAUGH...

...IN MY MEMORIES OF THE *FIRST.*

BEHOLD, DAUGHTER. THE MAN YOU PROFESS TO LOVE IS *NO* MAN AT ALL.

GAZE UPON HIM, *MARIKO!* AN *ANIMAL* CAST IN A SEMBLENCE OF HUMAN FORM! AN *ANIMAL!* AN...

...ANIMAL!

RAIN. IT DOES WHAT I CAN'T DO FOR MYSELF... FORGIVES.

WASHING, CLEANSING, THE STAINS OF MY KILL..

RAIN...

IN THE AUSTRALIAN OUTBACK... *THIS* TIME OF YEAR?

STORM! YOU... *SAW*?

THIS... THIS IS NOTHIN' FOR *YOU* OR ANY OF THE *OTHERS*!

WE ARE ALL *X-MEN*. WE ALL HAVE MUTANT ABILITIES, WOLVERINE. YOURS INCLUDE THE INSTINCTS, THE SENSES OF A CREATURE OF THE WILD--

THEY HAVE *SAVED* US MANY TIMES.

HOW COULD WE NOT *ACCEPT* THEM--?

-- AS WE ACCEPT THAT YOU ARE *MORE* THAN YOUR WILD SIDE, LOGAN... *BETTER*. THAT *TOO* HAS BEEN PROVEN MANY TIMES.

BUT THE ANIMAL'S ALWAYS *THERE*, DARLIN'... AND NEEDS *OUT* ON OCCASION. STUFF LIKE TONIGHT'S *HUNT* IS USUALLY HOW IT STARTS.

X-MEN ARE *FAMILY* TO ME, ORORO. I CAN'T PARADE THE ANIMAL IN FRONT OF FAMILY...

"...BEST TO HEAD WHERE I CAN LET OUT THE *LEASH*, ALLOW THE BEAST TO *RUN* A LITTLE."

AND IF *WE* NEED YOU, LOGAN...?

PSYLOCKE CAN FIX ME. AN' WITH *GATEWAY* AROUND... I'M NEVER *REALLY* VERY FAR.

YEP. 'NOTHER OF *THOSE* TRIPS, OLD TIMER. BUT YOU *KNOW* THAT, DON'T YOU?

SILENT OLD ABORIGINE. WE'LL NEVER KNOW *HOW MUCH* HE KNOWS.

JUST THAT HE WHIRLS THAT *BULL-ROARER* OF HIS... AND IT'S THERE.

CALL IT AN INTERDIMENSIONAL DOOR.

CALL IT A MYSTIC PORTAL.

SOMEHOW GATEWAY CREATES IT. X-MEN ALL USE IT. MAKES COMIN' AN' GOIN' FROM OUR SECRET BASE *REAL* CONVENIENT.

IN FACT, THE ONLY *PROBLEM* MAY BE...

...WHAT HAPPENS INBETWEEN.

THE PRESENT...

MADRIPOOR.

BE IT EVER SO HUMBLE...

KRAASH!

...IT'S *NO PLACE* LIKE HOME.

AT LEAST NOT WHAT ANY PROPER, UPSTANDING CITIZEN WOULD WANT TO CALL HOME.

WRAAAM!

MAYBE THAT'S ITS APPEAL.

THEN AGAIN...

C'MON BACK, LITTLE MAN! I'M BARELY STARTED! GONNA RIP YOUR BONES OUT, POUND YOU TO BITS WITH 'EM--

--AN' FEED WHAT'S LEFT TO THE NEIGHBORHOOD CATS 'N' DOGS!

...IT MIGHT BE THE FRIENDLY NATIVES.

OUTLININ' YOUR GAME PLAN, GIVIN' ME TIME TO SHRUG OFF MY COAT...?

BWOK!

YOU'VE GOTTEN SOFT IN MY ABSENCE, ROUGHOUSE!

RIGHT. SOFT AS A MOUNTAIN. A BIG MEAN MOUNTAIN. ONE WITH...

WUDDD!

...A COUNTER-PUNCH.

EITHER HAND.

WUNK!

MAKES THE ANIMAL RAGE. INSIDE ME. HOWLING.

THE CLAWS. USE THE CLAWS.

BUT THAT'S WHAT THIS IS ABOUT. BEIN' PUSHED TO THE EDGE, STARIN' INTO THE ABYSS...

KA-ROKK!

...AND FINDIN' IT IN YOU NOT TO GO OVER.

THAT'S WHY ROUGHOUSE IS MY FAVORITE SPARRING PARTNER.

BA-RAAAM!

I CAN GO ALL OUT...

...WITHOUT GOIN' BERSERK.

AND THERE'S NO UNDERESTIMATIN' THE BIG BRUISER. HE CAN SURE TAKE A PUNCH...

RRRRAKKK

...OR ANY-THING ELSE I CAN THROW.

WELL...

...LONGER THAN MOST.

WHAAALOM

GOOD SHOW, PATCH!

TRES BIEN!

DING HAO!

EVERYBODY LOVES A WINNER...

...'SPECIALLY WHEN THEY'VE *BET* ON HIM. AND IN MADRIPOOR'S *LOWTOWN,* A LOT OF LOCALS BACK ME. SINCE WORD'S NOT OUT THAT I'M *WOLVERINE,* ('CEPT TO A FEW CLOSE FRIENDS) COMPLETE WITH MUTANT HEALING FACTOR AND INDESTRUCTABLE ADAMANTIUM SKELETON...

...THEY EVEN GET REASONABLE *ODDS.*

YOU'D THINK ROUGHOUSE'S *BOSS* WOULD LEARN NOT TO OFFER 'EM.

ENOUGH OF THIS! BLOODSCREAM...

MOVE FOR THE GENERAL ...OR SUFFER FOR ME.

NGUYEN NGOC COY. LATE OF THE SOUTH VIETNAMESE ARMY, NOW ONE OF MADRIPOOR'S TWO CRIMELORDS.

IF GENERAL COY HAS SCRUPLES, HE DOESN'T STORE THEM ON *THIS* ISLAND. FOR *HONOR* AMONG THIEVES, THE CLASS ACT IS THE COMPETITION... *TYGER TIGER.*

CONGRATULATIONS, O'DONNELL... YOUR *LEASE* HAS JUST BEEN *RENEWED.*

COY SHADED YOU ON THE *REAL ESTATE,* BUT YOU GOT HIM TO *GAMBLE* IT *BACK* ON THIS FIGHT...?

CONGRATULATIONS TO *YOU,* LOVE.

WHEELIN' AN' DEALIN' NEVER STOPS AT *THE PRINCESS BAR.* GUESS I BOUGHT *HALF INTEREST* FROM O'DONNELL FOR THE ACTION. THAT AND THE *GOOD COMPANY...*

...IF YOU WATCH YOUR WALLET.

Y-YOUR *MONEY,* MR. CORRIGAN...

OBLIGED, SENATOR. MY GUIDED TOUR OF THE CITY'S SEAMY SIDE COMES *FREE* WITH CHARTERING MY PLANE... *SIDE BETS* ARE ANOTHER MATTER.

INCREDIBLE! SUCH A *SMALL MAN...* DEFEATING A *GIANT...!*

THE *MAGIC* OF MADRIPOOR, SENATOR... *NOTHING* IS QUITE WHAT IT SEEMS...

YEP. EVERYBODY LOVES A WINNER.

...BUT *LOSIN'*?

MY PAL, *ARCHIE CORRIGAN,* OWNER AN' SOLE EMPLOYEE OF *SOUTH SEA AIRWAYS,* WILL TELL YOU...

...IT'S ONE THING THIS TOWN *DOESN'T* FORGIVE.

YOU ARE STILL *INTERESTED*?

AFTER TONIGHT'S... *ENTERTAINMENT*?

OF *COURSE,* GENERAL COY. I DIDN'T *BET* ON HIM.

ROUGHOUSE SERVED LONG AND WELL AS MY *ENFORCER.* DESPITE *RECENT* DISAPPOINTMENTS, I CANNOT INSULT SUCH *LOYALTY--*

--BY ACCEPTING ANY *LESS* THAN YOUR *ORIGINAL* OFFER.

I NEVER *HAGGLE,* GENERAL.

BUSINESS DEALINGS SHOULD BE LIKE A *GOOD* SHAVE, YES...? *CLEAN* AND *SMOOTH.*

IF THIS IS *CORRECT,* THEN--

SOLD!

LATER...THE ROYAL PALACE.

A MAGNIFICENT *DINNER*, PRINCE BARAN. THE FLOW OF ONE COURSE TO ANOTHER... *ARTISTRY*.

YOUR SENSITIVITY TO SUCH NUANCES IS WHAT MAKES YOU AN EXCELLENT *CHIEF OF POLICE*, MY DEAR *TAI*... I STRIVE FOR *SIMILAR* ARTISTRY IN THE FLOW OF *EVENTS* ON OUR CHARMING ISLAND.

STILL, *DISRUPTIONS* OCCUR. TAKE THE RECENT *SEIZURE* MADE BY YOUR MEN AT CUSTOMS...

IMPORTS FOR *GENERAL COY*...FROM *CENTRAL AMERICA*. AN EMBARRASSING MATTER, YOUR HIGHNESS... HIDDEN WITHIN THEM WERE QUANTITIES OF *COCAINE*.

DOUBLY EMBARRASSING, THIS WAS *PUBLICLY* UNCOVERED BY THE MAN KNOWN LOCALLY AS *PATCH*...HE HAS A USEFUL *NOSE* FOR THIS SORT OF THING.

SPECULATION NOW ABOUNDS THAT-- WITH THIS *NEW* DRUG SOURCE-- THE GENERAL LOOKS TO MAKE *CRACK* HIS LATEST INROAD INTO THE PURSES OF MADRIPOOR.

OUR COUNTRY *THRIVES* ON A WICKED REPUTATION, *TAI*. BUT I *KNOW* THE DIFFERENCE BETWEEN TOLERATING A *VICE*...AND UNLEASHING A *PLAGUE*.

IN THE FLOW OF EVENTS I ENVISION, GENERAL COY'S *IMPORTS* WOULD RETURN TO THEIR POINT OF *ORIGIN*...

REASSURING, MY PRINCE... PARTICULARLY SINCE MY FORCE IS STRETCHED QUITE THIN. LAPSES IN SECURITY ARE *INEVITABLE*. DURING SUCH TIMES--

--ANYTHING MIGHT VANISH FROM CUSTODY.

WELL...WERE YOU ABLE TO OBSERVE *ENOUGH* FROM HIDING...? ARE YOU *ALSO* REASSURED?

INTRIGUING, YOUR POLICE CHIEF. BENEATH THE CIRCUMSPECTION, THE AIR OF CORRUPTION--

--MAY WELL LURK A DEDICATED, EVEN *HONEST* MAN, YES?

A MAN WHO HONESTLY UNDERSTANDS THE *LIMITS* OF HIS POSITION IN MADRIPOOR... UNLIKE *YOUR* ASSOCIATE!

GENERAL COY CROSSED A *LINE* WITH THIS BUSINESS. HE *VIOLATED* THE BALANCE OF POWER, OF VICES AND VIRTUE, I VERY *CARE-FULLY* MAINTAIN HERE.

OUR SHIPMENT TO COY WAS *DEFINITELY* A MISTAKE, YOUR *HIGHNESS*--

--FOR WHICH MY EMPLOYER HAS AGREED TO PAY QUITE *HANDSOMELY*, YES?

AND WITH THE *RETURN* OF THE CONFIS-CATED MATERIAL, MY GUAR-ANTEE--

--ITS LIKE WILL *NEVER* COME TO MADRIPOOR AGAIN.

THEN WE HAVE NOTHING *FURTHER* TO DISCUSS.

SO IT WOULD *SEEM*, PRINCE BARAN. BUT, WITH YOUR CONCERN FOR BALANCE OF POWER, PER-HAPS YOU WILL PERMIT AN *OBSERVATION*--

--FROM ONE WHO HAS SEEN POWER *LOST* AND POWER *GAINED* OVER THE YEARS.

IF EVER THERE WAS A NATURAL-BORN *BALANCE-TIPPER* ON THE JOB... HE IS ALREADY HARD AT WORK IN *YOUR* PRINCIPALITY.

WAIT! YOU MEAN--

CLICK

OF COURSE....! THE MAN *PATCH*, YES?

A PLEASANT EVENING, YOUR HIGHNESS.

A GOOD MORNING.

QUIET. CITY'S NOT AWAKE YET.

AIR'S STILL CLEAN. HEAVY WITH THE SMELL OF THE SEA, TINGED WITH *SCENTS* OF THE JUNGLE.

AT DAWN, A MAN COULD ALMOST BELIEVE MADRIPOOR ISN'T *REALLY* GOMORRAH ON THE PACIFIC RIM...

...UNLESS, LIKE *MOST* OF LOWTOWN, THAT MAN WAS HELPIN' TYGER AN' ME WITH LAST NIGHT'S *VICTORY CELEBRATION* DOWNSTAIRS IN THE PRINCESS BAR.

SLEEP WELL, DARLIN'. GOT A WORLD CLASS *HANGOVER* TO FACE.

BE WISHIN' FOR MY *HEALING FACTOR* INSTEAD'A MY *PATCH.*

THAT THING. *FUN* IN THE BEGINNING. NEW IDENTITY, NEW LOOK. NEW PART OF MY LIFE.

LIKE TYGER, MOST WHO KNOW ME AREN'T *DE-CEIVED*... JUST WILLING NOT TO *QUESTION* AS LONG AS I OBVIOUSLY *WANT* IT THAT WAY.

I *STARTED* IN MADRIPOOR TAKING THE ROLE OF TYGER'S *CONSCIENCE*. IS *THAT* WHAT I WAS DOIN' LAST N'GHT...?

OTHERWISE, I GUESS IT HELPS MAIN-TAIN THE *SECRECY*...OUR ILLUSION THAT WOLVERINE AND ALL THE X-MEN ARE *DEAD*.

BUT MAYBE WHAT IT *REALLY* HELPS IS ME...TO FOOL MY-SELF.

OR DOES BEIN' *PATCH* ALLOW ME TO GIVE THE *ANIMAL* SUCH A LONG LEASH...I NEED SOMEONE TO PLAY CONSCIENCE FOR *ME*?

TRIED TO BE A *SAMURAI* FOR MARIKO. WHAT'S *PATCH* TRIED?

THAT *SMELL*....!

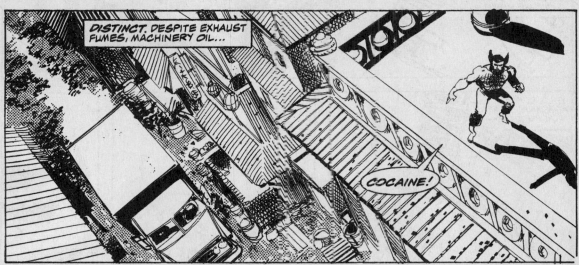

DISTINCT. DESPITE EXHAUST FUMES, MACHINERY OIL...

COCAINE!

TRUCK'S CARRYING THE *SAME* COCAINE I HELPED UNCOVER YESTERDAY.

...I'D HAVE TO STAY ON MY BALCONY AND *WONDER.*

WHERE?

AND *WHY?*

IF THIS WERE *HIGHTOWN,* ALL *MODERN* SKYSCRAPERS, SMOOTH GLASS TOWERS...

BUT LOWTOWN IS *OLD,* A SPRAWLING MAZE OF NARROW STREETS AND CONNECTING ROOFTOPS.

'COURSE, THIS KIND'A *WORK OUT--*

--CUTS SERIOUSLY INTO MY *SELF-AGONIZING.*

THOUGHT I WAS *LUCKY* SNIFFING OUT GENERAL COY'S LOAD OF JUNK SO SOON AFTER GATEWAY *GOT* ME HERE--!

SHOULD'VE *KNOWN* THAT IN MADRIPOOR--

--NOTHING'S *EVER* THAT SIMPLE!

RIGHT.

LOCAL MUSCLE. BUSH LEAGUE FREELANCERS.

NOT LIKE COY TO LET OTHERS--

--HANDLE ANY-THING OF HI--

ROUGHOUSE!

SOME CARE WITH YOUR BURDEN, YES?

I WISH THE GENTLEMAN JUST AS UNDAMAGED AS THE CRATES--

--EVEN IF HE COST SOMEWHAT LESS.

NOW...YOUR PAY, PLUS BONUS FOR SWIFT SERVICE--

--LESS DEDUCTIONS FOR CLUMSINESS WITH MY PUR-CHASE. I NEVER HAGGLE... OR REWARD INEPTITUDE.

GLINT OF SOMETHING AS HE TURNED... METAL COLLAR?

LET'S GO... SWIFTLY! BEFORE WE LOSE COVER OF THE MORNING MISTS!

GONE. AND INSTEAD OF ANSWERS...

...ALL I'VE GOT ARE MORE QUESTIONS.

"HOW BEST TO EX-PLAIN? PERHAPS THE INCIDENT IN NEW YORK...

"...HELL'S KITCHEN.

"THE ARMORED DOOR OF ONE OF THOSE TENEMENTS-TURNED-ILLICIT-FORTRESSES CALLED A CRACK HOUSE...

WRAAM!

"...PROVED NO RESTRAINT TO A CERTAIN CUSTOMER.

"HAMMER CODY. A ONCE PROMISING HEAVYWEIGHT REDUCED TO FIGHTING FOR HIS NEXT FIX.

YAAAGH!

"THIS DAY HE WON THE BIGGEST FIGHT OF HIS LIFE...

"...AND LEFT THE DEALERS WHO GAVE IT TO HIM DEAD. THE PRICE...? MULTI-PLE GUNSHOT AND STAB WOUNDS...AS WELL AS HIS SANITY.

"NONE OF WHICH SLOWED THE RAMPAGE THAT FOLLOWED.

"IN FACT, IT SEEMED NOTHING COULD.

BRAASH!

"UNTIL...

PCP, MAYBE...? SOME DESIGNER DRUG NEW TO THE STREET...? IF I READ YOU RIGHT--

--REASONING IS A WASTE OF BREATH. BEST I CAN OFFER IS TO TAKE YOU DOWN FAST.

"BRAVADO WORTHY OF A MAN WHO CALLS HIM-SELF DAREDEVIL...

"...AND SOMEWHAT *MISPLACED*.

RRRAARGH!

WRAAM!

"PUBLIC RECORD CANNOT CONFIRM IF THE COSTUMED CRIMEFIGHTER ACTUALLY HAS *SUPER POWERS*...

"...BUT STRENGTH, SPEED, AGILITY? *SUPERB*.

"PLUS...

"...NEARLY RADAR-LIKE *INSTINCT*.

WROK!

"YET ALL *MATCHED* BY HIS WOUNDED, DERANGED FOE!

WUNK!

"IN THE END...

"...ONLY TACTICS, SKILL AND...

"...*NCREDIBLE, BLIND DETERMINATION*...

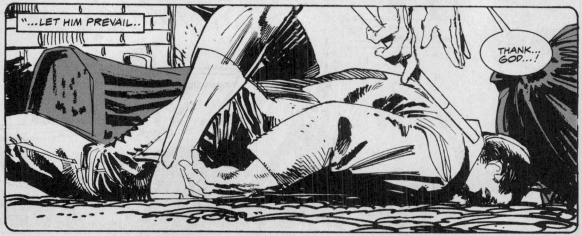

"...LET HIM PREVAIL...

THANK... GOD...!

"THOUGH BATTERED, DAREDEVIL STOOD OVER THE FALLEN MAN STILL, INTENSE... LIKE ONE LISTENING FOR A SOUND OTHERS CANNOT HEAR.

"THEN, SIRENS FILLED THE AIR.

IT'S OVER, GUYS... FINALLY.

BUT HE NEEDS EMERGENCY CARE FAST OR--

YAAAHH!

"AND FROM THIS PARTICULAR MOMENT...

WHAM!

"...THE CONVICTION AROSE THAT FATE HAD GIFTED US...

KRUNNK!

"...WITH SOMETHING MONUMENTAL...

STOP WHERE YOU ARE! STOP NOW!

THIS AIN'T POSSIBLE! IT JUST AIN'T--

"BUT JUST WHAT *WAS* POSSIBLE FROM SUCH A CONFRONTATION...

"...WOULD NEVER BE LEARNED.

HE...HE'S *DEAD.*

I KNOW.

BUT *WHY?*

"AN ANSWER *DENIED* DAREDEVIL. DISPOSITION OF HAMMER CODY'S *BODY* AND THE DRUGS WHICH *FUELED* HIM BECAME PART OF A COMPLICATED *JURISDICTIONAL DISPUTE* BETWEEN NUMEROUS LOCAL AND FEDERAL LAW AGENCIES AND ULTIMATELY...*DISAPPEARED."*

INTO *OUR* HANDS, HAPPILY. LESS HAPPILY, SOMETHING WAS ALL TOO *OBVIOUS*--

-- FATE'S MONUMENTAL *GIFT* TO US STILL HAD SOME *BUGS* TO BE WORKED OUT.

OF COURSE, WORKING OUT THE BUGS, FOLLOWING THROUGH... THIS WAS *ALWAYS* MY SPECIALTY.

IT'S ONE OF THE REASONS I'VE SURVIVED AS *LONG* AS I HAVE.

NATURALLY, *MODERN SCIENCE*-- THE WONDERS OF *CYBERNETICS* --HAS HAD A *BIT* TO DO WITH MY SURVIVAL AS WELL.

YOU CAN'T CARE *MUCH* ABOUT SURVIVIN', OL' MAN, OR YOU'D HAVE NEVER *DONE* THIS TO ME!

I EVER GET *LOOSE*...YOU AN' THAT FANCY *TIN SUIT* ARE GONNA LOOK LIKE A *BEER CAN* RUN OVER BY A *ROAD GRADER!*

I UNDER- STAND, MY FRIEND--

--YOU ARE NOT YET *RECON- CILED* TO MY BUSINESS AR- RANGEMENT WITH *GENERAL COY*, YES?

BUSINESS ARRANGEMENT?! I'M THE BEST BLASTED *ENFORCER* T'EVER HIT THE *SOUTH PACIFIC*...MEANEST, TOUGHEST *HIRED MUSCLE* T'BE FOUND!

NO WAY I CAN BE BOUGHT 'N' SOLD LIKE SOME *COOLIE SLAVE*, PRUNEFACE!

I AM *GEIST*--

--AND RELUCTANT TO ACCEPT NAME-CALLING FROM ANYONE WHO WOULD STYLE HIMSELF *ROUGHOUSE*.

BUT YOU ARE *FULL* OF *AMUSING* CONTRADICTIONS, YES?

GENERAL COY'S ENTERPRISES INCLUDE A VERY ACTIVE *SLAVE TRAFFIC*--

--YOU *PARTICIPATED*, BUT NOW RESENT BEING TREATED THE *SAME*?

YET *SLAVE* YOU ARE...COY AND I KNOW YOU HELP YOUR-SELF TO *THIS* FROM TIME TO TIME.

YOU MAY THINK IT *RECREATIONAL*... PART OF A LARGE MAN'S LARGE *APPE-TITES*. IT IS BE-YOND THAT.

WE WILL SEE HOW *FAR* BEYOND WITH AN *EXPERIMENT*. IT IN-VOLVES THE *SAME BATCH* OF COCAINE I TOLD YOU ABOUT. SHIPMENTS OF WHICH WE'VE GONE TO *RIDICULOUS* LENGTHS TO RECLAIM.

WAIT...! THE *BLACK* DUDE...*CODY*! HE--

KLIK

THERE IS A REASON TO BELIEVE YOU MAY FARE *BETTER* AS A TEST SUBJECT. HOWEVER--

--BEFORE OUR EXPERIMENT BEGINS, CERTAIN *ADJUSTMENTS* ARE NECESSARY--

--YES?

COMPLICATIONS. SUDDENLY THIS IS A LOT *MORE* THAN YOUR USUAL MADRIPOOR INTRIGUE. MIST IS HIDING THE *MARKINGS* ...BUT FROM THE *LINES* OF THIS BABY, IT'S OBVIOUSLY A *U.S. NAVY* VESSEL.

WHO SMUGGLES COCAINE ON AN AMERICAN *WARSHIP* AN' WHAT THE DEVIL DO THEY NEED WITH *ROUGHHOUSE?* SOME *PART* OF ME--MAYBE THE PART THAT WOULD BE *SAMURAI* INSTEAD OF ANIMAL--*HAS* TO KNOW.

SURE, HE'S AN *ENEMY,* BUT ONE WHO'S FOUGHT ME WELL. IT'S EARNED HIM *SOMETHING,* IF ONLY SO WE CAN FIGHT *AGAIN* SOMEDAY. EXCEPT...

...THAT DAY MAY NOT *COME.* BECAUSE OF A *SOUND* IN THE AIR. ONE I'VE *NEVER* HEARD.

THE SOUND OF ROUGHHOUSE SCREAMING.

NEXT ISSUE: ALL AT SEA

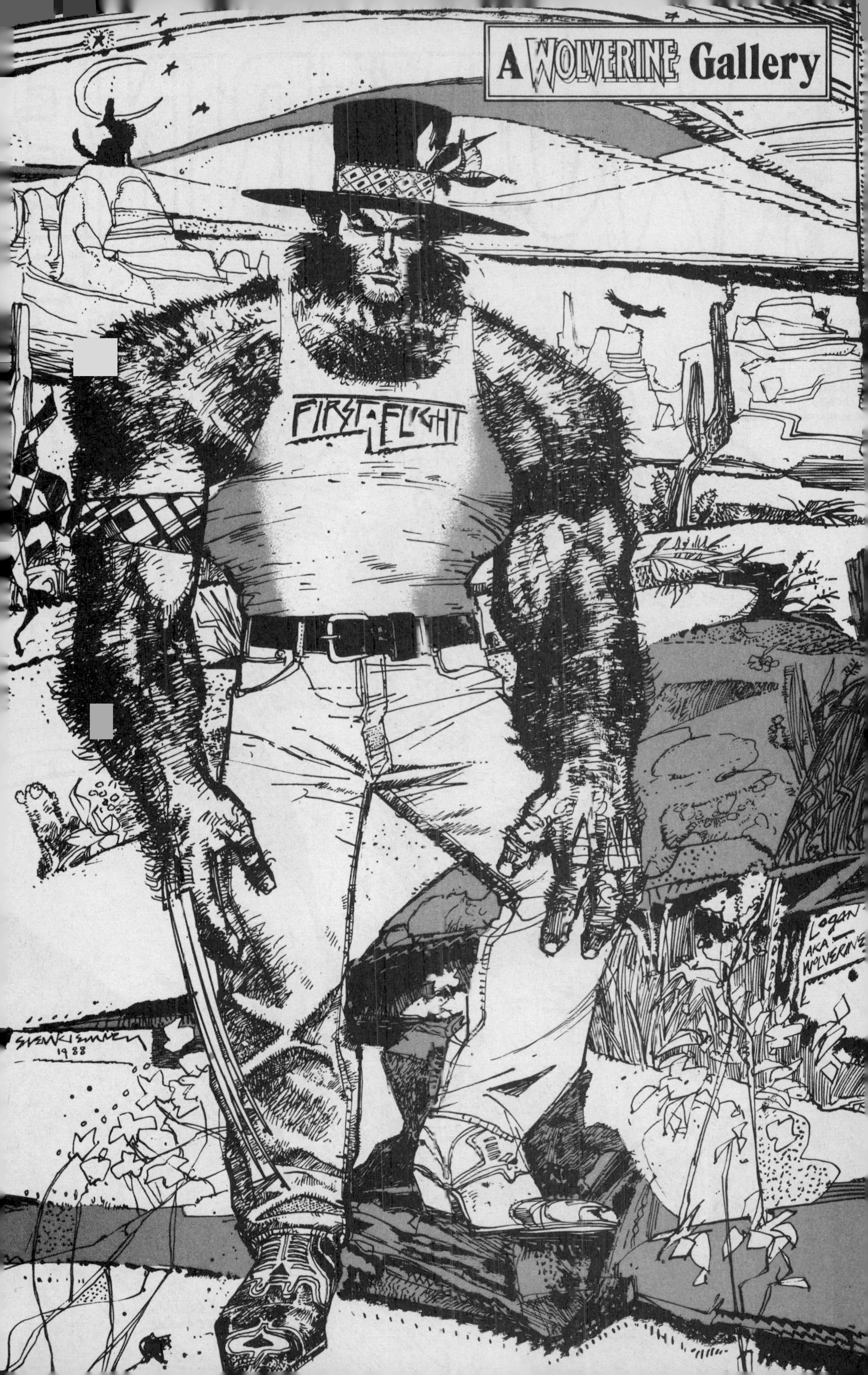
A WOLVERINE Gallery
FIRST FLIGHT
Logan AKA WOLVERINE
SIENKIEWICZ 1988

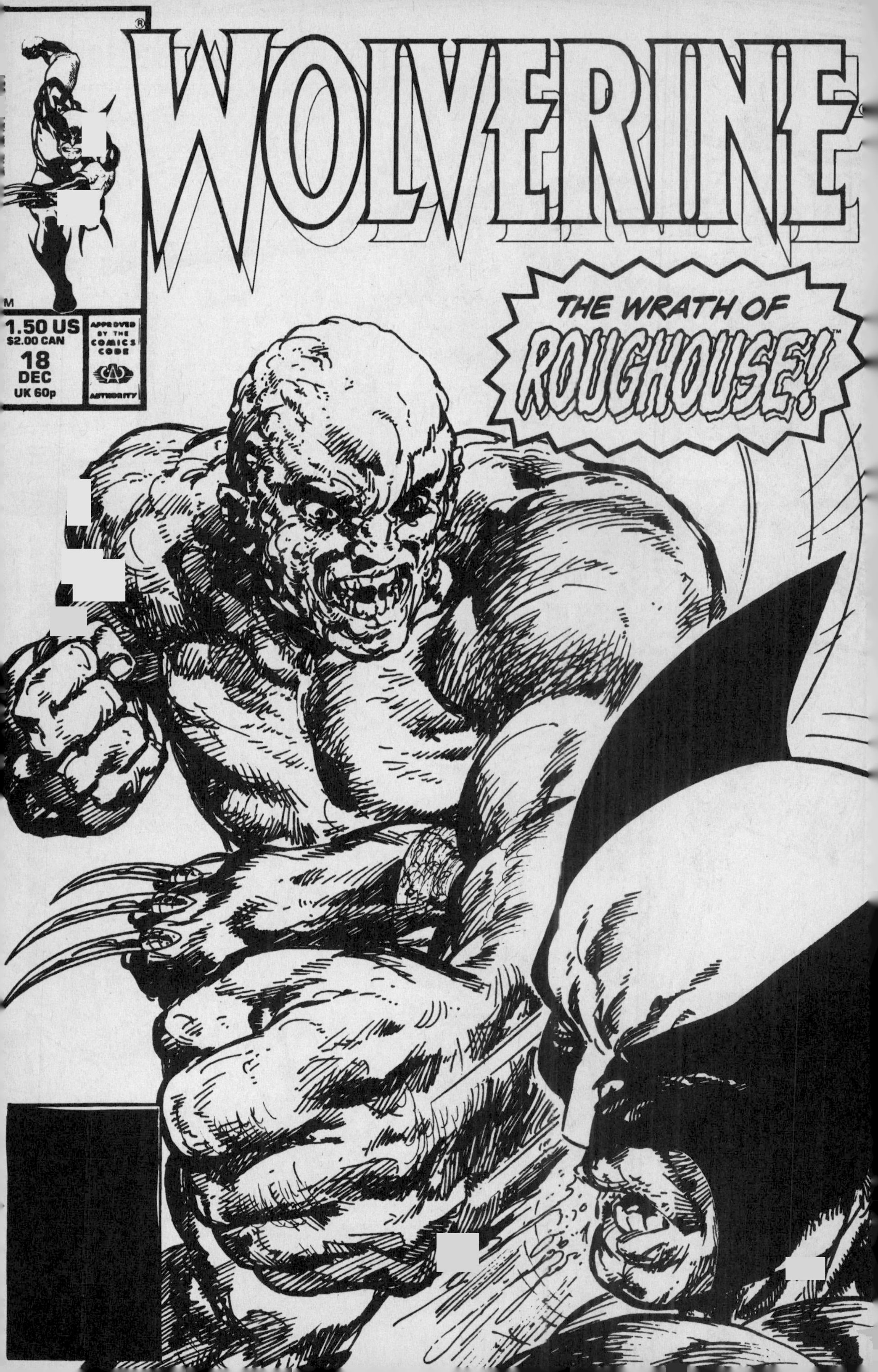
WOLVERINE
1.50 US
$2.00 CAN
18
DEC
UK 60p
APPROVED BY THE COMICS CODE AUTHORITY
THE WRATH OF
ROUGHOUSE!

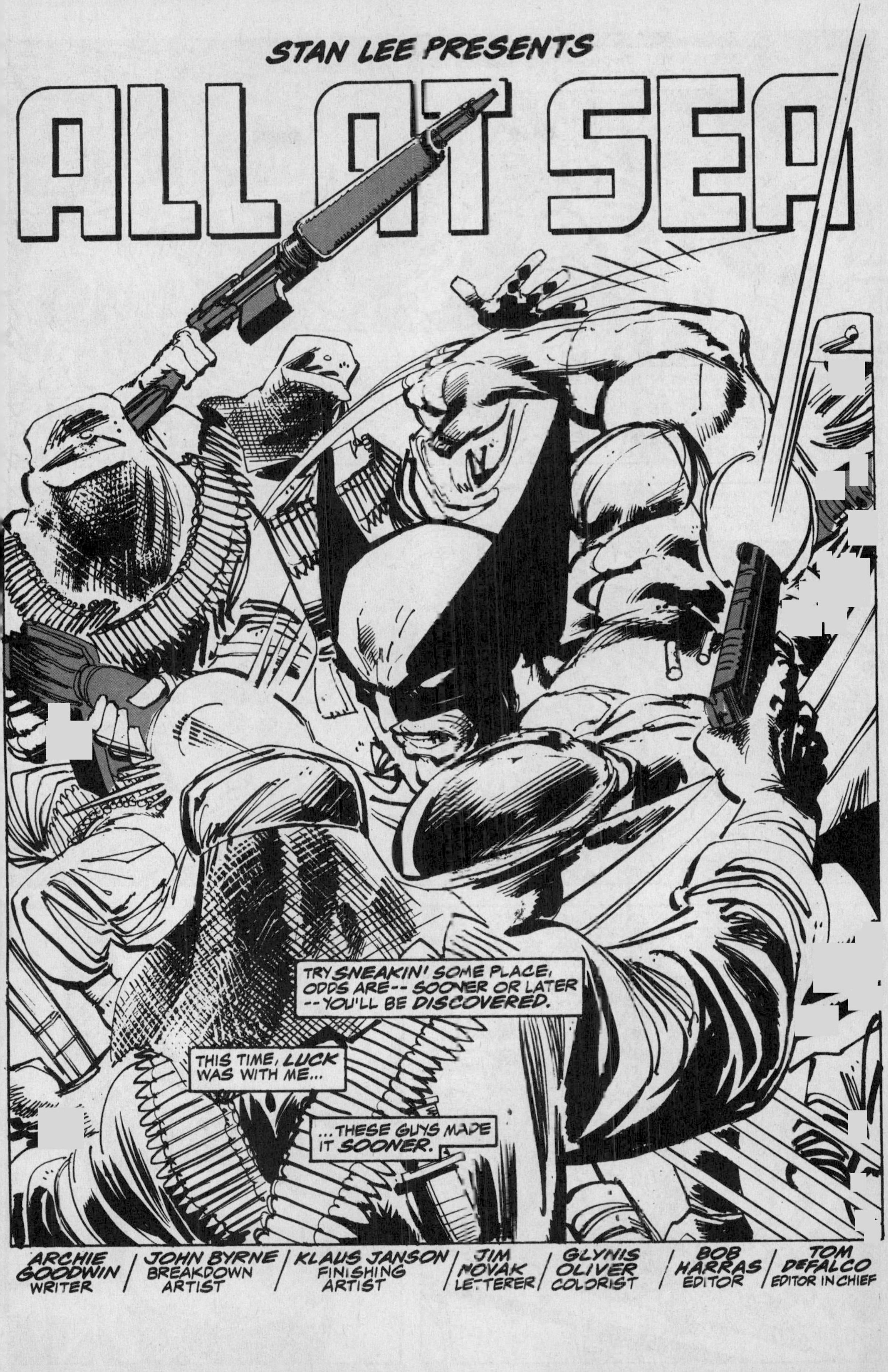
STAN LEE PRESENTS
ALL AT SEA
TRY SNEAKIN' SOME PLACE, ODDS ARE-- SOONER OR LATER --YOU'LL BE DISCOVERED.
THIS TIME, LUCK WAS WITH ME...
...THESE GUYS MADE IT SOONER.
ARCHIE GOODWIN WRITER
JOHN BYRNE BREAKDOWN ARTIST
KLAUS JANSON FINISHING ARTIST
JIM NOVAK LETTERER
GLYNIS OLIVER COLORIST
BOB HARRAS EDITOR
TOM DEFALCO EDITOR IN CHIEF

BETTER YET, THOUGH THIS SEEMS TO BE A *U.S. NAVY* VESSEL...

...WHOEVER I'M FIGHTIN' HIT LIKE *KILLERS* NOT A MILITARY TEAM. TO THEM, THAT MIGHT BE GIVIN' *NO QUARTER*. TO ME...

...IT'S GIVIN' *CARTE BLANCHE.*

SUDDENLY, SOMEONE'S *SHOUTING.* FIRST IN *SPANISH,* THEN...

THESE RIFLES HAVE *LASER-SIGHTS*--

--AND WITH OUR OVER-EAGER DECK GUARDS EITHER *DEAD* OR WITH-DRAWING...THOSE SIGHTS ARE ZEROED UPON *YOU,* YES?

I WOULD SAY YOUR POSITION HAS BECOME *IMPOSSIBLE.*

FUNNY. *I'D* SAY IT JUST GOT MORE *INTERESTING.*

ALL RIGHT...I'M *IMPRESSED.* BUT WHAT WOULD *DRIVE* YOU TO PUT ON THE CLOTHING OF A *DEAD MAN* AND COME ABOARD THIS SHIP SO WILLING TO *DIE?*

THE WORLD KNOWS THE X-MEN ARE DEAD. IS THIS SOME *PSYCHOLOGICAL TRICK?* A CHEAP ATTEMPT TO STRIKE FEAR--

--BY MAKING US BELIEVE *ONE* OF THAT NOTORIOUS MUTANT GROUP STILL *SURVIVES?*

MAYBE I FELT IF NO ONE *ELSE* WAS USIN' THE OUTFIT... I MIGHT AS WELL.

MAYBE I TRADED MY *PATCH* FOR IT. WHAT'S *IMPORTANT*--

--ARE SOME *PURCHASES* YOU MADE IN MADRIPOOR. ALONG WITH A SHIPMENT OF *BAD COCAINE,* YOU BOUGHT A *MAN.*

NOT A SWELL PERSON, BUT A GOOD ENOUGH *ENEMY*--

--THAT HE DOESN'T DESERVE WHATEVER YOU WERE *DOIN'* TO HIM WHEN I *BOARDED* THIS TUB.

AH! THE *SCREAMING* EARLIER FROM OUR MUTUAL FRIEND... *ROUGHHOUSE.*

COME!

JOIN ME. MY GUARDS WILL DISPERSE.

PERHAPS I CAN *EASE* YOUR FEARS--

--AND *SPARE* WHAT REMAINS OF OUR CREW, YES?

GAMES. DON'T LIKE 'EM. NOT CRAZY ABOUT CYBORGS EITHER. LIKE ONES I'VE FACED WITH THE X-MEN, THIS GUY SMELLS TOO MUCH OF *MACHINE OIL*, NOT ENOUGH OF HUMANITY.

BUT IF PLAYIN' ALONG GETS ME TO--

ROUGHOUSE!

YOU'VE MADE HIM--

NEATER, YES...? A MORE *DISCIPLINED* LOOK FOR A MORE *CONTROLLED* PHASE OF HIS LIFE.

BUT SHAVING PROVED A BIT *TRAUMATIC.* HE'S SELF-CONSCIOUS ABOUT THOSE OLD *SCARS,* PERHAPS.

SO ALONG WITH *HUMILIATING* THE BIG OX, YOU *DOPED* HIM INTO A STUPOR!

USED THAT *GARBAGE* FROM MADRIPOOR ...CABIN *REEKS* OF IT.

WHY...?! WHAT'RE YOU *DOIN'* HERE?

ANSWERS, OLD MAN...! OR A SUDDEN *PAIN* IN THE NECK. YOUR DECISION.

HE RELAXES. ALMOST BORED. A MAN ON FAMILIAR GROUND. VERY.

MY NAME IS *GEIST*. MY BUSINESS IS *SURVIVAL*. MY BODY—OBVIOUSLY—HAS BECOME A *MONUMENT* TO IT.

I SURVIVE BY BEING *USEFUL*...

'...CURRENTLY I AM USEFUL TO *FELIX GUILLERMO CARIDAD*. HE CURRENTLY...

"...IS *PRESIDENT* OF THE CENTRAL AMERICAN REPUBLIC OF *TIERRA VERDE*. A POSITION ATTAINED THROUGH MILITARY SUCCESS, ANTI-COMMUNIST POLITICS...

"...AND A PERSONAL FORTUNE FROM THE TRAFFIC OF COCAINE.

BUENO!

"SOME MONTHS AGO, MY PRESIDENT HIT UPON A *NEW GOAL*.

YOUR MAN HAS PENETRATED THE REBEL *STRONGHOLD*, COLONEL. NOW HE WILL *TRULY* BE PUT TO THE TEST, THIS... THIS...

NUKE. WE CALL 'IM *NUKE*, SIR.

"A CODE-NAME.

BA-VOM!

"MELODRAMATIC. TO BE EXPECTED IN A *SECRET PROJECT* OF U.S. MILITARY INTELLIGENCE, YES?

"BUT QUITE *APT.* A *SUPER-SOLDIER* THEY CALLED HIM, CREATED OUT OF *CHEMICAL* EXPERIMENTATION. TO THE BODY...

OUR BOYS...! OUR BOYS...!

BRRRAAAAAPP

THEY'RE HOLDIN' OUR BOYS!

"...AND THE MIND.

GIMME A RED.

FOR OUR BOYS!

"CARIDAD PROVIDED HIS ALLIES WITH A *PROVING GROUND...*

"...AND IF THE 'REBEL STRONGHOLD' ALSO HOUSED A RIVAL *COCAINE* PROCESSING FACTORY...

WUM!

OUR BOYS!

"...THE OVERALL *RESULT* WAS THE SAME.

NOTHING STANDS... NOTHING MOVES! *MAG-NIFICENT,* COLONEL! I *ENVY* YOUR *ACCOMPLISHMENT!*

YOUR LESS FRIENDLY *NEIGHBORS* WON'T, SENOR PRESIDENT... *GUARANTEED.*

"BUT MY EMPLOYER'S THOUGHTS WERE *BEYOND* NUKE'S POSSIBLE INVOLVEMENT ELSEWHERE IN CENTRAL AMERICA.

THAT WASN'T IDLE *FLATTERY* TO THE NORTEAMERICANO, GEIST. BACK AT THE *PALACE--*

--WE WILL *TALK.*

"WE ALSO VIEWED *VIDEOTAPES.* ALL CENTERED UPON...

...*SUPER HEROES,* GEIST! LOOK... *CAPTAIN AMERICA!* A LIVING *SYMBOL* OF HIS COUNTRY! A *PURER* VERSION OF WHAT WE SAW TODAY!

I WANT THAT FOR *ME,* GEIST...FOR *TIERRA VERDE.*

DIFFICULT, MY PRESIDENT. ANY *AVENGER* WOULD BE *ABOVE* POLITICAL ALLIANCES, YES?

BUT LET'S NOT DISCOUNT THIS *NUKE.* WITH OUR CIA AND U.S. MILITARY CONTACTS, PERHAPS...

NO! I DON'T WANT AN ITEM ON *LOAN*... AS THEY LOAN US ARMS, SHIPS, AND HELICOPTERS...

PATS ON THE HEAD FOR STANDING AGAINST *COMMUNISM*... EVEN AS THEIR *PRESS* BRANDS ME A BANANA REPUBLIC *DRUG CZAR!*

WELL, *WHATEVER* I AM... I AM FOR *TIERRA VERDE,* GEIST!

IT IS THE NORTEAMERICANOS WHO *WALLOW* IN MY DRUGS... YET THEY MAKE FUN OF *US!*

NO *MORE.* I WILL GIVE MY COUNTRY ITS *OWN* SUPER HERO... A SYMBOL OF PRIDE... EQUAL TO ANY SO-CALLED *IMPORTANT* NATION!

HOLD IT, GEIST!

THIS POOR SLOB IS YOUR *SOLUTION* FOR SOME THIRD RATE NAPOLEON WITH A CASE OF *SUPER HERO ENVY?!*

SNIKT!

LESS A SOLUTION THAN A *STEP* TOWARD IT.

CERTAIN TIERRA VERDE *COCAINE* SEEMS TO CAUSE INTERESTING... *SIDE* EFFECTS. I RECOVERED SOME IN MADRIPOOR AND...

YOU WANT *GUINEA PIGS,* OLD MAN... FIND SOME *VOLUNTEERS!*

SHRAAK!

BETTER YET--

--EXPERIMENT ON *YOURSELF.*

YOU ALREADY GOT A *START* BEIN' SOMETHIN' NOT QUITE *HUMAN.*

BUT NOT AT BEING *IRON MAN.* AS YOU SO READILY POINT OUT--

--I'M *OLD.* THIS RIDICULOUSLY EXPENSIVE *SHELL*--ACQUIRED GRADUALLY WITH THE COOPERATION OF SEVERAL GOVERNMENTS-- PRESERVES MY *LIFE.*

WHATEVER ITS *POWERS,* IT WAS NEVER INTENDED FOR THE CONSTANT *BATTLE* I GATHER IS A SUPER HERO'S *LOT,* YES?

SO YOU'LL KEEP CLEAR AN' PUMP DUMB *LUNKS* LIKE *ROUGHOUSE*--

--FULL OF WHAT-EVER'S *WEIRD* IN THOSE DRUGS, HOPIN' EVENTUALLY *ONE* OF 'EM TURNS INTO WHAT YOU *WANT.*

A MAN WHO PLAYS *ROULETTE* WITH HUMAN *LIVES* BETTER LEARN TO *FIGHT,* GEIST... OR AT *LEAST* HOW TO GET OUT OF THE WAY *FAST!*

GOOD EXIT LINE.

BUT--

--BAD EXIT.

KIND'A LIKE THIS *RESCUE.* NOBLE INTENTION, AIDIN' AN OLD *FOE...*

...MAYBE I SHOULD'VE *CHECKED* FIRST WITH *ROUGHHOUSE.*

YAARRRRG!

THEN AGAIN...

BRAAAASH!

...WE'RE A BIT *BEYOND* THE GENTLE ART OF REASON HERE.

CAPTAIN...? *NOW* WE CAN GET UNDERWAY.

AND HAVE *COMMUNICA-TIONS* SEND THE MES-SAGES I LEFT EARLIER.

IN THE PROPER *ORDER*, YES?

SO MUCH *DATA*, SO MANY *COMPLICATIONS*! HOW DID WE MANAGE IN THE OLD DAYS... *BEFORE* COMPUTERS?

MARK HOW *LONG* BEFORE THE DRUG BROUGHT ROUGHOUSE TO THE *ACTIVE* PHASE...

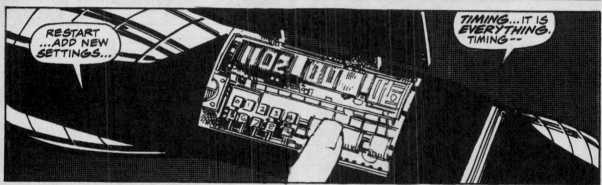

RESTART ...ADD NEW SETTINGS...

TIMING...IT IS *EVERYTHING.* TIMING--

"--AND *EXE-CUTION.*"

EEEEE--

--YAH!

KRAKRAAAMM.

A PROMISING *START!* STILL, WE CANNOT LEAVE *EVERY-THING* TO THE TEST ANIMALS--

--I HAVE MY *OWN* ROLE TO PLAY.

CH-KLAK

SENOR GEIST! I *PROTEST* THIS DESTRUCTION! IT IS--

NOTHING TO *CONCERN* YOU, CAPTAIN... SO LONG AS MY *MESSAGES* WERE SENT.

NOTHING...?!

BAD ENOUGH THAT MY *SHIP* --MEANT TO PROTECT TIERRA VERDE'S COAST-- IS USED FOR COLLECTING *DRUGS!* BUT YOU CAN-- NOT *JUSTIFY*--

I CAN... IT'S WHAT A PRESIDENTIAL ADVISER DOES BEST. JUST DRIVE THE *BOAT*, CAPTAIN--

"--LEAVE MATTERS OF *PHILOSOPHY* TO ME."

ROUGHOUSE! LISTEN! YOU--

TH-WAP!

YEAH. LISTEN--

--AS IF YOU *EVER* LISTENED--

--AS IF WHATEVER YOU'RE SHOT *FULL OF* WEREN'T MAKIN' YOU S*TRONGER*, MEANER, AND MORE *BULLHEADED CRAZY* THAN ANY *OTHER* TIME WE FOUGHT!

SORRY, ROUGHOUSE--

WRRRRAAMMM

WORDS AIN'T *DOIN'* IT...ALL I GOT LEFT ARE *CLAWS*.

SNIKT!

WHONNG!

STAY *DOWN,* BIG GUY! DON'T--

BUT OF COURSE--

--HE DOES.

AND THE *BEAST* IN ME RISES TO *MEET* HIM--

--RAGING TO *KILL* THE MAN I CAME INTO THIS MESS TO *SAVE.* ONLY--

WIK WIK WIK WIK WIK

--THIS KILLING EDGE--

--TURNS SUDDENLY SOFT.

A GOOD *TEST* MUST HAVE CERTAIN *CONTROLS,* YES?

ROUGHHOUSE IS OUR MOST **SUCCESSFUL** SUBJECT TO DATE. WE CANNOT HAVE HIM SLICED LIKE **BRATWURST**--

--AT LEAST NOT WHILE HIS **LIMITS** ARE STILL BEING CHARTED. INSTEAD, WE WILL NOTE THE **EFFECTS**--

--OF BEING RIDDLED WITH **TRANQUILIZER** DARTS UPON YOUR **OWN** FIGHTING SKILLS.

AH! **SLUGGISH-NESS.**

FAULTY REFLEXES.

LOSS OF **DEFENSIVE** SKILLS--

--PERHAPS EVEN, THE ABILITY TO **SURVIVE.**

THUD!

I'D SAY GEIST IS **WRONG** 'BOUT THAT LAST BIT. GOT AN UNBREAKABLE **ADAMANTIUM SKELE-TON**, AFTER ALL.

I'D SAY THAT--

WOM!

--BUT EVERY OUNCE'A FLESH'N'BLOOD *AROUND* THAT SKELETON IS *SCREAMIN'* GEIST IS *RIGHT.*

ONE CONSOLATION: MY MUTANT *HEALIN' FAC-TOR* HASN'T BEATEN THOSE *TRANQUILIZERS* YET. GONNA BE TOO *UNCONSCIOUS*--

--T'KNOW WHEN I *DROWN.*

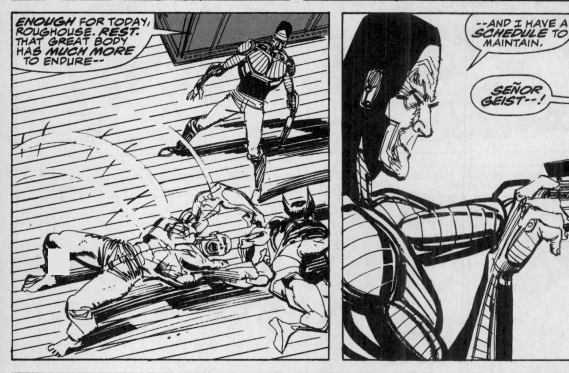

ENOUGH FOR TODAY, ROUGHHOUSE. *REST.* THAT GREAT BODY HAS *MUCH MORE* TO ENDURE--

--AND I HAVE A *SCHEDULE* TO MAINTAIN.

SEÑOR GEIST--!

THAT *HELICOPTER* IS--

--*PRECISELY* ON TIME,

THE *FIRST* OF MY EXPECTED GUESTS.

GENERAL COY! I APPRECIATE A MAN PREPARED TO *ACT* ON SHORT NOTICE.

AN OLD SOLDIER'S *NATURE*, GEIST. EVEN IF MY *ARMY* IS NOW MADRIPOOR'S *CRIMINAL CLASS*--

--AND MY *FOE* THAT INTERLOPING SHE-DEVIL, *TYGER TIGER.*

THIS MORNING'S *DEVELOPMENTS* WILL *PLEASE* YOU, GENERAL, AS THEY INVOLVE YOUR FORMER *BODYGUARD*--

--AND THE *SELF-STYLED PROTECTOR* OF YOUR LOVELY *RIVAL*, YES?

PATCH!

AN IDENTITY HE SEEMS *TIRED* OF...THOUGH IMITATING THE *WOLVERINE* SEEMS A MOST *PAINFUL* ALTERNATIVE.

AND DUE TO *ROUGHOUSE*...?! I WOULD SAY I *SOLD* HIM TOO QUICKLY--

--IF YOU WEREN'T SHARING THE *CATALYST* BEHIND THIS MIRACLE, GEIST.

A *SMALL* SHARE...FOR A *GOOD* PRICE. WHAT I PAID FOR *ROUGHOUSE*, I BELIEVE.

BUT BE *WARNED*, GENERAL--

--THE MAIN *PROPERTY* OF YOUR PURCHASE IS THAT IT DRIVES ANY *USER* TO INSANE *VIOLENCE* AND ULTIMATE *DEATH.*

INTERESTING *QUALITIES*, GEIST...IF ONE CAN CONTROL *WHERE* AND IN *WHOM* THEY APPEAR.

SOUNDS. FADIN' IN AN' OUT. HELICOPTER, NO. NOW... PLANE, SOMEONE BOARDING... *SECOND* VISITOR.

...APPEARS NEARLY *DEAD,* GEIST.

PRINCE BARAN. MADRIPOOR'S RULER IN THIS...?

BETTER *HE* SERVED AS AN OBJECT FOR ROUGHOUSE TO FOCUS HIS VIOLENCE UPON--

--THAN *ME* OR MY EMPLOYER'S MEN. THAT'S WHY I LET HIM SPY US *TAKING* ROUGHOUSE AND *FOLLOW* FROM YOUR ISLAND.

HIS *FUTURE*--

--I LEAVE TO YOU AND *YOUR* MEN.

AT A *PRICE!* ONE THAT SO CONVENIENTLY *DUPLICATES* THE TRIBUTE GIVEN ME TO RECLAIM YOUR *COCAINE*--

--IT IS STILL IN THE *BAG* IN WHICH YOU *DELIVERED* IT, GEIST!

ALL *RELATIVE,* YES? MAINTENANCE ON THIS METAL SHELL IS AN INCREDIBLE *EXPENSE*--

--BUT *ANY SUM* THAT REMOVES A MAN SO THREATENING TO YOUR CAREFULLY MAINTAINED *BALANCE OF POWER* IN MADRIPOOR IS *MODEST* INDEED.

FAREWELL, YOUR HIGHNESS.

PRESIDENT CARIDAD *TOLERATES* THIS SIDE BARGAINING, SEÑOR GEIST...?

AS I TOLERATE YOUR *DISAPPROVAL*, CAPTAIN... PROVIDED IT DOESN'T INTERFERE WITH OUR ULTIMATE GOAL. NOW *FULL SPEED*--

MADRE DE DIOS!

THE MAN *ROUGHHOUSE* FOUGHT...! THEY... THEY...

YES. IT SHOCKS *ME* AS WELL, CAPTAIN ...I'D HAVE WAITED UNTIL THE AIRCRAFT WAS *MUCH* HIGHER.

PRINCE BARAN OBVIOUSLY *FEARED* THE FERAL LITTLE GENTLEMAN EVEN *MORE* THAN HE LET ON... I MAY HAVE *UNDERCHARGED!*

AH, WELL. AT LEAST OUR *MISSION* IS ACCOMPLISHED. IN ROUGHHOUSE, THE PRESIDENT HAS A LAB RAT WHO CAN *SURVIVE* THE TESTING THAT MUST BE DONE...THOUGH THE DEVIL KNOWS *WHAT* IT WILL MAKE OF HIM!

TIERRA VERDE.

YOUR *TOUCH*....! BETTER THAN MY *BEST* MEMORIES!

TRULY YOU ARE A *MIRACLE WORKER*, MY LOVE. THE FOREIGN PRESS, THEY CALL ME THIS COUNTRY'S *STRONG MAN*--

THEY DON'T SEE MY *PAIN*. THEY DON'T KNOW THAT AGAINST MY CONSTANT *MIGRAINE ATTACKS*--

--ONLY *YOU* CAN SAVE ME.

COME BACK... TO *ME*, TO THE *CAPITAL!* I HAVE BUILT A *HOSPITAL* THERE... *MAGNIFICENT!*

A PLACE TO *SHARE* YOUR TALENT FOR HEALING WITH *EVERYONE*...NOT JUST INDIANS AT SOME *BACKRIVER* MISSION. *SAVAGES* WHO CALL YOU--

SISTER SALVATION.

THEY ARE *GENTLE, FELIX. ACCEPTING.* UNLIKE YOU--

--WHO CAN'T FORGET THAT *BEFORE* I WAS SISTER SALVATION, I WAS YOUR *WIFE.*

MAY I LEAVE THE *YACHT* NOW?

HEAR ME, DARLING--

--YOU FLED TO THE *CHURCH* BECAUSE I BECAME *CORRUPT*, NO?

WELL, *OUT OF* THAT *CORRUPTION* HAS COME SOMETHING THAT CAN BRING *PRIDE* TO TIERRA VERDE.

BUT I NEED *YOUR* GIFT TO COMPLETE THIS MIRACLE!

MIRACLES DON'T SPRING OUT OF CORRUPTION, FELIX--

--AND WHATEVER MY GIFT, THERE IS NEED ENOUGH FOR IT HERE.

I WAS AFRAID THAT WOULD BE YOUR ANSWER.

SHORE PARTY ABOARD, MY PRESIDENT...! READY TO CAST OFF!

IN HEAVEN'S NAME, FELIX! PUT ME ASHORE! EVEN YOU CAN'T--

MY LOVE--

--YOU'VE LEFT ME NO CHOICE!

KA-WHOOM!

THE PACIFIC. A SOUTH SEA AIRWAYS PLANE CIRCLES A LAUNCH BELOW...

...MAN TOLD ME TO KEEP MY *DISTANCE* BUT TRACK THE *SHIP* IF IT MOVED. WHO KNEW ANYTHING LIKE *THIS'D* HAPPEN?

YOU RUN AN *AIRLINE*, ARCHIE ...NOT A *CRYSTAL BALL GAZING SERVICE*. VISUAL FIX WAS *GOOD*--

--THE REST IS UP TO *US.*

O'DONNELL...! HAVE YOU--?

GOT 'IM, TIGER! CAN'T BE MUCH *LEFT* OF HIM--

--BUT IT'S *SURE HEAVY!*

EVEN IF HE'S *ALIVE*...MUST'VE BROKEN EVERY *BONE* IN HIS BODY!

TRUST SOMEONE WHO *KNOWS*, MR. CORRIGAN...HE DOESN'T *BREAK* EASILY AS *MOST.*

WELL, HE'S STILL *BREATHING*, DARLIN'... SEEMS *DOUBTFUL* HE'LL EVER DO ANYTHING *ELSE.*

...ONE...!

W-WHAT...?

...GONNA DO ONE OTHER THING... INVADE TIERRA VERDE...!

NEXT MONTH: *TIGER SHARK!*

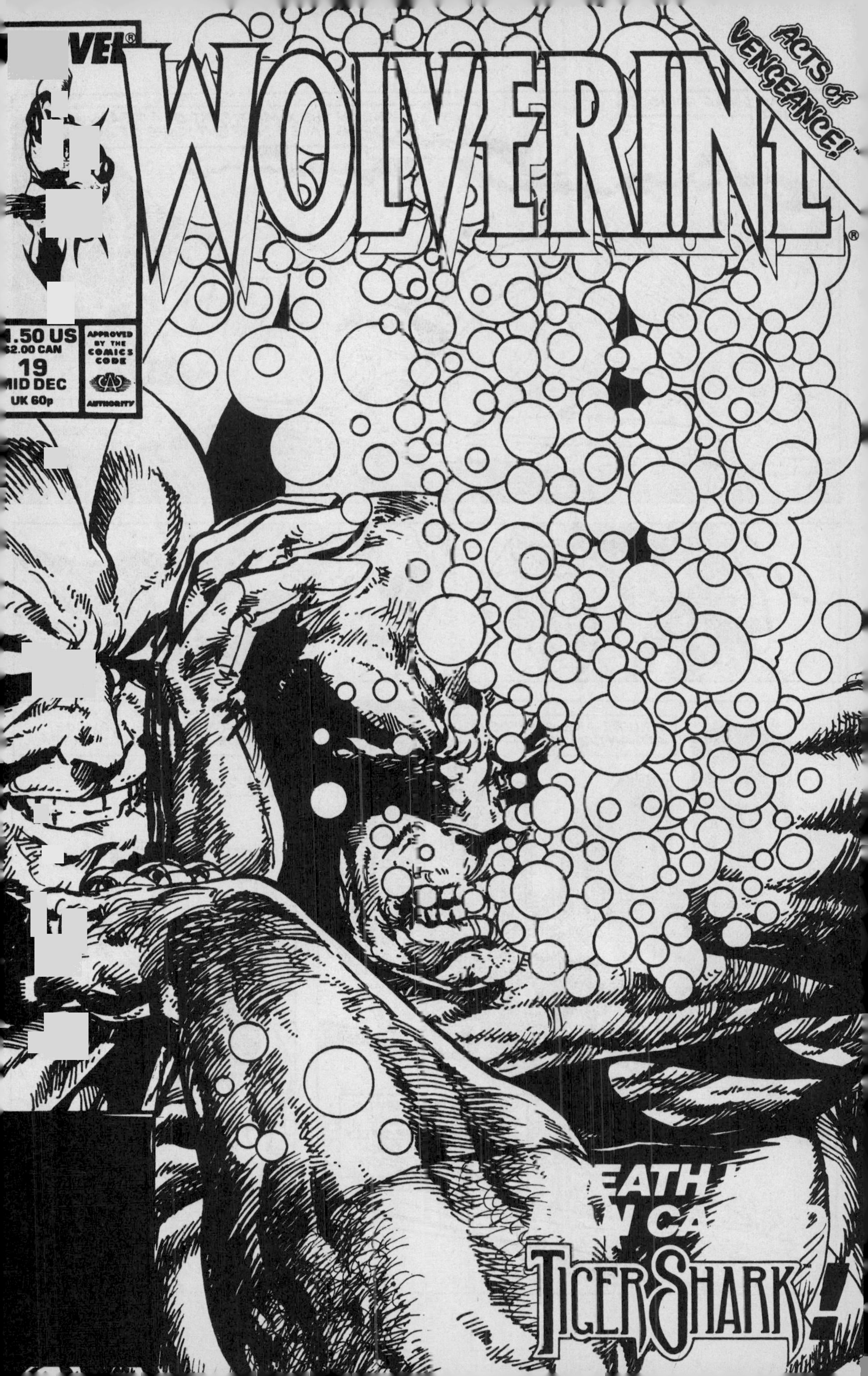
WOLVERINE
ACTS OF VENGEANCE!
1.50 US
$2.00 CAN
19
MID DEC
UK 60p
APPROVED BY THE COMICS CODE AUTHORITY
TIGER SHARK!

TIME WAS I WAS STRICTLY A LONER.

NOW I'M ONE OF THE *X-MEN*. PART OF A *TEAM*. AND SINCE ALL OF US HAVE DIFFERENT KINDS OF *MUTANT POWERS...*

HEY!

W-WHAT--?!

...THERE ARE SURPRISING *ADVANTAGES.*

'COURSE, THE NEWLY-WEDS HERE MIGHT *DISAGREE.* 'SPECIALLY IF THEY LOOK BACK TO WHERE MY *FOOT-PRINTS* START.

GATEWAY'S WORK. HE'S KINDA OUR INSTANT TRAVEL SERVICE. YEP. NICE BEING PART OF A TEAM.

STILL...

...SOME THINGS YOU HANDLE *ALONE.*

FIRST GLANCE, PLACE MIGHT BE MIAMI BEACH.

BUT MOVIN' BEYOND THE HOTELS AND TOURISTS...

...EACH NEW BLOCK FITS MORE WITH MY RESEARCH.

DID IT WHILE MY *MUTANT HEALING FACTOR* FIXED A FEW *INJURIES* OF MINE...

...FROM A WORLD CLASS BEATING AND BEING DUMPED FROM A PLANE.

YEP. WATCHIN' GOVERNMENT TROOPS REASON WITH THE PRESS MAKES IT CERTAIN.

I'M IN *PUERTO VERDE*...

...CAPITAL CITY OF *TIERRA VERDE*.

MY *INVASION* HAS BEGUN.

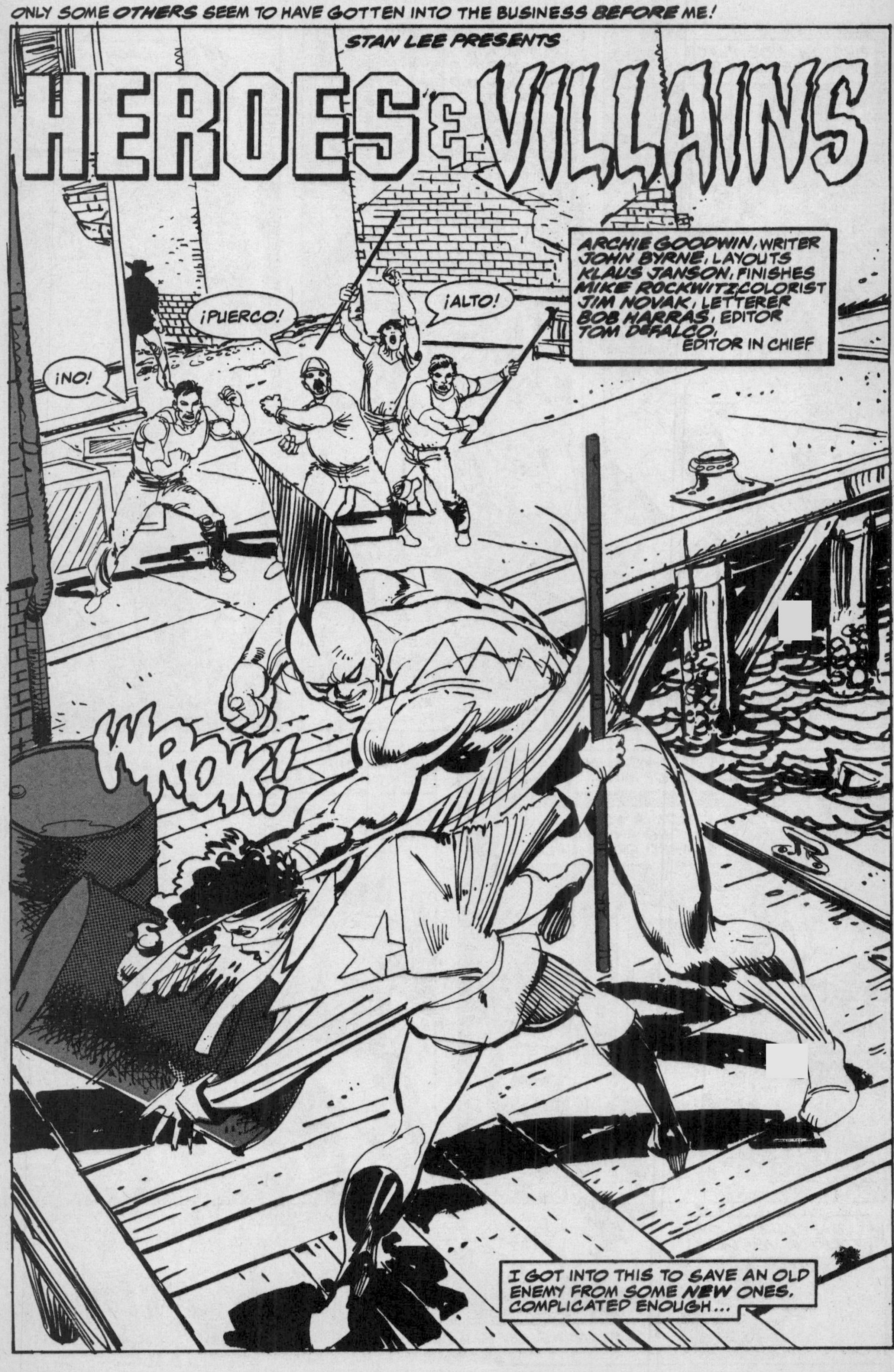
ONLY SOME OTHERS SEEM TO HAVE GOTTEN INTO THE BUSINESS BEFORE ME!
STAN LEE PRESENTS
HEROES & VILLAINS
ARCHIE GOODWIN, WRITER
JOHN BYRNE, LAYOUTS
KLAUS JANSON, FINISHES
MIKE ROCKWITZ, COLORIST
JIM NOVAK, LETTERER
BOB HARRAS, EDITOR
TOM DEFALCO, EDITOR IN CHIEF
¡NO!
¡PUERCO!
¡ALTO!
WROK!
I GOT INTO THIS TO SAVE AN OLD ENEMY FROM SOME NEW ONES. COMPLICATED ENOUGH...

...WITHOUT ADDING *NEW* TROUBLE TO COMPLICATE IT *MORE.*

DON'T KNOW THE PLAYERS. NOT MY GAME. WAY THINGS *LOOK...*

...GIRL SHOULDN'T HAVE MADE IT *HERS.*

DADE COUNTY, FLORIDA TO CENTRAL AMERICA. LONG TRIP, CHIQUITA... JUST TO *DIE.*

DON'T BOTHER GETTING UP... IT'S ALREADY *OVER.* YOU'RE FIGHTING *TIGER SHARK--*

--NOT STRUNG. OUT *CRACK PEDDLERS* LIKE YOU TACKLED AT HOME.

YOU'RE AN *ASSASSIN...* NOTHING MORE! A *TOOL* OF THE CORRUPTION THAT I FOUGHT IN THE BARRIO--

--THAT I HAVE COME TO *CHALLENGE HERE!*

AND SHE WILL NOT FIGHT ALONE, YANQUI! *RALLY,* AMIGOS--

RALLY TO *LA BANDERA!*

SURE. RALLY 'ROUND *THE FLAG*, BOYS--

BWAK!

--MIGHT AS WELL OFF A *DOZEN* WASTES AS *ONE*!

THEY ARE *THE PEOPLE*, TIGER SHARK! WHEN THE *SPIRIT* MOVES THEM--

--YOU DON'T *KNOW* WHAT THEY CAN DO!

I KNOW WHAT *I* CAN DO!

YOU CAN SUFFER THE *DEFEAT* YOUR KIND *ALWAYS* DOES!

WHOA! KID'S GOT MOVES AND SURPRISES...

...CAN'T *HELP* BUT BE *DRAWN* TO HER.

VIVA *LA BANDERA*!

COMPADRES, WITHOUT YOU I COULDN'T HAVE--

WON! GUTSY KID, *REALLY*--

WAIT! A GUY LIKE *THAT*...?! IT'S TOO *EASY*, GIRL!

NOW, CHIQUITA... IT GETS *UGLY*!

LOOK OU--

WHA-RAAK!

BAD TIME FOR THAT *STAFF* OF YOURS TO BE RUNNING OUT OF WHATEVER *POWERS* IT--

--BUT THEN THOSE PRECIOUS *"PEOPLE"* OF YOURS SEEM TO BE *RUNNING OUT*, TOO!

SMART! THEY *RECOGNIZE* WHO'S A RUN-OF-THE-MILL *ASSASSIN* AND WHO'S *NOT*--

--EVEN IF *YOU* DON'T!

FWAK!

YOU STEPPED ON SOME *BIG TOES* PLAYING *MS. COMMUNITY INSPIRATION* BACK IN FLORIDA. THAT *NETTED* YOU THE *DEATH WARRANT*--

--FULFILLING IT'S A *PERSONAL* PLEASURE!

SNIKT!

NOT FOR A *MAN* WHO *TALKS* WHEN HE SHOULD BE WATCHIN' HIS *BACK!*

WHUMP!

ANOTHER HERO--?

--GOOD!

THAT'S WHAT THIS IS REALLY ABOUT!

I HATE HEROES!

FWOM!

EVERYTHING I AM TODAY IS BECAUSE SOME IDIOT TRIED TO BE A HERO...AND WOUND UP A CRIPPLE!

I WAS THAT IDIOT, LITTLE GIRL... NO MORE!

NOW I'M A SHARK. BADDEST SHARK IN THE OCEAN. AND HEROES LIKE YOU--

--ARE MY FAVORITE PREY! MY--

W-WHAT--?!

'FRAID I CAUSED A LEAK, BUB--

NOBODY TOSSES ME AROUND AND GETS OFF *FREE.*

LA BANDERA, IF HE'S GOT *WATER* CIRCULATIN' THROUGH THAT SUIT--

IT MUST BE *VITAL* TO HIM! BY KEEPING HIM *BETWEEN* US, CUT OFF FROM THE *SEA,* WE CAN--

WEAKEN ME--?

BEAT ME--?

NOT--

--TODAY!

I'LL *SETTLE* FOR THAT. GUY HAS THE STRENGTH, THE POWER TO BE IN *SUB-MARINER'S* CLASS...

...I'LL SETTLE AND COUNT MYSELF...

...*LUCKY. THE SHIP.* THE SHIP WHERE I TOOK ALL MY *LUMPS.* IF IT'S ANCHORED HERE, THEN...

HEY!

VICTORY, COMPADRE! YOU HAVE HELPED ME TO *VICTORY...* AND I *LOVE* YOU FOR IT!

KID, YOU DON'T EVEN *KNOW* ME! OR THE *DIFFERENCE* 'TWEEN A *VICTORY*... AN' A *BREATHER*!

THIS AIN'T THE TIME TO *CELEBRATE*... ONLY TO *HIDE*.

I DIDN'T *COME* HERE TO *HIDE*--

--I CAME TO *FIGHT*! AND TO *INSPIRE OTHERS* TO DO THE SAME!

YEAH, I FELT THAT... *TOO MUCH*! SAYS MUTANT ABILITY T'ME, KID--

--'BOUT THE MOST *DANGEROUS* I'VE COME ACROSS. TRUST A *FELLOW* MUTANT!

IT IS A *GIFT*... A *WONDERFUL* GIFT! AND IT MAKES ME *MORE* THAN A "KID!"

DRUG TRAFFIC SUPPORTED BY THIS COUNTRY'S *GOVERN-MENT* DESTROYED MY *FAMILY* AND--

AN' YOU'RE GONNA *INSPIRE* A *REVOLU-TION* TO BRING IT DOWN.

INSPIRATION FADES, KID. *FAST*... WHEN YOU'RE ALSO *DRAW-IN'* ON IT, TURNIN' IT INTO A *PHYSICAL FORCE*--

--T'CHANNEL THROUGH THAT *STAFF* OF YOURS.

PITCH THE *COSTUME*. THIS OLD SEC-TION'S A *MAZE*. LOSE YOURSELF 'TIL YOU CAN MAKE IT *HOME*.

YOU GOT IT IN YOU TO *HURT* A WHOLE LOTTA PEOPLE, LA BANDERA--

--*DON'T*.

SHE GOES. WILL SHE LISTEN? MAYBE. IF SHE'S NOT AS STUBBORN AS *I* WAS AT HER AGE...

...AS I AM *NOW*. AS I *HAVE* TO BE...

...WITH ALL THE *DETOURS* POPPIN' UP 'TWEEN ME AN' WHAT I *CAME* FOR.

LOOK *UP,* HOSER--

YOU'RE BY-PASSIN' A *FREE BEER.*

FACE FROM MY PAST. MY DAYS WITH CANADIAN INTELLIGENCE. *JACK BASCOMB, CIA.*

THAT WATERFRONT SET-TO CAUGHT MY *ATTENTION,* LOGAN. *FEISTY* AS ALWAYS--

--AN' A TAD *MISGUIDED.*

LITTLE LADY YOU HELPED HAS *QUESTIONABLE* ROOTS, OL' SON. *CUBAN.* HER FATHER WAS A BIG DEAL IN *FIDEL'S* REVOLUTION.

SUPPOSEDLY GOT *DISILLU-SIONED* LATER...FLED TO *FLORIDA.* STAYED BITTER. FOUND *DRUGS.* DIED A *JUNKIE.*

PRETTY *SAD,* JACK. AN' SOMEHOW YOU SEE HIS *DAUGHTER* AS A BIG, BAD COMMUNIST *THREAT?*

I SEE *YOU* AS A THREAT, LOGAN--

--GETTIN' ALL *INVOLVED* IN SOMETHIN' YOU'VE BEEN *OUT* OF TOO LONG. THERE ARE *WHEELS* WITHIN *WHEELS* SPINNIN' IN TIERRA VERDE--

--AN' *YOU* ARE JUST NATURAL BORN *GRIT* IN THE GEARS.

DISAPPEAR AGAIN, OL' SON. *POR FAVOR.*

NEW YORK.

...I BELIEVE, SIR, THIS MATTER REQUIRES A *BROADER* VIEW.

MY **ONLY** VIEW, **SEÑOR**, IS THAT YOU ACTED WITHOUT **CONSULTING** ME!

THIS... THIS **TIGER SHARK** VIOLATED TIERRA VERDE'S BORDERS TO INFLICT **PERSONAL** PUNISHMENT ON YOUR BEHALF!

--BUT THIS IS STILL THE INTRICATE PART OF A **GRANDER SCHEME**. AND ALL THOSE INDIVIDUALS DUBBED **SUPER HEROES** WILL EVENTUALLY SUFFER.

THE **LONG RANGE BENEFITS**--EVEN IN OUR RELATIVELY UNCOMPLICATED **DRUG TRANSACTIONS**--SURELY DO NOT **ESCAPE** YOU, SIR?

SO IT **APPEARS**, CARIDAD. YES, THE YOUNG LADY ATTACKED HAS RASHLY **INTERFERED** WITH MY FLORIDA OPERATIONS--

AS TIGER SHARK'S **TARGET** ESCAPED **HIM**...? YOU MAY BE THE **KINGPIN OF CRIME**, WILSON FISK--

--BUT IT IS STILL **PRESUMPTUOUS** TO EXPECT A **WORLD LEADER** TO SHELTER YOUR **ASSASSIN** UNTIL--

GREATLY **APPRECIATED**, MR. PRESIDENT. NOW IF YOU'LL **EXCUSE** ME... I HAVE A **MEETING** THAT CANNOT WAIT.

KLIK

COMIC OPERA **FOOL**.

BUT HIS COCAINE TRADE IS A NECESSARY **HEDGE** AGAINST THE POWER OF THE COLUMBIA CARTEL--

--FOR **NOW**.

AH...! GENTLEMEN--

--EAGER FOR FURTHER **ACTS OF VENGEANCE**, I SEE.

GANGSTER PIG!

WAM!

THE *ARROGANCE* OF THAT *SLAB OF PORK*....! OF HIS *SCHEME!* DID YOU *HEAR,* GEIST...?

HE--AND WHATEVER MAD *PARTNERS* HE HAS--WOULD *DESTROY* THE WORLD'S HEROES! *HOW,* GEIST?!

YOU *CANNOT!* NO MATTER HOW *MANY* YOU DESTROY ...THE *PEOPLE* WILL ONLY CREATE *NEW* ONES!

THAT IS THE *TRUTH,* GEIST...AND WHY TIERRA VERDE WILL *REMEMBER* FELIX GUILLERMO CARIDAD! NOT BECAUSE I WAS A DRUG-TRAFFICKING *DICTATOR*--

--BUT BECAUSE I GAVE THEM THEIR OWN SYMBOL OF NATIONAL HONOR... A *SUPER HERO!* EQUAL TO *ANY* IN THE WORLD!

BUT WHEN I SHOULD *CONCENTRATE MOST* ON THIS...I HAVE *TIGER SHARK!* I HAVE *LA BANDERA!* I HAVE *REBELLION* AND... AND...

MIGRAINE! ANOTHER... SO *SOON!* MY *WIFE,* GEIST...! SHE'S THE ONLY ONE WHO CAN--

SHE STILL REFUSES TO *SEE* YOU, MY PRESIDENT. BUT...A *SUGGESTION,* YES?

AS YOU'VE SAID IN THE *PAST*--

BARRING YOUR *LADY'S* AMAZING TOUCH--

--THERE'S NOTHING SO RELAXING AS A CLEAN, CLOSE SHAVE.

KNOWING THE *URGENCY* OF YOUR INTERESTS, SENOR PRESIDENT--

CH-KLIK!

--I TOOK THE LIBERTY OF SENDING FOR YOUR RESEARCH TEAM. AS I SHAVE YOU--

--THEIR LATEST *FINDINGS* CAN BE REPORTED.

AFTER...AH...*EXHAUSTIVE* TESTS, WE HAVE...AH...*ISOLATED* THE SO-CALLED... AH...*MIRACLE COCAINE* TO...AH...

THE COCAINE IS FROM *ONE* FIELD ONLY, PRESIDENT CARIDAD... *EL JARDÍN DEL REY.*

NOT ONLY ONE...AH... FIELD, BUT ONE PARTICULAR...AH...*CROP* WHICH ...AH... SINCE...

SINCE THAT CROP'S *HARVEST*, PRESIDENT CARIDAD... *EL JARDÍN DEL REY* HAS BEEN *BARREN.*

GIFTS FROM THE GODS ARE ALWAYS *RARE*...SELDOM *LIMITLESS.*

THE *IMPORTANT* THING IS THAT WE RECOGNIZE THEM FOR *WHAT* THEY ARE...AND USE THEM *WELL.*

I KNOW, EL JARDÍN DEL REY!

"A JUNGLE MOUNTAINSIDE... A PLACE OF MANY *LEGENDS.*

"SOME SAY THAT BACK IN PREHISTORY, THE SITE WAS BOMBARDED BY *FALLING STARS*...

"OTHER STORIES HAVE IT THAT IN THE MOST *ANCIENT OF DAYS*, MIGHTY *GODS* MADE WAR..."

"...AND ONE SUCH *GOD* FOUGHT TO HIS *DEATH* ON THE MOUNTAINSIDE."

"*WHATEVER*.

"MANY CAME TO *FEAR EL JARDÍN DEL REY* AND MOST TRY TO *AVOID* IT.

"AN IDEAL *PLACE* THEN, FOR GROWING *COCAINE*... OR FINDING A *MIRACLE*."

BUT SUCH...AH...*TALES* CANNOT...AH...*ACCOUNT*, SENOR PRESIDENT, FOR...AH...

WHY THE COCAINE INDUCES *HYPER-ABILITIES*--

--OR HOW TO *CONTROL* THOSE EFFECTS SO THE TEST SUBJECT DOESN'T *DIE!*

SCIENTISTS ...HAH!

MY *ADVISOR* HERE HAS *FOUND* A MAN APPARENTLY *STRONG* ENOUGH TO SURVIVE *NUMEROUS* DOSES OF THE DRUG!

AND I HAVE REALIZED A MOST *OBVIOUS* MEANS FOR ASSURING CONTROL--

--MY WIFE.

SHE IS BLESSED WITH A TALENT FOR *HEALING.* SUCH A TALENT THAT SHE LEFT ME FOR THE *CHURCH*...AND *SERVICE* IN A JUNGLE *MEDICAL MISSION.*

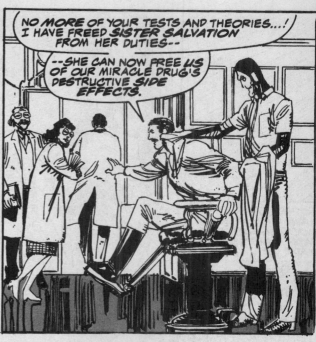

NO MORE OF YOUR *TESTS* AND *THEORIES*...! I HAVE FREED *SISTER SALVATION* FROM HER DUTIES--

--SHE CAN NOW FREE *US* OF OUR MIRACLE DRUG'S *DESTRUCTIVE SIDE EFFECTS.*

WE WILL HAVE THE *MEANS* OF CREATING THE SUPER HERO I *DESIRE* FOR TIERRA VERDE!

HAH...! GEIST, A CLEAN, CLOSE SHAVE *DOES* MAKE ME FEEL BETTER!

I WONDER, MY PRESIDENT...THE *MOUSTACHE?* PERHAPS *THAT* SHOULD GO AS WELL.

YOU'VE THE REMARKABLE ABILITY TO INSPIRE *TRUST* IN THOSE YOU SERVE, GEIST. WHO *ELSE* WOULD I LET PUT A *RAZOR* TO MY THROAT?

BUT I THINK YOU WON'T BE *HAPPY* UNTIL EVERYONE IS SHAVED SMOOTH AS THAT *ARMOR* YOU WEAR.

IS IT *TRUE* YOU ONCE SHAVED *ADOLF HITLER*...?

DID *HE* HAVE TO FIGHT FOR HIS MOUSTACHE AS I DO, AMIGO?

I AM *REVITALIZED,* GEIST... DESPITE THE LATE HOUR. IT IS TIME TO *FACE* MY WIFE--

--TO MAKE PERFECTLY *CLEAR* WHY SHE MUST LEND HER *GIFTS* TO MY *PROJECT.*

GOOD LUCK, SEÑOR PRESIDENT.

ALONE AT LAST.

TIME FOR A LITTLE *PAYBACK*--

WROK!

--FOR OUR PREVIOUS MEETIN'!

KRAASH!

BUT FROM WHAT I'VE LEARNED SINCE--

--WHEN IT COMES TO PAYIN' YOU BACK, GEIST, THERE'S LOTS'A *OTHERS* WITH *BIGGER* CLAIMS--

SNIKT!

--BUT NO ONE BETTER EQUIPPED FOR THE JOB!

AN' UNLESS YOU BEAT ME TO THAT *MACHINE PISTOL*--

--WE'RE GONNA TALK ABOUT MY MISSING *SPARRING PARTNER*--

WUNK!

"--ROUGHOUSE."

YAAAAARRRRGHHHH

SAD...YES, MY LOVE? HE GETS *STRONGER* WITH EACH DOSE OF THE COCAINE... BUT GROWS MORE UNCONTROLLABLY *VIOLENT* AS WELL.

THE SCARS ARE *OLD*-- PERHAPS EVEN FROM CHILDHOOD--BUT THE *SORES*? A NEW DEVELOPMENT...

FELIX...

IF ANYTHING *EVER* REQUIRED THE TOUCH OF *SISTER SALVATION*...

FELIX... HOW *COULD* YOU?! TO DO THIS TO ANOTHER HUMAN BEING...!

TO IMAGINE I WOULD *AID* IN SUCH A *BLASPHEMY*... ESPECIALLY AFTER YOU RUTHLESSLY *DESTROYED* MY MISSION...!

ALL FOR *TIERRA VERDE*. ONLY MY *METHODS* ARE BRUTAL...MY *GOAL* IS GREAT. BUT IF PATRI- OTISM DOESN'T MOVE YOU, MY ANGEL--

--WHAT ABOUT OUR *SON*?

FELIX... IN HEAVEN'S NAME! I--

KA-WHOM!

ATTACK, COMPADRES!

YOU'VE FOUGHT AS SMALL, ISO-LATED GROUPS IN THE SLUMS AND ON THE FARM-LANDS--

TONIGHT... YOU ARE AN **ARMY!**

!VIVA LA REVOLUCIÓN!

!VIVA LA BANDERA!

WHERE ARE WE **NOW**, GEIST? ANY **TRICKS...** I'LL PUNCTURE MORE THAN YOUR MECHA-NICAL HAND.

WE'RE NEARING THE **MEDICAL CENTER.** YOU DEMANDED I TAKE YOU TO **ROUGHOUSE**--

FOR A MAN IN A **WOLVERINE** COSTUME ... A ROUTE WHERE ATTENTION IS UNLIKE-LY SEEMS BEST, YES?

BUT THE **CAN OPENER'S** READY... JUST IN CASE.

THESE THREATS... UNNECESSARY. I AM A MAN DEDICATED TO **SURVIVING.** MY CYBERNETIC ARMOR IS A VITAL-- AND **EXPENSIVE**-- PART OF THAT.

REPLACING THIS **HAND** WILL EAT ANY **PROFIT** I MADE SETTING YOU UP FOR YOUR ENEMIES... **GENERAL COY** AND **PRINCE BARAN.**

THEIR DAY'LL COME...BUT YOU'RE *LONG* OVERDUE FOR SOME LOSSES.

WITH THE RIGHT *COMPUTER*...RIGHT *SENSE* OF WHAT *INTELLIGENCE* FILES TO TAP...I'VE COME TO *KNOW* YOU, TIN MAN.

WHAT A *PACKAGE* YOU ARE!

"UP TO YOUR EL- BOWS IN BLOOD AS ONE OF THE FÜHRER'S *INNER- CIRCLE*...

"BARTERIN' GER- MAN ROCKET SCI- ENTISTS TO THE AMERICAN OSS TO ESCAPE *WAR CRIMES* PROSE- CUTION...

"MAKIN' YOURSELF *USEFUL* IN QUES- TIONABLE CIA OPERATIONS...

"--AND TO NEW WORLD *FACISTS* LIKE CARIDAD."

A LONG, PROUD *TRADITION*, GEIST.

THE *NAZI GHOST* WHO STILL *HAUNTS* THE FREE WORLD...AN EMBARRASSING CLICHÉ, YES? BUT WHY SUCH *OUTRAGE*?

THE NOTION *THRILLS* MOST PEOPLE. LOOK IN ANY BOOKSTORE... FROM ALL THE SWAS- TIKAS DECORATING THE COVERS, YOU'D THINK WE WON THE WAR.

SPEAKING OF *WAR*, THIS TUNNEL WAS BUILT IN CASE THE PRESIDENT EVER HAD TO FLEE THE *PALACE*--

BA-DUM!

ANNOYING! OUR ENEMIES ARE APPAR- ENTLY *ATTACKING*... BUT AT THE *WRONG* END!

MUST BE USIN' *ROCKETS*!

THIS WAY!

TO SHAKE *THIS* SUB-LEVEL... THEY'VE GREATER *FIREPOWER* THAN I'D EXPECT. THE COMPLEX'S *FILTRATION SYSTEM* IS HOUSED HERE.

THE MEDICAL CENTER USES *REPROCESSED SEAWATER* FOR MOST OF ITS NEEDS... THAT'S WHAT ALL THESE *TANKS* ARE.

FORGET THE *INDUSTRIAL TOUR,* GEIST... WHY WOULD A *HOSPITAL* DRAW THIS *KIND'A ATTACK?*

WORD MUST HAVE *LEAKED* THIS WING IS USED FOR *EXPERIMENTATION* ON *POLITICAL PRISONERS*--

--JUST THE *SORT* OF *NEWS* TO FIRE *REBEL IDEALISTS* INTO *ACTION.*

WHY SO *CHEERY* ABOUT IT, GEIST? WHAT DO *YOU* KNOW THAT I--

MY *ANSWER* COMES BEFORE I FINISH MY *QUESTION.*

:WUGHK!:

THEN I'M TASTIN' SALTWATER AN' FACIN' DEATH.

HERO!

IN MY *ELEMENT*...PLAYING TO MY *STRENGTHS*.

IF IT ISN'T *SPORT*...IT'LL STILL BE *FUN*.

SWIFTLY, TIGER SHARK! YOUR ORIGINAL TARGET--LA BANDERA--CAN'T BE FAR.

AFTER I CAREFULLY LEAKED WORD ABOUT THE POLITICAL PRISONER SITUATION TO LURE THE GIRL--

--YOU MUSN'T BE TOO PREOCCUPIED TO FINISH HER, YES?

HE *EXPECTS* ME TO FIGHT FOR THE SURFACE.

I TRY--

--KICKIN' FOR THE DEPTHS!

PUTS ME *FREE* OF TIGER SHARK...AN' INTO *SOMETHIN' ELSE!*

UNDERTOW!

HAULIN' ME LIKE A FREIGHT TRAIN--

GONNA BE SMASHED OR SHREDDED--

--IF MY CLAWS DON'T DO IT *FIRST!*

SHRAAAKK!

ADAMANTIUM. WONDER STUFF.

'COURSE IT CAN'T *SLICE* AN UNDERTOW--

--OR CUT YOU EXTRA AIR.

I'M INTO THE *PIPELINE.* NO WORRIES BUT *ONE.*

WHICH ENDS *FIRST?*

ME OR--

--IT?

OCEAN. ALL I HAVE TO DO IS REACH THE *SURFACE.* THEN I CAN BREATHE. THEN I CAN WARN LA BANDERA.

EXCEPT--

--THA'S *NOT* ALL I HAVE TO DO.

NEXT: BURIED AT SEA!

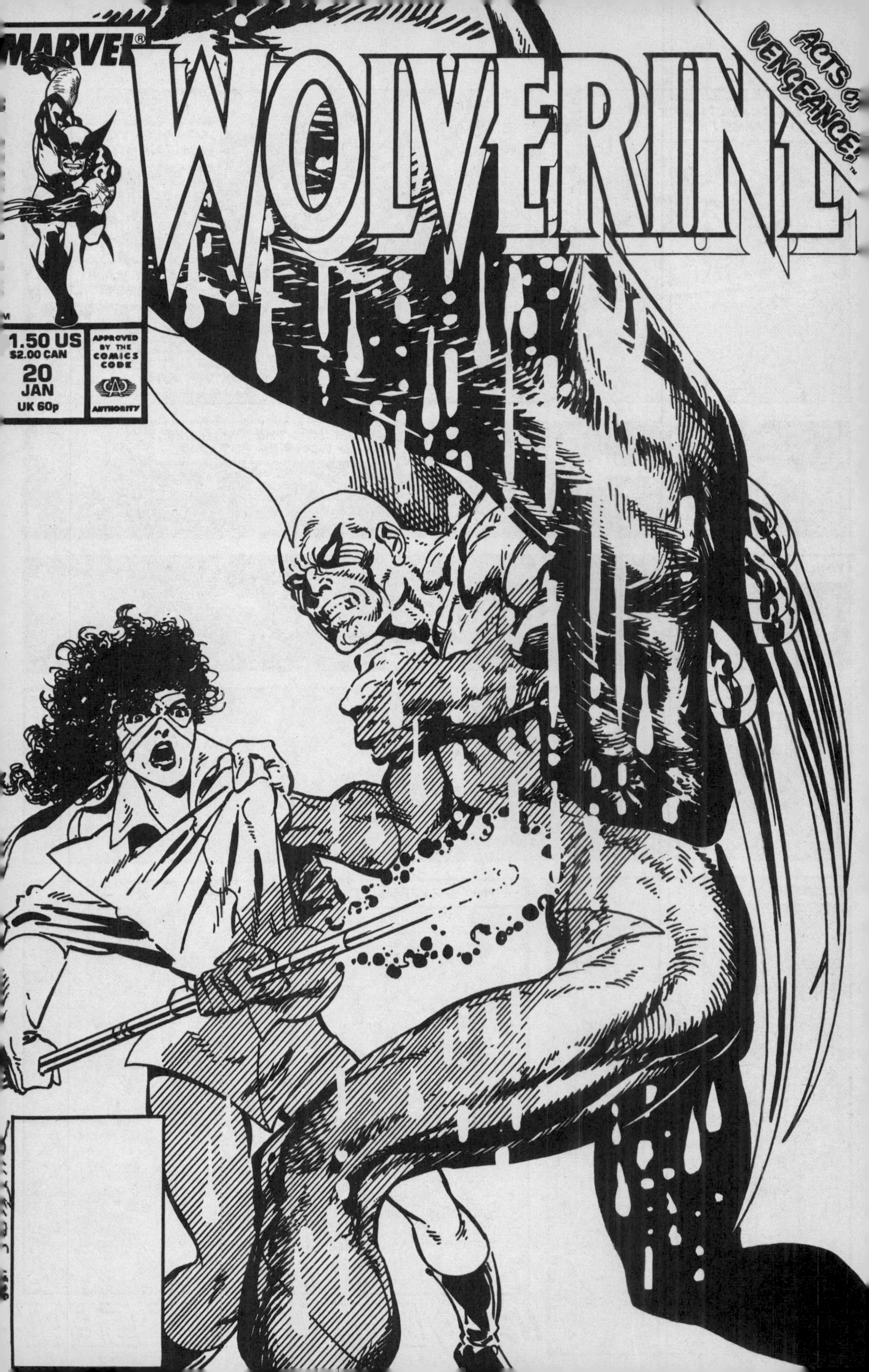
MARVEL
WOLVERINE
ACTS OF VENGEANCE!
1.50 US
$2.00 CAN
20
JAN
UK 60p
APPROVED BY THE COMICS CODE AUTHORITY

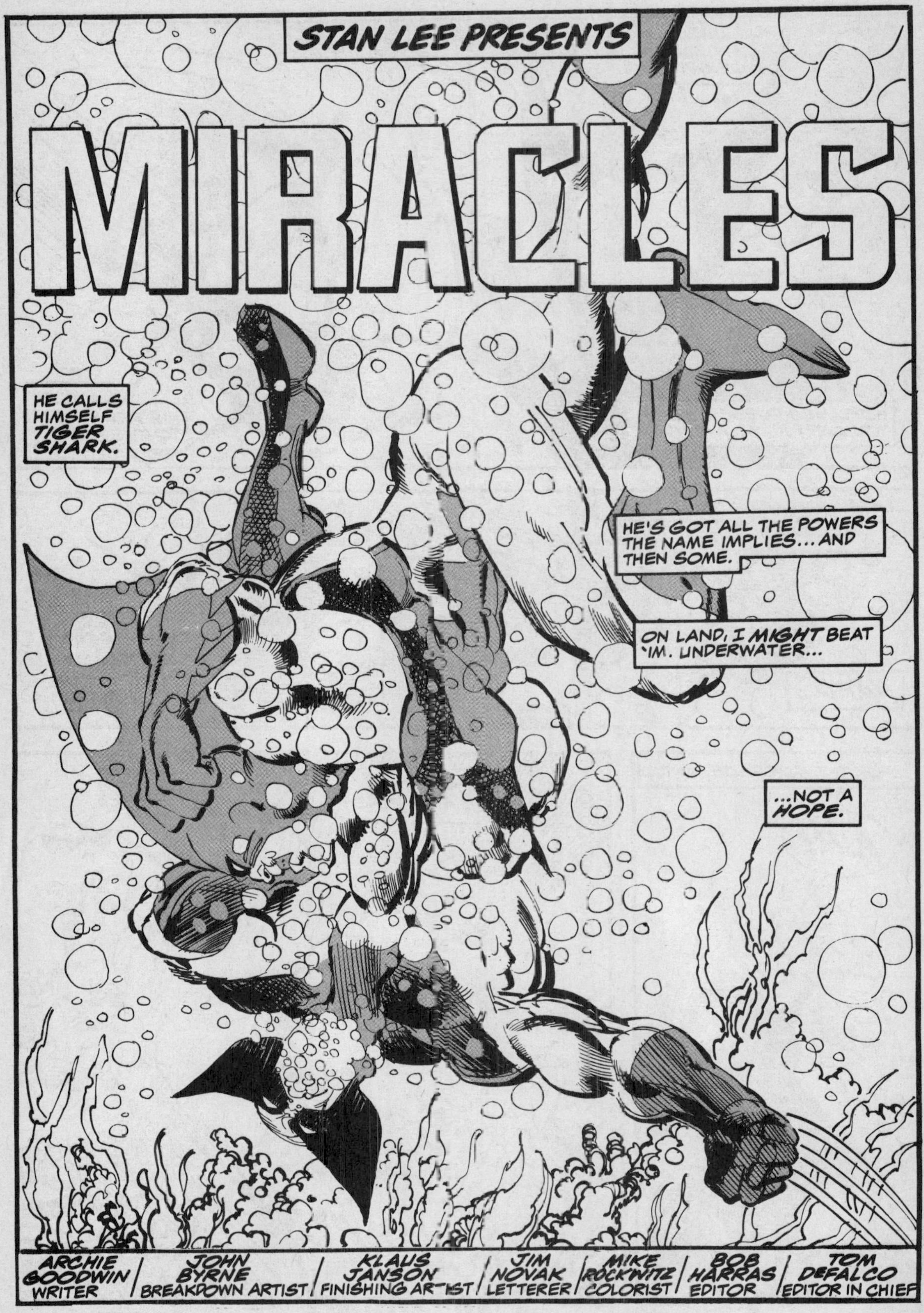
STAN LEE PRESENTS
MIRACLES
HE CALLS HIMSELF TIGER SHARK.
HE'S GOT ALL THE POWERS THE NAME IMPLIES... AND THEN SOME.
ON LAND, I MIGHT BEAT 'IM. UNDERWATER...
...NOT A HOPE.
ARCHIE GOODWIN WRITER
JOHN BYRNE BREAKDOWN ARTIST
KLAUS JANSON FINISHING ARTIST
JIM NOVAK LETTERER
MIKE ROCKWITZ COLORIST
BOB HARRAS EDITOR
TOM DEFALCO EDITOR IN CHIEF

MY KIND OF ODDS.

HOPELESS DOESN'T MEAN YOU CAN'T MAKE HIM *HURT.*

HIS REACTION TO THE *PAIN*...

...LETS ME REACT WITH A *KICK!*

HARD...

...FOR THE *SURFACE!* AND...

AIR!

BIG, TASTY *LUNG FULLS!* ENOUGH SO I CAN REACH *SHORE!* ENOUGH SO I CAN--

DON'T MAKE *PLANS*, HERO--

--WE'RE NOT *FINISHED!*

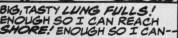

IT'S THE *SHARK* IN ME... IMPRINTED OVER MY HUMAN INSTINCTS.

WE *FIX* ON A CERTAIN PREY... WE JUST *CAN'T* LET IT GO.

ESPECIALLY NOT A *HERO*, LITTLE MAN... THE THING I HATE *MOST.*

HIS GRIP IS STEEL, STRENGTH INCREDIBLE.

WE PLUNGE AT TORPEDO SPEED.

HOW DEEP BEFORE MY EARDRUMS EXPLODE, MY LUNGS BURST?

NEED A *MIRACLE.*

GOTTA MAKE DO WITH...

...*CLAWS!*

GOTTA *HURT* HIM.

LIKE BEFORE.

HURT HIM *ENOUGH,* HE'LL--

THE CORAL SHELF! WE'RE GONNA RAM I--

WE DO.

BUT NOT LIKE I EXPECT.

EVEN WITHOUT KNOWIN' ABOUT MY UNBREAKABLE, ADAMANTIUM-LACED SKELETON... TIGER SHARK HAS *MORE* IN MIND THAN PULPIN' ME AGAINST SOME ROCKS.

PROUD OF THOSE *CLAWS*, AREN'T YOU, HERO?

PRETTY EFFECTIVE AGAINST ME.

ONLY NOW... YOU'RE *STUCK* WITH 'EM!

EERIE, HEARIN' SOMEONE TALK WHERE IT SHOULDN'T BE POSSIBLE. WORSE, HEARIN' *WHAT* HE SAYS.

MY *REAL* BUSINESS IS UPSTAIRS, RUNT... THE LITTLE GIRL PLAYING REVOLUTIONARY. OTHERWISE...

--I'D STAY AND GIVE LESSONS HOW TO *BREATHE* UNDER-WATER.

GOOD LUCK LEARNING ON YOUR OWN!

AND HE'S *GONE.* LIKE *AIR* LEAVIN' MY BODY. ALL THAT AIR HE *LET* ME GULP. TO MAKE THIS *LAST* LONGER. TO--

DON'T *THINK* ABOUT IT!

FIGHT!

HEAVE!

KICK!

STRAIN!

NOTHING, CLAWS IMBEDDED TOO DEEP, TOO TIGHT, CAN'T RETRACT 'EM, CAN'T SLASH, CAN'T--

DON'T THINK ABOUT IT!

FIGHT!

MUTANT HEALING FACTOR CAN'T COUNTER DROWNING... WILL IT PROLONG THE EFFECTS...? EXTEND THE AGONY...? ADD TO THE--

DON'T THINK ABOUT IT!

DON'T THINK--

DON'T--

DON'T

...

KEEP FIGHTING, COMPADRES!

WE'RE CLOSE TO OUR GOAL!

THE TIERRA VERDE MEDICAL CENTER, ONE OF THE FINEST FACILITIES IN CENTRAL AMERICA, SOME SAY...

...AND PERHAPS, SAY OTHERS, THE MOST MISUSED.

LEAVE A REAR GUARD IN THE LOBBY! EVERYONE ELSE....STAY WITH ME! THE POLITICAL PRISONERS WARD SHOULD BE--

--HERE!

AMIGOS! WE'VE COME TO FREE YOU!

FREE YOU FROM THE TORTURE AND SICK EXPERIMENTATION OF...OF...

AMIGOS...?

OUR INFORMATION WAS OBVIOUSLY CORRECT THAT THE PRISONERS WERE KEPT HERE, BUT--

THEY WERE MOVED--

--JUST BEFORE YOUR ATTACK.

I AM GEIST, DEAR LADY. SPECIAL ADVISER TO PRESIDENT CARIDAD--

--AND THE ONE WHO LEAKED THE INFORMATION THAT BROUGHT YOU.

SOMETHING OF A TRAP, YES?

NO! I BECAME *LA BANDERA* TO INSPIRE *WAR* AGAINST DRUG LORDS LIKE CARIDAD.

WHILE I WIELD THIS *STAFF*, I CAN--

IT'S *POWER* DEAR LADY--

--SEEMS TO *FADE.*

ALONG WITH HER *FELLOW* REBELS, GEIST.

COULD BE A *CONNECTION.* INTERESTING--

TIGER *SHARK!* STILL PLAYING *ASSASSIN* FOR THE DRUG INTERESTS I ATTACKED IN FLORIDA!

--IF SHE WERE *SURVIVING* THIS ENCOUNTER.

NO *PLAY* TO IT!

WROK!

THERE'S ONE BIG *ACT* OF *VENGEANCE* GOING DOWN AGAINST ALL *SUPER HEROES--*

--AND **YOU** POPPED UP WITH A FEW **FEEBLE** POWERS JUST IN TIME TO **QUALIFY!**

YOU'RE **SMALL FISH**, LA BANDERA, BUT HATING **HEROES** LIKE I DO--

--EVERY **LITTLE** BIT HEL--

PAUGK!

WHAT-EVER I AM OR **YOU** ARE--

--I WON'T BE **PARALYZED**, I WON'T JUST LIE HERE AND **DIE!**

TIGER SHARK... **NO!** SHE'S--

DEAD! YOU'RE ALREADY **DEAD**, GIRL! RUNNING WON'T **CHANGE** IT...NOT WITH **ME** BEHIND!

LONGER WE **TAKE**...THE MORE **HORRIBLE** IT'LL BE!

THE HELICOPTER WAITS *UPSTAIRS*, MY PRESIDENT... READY TO CARRY YOU *SAFELY* FROM THE MEDICAL CENTER.

THE *REBELS*, COLONEL...?

STILL CONFINED TO THE AREAS GEIST *PREDICTED* THEY WOULD HIT?

TO ALL *APPEARANCES* ...YES. BUT, AS A *PRECAUTION--*

AND THE *POLITICAL PRISONERS...*? ON THE ROOFTOP TO DISCOURAGE *SNIPING* AT OUR *ESCAPE* CRAFT...?

YES, MY PRESIDENT. THERE IS NO *IMMEDIATE* DANGER, BUT--

THAT IS GUARANTEE *ENOUGH,* COLONEL. RETURN TO YOUR *POST--*

WE MUST RETURN TO MAKING *HISTORY--*

--NOW THAT MY *WIFE* AT LAST REALIZES HER *DUTY* TO HER *COUNTRY* AND HER *HUSBAND.*

THE LAST DOSAGE OF THE...AH... *TAINTED* COCAINE WE ARE TESTING HAS MADE THE... AH... SUBJECT, *ROUGHHOUSE,* PARTICULARLY *VIOLENT,* SEÑOR PRESIDENT.

SINCE *SISTER SALVATION* IS SUCH AN...AH....*UNPREDICTA-BLE* FACTOR, SOME...AH... *DELAY* IS JUSTIFIABLE... AH... PERHAPS.

NO *DELAYS*. PLEASE... NO MATTER *HOW* SCIENTIFICALLY QUESTIONABLE THIS SEEMS. MY ABILITY *TO HEAL* IS A MIRACLE I DON'T UNDERSTAND MYSELF.

I ACCEPT IT AND TRY TO USE IT UNSELFISHLY. EXCEPT *TONIGHT*. DON'T SAY THIS IS FOR TIERRA VERDE *OR YOU*, FELIX GUILLERMO CARIDAD--

TONIGHT... IT'S FOR MY *SON*.

TO *SEE* THE SON YOU'VE *KEPT* FROM ME SINCE I LEFT YOU TO JOIN THE CHURCH.

YOUR *TERMS*, FELIX... AND MY *RISK*.

DEAR HEAVEN...! FELIX... WHAT *HAVE* YOU DONE?

I'M READY IF HE BREAKS *FREE*, SISTER. WE DON'T KNOW THE LIMITS OF HIS STRENGTH ... OR HIS MADNESS.

OR HIS *PAIN*. HOW CAN YOU *IGNORE* THAT? THOSE TERRIBLE *SORES*... ALMOST AN *EXPRESSION* OF IT.

LIKE A *DEMON* INSIDE HIM... TRYING TO BURST OUT.

SEÑOR PRESIDENT, SHE SHOULDN'T... AH... *TOUCH* ROUGHHOUSE. THAT--

HER TOUCH *IS* HER MIRACLE, FOOL! I *KNOW*... I HAVE *FELT* IT! WATCH, SCIENTIST... *LEARN!*

AS SHE CURES MY MIGRAINES ...SHE'LL PURGE THE COCAINE'S *DEVASTATIONS*, LEAVING ITS *MUTAGENIC* EFFECTS.

FROM *THAT*...WE'LL CREATE THE *SUPER HERO* I WANT. A SOURCE OF *PRIDE* FOR TIERRA VERDE... OF *REDEMPTION* FOR ME!

TIGER SHARK, HAVE YOU *FOUND* LA BANDERA...? *TIGER SHARK?!*

NO RESPONSE...? PERHAPS IT IS TIME THEN TO LEAVE *WAR* TO THE *WARRIORS*--

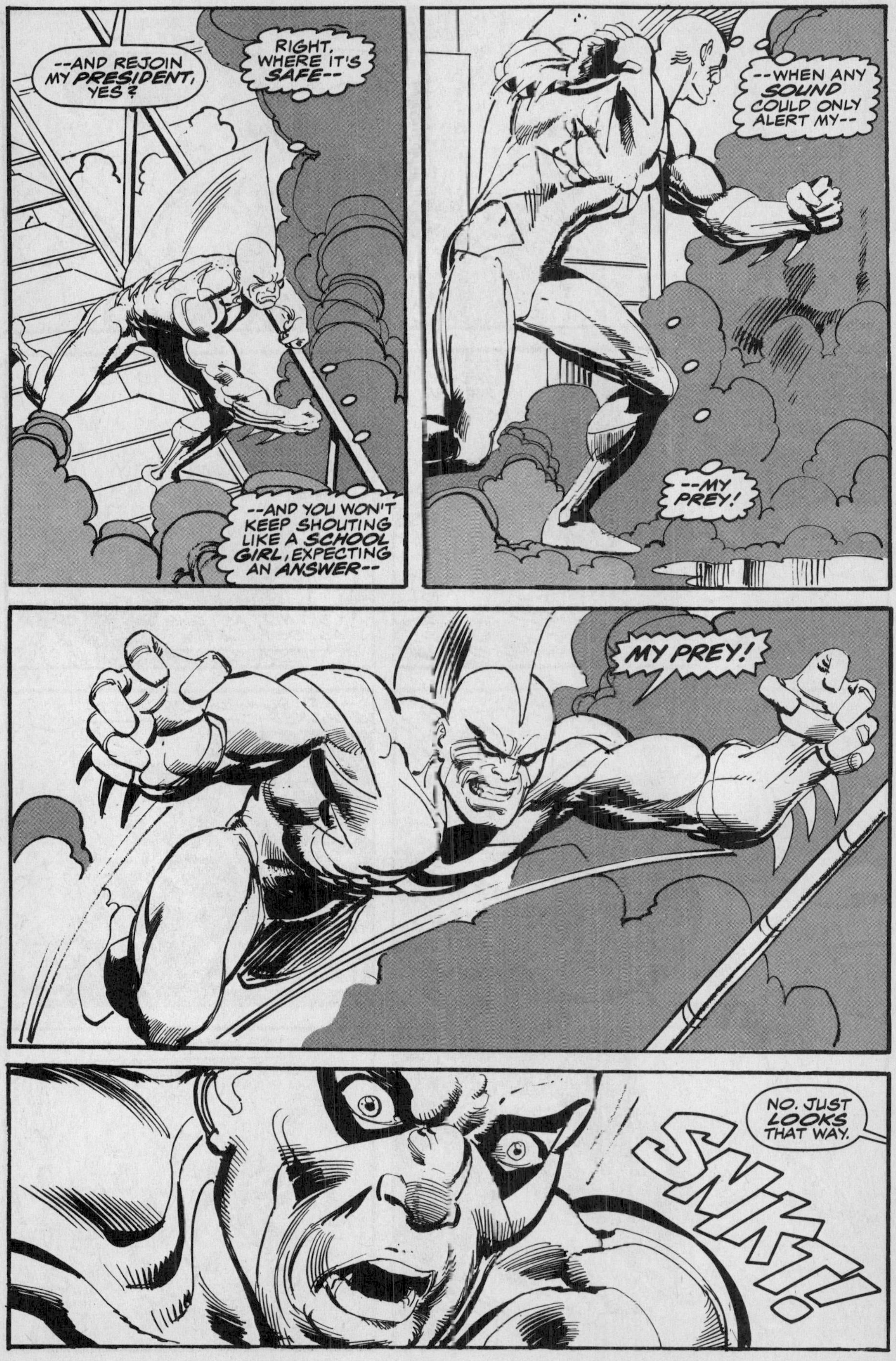
--AND REJOIN MY PRESIDENT, YES?
RIGHT, WHERE IT'S SAFE--
--AND YOU WON'T KEEP SHOUTING LIKE A SCHOOL GIRL, EXPECTING AN ANSWER--
--WHEN ANY SOUND COULD ONLY ALERT MY--
--MY PREY!
MY PREY!
NO. JUST LOOKS THAT WAY.
SNIKT!!

IN A REAL *KILLIN'* FRENZY, SHARK?

YOU FOUND THE *RIGHT* MAN.

KIND'A *BERSERK* MYSELF.

TOO LONG UNDER-WATER.

"BUT *NOT* AS LONG AS YOU FIGURED."

SEEMS YOU RAMMED ME INTO A *THIN* SECTION OF THE CORAL SHELF--

"--WITH SO MUCH *FORCE*, YOU *CRACKED* IT.

"AN' ALL MY *KICKIN'* AN' *STRAININ'*--"

--MADE IT GIVE!

"REAL *MIRACLE* FOR ME--"

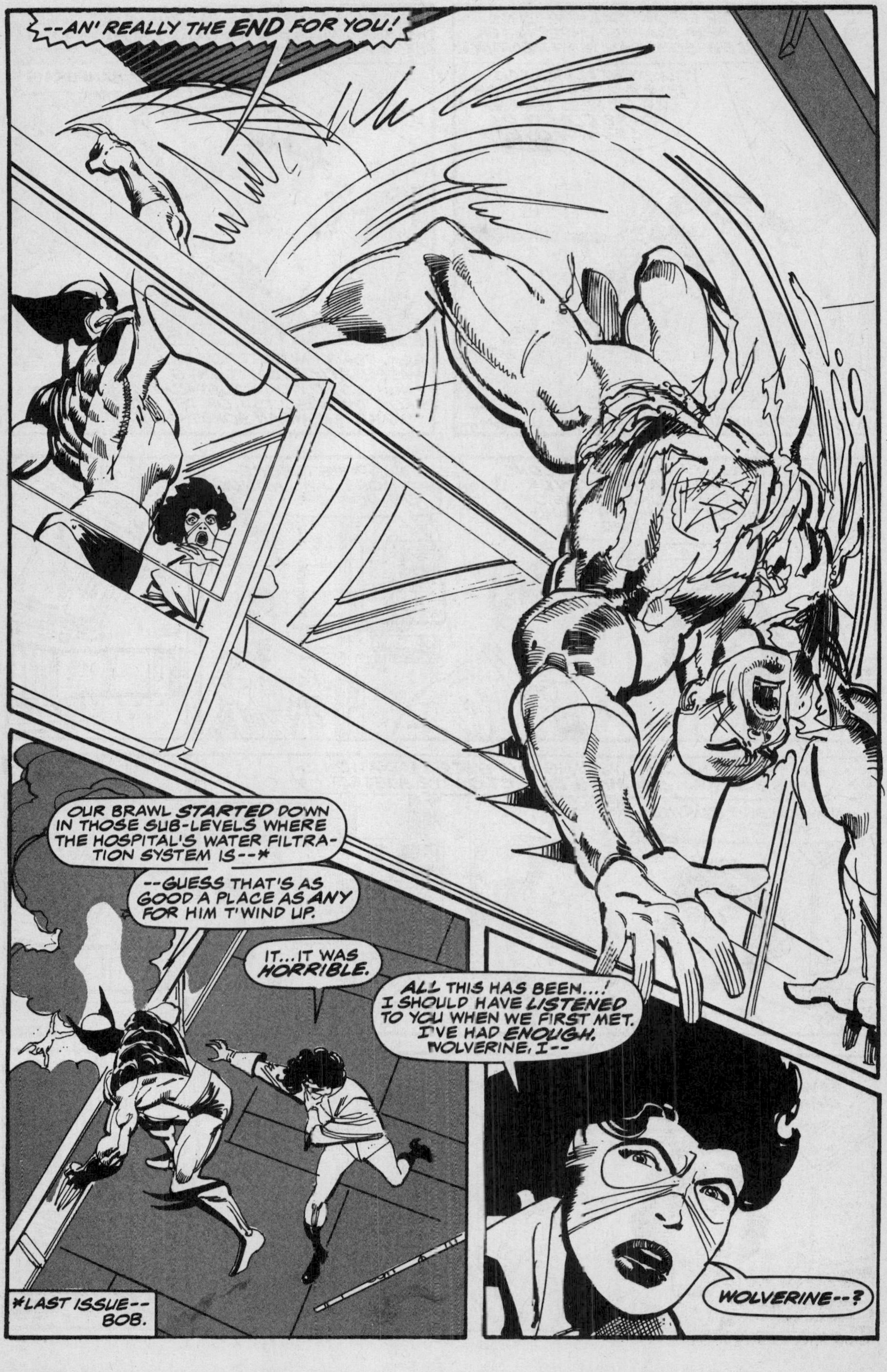
--AN' REALLY THE END FOR YOU!
OUR BRAWL STARTED DOWN IN THOSE SUB-LEVELS WHERE THE HOSPITAL'S WATER FILTRATION SYSTEM IS--*
--GUESS THAT'S AS GOOD A PLACE AS ANY FOR HIM T'WIND UP.
IT...IT WAS HORRIBLE.
ALL THIS HAS BEEN...! I SHOULD HAVE LISTENED TO YOU WHEN WE FIRST MET. I'VE HAD ENOUGH. WOLVERINE, I--
WOLVERINE--?
*LAST ISSUE--BOB.

WASTED EFFORT *TALKIN'* TO ME, KID... BEIN' TRAPPED UNDERWATER *BLEW* SOMETHIN' IN MY *HEARING.*

'TILL MY *HEALING FAC-TOR* SOLVES THE PROBLEM.... I NEED *EARS!* YOU'RE *ELECTED!* C'MON! *MOVE!*

MY *OTHER* ANIMAL SENSES ARE STILL KEEN...

...GOT A *SCENT.* MAN; MACHINE. *GEIST.* AND HIS TRAIL WILL LEAD TO WHAT I'M *REALLY* HERE FOR.

THEN I SEE LA BANDERA'S *PROBLEM.*

REAL DEADLY MUTANT POWER... *INSPIRATION.* CAN'T UNDO HAVIN' *USED* IT, KID. JUST *RUN* FROM THE RESULTS... OR TRY T'MAKE 'EM *MEAN* SOMETHIN'.

NOTHING MEANINGFUL CAN COME FROM THIS, DOCTOR. WHATEVER WORKED AT HER JUNGLE MISSION, THIS NUN ISN'T DOING ANYTHING WE HAVEN'T TRIED.

BUT SHE DOES IT SOME-WHAT MORE...AH... *HANDS ON,* DOCTOR.

AND THERE'S NO...AH...DENYING THAT SISTER SALVATION IS HAVING A...AH... *CALMING EFFECT* ON THE SUBJECT.

CALMING ISN'T *CURING,* DOCTOR.

HOWEVER EFFECTIVE WITH HYSTERICAL SAVAGES...PSEUDO-RELIGIOUS NONSENSE CANNOT COUNTER THE MADNESS THIS *COCAINE* UNLEASHES.

AND IF OUR COUNTRY'S LEADER BELIEVES IN *THIS*--

"--WHO KNOWS WHAT WILL INVADE OUR LABORATORY *NEXT?*"

SEÑOR PRESIDENT--!

LA BANDERA AND THE MAN WHO CALLS HIMSELF *WOLVERINE...!* THEY'RE HEADED *HERE!*

WHERE A *MIRACLE* IS UNDERWAY, *GEIST!* I WILL NOT *MISS* IT BECAUSE OF HYSTERIA--

"--WE HAVE *GUARDS* TO DEAL WITH SUCH MATTERS!"

NO MORE *DISTRACTIONS!* MY WIFE MUST BE ALLOWED TO--

FELIX--?

I'VE MINISTERED. I'VE PRAYED. I'VE DONE ALL I KNOW TO DO.

LET ME SEE MY SON.

LET ME SEE MY *MIRACLE!* LET ME-- *WHAT IS THIS?!*

HE IS *UNCHANGED!* THE *DOCTORS* HAVE ACCOMPLISHED AS MUCH BY SHOOTING HIM FULL OF *TRANQUILIZERS!*

IS THIS HOW YOU REWARD MY *FAITH,* WOMAN? IS THIS--

HIS *EYES...!* AWAKE... BUT THE MADNESS DOESN'T *BURN* THERE!

THE *TRUE TEST* WILL BE HIS REACTION WHEN *FREE!*

SOMEONE GET RID OF HIS *RESTRAINTS!*

DON'T BOTHER *COMPLAININ'* YOU DIDN'T *GESTURE* FOR *ME,* BIG SHOT--

--I CAN'T *HEAR.*

BUT I *SEE* WHAT HAS TO BE DONE--

WRAAK!

--AN' WHAT HAS TO BE *ANSWERED* FOR!

WE'RE A LONG WAY FROM WHERE WE *STARTED,* ROUGHHOUSE--

--BUT I'M TAKIN' YOU *HOME.*

LA BANDERA... GET A *VOLUNTEER* TO SHOW US THE SAFEST WAY *OUTTA* THIS *HORROR SHOW.*

ANYBODY'S *UNCOOPERATIVE...* SWELL! I'M IN THE MOOD T'DO SOME VERY *POINTED REASONING!*

YOUR PARTNER IS DEAF IN THE *BRAIN* AS WELL AS HIS EARS, GIRL! YOU WILL GO *NOWHERE...* NOT WITH *ROUGHHOUSE.*

THAT ONE IS A *HUMAN TIME BOMB!* HE WILL *EXPLODE* THE MOMENT MY WIFE'S HEALING TOUCH WEARS OFF!

AS FOR HOW TO GET *OUT--*

COME UP TO THE *ROOF* AS I DID, DEAR LADY...WHEN IT BECAME *OBVIOUS* YOU WOULD BREACH THE GAP.

PLEASE DON'T *DELAY.* THE LONGER YOU TAKE FOR THIS *SURRENDER--*

--THE MORE *POLITICAL PRISONERS* WE WILL HAVE TO *EXECUTE,* YES?

SEÑOR GEIST...! THE REBEL GIRL AND HER COMPANION HOLD *PRESIDENT CARIDAD*...A STRONGER BARGAINING *CHIP* THAN OUR *THREATS!*

TRUE, COLONEL...BUT IT IS IMPORTANT TO GO THROUGH THE *MOTIONS!*

SECURE IN THE BELIEF THAT THEY HAVE *WON* THEIR DEMANDS, THEY WILL BE *UNPREPARED*--

--WHEN I USE *THIS!*

MY DART GUN ATTACHMENT...FROM THE LAB, YES? EACH DART LOADED WITH THE *TAINTED COCAINE* USED ON *ROUGHOUSE.* ONE SHOT--

"...AND INSTEAD OF A HELICOPTER ESCAPE, THEY WILL FACE *INSANE* ATTACK BY THE VERY *MONSTROSITY* THEY HOPE TO SAVE."

KEEP CARIDAD AND HIS LADY *CLOSE,* KID...'TWEEN US AN' THE *GUARDS.* THEY LOOK *ANXIOUS...*

THIS PAIR...YOU THINK THEY PLAN TO INCLUDE SOME OF *US* IN THEIR ESCAPE, ENRIQUE?

MY BELIEF, AMIGO--

--IS THAT RATHER THAN WONDER--

--IT IS BETTER TO *ACT!*

BREAK FOR IT, COMPADRES ...*BREAK!*

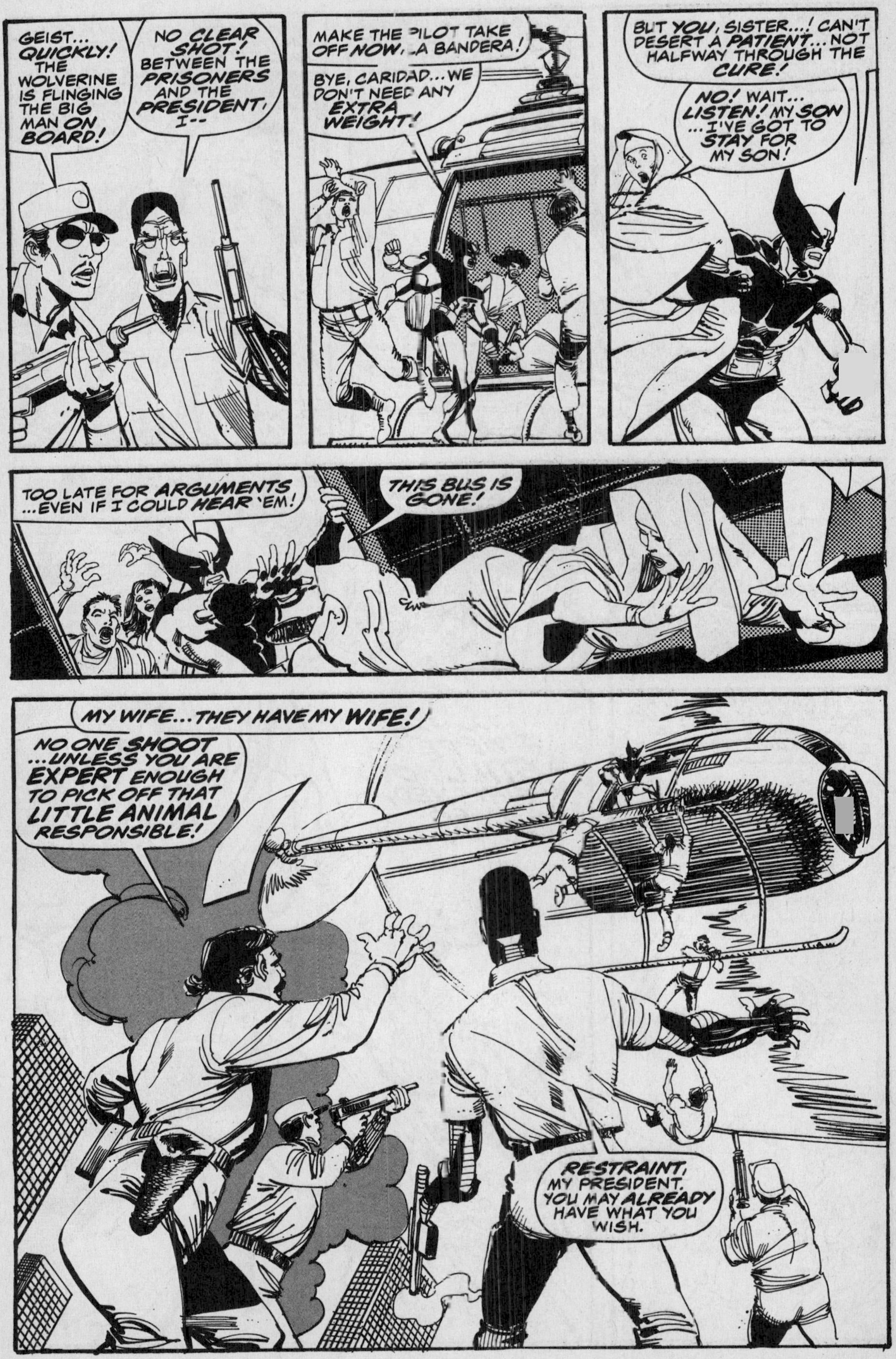
GEIST... QUICKLY! THE WOLVERINE IS FLINGING THE BIG MAN ON BOARD!
NO CLEAR SHOT! BETWEEN THE PRISONERS AND THE PRESIDENT, I--
MAKE THE PILOT TAKE OFF NOW, LA BANDERA!
BYE, CARIDAD... WE DON'T NEED ANY EXTRA WEIGHT!
BUT YOU, SISTER...! CAN'T DESERT A PATIENT... NOT HALFWAY THROUGH THE CURE!
NO! WAIT... LISTEN! MY SON ...I'VE GOT TO STAY FOR MY SON!
TOO LATE FOR ARGUMENTS ...EVEN IF I COULD HEAR 'EM!
THIS BUS IS GONE!
MY WIFE... THEY HAVE MY WIFE!
NO ONE SHOOT ...UNLESS YOU ARE EXPERT ENOUGH TO PICK OFF THAT LITTLE ANIMAL RESPONSIBLE!
RESTRAINT, MY PRESIDENT. YOU MAY ALREADY HAVE WHAT YOU WISH.

DROPPIN' LIKE A ROCK WITH THIS LOAD...!

LA BANDERA, IF EVER YOU USED YOUR POWER TO INSPIRE--

"--WORK ON THE PILOT!"

DOING MY BEST, SEÑORITA!

OUR GOVERNMENT HAS FINE AIRCRAFT, SHODDY MAINTENANCE--

--NOT UP TO THIS STRAIN!

IT'S ALL COMIN' APART--

--'CEPT FOR SISTER SALVATION! SPITE'A BEIN' FORCED ALONG--

--SHE RADIATES A KIND'A PEACE. MAYBE SOME LUCK TOO... GAINED A LITTLE ALTITUDE. WE'RE--

WE'RE STILL NOT FINISHED, HERO!

KWOM!

MADE THE WORST *MISTAKE* OF YOUR LIFE, LITTLE MAN... YOU *ALMOST* KILLED ME.

BUT I CRAWLED TO THE *SEA*...AND THE SEA MADE ME *STRONG!*

KRAK!

STRONG ENOUGH TO HAUL US *DOWN!*

HE LAUGHS AT MY *KICKS.* CAN'T *REACH* 'IM WITH MY *CLAWS*

WUD!

YOU'RE *BACK,* HERO... MY *DOMAIN.* AND NO MORE *MIRA-CLES* TO SAVE YOU.

TO THINK I TRIED TO BE *LIKE* YOU ONCE... WOUND UP *CRIPPLED* AND *WEAK* INSTEAD.

NOW I *HATE* YOUR KIND, *KILL* YOUR KIND... SO I'LL *NEVER* BE LIKE YOU AGAIN!

I *LIVE* FOR BEING A *SHARK!* YOU'LL *DIE* FOR BEING A HE--

RAAAHH!

W-WHAT--?!

WITHOUT HIS GRIP, THE 'COPTER *BUOYS UP,* AND I SEE...

ONE MORE MIRACLE...!

SHARKS. STRONG AND DEADLY. BUT THEY FEED ON THEIR OWN.

BLOOD FROM THE *WOUNDS* I GAVE TIGER SHARK MUST'VE ATTRACTED THEM. PROBABLY CAN'T *FINISH* A GUY LIKE THAT...

...BUT THEY'LL STAY *BUSY.* AWAY FROM ANY *PRISONERS* WHO FELL OFF THE CHOPPER.

READY TO RIDE *INSIDE* FOR A CHANGE, COMPADRE...? WE CAN'T MAKE IT *TOO FAR*--

--BUT WE'LL PUT PRESIDENT CARIDAD'S *CITY* BEHIND US!

I GET THE IDEA IT'S *GOOD NEWS.*

AND IN THE HOLD... I FIND *BETTER.*

ROUGHHOUSE...! HIS *FACE*...! THOSE WEIRD SORES, GROWTHS ...*FADED!*

YOUR HUSBAND HAD IT *RIGHT*...YOU'RE A *MIRACLE WORKER,* LADY.

I HAVE A *GIFT.* PERHAPS WE SHOULDN'T BE TOO *SWIFT* TO LABEL ANYTHING A *MIRACLE*--

--UNTIL WE KNOW THE *SACRIFICE* INVOLVED.

HEY, WE SHOULDN'T BE SWIFT TO *DISCOUNT* 'EM EITHER.

LONG WITH EVERYTHING *ELSE* TODAY... MY *HEARING'S* COMIN' BACK!

NOT A MOMENT TOO SOON. THING LIKE *THAT*--

--CAN THROW ALL YOUR SENSES OFF!

NEXT ISSUE:

BATTLE GROUND

THE SECRET OF CARIDAD'S COCAINE

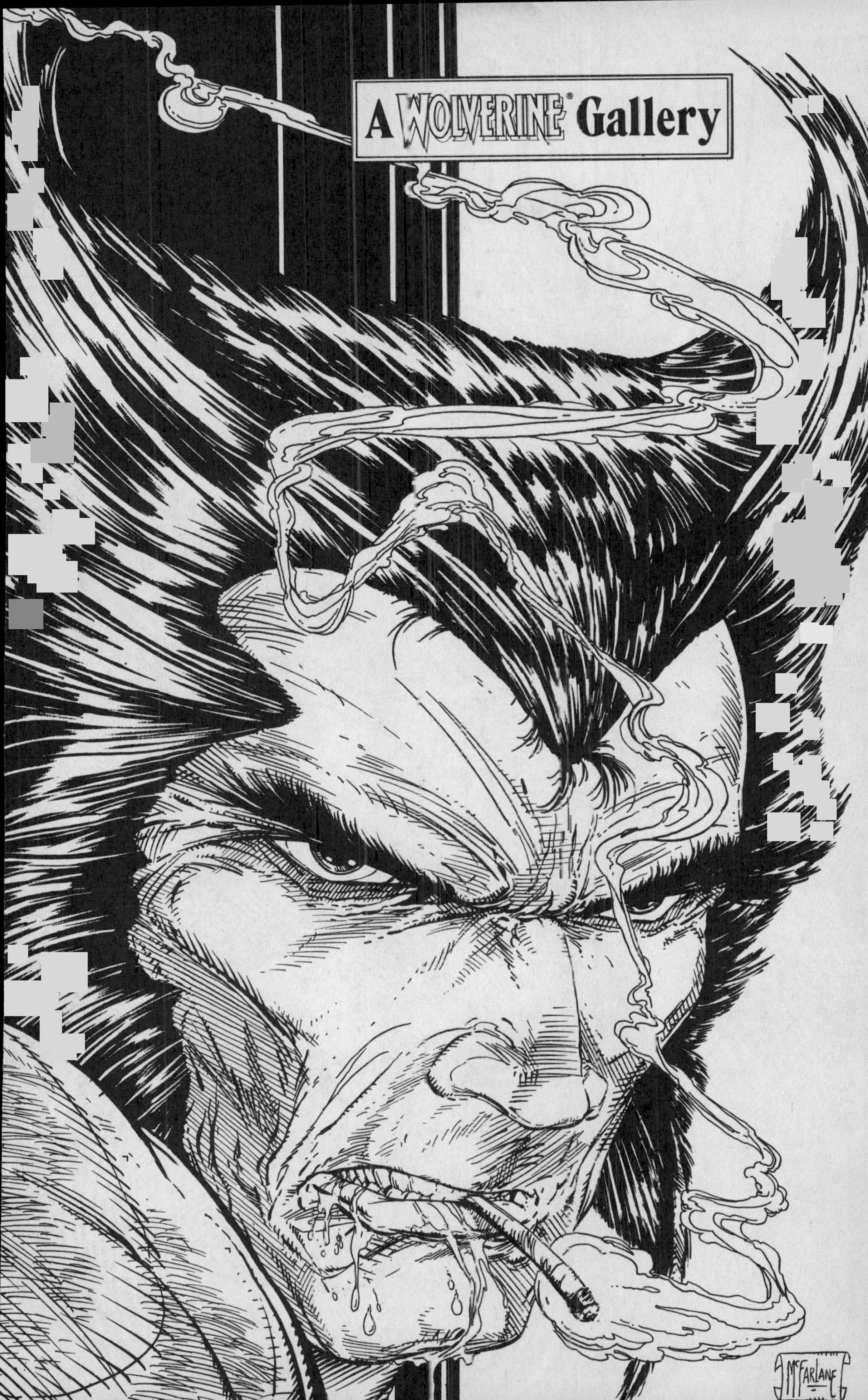
A WOLVERINE® Gallery
McFARLANE

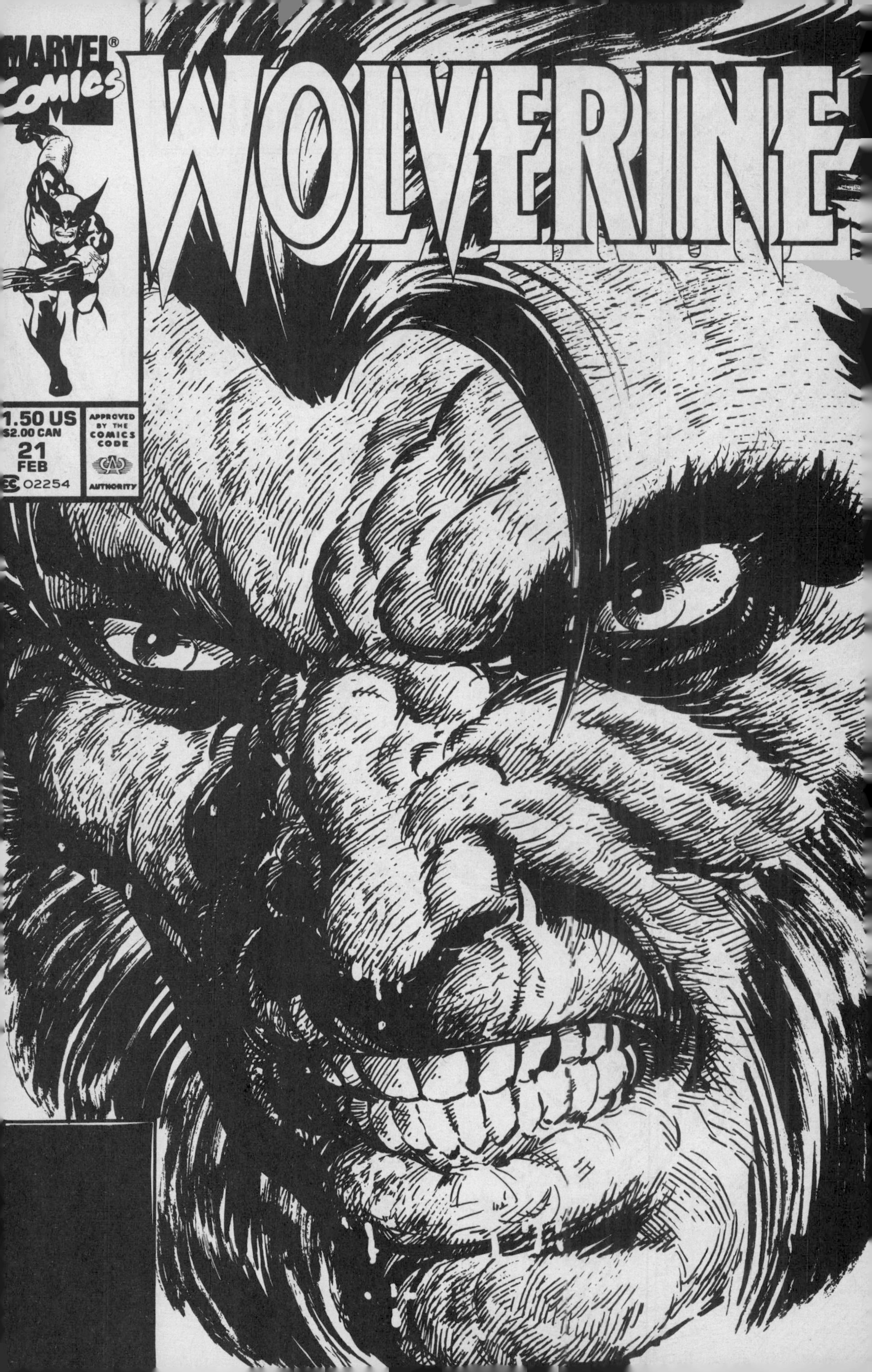

MARVEL® COMICS
WOLVERINE
1.50 US
$2.00 CAN
21
FEB
02254
APPROVED BY THE COMICS CODE AUTHORITY

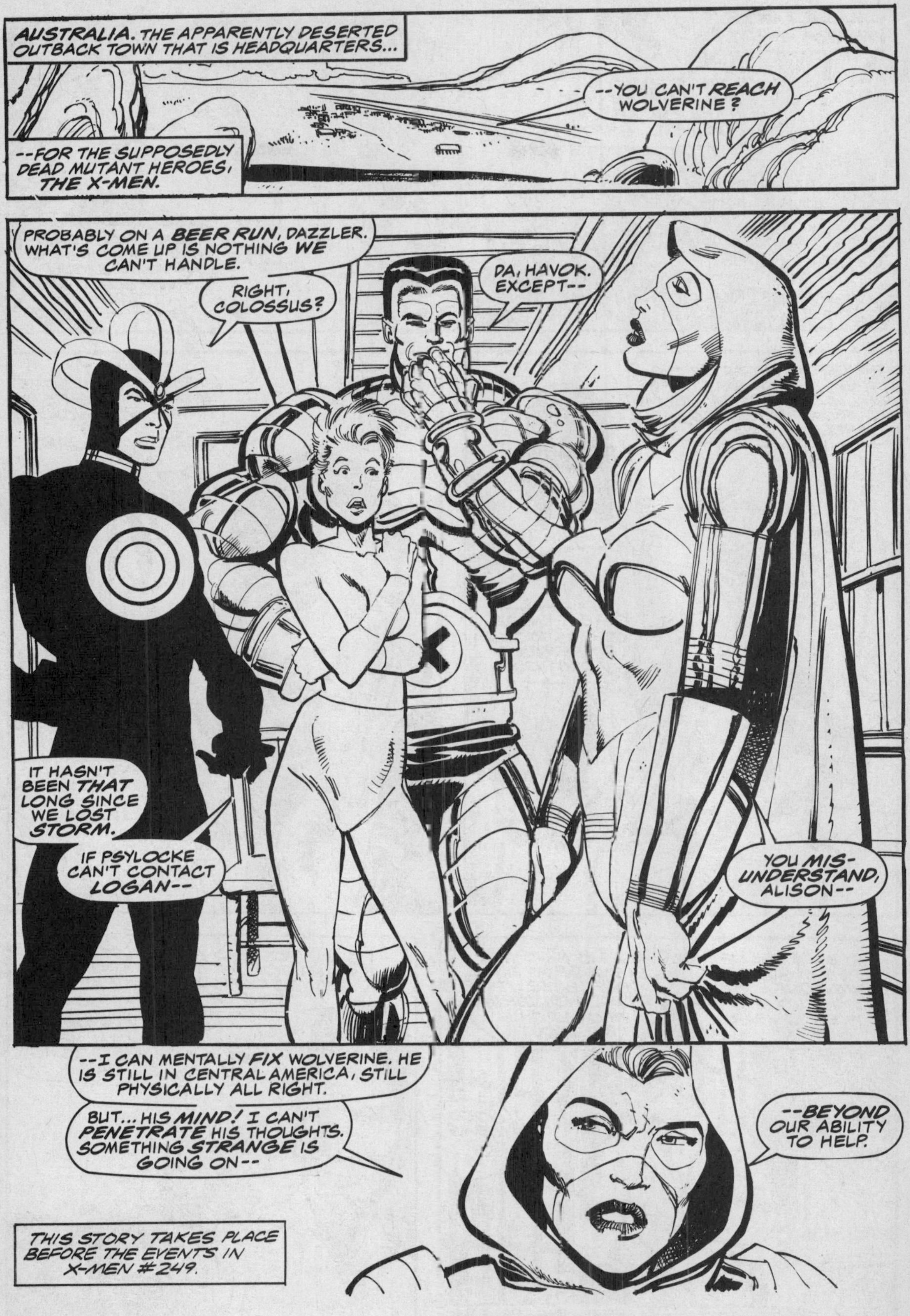
AUSTRALIA. THE APPARENTLY DESERTED OUTBACK TOWN THAT IS HEADQUARTERS...
--FOR THE SUPPOSEDLY DEAD MUTANT HEROES, THE X-MEN.
--YOU CAN'T REACH WOLVERINE?
PROBABLY ON A BEER RUN, DAZZLER. WHAT'S COME UP IS NOTHING WE CAN'T HANDLE.
RIGHT, COLOSSUS?
DA, HAVOK. EXCEPT--
IT HASN'T BEEN THAT LONG SINCE WE LOST STORM.
IF PSYLOCKE CAN'T CONTACT LOGAN--
YOU MISUNDERSTAND, ALISON--
--I CAN MENTALLY FIX WOLVERINE. HE IS STILL IN CENTRAL AMERICA, STILL PHYSICALLY ALL RIGHT.
BUT... HIS MIND! I CAN'T PENETRATE HIS THOUGHTS. SOMETHING STRANGE IS GOING ON--
--BEYOND OUR ABILITY TO HELP.
THIS STORY TAKES PLACE BEFORE THE EVENTS IN X-MEN #249.

TIERRA VERDE.

WE'VE FOUND THE *HELICOPTER* USED IN THE *ESCAPE*, MY PRESIDENT... *EMPTY*.

OUR TRACKERS ARE EXAMINING THE AREA. WE SHOULD HAVE SOMETHING SOO--

THEY *SPLIT UP* AFTER THE CRASH, SENOR GEIST. THE GIRL, *LA BANDERA*, LED THE POLITICAL PRISONERS SHE FREED *ONE WAY*--

--BUT *THREE* OTHERS TOOK A *DIFFERENT* DIRECTION.

YOU HEAR, PRESIDENT CARIDAD?

I AM *NOT* INTERESTED IN SOME *BRAT* WHO FIGHTS MY *DRUG-TRAFFICKING* BY PLAYING *REVOLUTIONARY*, GEIST!

WHO ARE THESE *OTHERS?!*

IS MY *WIFE* ONE OF THEM? DOES MY GUINEA PIG, *ROUGHHOUSE*, STILL SURVIVE?! THAT IS WHAT I *WISH* TO HEAR, GEIST!

THAT IS WHAT WILL *SALVAGE* MY PLAN... DESPITE THE LITTLE *ANIMAL*, *WOLVERINE*, WHO LED THIS BREAKOUT!

GOOD NEWS THEN, YES?

SIGNS NOT ONLY SHOW *SISTER SALVATION* AND THE HULKING *TEST SUBJECT* OF OUR EXPERIMENTS AS TWO OF THE TRIO--

--BUT THAT THE *THIRD*, WHATEVER ANIMAL HE *STYLES* HIMSELF, IS NOW ALSO A GUINEA PIG.

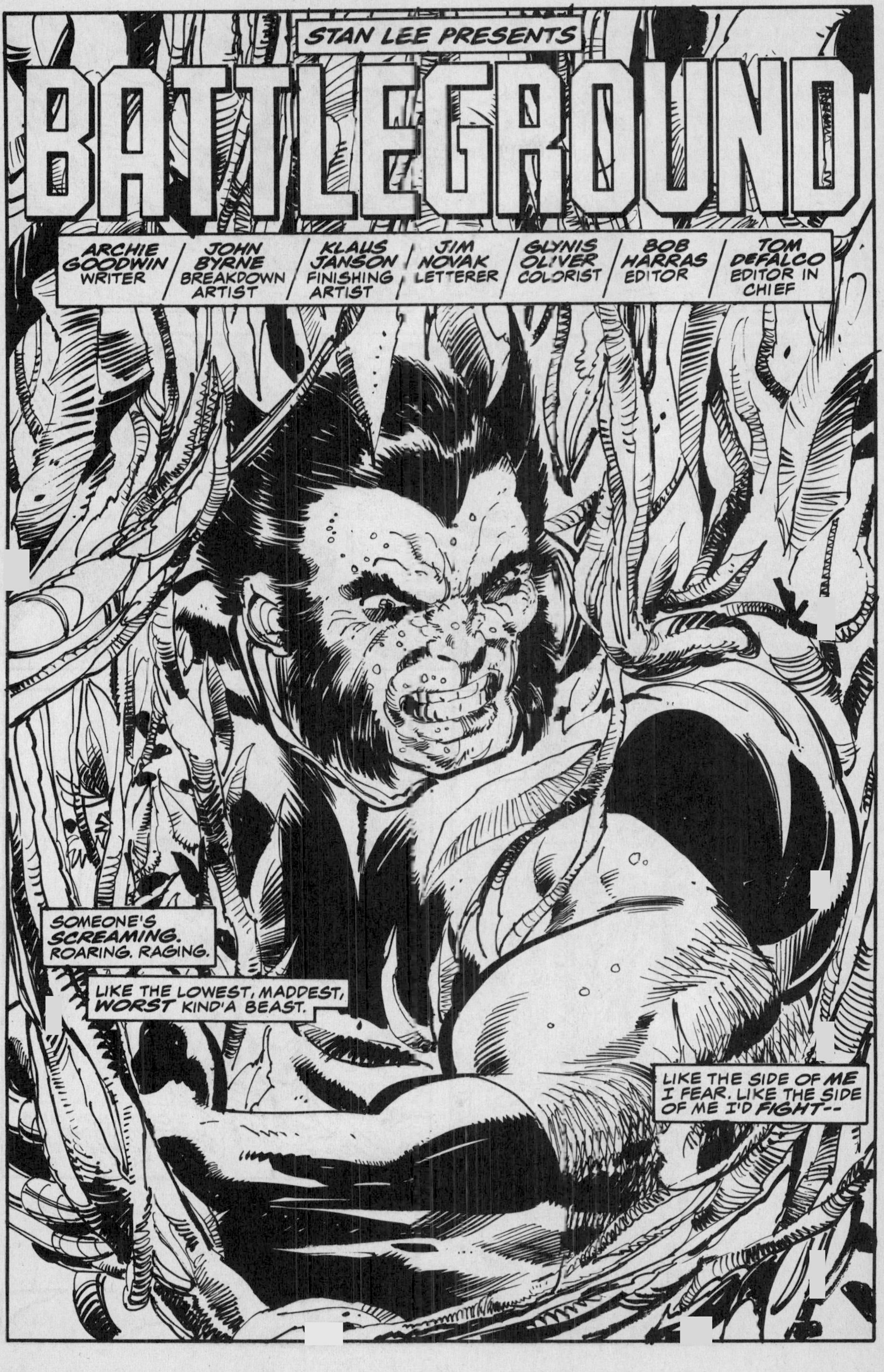
STAN LEE PRESENTS
BATTLEGROUND
ARCHIE GOODWIN WRITER
JOHN BYRNE BREAKDOWN ARTIST
KLAUS JANSON FINISHING ARTIST
JIM NOVAK LETTERER
GLYNIS OLIVER COLORIST
BOB HARRAS EDITOR
TOM DEFALCO EDITOR IN CHIEF
SOMEONE'S SCREAMING. ROARING. RAGING.
LIKE THE LOWEST, MADDEST, WORST KIND'A BEAST.
LIKE THE SIDE OF ME I FEAR. LIKE THE SIDE OF ME I'D FIGHT--

-- IF ONLY I WEREN'T *SO FAR* AWAY.

GOT 'IM--

THINK I CAN *HOLD* 'IM--

--BUT I CAN'T HELP HIS *PAIN.* YOU GOT THE *MIRACLES,* SISTER. YOU CAN *HEAL* 'IM... LIKE YOU DID *ME.*

HE *KIDNAPED* ME, ROUGHOUSE--

--FOR *YOUR* SAKE. I *UNDERSTAND.* BUT WHAT ABOUT *MY* SAKE? MUST THIS *GIFT* ALWAYS--

I ONLY KNOW HE'S *HURTIN',* SISTER. *BAD.* MAYBE WORSE'N *I* DID. DON'T THAT MATTER?

YES, IN THE END...

UH...
UH...

EASY. YOU'RE OKAY. SISTER PULLED YOU BACK.

UH...I...I MADE US...*STOP*...? CAN'T...*DO* THAT...! GOTTA KEEP *MOVIN'*...! REACH *BORDER*...'FORE CARIDAD'S ARMY... REACHES *US*...!

MADNESS.

THOSE *NEEDLES* WE FOUND IN YOUR BACK AFTER THE CRASH WERE OBVIOUSLY *LOADED* WITH THE SAME *TAINTED COCAINE* USED TO MAKE ROUGHHOUSE A RAGING *MONSTER*--

--AND YOU'RE HAVING A *STRONGER REACTION*. MY TOUCH ONLY *SLOWED* WHAT'S HAPPENING. THERE'S ONLY ONE WAY TO PROPERLY CARE FOR YOU.. *SURRENDER*.

NOT AN *ALTERNATIVE*, LADY... NOT AFTER WHAT YOUR *HUSBAND* AND THAT CYBORG NAZI HE CALLS AN *AIDE* HAVE *ALREADY* PUT US THROUGH.

I GOT THE *STRENGTH* T'KEEP US GOIN', SISTER... BUT WE NEED *MORE*. WE NEED *YOU*. HELPIN' TO *CONTROL* HIM--

--AGAINST KILLIN' *HIM-SELF* OR ME WHILE *FIGHTIN'* WHAT'S *INSIDE* 'IM.

STILL MADNESS.

ALWAYS. BUT MAYBE--

--NOT AS MUCH PAIN.

AND IN THE END...

...THAT STILL MATTERS MOST.

SEÑOR GEIST! IT IS *PRESIDENT CARIDAD!* HE WISHES A *PROGRESS REPORT!*

THOUSANDS OF *VINES* SLASHED... TONS OF *JUNGLE VERMIN* CRUSHED UNDERFOOT! CYBERNETICS HAVE *PROLONGED* MY LIFE--

--BUT TO WORK AS AN *ADVISOR,* NOT SLOGGING IN SOME *GREEN PURGATORY!*

NOTHING *YET,* MY PRESIDENT ...BUT OVERTAKING THE *FUGITIVES* IS *INEVITABLE.* IT MAKES MY PRESENCE *SUPERFLUOUS,* YES?

BUT *GOOD TRAINING,* MI *AMIGO...* NOT TO BE *TOO CLEVER.* YOUR SCHEME TO TRICK THE REBELS INTO *ATTACKING* MY MEDICAL CENTER--

--BROUGHT AN *ESCAPE* INSTEAD OF THEIR *DEFEAT.* SINCE I'M JOINING THE HUNT UP *HERE--*

WHY NOT STAY *BELOW...* AND MAKE *CERTAIN* OF THE 'INEVITABLE?'

THE GOVERNMENT FORCES ARE MOVING *WOLVERINE'S* WAY... IGNORING US.

S S SSSSS96'SS SSS

WE CAN'T LET SUCH A *SACRIFICE* BE IN VAIN!

WHAT *CHOICE* DO WE HAVE?

TO *CONTINUE* OUR WAR AGAINST *CARIDAD!*

REVOLUTIONS ARE MADE WITH *ARMIES,* LA BANDERA. IN THE CITY, YOU SOMEHOW *INSPIRED* OTHERS TO JOIN YOU.

THIS JUNGLE IS *WILD! SAVAGE!* EVEN UNPURSUED, THERE IS BUT *ONE THING* TO INSPIRE IN SUCH A PLACE--

"--SUDDEN DEATH!"

SEÑOR GEIST! THE PRESIDENT GROWS IMPATIENT. HE WANTS--

ANOTHER *PROGRESS REPORT?* WE HAVE ADDED *SWAMP* TO OUR CATALOGUE OF INDIGNITIES... *NOTHING ELSE?*

NO *WIFE* TURNED SISTER OF MERCY... NO HUMAN *TEST ANIMALS* FOR OUR LEADER'S PROJECT TO PRODUCE A *SUPERHERO* FOR *TIERRA VERDE.*

BY *EVERY COMPUTER CALCULATION* ... THE COCAINE INFECTING WOLVERINE FROM THE DARTS I FIRED INTO HIM DURING THE ESCAPE SHOULD BE RAGING AT ITS *WORST* NOW!

EVEN WITH THE GOOD *SISTER'S* HELP... THERE IS *NO WAY* HE COULD KEEP MOVING!

WHY HAVEN'T WE *HEARD* HIS RANTING AND RAVING?

WHY HAVEN'T WE *DISCOVERED* THEM YET?!

THE *BEAST* IS BACK.

SOUND'S MUFFLED. DISTANT.

BUT I *KNOW* HE'S BACK.

MADDER THAN BEFORE.

I KNOW *HE'S* BACK, BUT... WHERE AM *I*?

FIGHTIN' FOR MY LIFE... WHAT *ELSE*?

KER-RAASH!

SOME KIND'A ATTACK... CAUGHT ME *NAPPIN'*! COULD'A BURNED WITH TH' BUILDING!

SOLDIERS! STREETS'RE CRAWLIN', LIKE... A *FULL-SCALE* INVASION!

BRRRT!

VEEOW! ZING!

PDUM!

GRENADES! GOTTA GET SOME *DISTANCE* OR--

DEAD END!

NO TIME TO BE CLEVER--

--THEY'RE RIGHT ON MY *TAIL*!

WAS IST DIES?!

YOU CAN'T BE CLEVER, ONLY LEAVES *QUICK*—

ACHTUNG! ACH—

—AND *BRUTAL*.

I DO 'EM WELL.

SOLDIERS PILE INTO THE CUL-DE-SAC.

GERMAN SOLDIERS. CIRCA WORLD WAR II.

SS TROOPERS. NAZI ELITE.

HOW CAN IT *BE*? I DON'T KNOW.

BUT THEY'RE PLAYIN' *MY* GAME—

SCHWEINHUND! SIE SIND TODT!

--AND I'M PLAYIN' IT *ROUGH.*

ONCE I'M STARTED... I HATE TO *STOP.*

C'MON! GOTTA BE *MORE* OF YOU! THINK YOU'VE *TAKEN* OVER? FIGHT'S JUST *HEATIN'* U--

BA-WOM!

THEY *NEARLY* ENDED IT. TAKE AWAY THE ALL BUT INDESTRUCTIBLE ADAMANTIUM SKELETON INSIDE ME...

...THE MUTANT HEALING FACTOR ALREADY TRYIN' TO DO ITS WORK, I'M *DEAD.*

BOM!

AS IS... DESPITE THE PAIN, THE HURT...

I CAN STILL *MOVE...* STILL *SHOW* YOU...

...HOW FAR *SHORT* 'NEARLY' IS!

BRAAAP

BRRRT

SOME OF THEIR MACHINE GUN FIRE MISSES...

...LOT OF IT DOESN'T. I GO DOWN.

BUT THE WAY I WANT...

...AN' WHERE I WANT TO BE.

SHRAAAK!

BELLY OF THE BEAST! EVEN AN IRON MONSTER--

WHATANG!

BRAANK!

--HAS SOFT SPOTS!

BUT LIKE ME...

...IT'S ONLY CRIPPLED. GOTTA SCRAMBLE FAST...

...'FORE THEY RALLY ALL THAT FIREPOWER.

TCHAAK

I BEAT 'EM.

BUT THEIR EXPLODING AMMO STORES...

KA-BWOM!

...BEAT ME.

I'M MID-LEAP, NOT FAR ENOUGH.

SHRAPNEL TEARS MY BODY. A HUNDRED NEW WOUNDS TO GO WITH THOSE I HAVE.

MORE THAN MY HEALING FACTOR CAN EVER DEAL WITH BEFORE SNOW AN' ICY COLD BEYOND THE BLAST...

...DEAL WITH ME.

...'LEAST INVADERS KNOW... THEY HAD... A FIGHT...!

THAT'S NOT GOOD ENOUGH.

LISTEN TO ME, WOLVERINE... RIGHT NOW, YOU ARE YOUR HEALING FACTOR.

YOU HAVE IT IN YOU TO SAVE YOURSELF--

SISTER SALVATION...? THE SNOW...

-- AND THAT SEEMS TO BE LIMITING MY ABILITY TO HELP YOU.

SO MUCH SNOW... OVERWHELMING... I CAN'T...

YOU CAN.

LADY... *ANY* HELP YOU GOT, I NEED. EVEN JUST KNOWIN' I'M NOT GOIN' THROUGH THIS--

--ALONE.

N-NO, PLEASE...! PLEASE... LISTEN.

YOU HAVE TO CARRY THE FIGHT *TO THE INVADER... UP THERE!*

I *CAN'T BE WITH* YOU. THERE'S *NO WAY.* NO--

W-WHAT...?!

MUST'A *DOZED!* MUST'A--

SISTER...? DID YOU... DID YOU *SAY* SOMETHIN'?

I SAID *YOU'D* BETTER TAKE HIM, ROUGHHOUSE. I BELIEVE ANOTHER *VIOLENT SPELL* IS COMING--

--THERE'S *NO WAY I CAN BE WITH HIM.*

YEAH. GONNA NEED ANOTHER *HIDIN' SPOT* TOO.

SHOULDN'T HAVE LET ME *NOD OFF*... WE OUGHTTA BEEN *COVERIN'* GROUND WHILE HE WAS *CALM*.

FUNNY THOUGH, SISTER...TRICKS YOUR *MIND* PLAYS WHEN YOU'RE RUNNIN'... DOZIN'.

SEEMED LIKE YOU TWO WAS *TALKIN'* AND THEN I HEARD, WELL... ALMOST LIKE... A *KISS*.

STUPID, HUH?

SOMEHOW I'M HERE.

SOMEHOW THE SNOW, THE COLD COULDN'T STOP ME.

UNREAL.

EVERYTHING I'M DOIN' SEEMS UNREAL. EXCEPT--

--THE KISS. I STILL *FEEL* IT. FIRIN' ME. MAKIN' ME GO ON. AGAINST THE SNOW, AGAINST--

VOICES! DRIFTIN' UP FROM SOMEWHERE INSIDE. *RECOGNIZE* ONE. IT'S--

--*GEIST!*

--*NUMBERS* ARE A PROBLEM. PARTICULARLY IF THEY *SUSPECT* WHERE THEY'RE BEING LED. BUT SUPPOSE YOU TOLD THEM--

--SOMETHING OF A *CALMING NATURE*. FOR INSTANCE, THE PROSPECT OF A CLEAN, CLOSE *SHAVE* SUCH AS THIS IS *RELAXING*, YES?

HOWEVER, SINCE **WOMEN** AND **CHILDREN** ARE ALSO INVOLVED... PERHAPS THE NOTION THAT THEY ARE GOING FOR **SHOWERS** IS THE FINAL SOLUTION.

YES, MY **FUHRER?**

NOOOOOO!

ANYTHING TO PLEASE A **LEADER,** GEIST?

ANYTHING?!

HOW PLEASED ARE **YOU** GONNA BE--

--WHEN I **TAKE OUT** THAT LEADER BEFORE YOUR **EYES?!**

WHEN I **SLICE** 'IM TO-- TO--

S-SNOW...?!

CONFUSING, YES? YOU DON'T QUITE **KNOW** WHAT YOU'RE FIGHTING.

BUT REST ASSURED, ALTHOUGH WE'RE NOT DEALING IN STRICTEST **REALITY**--

--OUR SITUATION IS VERY MUCH GROUNDED IN **TRUTH.**

TRUTH IS... I'VE HAD **ENOUGH**, CYBORG!

YOU'RE ALL **MICRO-CIRCUITS** AN' MECHANIZED **DOODADS**... MAYBE **YOU** WON'T **MELT**!

CHUKT!

MAYBE IF I LAY OPEN ENOUGH **CLOCKWORK**--

WRRIIIIPP!

--WE'LL SEE IF THERE'S ANY **HUMANITY** LEFT TO STAND ON ITS **OWN**.

I'M BETTIN' 'IT **ROTTED** LONG AGO, GEIST!

AND **THAT'S** THE TRUTH.

WOLVERINE--

YOU--

YOU--

YOU **STILL** DON'T KNOW WHAT YOU'RE FIGHTING. BUT DON'T WORRY, I'M GOING TO **SHOW** YOU--

--NOW!

I AM *SPORE*.

I *GROW*.

AND THE *KNOWLEDGE* I IMPART--

--IS GOING TO *CONSUME* YOU.

THIS FIT SEEMS T'BE *KILLIN'* 'IM, SISTER!

SUDDEN *STORM* AIN'T HELPIN'... BUT THE *BORDER'S* NOT FAR ACCORDIN' TO WOLVERINE'S *DIRECTIONS* 'FORE ALL THIS CAME ON 'IM.

AIN'T THERE ANY *MORE* YOU CAN DO?

WE'RE SO *CLOSE*...BUT IT'S SO *BAD!* LOOK AT 'IM, SISTER... JUST *LOOK* AT 'IM!

HE'S...NOT *LIKE* OTHER MEN, ROUGHOUSE--

--I'M NOT CERTAIN ANYTHING *ELSE* CAN WORK. EXCEPT--

EXCEPT--

--LET *ME* HOLD HIM.

NOTHIN' HELPS...

-- HE'S *EVERYWHERE*, HIS VOICE A NASTY WHISPER INSIDE MY BRAIN.

THIS LAST, FUTILE BIT OF RESISTANCE WILL *FADE*, WOLVERINE... ONCE YOU *UNDERSTAND* WHAT'S AGAINST YOU.

"I AM *SPORE*. I AM ANCIENT. BORN IN PREHISTORY, WHEN TWO GREAT RACES WARRED. THE *ETERNALS*...

"...AND MY *CREATORS*, THE *DEVIANTS*.

"MASTERS OF TECHNOLOGY WHILE MANKIND STILL LIVED IN CAVES, THEIR SCIENTISTS TWISTED GENETICS TO GIVE BIRTH TO AN *ULTIMATE WEAPON* AGAINST THEIR UNDYING FOES.

"FROM A HUMAN TEMPLATE... I ROSE, A *LIVING DISEASE* WHO COULD CONSUME, ABSORB, AND GROW.

"THESE WERE MY POWERS. THIS WAS MY GLORY. ETERNALS FELL. THEIR GENES FOR IMMORTALITY BECAME *PART OF ME.* AND STILL...

"...MY *HUNGER* SWELLED. UNTIL...

"...ONLY THE GODS COULD CUT IT SHORT.

"THE CELESTIALS. THEY WHO FORGED ETERNALS AND DEVIANTS FROM THE MATRIX OF HUMANITY. THEY WHO RETURNED FROM THE STARS TO JUDGE THEIR EXPERIMENT...

"...AND FOUND ME AMONG THEIR DISPLEASURES.

"JUDGMENT WAS SWIFT. I WAS A ROGUE, PREYING BY NOW ON DEVIANT AS WELL AS HUMAN AND ETERNAL...

"...AN ABOMINATION TO BE PURGED FROM THEIR COSMIC SCHEME...

"...SCORCHED BACK TO THE VISCERAL SLIME FROM WHICH I GREW.

"AND THE SOIL OF CENTRAL AMERICA ABSORBED ME AS I HAD ABSORBED SO MANY. EXCEPT...

"...I STILL LIVED. MY STOLEN IMMORTALITY LEAVING ME AWARE THROUGH THE EONS BUT-- WITHOUT LIVING FLESH AND BLOOD TO ABSORB --TRAPPED. UNTIL--

"...THE MICROSCOPIC PARTICLES OF MY CONSCIOUSNESS SENSED A PATHWAY INTO THE HUMAN BLOOD I NEEDED TO TRULY LIVE.

"FRUSTRATION.

"...A CROP WAS PLANTED IN THE EARTH LONG BARREN FROM MY DEMISE. COCAINE. AND IN THIS ADDICTIVE GROWTH...

"MOST BODIES COULD NOT SURVIVE THE SHOCK OF AN ALIEN PRESENCE RAGING, GROWING WITHIN THEM.*

*WOLVERINE #17.--BOB.

BUT NOW I HAVE *YOU*, WOLVERINE... SO *DRIVEN*, SO *DETERMINED!* A *FIGHTER*... AND POSSESSED OF A *FACTOR* TO KEEP *HEALING* YOURSELF.

YOURS IS A BODY THAT CAN STAY *ALIVE* UNTIL I *GROW!* GROW FROM MERE PARTICLES IN YOUR *BLOODSTREAM*--

--TO *OOZE* FROM YOUR EVERY PORE, *CONSUME* YOUR VERY BEING... AND *EMERGE*... FINALLY, FULLY *FREE!*

ALWAYS WAS A *LONER* 'TIL THE X-MEN. ALWAYS FIGURED TO *DIE* ALONE.

BUT NOT LIKE *THIS!* SHRINKIN' INSIDE SOME *MONSTER!* CAN'T *SCREAM*... *STRUGGLE*... DO *ANYTHING* EXCEPT GO STARK, RAVIN'--

NO. THIS IS HOW *HE* WANTS YOU TO SEE WHAT'S GOIN' ON IN YOUR OWN BODY--

WHAT'D *SALVATION* SAY...?

I *AM* MY HEALING FACTOR--

I *AM* MY HEALING FACTOR--

WH-WHAT...?!

--AND I'M *NOT* ALONE!

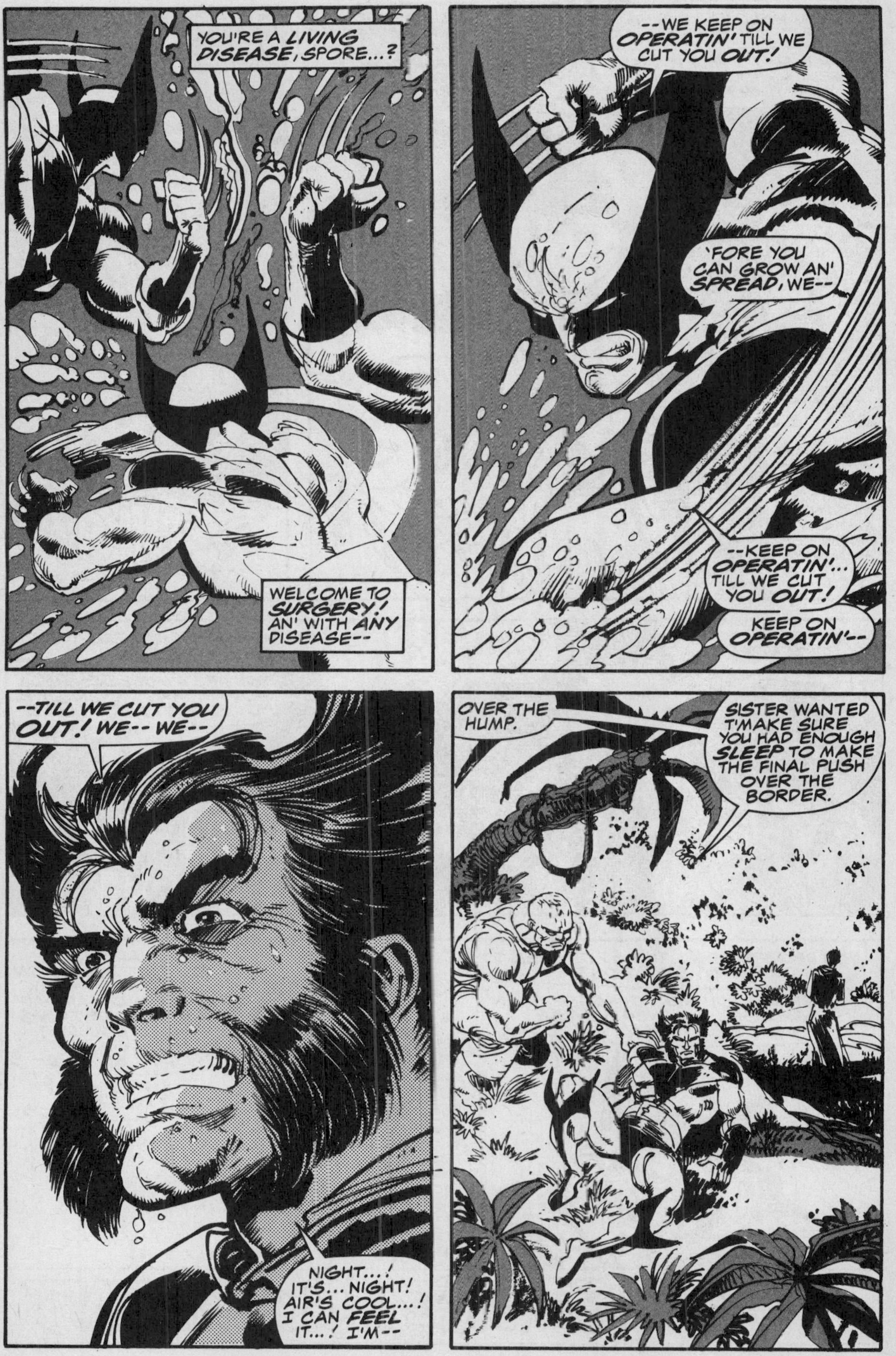
YOU'RE A LIVING DISEASE, SPORE...?
WELCOME TO SURGERY! AN' WITH ANY DISEASE--
--WE KEEP ON OPERATIN' TILL WE CUT YOU OUT!
'FORE YOU CAN GROW AN' SPREAD, WE--
--KEEP ON OPERATIN'... TILL WE CUT YOU OUT!
KEEP ON OPERATIN'--
--TILL WE CUT YOU OUT! WE-- WE--
NIGHT...! IT'S... NIGHT! AIR'S COOL...! I CAN FEEL IT...! I'M--
OVER THE HUMP.
SISTER WANTED T'MAKE SURE YOU HAD ENOUGH SLEEP TO MAKE THE FINAL PUSH OVER THE BORDER.

YOU *HELD* ME...DURING THE WORST OF IT. SO I WASN'T *ALONE.*

THOUGHT I *FELT* IT THEN... SMELLING YOU ON ME NOW MADE IT *CERTAIN.*

WOLVERINE, YOU...YOU MUSTN'T MAKE IT SOUND SO... *PERSONAL.* ANYTHING I DID--

--I DID TO EASE YOUR *SUFFERING.* I SAID I COULDN'T ABANDON *ANY-ONE* WHILE THERE WAS THAT CHANCE.

STAND WHERE YOU ARE! NO ONE MOVE! ESPECIALLY *YOU,* WOLVERINE--

SNIKT!

--YOU ARE *SURROUNDED,* YES?

THANKS TO MY *WIFE,* GEIST--

--FOR MARKING THE *TRAIL* THEY'D TAKE ON *THIS.*

YOU ARE A MORE *SENSIBLE* WOMAN THAN I EVER GAVE YOU *CREDIT* FOR, MY LOVE.

YOU DROPPED THAT THING FOR THEM TO FIND...? *WHY,* SALVATION?!

AFTER *ALL* YOU WENT THROUGH SAVIN' ROUGHHOUSE...AN' EVEN *WORSE* SAVIN' ME...*WHY?!*

YOU HAD *PAIN.* I COULDN'T *ABANDON* YOU TO IT. BUT FELIX GUILLERMO CARIDAD HAS THE *ONE THING* WHICH I COULDN'T ABANDON FOR YOUR *ESCAPE*--

--HE HAS MY *SON.*

NEXT ISSUE: SPORE ASCENDENT

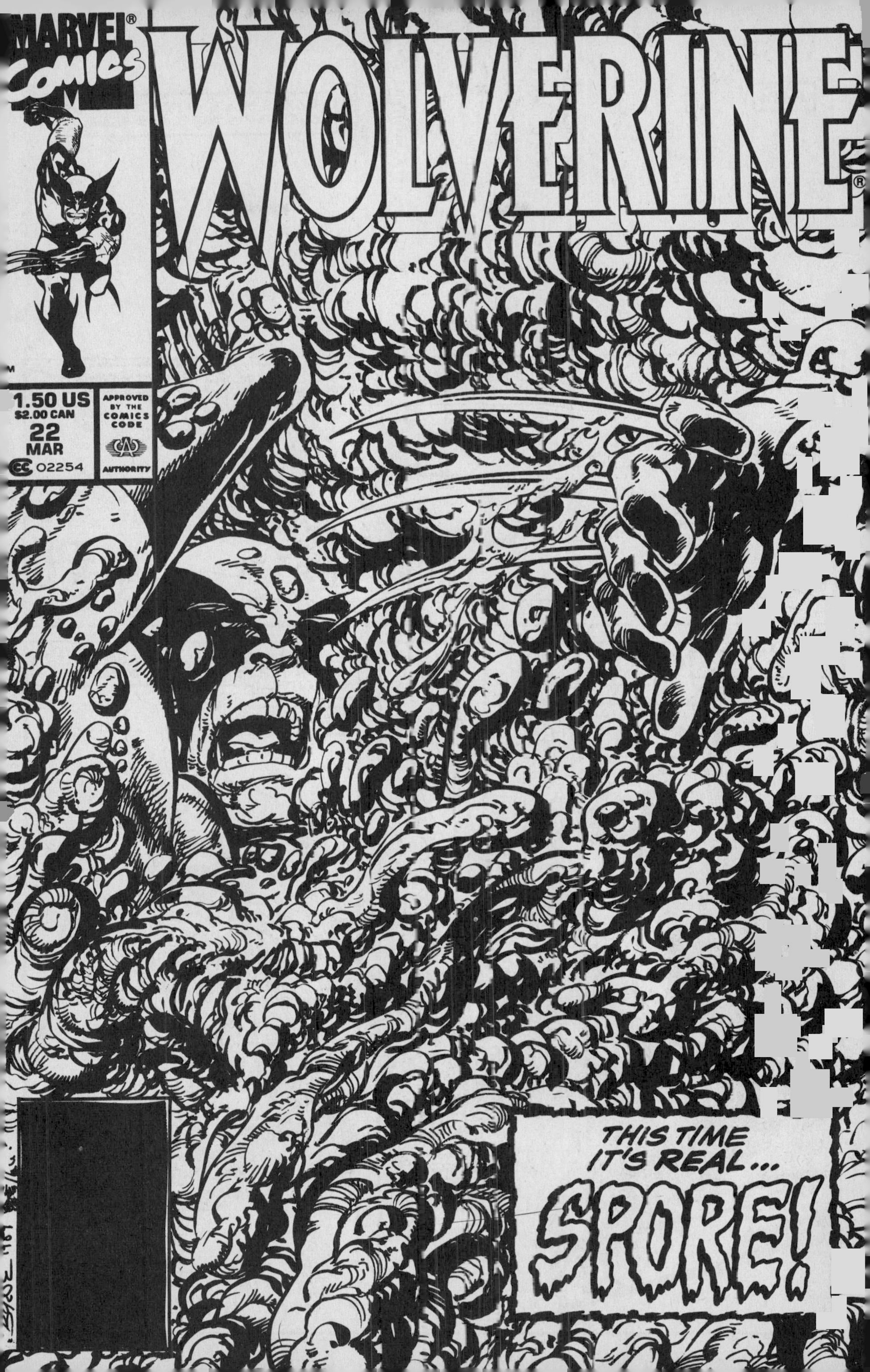
MARVEL COMICS
WOLVERINE
1.50 US
$2.00 CAN
22
MAR
02254
APPROVED BY THE COMICS CODE AUTHORITY
THIS TIME IT'S REAL...
SPORE!

PAIN.

TRICK IS, YOU GO BEYOND IT. PUT YOUR MIND SOMEPLACE ELSE.

'COURSE, THERE'S ALL KINDS OF PAIN. SOME HURT WORSE THAN OTHERS. LEAVE DEEPER WOUNDS.

LIKE *MARIKO*.

HER FATHER, *LORD YASHIDA*, SHOWED HER THE ANIMAL IN ME... AND LAUGHED.

BUT SHE LOOKED DEEPER.

...AND *LOVED*. STILL, DUTY BINDS HER, HONOR HOLDS HER... AWAY. NOBLE. ROMANTIC.

IMPOSSIBLE.

DOESN'T STOP ME. DRAWS ME ON.

STAN LEE PRESENTS

OUTBURST!

LIKE *SISTER* SALVATION.

MARRIED. FIRST TO A DICTATOR. NOW TO THE CHURCH.

IMPOSSIBLE.

HAS TO END IN--

ARCHIE GOODWIN
WRITER

JOHN BYRNE
BREAKDOWN ARTIST

KLAUS JANSON
FINISHING ARTIST

JIM NOVAK
LETTERER

GLYNIS OLIVER
COLORIST

BOB HARRAS, EDITOR

TOM DEFALCO, EDITOR IN CHIEF

--PAIN.

HE DOESN'T SCREAM.

LONG PAST THE POINT WHEN OTHER MEN-- *STRONG MEN* --HAVE HOWLED LIKE ANIMALS... BEGGED... WHIMPERED... BROKEN...

ENOUGH... *ENOUGH,* GEIST. WE MUST FACE AN UNPLEAS-ANT POSSIBILITY--

HE HAS BEEN TELLING US THE *TRUTH.*

A *MOMENT,* MY PRESIDENT.

OUR INTERROGATION SUBJECT MAY OR MAY NOT BE THE LEGENDARY *WOLVERINE*... ALL OF THOSE MUTANT SUPER HEROES, THE X-MEN, ARE SUPPOSEDLY DEAD.

BUT OBVIOUSLY, HE EXHIBITS MORE THAN *HUMAN* RESISTANCE.

PERHAPS GREATER EFFORT IS REQUIRED. PERHAPS IF THAT HAIRY BODY WERE... MORE *CLEANLY SHAVEN,* BETTER *CONTACT* COULD BE ACHIEVED.

AND BETTER *RESULTS,* YES?

PERHAPS SOMEDAY WE WILL ALL BE SMOOTH, SLEEK CYBORGS, GEIST ...AND YOU WILL *FORGET* THIS OBSESSION FOR SHAVING.

I HAVE *OTHER* GOALS. WE'VE WASTED ENOUGH TIME... RETURN OUR PERSISTENT FRIEND TO HIS CELL.

THE DREAM OF MY LIFE...SO *CLOSE!* YET WHENEVER I AM READY TO *SEIZE* IT--

--ANOTHER COMPLICATION ARISES!

MY HEAD...! THE MIGRAINES THIS BUSINESS HAS GIVEN ME...!

THE PRICE OF BEING *FELIX GUILLERMO CARIDAD*... THE PRICE OF POWER. A HARD DECISION IS NEEDED--

--AND I DID NOT BECOME "STRONGMAN OF TIERRA VERDE" BY FLEEING SUCH DECISIONS.

FELIX! HOW DARE YOU SHUT ME *AWAY!* YOU MADE A *PROMISE*... AND I *BETRAYED* WOLVERINE AND ROUGHOUSE TO SEE IT *FULFILLED!*

I WANT MY *SON*, FELIX... NOT TO *LANGUISH* IN SOME JUNGLE MONUMENT TO YOUR ARMY'S OPPRESSION.

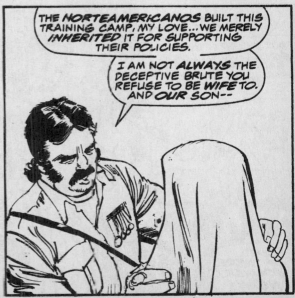

THE *NORTEAMERICANOS* BUILT THIS TRAINING CAMP, MY LOVE...WE MERELY *INHERITED* IT FOR SUPPORTING THEIR POLICIES.

I AM NOT *ALWAYS* THE DECEPTIVE BRUTE YOU REFUSE TO BE *WIFE* TO. AND *OUR SON*--

"-- IS NEARER THAN YOU KNOW."

WUD!

WUMPF!

SPLUSH!

SEÑOR PRESIDENT! HE...HE ALMOST HAD ME!

BUT *DIVED* IN THE MUD SO YOU DIDN'T *LOOK BAD,* SERGEANT?

OUT OF THERE, SOLDIER! NOW!

PALO?

YOUR PARDON, SISTER. DO I--

PALO! DEAR HEAVEN...! AFTER FIVE YEARS...!

FIVE *LONG* YEARS...!

M-MOTHER...?

LOOK AT YOU, LOOK HOW YOU'VE *GROWN!* YOU WERE JUST A BOY WHEN I HAD TO LEAVE YOU. NOW ...YOU'RE NEARLY A MAN.

HE *IS* A MAN, SALVATION.

AND HE IS A *SOLDIER* OF TIERRA VERDE... AS I WAS AT HIS AGE. BUT *UNLIKE* ME... PALO HAS NOT HAD TO *CLAW* HIS WAY UP OUT OF *POVERTY.*

THAT DOESN'T MEAN I DON'T *TRY,* PAPA. MY RANKING IN THIS TRAINING CYCLE HAS GONE FROM--

LIFE IS NOT *TRAINING!* IF YOU HAD *FOUGHT* FOR EVERY OPPORTUNITY AS I WAS DRIVEN TO DO--

--THE *SERGEANT* WOULD REEK OF THE MUDP.T. NOT MY *SON.*

BUT BECAUSE YOU *ARE* MY SON, YOU WILL HAVE *OTHER WAYS* TO PROVE YOURSELF AS I DID, PALO. MEANTIME--

--HE IS *YOUR* SON FOR THE AFTERNOON, SALVATION. TONIGHT... WE WILL DISCUSS FAMILY RELATIONSHIPS *FURTHER.*

BOLT HIS MANACLES *TIGHT* TO THE WALL. SO IF HE POPS THOSE *CLAWS*... HE STILL CAN'T *WIELD* THEM, YES?

HE HAS BEEN INTERROGATED BRUTALLY, BEATEN EXHAUSTIVELY, SENOR GEIST.

NOTHING WILL POP.

I WONDER, LIEUTENANT. MOMENTS SUCH AS THIS ARE WHEN HE IS MOST *DANGEROUS.*

SI... TO *HIMSELF.*

COME.

WOLVERINE?

YOU... ALIVE?

ROUGHOUSE...? SOME BODY PARTS AIN'T... CHECKED IN YET. GUESS ...I'M OKAY. BUT YOU SOUND... WEAK.

YOU GET PUT THROUGH THE MEAT-GRINDER TOO...?

DIDN'T WASTE... ELECTRI-CITY ON ME. JUST... USED *STICKS.* FUNNY...

SAME WAY... MY *DAD* USED TA BEAT ME.

ONLY WAY I'D MIND, HE SAID. MAKE ME A MAN, HE SAID. AN' HE'D *WHACK* ME.

S'HOW I GOT... *SCARS* ON MY HEAD. WHACK. WHACK. WHACK. *GOOD OL' DAD.*

SCARS, MADE ME SO... *ANGRY,* ASHAMED.

I GOT BIGGER, STRONGER, *ANGRIER,* SWORE... *I'D GIVE THE SCARS.*

DID IT SO WELL--

MEN LIKE GENERAL COY IN MADRIPOOR... PAID ME TO DO IT *MORE.*

WORLD'S FULL'A *USERS,* ROUGHOUSE. BUT RAGE AIN'T ALL BAD... NOT IF YOU CAN GET MAD ENOUGH TO *BREAK US FREE.*

BUT... IT'S *CHANGED.*

SOMEHOW WHEN SISTER SALVATION *CURED* ME... THE ANGER *WENT AWAY* ... 'LONG WITH THE *MADNESS* FROM THAT TAINTED COCAINE.

TRY ANYWAY! STRUNG UP IN THAT POSITION... YOU'LL *DIE,* ROUGHOUSE! IF CARIDAD DOESN'T CARE 'BOUT HIS FAVORITE *GUINEA PIG...* THEN HE'S DECIDED THE *TEST PHASE* IS OVER.

HE'S READY TO *ROLL* WITH THAT JUNK ...AN' HE DOESN'T WANNA *KNOW* WHAT'LL BE UNLEASHED.

"ITS NAME IS *SPORE.* A LIVIN' DISEASE. CREATED BACK IN PREHISTORY BY A WARPED RACE CALLED THE *DEVIANTS.*

"TOOK SOME GOD-LIKE ALIENS--THE *CELESTI-ALS,* CREATORS OF THE DEVIANTS--TO PUT 'IM OUTTA BUSINESS BACK THEN.

SPORE WAS BLASTED INTO OOZE, ABSORBED INTO THE EARTH. ETERNAL, BUT *DORMANT*...UNTIL HE FOUND A NEW CHANCE TO GROW AN' LIVE. CARIDAD'S *COCAINE*, ROUGHOUSE!

THROUGH IT, SPORE CAN REACH WHAT HE *NEEDS*...HUMAN FLESH, HUMAN BLOOD. I FOUGHT WITH 'IM THROUGH MY *HEALING FACTOR* WHEN I WAS INFECTED...I *KNOW!*

IF THE SHOCK DOESN'T KILL THE USER, THAT THING IS *FREE* AGAIN--

"-- WITH NO *CELESTIALS* TO STOP 'IM!"

THE *LAST* OF THE EL JARDÍN DEL REY HARVEST, GEIST. CAN *YOU* SEE MONSTERS IN IT?

CREATING A *SUPER* HERO FOR TIERRA VERDE WAS GOING TO SAVE ME FROM HISTORY... *JUSTIFY* ALL ELSE IN THE WAY I LIVED MY LIFE.

THE STORY WOLVERINE CLINGS TO ONLY JUSTIFIES *BURNING* THAT COCAINE.

AS YOUR ADVISER, MY PRESIDENT, I MUST--

PREPARE IT FOR *USE*, GEIST. MONSTERS CAN BE *VANQUISHED*--

"-- WITH A *MIRACLE* ON YOUR SIDE!"

A BEAUTIFUL SUNSET, PALO, BUT...I'D HOPED WE'D *TALK* MORE. SO LONG APART, I SUPPOSE IT'S *AWKWARD*--

WHAT DID YOU WISH TO HEAR, MOTHER?

THAT I AM *UNHAPPY* AS A SOLDIER AND DO IT ONLY TO PLEASE PAPA...? HE IS *DEMANDING*, YES. AND I KNOW I *DISAPPOINT* HIM.

BUT I WOULD NOT *ABANDON* HIM....AS *YOU* ABANDONED BOTH OF US.

OH, PALO....! I ABANDONED YOUR FATHER'S WAY OF *LIFE*...THE BRUTALITY, THE COR-RUPTION. NOT *YOU*... *NEVER* YOU!

I WOULD DO *ANY-THING* NOT TO BE SEPARATED FROM YOU AGAIN.

SISTER SALVATION! PRIVATE CARIDAD!

THIS WAY!

THE *PRESIDENT* WAITS!

AH! COME...JOIN ME, *JOIN ME!* IT IS TIME TO *CELEBRATE!* I HAVE MADE AN IMPORTANT *DECISION*--

--AND, WHATEVER OUR *DIFFERENCES*, MY *FAMILY* IS TOGETHER AGAIN!

I WANT TO KEEP US *TOGETHER*, PALO...THAT WOULD *PLEASE* ME. YOU WANT TO PLEASE YOUR FATHER, YES, BOY?

OF COURSE, PAPA. BUT... SO LITTLE SEEMS TO DO IT. ALWAYS, THERE ARE NEW *DEMANDS*...YOU DON'T MAKE IT *EASY*.

EASY IS FOR THE *WEAK*, PALO. TONIGHT, YOU MUST BE *STRONG*. TONIGHT, I MAKE MY *GREATEST* DEMAND.

IT INVOLVES VAST *DANGER*, BUT IT WILL BIND OUR FAMILY... AND MAKE YOU A *HERO!*

CH-K-LIK!

ROUGHHOUSE...LISTEN. PLEASE.

CARIDAD MAY ALREADY BE MAKIN' HIS MOVE. AN' THE LONGER WE'RE CHAINED UP...THE WEAKER YOU GET.

I'M TRYIN', WOLVERINE. BUT...I'M AFRAID.

THE LADY HEALED SOMETHIN' UGLY IN ME...I DON'T WANNA BRING IT BACK. EVEN IF I DI--

EEEEEEE!

THAT'S--
THE LADY!

WRRAAANK!

THE LADY!

KRIINK! SNING!

SHE NEEDS US, WOLVERINE!

NOTHIN' UGLY IN THAT!

FROM THIS ANGLE--

RRATCH!

--STRICTLY BEAUTIFUL, BUB!

SHRRRAK!

GOTTA SAVE S·STER SALVATION, WOLVERINE, BUT...I WON'T HURT ANYBODY.

THAT SIDE'A ME'S GONE...'LONG WITH HAVIN' THAT LIVIN' DISEASE IN ME.

FAIR ENOUGH. WHEN IT COMES TO HURTIN' IN THIS PLACE--

--I OWE 'EM DOUBLE ANYWAY!

EMPTY?!

OUGHTTA BE SOMEBODY ON DUTY... AIN'T RIGHT THAT THEY'RE NOT.

THEY LEFT THIS. SOMETHING YOU'LL NEED?

SECOND NATURE, ROUGHOUSE. I COME TO DO BUSINESS--

"--I DO IT BETTER IN A BUSINESS SUIT."

THE GUARDS--!

WENT OUT TO INVESTIGATE... WEREN'T READY FOR WHAT THEY FOUND.

THEIR WEAPONS ARE GONE, WOLVERINE.

SOMEONE'S ARMIN' THEMSELVES FOR A MAJOR ATTACK. PROBABLY SOON... WHILE MOST'A CARIDAD'S TROOPS ARE STILL AT EVENIN' MESS.

WE DON'T REACH SISTER SALVATION BEFORE THAT HAPPENS... WE MAY NOT REACH HER AT ALL.

RESTRAIN YOURSELF, WOMAN! YOU REWARD MY FRANKNESS WITH SCREAMS AND ABUSE?!

YOU'RE OBSCENE, FELIX! SO OBSESSED, YOU'D INFECT OUR CHILD... RELEASE A MONSTROSITY TO GROW INSIDE HIM!

MOTHER...! PAPA...! PLEASE...

SELF-RIGHTEOUS WITCH! YOUR HEALING TOUCH CAN NEUTRALIZE ANY RISK... AND LEAVE ONLY THE ENHANCEMENTS, POWERS WORTHY OF A SUPER HERO!

WILL YOU DENY OUR SON WHAT YOU'D WASTE ON ANY AILING SAVAGE?!

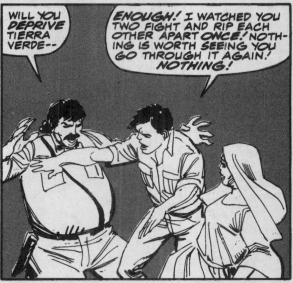

WILL YOU DEPRIVE TIERRA VERDE--

ENOUGH! I WATCHED YOU TWO FIGHT AND RIP EACH OTHER APART ONCE! NOTHING IS WORTH SEEING YOU GO THROUGH IT AGAIN! NOTHING!

PALO...! THERE'S NO GUARANTEE MY GIFT WILL ALWAYS WORK OR--

I WANT TO END THIS! NOW! DO WHATEVER MUST BE DONE!

THAT DUTY IS MINE. BUT PAINLESS, YES? LIKE A CLEAN, CLOSE SHAVE...

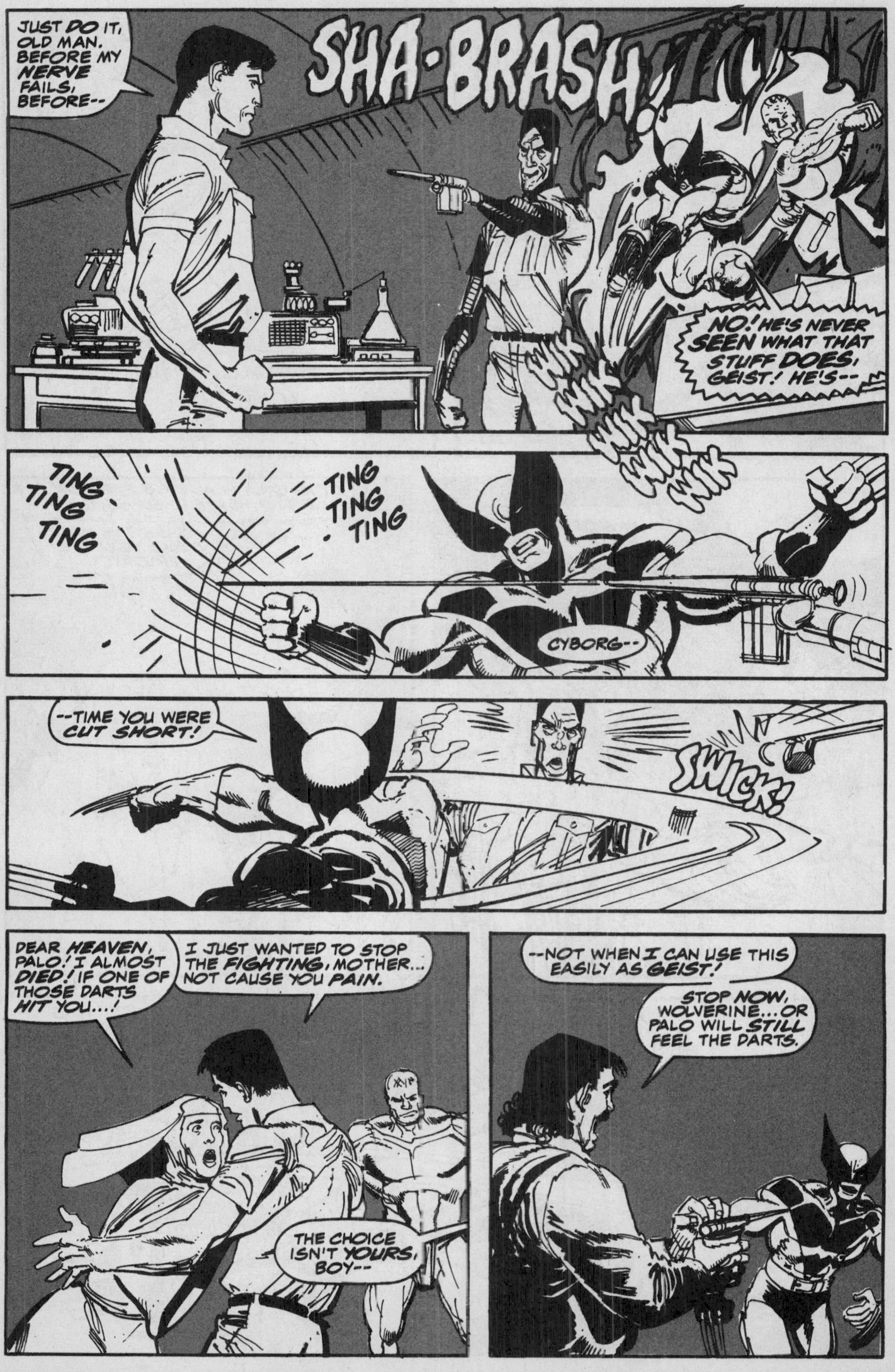

JUST DO IT, OLD MAN. BEFORE MY NERVE FAILS, BEFORE--
SHA-BRASH!
NO! HE'S NEVER SEEN WHAT THAT STUFF DOES, GEIST! HE'S--
SNIKT SNIKT SNIKT
TING TING TING
TING TING TING
CYBORG--
--TIME YOU WERE CUT SHORT!
SWICK!
DEAR HEAVEN, PALO! I ALMOST DIED! IF ONE OF THOSE DARTS HIT YOU....!
I JUST WANTED TO STOP THE FIGHTING, MOTHER... NOT CAUSE YOU PAIN.
THE CHOICE ISN'T YOURS, BOY--
--NOT WHEN I CAN USE THIS EASILY AS GEIST!
STOP NOW, WOLVERINE...OR PALO WILL STILL FEEL THE DARTS.

THREATENIN' YOUR *SON* DOESN'T SEEM THE BEST WAY TO STAY IN YOUR WIFE'S *GOOD GRACES,* CARIDAD. AN' FROM HERE, I'D SAY YOU'LL *NEED* 'EM--

--OR DON'T YOU *FEEL* IT YET?

SALVATION...

I'M SORRY, FELIX...

I CAN ONLY HEAL *ONE PERSON* AT A TIME. AND, HEAVEN HELP US BOTH--

--IT ISN'T IN ME TO MAKE *YOU* THE PRIORITY.

KWUD!

SO! IT IS EVERYONE FOR HIMSELF, YES?

AND THE ART OF *SURVIVING* SO MANY YEARS, SO MANY MASTERS--

--IS THE ART OF THE *WELL-TIMED EXIT!*

BOUM!

PWOM!

WH-WHAT...?

FALL BACK! WE CAN'T FIGHT OUR OWN *MORTARS* AND *ROCKETS!*

THEY'RE *DEVILS,* THOSE INDIANS! INFILTRATING *BEFORE* THE ATTACK ...LOOTING OUR *ARMS DEPOTS!*

BRRRT

VRIIT

INDIANS....? THE LOCAL TRIBES ARE TOO PRIMITIVE, TOO DISORGANIZED FOR SUCH ACTION.

HOW CAN IT--

--BE?!

WUD!

VIVA LA BANDERA!

VIVA LA BANDERA AND THE REVOLUTION!

THEY ARE INSPIRED, THIS BAND OF MEN ONCE POLITICAL PRISONERS OF THE DICTATOR CARIDAD.

SO TOO ARE THEIR UNLIKELY ALLIES...WAVE AFTER WAVE OF THE JUNGLE'S FINEST WARRIORS.

BLADAM!

AND SHE HAS DONE IT. DESPITE DISSIDENT VIEWS, TRIBAL FACTIONS... SHE HAS INSPIRED THEM TO BE AN ARMY.

EVEN ENRIQUE, A DOUBTER BY NATURE, GRINS AT THE PROSPECT OF VICTORY.

AND THEIR INSPIRATION IN TURN FEEDS HER.

SHE DRAWS UPON IT, TURNS IT TO ENERGY, AND, WITH HER STAFF TO CHANNEL IT, LETS IT EXPLODE AS A PHYSICAL FORCE.

SHE IS LA BANDERA. SHE IS A MUTANT WITH THE ABILITY TO INSPIRE.

AND IN ALL HER YOUNG LIFE... IT HAS NEVER WORKED MORE WONDERFULLY THAN TONIGHT.

SO FAR.

LISTEN, CARIDAD...! OUTSIDE! IF I CAN HEAR AFTER TAKIN' THAT SHOT FROM GEIST... YOU CAN, TOO.

A LITTLE GIRL, WHOSE FATHER WAS A VICTIM OF YOUR DRUG TRAFFIC IS ABOUT T'BRING EVERYTHING DOWN.

BEST YOU CAN DO NOW IS LET US GET MEDICAL HELP 'FORE THAT JUNK RACIN' IN YOUR BLOODSTREAM KILLS YOU.

NOT... IF I'M... STRONG.

LIKE YOU... LIKE ROUGHHOUSE... LIKE SUPER HERO.

GIVE MY COUNTRY... SHOW THE WORLD.

STRONG MAN... OF TIERRA VERDE....! SUPER HERO....!

CARIDAD! THAT'S CRAZY! THAT'S--

KRAASH!

CARIDAD!

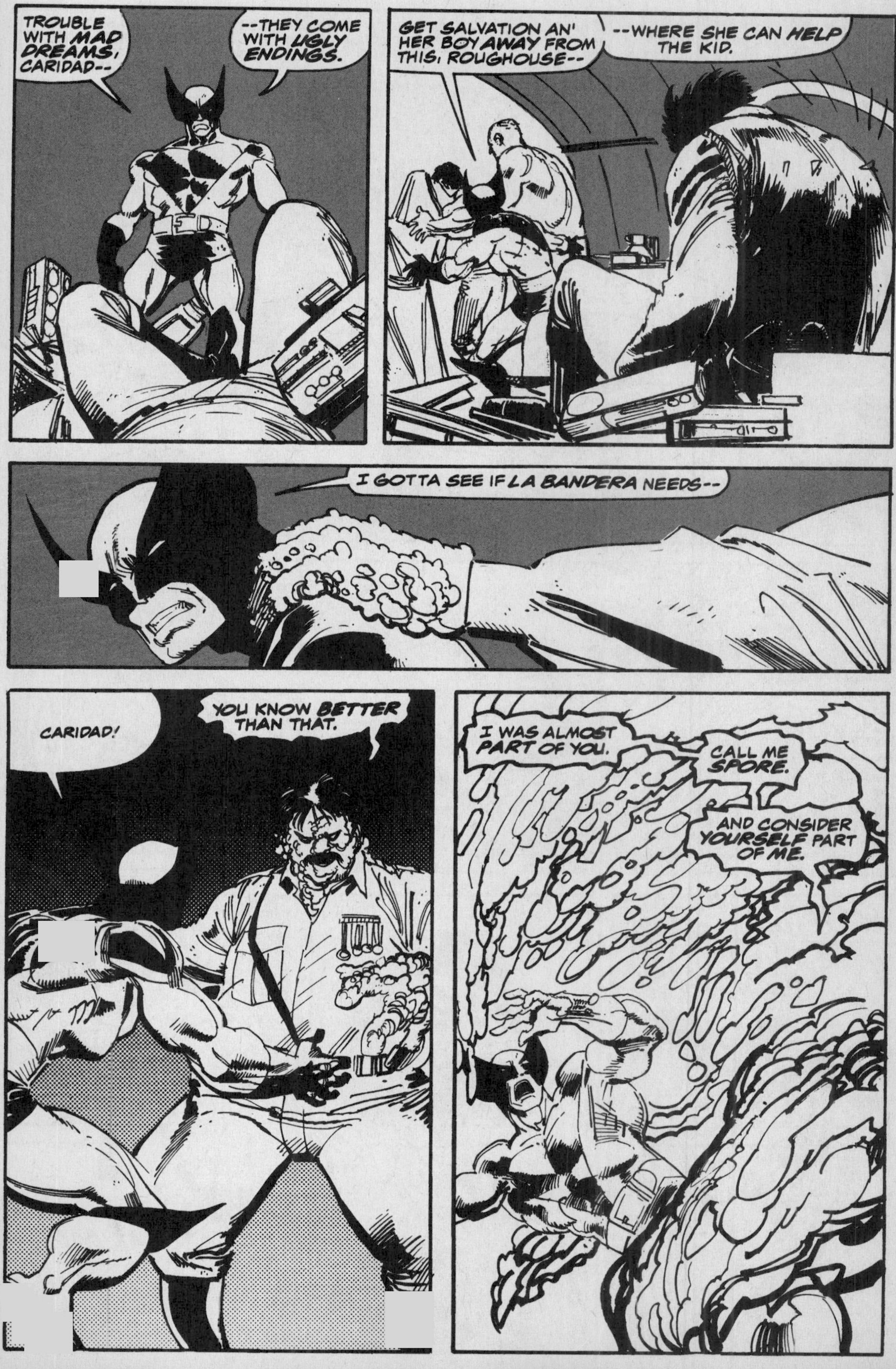
TROUBLE WITH MAD DREAMS, CARIDAD--
--THEY COME WITH UGLY ENDINGS.
GET SALVATION AN' HER BOY AWAY FROM THIS, ROUGHOUSE--
--WHERE SHE CAN HELP THE KID.
I GOTTA SEE IF LA BANDERA NEEDS--
CARIDAD!
YOU KNOW BETTER THAN THAT.
I WAS ALMOST PART OF YOU.
CALL ME SPORE.
AND CONSIDER YOURSELF PART OF ME.

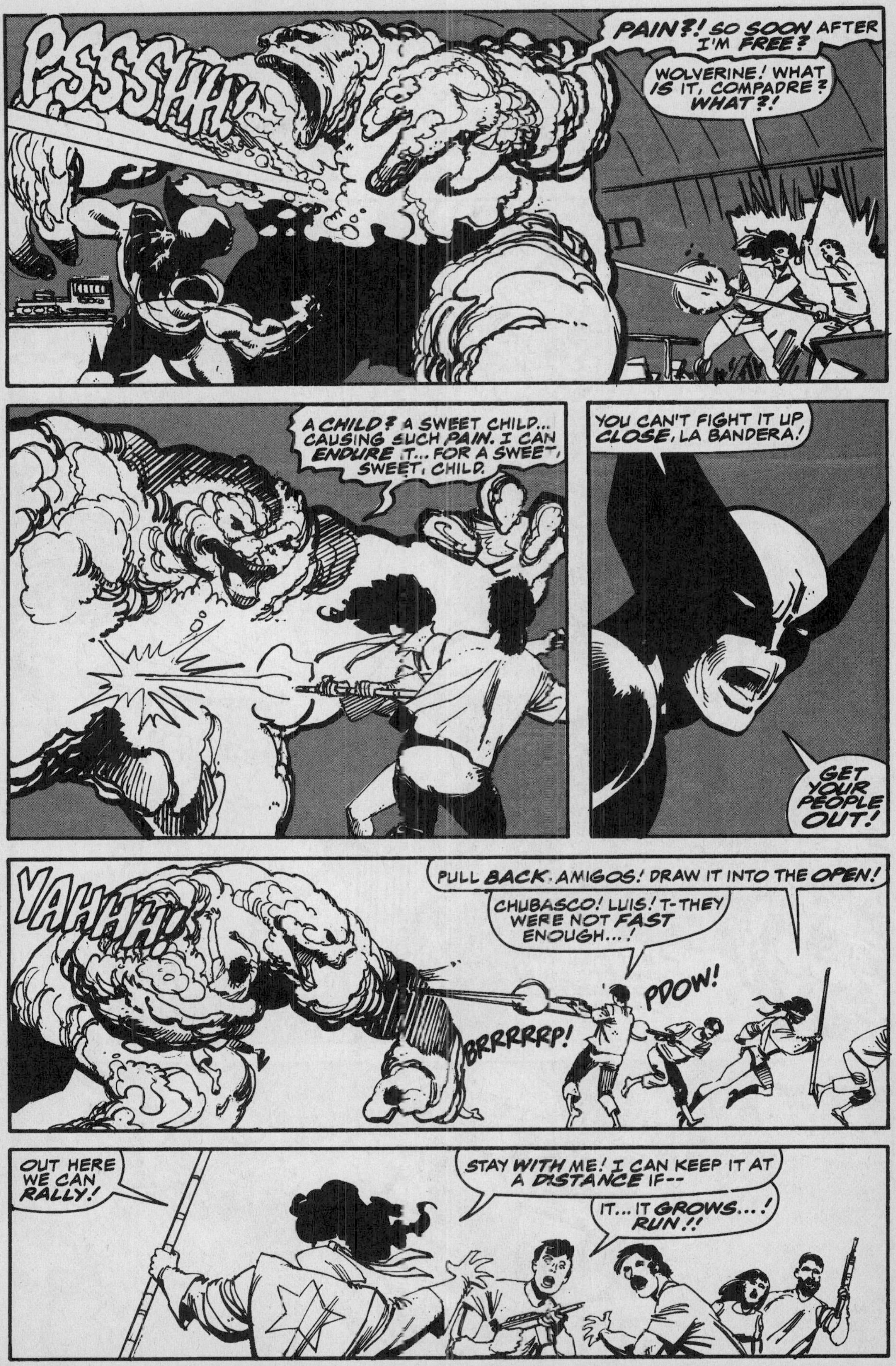
PSSSHH!
PAIN?! SO SOON AFTER I'M FREE?
WOLVERINE! WHAT IS IT, COMPADRE? WHAT?!
A CHILD? A SWEET CHILD... CAUSING SUCH PAIN. I CAN ENDURE IT... FOR A SWEET, SWEET, CHILD.
YOU CAN'T FIGHT IT UP CLOSE, LA BANDERA!
GET YOUR PEOPLE OUT!
YAHHH!
PULL BACK, AMIGOS! DRAW IT INTO THE OPEN!
CHUBASCO! LUIS! T-THEY WERE NOT FAST ENOUGH...!
PDOW!
BRRRRRP!
OUT HERE WE CAN RALLY!
STAY WITH ME! I CAN KEEP IT AT A DISTANCE IF--
IT... IT GROWS...! RUN!!

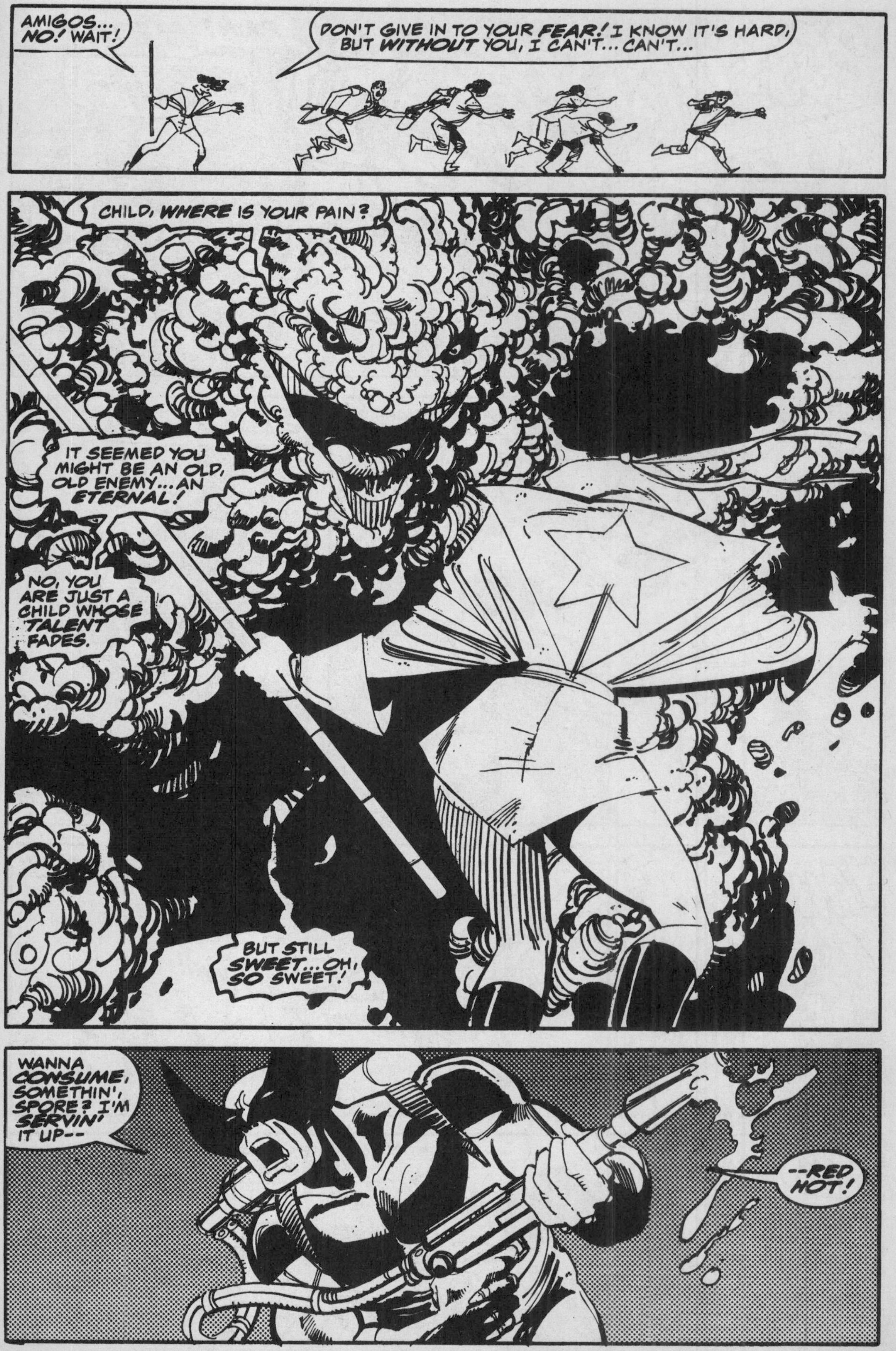
AMIGOS... NO! WAIT!
DON'T GIVE IN TO YOUR FEAR! I KNOW IT'S HARD, BUT WITHOUT YOU, I CAN'T... CAN'T...
CHILD, WHERE IS YOUR PAIN?
IT SEEMED YOU MIGHT BE AN OLD, OLD ENEMY... AN ETERNAL!
NO, YOU ARE JUST A CHILD WHOSE 'TALENT' FADES.
BUT STILL SWEET...OH, SO SWEET!
WANNA CONSUME SOMETHIN', SPORE? I'M SERVIN' IT UP--
--RED HOT!

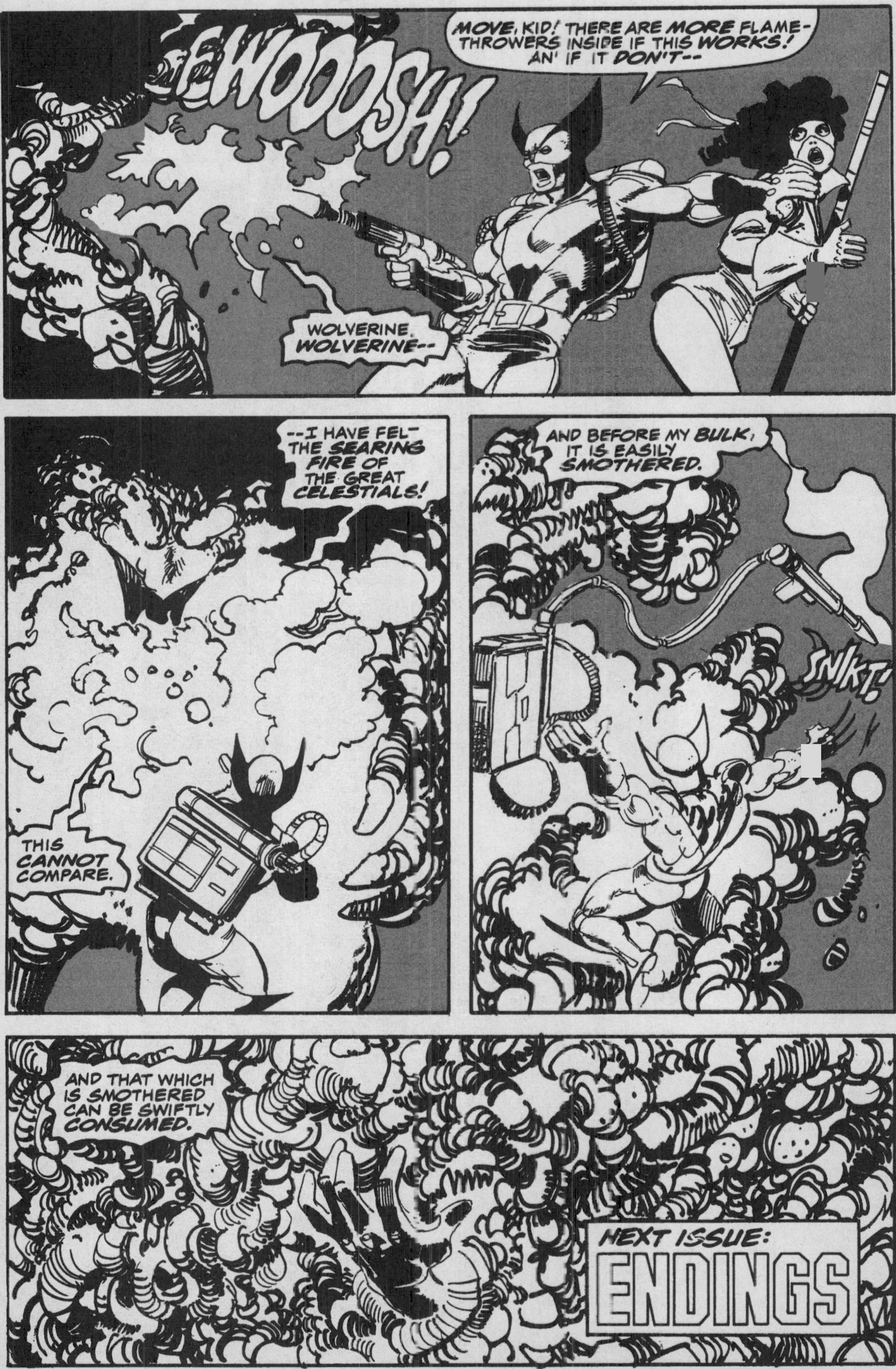
FWOOOSH!
MOVE, KID! THERE ARE MORE FLAME-THROWERS INSIDE IF THIS WORKS! AN' IF IT DON'T--
WOLVERINE, WOLVERINE--
--I HAVE FELT THE SEARING FIRE OF THE GREAT CELESTIALS!
THIS CANNOT COMPARE.
AND BEFORE MY BULK, IT IS EASILY SMOTHERED.
SNIKT!
AND THAT WHICH IS SMOTHERED CAN BE SWIFTLY CONSUMED.
NEXT ISSUE:
ENDINGS

MARVEL® COMICS

1.50 US
$2.00 CAN
23
APR

APPROVED
BY THE
COMICS CODE
AUTHORITY

02254

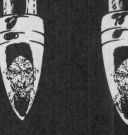

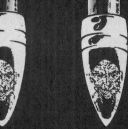

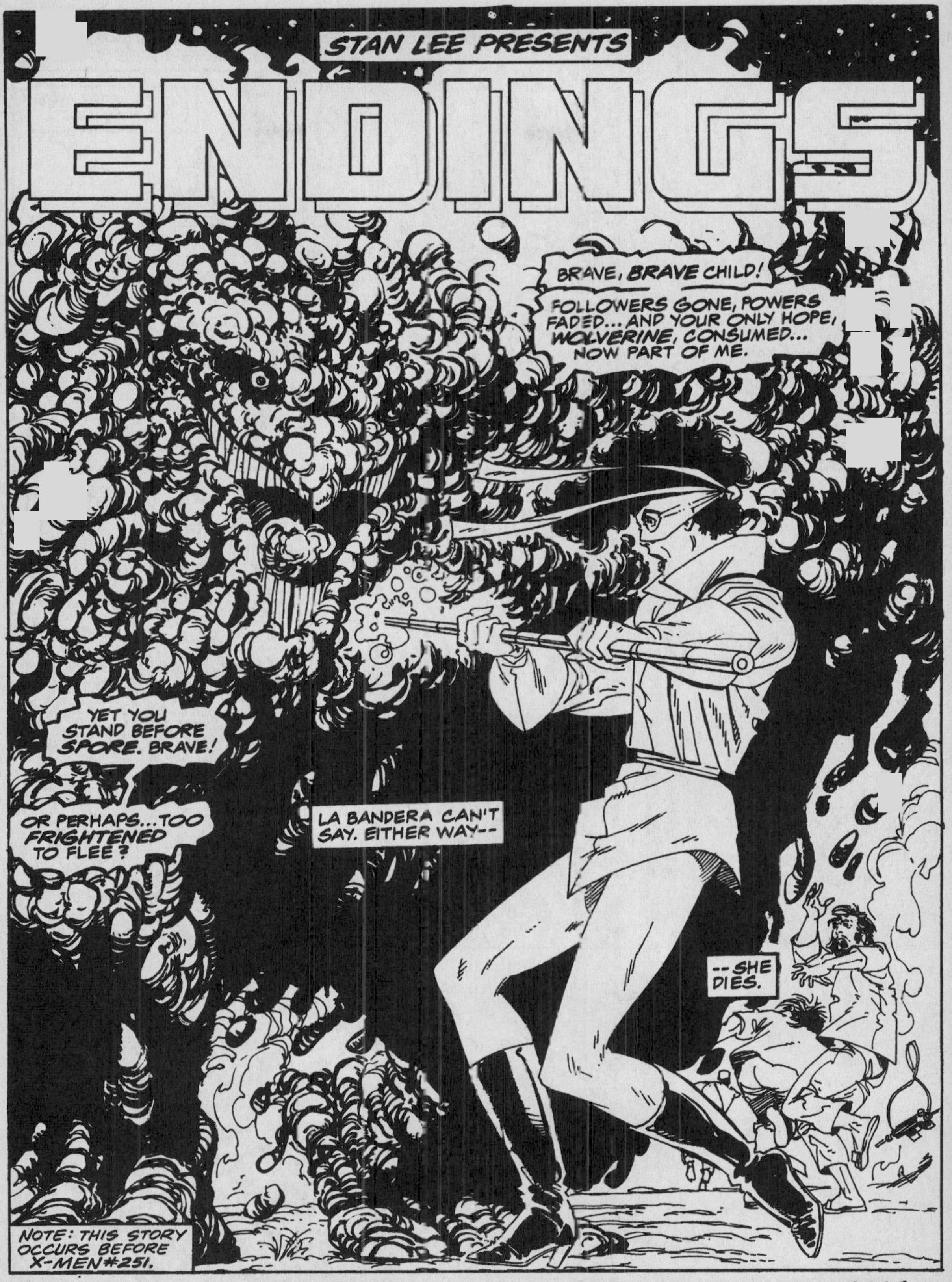

STAN LEE PRESENTS
ENDINGS
BRAVE, BRAVE CHILD!
FOLLOWERS GONE, POWERS FADED... AND YOUR ONLY HOPE, WOLVERINE, CONSUMED... NOW PART OF ME.
YET YOU STAND BEFORE SPORE. BRAVE!
OR PERHAPS... TOO FRIGHTENED TO FLEE?
LA BANDERA CAN'T SAY. EITHER WAY--
--SHE DIES.
NOTE: THIS STORY OCCURS BEFORE X-MEN #251.

ARCHIE GOODWIN WRITER | JOHN BYRNE ARTIST | JIM NOVAK LETTERER | GLYNIS OLIVER COLORIST | BOB HARRAS EDITOR

TOM DeFALCO, EDITOR IN CHIEF

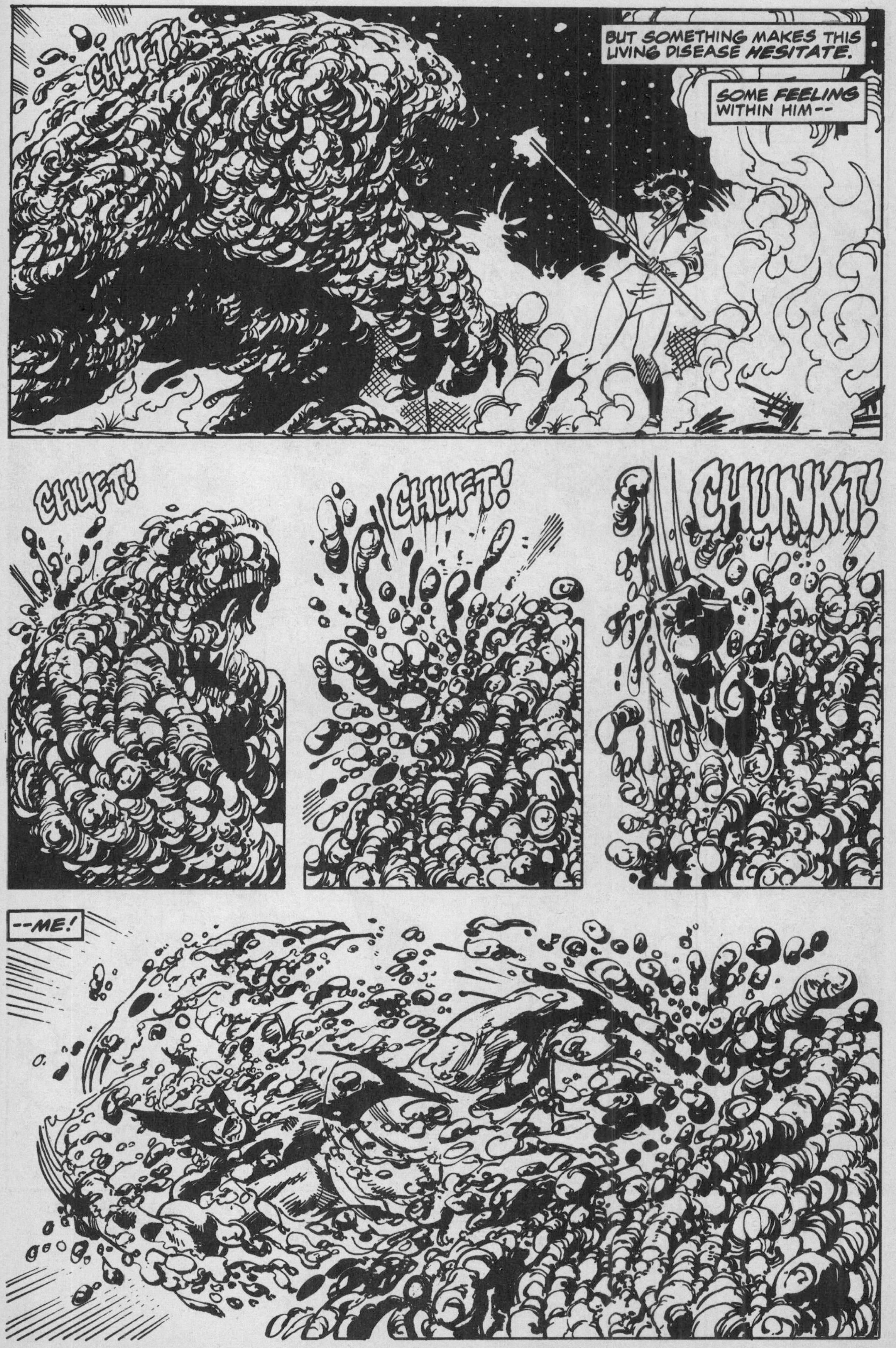

CHUFT!
BUT SOMETHING MAKES THIS LIVING DISEASE HESITATE.
SOME FEELING WITHIN HIM--
CHUFT!
CHUFT!
CHUNKT!
--ME!

WOLVERINE...! WHY AREN'T YOU **DEAD**?!

NO ONE **SURVIVES** BEING ABSORBED INTO ME... BECOMING THE **GRIST** FROM WHICH I THRIVE AND **GROW**.

NOT THE **ETERNALS** WHOM I BATTLED IN PREHISTORY... NOT EVEN THEIR FOES, THE **DEVIANTS**, WHO CREATED ME. **NO ONE**!

THEN YOU'RE **OVERDUE**.

I GOT AN UNBREAKABLE **ADAMANTIUM**-LACED SKELETON AN' **CLAWS** TO MATCH. GOT A MUTANT **HEALIN'** FACTOR BESIDES.

GOT ME THROUGH THE BELLY OF TH' **BEAST** IN A PLACE CALLED THE SAVAGE LAND, SPORE.* SHOULD BE GOOD FOR A COUPLE MORE TRIPS **HERE**.

MAYBE I CAN'T **FINISH** YOU LIKE THOSE OUTERSPACE HEAVYWEIGHTS, THE **CELESTIALS**, DID EONS AGO--

--BUT YOU'RE GONNA FIND ME **PAINFUL** TO **DIGEST**!

* WOLVERINE SPECIAL. --BOB

I LET IT GO. THE ANIMAL. THE BERSERKER. THE MAD RAGE INSIDE ME THAT MAKES MY LIFE A WAR FOR CONTROL.

IT...IT CAN BE HURT!

AND IF *THAT* IS SO--

NO NEED TO HOLD BACK. I WON'T SURVIVE TO FEEL THE SHAME. AND UNTIL THEN...

IT CAN BE FOUGHT, COMPADRES!

DON'T LET WOLVERINE DO IT ALONE! HIDING IN FEAR WON'T SAVE US!

WE RALLIED *TOGETHER* AGAINST THIS STRONGHOLD OF THE DICTATOR CARIDAD! *RALLY AGAIN!*

INSPIRATION. PRETTY DANGEROUS MUTANT POWER LA BANDERA HAS. LOTTA WAYS TO LEAD FOLKS WRONG.

BUT AGAINST *SPORE?* COULD BE THEIR ONLY CHANCE--

--AN' MAYBE *MINE* AS WELL.

POWER *BLASTS* WORKIN' AGAIN, KID? I CAN USE ALL OF 'EM YOU CAN DELIVER!

WHEN MY FOLLOWERS' INSPIRATION FALTERED, I HAD NOTHING TO DRAW UPON... TO RECHANNEL AS ENERGY BURSTS THROUGH MY STAFF.

BUT LOOK NOW, WOLVERINE!

YEAH. EVEN CARIDAD'S TROOPS ARE LEAPIN' TO JOIN US. WITH ALL THAT, WE'RE DOIN' SOME REAL DAMAGE--

--BUT THE COST IS TOO HIGH, KID!

SPORE'S STILL GROWIN'! TOO MANY FOLKS ARE FALLIN' TO 'IM!

PULL YOUR PEOPLE BACK! EVERYONE!

WE'LL REAR GUARD FOR 'EM TILL WE FIND SOME COVER--

--A PLACE TO MAKE A STAND!

SPORE DIDN'T *FOLLOW*. PERHAPS--

YEAH, WE *HURT* HIM. SO HE'LL TAKE HIS TIME. ABSORB BODIES, STRAGGLERS--

--GET BIGGER, STRONGER, UNSTOPPABLE. *THEN* HE'LL COME, LA BANDERA.

NICE TIME FOR AN *AIRSTRIKE*. ONLY WE CAN'T GET--

SPORE IS A *DISEASE*--

--GROWN OUT OF MY *HUSBAND* AND THE TAINTED *COCAINE* HE MADLY EXPERI-MENTED WITH.

BUT A DISEASE CAN BE *HEALED*. AND I AM THE ONE BLESSED WITH A *HEALING TOUCH*.

SALVATION! WHY DIDN'T YOU GET TO *SAFETY* WHEN YOU HAD THE CHANCE--

--ESPECIALLY WITH YOUR OWN *SON* INFECTED BY HIS DIC-TATOR POPPA'S EXPERIMENT?

FOR THE MOMENT--

--I'VE DONE ALL I CAN FOR PALO. WHY NOT SEE IF MY GIFT CAN SERVE AN EVEN *GREATER* NEED?

YOU WERE SAPPY ENOUGH TO *FALL* FOR THAT, ROUGHOUSE... TO LET HER COME *BACK* TO THIS MESS?! I *TRUSTED* YOU--

--FIGURED YOU *CARED* ABOUT SISTER SALVATION!

GUESS WE *BOTH* CARE FOR THE LADY, WOLVERINE. DIFFER-ENCE IS... ONLY *ONE* OF US SEEMS T'HAVE *FAITH* IN HER TOO.

DUTY. HONOR. THE GOOD FIGHT. A WORTHY DEATH. THOSE ARE PART OF ME. BUT *FAITH...?* NOT REALLY MY NATURE. IT COMES HARD. TAKES TIME. BUT *SPORE* HAS GIVEN US THAT--

--UNTIL HE'S *READY.*

NOW, WOLVERINE--!

FIRST *YOU* AND THAT SWEET CHILD, *LA BANDERA*--

--THEN YOUR *PITIFUL RABBLE* OF AN ARMY SCATTERED TO ANNOY ME.

WE'RE *ALL* WAITING, MONSTER! IS *THIS*--

--ANNOYING ENOUGH?!

LIGHTS ENABLE THE KID TO GET IT IN ONE SHOT.

SPORE REELS, TEMPORARILY BLINDED.

MY TURN!

THE BEAST WITHIN ME REJOICES, HOWLING FOR CARNAGE.

I OBLIGE.

WRAASK

BUT SPORE IS A MASS OF WILDLY MULTIPLYING CELLS, REPAIRING ALMOST AS QUICKLY AS I DESTROY--

--BUT NOT WITHOUT PAIN.

AND NOT WITHOUT DANGER. IF I STRIKE SWIFTLY ENOUGH, DEEPLY ENOUGH... THE MIND THAT DRIVES THIS ENGINE OF DISEASE MIGHT BE PIERCED.

IT MAKES SPORE FLAIL AT ME, AWKWARDLY STAGGER--

--AND FALL.

YOU'VE DONE IT, WOLVERINE! YOU'VE DONE IT!

YEAH. ACCORDING TO PLAN. THE REST IS--

--A MATTER OF FAITH.

SPORE LAUGHS.

I SCREAM AND MOVE, KNOWING I CAN NEVER BEAT THE FLOWING TENDRILS OOZING TOWARD THEIR PREY.

THEN...THE *HEALING* BEGINS.

HER TOUCH...! HER *TOUCH!*

IT... *SEARS!!*

IT SEARS LIKE THE FIRE THE *CELESTIALS* RAINED UPON ME!

AND AS WHEN HE FIRST FELT THE TOUCH OF THAT FIRE BACK IN PREHISTORY--

--SPORE IS CONSUMED.

LIKE MOST VICTORIES, THERE'S A PRICE.

TAKES SOMEONE REVIVING FROM A *DIFFERENT* COMBAT TO NOTICE.

M-MOTHER....! YOUR... *HANDS!*

NUMB...NOT LIKE *OTHER* BURNS I'VE TREATED...

HAVE A MEDICAL KIT BROUGHT *ANYWAY,* BANDERA...*FAST.*

WHY TAKE CHANCES? WE DON'T *KNOW* WHAT REALLY HAPPENED TONIGHT.

MAYBE THE CELESTIALS *FIGURED* SPORE MIGHT RISE AGAIN... AN' IMBUED SOME OF HUMANITY WITH A GENETIC TALENT FOR "CURING," JUST IN CASE.

OR PERHAPS I'M A *MUTANT*... WITH SPECIAL POWERS LIKE YOU AND LA BANDERA?

NOT SHARING MY FAITH, WOLVERINE, YOU WON'T SHARE ANOTHER *SIMPLER* EXPLANATION.

GOTTA ACCEPT WHAT WORKS FOR *ME,* SALVATION--

--IMPORTANT THING'S THE JOB GOT DONE.

YES...THOUGH I CAN'T HELP WONDERING. IF I'VE FULFILLED MY GIFT'S *TRUE PURPOSE* ...DOES IT *EXIST* ANY LONGER AT ALL?

MORNING.

WE'RE A REAL *ARMY* NOW, WOLVERINE--

--JOIN IN! YOU'LL MISS THE *REVOLUTION!*

WORD SPREADS ABOUT *CARIDAD'S* DEATH--

--YOU WON'T *LACK HELP* FOR THE CAUSE, KID!

SEE YOU IN PUERTO VERDE!

I DON'T WATCH LA BANDERA'S CARAVAN DEPART. ACROSS THE JUNGLE MILITARY BASE, ANOTHER GROUP IS ABOUT TO DO THE SAME.

PALO'S STRAPPED DOWN... EFFECTS OF THAT *POISON* INFLICTED ON 'IM ARE COMIN' *BACK?*

HE'S NOT *CURED* YET.

I WAS ABLE TO HELP *SOME* BEFORE THE CLASH WITH SPORE. PERHAPS WHEN MY *HANDS* MEND--

--I CAN HELP HIM *AGAIN.*

AND IF THE *HEALING TOUCH* IS *GONE--?*

I STILL HAVE *MEDICAL SKILLS.* AT LEAST MY SON AND I WILL BE TOGETHER. MEANWHILE... THERE'S A *MISSION* TO REBUILD.

WHATEVER HAPPENS, I'LL BE AROUND TO *PROTECT* THE BOY... *AND* THE *LADY.*

I GOT INTO THIS T'SAVE A GOOD SPAR-RIN' PARTNER AN' WORTHWHILE ENEMY, ROUGHHOUSE. LOOKS LIKE I'VE LOST BOTH--

--TO SOMETHIN' BETTER.

HEY, THERE'S WORK FOR MORE'N ONE STRONG MAN REBUILDIN' THAT MISSION HER HUSBAND DESTROYED.

BUT THAT'S ALL THERE CAN BE, WOLVERINE.

AND MUCH AS I'LL CHERISH THAT OUR PATHS CROSSED, I DON'T BELIEVE--

NO, SISTER, I DON'T BELIEVE EITHER.

MAYBE SOMEDAY I'LL BE A REBUILDER. FOR NOW--

--MY SKILLS AN' NEEDS RUN IN THE OPPOSITE DIRECTION.

MY ANIMAL SENSES ARE ALREADY ON THE JOB. UNFINISHED BUSINESS. PART MAN, MORE MACHINE--

"--GEIST."

TOO LATE! THE REVOLUTION HAS REACHED THE CAPITAL....! MOBS HAVE ALREADY SWEPT THE PRESIDENTIAL PALACE!

BUT THERE IS STILL HOPE IF--

BARBARIAN RABBLE!

THEY'VE SAVAGED MY *HIDING PLACE* IN THEIR *RAMPAGING*...! MY *EMERGENCY CACHE*... GONE!

AH! THEY OVERLOOKED *SOMETHING* OF USE, YES...? ONE OF MY *RAZOR* ATTACHMENTS!

CH-KLIK

ACTUALLY, THE *LOOTERS* MISSED YOUR *GETAWAY STASH*--

--BUT NO PROBLEM. MONEY, RECORDS, SAMPLES OF CARIDAD'S SPECIAL COCAINE... I *BURNED* IT ALL.

NO! NOT--

YEAH. GUESS WITH *SPORE* LOOSE LAST NIGHT, STEALIN' A *TRUCK* WAS THE BEST YOU COULD DO... THIS MORNIN', I JUST GRABBED A *HELICOPTER.*

EVEN HAD TIME TO DROP *LEAF-LETS* ALERTIN' THE CITY TO YOUR BOSS'S DOWNFALL.

ANIMAL!

FED UP WITH *POLITICS*, GEIST? HERE'S SOMETHIN' YOU CAN REALLY *RELATE* TO--

--A *CLEAN, CLOSE SHAVE!*

YOU...YOU DIDN'T *TOUCH M--*

KRIII-KRIIIII

SNAP! KRING!

N-NO!

KRAK! PING! RIIPPT!

YOU CANNOT *LEAVE* ME LIKE THIS...! I'LL *DIE* WITHOUT THE *SUPPORT* OF MY ARMOR...!

SEEMS FAIR.

LOTS OF OTHERS DIED OVER THE YEARS TO SUP-PORT IT!

WOLVERINE! YOU BEAT US HERE!

THE CITY'S OURS! ALMOST NO RESISTANCE! *WE'VE WON!*

THEN GET SOME *MEDICS.* IF THEY *HURRY,* YOU'LL HAVE THE NEW GOVERNMENT'S VERY FIRST *WAR CRIMINAL.*

VIVA LA BANDERA

VIVA LA REVOLUCC

FIRST PRIORITY, ELECTIONS

TOO SOON, RESTORE ORDER

NEED FREE PRESS

HAMPERS ARMY'S JOB

LAND REFORMS, THE INDIANS

FRIGHTEN DEVELOPERS

OK TOK TOK TOK TOK TOK TOK

SEÑOR WOLVERINE! YOU DISRUPT OUR FIRST *CABINET MEETING* AND--

WAM!

WHILE YOU GENIUSES ARE BUSY SPLITTIN' THE POT, SOME-ONE'S SPIRITED *GEIST* OUTTA THE HOSPITAL PRISON WARD-- --AN OUTTA THE *COUNTRY.*

THIS WAS AN *EXTRADITION MATTER,* SETTLED TO TIERRA VERDE'S BENEFIT. NOTHING TO INVOLVE SOMEONE--

--WITH NO TRUE *POLITICAL STATUS* IN THE NEW REVOLUTION.

ENRIQUE.

SURE. FREEIN' WHAT YOU *FOUGHT* AGAINST...? HOPE IT'S A *BIG* BENEFIT.

WOLVERINE! *WAIT!* PLEASE!

I DIDN'T KNOW THINGS WOULD *GO* THIS WAY...! THERE'S SO MUCH TO SETTLE ...SO MANY DIFFERENT FACTIONS...! I DIDN'T *KNOW...!*

GUESS THIS IS *PART'A* WHAT I WAS *WARNIN'* YOU ABOUT IN THE *BEGINNIN'*, BANDERA.

INSPIRIN' PEOPLE TO *FIGHT*, THAT'S THE *EASY* PART. INSPIRIN' 'EM TO *PEACE--?*

WELL, THE WHOLE *WORLD'S* STILL WORKIN' ON THAT ONE.

MAYBE YOU GOT THE *KIND'A* POWER T'MAKE THE *DIFFERENCE* HERE. ME, I TEND T'MOVE ON WHEN THE *ACTION* STOPS.

SO...SOME LAST *ADVICE.* MOST'A US *SUPERHERO* TYPES REMOVE OUR MASKS *BEFORE* WE CRY--

--AVOIDS *STAINS.*

I LEAVE HER.

A *TEENAGE* GIRL, SUDDENLY ALONE, SUDDENLY *AWARE--*

--OF THE *NIGHT,* THE *CELEBRATION--*

--OF THE FULL WEIGHT OF HER *VICTORY* IN TIERRA VERDE.

I'M MORE THAN READY TO BE *QUITS* WITH THE PLACE. BUT--

SNEAKIN' OUT, HOSER?

--TIERRA VERDE AND AN OLD ACQUAINTANCE FROM THE *CIA* AREN'T QUITE FINISHED WITH *ME.*

HAVE A *CERVEZA* WITH A FELLOW *NORTEAMERICANO,* LOGAN. SHOW THE WORLD YOU'RE NOT A *BAD LOSER.*

LAST TIME WE TALKED, YOUR PEOPLE WERE BACKIN' *CARIDAD.* SEEMS T'ME, THEY'RE THE *LOSERS.*

NOW CARIDAD WAS USEFUL IN HIS *DAY,* OL' SON... BUT HIS *COCAINE* DEALIN' HAD BECOME AN *EMBARRASSMENT.*

'SPECIALLY THAT *WEIRD* STUFF.

THE *TAINTED* COCAINE...! THE CROP *SPORE* GREW FROM! YOU COULDN'T KNOW ABOUT *THAT*, UNLESS--

WE HAD A *MOLE*, INFORMIN' US EVERY STEP...*GEIST*.

IT'S WHY WE GOT HIM OUTTA THE *COUNTRY* AN' THREW SOME SUPPORT TO YOUR *REBEL* PALS.

IF YOU COULD'A *CONTROLLED* SPORE, WOULD YOU HAVE GOTTEN *HIM* OUT TOO, BASCOMB?!

GEIST IS JUST AS MUCH A *DISEASE!* AN EX-NAZI GHOUL! AN' YOU GUYS ARE *PROTECTIN'* 'IM... KEEPIN' 'IM IN *BUSINESS!*

WHEELS WITHIN WHEELS, OL' SON. I *WARNED* YOU!

REAL WORLD'S MORE *COMPLICATED* THAN PERSONAL FEUDS. TIME YOU *LEARNED* THAT.

TIME YOU LEARNED THERE ARE *WORSE* ENEMIES THAN YOUR *OLD* ENEMIES.

I CARRY THE THOUGHT. ALL THE WAY BACK. TO WHERE THIS BEGAN. BACK TO... *MADRIPOOR.*

HIGHTOWN AT DAWN.

IN ITS GLITTERING TOWERS, MADRIPOOR'S PRIVILEGED STILL SLEEP.

LIKE CRIMELORD *GENERAL COY.* SAFE, SECURE IN HIS WEALTH AND POWER.

UNTIL--

SOMETHING DROPPED... ON COVERS. W-WHAT...?

LITTLE REMINDER--

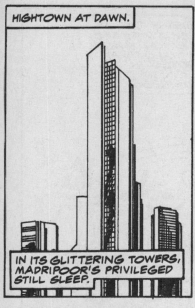

--OF A MAN NAMED *PATCH.* HE'S GONE. I'M HERE. NOT AN *IMPROVEMENT* FOR YOU.

MY BODY-GUARDS--!

YOU CAN CALL--

--THEY CAN'T COME. BESIDES ...I'VE ALREADY *FOUND* WHAT I'M AFTER.

LUCKY IT HASN'T BEEN *USED* YET.

I'VE GOT *PLANS.* FOR IT--

--AND *YOU.*

ONE HOUR LATER.

AS IS HIS HABIT, *BARAN,* MADRIPOOR'S RULING PRINCE--

--STARTS THE DAY WITH A RIDE.

HE DOESN'T FINISH IT.

"...SO IF YOU DON'T *DIE* FROM THE *MADNESS,* REDUCED TO *ANIMAL FRENZY,* THIS... *THING* GROWS INSIDE YOU.

"UNTIL *YOU'RE* CONSUMED... AN' IT'S *FREE.* NICE STUFF. FELIX GUILLERMO CARIDAD'S *COCAINE.*

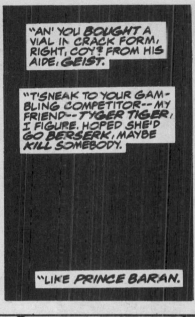

"AN' YOU *BOUGHT* A VIAL IN CRACK FORM, RIGHT, COY? FROM HIS AIDE, *GEIST.*

"T'SNEAK TO YOUR GAMBLING COMPETITOR-- MY *FRIEND*--*TYGER TIGER,* I FIGURE. HOPED SHE'D GO BERSERK, MAYBE KILL SOMEBODY.

"LIKE *PRINCE BARAN.*

"NOT THAT I *CARE.* NOT AFTER HE PAID GEIST FOR A SHOT AT MURDERIN' *ME.*

"YOU'D BE FREE OF PAYIN' BARAN *TRIBUTE,* COY... AN' RID OF A *RIVAL.* EXCEPT I'M NOT ABOUT TO LET IT *HAPPEN.*

"NO--

--I GOT A *BETTER* USE FOR CARIDAD'S POISON. FITTING. *IRONIC.*

WELCOME TO MADRIPOOR'S *SEWER SYSTEM.* FUN'S ABOUT TO BEGIN!

WHILE WE WERE *UNCONSCIOUS*--

YOU *DIDN'T*--

YEAH. I *COULD'VE* GIVEN IT TO YOU TWO.

SPLASH

BUT I'VE GOT THIS MUTANT *HEALING FACTOR.* PROBABLY THE ONE GUY--

--WHO CAN ACTUALLY *SURVIVE* THE STUFF.

LIKE BOTH OF *YOU* MIGHT SURVIVE BEIN' *TRAPPED* DOWN HERE WITH *ME*--

--IF YOU *RUN FAST* ENOUGH, *FAR* ENOUGH.

NOW!

SNIKT

SNIKT

I *HOWL* AS I LEAP. THE SOUND ECHOES LOUD AND RAW. THERE IS *MADNESS* IN IT.

USED TO COME TO *MADRIPOOR* TO GIVE REIN TO MY *ANIMAL* SIDE.

AT THIS INSTANT, IT DOESN'T SEEM THERE WAS *EVER* ANY OTHER.

AN' THE SEWERS OF MADRIPOOR ARE OVERWHELMED WITH THE RANK STENCH OF *FEAR.*

THE SYSTEM'S ANCIENT, VAST. BUT WITH THE HOURS, THE DESPERATION... ESCAPE IS POSSIBLE.

BUT IT'S RARELY CONVENIENT--

--AN' *NEVER* DIGNIFIED. THAT'S 'CAUSE NO AMOUNT OF CLEANSING EVER QUITE REMOVES--

--STAINS TO THE PRIDE.

AUSTRALIA. MY OUTBACK DESTINATION'S A LONG, SCORCH N' DRIVE AWAY. THINKIN' ABOUT COY AN' BARAN WILL FILL MY TIME. THINKIN' ABOUT WHAT THEY'LL NEVER KNOW.

I DIDN'T *USE* THE TAINTED COCAINE. JUST DESTROYED IT... AN' LET LOOSE WHAT'S *ALWAYS* INSIDE ME.

JUST FOR AN *INSTANT.* LENGTH OF A HOWL. BUT AN INSTANT THOSE TWO WILL TAKE TO THE GRAVE.

FOR ME, FOR NOW... I'M SICK OF THE BEAST.

I DON'T HAVE MARIKO. I DON'T HAVE SALVATION. BUT THE *X-MEN* ARE WAITING.

I HAVE *FAMILY* TO REJOIN.

EPILOGUE.

WHRR KLAK WHRR KLAK

WASHINGTON, DC.

WHRR KLAK BIP

GUTEN ABEND, HERR GEIST.

WHO--?

I'VE *STARTLED* YOU...DESPITE SENDING THE LITTLE *TOY* AHEAD AS A SCOUT. A VENDOR WAS SELLING THEM IN DUPONT CIRCLE...IT SEEMED *APPROPRIATE*.

DON'T WORRY, HERR GEIST...I *UNDER-STAND* YOUR NERVOUSNESS.

OBVIOUSLY THE CIA HAS GONE TO GREAT LENGTHS ARRANGING A *SAFE HOUSE*...FOR A MAN GENERALLY BELIEVED *DEAD*.

WHAT *IS* THIS GAME?! YOU WILL TELL *WHO* YOU ARE OR--

SOMEONE WHO REMEMBERS YOU FROM THE *PAST*. YOU USED A *DIFFERENT NAME*...

...WHILE VISITING A CERTAIN *CONCENTRATION CAMP* DURING WORLD WAR II. A CAMP WHERE MY *WIFE* DIED.

I USED A DIFFERENT NAME THEN AS WELL. NOW...I AM CALLED *MAGNETO*.

MASTER OF *MAGNETISM*, SOME SAY. EVIL MUTANT IS ANOTHER FAVORITE.

WHATEVER. I HAVE EXCELLENT RESOURCES *BEYOND* THIS EXHIBI-TION. SUCH AS *INFORMATION*--

SO, WHEN *ANONYMOUSLY* ALERTED TO YOUR POSSIBLE SURVIVAL...IT WAS NO *MAJOR* DIFFICULTY TO HUNT YOU DOWN.

LEIBER GOTT!

AH! YOUR *GERMAN* COMES BACK! LET'S TALK *INSIDE* YOUR SAFE HOUSE...UNDIS-TURBED. I ENJOY CONVERSING WITH FORMER NAZIS, HERR GEIST--

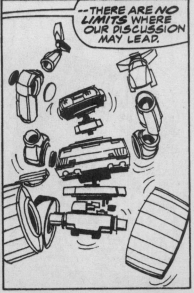

--THERE ARE *NO LIMITS* WHERE OUR DISCUSSION MAY LEAD.

FIN.